Mobil
Travel Guide

Northern California

2006

ExxonMobil
Travel Publications

Acknowledgements

We gratefully acknowledge the help of our representatives for their efficient and perceptive inspections of the lodging and dining establishments listed; the establishments' proprietors for their cooperation in showing their facilities and providing information about them; and the many users of previous editions who have taken the time to share their experiences. Mobil Travel Guide is also grateful to all the talented writers who contributed entries to this book.

www.mobiltravelguide.com

Front cover photo: Big Sur, California

ISBN: 0-7627-3928-2

ISSN: 1550-1930

Manufactured in the United States of America.

10 9 8 7 6 5 4 3 2 1

Contents

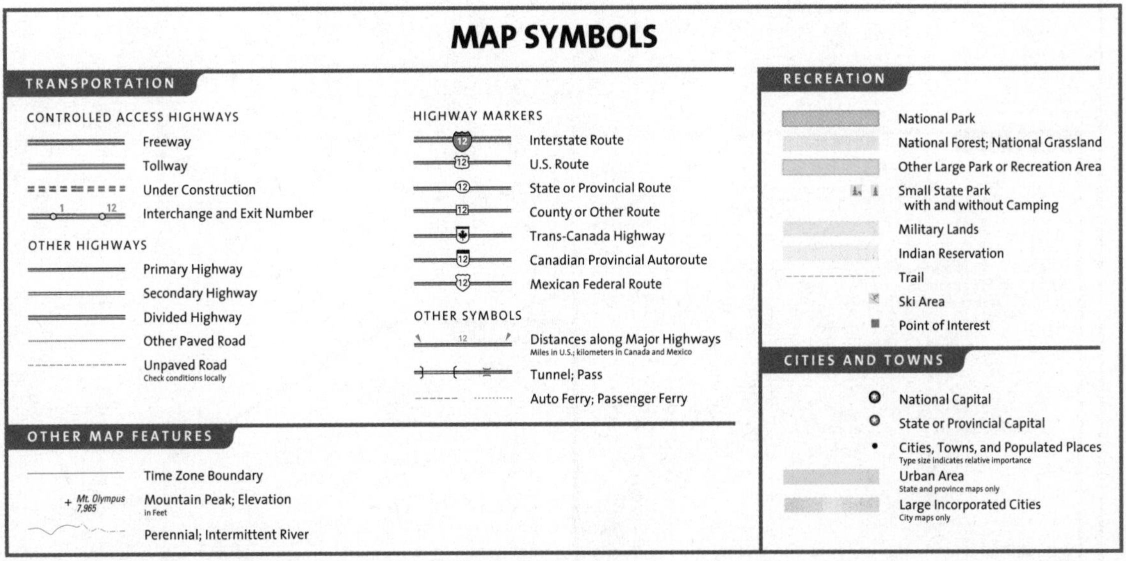

MAP SYMBOLS
TRANSPORTATION
CONTROLLED ACCESS HIGHWAYS
Freeway
Tollway
Under Construction
Interchange and Exit Number
OTHER HIGHWAYS
Primary Highway
Secondary Highway
Divided Highway
Other Paved Road
Unpaved Road
Check conditions locally
HIGHWAY MARKERS
Interstate Route
U.S. Route
State or Provincial Route
County or Other Route
Trans-Canada Highway
Canadian Provincial Autoroute
Mexican Federal Route
OTHER SYMBOLS
Distances along Major Highways
Miles in U.S.; kilometers in Canada and Mexico
Tunnel; Pass
Auto Ferry; Passenger Ferry
OTHER MAP FEATURES
Time Zone Boundary
Mt. Olympus 7,965
Mountain Peak; Elevation
in Feet
Perennial; Intermittent River
RECREATION
National Park
National Forest; National Grassland
Other Large Park or Recreation Area
Small State Park with and without Camping
Military Lands
Indian Reservation
Trail
Ski Area
Point of Interest
CITIES AND TOWNS
National Capital
State or Provincial Capital
Cities, Towns, and Populated Places
Type size indicates relative importance
Urban Area
State and province maps only
Large Incorporated Cities
City maps only

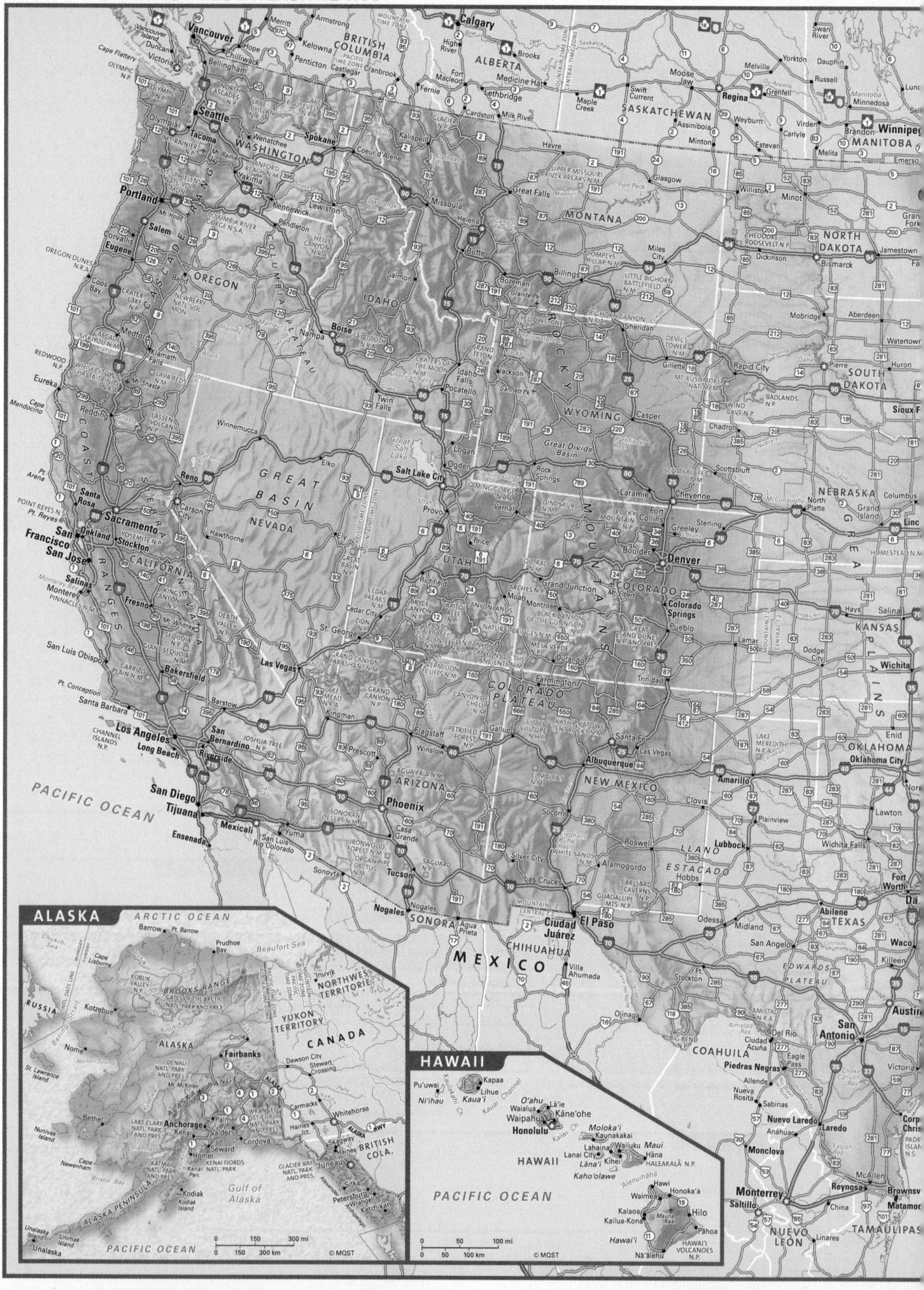

BRITISH COLUMBIA
ALBERTA
SASKATCHEWAN
MANITOBA
Vancouver
Calgary
Regina
Winnipeg
WASHINGTON
Seattle
Spokane
OREGON
Portland
Salem
IDAHO
Boise
MONTANA
Helena
Great Falls
Billings
NORTH DAKOTA
Bismarck
SOUTH DAKOTA
Pierre
WYOMING
Cheyenne
NEBRASKA
CALIFORNIA
Sacramento
San Francisco
San Jose
Fresno
Los Angeles
San Diego
NEVADA
Reno
Las Vegas
UTAH
Salt Lake City
COLORADO
Denver
ARIZONA
Phoenix
Tucson
NEW MEXICO
Albuquerque
Santa Fe
KANSAS
Wichita
OKLAHOMA
Oklahoma City
TEXAS
El Paso
San Antonio
MEXICO
Tijuana
Ciudad Juárez
Monterrey
CHIHUAHUA
COAHUILA
NUEVO LEÓN
TAMAULIPAS
SONORA
GREAT BASIN
COLORADO PLATEAU
ROCKY MOUNTAINS
CASCADE RANGE
COLUMBIA PLATEAU
COAST RANGES
SIERRA NEVADA
GREAT PLAINS
LLANO ESTACADO
EDWARDS PLATEAU
PACIFIC OCEAN
ALASKA
ARCTIC OCEAN
Barrow
Prudhoe Bay
BROOKS RANGE
Kotzebue
Nome
Fairbanks
Anchorage
Juneau
Kodiak
ALASKA PENINSULA
Gulf of Alaska
YUKON TERRITORY
NORTHWEST TERRITORIES
CANADA
BRITISH COLA.
RUSSIA
PACIFIC OCEAN
HAWAII
Kaua'i
O'ahu
Honolulu
Moloka'i
Lāna'i
Maui
Kaho'olawe
Hawai'i
Hilo
PACIFIC OCEAN
© MQST

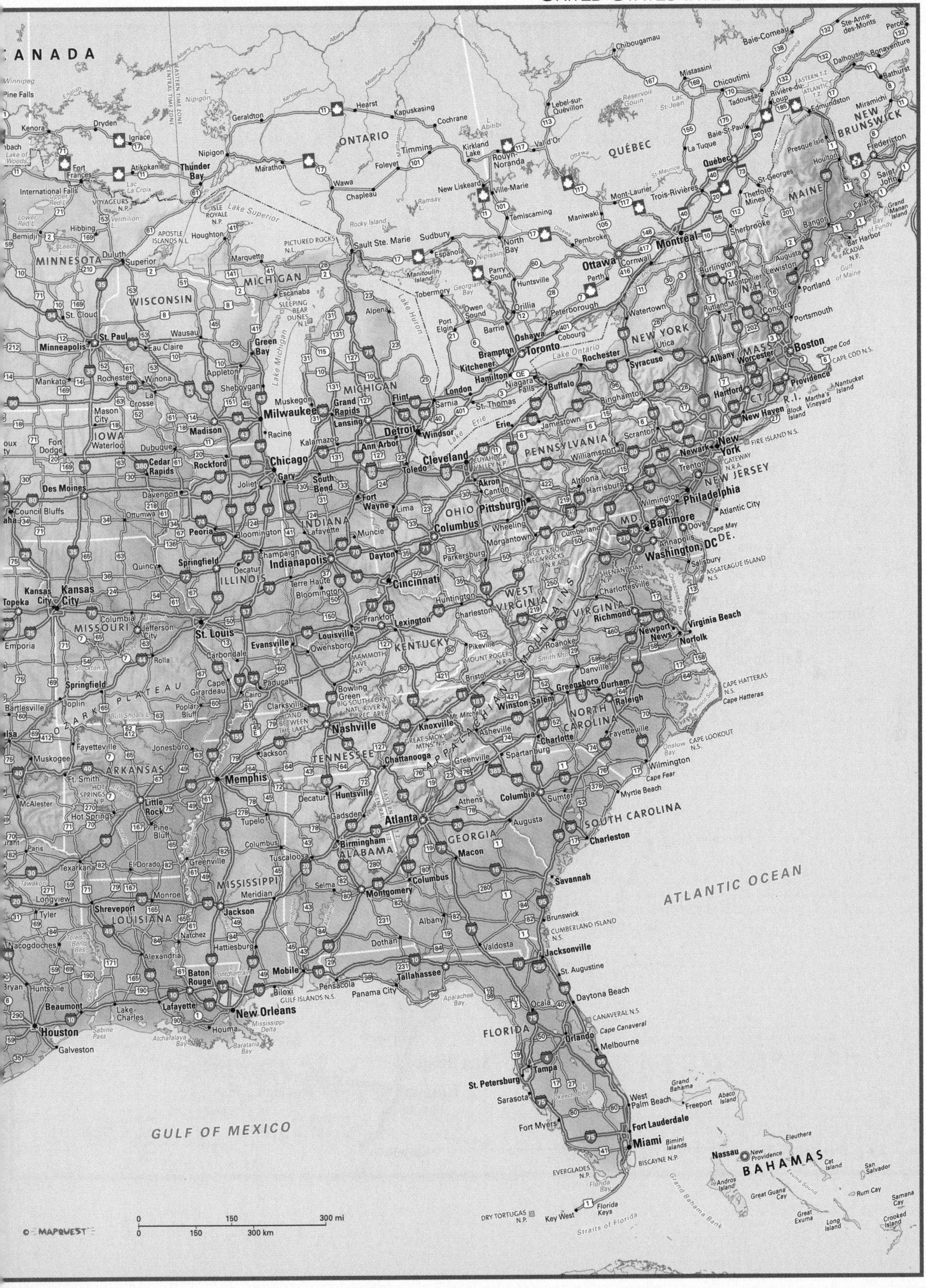
CANADA
ONTARIO
QUÉBEC
NEW BRUNSWICK
MAINE
MINNESOTA
WISCONSIN
MICHIGAN
IOWA
ILLINOIS
INDIANA
OHIO
PENNSYLVANIA
NEW YORK
VT.
N.H.
MASS.
CT.
R.I.
NEW JERSEY
MD.
DE.
WEST VIRGINIA
VIRGINIA
KENTUCKY
TENNESSEE
NORTH CAROLINA
SOUTH CAROLINA
GEORGIA
ALABAMA
MISSISSIPPI
LOUISIANA
ARKANSAS
MISSOURI
FLORIDA
BAHAMAS
OZARK PLATEAU
APPALACHIAN MOUNTAINS
ATLANTIC OCEAN
GULF OF MEXICO
Lake Superior
Lake Michigan
Lake Huron
Lake Ontario
Lake Erie
Chicago
Detroit
Cleveland
Pittsburgh
Toronto
Ottawa
Montréal
Québec
Boston
New York
Philadelphia
Baltimore
Washington, DC
Richmond
Norfolk
Virginia Beach
Columbus
Cincinnati
Indianapolis
St. Louis
Kansas City
Memphis
Nashville
Atlanta
Charlotte
Jacksonville
Orlando
Tampa
Miami
New Orleans
Houston
Milwaukee
Minneapolis
St. Paul
Des Moines
Louisville
Lexington
Knoxville
Chattanooga
Birmingham
Montgomery
Mobile
Tallahassee
Savannah
Charleston
Columbia
Raleigh
Durham
Greensboro
Buffalo
Rochester
Syracuse
Albany
Hartford
Providence
Portland
Bangor
Fredericton
Thunder Bay
Sault Ste. Marie
Sudbury
Nassau
Key West
0 150 300 mi
0 150 300 km
© MAPQUEST

Eugene
Bend
OREGON DUNES N.R.A.
Coos Bay
CASCADE RANGE
NEWBERRY NATL. VOL. MON.
CRATER LAKE N.P.
OREGON
Malheur L.
Harney L.
Upper Klamath L.
L. Abert
Medford
CASCADE-SISKIYOU N.M.
Klamath Falls
COLUMBIA PLATEAU
Owyhee
Nampa
Boise
SAWTOOTH N.R.A.
IDAHO
CRATERS OF THE MOON N.M.
American Falls Res.
Snake
Twin Falls
Pocatello
Idaho Falls
GRAND TETON N.P.
Jackson
Klamat
Goose L.
LAVA BEDS N.M.
REDWOOD N.P.
WHISKEYTOWN-SHASTA-TRINITY N.R.A.
Mt. Shasta
LASSEN VOLCANIC N.P.
Eureka
Redding
Shasta L.
Cape Mendocino
COAST RANGES
Pyramid L.
Winnemucca
Elko
GREAT BASIN
NEVADA
Reno
Carson City
L. Tahoe
SIERRA NEVADA
Point Arena
Clear L.
Santa Rosa
Sacramento
Walker L.
Hawthorne
Ely
PACIFIC TIME ZONE
MOUNTAIN TIME ZONE
GREAT BASIN N.P.
Logan
Great Salt Lake
Ogden
Salt Lake City
Utah L.
Provo
UTAH
Richfield
POINT REYES N.S.
Point Reyes
Oakland
Stockton
YOSEMITE N.P.
Mono L.
San Francisco
GOLDEN GATE N.R.A.
CALIFORNIA
San Jose
Salinas
Monterey Bay
Monterey
San Joaquin
KINGS CANYON N.P.
Fresno
Mt. Whitney 14,494
DEATH VALLEY N.P.
PINNACLES N.M.
SEQUOIA N.P.
GIANT SEQUOIA N.M.
Bakersfield
San Luis Obispo
CARRIZO PLAIN N.M.
Las Vegas
Henderson
Lake Mead
LAKE MEAD N.R.A.
CEDAR BREAKS N.M.
BRYCE CANYON N.P.
Cedar City
ZION N.P.
GRAND STAIRCASE/ESCALANTE N.M.
St. George
VERMILION CLIFFS N.M.
GRAND CANYON-PARASHANT N.M.
Colorado
GRAND CANYON N.P.
Kingman
Barstow
Prescott
Point Conception
SANTA MONICA MTS. N.R.A.
Santa Barbara
San Bernardino
JOSHUA TREE N.P.
ARIZONA
Santa Rosa I.
CHANNEL ISLANDS N.P.
Los Angeles
Long Beach
Riverside
Phoenix
Santa Catalina I.
SANTA ROSA & SAN JACINTO MOUNTAINS N.M.
Salton Sea
SONORAN DESERT N.M.
PACIFIC OCEAN
San Diego
Gila
Casa Grande
Yuma
ORGAN PIPE CACTUS N.M.
IRONWOOD FOREST N.M.
Tijuana
Rosarito
Tecate
Mexicali
San Luis Rio Colorado
BAJA CALIFORNIA
MEXICO
Sonoyta
Ensenada
© MAPQUEST
100 200 mi
100 200 km

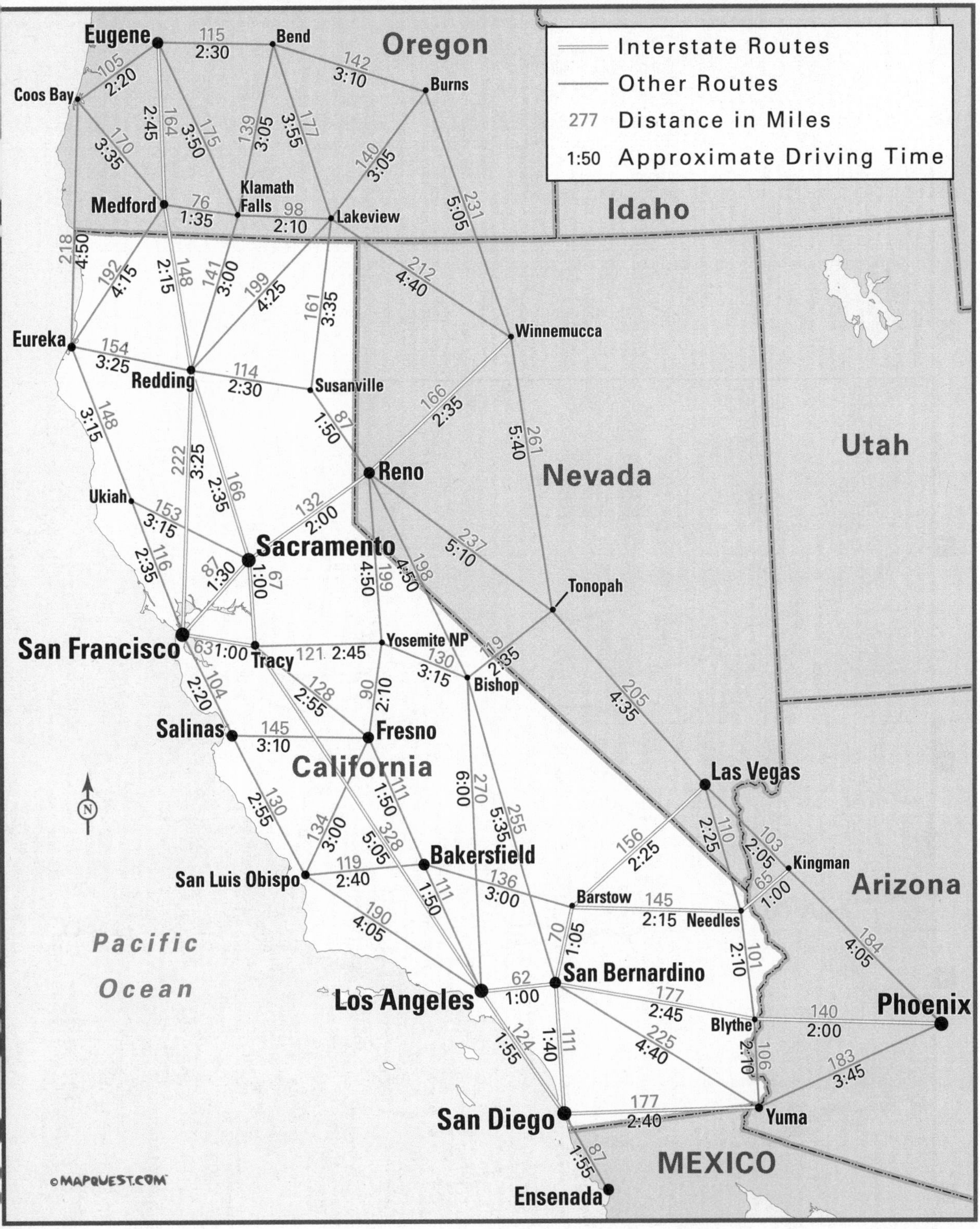
Interstate Routes
Other Routes
277 Distance in Miles
1:50 Approximate Driving Time
Oregon
Idaho
Nevada
Utah
California
Arizona
MEXICO
Pacific Ocean
Eugene
Bend
Burns
Coos Bay
Medford
Klamath Falls
Lakeview
Eureka
Redding
Susanville
Winnemucca
Reno
Ukiah
Sacramento
Tonopah
San Francisco
Tracy
Yosemite NP
Bishop
Salinas
Fresno
Las Vegas
Bakersfield
San Luis Obispo
Kingman
Barstow
Needles
San Bernardino
Los Angeles
Blythe
Phoenix
Yuma
San Diego
Ensenada

CALIFORNIA

POP: 33,871,648, rank 1

AREA: 158,706 sq mi, rank 3

Adelanto, 18130 .... H4
Alpine, 13143 .... K4
Alturas, 2892 .... B3
Anaheim, 328014 .... J4
Anderson, 9022 .... B2
Angels Camp, 3004 .... E3
Antioch, 90532 .... E2
Apple Valley, 54239 .... H4
Aptos, 9396 .... E2
Arcata, 16651 .... B1
Arnold, 4218 .... E3
Arroyo Grande, 15851 .... G2
Arvin, 12956 .... H3
Atascadero, 26411 .... G2
Atwater, 23113 .... E3
Auburn, 12462 .... D3
Avalon, 3127 .... J3
Avenal, 14674 .... G3
Bakersfield, 247057 .... G3
Barstow, 21119 .... H5
Berkeley, 102743 .... E2
Big Bear Lake, 5438 .... J4
Bishop, 3575 .... F4
Blythe, 12155 .... K6
Brawley, 22052 .... K5
Buellton, 3828 .... H2
Burney, 3217 .... B3
Calexico, 27109 .... K5
California City, 8385 .... H4
Calipatria, 7289 .... K5
Calistoga, 5190 .... D2
Camarillo, 57077 .... H3
Cambria, 6232 .... G2
Carlsbad, 78247 .... K4
Carmel-by-the-Sea, 4081 .... F2
Carmel Valley, 4700 .... F2
Carpinteria, 14194 .... H3
Castroville, 6724 .... F2
Cathedral City, 42647 .... J5
Cayucos, 2943 .... G2
Ceres, 34609 .... E2
Chico, 59954 .... C2
Chowchilla, 11127 .... F3
Chula Vista, 173556 .... K4
Citrus Hts., 85071 .... D2
Clearlake, 13142 .... D2
Cloverdale, 6831 .... D1
Clovis, 68468 .... F3
Coachella, 22724 .... J5
Coalinga, 11668 .... F3
Colusa, 5402 .... C2
Concord, 121780 .... E2
Corcoran, 14458 .... G3
Corning, 6741 .... C2
Coronado, 24100 .... K4
Cotati, 6471 .... D2
Cottonwood, 2960 .... B2
Crescent City, 4006 .... A1
Crestline, 10218 .... J4
Davis, 60308 .... D2
Delano, 38824 .... G3
Del Mar, 4389 .... K4
Desert Hot Sprs., 16582 .... J5
Dinuba, 16844 .... F3
Dixon, 16103 .... D2
Dos Palos, 4581 .... F3
Earlimart, 6583 .... G3
El Cajon, 94869 .... K4
El Centro, 37835 .... K5
Elk Grove, 59984 .... D2
Encinitas, 58014 .... K4
Escondido, 133559 .... K4
Eureka, 26128 .... B1
Exeter, 9168 .... G3
Fairfield, 96178 .... D2
Fallbrook, 29100 .... J4
Fillmore, 13643 .... H3
Firebaugh, 5743 .... F3
Florin, 27653 .... D2
Ford City, 3512 .... G3
Ft. Bragg, 7026 .... C1
Fortuna, 10497 .... B1
Fremont, 203413 .... E2
Fresno, 427652 .... F3
Galt, 19472 .... D2
Gilroy, 41464 .... E2
Gonzales, 7525 .... F2
Greenacres, 7400 .... G3
Greenfield, 12583 .... F2
Gridley, 5382 .... C2
Groveland, 3388 .... E3
Grover Beach, 13067 .... G2
Guadalupe, 5659 .... G2
Half Moon Bay, 11842 .... E2
Hanford, 41686 .... F3
Healdsburg, 10722 .... D1
Hemet, 58812 .... J4
Hesperia, 62582 .... H4
Hollister, 34413 .... F2
Holtville, 5612 .... K5
Huntington Beach, 189594 .... J4
Huron, 6306 .... F3
Imperial Beach, 26992 .... K4
Indio, 49116 .... J5
Ione, 7129 .... D3
Irvine, 143072 .... J4
Isla Vista, 18344 .... H3
Jackson, 3989 .... D3
Joshua Tree, 4207 .... J5
Kelseyville, 2928 .... C2
Kerman, 8551 .... F3
King City, 11094 .... F2
Kingsburg, 9199 .... F3
Lake Elsinore, 28928 .... J4
Lake Isabella, 3315 .... G4
Lakeport, 4820 .... C2
Lamont, 13296 .... G3
Lancaster, 118718 .... H4
Lemoore, 19712 .... F3
Lincoln, 11205 .... D3
Lindsay, 10297 .... G3
Livingston, 10473 .... E3
Lockeford, 3179 .... E2
Lodi, 56999 .... D2
Lompoc, 41103 .... H2
Long Beach, 461522 .... J4
Los Angeles, 3694820 .... J4
Los Banos, 25869 .... F2
Los Osos, 14351 .... G2
Madera, 43207 .... F3
Mammoth Lakes, 7093 .... E4
Manteca, 49258 .... E2
Marina, 25101 .... F2
Martinez, 35866 .... D2
Marysville, 12268 .... D2
McFarland, 9618 .... G3
McKinleyville, 13599 .... A1
Mecca, 5402 .... J5
Mendota, 7890 .... F3
Merced, 63893 .... E3
Milpitas, 62698 .... E2
Mission Viejo, 93102 .... J4
Modesto, 188856 .... E2
Mojave, 3836 .... H4
Monterey, 29674 .... F2
Moreno Valley, 142381 .... J4
Morgan Hill, 33556 .... E2
Morro Bay, 10350 .... G2
Mt. Shasta, 3621 .... A2
Napa, 72585 .... D2
Needles, 4830 .... H6
Nevada City, 3001 .... D3
Newport Beach, 70032 .... J4
Nipomo, 12626 .... G2
Oakdale, 15503 .... E3
Oakhurst, 2868 .... E3
Oakland, 399484 .... E2
Oceanside, 161029 .... K4
Oildale, 27885 .... G3
Ojai, 7862 .... H3
Olivehurst, 11061 .... D2
Orland, 6281 .... C2
Oroville, 13004 .... C2
Oxnard, 170358 .... H3
Pacifica, 38390 .... E1
Pacific Grove, 15522 .... F2
Palermo, 5720 .... C2
Palmdale, 116670 .... H4
Palm Desert, 41155 .... J5
Palm Sprs., 42807 .... J5
Palo Alto, 58598 .... E2
Paradise, 26408 .... C3
Pasadena, 133936 .... J4
Paso Robles, 24297 .... G2
Patterson, 11606 .... E2
Petaluma, 54548 .... D2
Pismo Beach, 8551 .... G2
Placerville, 9610 .... D3
Planada, 4369 .... E3
Porterville, 39615 .... G3
Poway, 48044 .... K4
Prunedale, 16432 .... F2
Quartz Hill, 9890 .... H4
Ramona, 15691 .... K4
Red Bluff, 13147 .... C2
Redding, 80865 .... B2
Redlands, 63591 .... J4
Redwood City, 75402 .... E2
Reedley, 20756 .... F3
Richgrove, 2723 .... G3
Richmond, 99216 .... D2
Ridgecrest, 24927 .... G4
Rio Dell, 3174 .... B1
Riverside, 255166 .... J4
Rocklin, 36330 .... D3
Rosamond, 14349 .... H4
Roseville, 79921 .... D2
Sacramento, 407018 .... D2
Salinas, 151060 .... F2
San Bernardino, 185401 .... J4
San Clemente, 49936 .... J4
San Diego, 1223400 .... K4
San Fernando, 23564 .... H3
San Francisco, 776733 .... E2
Sanger, 18931 .... F3
San Joaquin, 3270 .... F3
San Jose, 894943 .... E2
San Juan Capistrano, 33826 .... J4
San Luis Obispo, 44174 .... G2
San Mateo, 92482 .... E2
San Rafael, 56063 .... D2
Santa Ana, 337977 .... J4
Santa Barbara, 92325 .... H3
Santa Clarita, 151088 .... H3
Santa Cruz, 54593 .... E2
Santa Maria, 77423 .... G2
Santa Monica, 84084 .... J3
Santa Paula, 28598 .... H3
Santa Rosa, 147595 .... D2
Santa Ynez, 4584 .... H2
Scotts Valley, 11385 .... E2
Sebastopol, 7774 .... D1
Selma, 19444 .... F3
Shafter, 12736 .... G3
Shasta Lake, 9008 .... B2
Simi Valley, 111351 .... H3
Solana Beach, 12979 .... K4
Soledad, 11263 .... F2
Solvang, 5332 .... H2
Sonoma, 9128 .... D2
Sonora, 4423 .... E3
S. Lake Tahoe, 23609 .... D3
Squaw Valley, 2691 .... F3
Stockton, 243771 .... E2
Sunnyvale, 131760 .... E2
Susanville, 13541 .... C3
Taft, 6400 .... G3
Tehachapi, 10957 .... H4
Temecula, 57716 .... J4
Templeton, 4687 .... G2
Terra Bella, 3466 .... G3
Thermalito, 6045 .... C2
Thousand Oaks, 117005 .... H3
Torrance, 137946 .... J3
Tracy, 56929 .... E2
Truckee, 13864 .... D3
Tulare, 43994 .... G3
Turlock, 55810 .... E3
Twentynine Palms, 14764 .... J5
Ukiah, 15497 .... C1
Vacaville, 88625 .... D2
Vallejo, 116760 .... D2
Vandenberg Vil., 5802 .... H2
Ventura, 100916 .... H3
Victorville, 64029 .... H4
Visalia, 91565 .... F3
Vista, 89857 .... K4
Wasco, 21263 .... G3
Watsonville, 44265 .... F2
Weaverville, 3554 .... B2
Weed, 2978 .... A2
Williams, 3670 .... C2
Willits, 5073 .... C1
Willows, 6220 .... C2
Windsor, 22744 .... D1
Woodlake, 6651 .... F3
Woodland, 49151 .... D2
Wrightwood, 3837 .... H4
Yreka, 7290 .... A2
Yuba City, 36758 .... D2
Yucaipa, 41207 .... J4

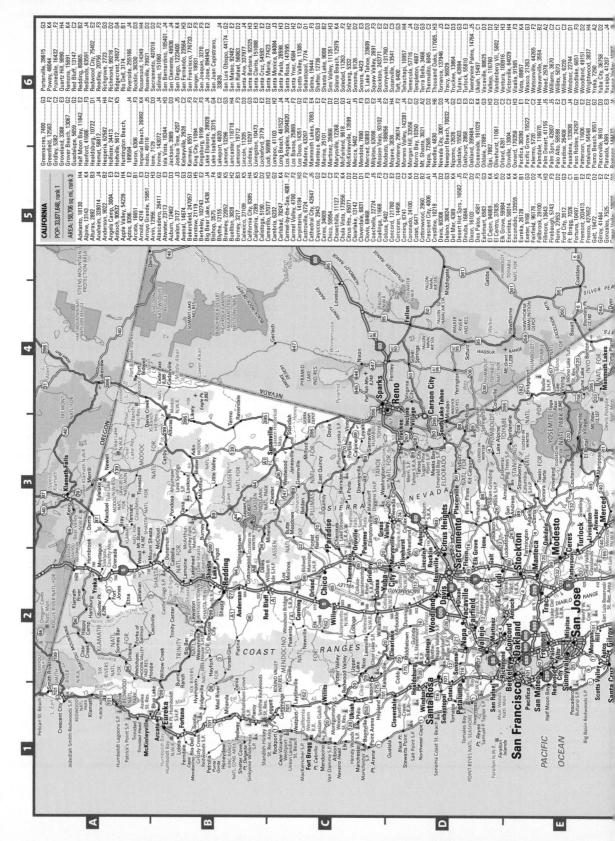

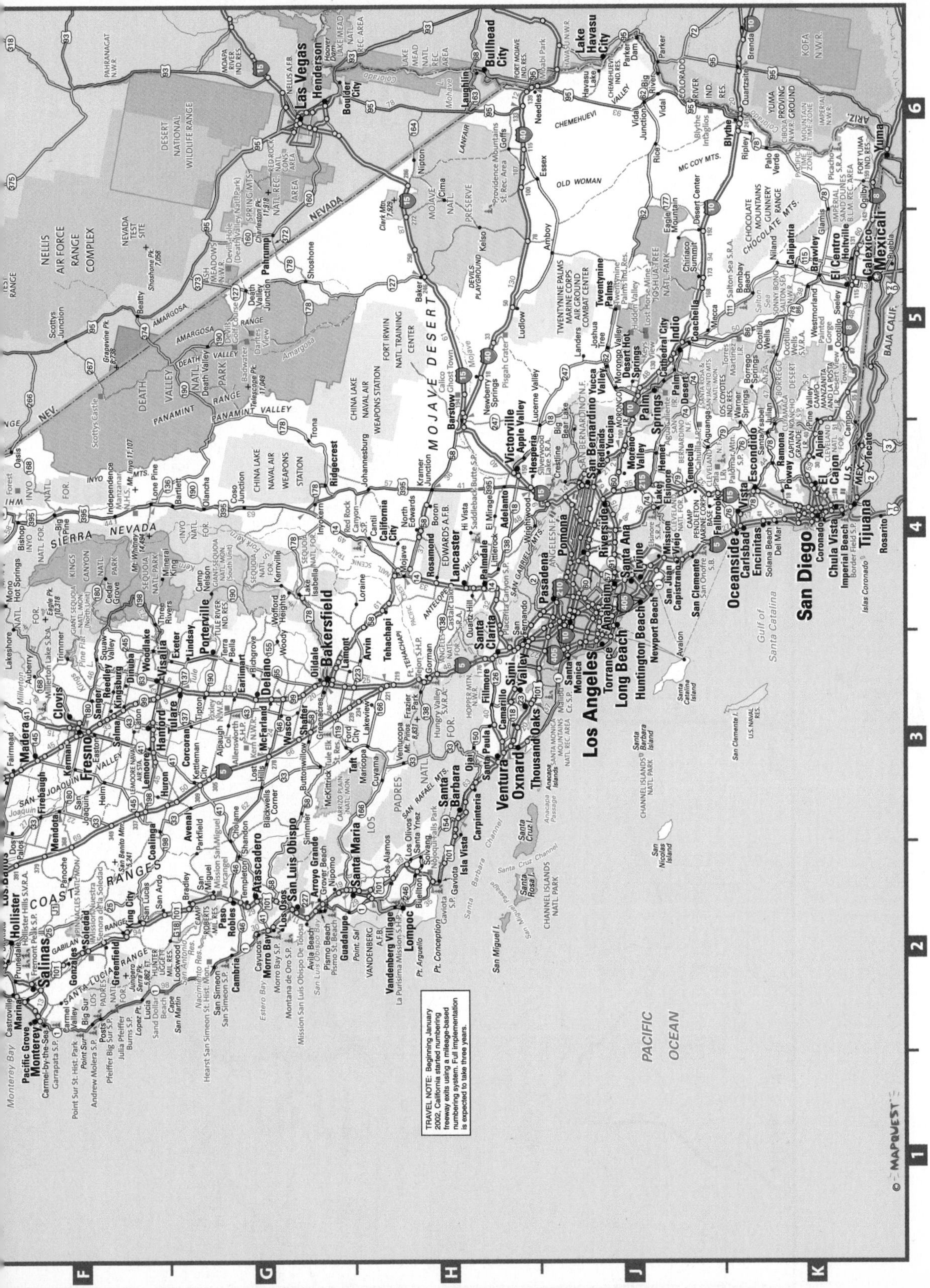
TRAVEL NOTE: Beginning January 2002, California started numbering freeway exits using a mileage-based numbering system. Full implementation is expected to take three years.
Las Vegas
Henderson
Bullhead City
Lake Havasu City
Needles
Blythe
MOJAVE DESERT
Barstow
Victorville
Bakersfield
Fresno
Los Angeles
Long Beach
San Diego
Santa Barbara
San Luis Obispo
Salinas
Monterey
Ventura
Oxnard
Riverside
San Bernardino
Palm Springs
Indio
El Centro
Mexicali
Tijuana
Yuma
PACIFIC OCEAN
NEVADA
MAPQUEST

SAN FRANCISCO, CA & VICINITY
Petaluma
Novato
Napa
American Canyon
Vallejo
Benicia
Fairfield
Cordelia
Birds Landing
Collinsville
MONTEZUMA HILLS
Antioch
Oakley
Brentwood
Pittsburg
Bay Point
Concord
Clayton
Walnut Creek
Pleasant Hill
Martinez
Pacheco
Vine Hill
Clyde
Lafayette
Orinda
Moraga
Alamo
Danville
San Ramon
Diablo
Mt. Diablo 3,849
Mt. Diablo State Park
BLACK HILLS
Crockett
Port Costa
Rodeo
Hercules
Pinole
El Sobrante
San Pablo
Richmond
North Richmond
El Cerrito
Kensington
Albany
Berkeley
Emeryville
Piedmont
Oakland
Alameda
San Francisco
Sausalito
Tiburon
Belvedere
Mill Valley
Corte Madera
Larkspur
Kentfield
Ross
San Anselmo
Fairfax
San Rafael
Santa Venetia
Marinwood
Ignacio
Black Point
Tamalpais Valley
Homestead Valley
Muir Beach
Stinson Beach
Bolinas
Woodacre
San Geronimo
San Pablo Bay
Grizzly Bay
Suisun Bay
Carquinez Strait
Mare Island
Alcatraz Island
Treasure Island
Angel Island State Park
Skaggs Island
Tubbs Island
Russ Island
Joyce Island
Grizzly Island
Simmons Island
Wheeler Island
Van Sickle Island
Chipps Island
Winter Island
Browns Island
Ryer Island
Roe Island
Morrow Island
Sherman Island
Decker Island
Jersey Island
Golden Gate National Recreation Area
Muir Woods Natl. Mon.
Mt. Tamalpais State Park
Mt. Tamalpais 2,571
Point Bonita
Point Lobos
SONOMA CO.
NAPA CO.
SOLANO CO.
CONTRA COSTA CO.
MARIN CO.
ALAMEDA CO.
SAN FRANCISCO CO.
SACRAMENTO CO.
San Rafael Bridge
Golden Gate Bridge
Bay Bridge

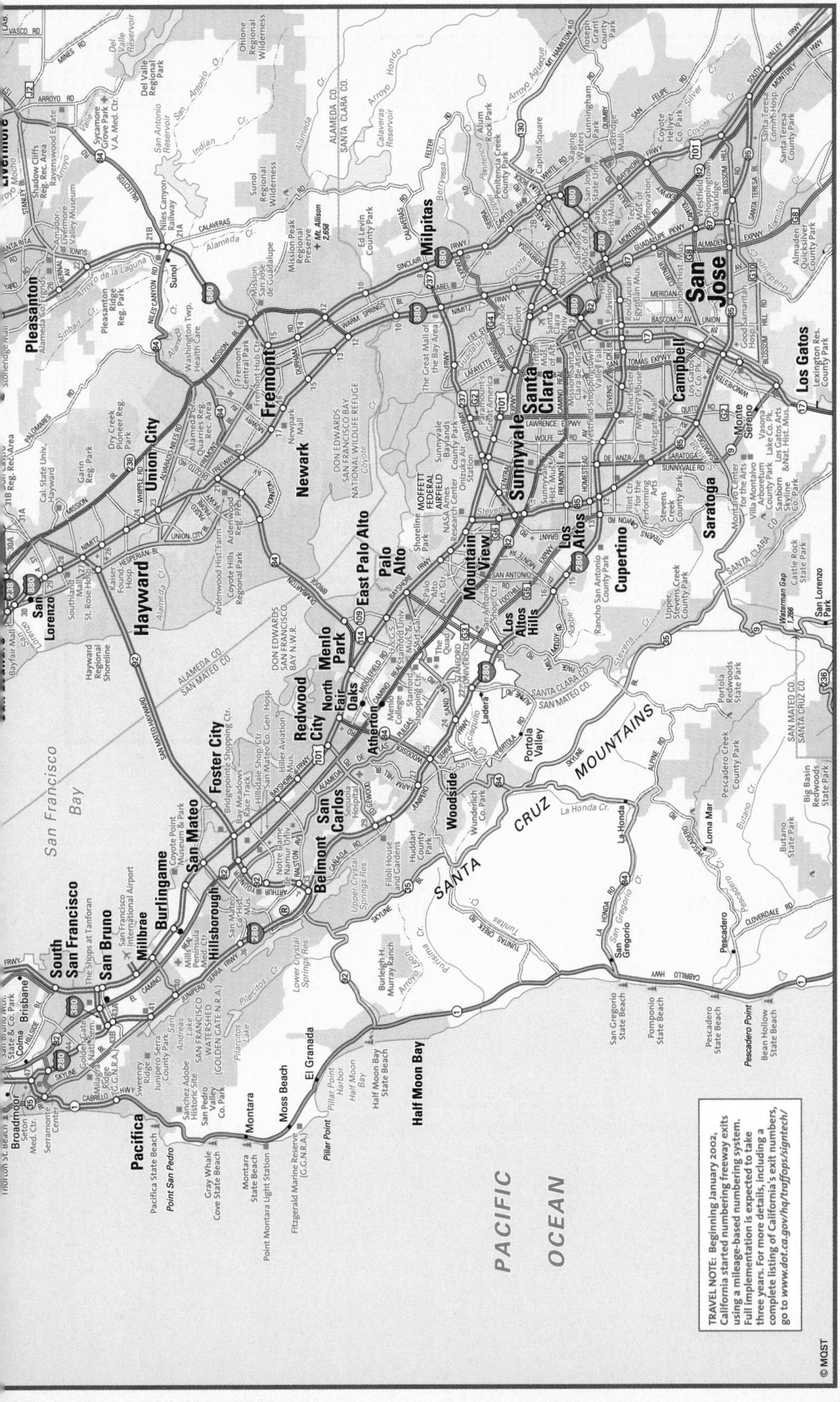
PACIFIC
OCEAN
San Francisco Bay
SANTA CRUZ MOUNTAINS
Pleasanton
Fremont
Union City
Newark
Hayward
San Lorenzo
Milpitas
San Jose
Santa Clara
Sunnyvale
Mountain View
Palo Alto
East Palo Alto
Menlo Park
North Fair Oaks
Atherton
Redwood City
Foster City
San Mateo
Belmont
San Carlos
Woodside
Portola Valley
Los Altos
Los Altos Hills
Cupertino
Campbell
Saratoga
Monte Sereno
Los Gatos
Burlingame
Hillsborough
Millbrae
San Bruno
South San Francisco
Brisbane
Colma
Broadmoor
Pacifica
Montara
Moss Beach
El Granada
Half Moon Bay
San Gregorio
La Honda
Loma Mar
Pescadero
Sunol
ALAMEDA CO.
SANTA CLARA CO.
SAN MATEO CO.
SANTA CRUZ CO.
TRAVEL NOTE: Beginning January 2002, California started numbering freeway exits using a mileage-based numbering system. Full implementation is expected to take three years. For more details, including a complete listing of California's exit numbers, go to www.dot.ca.gov/hq/traffops/signtech/
© MOST

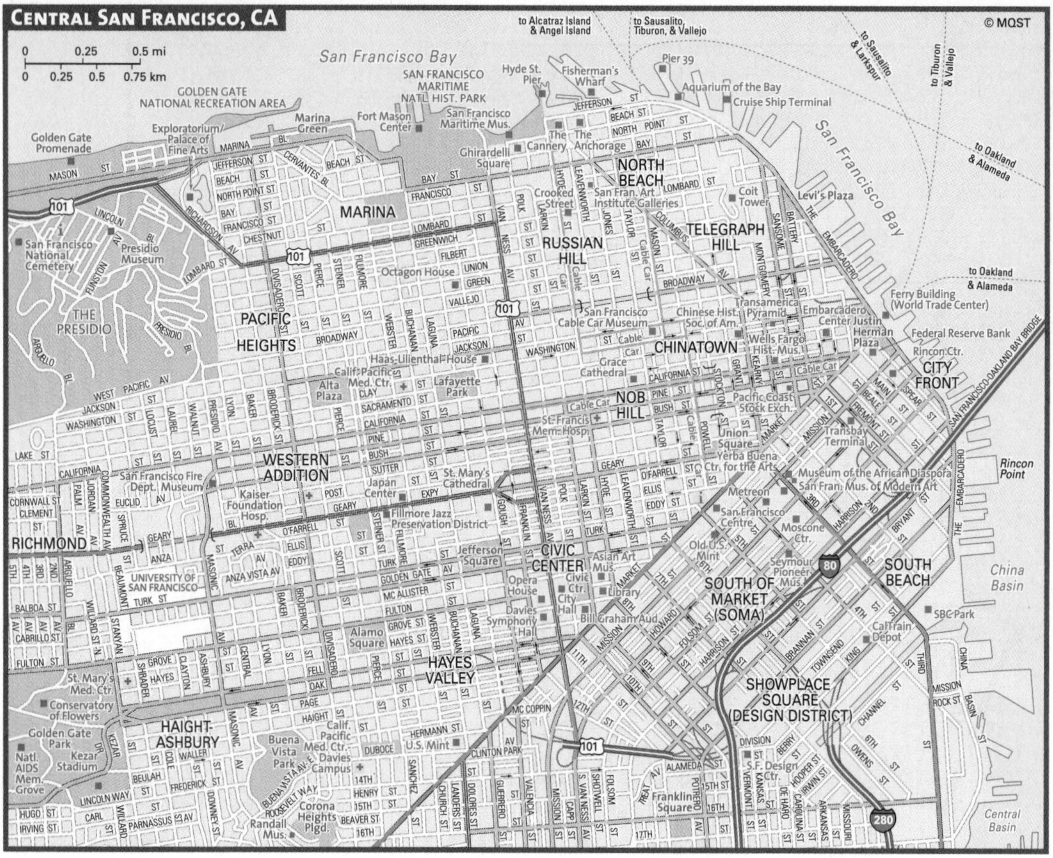

CENTRAL SAN FRANCISCO, CA
© MQST
0 0.25 0.5 mi
0 0.25 0.5 0.75 km
San Francisco Bay
to Alcatraz Island & Angel Island
to Sausalito, Tiburon, & Vallejo
to Sausalito & Larkspur
to Tiburon & Vallejo
to Oakland & Alameda
to Oakland & Alameda
GOLDEN GATE NATIONAL RECREATION AREA
SAN FRANCISCO MARITIME NATL. HIST. PARK
Hyde St. Pier
Fisherman's Wharf
Pier 39
Aquarium of the Bay
Cruise Ship Terminal
Golden Gate Promenade
Exploratorium/Palace of Fine Arts
Marina Green
Fort Mason Center
San Francisco Maritime Mus.
Ghirardelli Square
The Cannery
The Anchorage
NORTH BEACH
San Fran. Art Institute Galleries
Crooked Street
Coit Tower
Levi's Plaza
San Francisco Bay
MARINA
TELEGRAPH HILL
RUSSIAN HILL
San Francisco National Cemetery
Presidio Museum
THE PRESIDIO
Octagon House
PACIFIC HEIGHTS
San Francisco Cable Car Museum
Chinese Hist. Soc. of Am.
Transamerica Pyramid
Embarcadero Center
Justin Herman Plaza
Ferry Building (World Trade Center)
Federal Reserve Bank
Rincon Ctr.
CITY FRONT
Wells Fargo Hist. Mus.
CHINATOWN
Grace Cathedral
Haas-Lilienthal House
Calif. Pacific Med. Ctr.
Alta Plaza
Lafayette Park
NOB HILL
Pacific Coast Stock Exch.
St. Francis Mem. Hosp.
Union Square
Transbay Terminal
Yerba Buena Ctr. for the Arts
WESTERN ADDITION
San Francisco Fire Dept. Museum
Kaiser Foundation Hosp.
Japan Center
St. Mary's Cathedral
Museum of the African Diaspora
San Fran. Mus. of Modern Art
Metreon
San Francisco Centre
Moscone Ctr.
Rincon Point
Fillmore Jazz Preservation District
RICHMOND
Jefferson Square
CIVIC CENTER
Asian Art Mus.
Old U.S. Mint
Seymour Pioneer Mus.
SOUTH BEACH
UNIVERSITY OF SAN FRANCISCO
Opera House
Civic Ctr.
City Hall
Library
Bill Graham Aud.
SOUTH OF MARKET (SOMA)
China Basin
SBC Park
CalTrain Depot
Davies Symphony Hall
Alamo Square
HAYES VALLEY
SHOWPLACE SQUARE (DESIGN DISTRICT)
St. Mary's Med. Ctr.
Conservatory of Flowers
Golden Gate Park
Natl. AIDS Mem. Grove
Kezar Stadium
HAIGHT-ASHBURY
Buena Vista Park
Calif. Pacific Med. Ctr. Davies Campus
U.S. Mint
S.F. Design Ctr.
Franklin Square
Corona Heights Plgd.
Randall Mus.
Central Basin
101
80
280
SAN FRANCISCO-OAKLAND BAY BRIDGE
THE EMBARCADERO

Distances in chart are in miles.
To convert miles to kilometers, multiply the distance in miles by 1.609

Example:
New York, NY to Boston, MA
= 215 miles or 346 kilometers
(215 x 1.609)

	ALBUQUERQUE, NM	ATLANTA, GA	BALTIMORE, MD	BILLINGS, MT	BIRMINGHAM, AL	BISMARCK, ND	BOISE, ID	BOSTON, MA	BUFFALO, NY	BURLINGTON, VT	CHARLESTON, SC	CHARLESTON, WV	CHARLOTTE, NC	CHEYENNE, WY	CHICAGO, IL	CINCINNATI, OH	CLEVELAND, OH	DALLAS, TX	DENVER, CO	DES MOINES, IA	DETROIT, MI	EL PASO, TX	HOUSTON, TX	INDIANAPOLIS, IN	JACKSON, MS	KANSAS CITY, MO	LAS VEGAS, NV	LITTLE ROCK, AR	LOS ANGELES, CA
ALBUQUERQUE, NM		1490	1902	991	1274	1333	966	2240	1808	2178	1793	1568	1649	538	1352	1409	1619	754	438	1091	1608	263	994	1298	1157	894	578	900	806
ATLANTA, GA	1490		679	1889	150	1559	2218	1100	910	1158	317	503	238	1482	717	476	726	792	1403	967	735	1437	800	531	386	801	2067	528	2237
BALTIMORE, MD	1902	679		1959	795	1551	2401	422	370	481	583	352	441	1665	708	521	377	1399	1690	1031	532	2045	1470	600	1032	1087	2445	1072	2705
BILLINGS, MT	991	1889	1959		1839	413	626	2254	1796	2181	2157	1755	2012	455	1246	1552	1597	1433	554	1007	1534	1255	1673	1432	1836	1088	965	1530	1239
BIRMINGHAM, AL	1274	150	795	1839		1509	2170	1215	909	1241	466	578	389	1434	667	475	725	647	1356	919	734	1292	678	481	241	753	1852	381	2092
BISMARCK, ND	1333	1559	1551	413	1509		1039	1846	1388	1773	1749	1347	1604	594	838	1144	1189	1342	693	675	1126	1597	1582	1024	1548	801	1378	1183	1702
BOISE, ID	966	2218	2401	626	2170	1039		2697	2239	2624	2520	2182	2375	737	1708	1969	2040	1711	833	1369	1977	1206	1952	1852	2115	1376	760	1808	1033
BOSTON, MA	2240	1100	422	2254	1215	1846	2697		462	214	1003	741	861	1961	1003	862	654	1819	2004	1326	741	2465	1890	940	1453	1427	2757	1493	3046
BUFFALO, NY	1808	910	370	1796	909	1388	2239	462		375	899	431	695	1502	545	442	197	1393	1546	868	277	2039	1513	508	1134	995	2299	1066	2572
BURLINGTON, VT	2178	1158	481	2181	1241	1773	2624	214	375		1061	782	919	1887	930	817	567	1763	1931	1253	652	2409	1916	878	1479	1366	2684	1437	2957
CHARLESTON, SC	1793	317	583	2157	466	1749	2520	1003	899	1061		468	204	1783	907	622	724	1109	1705	1204	879	1754	1110	721	703	1102	2371	900	2554
CHARLESTON, WV	1568	503	352	1755	578	1347	2182	741	431	782	468		265	1445	506	209	255	1072	1367	802	410	1718	1192	320	816	764	2122	745	2374
CHARLOTTE, NC	1649	238	441	2012	389	1604	2375	861	695	919	204	265		1637	761	476	520	1031	1559	1057	675	1677	1041	575	625	956	2225	754	2453
CHEYENNE, WY	538	1482	1665	455	1434	594	737	1961	1502	1887	1783	1445	1637		972	1233	1304	979	100	633	1241	801	1220	1115	1382	640	843	1076	1116
CHICAGO, IL	1352	717	708	1246	667	838	1708	1003	545	930	907	506	761	972		302	346	936	1015	337	283	1543	1108	184	750	532	1768	662	2042
CINCINNATI, OH	1409	476	521	1552	475	1144	1969	862	442	817	622	209	476	1233	302		253	958	1200	599	261	1605	1079	116	700	597	1955	632	2215
CLEVELAND, OH	1619	726	377	1597	725	1189	2040	654	197	567	724	255	520	1304	346	253		1208	1347	669	171	1854	1328	319	950	806	2100	882	2374
DALLAS, TX	754	792	1399	1433	647	1342	1711	1819	1393	1763	1109	1072	1031	979	936	958	1208		887	752	1218	647	241	913	406	554	1331	327	1446
DENVER, CO	438	1403	1690	554	1356	693	833	2004	1546	1931	1705	1367	1559	100	1015	1200	1347	887		676	1284	701	1127	1088	1290	603	756	984	1029
DES MOINES, IA	1091	967	1031	1007	919	675	1369	1326	868	1253	1204	802	1057	633	337	599	669	752	676		606	1283	992	481	931	194	1429	567	1703
DETROIT, MI	1608	735	532	1534	734	1126	1977	741	277	652	879	410	675	1241	283	261	171	1218	1284	606		1799	1338	318	960	795	2037	891	2310
EL PASO, TX	263	1437	2045	1255	1292	1597	1206	2465	2039	2409	1754	1718	1677	801	1543	1605	1854	647	701	1283	1799		758	1489	1051	1085	717	974	801
HOUSTON, TX	994	800	1470	1673	678	1582	1952	1890	1513	1916	1110	1192	1041	1220	1108	1079	1328	241	1127	992	1338	758		1033	445	795	1474	447	1558
INDIANAPOLIS, IN	1298	531	600	1432	481	1024	1852	940	508	878	721	320	575	1115	184	116	319	913	1088	481	318	1489	1033		675	485	1843	587	2104
JACKSON, MS	1157	386	1032	1836	241	1548	2115	1453	1134	1479	703	816	625	1382	750	700	950	406	1290	931	960	1051	445	675		747	1735	269	1851
KANSAS CITY, MO	894	801	1087	1088	753	801	1376	1427	995	1366	1102	764	956	640	532	597	806	554	603	194	795	1085	795	485	747		1358	382	1632
LAS VEGAS, NV	578	2067	2445	965	1852	1378	760	2757	2299	2684	2371	2122	2225	843	1768	1955	2100	1331	756	1429	2037	717	1474	1843	1735	1358		1478	274
LITTLE ROCK, AR	900	528	1072	1530	381	1183	1808	1493	1066	1437	900	745	754	1076	662	632	882	327	984	567	891	974	447	587	269	382	1478		1706
LOS ANGELES, CA	806	2237	2705	1239	2092	1702	1033	3046	2572	2957	2554	2374	2453	1116	2042	2215	2374	1446	1029	1703	2310	801	1558	2104	1851	1632	274	1706	
LOUISVILLE, KY	1320	419	602	1547	369	1139	1933	964	545	915	610	251	464	1197	299	106	356	852	1118	595	366	1499	972	112	594	516	1874	526	2126
MEMPHIS, TN	1033	389	933	1625	241	1337	1954	1353	927	1297	760	606	614	1217	539	493	742	466	1116	720	752	1112	586	464	211	536	1611	140	1839
MIAMI, FL	2155	661	1109	2554	812	2224	2883	1529	1425	1587	583	994	730	2147	1382	1141	1250	1367	2069	1632	1401	1959	1201	1196	915	1466	2733	1190	2759
MILWAUKEE, WI	1426	813	805	1175	763	767	1748	1100	642	1027	1003	601	857	1012	89	398	443	1010	1055	378	380	1617	1193	279	835	573	1808	747	2082
MINNEAPOLIS, MN	1339	1129	1121	839	1079	431	1465	1417	958	1343	1319	918	1173	881	409	714	760	999	924	246	697	1530	1240	596	1151	441	1677	814	1951
MONTRÉAL, QC	2172	1241	564	2093	1289	1685	2535	313	397	92	1145	822	1003	1799	841	815	588	1772	1843	1165	564	2363	1892	872	1514	1359	2596	1446	2869
NASHVILLE, TN	1248	242	716	1648	194	1315	1976	1136	716	1086	543	395	397	1240	474	281	531	681	1162	725	541	1328	801	287	423	559	1826	355	2054
NEW ORLEANS, LA	1276	473	1142	1955	351	1734	2234	1563	1254	1588	783	926	713	1502	935	820	1070	525	1409	1117	1079	1118	360	826	185	932	1854	455	1917
NEW YORK, NY	2015	869	192	2049	985	1641	2491	215	400	299	773	515	631	1755	797	636	466	1589	1799	1121	622	2235	1660	715	1223	1202	2552	1262	2820
OKLAHOMA CITY, OK	546	944	1354	1227	729	1136	1506	1694	1262	1632	1248	1022	1102	773	807	863	1073	209	681	546	1062	737	449	752	612	348	1124	355	1352
OMAHA, NE	973	989	1168	904	941	616	1234	1463	1005	1390	1290	952	1144	497	474	736	806	669	541	136	743	1236	910	618	935	188	1294	570	1567
ORLANDO, FL	1934	440	904	2333	591	2003	2662	1324	1221	1383	379	790	525	1926	1161	920	1045	1146	1847	1411	1180	1738	980	975	694	1245	2512	969	2538
PHILADELPHIA, PA	1954	782	104	2019	897	1611	2462	321	414	371	685	454	543	1725	768	576	437	1501	1744	1091	592	2147	1572	655	1135	1141	2500	1175	2760
PHOENIX, AZ	466	1868	2366	1199	1723	1662	993	2706	2274	2644	2184	2035	2107	1004	1819	1876	2085	1077	904	1558	2074	432	1188	1764	1482	1360	285	1367	369
PITTSBURGH, PA	1670	676	246	1719	763	1311	2161	592	217	587	642	217	438	1425	467	292	136	1246	1460	791	292	1893	1366	370	988	857	2215	920	2476
PORTLAND, ME	2338	1197	520	2352	1313	1944	2795	107	560	233	1101	839	959	2059	1101	960	751	1917	2102	1424	838	2563	1988	1038	1550	1525	2855	1590	3144
PORTLAND, OR	1395	2647	2830	889	2599	1301	432	3126	2667	3052	2948	2610	2802	1166	2137	2398	2469	2140	1261	1798	2405	1767	2381	2280	2544	1805	1188	2237	971
RAPID CITY, SD	841	1511	1626	379	1463	320	930	1921	1463	1848	1824	1422	1678	305	913	1219	1264	1077	404	629	1201	1105	1318	1101	1458	710	1035	1093	1309
RENO, NV	1020	2440	2623	960	2392	1372	430	2919	2460	2845	2741	2403	2595	959	1930	2191	2262	1933	1054	1591	2198	1315	2072	2073	2337	1598	442	2030	519
RICHMOND, VA	1876	527	152	2053	678	1645	2496	572	485	630	428	322	289	1760	802	530	471	1309	1688	1126	627	1955	1330	641	914	1085	2444	983	2682
ST. LOUIS, MO	1051	549	841	1341	501	1053	1628	1181	749	1119	850	512	704	892	294	350	560	635	855	436	549	1242	863	239	505	252	1610	416	1856
SALT LAKE CITY, UT	624	1916	2100	548	1868	960	342	2395	1936	2322	2218	1880	2072	436	1406	1667	1738	1410	531	1067	1675	864	1650	1549	1813	1074	417	1507	691
SAN ANTONIO, TX	818	1000	1671	1500	878	1599	1761	2092	1665	2036	1310	1344	1241	1046	1270	1231	1481	271	946	1009	1490	556	200	1186	644	812	1272	600	1356
SAN DIEGO, CA	825	2166	2724	1302	2021	1765	1096	3065	2632	3020	2483	2393	2405	1179	2105	2234	2437	1375	1092	1766	2373	730	1487	2122	1780	1695	337	1703	124
SAN FRANCISCO, CA	1111	2618	2840	1176	2472	1749	646	3135	2677	3062	2934	2620	2759	1176	2146	2407	2478	1827	1271	1807	2415	1181	1938	2290	2232	1814	575	2012	385
SEATTLE, WA	1463	2705	2775	816	2657	1229	500	3070	2612	2997	2973	2571	2827	1234	2062	2368	2413	2208	1329	1822	2350	1944	2449	2249	2612	1872	1256	2305	1148
TAMPA, FL	1949	455	960	2348	606	2018	2677	1380	1276	1438	434	845	581	1941	1176	935	1101	1161	1862	1426	1194	1753	995	990	709	1259	2526	984	2553
TORONTO, ON	1841	958	565	1762	958	1354	2204	570	106	419	1006	537	802	1468	510	484	303	1441	1512	834	233	2032	1561	541	1183	1028	2265	1115	2538
VANCOUVER, BC	1597	2838	2908	949	2791	1362	633	3204	2745	3130	3106	2705	2960	1368	2196	2501	2547	2342	1463	1956	2483	2087	2583	2383	2746	2007	1390	2439	1291
WASHINGTON, DC	1896	636	38	1953	758	1545	2395	458	384	517	539	346	397	1659	701	517	370	1362	1686	1025	526	2008	1433	596	996	1083	2441	1036	2702
WICHITA, KS	707	989	1276	1067	838	934	1346	1616	1184	1554	1291	953	1145	613	728	785	995	367	521	390	984	898	608	674	771	192	1276	464	1513

	LOUISVILLE, KY	MEMPHIS, TN	MIAMI, FL	MILWAUKEE, WI	MINNEAPOLIS, MN	MONTRÉAL, QC	NASHVILLE, TN	NEW ORLEANS, LA	NEW YORK, NY	OKLAHOMA CITY, OK	OMAHA, NE	ORLANDO, FL	PHILADELPHIA, PA	PHOENIX, AZ	PITTSBURGH, PA	PORTLAND, ME	PORTLAND, OR	RAPID CITY, SD	RENO, NV	RICHMOND, VA	ST. LOUIS, MO	SALT LAKE CITY, UT	SAN ANTONIO, TX	SAN DIEGO, CA	SAN FRANCISCO, CA	SEATTLE, WA	TAMPA, FL	TORONTO, ON	VANCOUVER, BC	WASHINGTON,DC	WICHITA, KS
ALBUQUERQUE, NM	1320	1033	2155	1426	1339	2172	1248	1276	2015	546	973	1934	1954	466	1670	2338	1395	841	1020	1876	1051	624	818	825	1111	1463	1949	1841	1597	1896	707
ATLANTA, GA	419	389	661	813	1129	1241	242	473	869	944	989	440	782	1868	676	1197	2647	1511	2440	527	549	1916	1000	2166	2618	2705	455	958	2838	636	989
BALTIMORE, MD	602	933	1109	805	1121	564	716	1142	192	1354	1168	904	104	2366	246	520	2830	1626	2623	152	841	2100	1671	2724	2840	2775	960	565	2908	38	1276
BILLINGS, MT	1547	1625	2554	1175	839	2093	1648	1955	2049	1227	904	2333	2019	1199	1719	2352	889	379	960	2053	1341	548	1500	1302	1176	816	2348	1762	949	1953	1067
BIRMINGHAM, AL	369	241	812	763	1079	1289	194	351	985	729	941	591	897	1723	763	1313	2599	1463	2392	678	501	1868	878	2021	2472	2657	606	958	2791	758	838
BISMARCK, ND	1139	1337	2224	767	431	1685	1315	1734	1641	1136	616	2003	1611	1662	1311	1944	1301	320	1372	1645	1053	960	1599	1765	1749	1229	2018	1354	1362	1545	934
BOISE, ID	1933	1954	2883	1748	1465	2535	1976	2234	2491	1506	1234	2662	2462	993	2161	2795	432	930	430	2496	1628	342	1761	1096	646	500	2677	2204	633	2395	1346
BOSTON, MA	964	1353	1529	1100	1417	313	1136	1563	215	1694	1463	1324	321	2706	592	107	3126	1921	2919	572	1181	2395	2092	3065	3135	3070	1380	570	3204	458	1616
BUFFALO, NY	545	927	1425	642	958	397	716	1254	400	1262	1005	1221	414	2274	217	560	2667	1463	2460	485	749	1936	1665	2632	2677	2612	1276	106	2745	384	1184
BURLINGTON, VT	915	1297	1587	1027	1343	92	1086	1588	299	1632	1390	1383	371	2644	587	233	3052	1848	2845	630	1119	2322	2036	3020	3062	2997	1438	419	3130	517	1554
CHARLESTON, SC	610	760	583	1003	1319	1145	543	783	773	1248	1290	379	685	2184	642	1101	2948	1824	2741	428	850	2218	1310	2483	2934	2973	434	1006	3106	539	1291
CHARLESTON, WV	251	606	994	601	918	822	395	926	515	1022	952	790	454	2035	217	839	2610	1422	2403	322	512	1880	1344	2393	2620	2571	845	537	2705	346	953
CHARLOTTE, NC	464	614	730	857	1173	1003	397	713	631	1102	1144	525	543	2107	438	959	2802	1678	2595	289	704	2072	1241	2405	2759	2827	581	802	2960	397	1145
CHEYENNE, WY	1197	1217	2147	1012	881	1799	1240	1502	1755	773	497	1926	1725	1004	1425	2059	1166	305	959	1760	892	436	1046	1179	1176	1234	1941	1468	1368	1659	613
CHICAGO, IL	299	539	1382	89	409	841	474	935	797	807	474	1161	768	1819	467	1101	2137	913	1930	802	294	1406	1270	2105	2146	2062	1176	510	2196	701	728
CINCINNATI, OH	106	493	1141	398	714	815	281	820	636	863	736	920	576	1876	292	960	2398	1219	2191	530	350	1667	1231	2234	2407	2368	935	484	2501	517	785
CLEVELAND, OH	356	742	1250	443	760	588	531	1070	466	1073	806	1045	437	2085	136	751	2469	1264	2262	471	560	1738	1481	2437	2478	2413	1101	303	2547	370	995
DALLAS, TX	852	466	1367	1010	999	1772	681	525	1589	209	669	1146	1501	1077	1246	1917	2140	1077	1933	1309	635	1410	271	1375	1827	2208	1161	1441	2342	1362	367
DENVER, CO	1118	1116	2069	1055	924	1843	1162	1409	1799	681	541	1847	1744	904	1460	2102	1261	404	1054	1688	855	531	946	1092	1271	1329	1862	1512	1463	1686	521
DES MOINES, IA	595	720	1632	378	246	1165	725	1117	1121	546	136	1411	1091	1558	791	1424	1798	629	1591	1126	436	1067	1009	1766	1807	1822	1426	834	1956	1025	390
DETROIT, MI	366	752	1401	380	697	564	541	1079	622	1062	743	1180	592	2074	292	838	2405	1201	2198	627	549	1675	1490	2373	2415	2350	1194	233	2483	526	984
EL PASO, TX	1499	1112	1959	1617	1530	2363	1328	1118	2235	737	1236	1738	2147	432	1893	2563	1767	1105	1315	1955	1242	864	556	730	1181	1944	1753	2032	2087	2008	898
HOUSTON, TX	972	586	1201	1193	1240	1892	801	360	1660	449	910	980	1572	1188	1366	1988	2381	1318	2072	1330	863	1650	200	1487	1938	2449	995	1561	2583	1433	608
INDIANAPOLIS, IN	112	464	1196	279	596	872	287	826	715	752	618	975	655	1764	370	1038	2280	1101	2073	641	239	1549	1186	2122	2290	2249	990	541	2383	596	674
JACKSON, MS	594	211	915	835	1151	1514	423	185	1223	612	935	694	1135	1482	988	1550	2544	1458	2337	914	505	1813	644	1780	2232	2612	709	1183	2746	996	771
KANSAS CITY, MO	516	536	1466	573	441	1359	559	932	1202	348	188	1245	1141	1360	857	1525	1805	710	1598	1085	252	1074	812	1695	1814	1872	1259	1028	2007	1083	192
LAS VEGAS, NV	1874	1611	2733	1808	1677	2596	1826	1854	2552	1124	1294	2512	2500	285	2215	2855	1188	1035	442	2444	1610	417	1272	337	575	1256	2526	2265	1390	2441	1276
LITTLE ROCK, AR	526	140	1190	747	814	1446	355	455	1262	355	570	969	1175	1367	920	1590	2237	1093	2030	983	416	1507	600	1703	2012	2305	984	1115	2439	1036	464
LOS ANGELES, CA	2126	1839	2759	2082	1951	2869	2054	1917	2820	1352	1567	2538	2760	369	2476	3144	971	1309	519	2682	1856	691	1356	124	385	1148	2553	2538	1291	2702	1513
LOUISVILLE, KY		386	1084	394	711	920	175	714	739	774	704	863	678	1786	394	1062	2362	1215	2155	572	264	1631	1125	2144	2372	2364	878	589	2497	596	705
MEMPHIS, TN	386		1051	624	940	1306	215	396	1123	487	724	830	1035	1500	780	1451	2382	1247	2175	843	294	1652	739	1841	2144	2440	845	975	2574	896	597
MIAMI, FL	1084	1051		1478	1794	1671	907	874	1299	1609	1654	232	1211	2390	1167	1627	3312	2176	3105	954	1214	2581	1401	2688	3140	3370	274	1532	3504	1065	1655
MILWAUKEE, WI	394	624	1478		337	939	569	1020	894	880	514	1257	865	1892	564	1198	2063	842	1970	899	367	1446	1343	2145	2186	1991	1272	607	2124	799	769
MINNEAPOLIS, MN	711	940	1794	337		1255	886	1337	1211	793	383	1573	1181	1805	881	1515	1727	606	1839	1216	621	1315	1257	2014	2055	1654	1588	924	1788	1115	637
MONTRÉAL, QC	920	1306	1671	939	1255		1094	1632	383	1625	1300	1466	454	2637	607	282	2963	1758	2756	714	1112	2232	2043	2931	2972	2907	1522	330	3041	600	1547
NASHVILLE, TN	175	215	907	569	886	1094		539	906	703	747	686	818	1715	569	1234	2405	1269	2198	626	307	1675	954	2056	2360	2463	701	764	2597	679	748
NEW ORLEANS, LA	714	396	874	1020	1337	1632	539		1332	731	1121	653	1245	1548	1108	1660	2663	1643	2431	1002	690	1932	560	1846	2298	2731	668	1302	2865	1106	890
NEW YORK, NY	739	1123	1299	894	1211	383	906	1332		1469	1258	1094	91	2481	367	313	2920	1716	2713	342	956	2189	1861	2839	2929	2864	1150	507	2998	228	1391
OKLAHOMA CITY, OK	774	487	1609	880	793	1625	703	731	1469		463	1388	1408	1012	1124	1792	1934	871	1727	1331	505	1204	466	1370	1657	2002	1403	1295	2136	1350	161
OMAHA, NE	704	724	1654	514	383	1300	747	1121	1258	463		1433	1228	1440	928	1561	1662	525	1455	1263	440	932	927	1630	1672	1719	1448	971	1853	1162	307
ORLANDO, FL	863	830	232	1257	1573	1466	686	653	1094	1388	1433		1006	2169	963	1422	3091	1955	2884	750	993	2360	1180	2467	2918	3149	82	1327	3283	860	1434
PHILADELPHIA, PA	678	1035	1211	865	1181	454	818	1245	91	1408	1228	1006		2420	306	419	2890	1686	2683	254	895	2160	1774	2779	2900	2835	1062	522	2968	140	1330
PHOENIX, AZ	1786	1500	2390	1892	1805	2637	1715	1548	2481	1012	1440	2169	2420		2136	2804	1335	1308	883	2343	1517	651	987	358	750	1513	2184	2307	1655	2362	1173
PITTSBURGH, PA	394	780	1167	564	881	607	569	1108	367	1124	928	963	306	2136		690	2590	1386	2383	341	611	1859	1519	2494	2599	2534	1019	321	2668	240	1046
PORTLAND, ME	1062	1451	1627	1198	1515	282	1234	1660	313	1792	1561	1422	419	2804	690		3223	2019	3016	670	1279	2493	2189	3162	3233	3168	1478	668	3301	556	1714
PORTLAND, OR	2362	2382	3312	2063	1727	2963	2405	2663	2920	1934	1662	3091	2890	1335	2590	3223		1268	578	2925	2057	771	2322	1093	638	170	3106	2633	313	2824	1775
RAPID CITY, SD	1215	1247	2176	842	606	1758	1269	1643	1716	871	525	1955	1686	1308	1386	2019	1268		1151	1720	963	628	1335	1372	1368	1195	1970	1429	1328	1620	712
RENO, NV	2155	2175	3105	1970	1839	2756	2198	2431	2713	1727	1455	2884	2683	883	2383	3016	578	1151		2718	1850	524	1870	642	217	755	2899	2426	898	2617	1568
RICHMOND, VA	572	843	954	899	1216	714	626	1002	342	1331	1263	750	254	2343	341	670	2925	1720	2718		834	2194	1530	2684	2934	2869	805	660	3003	108	1274
ST. LOUIS, MO	264	294	1214	367	621	1112	307	690	956	505	440	993	895	1517	611	1279	2057	963	1850	834		1326	968	1875	2066	2125	1008	782	2259	837	441
SALT LAKE CITY, UT	1631	1652	2581	1446	1315	2232	1675	1932	2189	1204	932	2360	2160	651	1859	2493	771	628	524	2194	1326		1419	754	740	839	2375	1902	973	2094	1044
SAN ANTONIO, TX	1125	739	1401	1343	1257	2043	954	560	1861	466	927	1180	1774	987	1519	2189	2322	1335	1870	1530	968	1419		1285	1737	2275	1195	1714	2410	1635	624
SAN DIEGO, CA	2144	1841	2688	2145	2014	2931	2056	1846	2839	1370	1630	2467	2779	358	2494	3162	1093	1372	642	2684	1875	754	1285		508	1271	2481	2601	1414	2720	1531
SAN FRANCISCO, CA	2372	2144	3140	2186	2055	2972	2360	2298	2929	1657	1672	2918	2900	750	2599	3233	638	1368	217	2934	2066	740	1737	508		816	2933	2643	958	2834	1784
SEATTLE, WA	2364	2440	3370	1991	1654	2907	2463	2731	2864	2002	1719	3149	2835	1513	2534	3168	170	1195	755	2869	2125	839	2275	1271	816		3164	2577	140	2769	1843
TAMPA, FL	878	845	274	1272	1588	1522	701	668	1150	1403	1448	82	1062	2184	1019	1478	3106	1970	2899	805	1008	2375	1195	2481	2933	3164		1383	3297	916	1448
TORONTO, ON	589	975	1532	607	924	330	764	1302	507	1295	971	1327	522	2307	321	668	2633	1429	2426	660	782	1902	1714	2601	2643	2577	1383		2711	563	1217
VANCOUVER, BC	2497	2574	3504	2124	1788	3041	2597	2865	2998	2136	1853	3283	2968	1655	2668	3301	313	1328	898	3003	2259	973	2410	1414	958	140	3297	2711		2902	1977
WASHINGTON, DC	596	896	1065	799	1115	600	679	1106	228	1350	1162	860	140	2362	240	556	2824	1620	2617	108	837	2094	1635	2720	2834	2769	916	563	2902		1272
WICHITA, KS	705	597	1655	769	637	1547	748	890	1391	161	307	1434	1330	1173	1046	1714	1775	712	1568	1274	441	1044	624	1531	1784	1843	1448	1217	1977	1272	

Welcome

Dear Traveler,

Since its inception in 1958, Mobil Travel Guide has served as a trusted advisor to auto travelers in search of value in lodging, dining, and destinations. Now in its 48th year, the Mobil Travel Guide is the hallmark of our ExxonMobil family of travel publications, and we're proud to offer an array of products and services from our Mobil, Exxon, and Esso brands in North America to facilitate life on the road.

Whether you're looking for business or pleasure venues, our nationwide network of independent, professional evaluators offers their expertise on thousands of travel options, allowing you to plan a quick family getaway, a full-service business meeting, or an unforgettable Mobil Five-Star celebration.

Your feedback is important to us as we strive to improve our product offerings and better meet today's travel needs. Whether you travel once a week or once a year, please take the time to contact us at www.mobiltravelguide.com. We hope to hear from you soon.

Best wishes for safe and enjoyable travels.

Lee R Raymond

Lee R. Raymond
Chairman and CEO
Exxon Mobil Corporation

A Word to Our Readers

Travelers are on the roads in great numbers these days. They're exploring the country on day trips, weekend getaways, business trips, and extended family vacations, visiting major cities and small towns along the way. Because time is precious and the travel industry is ever-changing, having accurate, reliable travel information at your fingertips is critical. Mobil Travel Guide has been providing invaluable insight to travelers for more than 45 years, and we are committed to continuing this service well into the future.

The Mobil Corporation (known as Exxon Mobil Corporation since a 1999 merger) began producing the Mobil Travel Guide books in 1958, following the introduction of the US interstate highway system in 1956. The first edition covered only five Southwestern states. Since then, our books have become the premier travel guides in North America, covering all 50 states and Canada.

Since its founding, Mobil Travel Guide has served as an advocate for travelers seeking knowledge about hotels, restaurants, and places to visit. Based on an objective process, we make recommendations to our customers that we believe will enhance the quality and value of their travel experiences. Our trusted Mobil One- to Five-Star rating system is the oldest and most respected lodging and restaurant inspection and rating program in North America. Most hoteliers, restaurateurs, and industry observers favorably regard the rigor of our inspection program and understand the prestige and benefits that come with receiving a Mobil Star rating.

The Mobil Travel Guide process of rating each establishment includes:

- Unannounced facility inspections
- Incognito service evaluations for Mobil Four-Star and Mobil Five-Star properties
- A review of unsolicited comments from the general public
- Senior management oversight

For each property, more than 450 attributes, including cleanliness, physical facilities, and employee attitude and courtesy, are measured and evaluated to produce a mathematically derived score, which is then blended with the other elements to form an overall score. These quantifiable scores allow comparative analysis among properties and form the basis that we use to assign our Mobil One- to Five-Star ratings.

This process focuses largely on guest expectations, guest experience, and consistency of service, not just physical facilities and amenities. It is fundamentally a relative rating system that rewards those properties that continually strive for and achieve excellence each year. Indeed, the very best properties are consistently raising the bar for those that wish to compete with them. These properties proactively respond to consumers' needs even in today's uncertain times.

Only facilities that meet Mobil Travel Guide's standards earn the privilege of being listed in the guide. Deteriorating, poorly managed establishments are deleted. A Mobil Travel Guide listing constitutes a positive quality recommendation; every listing is an accolade, a recognition of achievement. Our Mobil One- to Five-Star rating system highlights its level of service. Extensive in-house research is constantly underway to determine new additions to our lists.

- The Mobil Five-Star Award indicates that a property is one of the very best in the country and consistently provides gracious and courteous service, superlative quality in its facility, and a unique ambience. The lodgings and restaurants at the Mobil Five-Star level consistently and proactively respond to consumers' needs and continue their commitment to excellence, doing so with grace and perseverance.
- Also highly regarded is the Mobil Four-Star Award, which honors properties for outstanding achievement in overall facility and for providing very strong service levels in all areas. These

award winners provide a distinctive experience for the ever-demanding and sophisticated consumer.

- The Mobil Three-Star Award recognizes an excellent property that provides full services and amenities. This category ranges from exceptional hotels with limited services to elegant restaurants with a less-formal atmosphere.
- A Mobil Two-Star property is a clean and comfortable establishment that has expanded amenities or a distinctive environment. A Mobil Two-Star property is an excellent place to stay or dine.
- A Mobil One-Star property is limited in its amenities and services but focuses on providing a value experience while meeting travelers' expectations. The property can be expected to be clean, comfortable, and convenient.

Allow us to emphasize that we do not charge establishments for inclusion in our guides. We have no relationship with any of the businesses and attractions we list and act only as a consumer advocate. In essence, we do the investigative legwork so that you won't have to.

Keep in mind, too, that the hospitality business is ever-changing. Restaurants and lodgings—particularly small chains and stand-alone establishments—change management or even go out of business with surprising quickness. Although we make every effort to double-check information during our annual updates, we nevertheless recommend that you call ahead to make sure the place you've selected is still open and offers all the amenities you're looking for. We've provided phone numbers; when available, we also list fax numbers and Web site addresses.

We hope that your travels are enjoyable and relaxing and that our books help you get the most out of every trip you take. If any aspect of your accommodation, dining, or sightseeing experience motivates you to comment, please drop us a line. We depend a great deal on our readers' remarks, so you can be assured that we will read your comments and assimilate them into our research. General comments about our books are also welcome. You can write to us at Mobil Travel Guide, 7373 N Cicero Ave, Lincolnwood, IL 60712, or send an e-mail to info@mobiltravelguide.com.

Take your Mobil Travel Guide books along on every trip you take. We're confident that you'll be pleased with their convenience, ease of use, and breadth of dependable coverage.

Happy travels!

How to Use This Book

The Mobil Travel Guide Regional Travel Planners are designed for ease of use. This book begins with a general introduction that provides a geographical and historical orientation to the state and gives basic statewide tourist information, from climate to calendar highlights to seatbelt laws. The remainder of the book is devoted to travel destinations within the state—mainly cities and towns, but also national parks and tourist areas—which are arranged in alphabetical order.

The following sections explain the wealth of information you'll find about those travel destinations: information about the area, things to see and do there, and where to stay and eat.

Maps and Map Coordinates

At the front of this book in the full-color section, we have provided state maps as well as maps of selected larger cities to help you find your way around once you leave the highway. You'll find a key to the map symbols on the Contents page at the beginning of the map section.

Next to most cities and towns throughout the book, you'll find a set of map coordinates, such as C-2. These coordinates reference the maps at the front of this book and help you find the location you're looking for quickly and easily.

Destination Information

Because many travel destinations are close to other cities and towns where travelers might find additional attractions, accommodations, and restaurants, we've included cross-references to those cities and towns when it makes sense to do so. We also list addresses, phone numbers, and Web sites for travel information resources—usually the local chamber of commerce or office of tourism—as well as pertinent statistics and, in many cases, a brief introduction to the area.

Information about airports, ground transportation, and suburbs is included for large cities.

Driving Tours and Walking Tours

The driving tours that we include for many states are usually day trips that make for interesting side excursions, although they can be longer. They offer you a way to get off the beaten path and visit an area that travelers often overlook. These trips frequently cover areas of natural beauty or historical significance.

Each walking tour focuses on a particularly interesting area of a city or town. Again, these tours can provide a break from everyday tourist attractions. The tours often include places to stop for meals or snacks.

What to See and Do

Mobil Travel Guide offers information about nearly 20,000 museums, art galleries, amusement parks, historic sites, national and state parks, ski areas, and many other types of attractions. A white star on a black background ★ signals that the attraction is a must-see—one of the best in the area. Because municipal parks, public tennis courts, swimming pools, and small educational institutions are common to most towns, they generally are not mentioned.

Following an attraction's description, you'll find the months, days, and, in some cases, hours of operation; the address/directions, telephone number, and Web site (if there is one); and the admission price category. The following are the ranges we use for admission fees, based on one adult:

- **FREE**
- **$** = Up to $5
- **$$** = $5.01-$10
- **$$$** = $10.01-$15
- **$$$$** = Over $15

Special Events

Special events are either annual events that last only a short time, such as festivals and fairs, or longer, seasonal events such as horse racing, theater, and summer concerts. Our Special Events listings also include infrequently occurring occasions that mark certain dates or events, such as a centennial or other commemorative celebration.

Listings

Lodgings, spas, and restaurants are usually listed under the city or town in which they're located. Make sure to check the related cities and towns that appear right beneath a city's heading for additional options, especially if you're traveling to a major metropolitan area that includes many suburbs. If a property is located in a town that doesn't have its own heading, the listing appears under the town nearest it, with the address and town given immediately after the establishment's name. In large cities, lodgings located within 5 miles of major commercial airports may be listed under a separate "Airport Area" heading that follows the city section.

LODGINGS

Travelers have different wants and needs when it comes to accommodations. To help you pinpoint properties that meet your particular needs, Mobil Travel Guide classifies each lodging by type according to the following characteristics.

Mobil Rated Lodgings

- **Limited-Service Hotel.** A limited-service hotel is traditionally a Mobil One-Star or Mobil Two-Star property. At a Mobil One-Star hotel, guests can expect to find a clean, comfortable property that commonly serves a complimentary continental breakfast. A Mobil Two-Star hotel is also clean and comfortable but has expanded amenities, such as a full-service restaurant, business center, and fitness center. These services may have limited staffing and/or restricted hours of use.
- **Full-Service Hotel.** A full-service hotel traditionally enjoys a Mobil Three-Star, Mobil Four-Star, or Mobil Five-Star rating. Guests can expect these hotels to offer at least one full-service restaurant in addition to amenities such as valet parking, luggage assistance, 24-hour room service, concierge service, laundry and/or dry-cleaning services, and turndown service.
- **Full-Service Resort.** A resort is traditionally a full-service hotel that is geared toward recreation and represents a vacation and holiday destination. A resort's guest rooms are typically furnished to accommodate longer stays. The property may offer a full-service spa, golf, tennis, and fitness facilities or other leisure activities. Resorts are expected to offer a full-service restaurant and expanded amenities, such as luggage assistance, room service, meal plans, concierge service, and turndown service.
- **Full-Service Inn.** An inn is traditionally a Mobil Three-Star, Mobil Four-Star, or Mobil Five-Star property. Inns are similar to bed-and-breakfasts (see below) but offer a wider range of services, most significantly a full-service restaurant that serves at least breakfast and dinner.

Specialty Lodgings

Mobil Travel Guide recognizes the unique and individualized nature of many different types of lodging establishments, including bed-and-breakfasts, limited-service inns, and guest ranches. For that reason, we have chosen to place our stamp of approval on the properties that fall into these two categories in lieu of applying our traditional Mobil Star ratings.

- **B&B/Limited-Service Inn.** A bed-and-breakfast (B&B) or limited-service inn is traditionally an owner-occupied home or residence found in a residential area or vacation destination. It may be a structure of historic significance. Rooms are often individually decorated, but telephones, televisions, and private bathrooms may not be available in every room. A B&B typically serves only breakfast to its overnight guests, which is included in the room rate. Cocktails and refreshments may be served in the late afternoon or evening.
- **Guest Ranch.** A guest ranch is traditionally a rustic, Western-themed property that specializes in stays of three or more days. Horseback riding is often a feature, with stables and trails found on the property. Facilities can range from clean, comfortable establishments to more luxurious facilities.

Mobil Star Rating Definitions for Lodgings

- ★★★★★ : A Mobil Five-Star lodging provides consistently superlative service in an exceptionally distinctive luxury environment, with expanded services. Attention to detail is evident throughout the hotel, resort, or inn, from bed linens to staff uniforms.
- ★★★★ : A Mobil Four-Star lodging provides a luxury experience with expanded amenities in a distinctive environment. Services may include, but are not limited to, automatic turndown service, 24-hour room service, and valet parking.
- ★★★ : A Mobil Three-Star lodging is well appointed, with a full-service restaurant and expanded amenities, such as a fitness center, golf course, tennis courts, 24-hour room service, and optional turndown service.
- ★★ : A Mobil Two-Star lodging is considered a clean, comfortable, and reliable establishment that has expanded amenities, such as a full-service restaurant on the premises.
- ★ : A Mobil One-Star lodging is a limited-service hotel, motel, or inn that is considered a clean, comfortable, and reliable establishment.

Information Found in the Lodging Listings

Each lodging listing gives the name, address/location (when no street address is available), neighborhood and/or directions from downtown (in major cities), phone number(s), fax number, total number of guest rooms, and seasons open (if not year-round). Also included are details on business, luxury, recreational, and dining facilities at the property or nearby. A key to the symbols at the end of each listing can be found on the page following the "A Word to Our Readers" section.

For every property, we also provide pricing information. Because lodging rates change frequently, we list a pricing category rather than specific prices. The pricing categories break down as follows:

- **$** = Up to $150
- **$$** = $151-$250
- **$$$** = $251-$350
- **$$$$** = $351 and up

All prices quoted are in effect at the time of publication; however, prices cannot be guaranteed. In some locations, short-term price variations may exist because of special events, holidays, or seasonality. Certain resorts have complicated rate structures that vary with the time of year; always confirm rates when making your plans.

Because most lodgings offer the following features and services, information about them does not appear in the listings:

- Year-round operation
- Bathroom with tub and/or shower in each room
- Cable television in each room
- In-room telephones
- Cots and cribs available
- Daily maid service
- Elevators
- Major credit cards accepted

Although we recommend every lodging we list in this book, a few stand out—they offer noteworthy amenities or stand above the others in their category in terms of quality, value, or historical significance. To draw your attention to these special spots, we've included the magnifying glass icon to the left of the listing, as you see here.

SPAS

Mobil Travel Guide is pleased to announce its newest category: hotel and resort spas. Until now, hotel and resort spas have not been formally rated or inspected by any organization. Every spa selected for inclusion in this book underwent a rigorous inspection process similar to the one Mobil Travel Guide has been applying to lodgings and restaurants for more than four decades. After spending a year and a half researching more than 300 spas and performing exhaustive incognito inspections of more than 200 properties, we narrowed our list to the 48 best spas in the United States and Canada.

Mobil Travel Guide's spa ratings are based on objective evaluations of more than 450 attributes. Approximately half of these criteria assess basic expectations, such as staff courtesy, the technical proficiency and skill of the employees, and whether the facility is maintained properly and hygienically. Several standards address issues that impact a guest's physical comfort and convenience, as well as the staff's ability to impart a sense of personalized service and anticipate clients' needs. Additional criteria measure the spa's ability to create a completely calming ambience.

The Mobil Star ratings focus on much more than the facilities available at a spa and the treatments it offers. Each Mobil Star rating is a cumulative score achieved from multiple inspections that reflects the spa management's attention to detail and commitment to consumers' needs.

Mobil Star Rating Definitions for Spas

- ★★★★★ : A Mobil Five-Star spa provides consistently superlative service in an exceptionally distinctive luxury environment with extensive amenities. The staff at a Mobil Five-Star Spa provides extraordinary service above and beyond the traditional spa experience, allowing guests to achieve the highest level of relaxation and pampering. A Mobil Five-Star spa offers an extensive array of treatments, often incorporating international themes and products. Attention to detail is evident throughout the spa, from arrival to departure.
- ★★★★ : A Mobil Four-Star spa provides a luxurious experience with expanded amenities in an elegant and serene environment. Throughout the spa facility, guests experience personalized service. Amenities might include, but are not limited to, single-sex relaxation rooms where guests wait for their treatments, plunge pools and whirlpools in both men's and women's locker rooms, and an array of treatments, including at a minimum a selection of massages, body therapies, facials, and a variety of salon services.
- ★★★ : A Mobil Three-Star spa is physically well appointed and has a full complement of staff to ensure that guests' needs are met. It has some expanded amenities, such as, but not limited to, a well-equipped fitness center, separate men's and women's locker rooms, a sauna or steam room, and a designated relaxation area. It also offers a menu of services that at a minimum includes massages, facial treatments, and at least one other type of body treatment, such as scrubs or wraps.

RESTAURANTS

All Mobil Star rated dining establishments listed in this book have a full kitchen and offer seating at tables; most offer table service.

Mobil Star Rating Definitions for Restaurants

- ★★★★★ : A Mobil Five-Star restaurant offers one of few flawless dining experiences in the country. These establishments consistently provide their guests with exceptional food, superlative service, elegant décor, and exquisite presentations of each detail surrounding a meal.
- ★★★★ : A Mobil Four-Star restaurant provides professional service, distinctive presentations, and wonderful food.
- ★★★ : A Mobil Three-Star restaurant has good food, warm and skillful service, and enjoyable décor.
- ★★ : A Mobil Two-Star restaurant serves fresh food in a clean setting with efficient service. Value is considered in this category, as is family friendliness.
- ★ : A Mobil One-Star restaurant provides a distinctive experience through culinary specialty, local flair, or individual atmosphere.

Information Found in the Restaurant Listings

Each restaurant listing gives the cuisine type, street address (or directions if no address is available), phone and fax numbers, Web site (if available), meals served, days of operation (if not open daily year-round), and pricing category. Information about appropriate attire is provided, although it's always a good idea to call ahead and ask if you're unsure; the meaning of "casual" or "business casual" varies widely in different parts of the country. We also indicate whether the restaurant has a bar, whether a children's menu is offered, and whether outdoor seating is available. If reservations are recommended, we note that fact in the listing. When valet parking is available, it is noted in the description. In many cases, self-parking is available at the restaurant or nearby.

Because menu prices can fluctuate, we list a pricing category rather than specific prices. The pricing categories are defined as follows, per diner, and assume that you order an appetizer or dessert, an entrée, and one drink:

- **$** = $15 and under
- **$$** = $16-$35
- **$$$** = $36-$85
- **$$$$** = $86 and up

Again, all prices quoted are in effect at the time of publication, but prices cannot be guaranteed.

Although we recommend every restaurant we list in this book, a few stand out—they offer noteworthy local specialties or stand above the others in their category in terms of quality, value, or experience. To draw your attention to these special spots, we've included the magnifying glass icon to the left of the listing, as you see here.

SPECIAL INFORMATION FOR TRAVELERS WITH DISABILITIES

The Mobil Travel Guide symbol indicates that an establishment is not at least partially accessible to people with mobility problems. When the symbol follows a listing, the establishment is not equipped with facilities to accommodate people using wheelchairs or crutches or otherwise needing easy access to doorways and rest rooms. Travelers with severe mobility problems or with hearing or visual impairments may or may not find the facilities they need. Always phone ahead to make sure that an establishment can meet your needs.

Understanding the Symbols

What to See and Do

☆	=	One of the top attractions in the area
$	=	Up to $5
$$	=	$5.01 to $10
$$$	=	$10.01 to $15
$$$$	=	Over $15

Lodgings

$	=	Up to $150
$$	=	$151 to $250
$$$	=	$251 to $350
$$$$	=	Over $350

Restaurants

$	=	Up to $15
$$	=	$16 to $35
$$$	=	$36 to $85
$$$$	=	Over $85

Lodging Star Definitions

★★★★★ A Mobil Five-Star lodging establishment provides consistently superlative service in an exceptionally distinctive luxury environment with expanded services. Attention to detail is evident throughout the hotel/resort/inn from the bed linens to the staff uniforms.

★★★★ A Mobil Four-Star lodging establishment is a hotel/resort/inn that provides a luxury experience with expanded amenities in a distinctive environment. Services may include, but are not limited to, automatic turndown service, 24-hour room service, and valet parking.

★★★ A Mobil Three-Star lodging establishment is a hotel/resort/inn that is well appointed, with a full-service restaurant and expanded amenities, such as, but not limited to, a fitness center, golf course, tennis courts, 24-hour room service, and optional turndown service.

★★ A Mobil Two-Star lodging establishment is a hotel/resort/inn that is considered a clean, comfortable, and reliable establishment, but also has expanded amenities, such as a full-service restaurant on the premises.

★ A Mobil One-Star lodging establishment is a limited-service hotel or inn that is considered a clean, comfortable, and reliable establishment.

Restaurant Star Definitions

★★★★★ A Mobil Five-Star restaurant is one of few flawless dining experiences in the country. These restaurants consistently provide their guests with exceptional food, superlative service, elegant décor, and exquisite presentations of each detail surrounding the meal.

★★★★ A Mobil Four-Star restaurant provides professional service, distinctive presentations, and wonderful food.

★★★ A Mobil Three-Star restaurant has good food, warm and skillful service, and enjoyable décor.

★★ A Mobil Two-Star restaurant serves fresh food in a clean setting with efficient service. Value is considered in this category, as is family friendliness.

★ A Mobil One-Star restaurant provides a distinctive experience through culinary specialty, local flair, or individual atmosphere.

Symbols at End of Listings

- Facilities for people with disabilities not available
- Pets allowed
- Ski in/ski out access
- Golf on premises
- Tennis court(s) on premises
- Indoor or outdoor pool
- Fitness room
- Major commercial airport within 5 miles
- Business center

Making the Most of Your Trip

A few hardy souls might look back with fondness on a trip during which the car broke down, leaving them stranded for three days, or a vacation that cost twice what it was supposed to. For most travelers, though, the best trips are those that are safe, smooth, and within budget. To help you make your trip the best it can be, we've assembled a few tips and resources.

Saving Money

ON LODGING

Many hotels and motels offer discounts—for senior citizens, business travelers, families, you name it. It never hurts to ask—politely, that is. Sometimes, especially in the late afternoon, desk clerks are instructed to fill beds, and you might be offered a lower rate or a nicer room to entice you to stay. Simply ask the reservation agent for the best rate available. Also, make sure to try both the toll-free number and the local number. You may be able to get a lower rate from one than from the other.

Timing your trip right can cut your lodging costs as well. Look for bargains on stays over multiple nights, in the off-season, and on weekdays or weekends, depending on the location. Many hotels in major metropolitan areas, for example, have special weekend packages that offer leisure travelers considerable savings on rooms; they may include breakfast, cocktails, and/or dinner discounts.

Another way to save money is to choose accommodations that give you more than just a standard room. Rooms with kitchen facilities enable you to cook some meals yourself, reducing your restaurant costs. A suite might save money for two couples traveling together. Even hotel luxury levels can provide good value, as many include breakfast or cocktails in the price of a room.

State and city taxes, as well as special room taxes, can increase your room rate by as much as 25 percent per day. We are unable to include information about taxes in our listings, but we strongly urge you to ask about taxes when making reservations so that you understand the total cost of your lodgings before you book them.

Watch out for telephone-usage charges that hotels frequently impose on long-distance, credit-card, and other calls. Before phoning from your room, read the information given to you at check-in, and then be sure to review your bill carefully when checking out. You won't be expected to pay for charges that the hotel didn't spell out. Consider using your cell phone if you have one; or, if public telephones are available in the hotel lobby, your cost savings may outweigh the inconvenience of using them.

Here are some additional ways to save on lodgings:

- Stay in B&B accommodations. They're generally less expensive than standard hotel rooms, and the complimentary breakfast cuts down on food costs.
- If you're traveling with children, find lodgings at which kids stay free.
- When visiting a major city, stay just outside the city limits; these rooms are usually less expensive than those in downtown locations.
- Consider visiting national parks during the low season, when prices of lodgings near the parks drop by 25 percent or more.
- When calling a hotel, ask whether it is running any special promotions or if any discounts are available; many times reservationists are told not to volunteer these deals unless they're specifically asked about them.
- Check for hotel packages; some offer nightly rates that include a rental car or discounts on major attractions.
- Search the Internet for travel bargains. Web sites that allow for online booking of hotel rooms and travel planning, such as *www.mobiltravelguide.com,* often deliver lower rates than are available through telephone reservations.

ON DINING

There are several ways to get a less expensive meal at an expensive restaurant. Early-bird dinners are popular in many parts of the country and offer considerable savings. If you're interested in visiting a Mobil Four- or Five-Star establishment, consider going at lunchtime. Although the prices are probably still relatively high at midday, they may be half of those at dinner, and you'll experience the same ambience, service, and cuisine.

ON ENTERTAINMENT

Although many national parks, monuments, seashores, historic sites, and recreation areas may be visited free of charge, others charge an entrance fee and/or a usage fee for special services and facilities. If you plan to make several visits to national recreation areas, consider one of the following money-saving programs offered by the National Park Service:

- **National Parks Pass.** This annual pass is good for entrance to any national park that charges an entrance fee. If the park charges a per-vehicle fee, the pass holder and any accompanying passengers in a private noncommercial vehicle may enter. If the park charges a per-person fee, the pass applies to the holder's spouse, children, and parents as well as the holder. It is valid for entrance fees only; it does not cover parking, camping, or other fees. You can purchase a National Parks Pass in person at any national park where an entrance fee is charged; by mail from the National Park Foundation, PO Box 34108, Washington, DC 20043-4108; by calling toll-free 888/467-2757; or at www.nationalparks.org. The cost is $50.
- **Golden Eagle Sticker.** When affixed to a National Parks Pass, this hologram sticker, available to people who are between 17 and 61 years of age, extends coverage to sites managed by the US Fish and Wildlife Service, the US Forest Service, and the Bureau of Land Management. It is good until the National Parks Pass to which it is affixed expires and does not cover usage fees. You can purchase one at the National Park Service, the Fish and Wildlife Service, or the Bureau of Land Management fee stations. The cost is $15.
- **Golden Age Passport.** Available to citizens and permanent US residents 62 and older, this passport is a lifetime entrance permit to fee-charging national recreation areas. The fee exemption extends to those accompanying the permit holder in a private noncommercial vehicle or, in the case of walk-in facilities, to the holder's spouse and children. The passport also entitles the holder to a 50 percent discount on federal usage fees charged in park areas, but not on concessions. Golden Age Passports must be obtained in person and are available at most National Park Service units that charge an entrance fee. The applicant must show proof of age, such as a driver's license or birth certificate (Medicare cards are not acceptable proof). The cost is $10.
- **Golden Access Passport.** Issued to citizens and permanent US residents who are physically disabled or visually impaired, this passport is a free lifetime entrance permit to fee-charging national recreation areas. The fee exemption extends to those accompanying the permit holder in a private noncommercial vehicle or, in the case of walk-in facilities, to the holder's spouse and children. The passport also entitles the holder to a 50 percent discount on usage fees charged in park areas, but not on concessions. Golden Access Passports must be obtained in person and are available at most National Park Service units that charge an entrance fee. Proof of eligibility to receive federal benefits (under programs such as Disability Retirement, Compensation for Military Service-Connected Disability, and the Coal Mine Safety and Health Act) is required, or an affidavit must be signed attesting to eligibility.

A money-saving move in several large cities is to purchase a **CityPass.** If you plan to visit several museums and other major attractions, CityPass is a terrific option because it gets you into several sites for one substantially reduced price. Currently, CityPass is available in Boston, Chicago, Hollywood, New York, Philadelphia, San Francisco, Seattle, southern California (which includes Disneyland, SeaWorld, and the San Diego Zoo), and Toronto. For more information or to buy one, call toll-free 888/330-5008 or visit www.citypass.net. You can also buy a CityPass from any participating CityPass attraction.

Here are some additional ways to save on entertainment and shopping:

- Check with your hotel's concierge for various coupons and special offers; they often have two-for-one tickets for area attractions and coupons for discounts at area stores and restaurants.

- Purchase same-day concert or theater tickets for half-price through the local cheap-tickets outlet, such as TKTS in New York or Hot Tix in Chicago.
- Visit museums on their free or "by donation" days, when you can pay what you wish rather than a specific admission fee.

ON TRANSPORTATION

Transportation is a big part of any vacation budget. Here are some ways to reduce your costs:

- If you're renting a car, shop early over the Internet; you can book a car during the low season for less, even if you'll be using it in the high season.
- Rental car discounts are often available if you rent for one week or longer and reserve in advance.
- Get the best gas mileage out of your vehicle by making sure that it's properly tuned up and keeping your tires properly inflated.
- Travel at moderate speeds on the open road; higher speeds require more gasoline.
- Fill the tank before you return your rental car; rental companies charge to refill the tank and do so at prices of up to 50 percent more than at local gas stations.
- Make a checklist of travel essentials and purchase them before you leave; don't get stuck buying expensive sunscreen at your hotel or overpriced film at the airport.

FOR SENIOR CITIZENS

Always call ahead to ask if a discount is being offered, and be sure to carry proof of age. Additional information for mature travelers is available from the American Association of Retired Persons (AARP), 601 E St NW, Washington, DC 20049; phone 202/434-2277; www.aarp.org.

Tipping

Tips are expressions of appreciation for good service. However, you are never obligated to tip if you receive poor service.

IN HOTELS

- Door attendants usually get $1 for hailing a cab.
- Bell staff expect $2 per bag.
- Concierges are tipped according to the service they perform. Tipping is not mandatory when you've asked for suggestions on sightseeing or restaurants or for help in making dining reservations. However, a tip of $5 is appropriate when a concierge books you a table at a restaurant known to be difficult to get into. For obtaining theater or sporting event tickets, $5 to $10 is expected.
- Maids should be tipped $1 to $2 per day. Hand your tip directly to the maid, or leave it with a note saying that the money has been left expressly for the maid.

IN RESTAURANTS

Before tipping, carefully review your check for any gratuity or service charge that is already included in your bill. If you're in doubt, ask your server.

- Coffee shop and counter service waitstaff usually receive 15 percent of the bill, before sales tax.
- In full-service restaurants, tip 18 percent of the bill, before sales tax.
- In fine restaurants, where gratuities are shared among a larger staff, 18 to 20 percent is appropriate.
- In most cases, the maitre d' is tipped only if the service has been extraordinary, and only on the way out. At upscale properties in major metropolitan areas, $20 is the minimum.
- If there is a wine steward, tip $20 for exemplary service and beyond, or more if the wine was decanted or the bottle was very expensive.
- Tip $1 to $2 per coat at the coat check.

AT AIRPORTS

Curbside luggage handlers expect $1 per bag. Car-rental shuttle drivers who help with your luggage appreciate a $1 or $2 tip.

Staying Safe

The best way to deal with emergencies is to avoid them in the first place. However, unforeseen situations do happen, so you should be prepared for them.

IN YOUR CAR

Before you head out on a road trip, make sure that your car has been serviced and is in good working order. Change the oil, check the battery and belts, make sure that your windshield washer fluid is full and your tires are properly inflated (which can also improve your gas mileage). Other inspections recommended by the vehicle's manufacturer should also be made.

Next, be sure you have the tools and equipment needed to deal with a routine breakdown:

- Jack
- Spare tire
- Lug wrench
- Repair kit
- Emergency tools
- Jumper cables
- Spare fan belt
- Fuses
- Flares and/or reflectors
- Flashlight
- First-aid kit
- In winter, a windshield scraper and snow shovel

Many emergency supplies are sold in special packages that include the essentials you need to stay safe in the event of a breakdown.

Also bring all appropriate and up-to-date documentation—licenses, registration, and insurance cards—and know what your insurance covers. Bring an extra set of keys, too, just in case.

En route, always buckle up! In most states, wearing a seatbelt is required by law.

If your car does break down, do the following:

- Get out of traffic as soon as possible—pull well off the road.
- Raise the hood and turn on your emergency flashers or tie a white cloth to the roadside door handle or antenna.
- Stay in your car.
- Use flares or reflectors to keep your vehicle from being hit.

IN YOUR HOTEL

Chances are slim that you will encounter a hotel or motel fire, but you can protect yourself by doing the following:

- Once you've checked in, make sure that the smoke detector in your room is working properly.
- Find the property's fire safety instructions, usually posted on the inside of the room door.
- Locate the fire extinguishers and at least two fire exits.
- Never use an elevator in a fire.

For personal security, use the peephole in your room door and make sure that anyone claiming to be a hotel employee can show proper identification. Call the front desk if you feel threatened at any time.

PROTECTING AGAINST THEFT

To guard against theft wherever you go:

- Don't bring anything of more value than you need.
- If you do bring valuables, leave them at your hotel rather than in your car.
- If you bring something very expensive, lock it in a safe. Many hotels put one in each room; others will store your valuables in the hotel's safe.
- Don't carry more money than you need. Use traveler's checks and credit cards or visit cash machines to withdraw more cash when you run out.

For Travelers with Disabilities

To get the kind of service you need and have a right to expect, don't hesitate when making a reservation to question the management about the availability of accessible rooms, parking, entrances, restaurants, lounges, or any other facilities that are important to you, and confirm what is meant by "accessible."

The Mobil Travel Guide [D] symbol indicates establishments that are not at least partially accessible to people with special mobility needs (people using wheelchairs or crutches or otherwise needing easy access to buildings and rooms). Further information about these criteria can be found in the earlier section "How to Use This Book."

A thorough listing of published material for travelers with disabilities is available from the Disability Bookshop, Twin Peaks Press, Box 129, Vancouver, WA 98666; phone 360/694-2462; disabilitybookshop.virtualave.net. Another reliable organization is the Society for Accessible Travel & Hospitality (SATH), 347 Fifth Ave, Suite 610, New York, NY 10016; phone 212/447-7284; www.sath.org.

Important Toll-Free Numbers and Online Information

Hotels

Adams Mark 800/444-2326
www.adamsmark.com
AmericInn 800/634-3444
www.americinn.com
AmeriHost Inn 800/434-5800
www.amerihostinn.com
Amerisuites 800/833-1516
www.amerisuites.com
Baymont Inns 877/229-6667
www.baymontinns.com
Best Inns & Suites 800/237-8466
www.bestinn.com
Best Value Inn 888/315-2378
www.bestvalueinn.com
Best Western 800/780-7234
www.bestwestern.com
Budget Host Inn 800/283-4678
www.budgethost.com
Candlewood Suites 888/226-3539
www.candlewoodsuites.com
Clarion Hotels 800/252-7466
www.choicehotels.com
Comfort Inns and Suites 800/252-7466
www.comfortinn.com
Country Hearth Inns 800/848-5767
www.countryhearth.com
Country Inns & Suites 800/456-4000
www.countryinns.com
Courtyard by Marriott 800/321-2211
www.courtyard.com
Cross Country Inns (KY and OH) 800/621-1429
www.crosscountryinns.com
Crowne Plaza Hotels and Resorts 800/227-6963
www.crowneplaza.com
Days Inn 800/544-8313
www.daysinn.com
Delta Hotels 800/268-1133
www.deltahotels.com
Destination Hotels & Resorts 800/434-7347
www.destinationhotels.com
Doubletree Hotels 800/222-8733
www.doubletree.com
Drury Inn 800/378-7946
www.druryinn.com
Econolodge 800/553-2666
www.econolodge.com
Embassy Suites 800/362-2779
www.embassysuites.com
ExelInns of America 800/367-3935
www.exelinns.com
Extended StayAmerica 800/398-7829
www.extendedstayhotels.com
Fairfield Inn by Marriott 800/228-2800
www.fairfieldinn.com
Fairmont Hotels 800/441-1414
www.fairmont.com
Four Points by Sheraton 888/625-5144
www.fourpoints.com
Four Seasons 800/819-5053
www.fourseasons.com
Hampton Inn 800/426-7866
www.hamptoninn.com
Hard Rock Hotels, Resorts, and Casinos 800/473-7625
www.hardrock.com
Harrah's Entertainment 800/427-7247
www.harrahs.com
Hawthorn Suites 800/527-1133
www.hawthorn.com
Hilton Hotels and Resorts (US) 800/774-1500
www.hilton.com
Holiday Inn Express 800/465-4329
www.hiexpress.com
Holiday Inn Hotels and Resorts 800/465-4329
www.holiday-inn.com
Homestead Studio Suites 888/782-9473
www.homesteadhotels.com
Homewood Suites 800/225-5466
www.homewoodsuites.com
Howard Johnson 800/406-1411
www.hojo.com
Hyatt 800/633-7313
www.hyatt.com
Inns of America 800/826-0778
www.innsofamerica.com
InterContinental 888/567-8725
www.intercontinental.com
Joie de Vivre 800/738-7477
www.jdvhospitality.com
Kimpton Hotels 888/546-7866
www.kimptongroup.com
Knights Inn 800/843-5644
www.knightsinn.com
La Quinta 800/531-5900
www.laquinta.com

Le Meridien 800/543-4300
www.lemeridien.com
Leading Hotels of the World 800/223-6800
www.lhw.com
Loews Hotels 800/235-6397
www.loewshotels.com
MainStay Suites 800/660-6246
www.mainstaysuites.com
Mandarin Oriental 800/526-6566
www.mandarin-oriental.com
Marriott Hotels, Resorts, and Suites 800/228-9290
www.marriott.com
Microtel Inns & Suites 800/771-7171
www.microtelinn.com
Millennium & Copthorne Hotels 866/866-8086
www.millenniumhotels.com
Motel 6 .... 800/466-8356
www.motel6.com
Omni Hotels 800/843-6664
www.omnihotels.com
Pan Pacific Hotels and Resorts 800/327-8585
www.panpac.com
Park Inn & Park Plaza 888/201-1801
www.parkinn.com
The Peninsula Group .... Contact individual hotel
www.peninsula.com
Preferred Hotels & Resorts Worldwide 800/323-7500
www.preferredhotels.com
Quality Inn 800/228-5151
www.qualityinn.com
Radisson Hotels 800/333-3333
www.radisson.com
Raffles International Hotels and Resorts ... 800/637-9477
www.raffles.com
Ramada Plazas, Limiteds, and Inns 800/272-6232
www.ramada.com
Red Lion Inns 800/733-5466
www.redlion.com
Red Roof Inns 800/733-7663
www.redroof.com
Regent International 800/545-4000
www.regenthotels.com
Relais & Chateaux 800/735-2478
www.relaischateaux.com
Renaissance Hotels 888/236-2427
www.renaissancehotels.com
Residence Inn 800/331-3131
www.residenceinn.com
Ritz-Carlton 800/241-3333
www.ritzcarlton.com
RockResorts 888/367-7625
www.rockresorts.com
Rodeway Inn 800/228-2000
www.rodeway.com
Rosewood Hotels & Resorts 888/767-3966
www.rosewoodhotels.com
Select Inn 800/641-1000
www.selectinn.com
Sheraton 888/625-5144
www.sheraton.com
Shilo Inns 800/222-2244
www.shiloinns.com
Shoney's Inn 800/552-4667
www.shoneysinn.com
Signature/Jameson Inns 800/822-5252
www.jamesoninns.com
Sleep Inn 877/424-6423
www.sleepinn.com
Small Luxury Hotels of the World 800/525-4800
www.slh.com
Sofitel 800/763-4835
www.sofitel.com
SpringHill Suites 888/236-2427
www.springhillsuites.com
St. Regis Luxury Collection 888/625-5144
www.stregis.com
Staybridge Suites 800/238-8000
www.staybridge.com
Summerfield Suites by Wyndham 800/833-4353
www.summerfieldsuites.com
Summit International 800/457-4000
www.summithotels.com
Super 8 Motels 800/800-8000
www.super8.com
The Sutton Place Hotels 866/378-8866
www.suttonplace.com
Swissôtel 800/637-9477
www.swissotel.com
TownePlace Suites 888/236-2427
www.towneplace.com
Travelodge 800/578-7878
www.travelodge.com
Vagabond Inns 800/522-1555
www.vagabondinns.com
W Hotels 888/625-5144
www.whotels.com
Wellesley Inn and Suites 800/444-8888
www.wellesleyinnandsuites.com
WestCoast Hotels 800/325-4000
www.westcoasthotels.com
Westin Hotels & Resorts 800/937-8461
www.westin.com

Wingate Inns 800/228-1000
www.wingateinns.com
Woodfin Suite Hotels 800/966-3346
www.woodfinsuitehotels.com
WorldHotels 800/223-5652
www.worldhotels.com
Wyndham Hotels & Resorts 800/996-3426
www.wyndham.com

Airlines

Air Canada 888/247-2262
www.aircanada.ca
AirTran 800/247-8726
www.airtran.com
Alaska Airlines 800/252-7522
www.alaskaair.com
American Airlines 800/433-7300
www.aa.com
America West 800/235-9292
www.americawest.com
ATA 800/435-9282
www.ata.com
Continental Airlines 800/523-3273
www.continental.com
Delta Air Lines 800/221-1212
www.delta.com
Frontier Airlines 800/432-1359
www.frontierairlines.com
Hawaiian Airways 800/367-5320
www.hawaiianair.com
Jet Blue Airlines 800/538-2583
www.jetblue.com
Midwest Express 800/452-2022
www.midwestexpress.com
Northwest Airlines 800/225-2525
www.nwa.com
Southwest Airlines 800/435-9792
www.southwest.com
Spirit Airlines 800/772-7117
www.spiritair.com
United Airlines 800/241-6522
www.united.com
US Airways 800/428-4322
www.usairways.com

Car Rentals

Advantage 800/777-5500
www.arac.com
Alamo 800/327-9633
www.goalamo.com
Avis 800/831-2847
www.avis.com
Budget 800/527-0700
www.budget.com
Dollar 800/800-4000
www.dollarcar.com
Enterprise 800/325-8007
www.enterprise.com
Hertz 800/654-3131
www.hertz.com
National 800/227-7368
www.nationalcar.com
Payless 800/729-5377
www.paylesscarrental.com
Rent-A-Wreck.com 800/535-1391
www.rent-a-wreck.com
Thrifty 800/847-4389
www.thrifty.com

Meet The Stars

Mobil Travel Guide 2006 **Five-Star** *Award Winners*

CALIFORNIA
Lodgings
The Beverly Hills Hotel, *Beverly Hills*
Chateau du Sureau, *Oakhurst*
Four Seasons Hotel San Francisco, *San Francisco*
Hotel Bel-Air, *Los Angeles*
The Peninsula Beverly Hills, *Beverly Hills*
Raffles L'Ermitage Beverly Hills, *Beverly Hills*
The Ritz-Carlton, San Francisco, *San Francisco*

Restaurants
Bastide, *Los Angeles*
The Dining Room, *San Francisco*
The French Laundry, *Yountville*
Gary Danko, *San Francisco*

COLORADO
Lodgings
The Broadmoor, *Colorado Springs*
The Little Nell, *Aspen*

CONNECTICUT
Lodging
The Mayflower Inn, *Washington*

DISTRICT OF COLUMBIA
Lodging
Four Seasons Hotel Washington, DC *Washington*

FLORIDA
Lodgings
Four Seasons Resort Palm Beach, *Palm Beach*
The Ritz-Carlton Naples, *Naples*
The Ritz-Carlton, Palm Beach, *Manalapan*

GEORGIA
Lodgings
Four Seasons Hotel Atlanta, *Atlanta*
The Lodge at Sea Island Golf Club, *St. Simons Island*

Restaurants
The Dining Room, *Atlanta*
Seeger's, *Atlanta*

HAWAII
Lodging
Four Seasons Resort Maui at Wailea, *Wailea, Maui*

ILLINOIS
Lodgings
Four Seasons Hotel Chicago, *Chicago*
The Peninsula Chicago, *Chicago*
The Ritz-Carlton, A Four Seasons Hotel, *Chicago*

Restaurant
Charlie Trotter's, *Chicago*

MAINE
Restaurant
The White Barn Inn, *Kennebunkport*

MASSACHUSETTS
Lodgings
Blantyre, *Lenox*
Four Seasons Hotel Boston, *Boston*

NEW YORK
Lodgings
Four Seasons, Hotel New York, *New York*
The Point, *Saranac Lake*
The Ritz-Carlton New York, Central Park, *New York*
The St. Regis, *New York*

Restaurants
Alain Ducasse, *New York*
Jean Georges, *New York*
Masa, *New York*
per se, *New York*

NORTH CAROLINA
Lodging
The Fearrington House Country Inn, *Pittsboro*

PENNSYLVANIA
Restaurant
Le Bec-Fin, *Philadelphia*

SOUTH CAROLINA
Lodging
Woodlands Resort & Inn, *Summerville*

Restaurant
Dining Room at the Woodlands, *Summerville*

TEXAS
Lodging
The Mansion on Turtle Creek, *Dallas*

VERMONT
Lodging
Twin Farms, *Barnard*

VIRGINIA
Lodgings
The Inn at Little Washington, *Washington*
The Jefferson Hotel, *Richmond*

Restaurant
The Inn at Little Washington, *Washington*

Mobil Travel Guide has been rating establishments with its Mobil One- to Five-Star system since 1958. Each establishment awarded the Mobil Five-Star rating is one of the best in the country. Detailed information on each award winner can be found in the corresponding regional edition listed on the back cover of this book.

Four- and Five-Star Establishments in Northern California

★★★★★ Lodgings

Chateau du Sureau, *Oakhurst*
Four Seasons Hotel San Francisco, *San Francisco*
The Ritz-Carlton, San Francisco, *San Francisco*

★★★★★ Restaurants

The Dining Room, *San Francisco*
The French Laundry, *Yountville*
Gary Danko, *San Francisco*

★★★★ Lodgings

Bernardus Lodge, *Carmel Valley*
Casa Palmero at Pebble Beach, *Pebble Beach*
The Inn at Spanish Bay, *Pebble Beach*
The Lodge at CordeValle, *San Martin*
The Lodge at Pebble Beach, *Pebble Beach*
Mandarin Oriental, San Francisco, *San Francisco*
Meadowood Napa Valley, *St. Helena*
Park Hyatt San Francisco, *San Francisco*
Post Ranch Inn, *Big Sur*
The Ritz-Carlton, Half Moon Bay, *Half Moon Bay*

★★★★ Spas

The Carneros Inn Spa, The Carneros Inn, *Napa*
The Ritz-Carlton Spa, Half Moon Bay, *Half Moon Bay*
The Spa at Bernardus, Bernardus Lodge, *Carmel Valley*
The Spa at CordeValle, The Lodge at CordeValle, *San Martin*
The Spa at Post Ranch Inn, *Big Sur*
Spa du Soleil, Auberge du Soleil, *Rutherford*

★★★★ Restaurants

Aqua, *San Francisco*
Auberge du Soleil, *Rutherford*
Campton Place Dining Room, *San Francisco*
Erna's Elderberry House, *Oakhurst*
Fifth Floor, *San Francisco*
Fleur De Lys, *San Francisco*
La Folie, *San Francisco*
Masa's, *San Francisco*
Sierra Mar, *Big Sur*
Terra, *St. Helena*
The Village Pub, *Woodside*

America's Byways™ are a distinctive collection of American roads, their stories, and treasured places. They are roads to the heart and soul of America. In this section, you'll find the nationally designated Byways in California.

Big Sur Coast Highway, Route 1

CALIFORNIA

Route 1 from Carmel south to the San Luis Obispo County line follows some of the most spectacular and highly scenic shoreline found along California's coast. Views include rugged canyons and steep sea cliffs, granite shorelines, sea lions and other marine life, windswept cypress trees, and majestic redwood forests.

This Byway also provides you with a lesson in California's rich Mission-era and natural history. The primary goal of the Byway is to preserve California's delicate and pristine coastal ecosystem for its natives, visitors, and future generations, while still providing opportunities to experience its wonder.

Travel the route that hugs the California coast, providing access to austere, windswept cypress trees, fog-shrouded cliffs, and the crashing surf of the Pacific Ocean.

QUICK FACTS

Length: 72 miles.

Time to Allow: 3 to 5 hours.

Best Time to Drive: Spring, summer, and fall. High season is during June, July, and August.

Byway Travel Information: Monterey Travel and Tourism Alliance: phone 831/626-1424; Monterey Peninsula Visitor and Convention Bureau: phone 831/372-9323.

Special Considerations: Fill your gas tank in Carmel before heading south or in San Simeon before heading north on Route 1, because you'll encounter few gas stations along the way. The road is narrow and curvy, and in some places it has narrow shoulders and sharp drop-offs to the ocean far below. Large, long vehicles may have trouble with this winding road. Drive with care and watch for pedestrians and bicyclists.

Restrictions: The road is open all year, except for occasional mudslides during severe rainstorms.

Bicycle/Pedestrian Facilities: This Byway is a major attraction to pedestrians and cyclists. You'll find many shoulders along the way (although in some areas, they're narrow with sharp drop-offs) and plenty of room where all can share.

The Byway Story

The Big Sur Coast Highway tells cultural, historical, natural, recreational, and scenic stories that make it a unique and treasured Byway.

CULTURAL

The Big Sur is an area whose culture is largely shaped by the region's geography. The awe-inspiring scenic beauty of the Big Sur has lured and inspired countless artists, authors, and poets. The literary works of Henry Miller are filled with vivid descriptions of the Big Sur, while the artwork of Emil White and others attempts to portray the breathtaking scenery of the Big Sur's rocky coast and coastal mountains.

The Carmel area and the Salinas valley, less rugged but no less scenic or inspiring, also have played a vital role in the area's culture. The region has been home to many artists, none more famous than John Steinbeck, whose novels vividly describe life in the fertile Salinas valley. Although Steinbeck is the most famous, the area has also been home to actor Clint Eastwood, photographer Ansel Adams, and poet Robinson Jeffers.

HISTORICAL

Written histories regarding the region now known as the Big Sur began to appear in the mid-1500s, when a Portuguese ship passed by the area's coastline. New groups of European explorers approached the area throughout the late 1500s and early 1600s, many anchoring for a time in Monterey Bay. However, it wasn't until 1770 that the first permanent settlement was established, when a Spanish group started a mission in Carmel. The Spaniards first called the area south of the Carmel settlement El Pais Grande del Sur, or "the Big Country of the South." These same Spanish settlers were quick to introduce themselves and their culture to the area natives, who had lived in the region for centuries.

For centuries before the Europeans discovered the Big Sur, the Esselen Indians had thrived in the area as hunters and gatherers, using land and sea animals and plants in the woodlands and coastal plains between Point Sur and Lopez Point. By the early 18th century, other Spanish missions followed the Carmel Mission. The missions had the dual purpose of claiming the land for Spain and teaching the natives the Europeans' message of Christianity. In the late 1700s, the Spanish missionaries and soldiers forced many of the Esselen and other native peoples to leave their villages and move into the missions. Smallpox, cholera, and other European diseases almost completely wiped out the Esselen people when they came in contact with the foreign settlers. Those who were left mixed with the other natives in the missions so that they ceased to maintain a separate existence. As a result, very little is known today about their way of life.

A colorful variety of settlers of various nationalities began to take notice of the scenic Big Sur area and its inviting foothills. The Spanish and Mexican history also heavily influenced the culture and history of the area. Monterey was soon an important port, bringing even more people to the area.

Until the late 1800s, a small, rough trail served as the best overland route to Monterey from the Big Sur. Eventually, the trail widened into a road of sorts, which was still frequently lost in landslides. This widening allowed the journey to Monterey to be made in just 11 hours, as opposed to the three or four days it had taken previously. After many years of difficult passage over poor roads between Big Sur and the rest of central California, Route 1 was completed in 1937. By its completion, 15 years of labor and $9 million had been expended.

NATURAL

The allure of the Big Sur Coast Highway comes not just from the sea and the mountains, but also from the convergence of the sea with the mountains. Many other destinations around the country feature beautiful mountains, and countless others offer beaches from which to enjoy the ocean. The Big Sur, however, is one of the few places in America where these two dominant features converge so dramatically. Travelers from around the world visit the Big Sur to experience its breathtaking scenery.

The Byway enables you to experience the Pacific Ocean in its most natural, prehistoric state. The endless blue horizon, as seen from the Byway, is most often void of any man-made floating vessels, unlike most other coastlines. Travelers are more likely, in fact, to witness a massive whale surfacing for air or some sea otters playing than to see a freighter waiting to port. Additionally, the Big Sur offers you the unique experience of enjoying the enchanting sounds of the sea, unhindered by any other noise. Many people find that time escapes them as they park on one of the many turnouts and take in the sounds of the sea.

The San Lucia coastal mountain range offers the other side of the Big Sur's natural beauty. The range is a natural paradise of cypress and redwood forests, waterfalls, and meadows full of colorful wildflowers, such as lupines and poppies. The mountains also host one of the Byway's most unique natural elements: the giant redwood tree. The redwoods stretch along a narrow strip of land from the Big Sur area to the southwest corner of Oregon; redwood trees thrive in the specific climate along this area and are not native to any other region in the world. Many of the oldest of the trees are around 2,000 years old. The tallest redwoods have reached heights of about 350 feet. Most redwoods average 50 to 250 feet in height. Such heights require solid foundations, with many of the giant trees' diameters spanning 10 to 15 feet.

The convergence of the Pacific Ocean with the San Lucia Mountains of the Big Sur coastline is the source of the inviting, often overwhelming scenery of the Big Sur. The ocean has helped to carve out the tantalizing craggy rock inlets along the corridor. The highway hugs steep, rocky cliffs on the east side of the road, while blunt drops to the west fall straight to the sea. The solid land mass of the shoreline holds strong as waves of the mighty Pacific push against its cliffs and crash against its rocks. The Big Sur offers a fulfilling blend of natural sights and sounds unlike anywhere else.

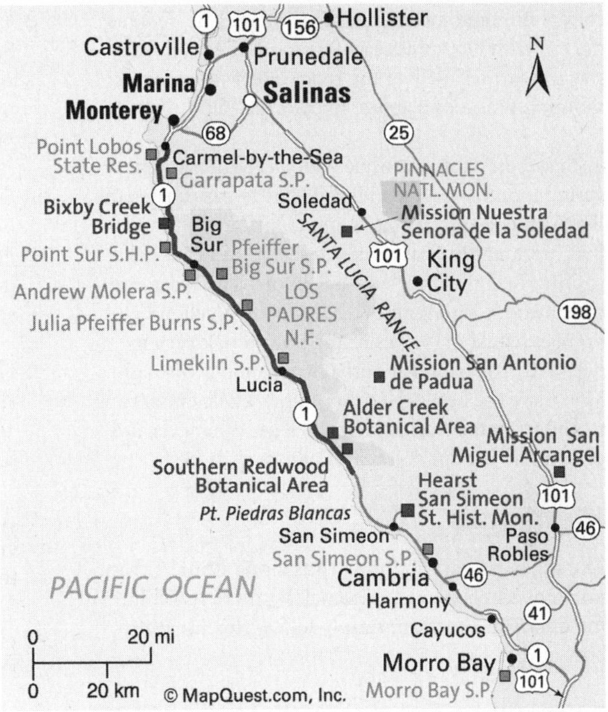

RECREATIONAL

While Big Sur's beaches hardly resemble the vast stretches of sun-baked sand that dot southern California's coastline, they do offer a wide variety of recreational possibilities. Even during the summer, Big Sur's beaches are subject to generally cool weather. Sunny days are sporadic because a blanket of seasonal fog often hugs the coastline, lowering the temperature in the process. To be prepared, bring a change of warm clothes. Also, bring a pair of sturdy shoes—getting to Big Sur's beaches requires at least a short hike.

Private property and Big Sur's steep terrain make most of its coastline inaccessible to the public. Fortunately, however, several state park and US Forest Service beaches are open to the public all year. These beaches are recommended due to easy access and breathtaking scenery. Located 23 miles south of Carmel, **Andrew Molera State Park** is the largest state park on the Big Sur coast. A wide, scenic, mile-long path leads to a sandy beach that's sheltered from the wind by a large bluff to the north. The path itself is as much a delight as the beach, taking you through a meadow filled with wildflowers and sycamore trees and offering fine views of the coastal mountain range to the east. The path parallels the Big Sur River, which enters the sea adjacent to Molera's beach.

Although **Pfeiffer Beach** is Big Sur's most popular coastal access point, this beach is hard to find if you've never been to it before. The trick is locating unmarked Sycamore Canyon Road. Here's a tip: Sycamore Canyon Road is the only paved, ungated road west of Route 1 between the Big Sur post office and Pfeiffer Big Sur State Park. After you find the turnout, make a very sharp turn and follow the road for about 2 miles until it ends. Drive carefully—this road is narrow and winding and is unsuitable for trailer traffic. From a large parking area at the end of the road, a short, well-marked path leads to the beach. Cliffs tower above this breathtaking stretch of sand, and a large arch-shaped rock formation just offshore makes for some dazzling sunsets.

Just a mile south of the US Forest Service Station in Pacific Valley and 14 miles north of the San Luis Obispo County line lies **Sand Dollar Beach.** From a large parking lot across Route 1 from Plaskett Creek Campground, a well-built stairway leads to a crescent-shaped beach that's protected from the wind by bluffs. Sand Dollar offers visitors the widest expanse of sand along the Big Sur Coast and, possibly, the mildest weather. Standing on the beach looking northeast, the towering 5,155-foot **Cone Peak** is visible. For an interesting side trip, visit **Jade Cove,** which is located 2 miles south of Sand Dollar Beach. Big Sur's south coast is famous for its jade reserves, and Jade Cove is a popular spot for beachcombers and rock hounds.

SCENIC

The Big Sur Coast Highway affords fantastic views of one of the nation's most scenic coastlines. (Keep in mind that the scenery can be overwhelming, and you may struggle to keep your eyes on the narrow, winding road.) At certain points along the Byway, the only way to get any closer to the Pacific is to get in it! Traveling Route 1 offers ample opportunity for experiencing the mighty ocean pounding against the pristine coastline, with waves crashing against the rocks and cliffs. Scenic overlooks are plentiful along the Byway, providing you with breathtaking views from safe turnouts.

If the vast blue waters of the Pacific aren't enough for you, direct your eyes inland, taking in the beautiful coastal hills and mountains. The inland side delights the eye with its cypress and redwood forests, impressive trees towering over the road. Other areas feature mountain meadows ablaze in colorful wildflowers.

Each season offers a unique scenic experience. The spring months are a wonderful time to experience the Big Sur's deep green colors and colorful wildflowers that brighten the grassy hillsides. Autumn in Big Sur country brings with it new fall colors. The sycamores, cottonwoods, and maples display golden yellows and oranges, while the leaves of the poison oak turn a deep red. The winter months of December through March are the best time to spot gray whales migrating to and from the warm waters of Baja. Whenever the season, the Big Sur showcases nature at its best.

Highlights

The Big Sur Coast Highway runs along Route 1 from north of San Simeon to Carmel. If you're traveling the opposite direction, simply follow this list from bottom up.

- **Ragged Point** marks the official entrance to the Big Sur Coast Highway. Ragged Point has incredible views in every direction and features a restaurant, gas station, and hotel.

- Not far after Ragged Point, the Byway enters **Los Padres National Forest.**

- Continuing north, the Byway travels past the **Southern Redwood Botanical Area** and then the **Alder Creek Botanical Area.**

- **Lucia,** consisting of a restaurant and a small motel, is the next major point of interest along the corridor.

- From Lucia, the Byway passes several state parks, including **Limekiln** and **Julia Pfeiffer Burns state parks.**

- Following Julia Pfeiffer Burns State Park, the corridor soon enters the expansive **Big Sur area.** This area consists of several inns, restaurants, and shops scattered along the corridor.

- An important point of interest near the Big Sur area is the **Point Sur State Historic Park,** home to the historic Point Sur Lighthouse.

- Historic **Bixby Bridge** lies farther north of Point Sur.

- From Bixby Bridge, the Byway continues north to its ending point in **Carmel,** known for its pristine beaches and charming shops, as well as its cozy cottages and extravagant mansions.

Tioga Road/Big Oak Flat Road

CALIFORNIA

Tioga Road/Big Oak Flat Road offers one of the most spectacular passages over the Sierra Nevada, making it the highest automobile pass in California, boasting an elevation change of over 1 mile from west to east. Along the route, views include towering granite peaks, pristine lakes, wildflower-covered meadows, and lush evergreen forests with Giant Sequoia groves. Tuolumne meadows offers visitors a chance to see how ancient glaciers created this serene and rugged landscape.

The Byway provides motorists with an opportunity to experience this scenery from a vehicle. For hiking enthusiasts, it offers some of the most beautiful High Sierra backcountry trails.

The Byway Story

The Tioga Road/Big Oak Flat Road tells historical, natural, recreational, and scenic stories that make it a unique and treasured Byway.

HISTORICAL

The area now encompassed by Yosemite National Park was once home to various nations of Native Americans. By the mid-1800s, when American explorers first caught sight of the area, the natives were primarily of Southern Miwok ancestry and called themselves the Ahwahneechee. The word "Yosemite" is in fact derived from the Ahwahneechee word for grizzly bear, *uzumati.* These earliest inhabitants of Yosemite soon found themselves at odds with the new settlers of the area. The Gold Rush of 1849 brought thousands of settlers to Yosemite, many crossing over the Sierra Nevada in search of their dreams.

Conflict between the natives and the new settlers followed, and eventually, California authorized the organization of the Mariposa Battalion to gather the Ahwahneechee and relocate them to various other locations in the state. Thus the Yosemite valley opened for tourism, which today brings more than 4 million visitors annually.

The many new visitors to the beautiful area did not come without impact, so citizens began a campaign to preserve the area. On June 30, 1864, President Abraham Lincoln signed a bill granting Yosemite Valley and the Mariposa Grove of Giant Sequoias to the state of California as an inalienable public trust. This marked the first time in history that the federal government set aside scenic lands simply to protect them and to allow for their enjoyment by all people. This act also paved the way for the establishment of the nation's first national park, Yellowstone, in 1872. Later, a concerned and energetic conservationist,

Quick Facts

Length: 64 miles.

Time to Allow: 3 hours.

Best Time to Drive: Mid- to late May through mid-November. Summer is the high season.

Byway Travel Information: Yosemite National Park: phone 209/372-0200.

Special Considerations: The maximum speed limit is 45 mph along the Byway. You'll find limited fueling opportunities.

Restrictions: Tioga Road is closed during the winter from Crane Flat Junction to Lee Vining due to snowfall. Call Yosemite National Park for updated road and weather information. Yosemite National Park charges an entrance fee.

Bicycle/Pedestrian Facilities: The Byway is well traveled by pedestrians and bicyclists. National Park entrance fees are reduced when entering on foot, bicycle, or motorcycle.

John Muir, brought about the creation of Yosemite National Park on October 1, 1890.

NATURAL

The Tioga Road crosses right through the middle of an area known worldwide for its unique natural features. Yosemite National Park includes three major natural features: forested mountains and bald granite domes, mountain meadows, and the Earth's largest living thing—the giant sequoia tree. Two hundred miles of roads help travelers enjoy all these features, whether by car or by the free shuttle buses offered in some areas. To get to know the real Yosemite, however, you must leave your car and take a few steps on a trail.

The Mountains and Granite Domes of the Sierra Nevada began to take shape about 500 million years ago, when the region lay beneath an ancient sea. The seabed consisted of thick layers of sediment, which eventually were folded, twisted, and thrust above sea level. At the same time, molten rock welled up from the earth and slowly cooled beneath the layers of sediment, forming granite. Over millions of years, erosion wore away most of the overlying rock, exposing the granite. While this continued, water and then glaciers shaped and carved the face of Yosemite, leaving massive peaks and bare granite domes. Today, the park ranges from 2,000 feet to more than 13,000 feet above sea level.

The meadows of Yosemite are natural wonders in their own right. They are the most diverse parts of Yosemite's ecosystem, providing food and shelter for nearly all the wildlife living in the park. In the summer, the meadows and lakes are busy with life, as the plants and animals take advantage of the short warm season to grow, reproduce, and store food. The meadows are also unique because they are immense fields of bliss recessed and secluded in the middle of towering granite mountains. The more popular and accessible meadows are found in Yosemite Valley, Tuolumne Meadows, and Wawona. The middle and upper elevations of the park also contain secluded, perfect mountain meadows.

The mighty sequoia is the largest living thing on Earth. Yosemite is one of the few locations where the sequoias can be found, growing in any of three sequoia groves. Mariposa Grove, 35 miles south of Yosemite Valley, is the largest of the groves. The oldest of the sequoia trees have been dated at over 2,700 years old. The greatest of the trees have trunk diameters of over 30 feet! Although the more slender redwood trees along California's coast surpass the sequoia in height, the much more robust sequoia is no shorty, with the highest measuring over 300 feet tall.

RECREATIONAL

For more than a century, Yosemite National Park has been a premier destination for recreation. Its unique natural qualities and breathtaking scenery provide the perfect backdrop for outdoor recreational activities. Put hiking on top of your to-do list, because just a bit of hiking can take you to sites more rewarding than sites just off of the highway.

The summer season, although short along the Sierra Nevada, offers the most accommodating environment for recreation. Hiking, enjoying the scenery, fishing, camping, wildlife viewing, mountain and rock climbing, backpacking, and photography are some activities available in the park. Yosemite's wilderness offers experiences for both seasoned hikers and novices. About 800 miles of trails offer a variety of climate, elevation, and spectacular scenery.

In the winter, Yosemite's high country is a serene, white wonderland. The land is covered by deep, undisturbed snow, creating a landscape far different than the summer's. The winter months in Yosemite are seeing increased amounts of mountaineering activities. Meanwhile, cross-country skiing and snowshoeing have grown in popularity and open up a new world for backpackers. Whether you visit in the winter or summer, Yosemite offers an unparalleled chance to get away from it all.

SCENIC

The Tioga Road traverses an area in which the most memorable features are remembered not only for their superb natural beauty but also for their unmatched size. Massive granite domes and cliffs take your breath away. Sequoia trees have branches that are larger than the largest of other tree species, while the park's famous waterfalls are remembered for their size and spectacle. For ages, Yosemite has lured and inspired painters, photographers, and writers. Yet most find that no work of art can adequately provide the sense of amazement and serenity granted to Yosemite's visitors.

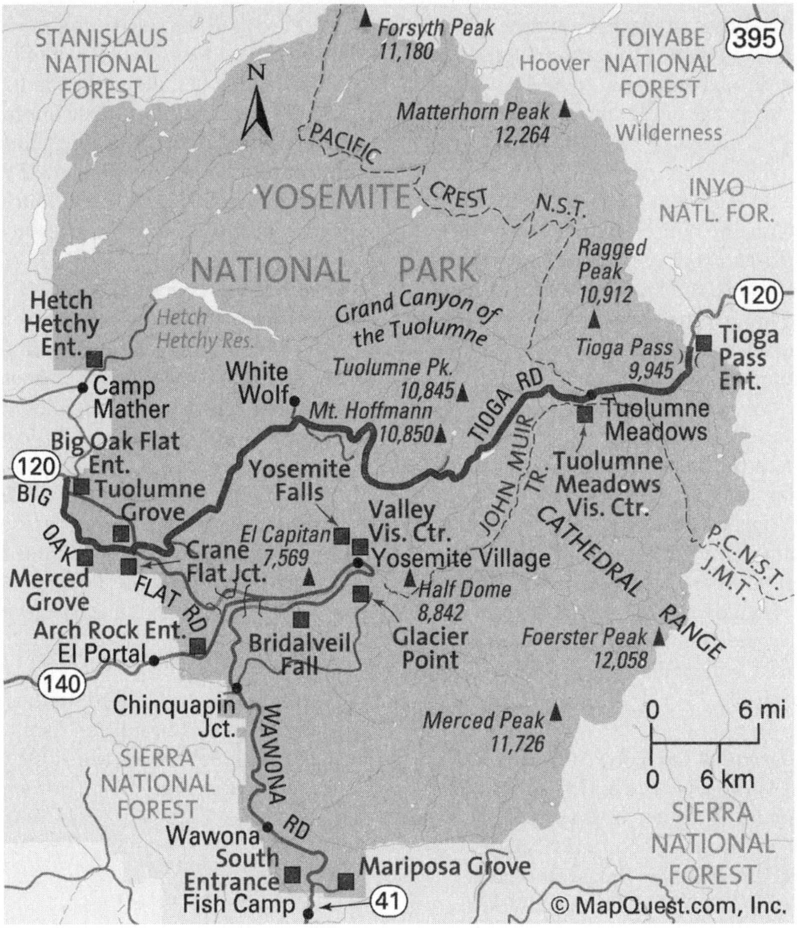

Spring provides the best time to see Yosemite's waterfalls, as the spring thaw brings with it an abundance of runoff water to fall from cliffs and peaks. Peak runoff typically occurs in May or June, with some waterfalls (including Yosemite Falls) often dwindling to only a trickle or even becoming completely dry by August. Yosemite Falls are the highest in the park at 2,452 feet and are the fifth highest falls in the world. You can walk to Lower Yosemite Fall (320 feet) in just a few minutes. A hike to the top of Upper Yosemite Fall (1,430 feet) is a strenuous, all-day hike. Other famous falls include the Bridaveil Falls (620 feet), Nevada Falls (594 feet), Ribbon Falls (1,612 feet), Staircase Falls (1,300 feet), and Horsetail Falls (1,000 feet). Horsetail Falls, on the east side of El Capitán, is famous for appearing to be on fire when it reflects the orange glow of sunset in mid-February.

The Tioga Road passes through an area of rugged mountain scenery mixed with sublime mountain meadows. The road continues through an area featuring sparkling mountain lakes; bare granite domes; and lofty, forested mountain peaks. Some of the best views are available on the many scenic overlooks along the road, while hiking is sometimes necessary to view that perfect mountainscape.

Highlights

Consider taking this tour of Yosemite National Park:

- Begin on the east end by ascending the **Tioga Pass** and entering the park. Be sure to have the entrance fee handy ($20 for a passenger car). This fee entitles you to seven days of entry into the park, coming and going as you please during that time.

- Enjoy the drive as you approach **Tuolumne Meadows.** Expect to spend several hours learning and exploring through tours and tram rides. You can also take advantage of the concessions offered by the park.

- Fifteen to twenty miles past Tuolumne Meadows, look to the south and notice **Tenaya Lake.** Look up to the north, and you see the towering peaks of **Mount Hoffmann** and **Tuolumne.** One of these peaks is just 5 feet shorter than the other; can you tell which one is which? Continue along the Tioga Road throughout most of the park, a fantastic drive.

- As you approach the junction of the Tioga and Big Oak Flat Roads, chances are, you'll want to get out and enjoy the sights. The Junction at Crane Flat is a good stopping place. To the north is **Tuolumne Grove,** a short hike onto a pretty grove of sequoia trees with a self-guided nature trail. A little down the road and to the south is **Merced Grove.** The trail into Merced is more difficult than at Tuolumne but just as enjoyable.

- As you near the end of the Byway at the **Big Oak Flat Entrance Station,** be sure to stop and gather information about Yosemite. As you exit the park, you may wish to turn to the north and take a side trip up to **Hetch Hetchy Reservoir.** This is an especially great idea if you like the outdoors and backcountry trails. Fishing is available at the reservoir.

- After a visit to the reservoir, turn back toward Big Oak Flat Road and head down into the **Yosemite Valley,** about 40 miles to the south. Stop at the visitors center for up-to-date information about activities and sights, including the famous **Half Dome, El Capitán,** and **Bridalveil Falls.** Hotels and restaurants are plentiful here, which makes the area an excellent place to stay the night.

- Continue south along Highway 41 (Wawona Road) into **Wawona.** Although smaller than Yosemite Valley, plenty of amenities are still to be found here, including the **Pioneer Museum and Visitors Center.** If you visit at the right time of the year (summer), hop on the free shuttle bus at the Wawona store, which will take you 7 miles away to the **Mariposa Grove.** The grove is famous for the "drive-through trees," the giant sequoias. Although cars no longer drive through these trees, feel free to explore by foot or tram (for a fee). Toward the top of the grove, a small museum and gift shop help orient you.

- The tour ends as you head south and out the South Entrance toward Fish Camp and into the **Sierra National Forest,** which is a whole new treasure to discover.

Volcanic Legacy Scenic Byway

CALIFORNIA

Quick Facts

Length: 360 miles.

Time to Allow: 1 day.

Best Time to Drive: Summer and fall provide for the best travel conditions. The winter months offer beautiful snowscapes. High season is June to September.

Byway Travel Information: Siskiyou County Visitor's Bureau: phone toll-free 888/66-BYWAY; Volcanic Legacy National Scenic Byway Information: phone toll-free 866/772-9929; Byway local Web site: www.volcaniclegacybyway.org.

Restrictions: The geometry of this Byway makes it the most restrictive of the routes with respect to large vehicles, including recreational vehicles (RVs) and tour buses. Tour buses are allowed on the Byway, subject to specific permitting by the park. All route segments of the Volcanic Legacy Scenic Byway are open to traffic year-round, with the exception of the roadway within Lassen Volcanic National Park. Portions of this road are subject to seasonal closures, typically from November through June. Other portions of the route may be subject to periodic temporary closures or restrictions due to inclement weather and maintenance. Small fees are collected at Lassen Volcanic National Park and Lava Beds National Monument.

Bicycle/Pedestrian Facilities: Bicyclists and pedestrians are permitted along the corridor route segments with the exception of I-5. Pedestrians are, however, discouraged from using some portions of the roadway, particularly in Lassen Volcanic National Park, due to the lack of sufficient shoulder area along the existing roadways. In several areas, particularly the National Park Service and Forest Service lands, trails leading off the Byway are used by bicyclists and pedestrians for recreation, as well as for travel to points of interest.

California's Volcanic Legacy Scenic Byway stretches from Mount Lassen in northern California to the California-Oregon border. From the border, the Byway continues north to Oregon's Crater Lake, making this Byway America's volcano-to-volcano highway. The volcanic activity of the past has created unique geological formations, such as wavy lava flows and lava tube caves. Surrounding this volcanic landscape is a wide diversity of scenery. The Byway travels through or near dense forests, broad wetlands and habitat areas, pastoral grasslands, farms and ranches, and well-managed timber resource lands.

The Volcanic Legacy Scenic Byway offers even more benefits than just the fascinating volcanic geology and scenery. Each season offers a different array of outdoor recreational opportunities. The beautiful green forests and mountains along the Byway are home to hiking trails, including the nationally recognized Pacific Crest Trail; ski slopes; and great fishing and kayaking in clear, cool mountain streams and lakes. Traveling the Byway, you can also enjoy viewing the hundreds of species of wildlife along the way.

The Byway Story

The Volcanic Legacy Scenic Byway tells historical, natural, recreational, and scenic stories that make it a unique and treasured Byway.

HISTORICAL

Although the name may not imply it, the Volcanic Legacy Scenic Byway contains not only natural and scenic qualities, but also rich historical qualities. Much of the historical significance of the Byway arises from its Native American roots, and the Byway is dotted with historic mining and logging towns. Many features along the Byway are listed as historical landmarks.

Captain Jack's Stronghold, a national monument located in the Lava Beds National Monument, is historically significant because it was the site of the Modoc War. During the Modoc War of 1872-1873, the Modoc Tribe took advantage of the unique geography of their homelands. Under the leadership of Kintuashk, who came to be known as Captain Jack, the Modoc people took refuge in a natural lava fortress. The site of the fortress is now known as Captain Jack's Stronghold. From this secure base, Captain Jack and his group of 53 fighting men and their families held off US Army forces, which numbered up to ten times more than Kintuashk's tribe. However, the tribe was still able to hold off the Army forces for five months.

Mount Shasta is another site of historical significance along this Byway. The major history of the mountain lies in its geological greatness. It also has a spiritual history. Native Americans of the area believed Mount Shasta to be the abode of the Great Spirit. Out of respect, the natives never ascended past the timberline. A long history of mythology surrounds the mountain, including legends of Lemurians, Atlanteans, secret commonwealth citizens, dwarfs, fairies, Bigfoot, and space beings that materialize at will. Mount Shasta draws visitors from all over the world, some seeking spiritual insight, others the experience of the beauty and natural wonders that Mother Nature has to offer here in this unique alpine region. The upper elevation of Mount Shasta Wilderness was designated in 1976 as a National Natural Historic Landmark.

The Volcanic Legacy Scenic Byway is dotted with historic towns, many of which began as logging communities. McCloud is one example, being a company-built mill town, still revealing its colorful railroad and logging history. The Heritage Junction Museum in the city offers exhibits displaying 100 years worth of historical artifacts and photographs depicting the region. The still-functioning McCloud Railway is also evidence of the logging history of the town. Likewise, the town of Weed was a logging town, built in 1897. The Weed Historic Lumber Museum helps to reveal the part Weed played in the logging industry of the time. Other historical towns along the Byway include Westwood, one of the largest company towns in the West during the early to mid-1900s, and Mount Shasta City.

Unfortunately, not all of the history along the Byway is bright. The Tulelake Relocation Center was one of ten American concentration camps established during World War II to incarcerate 110,000 persons of Japanese ancestry. The majority of these people were American citizens. A large monument of basalt rock and concrete along the north side of State Highway 139 commemorates the relocation center. The monument, dedicated in 1979, incorporates multiple levels of rock walls, a concrete apron, and a state historical marker. The Tule Lake Relocation Center is located off the Byway about 10 miles from the town of Tule Lake. The new Tule Lake Museum in the town of Tule Lake has a restored camp building and watch tower on display, as well as information about the relocation center.

NATURAL

The Volcanic Legacy Scenic Byway includes some of the most spectacular natural wonders in the nation and takes you around magnificent Mount Shasta, a solitary peak rising to a height of 14,162 feet. The Byway allows you to experience the effects of the geological and volcanic history of the region. These geological and volcanic natural wonders are reason enough to travel the Byway, but the Byway also contains an abundance of natural wildlife and vegetative habitats.

This Byway traverses two major geological areas. Lassen Volcanic National Park is located in the southern portion of the Byway. The park contains Lassen Peak, one of the largest plug dome volcanoes in the world. Lassen Peak was a major source of the many geological formations of the area. Lava Beds National Monument, located along the northern part of the Byway, near California's border with Oregon, is the site of the largest concentration of lava tube caves in the world. To finish this exciting volcano-to-volcano journey, continue north on Highway 97 to Crater Lake National Park.

The Volcanic Legacy Scenic Byway stretches across the convergence of the Nevada Mountains with the Great Basin. This convergence provides a vast diversity of habitats. The diversity allows for a significantly higher number of plant and animal species than most other regions of the West, with habitat for more than 360 species of animals and more than 1,000 plant species.

The many state parks, recreation areas, and wildlife reserves along the Byway provide the best opportunities to observe these natural living resources. At the refuges, such as the Lower Klamath National Wildlife Refuge, visitors can view the largest concentration of bald eagles in the lower 48 states during the winter, and the largest annual concentration of waterfowl in North America.

RECREATIONAL

The Volcanic Legacy Scenic Byway's length and vast diversity of landscapes provide a wide variety of year-round recreational opportunities. You can tour a lighted lava tube or spelunk on your own at Lava Beds National Monument, see bubbling mud pots and steam vents at Lassen Volcanic National Park, or drive to an elevation of 7,900 feet on Mount Shasta to view the surrounding landscape. The Byway offers hikes through national forest lands that cover much of the area along the Byway. Crisp lakes, streams, and rivers offer great fishing, boating, swimming, or quiet contemplation. Also available are cross-country skiing, snowshoeing, and snowmobiling in the winter months. If that isn't enough, hang gliding and parasailing are popular in the Hat Creek area of Lassen National Forest.

SCENIC

The volcanic landscape of the Volcanic Legacy Scenic Byway includes distinctive features of mountain lakes and streams, three

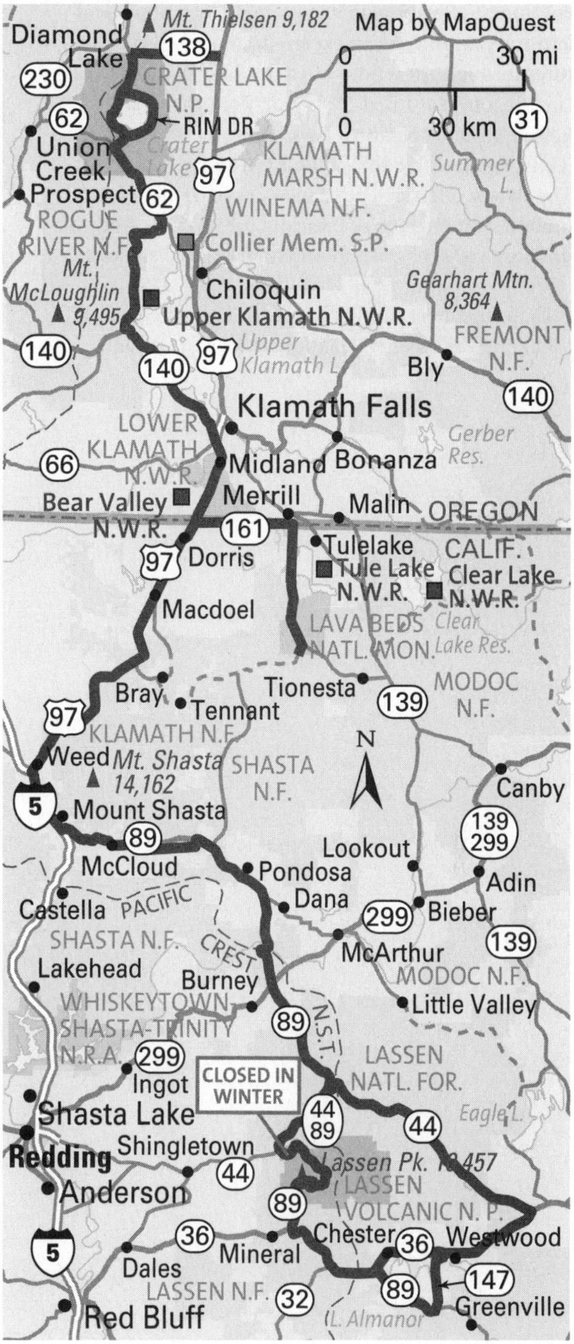

volcanoes (all nationally recognized), lava flows, and lava tube caves. You can experience these volcanic features through attractions at Crater Lake National Park (in Oregon), Lava Beds National Monument, and Lassen Volcanic National Park. However, the volcanic landscape is visible throughout the entire Byway. The Byway offers extended views of majestic volcano peaks, an abundance of beautiful forest vistas, and up-close views of crisp mountain lakes and streams.

Perhaps the most captivating of the Volcanic Legacy Scenic Byway's scenic qualities are its vast volcano mountain peaks. Mount Shasta is the tallest of the peaks. Others include Lassen Peak and Mount Scott on the rim of Crater Lake. The immensity of the peaks allows them to be viewed from hundreds of miles away. The Byway circles around Mount Shasta, providing views from every angle. The majority of peaks along the Byway are above the timberline and provide views of broad snowfields and craggy rock outcroppings. At lower elevations, broad grassy meadows with extensive wildflowers offer outstanding foreground settings for views of the more distant peaks.

Las Vegas Strip

NEVADA

An All-American Road

Often referred to as the Jewel of the Desert, Las Vegas has long been recognized as the entertainment vacation capital of the country, and the Las Vegas Strip—at the heart of this playland—sparkles like no other place on Earth. More than 31 million visitors from around the world are drawn to the lights of the Strip each year to experience its unique blend of exciting entertainment, scenic beauty, and lavishly landscaped resorts. An array of theme resorts can transport you to various exotic realms, from a medieval castle to a Parisian sidewalk café, a lakeside Italian village, or a pyramid in ancient Egypt.

The Las Vegas Strip hosts thousands of motorists a week; after you arrive on the Strip, however, you may be surprised to find that it's also a very enjoyable walking environment. The Strip is the only Byway that is more scenic at night than during the day. In fact, 365 days of the year, 24 hours a day, the Neon Trail offers a fascinating foray past spectacular resorts featuring a variety of visual delights. Whether it's pirates plundering, fiery volcanoes spouting, or tropical gardens luring the weary, the Las Vegas Strip offers a variety of fascinating visual experiences that enchant and mesmerize visitors of all ages. The many facets of this corridor make it truly a one-of-a-kind destination.

QUICK FACTS

Length: 4.5 miles.

Time to Allow: From half an hour to several hours.

Best Time to Drive: Las Vegas is warm year-round. The Strip is usually fairly crowded and congested. Nighttime is usually busier than daytime, and holidays are especially busy.

Byway Travel Information: Nevada Commission on Tourism: phone 775/687-4322.

Special Considerations: This is a pedestrian-rich environment, so be on the alert when driving. Consider driving the Byway once each direction. This way, you will be able to view all the sites that line both sides of the street and catch some that you may have missed.

Bicycle/Pedestrian Facilities: Sidewalks line the Strip and provide plenty of room for walking. Cyclists are welcome, but they must observe the same traffic laws as automobiles.

The Byway Story

The Las Vegas Strip tells cultural, historical, recreational, and scenic stories that make it a unique and treasured Byway.

CULTURAL

While Las Vegas is perhaps best known for its gaming culture—the popularity and influence of which have spread to cities all over the world—the Las Vegas Strip possesses many other outstanding cultural amenities. The diversity and virtuosity of the architecture of the hotels and resorts along the Strip are certainly worth noting. Some of the world's most talented architects have created complex fantasylands all along the Strip. Just a few of the more recent projects include reproductions of the streets of New York, a bayside Tuscany village, the canals of Venice, and a replica of the Eiffel Tower and the Arc de Triomphe.

Many of the resorts on the Las Vegas Strip also feature world-class art galleries full of paintings by world-renowned artists, such as Renoir, Monet, and Van Gogh. Other resorts hold galleries of other unique items, like antique automobiles or wax figures. The Guinness World of Records Museum offers an interesting array of the unusual, and the World of Coca-Cola Las Vegas features an interactive storytelling theater.

Various hotels on the Las Vegas Strip feature a variety of top-caliber theatrical and dance shows. Several hotels and casinos host world-class sporting events and concerts featuring top-name entertainers. And no matter where you go on the Strip, you are bound to run into the dazzling light displays that permeate the area. The magical re-creations found along the Byway are the symbols of our society's most fantastic dreams of luxury.

HISTORICAL

The Las Vegas Strip, world-renowned for its neon glitter, possesses an equally colorful historical past. The unique history of Las Vegas is undeniably entwined with the culture of gaming. Gambling was legalized in Nevada in 1931, and the first casino opened downtown that same year. Competition was intense, and casino builders soon were looking to land outside the city limits just south of downtown along Highway 91 (the Old Los Angeles Highway), which is now known as the Las Vegas Strip.

Most of the Las Vegas Strip is not really located within the Las Vegas city limits, but along a corridor of South Las Vegas Boulevard located in unincorporated Clark County. The area was sparsely developed until 1938, when the first resort property was built 4 miles south of downtown Las Vegas at the corner of San Francisco Avenue (now Sahara) and Highway 91 (South Las Vegas Boulevard). Reportedly, city officials had denied licenses to certain businessmen with questionable connections who had applied to build a casino downtown. Undaunted, they decided to build outside the city limits, just south of the downtown district.

In 1941, construction began on El Rancho Vegas resort at the corner of San Francisco Avenue and Highway 91. The original El Rancho Vegas introduced a new style of recreation and entertainment to the Nevada desert by combining lodging, gambling, restaurants, entertainment, shops, a travel agency, horseback riding, and swimming in one resort. El Rancho Vegas was followed a year later by the Last Frontier Resort Hotel & Casino. The well-known Little Church of the West was originally constructed in the resort's Frontier Village. Listed on the National Register of Historic Places, the small chapel has survived four moves on the Strip.

One of the Strip's more colorful (and infamous) characters, Ben "Bugsy" Siegel (reputed hit man for New York mobster Lucky Luciano), oversaw the construction of the fabulous Flamingo Hotel, the third major (and most extravagant) resort to be built on the Strip. Although Siegel met his unfortunate demise soon after the resort's 1946 opening, his prophecies for the future of Las Vegas came true. This new popular playground of Hollywood stars prospered, with the Flamingo setting the stage for the many luxurious resorts yet to be imagined.

As the 1950s began, only four major resorts stood along the Strip, but three more major players were about to hit the scene. The Desert Inn, the Sahara, and the Sands all arrived on the Strip in the early 1950s, further enhancing the Strip's image as a self-contained playground by featuring elaborate tennis courts, an 18-hole golf course, larger casinos, and fabulous showrooms with Broadway's and Hollywood's brightest stars. Las Vegas has continued to build on this legacy, developing newer and more elaborate resorts every year to make certain that Las Vegas retains the image of the most fabulous playground on Earth.

RECREATIONAL

The simplest and easiest recreation on the Strip is strolling and sightseeing along the Boulevard. Intriguing arrays of fantasylands in lush surroundings welcome you to the Strip. But the excitement only begins with sightseeing. From comfortable and plush hotels to exciting displays of lights and fountains, Las Vegas creates a dreamlike lifestyle with color, sound, and light all combined to make the experience on the Las Vegas Strip memorable.

For the more adventuresome, roller coasters featured at several hotels provide a ride that twists, loops, and turns to your delight. Other resorts provide 3-D ride films appealing to the senses of sight, sound, and motion. Many of these rides feature the latest technologies for extra thrills. Most of the resorts along the Strip offer displays of grandeur for every visitor to enjoy. Anyone driving the Byway can stop to see erupting volcanoes, dueling ships, dancing fountains, circus acts, and lush tropical gardens.

In addition to a variety of theatrical and dance shows, the resorts offer varied spectator sports, such as boxing matches. There isn't a resort on the Strip that doesn't offer visitors every amenity imaginable. World-class spas, pools, and exercise rooms are as enticing as the casinos. When you aren't searching for slot machines, you may choose to browse through the many stores and boutiques each resort has to offer. You will find everything from designer fashion to specialty candies to Las Vegas souvenirs. Whatever you choose to do, you can find it in Las Vegas.

SCENIC

As one of the most geographically isolated major cities in the continental United States, Las Vegas provides you with an extraordinary visual experience. The matchless Las Vegas Strip serves as the gateway to a host of memorable experiences that are distinctly Las Vegas. The Strip's incredible array of resorts are constructed around themes that transport visitors to different exotic realms, including a medieval castle, the Parisian Eiffel Tower, a lakeside Italian village, and a pyramid in ancient Egypt. Day or night, the Neon Trail provides a fascinating foray past spectacular resorts that offer a variety of visual delights to pedestrians and motorists alike.

Highlights

The Southern Las Vegas Strip Walking Tour begins at South Las Vegas Blvd and Russell Road, although you can go the opposite way by reading this list from the bottom up.

- The famous "Welcome to Fabulous Las Vegas" sign announces that you're on the right track. On the east side of the Strip, you see **The Little Church of the West,** the site of many celebrity weddings and a favorite place today to have the perfect wedding.

- Park the car at the free parking garage at **Mandalay Bay** (most of the large hotels offer plenty of covered free parking). Explore the tropical themed hotel, including a fun sand and surf beach. Mandalay Bay is one of the newest hotels on the Strip (built in 1999), and that makes it a popular attraction.

- From Mandalay Bay, you can walk north to **Luxor,** the great black glass pyramid. (If you prefer, hop on the free tram that takes you right to the front doors of Luxor—you may want to save your energy for later in the trip.) While at Luxor, don't miss the **King Tut Tomb exhibit**—an exact replica of the ancient Egyptian pharaoh's tomb. A rotating **IMAX** film experience is also a popular attraction here. This unique hotel is amazing and has one of the largest atriums in the world.

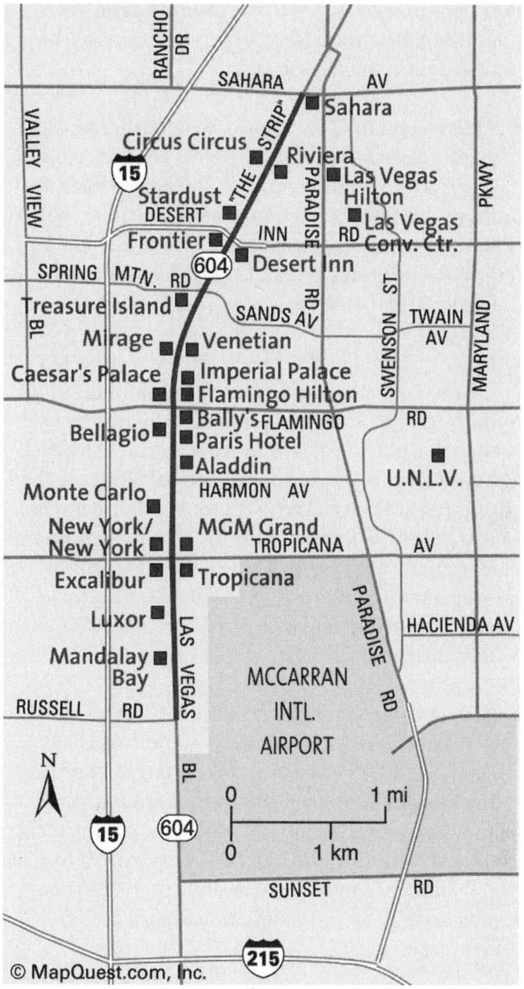

- After spending time at Luxor, hop on the tram that takes you over to **Excalibur.** This is the place for an exciting dinner and show. The majestic castle offers adventure at its **Fantasy Faire Midway**—an arena of games appropriate for everyone in the family.

- After spending time at the medieval castle, cross the over street walkway into 1930s- and '40s-inspired **New York-New York.** Billed as "the Greatest City in Las Vegas," New York-New York has attractions that are all themed to the New York life. Park Avenue shopping, a fast-paced Manhattan roller coaster, and Greenwich Village eateries help keep the theme intact.

- It's not time to stop yet. **The Monte Carlo,** just north of New York-New York, is just as classy, but with a purely European twist.

- After a jaunt to Monte Carlo, walk farther north, getting close to the halfway point. The big lake and fantastic fountains are part of **Bellagio,** a hotel that strives for utter perfection. Check out the art gallery here—it houses some fantastic pieces, including original paintings by Van Gogh, Monet, Renoir, Cezanne, and other masters.

- Now, at Flamingo Boulevard, cross the street to the east—over to **Paris.** This is the midpoint of the tour, and this area is full of areas to sit and rest or to grab a bite to eat. While at Paris, tour the **Eiffel Tower.** This is an exact replica, in half scale, of the original in France. The plans for the original were lent to the developers of the hotel so they could be as accurate as possible. There's also a two-thirds-scale replica of ***L'Arc de Triomphe*** near the hotel entrance—complete with Napoleon's victories inscribed on it.

- The next stop on this tour is the **MGM Grand.** This very large hotel strives to make visitors feel like stars. Elegance abounds at this hotel. Don't miss the **Lion Habitat** here: a walk-through tour that showcases some beautiful lions, some of which are descendants of Metro, the MGM marquee lion. The only thing separating you and the lions is a glass wall on both sides—an exciting experience.

- Just south of the MGM Grand is the famous **Tropicana,** home to the longest-running show on the Strip.

- After the Tropicana, cross the street again and take the tram from Excalibur to Mandalay Bay. At Mandalay Bay, get back in your car and cross the street to see the **Glass Pool Inn.** This motel was originally called The Mirage but sold the rights to its name to the much larger entity many years ago. The motel features an unusual above-ground pool with portal windows that has been featured in many movies.

- Finish off the tour of the Southern Las Vegas Strip by driving north back past the Tropicana and MGM Grand and beyond. The drive provides amazing views that you may have missed along the walk.

Northern California

California has the largest population of any state in the United States. Within it, only 80 miles apart, are the lowest and highest points in the contiguous United States—Death Valley and Mount Whitney. California has ski areas and blistering deserts, mountains and beaches, giant redwoods and giant missiles, Spanish missions and skyscrapers. The oldest living things on earth grow here—a stand of bristlecone pine said to be 4,600 years old. San Francisco, the key city of northern California, is cosmopolitan, beautiful, proud, and old-worldly. Los Angeles, in southern California, is bright and brazen, growing, and modern. California, with 1,264 miles of coastline and a width of up to 350 miles, does things in a big way.

Population: 33,871,648

Area: 158,693 square miles

Elevation: 282 feet below sea level–14,494 feet

Peak: Mount Whitney (between Inyo and Tulare counties)

Entered Union: September 9, 1850 (31st state)

Capital: Sacramento

Motto: Eureka (I have found it)

Nickname: The Golden State

Flower: Golden Poppy

Bird: California Valley Quail

Tree: California Redwood

Fair: Late August in Sacramento

Time Zone: Pacific

Web Site: www.gocalif.ca.gov

Fun Facts:

- More than 300,000 tons of grapes are grown in California annually.
- More turkeys are raised in California than in any other state in the country.
- The first motion picture theater opened in Los Angeles on April 2, 1902.

Almost every crop of the United States grows here. Prunes, oranges, bales of cotton, and tons of vegetables roll out from the factory farms in the fertile valleys. California leads the nation in the production of 75 crop and livestock commodities, including grapes, peaches, apricots, olives, figs, lemons, avocados, walnuts, almonds, rice, plums, prunes, dates, and nectarines. It also leads in the production of dried, canned, and frozen fruits and vegetables, wine, eggs, turkeys, safflower, beeswax, and honey. Homegrown industries include Hollywood movies, television, electronics, aircraft, and missiles.

Spaniards, Mexicans, English, Russians, and others helped write the history of the state. The first explorer to venture into the waters of California was Portuguese—Juan Rodriguez Cabrillo, in 1542. In 1579, Sir Francis Drake explored the coastal waters and is believed to have landed just northwest of what is now San Francisco. Beginning in 1769, Spanish colonial policy sprinkled a trail of missions around which the first towns developed. The Mexican flag flew over California after Mexico won independence from Spain in 1821. American settlers later wrenched the colony from Mexico and organized the short-lived Bear Flag Republic. On July 7, 1846, Commodore John D. Sloat raised the United States flag at Monterey. Under the Treaty of Guadalupe Hidalgo, California became part of what was to be the coastal boundary of the United States in 1848.

Perhaps the most important event in California's history was the discovery of gold in January of 1848, which set off a sudden mass migration that transformed the drowsy, placid countryside and

Calendar Highlights

FEBRUARY

Chinese New Year *(San Francisco). Chinatown. Contact the Chinese Chamber of Commerce, phone 415/982-3000.* The largest and most colorful celebration of this occasion held in the United States. Weeklong activities include the Golden Dragon Parade, lion dancing, carnival, and cultural exhibits.

MARCH

Whale Festival *(Mendocino). Contact the Mendocino Chamber of Commerce, phone 707/961-6300 or toll-free 800/726-2780.* Whale-watching walks, wine tasting, and chowder tasting.

APRIL

Monterey Wine Festival *(Carmel). Phone toll-free 800/656-4282.* Approximately 170 wineries participate in this food and wine-tasting festival.

JULY

San Jose America Festival *(San Jose). Phone 408/298-6861.* Food booths, arts and crafts, rides and games, and entertainment.

American Century Investments Celebrity Golf Championship *(Lake Tahoe Area). Edgewood Tahoe Golf Course. Phone toll-free 800/288-2463.* More than 70 sports and entertainment celebrities compete for a $500,000 purse.

AUGUST

California State Fair *(Sacramento). California Exposition grounds. Phone 916/263-3247.* Includes traditional state fair activities, exhibits, livestock, carnival food, entertainment on ten stages, thoroughbred racing, and a 1-mile monorail.

SEPTEMBER

Monterey Jazz Festival *(Monterey). County Fairgrounds. Phone 925/275-9255.* The oldest jazz festival in the United States. Reserved seats only.

accelerated the opening of the Far West by several decades. The 49ers who came for gold found greater riches in the fertile soil of the valleys and the markets of the young cities.

During and after World War II, California grew at an astounding pace in both industry and population. Jet travel across the Pacific makes the state a gateway to the Orient.

When to Go/Climate

We recommend visiting California in the mid- to late spring or early to mid-fall, when the fog generally lifts and the heavy tourist traffic is over. Winters are rainy; summers are dry and hot in much of the state.

AVERAGE HIGH/LOW TEMPERATURES (° F)

San Francisco

Jan 56/46	**May** 63/51	**Sept** 69/56
Feb 60/49	**June** 64/53	**Oct** 69/55
Mar 61/49	**July** 65/54	**Nov** 63/52
Apr 62/50	**Aug** 66/55	**Dec** 56/47

Parks and Recreation

Water-related activities, hiking, riding, various other sports, picnicking, nature trails, and visitor centers, as well as camping, are available in many of California's parks. Some parks limit camping to a maximum consecutive period of 7-30 days, depending on the season and the popularity of the area. Campsite charges are $10-$29 per night per vehicle; trailer hook-ups are $9-$25. For campsite reservations, phone toll-free 800/444-7275 from anywhere in the continental United States; outside the country, phone customer service at toll-free 800/695-2269. Day-use fee is $2-$6 per vehicle; vehicle with sailboat over 8 feet and all motor vessels, $3-$5 additional; all other boats, $1 additional; annual pass for $75 includes unlimited day use, $125 with boat; boat launching $3-$5. Fees may vary in some areas. There are also small fees for some activities at some areas. Pets on a leash permitted in campground and day-use areas only, $1 per night (camping), $1 (day-use). Reservations for Hearst-San Simeon State Historical Monument (Hearst Castle) (see) can be made by calling toll-free 800/444-4445. For a map folder listing and describing state parks ($2), contact the California State Parks Store, PO Box 942896, Sacramento 94296-0001; phone 916/653-4000; www.parks.ca.gov. For general park information, phone 916/653-6995.

FISHING AND HUNTING

Streams, rivers, canals, and lakes provide a great variety of freshwater fish. Salmon and steelhead trout run in great numbers in major coastal rivers north of San Francisco. Everything from barracuda to smelt may be found along or off the shore.

Hunting for deer, bear, and other big game is available in most national forests, other public lands, and some private lands (by permission), except in national and state parks, where firearms are prohibited. Waterfowl, quail, and dove shooting can be arranged at public management areas and in private shooting preserves. Tidepool collecting is illegal without a special permit.

A fishing license is required for all persons 16 and older to fish in either inland or ocean waters. Some public piers in ocean waters allow fishing without a license (a list is available on request). A hunting license is required to hunt any animal. For information, contact the California Department of Fish and Game, 3211 S St, Sacramento 95816. For general information, phone 916/653-7664; for license information, phone 916/227-2282.

Driving Information

Safety belts are mandatory for all persons anywhere in a vehicle. Children under 4 years and weighing under 40 pounds must be in approved safety seats anywhere in vehicle.

INTERSTATE HIGHWAY SYSTEM

Use the following list as a guide to access interstate highways in California. Consult a map to confirm driving routes.

Highway Number	Cities/Towns within 10 Miles
Interstate 5	Anaheim, Buena Park, Carlsbad, Costa Mesa, Del Mar, Dunsmuir, Fullerton, Garden Grove, Irvine, Lodi, Mount Shasta, Oceanside, Orange, Rancho Santa Fe, Red Bluff, Redding, Sacramento, San Clemente, San Diego, San Juan Capistrano, Santa Ana, Stockton, Valencia, Willows, Yreka
Interstate 8	Calexico, El Cajon, El Centro, Pine Valley, San Diego
Interstate 10	Beaumont, Blythe, Claremont, Desert Hot Springs, Indio, Ontario, Palm Desert, Palm Springs, Pomona, Redlands, San Bernardino, Santa Monica, West Covina
Interstate 15	Barstow, Corona, Escondido, Redlands, Riverside, San Bernardino, San Diego, Temecula, Victorville
Interstate 40	Barstow, Needles
Interstate 80	Auburn, Berkeley, Davis, Fairfield, Oakland, Sacramento, San Francisco, Truckee, Vacaville, Vallejo
Interstate 110	Arcadia, Beverly Hills, Burbank, Culver City, Glendale, Long Beach, Los Angeles, Los Angeles International Airport Area, Marina del Rey, Pasadena, Redondo Beach, San Gabriel, San Marino, San Pedro, Torrance, Westwood and Westwood Village

Additional Visitor Information

For material on northern California, contact the San Francisco Visitor Information Center, 900 Market St, San Francisco 94103, phone 415/391-2000, www.sfvisitor.org; or the Redwood Empire Association, Pier 39, Suite Q-5, San Francisco 94133, phone 415/956-3491, www.redwoodempire.com. Serious hikers should consult *Sierra North* or *Sierra South,* available from Wilderness Press, 1200 5th St, Berkeley 94710, phone toll-free 800/443-7227, www.wildernesspress.com. For general information, contact the California Division of Tourism, 801 K St, Suite 1600, Sacramento 95814, phone 916/322-2881 or toll-free 800/862-2543, gocalif.ca.gov. The monthly magazine *Sunset* gives special attention to West Coast travel and life. Contact Sunset Publishing Corporation, 80

THE BIG SUR COASTLINE

Hugging the rugged Big Sur coastline where cliffs fall to the sea, Highway 1 south of Monterey is often called the most scenic roadway in America. For sheer coastal beauty, it's hard to top. Development is sparse, so it's important to fill up on gas before starting out; a picnic lunch is a good option, too. From Monterey, it's less than 30 miles south to the most famous stretches of Big Sur, though the winding road and spectacular scenery call for taking it slow. Scenic turnouts dot the road along the way. Several state parks (Garrapata, Andrew Molera, Pfeiffer-Big Sur, and Julia Pfeiffer Burns) offer a combination of coastal access trails, waterfalls, and campgrounds. Rustic lodges and restaurants are also spread out along the route. Big Sur extends for about 90 miles south of Monterey, but for a one-day drive, a good turnaround point is the tiny hamlet of Lucia, about 50 miles south. The winding route is pitch black at night, so it's wise to return before dark. Those with two days can spend the night at Lucia in a modest lodge or continue south to San Simeon, where Hearst Castle perches high atop a mountain on the southern fringes of Big Sur. Those planning to tour Hearst Castle should reserve a time in advance and allow at least two hours. The town of Cambria, a few miles south of Hearst Castle, has plenty of lodging. Drivers have the option of returning to Monterey north on Highway 1 or looping back via Highway 101, a longer and less scenic (but potentially speedier) route that runs inland. To follow this option, take Highway 46 east off Highway 1 a few miles south of Cambria, reaching Highway 101 at Paso Robles. Continue north to Salinas, and take Highway 68 west to Monterey. **(Approximately 240 miles)**

DISCOVERING GOLD COUNTRY

This route combines California history with good scenery and a procession of colorful old towns. Allow plenty of time for negotiating the winding turns and for stops at historic sites along the way. From Sacramento, a 30-mile drive east along I-80 leads to Auburn, the gateway to Highway 49, which snakes north-south through the state's historic Gold Country. Old Town Auburn is well worth a stop. If you have more than one day, you can first head north from Auburn about 30 miles to Nevada City, an old mining town built on steep hills; nearby mines can be toured. The trip to Nevada City requires backtracking down Highway 49 again to Auburn. Those with only one day should forego Nevada City and turn south at Auburn onto Highway 49, proceeding to tiny Coloma, site of the Marshall Gold Discovery State Historic Park on the American River, where the gold rush was ignited in 1848. The historic sites can be visited; it's also a prime picnic spot. Highway 49 continues south through atmospheric 19th-century towns such as Placerville (or Hangtown), Amador City, Sutter Creek, Mokelumne Hill (once a top contender for state capital, but now a tiny burg), Angels Camp (site of Mark Twain's story, *The Celebrated Jumping Frog of Calaveras County*), Sonora, and Jamestown. All these towns are lined with Victorian residences and hotels, restaurants, and antique shops. Those staying overnight in Sonora can visit Columbia State Historic Park the next morning; it's just off Highway 49 a few miles north of Sonora. The living history park re-creates the life of bygone times; you can pan for gold there, or tour nearby mines–an indispensable stop for families. To return to Sacramento, go north again on Highway 49 to just north of Amador City, and then follow Highway 16 northwest about 35 miles to Sacramento. **(Approximately 225 miles, not including the 60-mile round-trip to Nevada City)**

EXPLORING LAKE TAHOE

Circumnavigating North America's largest alpine lake offers perspectives on four different sides of Tahoe and allows access to historic sites, hiking trails, ski resorts, restaurants, and casinos. Starting in the resort center of South Lake Tahoe, Highways 50 and 89 head west along the southern shore of the lake. From late spring through mid-fall, the Tallac Historic Site, a trio of opulent turn-of-the-century estates, is open for touring; beaches and nature trails are adjacent. Highway 89, turning north, leads to Emerald Bay, one of the most photographed sites in the state. The bay's emerald-green waters harbor tiny Fannette Island. A steep hiking trail leads a mile down to Vikingsholm, a replica of a medieval Scandinavian castle along Emerald Bay that is open for tours in summer. Farther north, Tahoe's rustic West Shore provides exceptional views of mountain peaks across the lake. State park shoreline campgrounds and hiking trails are exceptional. At Tahoe City, Highway 28 leads east around the lake's North Shore, site of numerous resorts, restaurants, and parks. At Crystal Bay, Highway 28 enters Nevada and then turns south, passing along the woodsy eastern shore back to South Lake Tahoe; casinos are clustered at Stateline, Nevada, just north of South Lake Tahoe. Though only 72 miles around, the lake's curvy roads require a minimum of three hours to navigate; a full day allows for several stops. In the winter, the three California sides of Tahoe are lined with ski resorts (some are located a few miles from the lake); four-wheel drive or tire chains may be necessary to negotiate snowy, icy roads at that time. **(Approximately 72 miles; add approximately 230 miles if originating in Sacramento)**

POSTCARDS FROM MARIN COUNTY

This tour packs in a remarkable amount of scenery: postcard views of San Francisco, the Pacific coastline, redwood forests, Tomales Bay, and the superb Point Reyes National Seashore. Allow a full day, especially if you want to stop and hike a bit. Cross over the Golden Gate Bridge to the Marin Headlands, where Conzelman Road runs along the cliffsides and offers panoramas of the bridge and the San Francisco skyline. After the roadway loops back to Highway 101, take that north past Sausalito, and then follow Highway 1 north toward the coast. Your first stop is Muir Woods, the state's most popular and accessible grove of virgin redwoods; short trails lead through the main groves. Continue north to Mount Tamalpais, and follow signs toward East Peak for picnic areas and dramatic views of the entire Bay Area. Farther north along Highway 1 is Point Reyes National Seashore. There are hiking trails near the Bear Valley Visitor Center (just off Highway 1), or, for a more complete tour of the park, go north about 22 miles on Sir Francis Drake Highway through the resort town of Inverness (where there are lodgings for overnight stays) all the way to the tip of the peninsula. There, a lighthouse is perched high over the Pacific (a top whale-watching site in the winter, although you may have to park and ride a shuttle bus at peak times on weekends). The entire peninsula is lined with often-deserted beaches, and there are forests, estuaries, wildlife, and rolling grasslands along the way. Doubling back to Highway 1, the town of Point Reyes Station offers several good restaurants. From there, follow the Point Reyes-Petaluma Road (and directional signs) across the rolling countryside to either Petaluma or Novato, both located on Highway 101, which heads south to San Francisco. **(Approximately 90-120 miles)**

RUSSIAN RIVER COUNTRY

This route combines rolling pastureland with spectacular coastal scenery and Russian River redwoods. Picturesque small towns dot the roadways. You can make the drive in one day or turn it into a leisurely two-day excursion. From San Francisco, follow Highway 101 north to Petaluma in Sonoma County. Then head west on Bodega Avenue and later Valley Ford Road, which cross through farmlands and old ranchos, to Highway 1 at the town of Valley Ford. Highway 1 then leads west and north to Bodega Bay, a coastal fishing village. Continue up the winding coastal road, perhaps stopping at one of the turnoffs to Sonoma Coast State Beach or to the town of Jenner, perched over the Pacific at the mouth of the Russian River. This is a good place to enjoy lunch with a spectacular view or to linger for an overnight stay. Next, head inland (east) for about 12 miles on Route 116 to Guerneville, a rustic Russian River resort town in the redwoods (Armstrong Redwoods State Reserve is just to the north). Bed-and-breakfasts and other lodging are available there. Route 116 heads southeast back to Highway 101, which then leads south to San Francisco. **(Approximately 175 miles)**

SANTA CRUZ COUNTY COASTLINE

This route hugs the coastline from San Francisco to the beach resort of Santa Cruz, passing often-deserted golden-sand beaches, and then back up through redwood forests. From San Francisco, Highway 1 leads south through Pacifica toward Half Moon Bay, at times winding along the tops of sheer cliffs. The small fishing village of Princeton makes a good stop for seafood. The road later passes strikingly beautiful state beaches such as San Gregorio, Pomponio, and Bean Hollow; Pigeon Point Lighthouse, occupying a peninsula, is one of the state's most photographed sites. About 50 miles south of San Francisco is the Ano Nuevo State Reserve, where thousands of massive elephant seals migrate annually in winter to mate and give birth (reservations for walking tours are essential from mid-December through March; allow two to three hours). The seaside town of Santa Cruz, with beaches and an old-fashioned boardwalk and wharf, is 75 miles south of San Francisco. This is a good place to spend the night if making a multiday drive. Return north from Santa Cruz via Route 9, which climbs through the redwoods (with a possible winding side trip to Big Basin State Park, a redwood haven), and continue north on Route 35 at the Saratoga Gap (elevation 2,600 feet). Farther along, Route 84 leads back east to I-280, which usually offers a speedy return north to San Francisco. **(Approximately 150 miles)**

THROUGH THE REDWOODS

This route takes in North Coast ocean scenery as well as redwoods, wineries, and state parks with forested hiking trails. It's important to get an early start, especially for a one-day tour. From San Francisco, follow Highway 101 north to the town of Cloverdale, and then take Route 128 northwest to Mendocino, passing Anderson Valley wineries and Hendy Woods State Park (featuring redwoods) along the way. Much of the route is winding. At the coast, meet up with Highway 1 and follow it north to the arty resort town of Mendocino, which resembles a New England fishing village perched upon cliff tops. Those with two days can spend the night here and linger at antique and art shops or at one of several nearby state parks. Those with only one day can return to San Francisco via Highway 20 east from the town of Fort Bragg (6 miles north of Mendocino), a scenic route that leads to Highway 101, which then heads south to San Francisco; the total distance for the day is about 350 miles. Otherwise, continue north the next day on Highway 1 through Fort Bragg up to Leggett, where those who wish can drive through a redwood tree. At Leggett, take Highway 101 north to Humboldt Redwoods State Park, home of the world's greatest redwood forests. The 30-mile-long

Avenue of the Giants runs north through the heart of the redwoods. After completing the Avenue of the Giants, reverse direction and follow Highway 101 south to San Francisco. **(Approximately 500 miles)**

TOURING THE WINE COUNTRY

Vineyards, wineries, restaurants, and all-around great scenery make this drive a must. From San Francisco, Highway 101 north and 37 east lead to Route 121, which goes north and then east toward the Napa Valley. Highway 29 is the main route heading north, but rather than driving it in both directions, head to the gently curving, seldom-crowded Silverado Trail, which parallels 29 just a few miles away and retains a more rural atmosphere. (The start of the roadway begins in the town of Napa.) Follow the Silverado Trail north, passing dozens of boutique wineries and hillside vineyards, to the town of Calistoga, which has hot springs resorts and good restaurants and is an ideal place to spend the night. Return south on Highway 29, which is lined with many big-name, popular wineries, most of them open for touring and tastings. Along the way, the towns of St. Helena and Rutherford have numerous excellent restaurants. At Oakville, turn west across the mountains via the Oakville Grade; the winding road is steep at times, but the scenery is worth it. It also serves as a shortcut to Sonoma County. At Highway 12, turn south toward the town of Sonoma, near the town of Glen Ellen; Jack London State Park, where the famed writer-adventurer once lived, is nearby. The town of Sonoma has a large, attractive central square, which is the site of the state's northernmost historic Franciscan mission, as well as historic homes, excellent shops, wineries, and lodgings. Routes 12 and 121 (south), Highway 37 (west), and Highway 101 (south) lead back to San Francisco. **(Approximately 150 miles)**

YOSEMITE VALLEY

This tour takes the most picturesque route into Yosemite Valley and includes the valley's most dramatic scenic points, as well as other beautiful stretches of the park. From Fresno, Highway 41 leads north toward the park. The route starts off flat but gets quite hilly and winding by the town of Oakhurst, the southernmost point on Highway 49. Follow Highway 49 northwest to the old mining town of Mariposa, where Highway 140 heads north and then east toward Yosemite. On the way into the park, Highway 140 runs along a very pretty stretch of the Merced River, popular with rafters in summer. From the park's western entrance, follow the signs leading to Yosemite Valley. Expect heavy traffic on a weekend in the height of summer or over a holiday (cars are occasionally banned from the valley on peak summer holidays); the best times to visit are fall and spring. Snowy winters can be beautiful, but the roads may be slick and require four-wheel drive or tire chains; some high-elevation roads typically close. Southside and northside drives make a loop around the valley, passing spectacular waterfalls (best in spring) and granite monoliths such as Half Dome and El Capitán. There are plenty of pullouts where tourists can stop to take pictures or embark on a short hike. If you want to stay overnight in the valley, make reservations in advance; otherwise, your chances of finding lodging here are slim. When leaving the valley, take Highway 41 south. If the access road to Glacier Point is open (it closes in winter) and you have an extra hour or two, follow the signs to Glacier Point for panoramic views of the valley, Yosemite Falls, and Half Dome. Continue south on Highway 41 through the park's Wawona section, where the Mariposa Grove of Big Trees awaits; a short hike leads to several ancient giant sequoias. Highway 41 then leads south out of the park and back to Fresno. **(Approximately 200 miles)**

Willow Rd, Menlo Park 94025-3691, phone toll-free 800/227-7346 outside California, 800/321-0372 in California, www.sunset.com.

Alturas (B-3)

Population 2,892
Elevation 4,366 ft
Area Code 530
Zip 96101
Information Chamber of Commerce, 522 S Main St; phone 530/233-4434
Web Site www.alturaschamber.org

What to See and Do

Modoc County Historical Museum. *600 S Main St, Alturas (96101). Phone 530/233-6328.* More than 4,000 Native American artifacts, including arrowheads, spear points, and many other items; exhibits of local history, including an antique gun collection. (May-Oct, Tues-Sat 10 am-4 pm) **$**

Modoc National Forest. *800 W 12th St, Alturas (96101). Sections surrounding Alturas reached via I-395 and Hwy 139/299. Phone 530/233-5811. www.fs.fed.us/r5/modoc/.* Scene of the Modoc Indian Wars, this forest of nearly 2 million acres is famous for its scenic trails through the South Warner Wilderness. In Medicine Lake Highlands Area, there is a spectacular flow of jumbled black lava surrounding islands of timber, with craters, cinder cones, and lava tube caves. For wildlife watchers, the forest is home to more than 300 species of wildlife; the Pacific Flyway for migratory waterfowl crosses directly over the forest, making this area a bird-watcher's paradise. Swimming, stream and lake fishing, and hunting are popular activities as well. A winter sports area provides activities in winter, and picnicking and camping occupy summertime visitors.

Modoc National Wildlife Refuge. *County Rd 115, Alturas (96101). 2 miles S on County Rd 115. Phone 530/233-3572. modoc.fws.gov.* Nesting habitat for the Great Basin Canada goose; also ducks, sandhill cranes, and other interesting birds. (Daily, daylight hours; Dorris Reservoir Recreation Area closed during waterfowl hunting season; inquire about fees. Refuge closed to public fishing except in the Dorris Reservoir Recreation Area.) **FREE**

Special Events

Fandango Days Celebration. *Veterans Park, 204 S Court St, Alturas (96101). Phone 530/233-4434.* Begin your day by grabbing a spot along Main Street for the parade, then move on to Veterans Park for the Classic car show, horseshoe games, and plenty of country music. July.

Modoc District Fair. *Modoc District Fairgrounds, 1 Center St, Cedarville (96104). Phone 530/279-2315.* The four-day fair holds daily equestrian events as well as a demolition derby, baseball tournament, and junior rodeo. Mid-Aug. **$**

Limited-Service Hotel

★ BEST WESTERN TRAILSIDE INN. *343 N Main St, Alturas (96101). Phone 530/233-4111; toll-free 800/780-7234; fax 530/233-3180. www.bestwestern.com.* 38 rooms, 2 story. Pets accepted, some restrictions; fee. Complimentary continental breakfast. Check-in 3 pm, check-out 11 am. Outdoor pool. **$**

Antioch (E-2)

See also Concord, Martinez, Oakland, Vallejo

Population 90,532
Elevation 25 ft
Area Code 925
Zip 94509
Information Chamber of Commerce, 301 W 10th St, Suite 1; phone 925/757-1800
Web Site www.antiochchamber.com

What to See and Do

Black Diamond Mines Regional Preserve. *5175 Somersville Rd, Antioch (94509). Phone 925/757-2620. www.ebparks.org/parks/black.htm.* Nearly 5,000 acres on flanks of Mount Diablo (see MOUNT DIABLO STATE PARK) contain coal, silica sand mines, and the Rose Hill Cemetery. Hiking, bicycle, bridle trails; picnicking. Naturalist programs. Preserve. (Daily 8 am-dusk) **$**

Contra Loma Regional Park. *1200 Frederickson Ln, Antioch (94509). From Hwy 4, S on Lone Tree Way to Golf Course Rd, then right on Frederickson Ln to park entrance. Phone 510/562-7275. www.ebparks.org/parks/conloma.htm.* Approximately 775 acres. Lake swimming (summer, daily, fee), sand beach, fishing, boating; hiking, bicycling, picnicking, concession. (Daily 5 am-10 pm) **$$**

Special Event

Contra Costa County Fair. *County Fairgrounds, 10th and L sts, Antioch (94509). Phone 925/779-7916. www.ccfair.org.* This fair provides fun for everyone with carnival rides, musical acts, and even a hypnosis show! Late May-early June. **$$**

Arcata (B-1)

Web Site www.arcatacityhall.org

What to See and Do

Humboldt Light Opera Company. *1482 Buttermilk Ln, Arcata (95521). www.hloc.org.* Since its inaugural production in 1973, the Humboldt Light Opera Company has staged about 100 musicals at venues in Humboldt County. The marquee has been graced by such titles as Handel's *Messiah*, *Guys and Dolls*, and *The Pirates of Penzance*. The company performs at the College of the Redwoods' Forum Theatre in Eureka and the John Van Dusen Theatre at Humboldt State University in Arcata.

Auburn (D-3)

See also Grass Valley, Mother Lode Country, Nevada City, Placerville, Sacramento

Settled 1848
Population 12,462
Elevation 1,297 ft
Area Code 530
Zip 95603
Information Auburn Area Chamber of Commerce, 601 Lincoln Way; phone 530/885-5616
Web Site www.auburnchamber.net

Here is a town with a split personality: the restored "old town" retains its gold rush boomtown flavor; the other Auburn, built on a hilltop, is a modern city. In 1848, a mining camp called North Fork Dry Diggins was renamed for Auburn, New York. It developed as a center for gold rush camps and survived when the railroad came through and orchards were planted after the gold gave out.

What to See and Do

Folsom Lake State Recreation Area. *7806 Folsom Auburn Rd, Auburn (95603). Near the town of Folsom. Phone 916/988-0205. www.parks.ca.gov.* This 17,545-acre area offers swimming, water-skiing, fishing, boating (rentals, marina); bicycle, hiking, bridle trails, picnicking, concession, camping (dump station). Historic Folsom Powerhouse (Wed-Sun afternoons). **$$**

Gold Country Museum. *Gold Country Fairgrounds, 1273 High St, Auburn. Phone 530/889-6500.* Exhibits depicting early days of Placer County; history of gold mining and lifestyle of gold miners. (Tues-Sun 11 am-4 pm; closed holidays) **$** Admission includes

> **Bernhard Museum Complex.** *291 Auburn-Folsom Rd, Auburn (95603). Phone 530/889-6500.* Restored 14-room house (1851), winery (1874), and art gallery. Living history programs. Guided tours. (Tues-Sun 11 am-4 pm; closed holidays).

Old Town. *Lincoln Way, Sacramento, Commercial and Court sts, Auburn (95603). Phone 530/885-5616. www.auburnchamber.net.* Take a walking tour of this restored gold rush town. Chamber of Commerce has information.

Special Events

Gold Country Fair. *Gold Country Fairgrounds, 1273 High St, Auburn (95603). Phone 530/823-4533.* Historic exhibits, entertainment, food, carnival, livestock shows, and agriculture exhibits. Weekend after Labor Day. **$$**

Placer County Fair. *Placer County Fair and Events Center, 800 All America City Blvd, Roseville (95678). 2 miles N off I-80, on Washington Blvd. Phone 916/786-2023. www.placercountyfair.org.* Come and join in the fun at this four-day event. Events and activities include car races, a destruction derby, carnival, parade, concerts, and the Placer County Idol Contest. Late June. **$$**

Restaurant

★ LOU LA BONTE'S. *13460 Lincoln Way, Auburn (95603). Phone 530/885-9193; fax 530/885-4378.* California, Mediterranean menu. Breakfast, lunch, dinner. Bar. Children's menu. Casual attire. Outdoor seating. **$$**

Berkeley (E-2)

See also Oakland, San Francisco, San Rafael, Sausalito, Vallejo, Walnut Creek

Settled 1841
Population 102,743
Elevation 152 ft
Area Code 510
Information Berkeley Convention & Visitors Bureau, 2015 Center St, 94704; phone 510/549-8710
Web Site www.berkeleycvb.com

Berkeley is the home of the principal campus of the University of California. With an average monthly high temperature of 64° F, Berkeley regards itself as "one of America's most refreshing cities."

Named for George Berkeley, Bishop of Cloyne, an 18th-century Irish philosopher, the area was once a part of the vast Rancho San Antonio. Shortly after a group of developers bought the townsite, the College of California was founded—later to become the University of California.

The town's population was increased by refugees from the San Francisco earthquake and fire of 1906. In September of 1923, 25 percent of Berkeley was destroyed by fire. Quickly rebuilt, the city government instituted one of the most efficient fire-prevention systems in the country.

What to See and Do

Bade Institute of Biblical Archaeology. *1798 Scenic Ave, Berkeley (94709). Phone 510/849-8272. bade.psr.edu/bade.* Devoted to the archaeology of Palestine from 3200 to 600 BC. The bible collection has documents from the 5th to 18th centuries (by appointment only). Museum (Tues-Thurs 10 am-3 pm, also by appointment; closed holidays). **FREE**

Berkeley Farmers' Market. *Center St and Martin Luther King Jr. Way, Berkeley (94704). Phone 510/548-3333.* There is a pair of outstanding farmers' markets in the East Bay college town of Berkeley, held year-round on Tuesdays, Thursdays and Saturdays. Local farmers and chefs set up booths vending a far-flung range of delicacies, including olives, avocadoes, coffee beans, and vegan Mexican food. In keeping with Berkeley's progressive culture, more than half of the produce at the markets is organically grown. (Sat 10 am-3 pm, Tues 2-6 pm, Thurs 2-7 pm)

Berkeley Marina. *201 University Ave, Berkeley (94710). 1/2 mile W of Eastshore Fwy, I-80, at W end of University Ave, on San Francisco Bay. Phone 510/981-6740. www.ci.berkeley.ca.us/marina.* Public fishing pier (free); bait and tackle shop; sportfishing boat; 950 berths, 25 visitor berths. Protected sailing basin; four-lane boat ramp (fee). Motel, restaurants.

Berkeley Rose Garden. *1200 Euclid Ave, Berkeley (94708). Phone 510/981-5150.* Collection of 4,000 roses; 200 varieties. (Daily 6 am-10 pm; best blooms mid-May-Sept) **FREE**

Grizzly Peak Blvd. A winding drive along the crest of hills behind the city; it offers views of most of San Francisco Bay and the surrounding cities.

Judah L. Magnes Museum. *2911 Russell St, Berkeley (94705). Phone 510/549-6950. www.magnes.org.* Artistic, historical, and literary materials, including ceremonial objects and textiles, trace Jewish life and culture throughout the world; the Western Jewish History Center houses documentation of Jewish contributions to the history of the American West; research library of rare and illustrated Jewish books and manuscripts; permanent collection and changing exhibits of traditional and contemporary Jewish artists and themes. (Sun-Wed 11 am-4 pm, Thurs to 8 pm; closed Jewish and federal holidays) **DONATION**

Sur La Table. *1806 Fourth St, Berkeley (94710). Phone 510/849-2252. www.surlatable.com.* In the 1970s, Seattle spawned this clearinghouse for hard-to-find kitchen gear, and it soon became known as a source for cookware, small appliances, cutlery, kitchen tools, linens, tableware, gadgets, and specialty foods. Sur La Table has since expanded to include cooking classes ($$$$), chef demonstrations, and cookbook author signings, as well as a catalog and online presence. Cooking connoisseurs discover such finds as cool oven mitts, zest graters, copper whisks, onion soup bowls, and inspired TV dinner trays. (Mon-Sat 10 am-7 pm, Sun 11 am-6:30 pm)

Tilden Park Golf Course. *Grizzly Peak and Shasta Rd, Berkeley (94708). Phone 510/848-7373.* Tilden Park isn't very long (a few yards under 6,300), but the process of club selection leads to challenging golf on many of the tees. Several holes dogleg, and most are lined with large trees that can eat errant drives for lunch. Three of the four par-threes measure greater than 200 yards and provide perhaps the biggest overall challenge to the layout. The course is usually very crowded (about 90,000 rounds are played there a year), so get a tee time early and hope that you play behind someone quick. **$$$$**

Tilden Regional Park. *2501 Grizzly Peak Blvd, Berkeley (94708). E on Hwy 24 to Fish Ranch Rd exit, then W to Grizzly Peak Blvd, right to park. Phone 510/562-7275. www.ebparks.org/parks/tilden.htm.* The park's 2,078 recreational acres include swimming (fee), a swimming beach, bathhouse, fishing at Lake Anza; nature, hiking, bicycle, and bridle trails; 18-hole golf (fee), picnicking, concessions. Environmental Education Center, Little Farm, Jewel Lake. Merry-go-round, pony and steam train rides (fee); botanical garden of native California plants. The park connects with East Bay Skyline National Trail at Inspiration Point. (Daily 8 am-10 pm) **FREE**

☆ **University of California, Berkeley.** *101 University Hall, Berkeley (94720). 2 miles E of Eastshore Frwy, I-80, at E end of University Ave. Phone 510/642-5215. www.berkeley.edu.* (1873) (33,000 students) This campus in the foothills of the east shore of San Francisco Bay covers more than 1,200 acres. Many fields of study are offered, including agriculture, zoology, art, and medicine. The oldest of the nine University of California campuses, its white granite buildings are surrounded by groves of oak trees; its 307-foot campanile (elevator, fee) can be seen from a great distance. On or near the campus are

Berkeley Art Museum. *2626 Bancroft Way, Berkeley (94704). Phone 510/642-0808. www.bampfa.berkeley.edu.* Includes Hans Hofmann paintings, an outdoor sculpture garden, and the Pacific Film Archive film program; 11 exhibition galleries. (Wed, Fri-Sun 11 am-5 pm, Thurs to 7 pm) **$$**

Botanical Garden. *200 Centennial Dr, Berkeley (94720). Phone 510/643-2755. botanicalgarden.berkeley.edu.* Features many unusual plants, including native, Asian, Australian, and South American collections and a redwood grove; visitor center. Tours. (Daily 9 am-5 pm; closed the first Tues of the month; also holidays) **$**

Hearst Greek Theatre. *Gayley Rd and Stadium Rim Way, Berkeley (94720). At E gate. Phone 510/642-9988.* Gift of William Randolph Hearst; an amphitheater where leading pop and jazz artists perform.

International House. *2299 Piedmont Ave, Berkeley (94704). Bancroft Way at Piedmont Ave. Phone 510/642-9490. ias.berkeley.edu/ihouse.* This Mission-Revival structure serves as a home and program center for 600 students from both the United States and abroad. Built in 1930, this was the second such institution in the world. Its impressive dome is visible for miles. (Daily)

Lawrence Hall of Science. *200 Centennial Dr, Berkeley (94720). Centennial Dr, S of Grizzly Peak Blvd. Phone 510/642-5132. www.lawrencehallofscience.org.* Hands-on exhibits and activities for all ages. Classes, films, planetarium shows, discovery labs, special events, and programs on a variety of scientific topics. (Daily 10 am-5 pm; closed school holidays, Labor Day, Thanksgiving, Dec 25) **$$**

Phoebe Apperson Hearst Museum of Anthropology. *102 Kroeber Hall, Berkeley (94720). On Bancroft Way, at the end of College Ave. Phone 510/642-3682. hearstmuseum.berkeley.edu.* Changing exhibits on ancient and modern lands and people. (Wed-Sat 10 am-4:30 pm, Sun noon-4 pm; closed school holidays) **$**

Wildcat Canyon Regional Park. *5755 McBride, Richmond (94806). N of Tilden Regional Park, access from Tilden Nature Area. Phone 510/635-0138. www.ebparks.org.* On 2,421 acres. Hiking, jogging, bicycle, and bridle trails; picnicking, interpretive programs, bird-watching. (Daily 5 am-10 pm) **FREE**

Special Event

Berkeley Free Folk Festival. *Ashkenaz Music and Dance Center, 1317 San Pablo Ave, Berkeley (94702). Phone 510/525-5054.* A celebration of folk music from all corners of the globe, the Berkeley Free Folk Festival attracts folkies of all stripes every year in November. More than 50 performers take to four stages at the Malcolm X School. The schedule also includes kids' events, musical workshops, and food stands. Mid-Nov.

Limited-Service Hotel

★★ DOUBLETREE HOTEL BERKELEY MARINA. *200 Marina Blvd, Berkeley (94710). Phone 510/548-7920; fax 510/548-7944. www.doubletree.com.* Directly on the water and facing the Berkeley Marina, this sprawling hotel is the only hotel on the San Francisco Bay. Shuttle service is available to the University of California campus and the nearest BART station. 369 rooms, 4 story. Check-in 3 pm, check-out noon. High-speed Internet access. Restaurant, bar. Fitness room. Indoor pool, children's pool, whirlpool.

Business center. **$**

Full-Service Resort

★ ★ ★ CLAREMONT RESORT AND SPA. *41 Tunnel Rd, Berkeley (94705). Phone 510/843-3000; toll-free 800/551-7266; fax 510/848-6208. www.claremontresort.com.* The magic of old-time resorts comes alive at The Claremont Resort and Spa. Nestled in Berkeley's Oakland Hills on 22 acres of lush gardens, this resort combines the best of a country retreat with proximity to the city. San Francisco is only 12 miles away, and the twinkling lights of the skyline and the glittering waters of the bay make for delightful views. The guest rooms and suites reflect the hotel's historic charm while incorporating modern amenities for business and leisure travelers. Two pools, tennis courts, a comprehensive fitness center, and a celebrated spa entertain and relax guests, and the resort's three eateries tempt diners with Pacific Rim and American cuisine. 279 rooms, 9 story. Check-in 4 pm, check-out noon. Restaurant, bar. Children's activity center. Fitness room, spa. Outdoor pool, whirlpool. Tennis. Business center. **$$$**

Specialty Lodging

The following lodging establishment is approved by Mobil Travel Guide, but due to its unique and individualized nature has not been given a traditional Mobil Star rating. Included in this listing you may find bed-and-breakfasts, limited-service inns, guest ranches, and other unique hotel properties.

ROSE GARDEN INN. *2740 Telegraph Ave, Berkeley (94705). Phone 510/549-2145; toll-free 800/992-9005; fax 510/549-1085. www.rosegardeninn.com.* Built in 1903, Berkeley's Rose Garden Inn has a somewhat serene, country feel despite its busy metropolitan locale. Two of the inn's five buildings are historic landmark mansions built by the Marshall brothers, turn-of-the-century real estate developers. Guest rooms vary in size and furnishings; the larger, more contemporary rooms are in the rear buildings. The rear courtyard, with extensive rose gardens, fountains, and patios, is relatively quiet and secluded from street noise. 40 rooms, 3 story. Complimentary continental breakfast. Check-in 3 pm, check-out noon. High-speed Internet access, wireless Internet access. **$**

Restaurants

★ ★ AJANTA. *1888 Solano Ave, Berkeley (94707). Phone 510/526-4373; fax 510/526-3885. www.ajantarestaurant.com.* Indian menu. Specials change monthly. Lunch, dinner. Closed Thanksgiving, Dec 25. **$$**

★ ★ CAFE ROUGE. *1782 4th St, Berkeley (94710). Phone 510/525-1440; fax 510/525-2776. www.caferouge.net.* Authentic meat market setting. Mediterranean menu. Lunch, dinner. Closed holidays; also one week in Aug. Bar. Outdoor seating. **$$$**

★ ★ CESAR. *1515 Shattuck Ave, Berkeley (94709). Phone 510/883-0222; fax 510/883-0227. www.barcesar.com.* Spanish menu. Lunch, dinner, late-night. Closed holidays. Bar. Outdoor seating. **$$**

★ ★ ★ CHEZ PANISSE CAFE AND RESTAURANT. *1517 Shattuck Ave, Berkeley (94709). Phone 510/548-5525. www.chezpanisse.com.* Celebrity chef Alice Waters is renowned for launching the movement toward organic, locally grown meat and produce and for creating dishes that allow seasonal ingredients to speak for themselves. Waters has created a restaurant that skillfully navigates between an inviting, cozy atmosphere and an elegant setting, with a décor that boasts a few subtle Asian touches. The service here is impeccable. The more casual café upstairs serves an à la carte menu; the more formal downstairs dining area is a prix fixe restaurant serving dinner only, with reservations booked up to a month in advance. The week's menu is posted on the restaurant's Web site. California, fusion menu. Lunch, dinner. Closed Sun; Jan 1, Dec 25. **$$$$**

★ ★ ★ JORDAN'S. *41 Tunnel Rd, Berkeley (94705). Phone 510/843-3000; fax 510/649-9563. www.claremontresort.com.* Part of the Claremont Resort and Spa (see), elegant Jordan's serves seasonal cuisine with a Pacific Rim influence. Come for brunch or lunch, when you can enjoy the "wall" of windows that give diners a spectacular view over Berkeley to San Francisco (a view of three bridges!). The dining room itself is peaceful, with soft yellow paint, formal table settings, and unobtrusive classical music; during brunch, a pianist adds to the relaxed atmosphere. Fresh lobster is flown in every Wednesday. California menu. Breakfast, lunch, dinner. Bar. Children's menu. **$$$**

★ ★ LALIME'S CAFE. *1329 Gilman St, Berkeley (94706). Phone 510/527-9838; fax 510/527-1350. www.lalimes.com.* Two-level dining area housed in a cottage. California, Mediterranean menu. Dinner. Closed holidays. Bar. **$$$**

★ ★ O CHAME. *1830 4th St, Berkeley (94710). Phone 510/841-8783.* Japanese menu. Lunch, dinner. Closed Sun; Memorial Day, July 4, Labor Day. Casual attire. **$$**

★ ★ ★ SKATES ON THE BAY. *100 Seawall Dr, Berkeley (94710). Phone 510/549-1900; fax 510/549-0257. www.skatesonthebay.com.* Offers spectacular views of the bay, the Golden Gate Bridge, Bay Bridge, and San Francisco. California, seafood menu. Lunch, dinner. Closed Thanksgiving, Dec 25. Bar. Children's menu. Casual attire. **$$$**

Big Basin Redwoods State Park (E-1)

See also Santa Cruz

23 miles N of Santa Cruz via Hwys 9, 236.

Web Site www.bigbasin.org

This 20,000-acre park is one of the most popular parks in California. The area was set aside as the state's first redwood preserve in 1902. Its redwood groves include trees 300 feet high. There are about 50 miles of hiking and riding trails, plus numerous picnic sites and campgrounds with full facilities (limit eight persons per site; reservations required in summer). Ranger-conducted nature programs, held in the summer, include campfire programs and guided hikes. Flora and fauna of the park are on display in exhibits at the nature lodge. Supplies are available at a concession and a store. Phone 831/338-8860.

Big Sur (F-2)

See also Carmel, Carmel Valley, Monterey, Pacific Grove, Salinas

Population 1,000
Elevation 155 ft
Area Code 831
Zip 93920
Information Pfeiffer-Big Sur State Park, Big Sur Ranger Station; phone 831/667-2315
Web Site www.bigsurcalifornia.org

Big Sur is 30 miles south of Monterey on Highway 1, with the Santa Lucia Range on the east and the Pacific Ocean on the west.

A scenic drive along Highway 1 provides 90 miles of views along the rocky Big Sur bluffs, past redwood forests, canyons, waterfalls, secluded beaches, and sheer mountains. This route provides access to many state parks south of Carmel. Garrapata State Park, 7 miles south of Carmel, offers hiking, mountain biking, fishing, coastal access, tide pools, canyons, and whale-watching in winter. Andrew Molera State Park, 21 miles south of Carmel, is Big Sur's largest state park and offers hiking and beach access along rugged headlands. Pfeiffer-Big Sur State Park contains a coastal redwood forest. Recreational opportunities include swimming and hiking. Picnicking and camping facilities are available (fee for camping). There is also a lodge, gift shop, and store. Naturalist programs are offered. Julia Pfeiffer Burns State Park, 36 miles south of Carmel, has a dramatic 80-foot waterfall accessed by a short trail. Camping facilities are available (fee).

What to See and Do

Bixby Bridge. The Bixby Bridge, completed in 1932, is a marvel of engineering and one of the ten highest single span bridges in the world. The bridge spans a large canyon along the Big Sur coastline. The weather conditions can have a noticeable impact on the bridge's appearance: clouds may partially hit it, or the sun may reflect off the gleaming white structural supports. That quality, combined with the massive appearance of the bridge, brings countless people to photograph the bridge. **FREE**

Julia Pfeiffer Burns State Park. *Big Sur Station 1, Big Sur (93920). Phone 831/667-2315. www.parks.ca.gov.* Julia Pfeiffer Burns State Park stretches from the Big Sur coastline into nearby 3,000-foot ridges. The park features redwood, tan oak, madrone, chaparral, and an 80-foot waterfall that drops from granite cliffs into the ocean from the Overlook Trail. A panoramic view of the ocean and miles of rugged coastline is available from the higher elevations along the trails east of Route 1. The park also has a 1,680-acre underwater reserve which protects a spectacular assortment of marine life. Special-use permits allow experienced scuba divers to explore the reserve. Seals, sea lions, and sea otters can be seen in the park's cove. Hikers can discover the park's backcountry via several trail systems. (Daily, dawn-dusk) **$$**

Point Sur State Historic Park. *On Rte 1, 19 miles S of Carmel and Monterey and 1/4 mile N of Point Sur Naval Facility. Phone 831/625-4419; toll-free www.pointsur.org.* Point Sur State Historic Park is the home of the historic Point Sur Light Station and an active US Coast Guard light station. The park sits 361 feet above the surf on a large volcanic rock. Point Sur has been a navigational landmark throughout history, and the nearby coastline has been the site of several notable shipwrecks, both before and after the installation of the lighthouse. Point Sur is on the National Register of Historic Places, and is a California State Historic Landmark. From the highway you can see the majestic stone buildings of the Point Sur Light Station that have been part of the Big Sur coast for almost 100 years. Lighthouses and lightships were an important part of coastal navigation. The facilities were established for the safety of seagoing vessels on August 1, 1889; it has remained in continuous operation. Four lighthouse keepers and their families lived at the site until 1974, when the light station was automated. Call for specific hours and tour times. Tours. **$**

Full-Service Resort

★★★★ **POST RANCH INN.** *Hwy 1, Big Sur (93920). Phone 831/667-2200; toll-free 800/527-2200; fax 831/667-2512. www.postranchinn.com.* Perched on the tip of a cliff overlooking the dramatic coastline of Big Sur, the Post Ranch Inn brings new meaning to living on the edge. This unique hideaway offers an experience far from the ordinary. Designed to live in harmony with the majestic natural setting, the architecture resembles a collection of sophisticated treehouses. Clean lines and simple interiors create an uncluttered appearance and state of mind. Floor-to-ceiling windows open to awe-inspiring views and enhance the subtle beauty of the accommodations, while two-sided fireplaces are the ultimate luxury, allowing guests to enjoy the warm glow from the bed or the bath. No televisions or alarm clocks disrupt the gentle rhythm of this place, where yoga and tai chi reawaken the soul, and the spa soothes the spirit. The Sierra Mar restaurant (see) is a triumph of California cuisine, and the extensive wine list is a perfect accompaniment to the superb dishes. 30 rooms, 2 story. No children allowed. Complimentary full breakfast. Check-in 4 pm, check-out 1 pm. Restaurant, bar. Fitness room, spa. Two outdoor pools. **$$$$**

Full-Service Inn

★★★ **VENTANA INN & SPA.** *Hwy 1, Big Sur (93920). Phone 831/667-2331; toll-free 800/628-6500; fax 831/667-0573. www.ventanainn.com.* Ventana Inn & Spa is the sophisticate's answer to rusticating. This stylish resort speaks to nature lovers with a penchant for luxury from its perch 1,200 feet above the Big Sur coastline. The dramatic views of the Pacific Ocean are unforgettable, and the property's 243 acres of towering redwoods, wildflower-filled meadows, and rolling hills instantly calm frayed nerves. Everything has been designed to live in harmony with the natural setting here, and the wood-paneled guest rooms and suites are no exception. After communing with nature, guests indulge with a sensational treatment at the spa or with a mouthwatering meal from the resort's restaurant, Cielo (see), where the inventive cuisine competes with the impressive view. 60 rooms, 2 story. Complimentary continental breakfast. Check-in 4 pm, check-out 1 pm. Bar. Fitness room, spa. Outdoor pool, whirlpool. **$$$$**

Spa

★★★★ **THE SPA AT POST RANCH INN.** *Hwy 1, Big Sur (93920). Phone 831/667-2927; toll-free 800/527-2200. www.postranchinn.com.* Eastern practices, Native American traditions, and nature-based therapies are the focus at the Post Ranch Inn's spa. The area's abundance of plants and flowers inspire the organic garden facial, which uses homemade honey, flower essences, and tomato sun cream, while the wildflower facial blends rose, chamomile, lavender, rosemary, or sage to refresh and heal the skin. The Hungarian herbal body wrap and lavender body exfoliation also celebrate the great outdoors. The crystal and gemstone therapy, a holistic treatment using aromatherapy, crystal quartz, and jade to awaken and balance, and the Big Sur jade therapy, a treatment using cooled jade and basalt river rocks to stimulate circulation and relaxation, are a nod to Native American traditions. For a truly unusual approach to well-being, book the Native American Shamanic Session. From reiki and Thai massage to craniosacral therapy, this spa also shares the wisdom of Asia with clients. Private hikes, meditation sessions, yoga, and couples massage instruction are also available. From its ridge top location amid towering redwoods, heaven does indeed seem reachable from this magical spa. The treatment rooms echo the inn's commitment to bringing the outdoors in, and many guests choose to book treatments in the privacy of their guest rooms or terraces. Two pools provide refreshing spots for relaxation or recreation, and a fitness room is also available.

Restaurants

★★★ **CIELO.** *Hwy 1, Big Sur (93920). Phone 831/667-4242; fax 831/667-2287. www.ventanainn.com.* Cielo is a magical place. Set on the cliffs of Highway 1, this restaurant affords breathtaking mountain views and heart-stopping peeks at the whitecapped, deep-blue ocean below. With nature's bounty on such magnificent display, outdoor dining on the wide, rustic, elegant patio is the way to go. Market umbrellas, sturdy redwood tables, teak chairs, and votive candles give this enchanted spot even more ambience. If you can't sit outside, though, don't fret. The dining room is warm and cozy, with tall windows, a large stone fireplace, wood-beamed ceilings, and a bird's-eye view of the sparkling exhibition kitchen, where you'll witness pristine California ingredients being transformed into sumptuous plates of New American fare. Nature does its part to make dining at Cielo an unforgettable experience, and the kitchen does its best to compete with the view. Let's call it a tie. California menu. Lunch, dinner. Bar. Casual attire. Reservations recommended. Outdoor seating. **$$$**

★★ **NEPENTHE.** *Hwy 1, Big Sur (93920). Phone 831/667-2345; fax 831/667-2394. www.nepenthebigsur.com.* American, California menu. Lunch, dinner. Bar. Casual attire. Outdoor seating. **$$$**

★★★★ **SIERRA MAR.** *Hwy 1, Big Sur (93920). Phone 831/667-2800; fax 831/667-2824. www.postranchinn.com.* Perched high over the Pacific Ocean on the Pacific Coast Highway is the highly acclaimed Sierra Mar restaurant, an elegant but comfortable space appointed with wood and chrome and, of course, surrounded by magnificent views of cliffs, mountains, and the wide ocean below. It's tough to compete with such incredible natural beauty, but the food at Sierra Mar does a winning job of it. Innovative and modern but grounded in precise French technique, the four-course prix fixe menu changes daily and utilizes seasonal organic products. You'll find seafood, lamb, and beef alongside luxurious ingredients like oysters, truffles, foie gras, and caviar. The restaurant has one of the most extensive wine cellars in North America, giving you many options for glass-clinking toasts. California menu. Lunch, dinner. Bar. Business casual attire. Reservations recommended. Valet parking. Outdoor seating. **$$$$**

Bishop (F-4)

See also Inyo National Forest, Mammoth Lakes

Population 3,575
Elevation 4,147 ft
Area Code 760
Zip 93514
Information Bishop Area Chamber of Commerce and Visitors Bureau, 690 N Main St; phone 760/873-8405
Web Site www.bishopvisitor.com

What to See and Do

Ancient Bristlecone Pine Forest. *798 N Main St, Bishop (93514). In the White and Inyo mountains of the Inyo National Forest (see). Hwy 168 E from Big Pine to White Mountain Rd to Schulman Grove and Patriarch Grove. Phone 760/873-8405.* These trees are estimated to be more than 4,600 years old, making them some of the oldest known living trees on Earth. Naturalist programs. White Mountain Road District Visitor Center (July 4-Labor Day, Mon-Fri).

Laws Railroad Museum & Historical Site. *Silver Canyon Rd, Bishop. 5 miles NE on Hwy 6, then 1/2 mile E on Silver Canyon Rd. Phone 760/873-5950.* Laws Post Office with old-fashioned equipment, 1883 depot, narrow-gauge locomotive, restored station agent's five-room house; hand-operated gallows-type turntable used 1883-1960; water tower, pump house; mining exhibits; library and arts building, Western building, pioneer building, firehouse, bottle house, doctor's office, country store; Native American exhibit. (Daily 10 am-4 pm, weather permitting; closed Jan 1, Thanksgiving, Dec 25) **DONATION**

Special Events

Eastern Sierra Tri-County Fair. *Fair Dr and Sierra St, Bishop (93515). Phone 760/873-3588. www.tricountyfair.com.* Thousands of homemade and homegrown goods—from fruits and flower arrangements to barbecued beef and baked treats—are displayed each year. Family activities include carnival rides, games, and a Destruction Derby (fee). Labor Day weekend. **$$**

Mule Days. *Bishop Fairgrounds, Hwy 395 and Hwy 6, Bishop (93515). Phone 760/872-4263.*

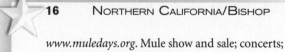

www.muledays.org. Mule show and sale; concerts; barbecue; parade. Memorial Day weekend.

Limited-Service Hotels

★ BEST WESTERN HOLIDAY SPA LODGE. *1025 N Main St, Bishop (93514). Phone 760/873-3543; toll-free 800/576-3543; fax 760/872-4777. www.bestwestern.com*. 89 rooms, 2 story. Pets accepted, some restrictions; fee. Complimentary continental breakfast. Check-in 3 pm, check-out 11 am. High-speed Internet access. Fitness room. Outdoor pool, whirlpool. Business center. **$**

★ COMFORT INN. *805 N Main St, Bishop (93514). Phone 760/873-4284; toll-free 800/576-4080; fax 760/873-8563. www.choicehotels.com*. 54 rooms, 2 story. Pets accepted; fee. Complimentary continental breakfast. Check-in 11 am, check-out 2 pm. Outdoor pool, whirlpool. **$**

Specialty Lodging

The following lodging establishment is approved by Mobil Travel Guide, but due to its unique and individualized nature has not been given a traditional Mobil Star rating. Included in this listing you may find bed-and-breakfasts, limited-service inns, guest ranches, and other unique hotel properties.

CHALFANT HOUSE BED & BREAKFAST. *213 Academy Ave, Bishop (93514). Phone 760/872-1790; toll-free 800/641-2996. www.chalfanthouse.com*. Built in 1898. 7 rooms, 2 story. Complimentary full breakfast. Check-in 3 pm, check-out 11 am. **$**

Restaurants

★ INYO COUNTRY STORE AND RESTAURANT. *177 Academy St, Bishop (93514). Phone 760/872-2552*. American menu. Breakfast, lunch. Closed Sun. Children's menu. Casual attire. **$**

★★ WHISKEY CREEK. *524 N Main St, Bishop (93514). Phone 760/873-7174; fax 760/934-8860*. American menu. Lunch, dinner. Bar. Children's menu. Casual attire. Reservations recommended. Outdoor seating. **$$**

Bodega Bay

See also Fort Ross State Historic Park, Guerneville, Healdsburg, Inverness, Santa Rosa

Settled 1835
Population 1,423
Elevation 120 ft
Area Code 707
Zip 94923
Web Site www.bodegabay.com

Limited-Service Hotel

★ BODEGA COAST INN. *521 Coast Hwy 1, Bodega Bay (94923). Phone 707/875-2217; toll-free 800/346-6999; fax 707/875-2964. www.bodegacoastinn.com*. 45 rooms, 3 story. Pets accepted; some restrictions. Complimentary continental breakfast. Check-in 3 pm, check-out noon. Whirlpool. **$$**

Full-Service Resort

★★★ BODEGA BAY LODGE AND SPA. *103 Coast Hwy 1, Bodega Bay (94923). Phone 707/875-3525; toll-free 800/368-2468; fax 707/875-2428. www.bodegabaylodge.com*. The Bodega Bay Lodge and Spa overlooks the ocean, Doran Beach State Park, and the bluffs of Bodega Head. 84 rooms, 2 story. Check-in 3 pm, check-out 11:30 am. Restaurant. Fitness room, spa. Outdoor pool, whirlpool. **$$$**

Full-Service Inn

★★★ INN AT THE TIDES. *800 Coast Hwy 1, Bodega Bay (94923). Phone 707/875-2751; toll-free 800/541-7788; fax 707/875-2669. www.innatthetides.com*. Sixty miles north of San Francisco on the Sonoma Coast is the quaint fishing village of Bodega Bay, home to the charming Inn at the Tides. Nestled above the sparkling bay from a hilltop locale, this inn perfectly captures the essence of the California coast with its laid-back attitude and serene views. From the dazzling bay and harbor views in the guest rooms to the casual and friendly mood of the staff, this resort is all about relaxation. Sunny days are best enjoyed by the indoor/outdoor heated pool, and in-room massages are a great way to savor the soothing feeling here. 86 rooms, 2 story. Complimentary continental breakfast. Check-in 3 pm, check-out

11 am. Restaurant, bar. Fitness room. Outdoor pool, whirlpool. **$$**

Specialty Lodgings

The following lodging establishments are approved by Mobil Travel Guide, but due to their unique and individualized nature have not been given a traditional Mobil Star rating. Included in this listing you may find bed-and-breakfasts, limited-service inns, guest ranches, and other unique hotel properties.

THE INN AT OCCIDENTAL. *3657 Church St, Occidental (95465). Phone 707/874-1047; toll-free 800/522-6324; fax 707/874-1078. www.innatoccidental.com.* The Inn at Occidental shares its quirky charms with visitors. Every corner of this delightful inn is filled with intriguing folk art and antiques. Handmade quilts, wooden roosters, and other pieces of Americana are just the beginning at this unique lodging in the funky wine country village of Occidental. The guest rooms and suites are individually designed, highly imaginative, and colorful, and their different themes are designed to inspire and enchant. Hearty breakfasts are a highlight of a visit to this inn—from fresh granola and homemade pastries to hot entrées. 18 rooms. Children over 10 years only. Complimentary full breakfast. Check-in 3 pm, check-out noon. **$$$**

SONOMA COAST VILLA INN AND SPA. *16702 Coast Hwy 1, Bodega (94922). Phone 707/876-9818; toll-free 888/404-2255; fax 707/876-9856. www.scvilla.com.* The Sonoma Coast Villa Inn and Spa feels like an enchanted Mediterranean village with its red-tile roofs and charming villa-style buildings. This family-owned and-run bed-and-breakfast is a particularly inviting spot for those visiting the California wine country and beyond. Just minutes from beautiful Bodega Bay, this resort is tucked away on 60 countryside acres in Sonoma County. A warm, hospitable attitude is felt throughout the resort, from the welcoming comfort of the guest rooms and suites to the daily breakfasts of freshly baked breads and muffins still warm from the oven. Its pastoral setting is perfect for unwinding, and the spa features wonderfully relaxing massages and body treatments. 18 rooms. Complimentary full breakfast. Check-in 3-6 pm, check-out 11 am. Outdoor pool, whirlpool. **$$$**

Restaurants

★ ★ **BAY VIEW.** *800 Hwy 1, Bodega Bay (94923). Phone 707/875-2751; toll-free 800/541-7788; fax 707/875-2119. www.innatthetides.com.* True to its name, this restaurant promises a fantastic view from every table in its warm, elegant dining room, accented with beamed ceilings and a cozy fireplace. The menu features recipes that highlight the best of California cuisine and takes advantage of the freshest produce, seafood, and poultry that have made Sonoma County so well known in the world of food fanatics. California menu. Dinner. Closed Mon-Tues. Bar. Children's menu. Outdoor seating. **$$**

★ ★ **THE DUCK CLUB.** *103 Coast Hwy 1, Bodega Bay (94923). Phone 707/875-3525; fax 707/875-2428. www.woodsidehotels.com.* California menu. Breakfast, dinner. Children's menu. **$$**

★ **LUCAS WHARF.** *595 Hwy 1, Bodega Bay (94923). Phone 707/875-3522; fax 707/875-3032.* On the waterfront of Bodega Bay, this simple, rustic seafood restaurant features great views of the Bay and the fishing boats that catch the fish and shellfish served here every day. With an open kitchen, nautical décor, and a working fireplace, the atmosphere is airy and comfortable. Seafood menu. Lunch, dinner. Closed Thanksgiving, Dec 25. Bar. Children's menu. Casual attire. Outdoor seating. **$$**

Bridgeport (E-4)

See also Coleville, Lee Vining

Population 500
Elevation 6,473 ft
Area Code 760
Zip 93517
Web Site www.bridgeportcalifornia.com

A Ranger District office of the Toiyabe National Forest is located here.

What to See and Do

Bodie State Historic Park. *7 miles S on Hwy 395, then 13 miles E on partially unpaved road; not cleared in winter (only accessible on foot). Phone 760/647-6445. www.parks.ca.gov.* An unrestored ghost town of the late 1800s. Between 1879 and 1881, more than 10,000 people lived here. Fires in 1892 and 1932 took their toll, and now only about 5 percent of the town remains. A self-guiding brochure takes you through the main part of town, consisting of a church (circa 1880), jail, a two-room school, Miners Union Hall (now a museum), and a hillside cemetery with a monument to James A. Garfield. Picnicking. (Memorial Day-Labor Day: daily 8 am-7 pm; rest of year: 9 am-4 pm) **$**

Specialty Lodging

The following lodging establishment is approved by Mobil Travel Guide, but due to its unique and individualized nature have not been given a traditional Mobil Star rating. Included in this listing you may find bed-and-breakfasts, limited-service inns, guest ranches, and other unique hotel properties.

CAIN HOUSE. *340 Main St, Bridgeport (93517). Phone 760/932-7040; toll-free 800/433-2246; fax 760/932-7419. www.cainhouse.com.* The house was originally built in 1925 and converted into a bed-and-breakfast in 1989. All rooms are well maintained and furnished in wicker and whitewashed woods. 7 rooms, 2 story. Complimentary full breakfast. Check-in 3-7 pm, check-out 11 am. **$**

Restaurant

★★ **BRIDGEPORT INN.** *205 Main St, Bridgeport (93517). Phone 760/932-7380; fax 760/932-1160. www.thebridgeportinn.com.* American menu. Breakfast, lunch, dinner. Bar. Children's menu. Casual attire. Reservations recommended. **$**

Burney (B-3)

See also Mount Shasta, Redding

Population 3,217
Elevation 3,130 ft
Area Code 530
Zip 96013
Information Chamber of Commerce, 37088 Main St, PO Box 36; phone 530/335-2111
Web Site www.burneychamber.com

All the attractions of outdoor living are in the area surrounding Shasta Lake, Mount Shasta (see), and Lassen Volcanic National Park (see).

What to See and Do

Hat Creek Recreation Area. *43225 CA 299 E, Fall River Mills (96028). 17 miles SE on Hwy 89. Phone 530/336-5521. www.fs.fed.us.* Located in Lassen National Forest, this recreation area offers fishing; picnicking, camping (fee). Geological sites include Subway Cave, a lava tube; and Spattercone, a guided volcanic nature trail. Camping and fishing facilities for the disabled.

McArthur-Burney Falls Memorial State Park. *24898 Hwy 89, Burney (96013). 5 miles E on Hwy 299, then 6 miles N on Hwy 89. Phone 530/335-2777. www.parks.ca.gov.* These 853 acres encompass Burney Falls (in season, water bubbles from underground springs, flows 1/2 mile, then drops over a precipice in 129-foot twin falls). Swimming, fishing, boat launching; nature and hiking trails, picnicking, concession, camping. Naturalist program.

Calistoga (D-2)

See also Napa, Petaluma, Rutherford, Santa Rosa, Sonoma, St. Helena

Founded 1859
Population 5,190
Elevation 362 ft
Area Code 707
Zip 94515
Information Chamber of Commerce, 1458 Lincoln Ave #9; phone 707/942-6333
Web Site www.calistogafun.com

Tucked away at the north end of Napa Valley, Calistoga is known for its geothermal hot springs and mineral water, as well as its wineries. California's first millionaire, Samuel Brannan, arrived here in the 1840s and opened a hot springs resort, hoping it would be California's equivalent of New York's Saratoga Springs; the city's name derives from this inspiration. Downtown Calistoga balances old and new, with 19th-century architecture housing restaurants, shops, and spas that offer decidedly 21st-century fare and amenities. Calistoga is also home to the Old Faithful Geyser of California. The geyser erupts every 30 minutes, beginning with bubbles and steam, and then shooting 350-degree water 60 feet into the air. Also here are the scenic trails of Robert Louis Stevenson State Park, named for the *Treasure Island* author who spent his honeymoon here in 1880. A 5-mile trail in the park leads to the 4,339-foot summit of Mount St. Helena. Good views of the mountain can be found at the Petrified Forest, where redwood trees, buried by volcanic ash when Mount St. Helena erupted 3 million years ago, became saturated by silica and ultimately turned to stone.

What to See and Do

Bale Grist Mill State Historic Park. *Hwy 29, Calistoga (94515). 3 miles N of St. Helena. Phone 707/942-4575. www.parks.ca.gov.* Once the center of social activity in the Napa Valley—the place where settlers gathered to have their corn and wheat ground into flour—the Bale Grist Mill State Historic Park is the site of a water-powered mill built in 1846. Today, visitors can visit this old stone mill (and, if they're lucky, get to watch the "run of the mill" turn wheat into flour) or simply enjoy hiking in nature and camping in the park. (Daily) **$**

Cedar Street Spa. *1107 Cedar St, Calistoga (94515). Phone 707/942-2947. www.cedarstreetspa.com.* If sitting up to your neck in a gooey bath isn't your thing, Cedar Street Spa provides a different way to get that Calistoga rejuvenation. Primarily a massage center (although it does also offer herbal facials and European body wraps, too), this spa offers a variety of massage techniques, from deep tissue to Shiatsu. Reservations are recommended. Like most of the spas in Calistoga, Cedar Street offers specials for couples. (Thurs-Mon) **$$$$**

Lavender Hill Spa. *1015 Foothill Blvd, Calistoga (94515). Phone 707/942-4495; toll-free 800/528-4772. www.lavenderhillspa.com.* Quieter and more out of the way than some of Calistoga's other spas, Lavender Hill offers massages and facials in the main house and other treatments in private, individual bathhouses that accommodate one or two people. Treatments include volcanic mud, seaweed, mineral salt, and herbal baths; foot reflexology; hot stone massage; and wraps. This day spa is clean, professional, and low-key, offering the latest spa services with just a hint of the California hippie vibe. (Daily; closed holidays) **$$$$**

Lincoln Avenue Spa. *1339 Lincoln Ave, Calistoga (94515). Phone 707/942-5296. www.lincolnavenuespa.com.* Offering its own variation on the mud bath, the Lincoln Avenue Spa coats guests in one of four natural muds—herbal, green tea, sea, or mint—and then ensconces them in special wraparound steam tables, with attendants close at hand, to let the mud seep in and work its magic. All this is done in private treatment rooms designed for both individuals and couples. Other options include facials and body wraps. Reservations are recommended. (Daily; closed Dec 25) **$$$$**

Mount St. Helena. *8 miles N on Hwy 29.* (4,344 feet). Extinct volcano where Robert Louis Stevenson honeymooned in 1880 and wrote *The Silverado Squatters.* Robert Louis Stevenson State Park, on Mount St. Helena, has a monument (a statue of the author holding an open book) located near the site of the Silverado mine; 3/4-mile hiking trail from parking lot.

Napa Valley Brewing Company. *1250 Lincoln Ave, Calistoga (94515). Phone 707/942-4101. www.calistogainn.com.* If wine isn't your thing, you can enjoy alternative Napa libations at the Napa Valley Brewing Company. Opened in 1987, the brewery was the first to brew beer commercially in Napa since Prohibition. With a full-time dedicated brewmaster, the brewery has developed award-winning beers and ales while limiting production to 450 barrels a year. Most of it is served on draft at the adjacent Calistoga Inn (see), where you'll find a restaurant, an English-style pub, and a beer garden. The pub features live music on weekends and an open mike night on Wednesdays for new musicians, while the beer garden features live music on Sunday afternoons. (Daily)

Napa Valley Railroad Depot. *1458 Lincoln Ave, Calistoga (94515).* The second-oldest remaining railroad station in California, the Calistoga Depot was built by millionaire and Calistoga founder Sam Brannan for the Napa Valley Railroad in 1868, a year before the transcontinental railroad was completed. The building was restored in 1978 and is now a California State Historic Landmark. Along with photos of the early days, the depot houses six retail stores and a restaurant. (Daily; closed Thanksgiving, Dec 25)

Old Faithful Geyser of California. *1299 Tubbs Ln, Calistoga (94515). Phone 707/942-6463. www.oldfaithfulgeyser.com.* One of only three regularly erupting geysers in the world, this Old Faithful spews approximately every 30 minutes for about three minutes at a time, unless an earthquake disrupts its timing. The spot is fed by an underground river that heats up to 350 degrees, causing vapor and steam to escape to heights of 60 feet. A favorite of families, the site also features picnic grounds. (Daily 9 am-6 pm) **$$**

Petrified Forest. *4100 Petrified Forest Rd, Calistoga (94515). 8 miles W. Phone 707/942-6667. www.petrifiedforest.org.* Children especially enjoy visiting this park dedicated to a natural phenomenon. Some 3 million years ago, a volcanic eruption literally petrified the giant redwoods that covered this part of northern California. As a result, the wood, coated in molecules of silica, turned to solid quartz and stone. Discovered around 1860, some trees are as large as 105 feet long and 8 feet in diameter, with details excellently preserved. Today, these preserved trees offer insight into geologic formations and give visitors a glimpse of a prehistoric world. The museum and rock shop offer a close-up look at some geological wonders. (Daily 9 am-7 pm; to 5 pm in winter; closed Dec 25) **$$**

Robert Louis Stevenson State Park. *7 miles N of Calistoga on Hwy 29. Phone 707/942-4575. www.parks.ca.gov.* Commemorating the famous author who spent his 1880 honeymoon here, the Robert Louis Stevenson State Park provides rugged respite from the wine crowds. Little of the park's 3,000 acres are developed, but there is a good trail up to the summit of Mount St. Helena, an extinct volcano and the highest peak in the Napa Valley at 4,343 feet. As you climb this 5-mile trail, look for the marker identifying the site of the bunkhouse of the abandoned Silverado Mine, where Stevenson and his bride Fanny Osbourne slept. It's believed that their stay here inspired Stevenson's book *The Silverado Squatters.* At the top, you'll have fantastic view of the valley, as well as of the Bay Area and Mount Shasta. (Daily, sunrise-sunset)

Sharpsteen Museum and Sam Brannan Cottage. *1311 Washington St, Calistoga (94515). Phone 707/942-5911. www.sharpsteen-museum.org.* Dedicated to presenting the story of Napa Valley from its prehistory to post-World War I, this small museum showcases complex dioramas, historical exhibits, and quarterly special exhibits. Special attention is paid to Calistoga's heyday in the 1860s, when it was an elegant hot springs resort developed by California's first millionaire, Sam Brannan. Founded in 1978, the museum is the brainchild of Ben and Bernice Sharpsteen, and one room features memorabilia from Ben's career as an animator, producer, and director for Walt Disney Studios. (Daily 11 am-4 pm; closed holidays) **FREE**

Sterling Vineyards. *1111 Dunaweal Ln, Calistoga (94515). Phone 707/942-3344; toll-free 800/726-6136. www.sterlingvineyards.com.* For some of the best panoramic views of the Napa Valley, take the aerial tramway up to Sterling Vineyards. A whitewashed building modeled after the villages on the Greek Island of Mykonos, Sterling was a pioneer of once-unknown chardonnay and merlot grapes. Once there, you can take a self-guided tour and view the winemaking operations from elevated walkways, sample current releases in the main tasting room, or check out the Reserve Tasting Room and Cellar Club Room. (Daily 10:30 am-4:30 pm; closed holidays) **$$$**

Special Event

Napa County Fair. *Napa County Fairgrounds, 1435 N Oak St, Calistoga (94515). Phone 707/942-5111. www.napacountyfairgrounds.com.* The Napa County Fairgrounds host numerous events year-round, from car races on the speedway to horse shows, festivals, and fundraisers, but the annual highlight is the County Fair. Over the July 4 weekend, visitors can enjoy fireworks, country music concerts, rides, a barbecue contest, exhibits, and a wide range of food concessions in a festive country atmosphere. A nine-hole public golf course and an RV park also share the grounds. July 4 weekend. **$$**

Limited-Service Hotel

★ CALISTOGA SPA HOT SPRINGS. *1006 Washington St, Calistoga (94515). Phone 707/942-6269; toll-free 866/822-5772; fax 707/942-4214. www.calistogaspa.com.* This motel-style lodging is just a block off Calistoga's main street, close to shopping and restaurants. It has some unique resortlike features, with its tapping of naturally heated mineral water for its four outdoor pools. Additionally, there are spa facilities offering massage therapy, mud baths, and mineral baths, plus a large exercise room. The guest rooms are simple and functional, with kitchenettes, which can support vacation-length stays. The property also has a picnic area and barbecue pits. 57 rooms, 2 story. Check-in 3 pm, check-out 11 am. Fitness room, spa. Two outdoor pools, children's pool, whirlpool. **$$**

Full-Service Inn

★★★ MOUNT VIEW HOTEL AND SPA. *1457 Lincoln Ave, Calistoga (94515). Phone 707/942-6877; toll-free 800/816-6877; fax 707/942-6904. www.mountviewhotel.com.* This charming, historic small hotel is located in the heart of downtown Calistoga. At the north end of the world-famous Napa Valley, the property offers a full range of guest accommodations, from cozy rooms to suites and cottages, each with a nice mix of Victorian antiques and modern amenities. An attractive garden area is at the rear of the property, along with a pool, Jacuzzi tub, and cabana. An upscale plus for travelers is an on-site, full-service Euro Spa featuring hydrotherapy baths, massage, and facials. There is also an excellent fine-dining restaurant off the lobby. 31 rooms. Complimentary continental breakfast. Check-in 4 pm, check-out noon. Restaurant. Spa. Outdoor pool, whirlpool. **$$**

Specialty Lodgings

The following lodging establishments are approved by Mobil Travel Guide, but due to their unique and individualized nature have not been given a traditional Mobil Star rating. Included in this listing you may find bed-and-breakfasts, limited-service inns, guest ranches, and other unique hotel properties.

CALISTOGA INN. *1250 Lincoln Ave, Calistoga (94515). Phone 707/942-4101; fax 707/942-4914. www.calistogainn.com.* This historic, century-old lodging is a good alternative for young or low-budget travelers. It's located on the main street of Calistoga, at the north end of the Napa Valley, and Calistoga's restaurants, shops, and attractions are all a short walk away. The guest rooms are on the second floor, above the inn's restaurant and bar. This is a traditional European-style small hotel, with communal bathroom facilities and basic rooms that feature attractive, freshly painted color schemes and comfortable beds with duvet covers. A continental breakfast with freshly baked breakfast breads is provided each morning. 18 rooms, 2 story. Complimentary continental breakfast. Check-in 3 pm, check-out 11 am. Restaurant, bar. **$**

CHELSEA GARDEN INN. *1443 Second St, Calistoga (94515). Phone 707/942-0948; toll-free 800/942-1515; fax 707/942-5102. www.chelseagardeninn.com.* 5 rooms. Complimentary full breakfast. Check-in 3 pm, check-out 11 am. Outdoor pool. **$$**

CHRISTOPHER'S INN. *1010 Foothill Blvd, Calistoga (94515). Phone 707/942-5755; toll-free 866/876-5755; fax 707/942-6895. www.chrisinn.com.* Situated on Highway 29, the main artery through the Napa Valley, this is a small, modern, country-style inn. It is only a short walk from the center of Calistoga, at the valley's north end. Having added a wing of luxury suites, the property has a range of quality accommodations. The guest rooms are quite spacious, feature Laura Ashley interiors, and include varying major features such as fireplaces, Jacuzzi tubs, 12-foot ceilings, private patios, and skylights. An expanded continental breakfast is provided to guests, along with an afternoon wine reception in the summertime. 21 rooms, 2 story. Complimentary continental breakfast. Check-in 2 pm, check-out 11 am. **$$**

COTTAGE GROVE INN. *1711 Lincoln Ave, Calistoga (94515). Phone 707/942-8400; toll-free 800/799-2284; fax 707/942-2653. www.cottagegrove.com.* The Cottage Grove Inn consists of a cluster of luxury private cottages, shaded by a grove of elm trees, on the north end of downtown Calistoga. Found at the upper end of the Napa Valley, the property is short walk from Calistoga's restaurants, shops, and hot mineral water spas and minutes from world-class wineries. Each cottage has a unique personality, individually decorated in varying fabrics and paint schemes. They share many modern comforts and distinctive features, including Jacuzzi soaking tubs, fireplaces, CD stereo systems, front porches with wicker rockers, skylights, hardwood floors, TVs/VCRs, robes, and down comforters and pillows. A wonderful spot for a romantic getaway, the inn also provides a complimentary breakfast and an afternoon wine reception. 16 rooms. Children over 12 years only. Complimentary continental breakfast. Check-in 3 pm, check-out 11 am. **$$$**

CULVER MANSION. *1805 Foothill Blvd, Calistoga (94515). Phone 707/942-4535; toll-free 877/281-3671; fax 707/942-4557. www.culvermansion.com.* Built in 1875. 4 rooms, 2 story. Closed Dec-Jan. Children over 16 years only. Complimentary full breakfast. Check-in 3-6 pm, check-out 11 am. Outdoor pool, whirlpool. **$$**

THE ELMS BED & BREAKFAST INN. *1300 Cedar St, Calistoga (94515). Phone 707/942-9476; toll-free 888/399-3567; fax 707/942-9479. www.theelms.com.* Although it is located in a quiet, tree-shaded, residential neighborhood, this bed-and-breakfast is only a short block off the main street of downtown Calistoga. Listed on the National Historic Registry, this fine old Victorian residence was built in 1871. In addition to the main house accommodations, a small carriage house is at the rear, with rooms facing the Napa River. The guest rooms offer an interesting blend of antique furnishings with modern amenities. Feather-top beds, down comforters, bathrobes, TVs with VCRs, and some spa tubs are mixed in varying degrees with claw-foot tubs, pedestal sinks, and fireplaces. A full gourmet breakfast and afternoon wine and refreshments are complimentary. 7 rooms, 3 story.

Pets accepted, some restrictions; fee. Complimentary full breakfast. Check-in 4-6 pm, check-out 11 am. Whirlpool. **$$**

FOOTHILL HOUSE BED AND BREAKFAST. *3037 Foothill Blvd, Calistoga (94515). Phone 707/942-6933; toll-free 800/942-6933; fax 707/942-5692. www.foothillhouse.com.* Located in the foothills off Highway 128 just north of Calistoga, this quality bed-and-breakfast looks out across the northern Napa Valley at Mount St. Helena. It is in a secluded country setting and entered through a large garden. The five guest rooms are spread out on the property, offering spacious privacy. The grounds include rock gardens, a small waterfall, and a gazebo. The guest rooms are replete with amenities, including Jacuzzi tubs, fireplaces, CD players, VCRs, bathrobes, and even cookies. A full complimentary breakfast is included in the room rate, plus soda and water in a common-area refrigerator. 5 rooms. Complimentary full breakfast. Check-in 3 pm, check-out 11 am. **$$**

GARNETT CREEK INN. *1139 Lincoln Ave, Calistoga (94515). Phone 707/942-9797; fax 707/942-8021. www.garnettcreekinn.com.* 5 rooms. Children over 12 years only. Complimentary continental breakfast. Check-in 3 pm, check-out 11 am. **$$**

MEADOWLARK COUNTRY HOUSE AND INN. *601 Petrified Forest Rd, Calistoga (94515). Phone 707/942-5651; fax 707/942-5023. www.meadowlarkinn.com.* Set amongst 20 acres of meadows and woodlands, this adult-oriented property is in the rolling hills to the west of Calistoga. With its tranquil sylvan setting, it provides privacy and seclusion. In addition to the converted farmhouse, accommodations are available in a separate guest room wing and in a poolside luxury cottage. The enclosed mineral pool and hot tub are available to all guests. Each guest room has a CD player, bathrobes, duvet bed covers, and a VCR; some rooms have deep soaking tubs and private decks. A full gourmet breakfast is served each morning. 8 rooms, 2 story. Pets accepted; restrictions. Complimentary full breakfast. Check-in 3:30 pm, check-out 11:30 pm. Outdoor pool, whirlpool. **$$**

PINK MANSION. *1415 Foothill Blvd, Calistoga (94515). Phone 707/942-0558; toll-free 800/238-7465; fax 707/942-0558. www.pinkmansion.com.* This bed-and-breakfast, a historic 1875 Victorian mansion, is located just north of Calistoga at the far end of the Napa Valley. It is set on a hillside with an elaborate front garden separating it from Highway 128. It has been called the Pink Mansion since the 1930s, and a fresh coat of paint vividly retains this tradition. Reached by a circular drive around an entry fountain, the lodging has six distinctive guest rooms, which have a number of antique furnishings and an Asian influence. A property trademark is a large handsome indoor pool, a unique feature in Napa County. The hospitable innkeepers provide a full complimentary breakfast, an afternoon wine and cheese reception, welcoming chocolates and roses, and guest bathrobes. 6 rooms, 3 story. Complimentary full breakfast. Check-in 3 pm, check-out 11 am. Indoor pool, whirlpool. **$$**

SILVER ROSE INN AND SPA. *351 Rosedale Rd, Calistoga (94515). Phone 707/942-9581; toll-free 800/995-9381; fax 707/942-5102. www.silverrose.com.* The Silver Rose Inn and Spa is a unique hideaway near the town of Calistoga in Napa Valley. This intimate bed-and-breakfast has just 20 rooms in two Tudor-style buildings. Each room here is one-of-a-kind, with thematic décors ranging from western, oriental, safari, and carousel rooms to Mardi Gras, nutcracker, celestial, and depot rooms. The spa is open only to hotel guests, ensuring privacy and availability, and many of the treatments reflect the locale with such favorites as the champagne facial and body treatment. The Silver Rose Inn even has its own winery complete with a tasting room for enjoying the property's bottles. 20 rooms, 2 story. Complimentary continental breakfast. Check-in 3 pm, check-out 11:30 am. Fitness room, spa. Two outdoor pools, two whirlpools. Tennis. **$$**

Restaurants

★★ ALL SEASONS CAFE. *1400 Lincoln Ave, Calistoga (94515). Phone 707/942-9111; fax 707/942-9420.* Contemporary California menu. Dinner. Closed Mon; Dec 24-25. Bar. **$$**

★★ BRANNAN'S GRILL. *1374 Lincoln Ave, Calistoga (94515). Phone 707/942-2233; fax 707/942-2299. www.brannansgrill.com.* Eclectic menu. Lunch, dinner. Bar. **$$**

★ CALISTOGA INN. *1250 Lincoln Ave, Calistoga (94515). Phone 707/942-4101; fax 707/942-4914. www.calistogainn.com.* American, California menu.

Lunch, dinner, brunch. Bar. Children's menu. Outdoor seating. **$$**

★ **FUENTES TAPAS.** *1458 Lincoln Ave, Calistoga (94515). Phone 707/942-8165.* Latin American, Tapas menu. Breakfast, lunch, dinner. Closed Tues. Children's menu. Casual attire. Outdoor seating. **$**

★ **HYDRO BAR AND GRILL.** *1403 Lincoln Ave, Calistoga (94515). Phone 707/942-9777; fax 707/942-9420.* American menu. Breakfast, lunch, dinner. Closed Dec 25. Bar. Children's menu. **$$**

★ **PACIFICO.** *1237 Lincoln Ave, Calistoga (94515). Phone 707/942-4400.* Vividly colored décor invites visitors to relax and enjoy a taste of the true flavors of Mexico. Mexican menu. Lunch, dinner, brunch. Closed Thanksgiving, Dec 24-25. Bar. Children's menu. **$$**

★★ **WAPPO BAR AND BISTRO.** *1226 Washington St, Calistoga (94515). Phone 707/942-4712; fax 707/942-4741. www.wappobar.com.* International menu. Lunch, dinner. Closed Tues; also Easter, Thanksgiving, Dec 25. Children's menu. Reservations recommended. Outdoor seating. **$$**

Capitola

See also Santa Cruz

Founded 1874
Population 10,500
Area Code 831
Information Capitola Chamber of Commerce, 716-G Capitola Ave, 95010; phone 831/475-6522
Web Site www.capitolachamber.com

Special Event

Capitola Begonia Festival. *716 Capitola Ave, Capitola (65010). 5 miles E. Phone 831/476-3566. www.begoniafestival.com.* Held during the height of blooming season, this festival features fishing derbies, rowboat races, sand sculptures, and a nautical parade. Sept.

Full-Service Inns

★★★ **INN AT DEPOT HILL.** *250 Monterey Ave, Capitola (95010). Phone 831/462-3376; fax 831/462-3697. www.innsbythesea.com/depot-hill/.* Snuggled in the Mediterranean-style village and artists' community of Capitola-by-the-Sea, the Inn at Depot Hill proposes a departure from the ordinary. Lovingly maintained, this former Southern Pacific Railroad Depot is only two blocks from the sandy beaches of this seaside retreat. This charming inn is a passport to luxury, where the rooms take visitors on a first-class journey around the world. The *je ne sais quoi* of the French Riviera is celebrated in the Cote d'Azur Room; the Railroad Baron Room is a resplendent sight with rich reds and a worldly ambience; and the Kyoto Room is a temple of serenity and simplicity. Playful and endearing, the décor allows guests to indulge in their fantasies, whether they opt to play the bon vivant in the Portofino Room or the budding Shakespeare in the Stratford-on-Avon Room. 12 rooms, 2 story. Complimentary full breakfast. Check-in 3 pm, check-out 11:30 am. Wireless Internet access. Whirlpool. **$$**

Restaurants

★★★ **SHADOWBROOK.** *1750 Wharf Rd, Capitola (95010). Phone 831/475-1511; toll-free 800/975-1511; fax 831/475-7664. www.shadowbrook-capitola.com.* Reached by its own trolley or a stroll through the lavish gardens, the old-world charm of Shadowbrook shines through the romantic dining rooms. American menu. Dinner, Sun brunch. Bar. Children's menu. **$$**

★★★ **THEO'S.** *3101 N Main St, Soquel (95073). Phone 831/462-3657; fax 831/462-9459. www.theosrestaurant.net.* Organic garden. Uses locally grown produce. California, French menu. Dinner. Closed Sun-Mon. Outdoor seating. **$$$**

Carmel (F-2)

See also Big Sur, Carmel Valley, Monterey, Pacific Grove, Pebble Beach, Salinas

Founded 1916
Population 4,081
Elevation 220 ft
Area Code 831
Information Carmel Business Association, San Carlos between 5th and 6th sts, PO Box 4444, 93921; phone 831/624-2522
Web Site www.carmelcalifornia.org

Situated on the Bay of Carmel, the town sits at one of the loveliest spots along the California coast. A center for artists and writers since the turn of the century, Carmel fiercely protects its individuality. The architecture is a mixture of every style and whim of the literary and artistic populace, creating a unique and enchanting setting with endless activities for tourists.

What to See and Do

Antique and Art Galleries. *San Carlos St and 5th Ave, Carmel. Phone 831/624-2522. www.carmelcalifornia.org.* More than 90 galleries display a wide variety of art and antiques in the Carmel area. A brochure, *The Guide to Carmel,* containing a list of galleries may be obtained from the Carmel Business Association, PO Box 4444, 93921.

Barnyard. *26400 Carmel Rancho Blvd, Carmel (93923). Hwy 1, Carmel Valley Rd exit, then take the first right and enter Barnyard from Carmel Rancho Blvd. Phone 831/624-8886. www.thebarnyard.com.* Shopping area with 1 1/2 acres of terraced flower gardens around rustic, old-style California barns housing a number of shops, galleries, and restaurants.

Beach areas. *Phone 831/624-3543 (Carmel City Beach).* **Carmel City Beach**, located at the foot of Ocean Ave, has easy accessibility, white sands, and beautiful sunsets. **Carmel River State Beach**, south of Carmel on Scenic Rd, offers calm waters, tide pools, and an adjacent bird sanctuary. **FREE**

Biblical Garden. *Church of the Wayfarer, Lincoln St and 7th Ave, Carmel. Phone 831/624-3550. www.churchofthewayfarer.com.* Founded in 1904. Stained-glass windows in the sanctuary depict Biblical and local scenes. Includes Gaza St. Galy mosaic, sundial on a granite boulder, mosaic cross in the garden, and a 32-rank pipe organ. Garden contains trees and plants mentioned in the Bible and indigenous to the Holy Land. Worship services Sun 10 am. (Daily) **FREE**

Mission San Carlos Borromeo del Rio Carmelo. *3080 Rio Rd, Carmel (93923). 1 mile S off Hwy 1, then W to Rio Rd. Phone 831/624-3600.* Basilica founded by Frey Junipero Serra in 1770; his burial place. Oldest church in Carmel. Headquarters for the California missions. (Mon-Fri 9:30 am-4:30 pm, Sat-Sun 10:30 am-4:30 pm; closed Thanksgiving, Dec 25) **$**

Pacific Repertory Theatre. *Monte Verde St, between 8th and 9th sts, Carmel (93922). Phone 831/622-0100 (tickets). www.pacrep.org.* Company performs dramas, comedies, and musicals in three venues: Golden Bough Playhouse, Circle Theatre, and outdoor Forest Theatre. (Schedule varies). **$$$$**

Point Lobos State Reserve. *Hwy 1, Carmel (93923). 3 miles S on Hwy 1. Phone 831/624-4909. pt-lobos.parks.state.ca.us.* Sea Lion Rocks, Bird Island just offshore. Natural grove of Monterey cypress. Picnic area (no fires or stoves), naturalist programs. No dogs. (Daily from 9 am; closing times vary) **$$**

Rancho Cañada Golf Club. *4860 Carmel Valley Rd, Carmel (93923). Carmel Valley Rd, 1 mile E of Hwy 1. Phone 831/624-0111; toll-free 800/536-9459. www.ranchocanada.com.* Two 18-hole championship courses; driving range. (Daily) **$$$$**

Seventeen-Mile Drive. Stretching from Carmel to Monterey, this is one of the most scenic drives in the world.

Special Events

Carmel Art Festival. *Various venues in downtown Carmel. Phone 831/642-2503. www.carmelartfestival.org.* Several artists and many different pieces of art are represented at this juried art show: paintings, sculptures, and even a "painting performance" with live music accompaniment. Mid-May.

Carmel Bach Festival. *San Carolos and 9th sts, Carmel (93921). Phone 831/624-2046. www.bachfestival.org.* Concerts, recitals, lectures, special events. Mid-July-early Aug.

Monterey Wine Festival. *140 W Franklin St #202, Carmel (93940). Phone toll-free 800/656-4282. www.montereywine.com.* Wine lovers will have the opportunity to taste more than 1,000 different wines, attend cooking demonstrations, and meet wine experts from around the globe. Late Apr.

Limited-Service Hotels

★ BEST WESTERN CARMEL BAY VIEW INN. *6th Ave and Junipero St, Carmel (93921). Phone 831/624-1831; toll-free 800/343-1831; fax 831/625-2336. www.bestwestern.com.* 59 rooms, 5 story. Complimentary continental breakfast. Check-in 3 pm, check-out 11 am. Outdoor pool. **$$**

★ ★ BEST WESTERN CARMEL MISSION INN. *3665 Rio Rd, Carmel (93923). Phone 831/624-1841; toll-free 800/348-9090; fax 831/624-8684. www.carmelmissioninn.com.* 165 rooms, 4 story. Pets accepted, some restrictions; fee. Check-in 4 pm, check-out noon. Restaurant, bar. Fitness room. Outdoor pool. Business center. **$**

★ **HORIZON INN.** *Junipero and 3rd St, Carmel (93921). Phone 831/624-5327; toll-free 800/350-7723; fax 831/626-8253. www.horizoninncarmel.com.* 19 rooms, 2 story. Pets accepted, fee. Complimentary continental breakfast. Check-in 3 pm, check-out noon. Whirlpool. **$$**

★ **LOBOS LODGE.** *Ocean Ave and Monte Verde St, Carmel (93921). Phone 831/624-3874; fax 831/624-0135. www.loboslodge.com.* 30 rooms, 3 story. Complimentary continental breakfast. Check-in 2 pm, check-out noon. **$**

★ **NORMANDY INN.** *Ocean Ave and Monte Verde St, Carmel (93921). Phone 831/624-3825; toll-free 800/343-3825; fax 831/624-4614. www.normandyinncarmel.com.* 48 rooms, 2 story. Complimentary continental breakfast. Check-in 3 pm, check-out 11 am. Outdoor pool. **$$**

★ ★ **PINE INN.** *Ocean Ave and Monte Verde, Carmel (93921). Phone 831/624-3851; toll-free 800/228-3851; fax 831/624-3030. www.pine-inn.com.* Although shops and contemporary restaurants surround it, the Pine Inn stays true to its history and character. The inn was built in 1889 and boasts of having been the first inn in Carmel-by-the-Sea. Elegant antiques appear throughout the property, which has a graceful lobby and an alluring red theme. The European- and Asian-themed guest rooms are comfortable and pretty, with canopy beds topped by plush red bedcovers, floral chairs, and marble bathroom floors. Il Fornaio is the inn's Italian restaurant; it serves full breakfasts to guests on weekdays. 49 rooms, 3 story. Check-in 4 pm, check-out 1 pm. Restaurant, bar. Whirlpool. **$$**

★ **WAYSIDE INN.** *Mission St and 7th Ave, Carmel (93921). Phone 831/624-5336; fax 831/626-6974. www.innsbythesea.com/wayside.* 22 rooms, 2 story. Pets accepted, some restrictions. Complimentary continental breakfast. Check-in 3 pm, check-out noon. **$**

Full-Service Hotels

★ ★ ★ **LA PLAYA HOTEL.** *Camino Real and 8th Ave, Carmel (93921). Phone 831/624-6476; toll-free 800/582-8900; fax 831/624-7966. www.laplayahotel.com.* Renovated Mediterranean-style villa (1904). 80 rooms, 4 story. Check-in 4 pm, check-out noon. Restaurant, bar. Outdoor pool. Business center. **$$**

★ ★ ★ **PARK HYATT CARMEL, HIGHLANDS INN.** *120 Highlands Dr, Carmel (93921). Phone 831/620-1234; fax 831/626-1574. www.hyatt.com.* Carmel's rustic beauty on California's Monterey Coast is legendary, and the Park Hyatt Carmel, Highlands Inn is the area's finest lodging. This sophisticated rendering of a mountain lodge has been a destination in its own right since opening in 1917. Now part of the exclusive Park Hyatt chain, the resort blends historic charm with full-service amenities. Wood and stone are used throughout the property to blend effortlessly with the rugged setting, and the rooms and suites are soothing havens with earth tones and majestic views. The vistas of the famous crashing Carmel surf are the hallmark of the resort; even dining is complemented by superlative views. 148 rooms, 3 story. Check-in 4 pm, check-out noon. Restaurant, bar. Fitness room. Outdoor pool, whirlpool. **$$$**

Full-Service Resort

★ ★ ★ **QUAIL LODGE RESORT AND GOLF COURSE.** *8205 Valley Greens Dr, Carmel (93923). Phone 831/624-2888; fax 831/624-3726.* Quail Lodge is a magnet for active travelers seeking the total resort experience. Set on 850 acres on the sunny side of the Carmel Valley, the grounds are a lovely mix of rolling hills, lakes, and gardens. It is no wonder that golf is a favorite pursuit here, with a fantastic 18-hole course designed by Robert Muir-Graves and a 7-acre driving range. The Carmel River gently snakes along the course, making it a particularly scenic round. Four tennis courts and two outdoor pools tempt others, while the spa alleviates aches and pains with its wonderful assortment of facials, massages, and hydrotherapy with Vichy showers. The guest accommodations are attractively appointed and cradle guests in comfort. All preferences are suited at the two restaurants, The Covey standing out for its charming lakeside setting, gourmet cuisine, and extensive wine list. 97 rooms, 2 story. Check-in 4 pm, check-out noon. High-speed Internet access, wireless Internet access. Two restaurants, two bars. Fitness room, fitness classes available, spa. Outdoor pool, whirlpool. Golf, 18 holes. Tennis. Airport transportation available. Business center. **$$$**

Full-Service Inn

★ ★ ★ **MISSION RANCH.** *26270 Dolores St, Carmel-by-the-Sea (93923). Phone 831/624-6436; toll-free 800/538-8221; fax 831/626-4163. www.missionranchcarmel.com.* It was the famous city mayor, Clint Eastwood, who saved this 1850s farmhouse from demolition in the 1980s. Since then, it has been restored, expanded, and filled with antiques and custom-designed rustic pieces. The tranquil sunset views are worth the trip. 31 rooms, 2 story. Complimentary continental breakfast. Check-in 3 pm, check-out 11 am. Restaurant, bar. Fitness room. Tennis. **$$**

Specialty Lodgings

The following lodging establishments are approved by Mobil Travel Guide, but due to their unique and individualized nature have not been given a traditional Mobil Star rating. Included in this listing you may find bed-and-breakfasts, limited-service inns, guest ranches, and other unique hotel properties.

ADOBE INN. *Dolores and 8th Ave, Carmel (93921). Phone 831/624-3933; toll-free 800/388-3933; fax 831/624-8636. www.adobeinn.com.* With a great location in Carmel Village close to shops, dining, and the beach, the Adobe is a pleasant inn. On the inn's exterior there are beautiful murals of local sites. The inn, which is clean and well maintained, proclaims that its rooms are the most spacious in town, and they are good-sized for Carmel. They are nicely furnished, with fireplaces and marble-topped work desks; some rooms have ocean views. 20 rooms, 2 story. Complimentary continental breakfast. Check-in 4 pm, check-out noon. Outdoor pool. **$$**

CANDLE LIGHT INN. *San Carlos St, between 4th and 5th Ave, Carmel (93921). Phone 831/624-6451; toll-free 800/433-4732; fax 831/624-6732. www.innsbythesea.com.* 20 rooms, 2 story. Complimentary continental breakfast. Check-in 3 pm, check-out noon. **$**

CARMEL GARDEN COURT INN. *4th and Torres sts, Carmel (93921). Phone 831/624-6926; toll-free 800/313-7770; fax 831/624-4935. www.carmelgardencourtinn.com.* Head here for a comfortable, intimate place to rest your head, four blocks from the heart of the village. Guest rooms come equipped with wood-burning fireplaces, flowery décor, and wood-paneled walls; some rooms have private patios with flowering plants. The common garden features oak trees, bougainvillea, and fountains. This casual inn attracts couples who enjoy the bed-and-breakfast atmosphere. Enjoy complimentary port and sherry in the lobby in the afternoons. 10 rooms, 2 story. Pets accepted, fee. Complimentary continental breakfast. Check-in 4-9 pm, check-out 11 am. **$$**

CARRIAGE HOUSE INN. *Junipero Ave, between 7th and 8th aves, Carmel (93921). Phone 831/625-2585; toll-free 800/433-4732; fax 831/624-0974. www.innsbythesea.com.* Village restaurants, galleries, and shops are a short walk away. 13 rooms, 2 story. Complimentary continental breakfast. Check-in 3 pm, check-out noon. **$$**

COBBLESTONE INN. *Junipero Ave, Carmel (93921). Phone 831/625-5222; toll-free 800/833-8836; fax 831/625-0478. www.cobblestoneinncarmel.com.* What must have been a run-of-the-mill motel has been transformed into a quaint inn, which gets its name from the real cobblestones—taken from the Carmel River—that cover most of the façade. Country fabrics, wall stenciling, and Shaker baskets complete the country theme. The inn has charm, although some might find the teddy bears a bit excessive. Guest rooms have fireplaces, TVs (small and tucked away in a cupboard), and refrigerators stocked with complimentary soft drinks. 24 rooms, 2 story. Complimentary full breakfast. Check-in 3 pm, check-out noon. Whirlpool. **$$**

CYPRESS INN. *Lincoln and 7th aves, Carmel (93921). Phone 831/624-3871; toll-free 800/443-7443; fax 831/624-8216. www.cypress-inn.com.* A landmark hotel built in 1929, the Cypress Inn is smack dab in the center of town, steps away from boutiques, art galleries, and great restaurants. Within the beautiful white Mediterranean exterior is an appealing lobby with a large fireplace, deep comfortable sofas, and a vaulted ceiling. A beautiful patio next to the lobby welcomes dogs and cats, and the inn also offers pet-sitting services (Doris Day, a part-owner, is involved with the Doris Day Animal Foundation). The guest rooms are spread out on two floors. They aren't especially spacious, but they're welcoming to both two-legged and four-legged guests, with pet blankets, fresh flowers, fruit bowls, and sherry decanters. 33 rooms, 2 story. Pets accepted; fee. Complimentary continental breakfast. Check-in 4 pm, check-out noon. Bar. Whirlpool. **$**

DOLPHIN INN. *San Carlos St and 4th Ave, Carmel (93921). Phone 831/624-5356; toll-free 800/433-4732; fax 831/624-4891. www.innsbythesea.com.* 27 rooms, 2 story. Complimentary continental breakfast. Check-in 3 pm, check-out noon. Outdoor pool. **$**

SANDPIPER COUNTRY INN. *2408 Bay View Ave, Carmel (93923). Phone 831/624-6433; toll-free 800/590-6433; fax 831/624-5964. www.sandpiper-inn.com.* Celebrating its 75th birthday in 2004, the Sandpiper resides in the most expensive neighborhood in Carmel: a tranquil setting next to the beach and a short drive to downtown. Inside, the inn has a mix of Craftsman and country styles. The guest rooms are pleasant; all have fresh flowers, while others offer ocean views and/or fireplaces. (Rooms do not have televisions or telephones.) 17 rooms, 2 story. Children over age 12 only. Complimentary continental breakfast. Check-in 3 pm, check-out noon. **$**

TICKLE PINK INN AT CARMEL HIGHLANDS. *155 Highland Dr, Carmel (93923). Phone 831/624-1244; toll-free 800/635-4774; fax 831/626-9516. www.ticklepinkinn.com.* This stone cottage has overlooked the rugged Pacific cliffs and Carmel Highlands since 1953. 34 rooms, 3 story. Complimentary continental breakfast. Check-in 3-10 pm, check-out noon. Whirlpool. **$$$**

Restaurants

★★★ **ANTON AND MICHEL.** *Mission St between Ocean and 7th aves, Carmel (93921). Phone 831/624-2406; toll-free 866/244-0645; fax 831/625-1542. www.antonandmichel.com.* French menu. Lunch, dinner. Bar. Business casual attire. Reservations recommended. Outdoor seating. **$$$**

★★ **BAJA CANTINA.** *7166 Carmel Valley Rd, Carmel (93923). Phone 831/625-2252.* Mexican menu. Lunch, dinner. Closed Thanksgiving, Dec 25. Bar. Children's menu. Casual attire. Reservations recommended. Outdoor seating. **$$**

★★★ **CASANOVA.** *5th Ave and Mission, Carmel (93921). Phone 831/625-0501; fax 831/625-9799. www.casanovarestaurant.com.* French, Italian menu. Lunch, dinner. Closed Dec 25. Bar. Outdoor seating. **$$$**

★ **COTTAGE RESTAURANT.** *Lincoln St, between Ocean and 7th aves, Carmel (93921). Phone 831/625-6260; fax 831/624-0989. www.cottagerestaurant.com.* American menu. Breakfast, lunch, dinner. Closed Dec 25. Children's menu. Casual attire. **$$**

★★★ **THE COVEY.** *8205 Valley Greens Dr, Carmel (93923). Phone 831/620-8860; fax 831/624-3726. www.quaillodge.com.* Fans of California coastal cuisine flock to The Covey, the upscale eatery within the Quail Lodge Resort and Golf Club (see). Regionally raised poultry and meats join locally caught fish and shellfish on the wine country menu. Indulgences abound, from red abalone in caper brown butter to butter-poached lobster and roast filet mignon with foie gras, truffles, and morel mushrooms. Don't miss the classic Caesar salad or steak tartare, both prepared tableside. Choose from a table in the handsome wood-trimmed dining room or out on the terrace; both overlook a tranquil lake and an arched bridge, site of many a Quail Ridge wedding. California menu. Breakfast, dinner. Bar. Children's menu. Reservations recommended. **$$$**

★★ **FLYING FISH GRILL.** *Carmel Plz, Carmel (93921). Phone 831/625-1962.* California, Japanese, seafood menu. Dinner. Casual attire. **$$**

★★ **THE FORGE IN THE FOREST.** *5th Ave and Junipero, Carmel (93921). Phone 831/624-2233; fax 831/624-1102. www.forgeintheforest.com.* Eclectic/International menu. Lunch, dinner, Sun brunch. Bar. Children's menu. Casual attire. Outdoor seating. **$$$**

★★★ **FRENCH POODLE.** *Junipero and 5th Ave, Carmel (93921). Phone 831/624-8643.* The French Poodle is an intimate hideaway set on the edge of Carmel-by-the-Sea that serves a sophisticated menu which includes lots of luxurious ingredients prepared with classic French technique. If you are looking for dishes dressed up with truffles, foie gras, filet mignon, or perhaps some luscious fresh local abalone, this is your place. The kitchen expertly coaxes subtle flavors to attention, offering perfectly balanced, artfully presented plates that taste as good as they look (if not better). This is a precious little restaurant that is one of the most charming, understated places to dine in Carmel. French menu. Dinner. Closed Sun; Dec 25; two weeks in Jan. Casual attire. **$$$**

★★ **GRILL ON OCEAN AVENUE.** *Ocean Ave between Dolores and Lincoln, Carmel (93921). Phone 831/624-2569; fax 831/624-5370. www.carmelsbest.com.* California, Pacific-Rim/Pan-Asian menu. Lunch, dinner. Bar. Children's menu. Casual attire. **$$**

★★ **LA BOHEME.** *Dolores and 7th Ave, Carmel (93921). Phone 831/624-7500. www.laboheme.com.* If you want to be surprised for dinner, visit this wonderful Carmel classic with its daily changing three-course prix-fixe menu. Eliminating the surprise factor is possible: visit the entertaining Web page, which previews the dinners of the month. French menu. Dinner. Closed Easter, Thanksgiving, Dec 25; three weeks in Jan. Children's menu. Casual attire. **$$**

★★ **LE COQ D'OR.** *Mission St and 5th Ave, Carmel (93921). Phone 831/626-9319. www.lecoqdor.com.* French, German menu. Dinner. Closed Jan 1, Dec 25. Casual attire. Outdoor seating. **$$**

★★ **LITTLE NAPOLI.** *Dolores St and 7th Ave, Carmel (93923). Phone 831/626-6335. www.littlenapoli.com.* Italian menu. Lunch, dinner. Closed Thanksgiving, Dec 25. Casual attire. **$$**

★★ **LUGANO SWISS BISTRO.** *3670 The Barnyard, Carmel (93923). Phone 831/626-3779; fax 831/626-6783. www.swissbistro.com.* Swiss menu. Lunch, dinner. Closed Mon; also Dec 25. Bar. Children's menu. Casual attire. Outdoor seating. **$$**

★★ **MISSION RANCH.** *26270 Dolores, Carmel (93923). Phone 831/625-9040; toll-free 800/538-8221; fax 831/626-4163. www.missionranchcarmel.com.* American menu. Dinner, Sun brunch. Closed Dec 25. Bar. Children's menu. Casual attire. Reservations recommended. Outdoor seating. **$$**

★★★ **PACIFIC'S EDGE.** *120 Highlands Dr, Carmel (93923). Phone 831/622-5445; fax 831/626-1574. www.mfandw.com.* The view at Pacific's Edge provides one of those "pinch-me-to-make-sure-I-am-not-dreaming" vistas. Perched high over the Pacific Ocean, this magical dining space, located in the Highlands Inn (see), is one of the culinary jewels of the Pacific coastline. The menu is rooted in local products—troll-caught Monterey Spot Prawns, Colorado lamb, and regional pork and beef are richly accented with fresh herbs, and plated with seasonal ingredients (and lots of passion) by the talented kitchen. The extensive, heavily American wine list gives your tall glasses lots of opportunities to clink. California menu. Dinner. Bar. Business casual attire. Reservations recommended. Valet parking. **$$$**

★★ **RIO GRILL.** *101 Crossroads Blvd, Carmel (93923). Phone 831/625-5436; fax 831/625-2950. www.riogrill.com.* California menu. Lunch, dinner, Sun brunch. Closed July 4, Dec 25. Bar. Children's menu. Casual attire. Reservations recommended. Outdoor seating. **$$**

★★ **ROBATA GRILL AND SAKE BAR.** *3658 The Barnyard, Carmel (93923). Phone 831/624-2643; fax 831/624-0360. www.robatacarmel.com.* Japanese, Sushi menu. Lunch, dinner. Closed Jan 1, July 4, Dec 25. Bar. Children's menu. Casual attire. Reservations recommended. Outdoor seating. **$$**

★★ **ROCKY POINT.** *Hwy 1 SE, Carmel (93922). Phone 831/624-2933; fax 831/624-4091. www.rocky-point.com.* American, seafood, steak menu. Breakfast, lunch, dinner. Bar. Casual attire. **$$$**

Carmel Valley (F-2)

See also Big Sur, Carmel, Monterey, Pacific Grove

Population 4,700
Elevation 400 ft
Area Code 831
Zip 93924
Web Site www.carmelcalifornia.com

Full-Service Resort

★★★ **CARMEL VALLEY RANCH RESORT.** *1 Old Ranch Rd, Carmel Valley (93923). Phone 831/625-9500; toll-free 800/996-3426; fax 831/624-2858. www.wyndham.com.* Carmel Valley Ranch is a luxury resort set on 400 acres in the Carmel Valley countryside. The Santa Lucia Mountains wink in the distance, and forests of oak trees enhance the beautiful surroundings of this comprehensive resort. The lodge-style architecture houses wonderfully spacious and inviting guest rooms. Vaulted ceilings and wood-burning fireplaces create a sense of warmth, while floor-to-ceiling windows and large decks focus attention on the spectacular scenery. This dynamic resort caters to guests of all interests, with an 18-hole Pete Dye-designed golf course, a tennis facility, a fitness center, and a shimmering outdoor pool. Stunning views accompany the delicious menus at the three dining venues. The Ranch House Café and Club Grille overlook the tennis courts and the 18th green and share a relaxed ambience, while the more formal Oaks Dining Room features stunning views of the forests and intriguing wildlife. 144 rooms. Check-in 4 pm, check-out noon. Restaurant, bar. Fitness room. Two outdoor pools, seven whirlpools. Golf, 18 holes. Tennis. **$$**

Full-Service Inn

★ ★ ★ ★ **BERNARDUS LODGE.** *415 Carmel Valley Rd, Carmel Valley (93924). Phone 831/658-3400; toll-free 888/648-9463; fax 831/659-3529. www.bernardus.com.* Bernardus Lodge offers a rare opportunity to those thirsty to unwind in the shadow of a revered vineyard. The Lodge, long considered one of the finest winemaking estates in California, welcomes visitors to its scenic, undulating landscape in the Carmel Valley. Stylish and sun-filled, the guest rooms combine subtle luxury and country chic. As the golden sunshine bathes the grounds, guests retire to the pool or wander about to take in the lovely scenery. This inn offers its visitors a taste of the good life, from its fine wines to its extraordinary wine-country cuisine. Marinus is an epicurean's delight, attracting diners with artfully prepared French-Californian dishes complemented by sensational wine selections. The spa figures largely in the experience here, too; guests are polished and pampered with an astonishingly wide variety of beautifying and rejuvenating treatments. 57 rooms, 2 story. Check-in 4 pm, check-out noon. Two restaurants, bar. Fitness room, fitness classes available, spa. Outdoor pool, whirlpool. Tennis. Airport transportation available. **$$$$**

Specialty Lodgings

The following lodging establishments are approved by Mobil Travel Guide, but due to their unique and individualized nature have not been given a traditional Mobil Star rating. Included in this listing you may find bed-and-breakfasts, limited-service inns, guest ranches, and other unique hotel properties.

CARMEL VALLEY LODGE. *Carmel Valley Rd at Ford Rd, Carmel Valley (93924). Phone 831/659-2261; toll-free 800/641-4646; fax 831/659-4558. www.valleylodge.com.* 27 rooms, 2 story. Pets accepted, some restrictions; fee. Complimentary continental breakfast. Check-in 3 pm, check-out noon. Fitness room. Outdoor pool, whirlpool. **$$**

LOS LAURELES LODGE. *313 W Carmel Valley Rd, Carmel Valley (93924). Phone 831/659-2233; toll-free 800/533-4404; fax 831/659-0481. www.loslaureles.com.* Main building built in 1890s; once home of Muriel Vanderbilt. 31 rooms. Pets accepted; fee. Check-in 3 pm, check-out noon. Restaurant. Outdoor pool. **$**

Spa

★ ★ ★ ★ **BERNARDUS LODGE SPA.** *415 Carmel Valley Rd, Carmel Valley (93924). Phone 831/658-3400; toll-free 888/648-9463. www.bernardus.com.* The spa's menu is dedicated to satisfaction and comfort. From therapeutic, aromatherapy, reflexology, and lomi lomi massages to those specially designed for golfers, athletes, and couples, tired muscles meet their match. Even the facials include a head, neck, and heated hand massage. Seaweed wraps and moor muscle soothers help rid the body of toxins and encourage renewal. The Bernardus revitalizer is a must-try, blending an herbal body polish, a botanical body mask and wrap, and an exfoliating facial into one treatment. Fitness sessions also are available and include stretch, yoga, tennis, meditation, croquet, and bocce lessons. This delightful facility offers a blend of local and exotic appeal, especially with its two signature treatments. Close your eyes and inhale the tropical scents during the taste of Hawaii treatment, and you just might think you have escaped to the islands. This luxurious body treatment buffs you with a luscious coconut-mango scrub; exfoliates you with a Hawaiian sea salt, red clay, and kukui-nut oil application; and relaxes you with the rhythmic strokes of a traditional lomi lomi massage while island music gently plays in the background. The vineyard romance treatment begins with a harvest crush body scrub, which uses crushed grape seeds and red wine to eliminate free radicals. Then dip in the outdoor lavender bath, where striking views of the Santa Lucia Mountains captivate you. This signature therapy, which is ideal for couples yet can be booked for one guest, ends with a wonderful full-body massage.

Restaurants

★ ★ ★ **MARINUS.** *415 Carmel Valley Rd, Carmel Valley (93924). Phone 831/658-3595; toll-free 888/648-9463; fax 831/659-3529. www.bernardus.com.* A warm, elegant, country inn-style restaurant boasting open-beamed ceilings, earth-toned walls, vintage tapestries, and a magnificent 12-foot-wide European limestone fireplace, Marinus is a charming spot to find yourself nibbling on glorious California-French fare. The lovely tables are set with silver dress plates, fresh meadow flowers, and pretty votive candles. An enchanting outdoor patio offers guests a chance to dine in closer proximity to the gardens and mountains. The seasonal menu puts to use an array of organic ingredients, as well as fresh herbs and vegetables from the chef's garden. A mesquite grill is also in house for patrons who crave smoky roasted meats. Seasonal signatures like turbot with caramelized endive and celery root purée, and local spot prawns with crispy marinated vegetables and truffle vinaigrette show off the chef's sophisticated hand. The impressive wine cellar boasts more than 1,000 selections. California menu. Dinner. Business casual attire. Reservations recommended. Valet parking. **$$$$**

★ ★ WILL'S FARGO. *Carmel Valley Rd, Carmel Valley (93924). Phone 831/659-2774; fax 831/659-2167. www.willsfargo.com.* American menu. Lunch Fri-Sun, dinner. Closed Tues; also Thanksgiving, Dec 25. Bar. Children's menu. Casual attire. Reservations recommended. Outdoor seating. **$$**

Chester (C-3)

See also Lassen Volcanic National Park, Quincy, Susanville

Population 2,316
Elevation 4,528 ft
Area Code 530
Zip 96020
Information Chester/Lake Almanor Chamber of Commerce, 529 Main St, PO Box 1198; phone 530/258-2426 or toll-free 800/350-4838
Web Site www.chester-lakealmanor.com

The Lake Almanor area offers both summer and winter sports. Mount Lassen is 30 miles north and west. Fishing is good in the lake and surrounding streams and is served by many boat landings and ramps. Deer, bear, waterfowl, and birds are plentiful in season. There are many resorts, tent and trailer sites, and two scenic golf courses around the lake, as well as a number of improved campsites within 5 miles of Chester. Chester is also the home of the Collins Pine Sawmill, one of the largest in the state. A Ranger District office of the Lassen National Forest (see SUSANVILLE) is located here.

What to See and Do

Lake Almanor. *Phone 530/258-2426. www.chester-lakealmanor.com.* Located about 20 miles southeast of Lassen Peak, Lake Almanor is a favorite vacation destination and summer-home spot for residents of north-central California. Tucked between Lassen and Plumas national forests, the lake and the surrounding area offer a mix of recreational opportunities from golf to fishing as well as a number of resorts and quaint lakeside towns. In winter, the area attracts snowmobilers and cross-country skiers.

Specialty Lodging

The following lodging establishment is approved by Mobil Travel Guide, but due to its unique and individualized nature has not been given a traditional Mobil Star rating. Included in this listing you may find bed-and-breakfasts, limited-service inns, guest ranches, and other unique hotel properties.

BIDWELL HOUSE BED AND BREAKFAST. *1 Main St, Chester (96020). Phone 530/258-3338. www.bidwellhouse.com.* Built in 1901. 14 rooms, 2 story. Complimentary full breakfast. Check-in 3-6 pm, check-out 11 am. **$**

Chico (C-2)

See also Oroville

Settled 1843
Population 59,954
Elevation 200 ft
Area Code 530
Information Chamber of Commerce, 300 Salem St, 95928; phone 530/891-5556 or toll-free 800/852-8570
Web Site www.chicochamber.com

Chico was originally settled in 1843 as Rancho Del Arroyo by General John Bidwell, a leading agriculturist of the 19th century as well as a gold miner, statesman, and a US congressman. Chico is now a city of diversified business, industry, and agriculture in an area that is said to produce 20 percent of the world's almonds.

What to See and Do

Bidwell Mansion State Historic Park. *525 Esplanade, Chico (95926). Phone 530/895-6144. www.parks.ca.gov.* (1868) This is the 26-room Victorian house of the founder of Chico (candidate for US president in 1892); the first, second, and third floors have been restored. Visitor center(Wed-Fri noon-5 pm, Sat-Sun from 10 am; closed Jan 1, Thanksgiving, Dec 25). Tours (Wed-Fri noon-4 pm). **$**

Bidwell Park. *Woodland and Mansinita aves, Chico. 1/2 mile E on E 4th St. Phone 530/896-7800.* Eleven-mile-long, 3,670-acre city park with stream; site of location shots for many movies including *The Adventures of Robin Hood.* Swimming pools; picnicking, 18-hole golf at northeast end of park; bridle, foot and nature trails; kiddie playland.

California State University, Chico. *400 W First St, Chico (95929). Phone 530/898-4636. www.csuchico.edu.* (1887) (16,232 students) On 119 tree-shaded acres; art galleries (Mon-Fri, Sun; closed during summer); "anthromuseum," campus tour. Nearby is a 1,000-acre college farm.

Chico Museum. *141 Salem St, Chico (95928). Phone 530/891-4336.* History museum housed in 1904 Carnegie Library; permanent and changing exhibits include local history artifacts and photos, Chinese Temple. Programs, activities. (Wed-Sun afternoons) **DONATION**

Sierra Nevada Brewing Company. *1075 E 20th St, Chico. Phone 530/896-2198. www.sierra-nevada.com.* One of the largest and best-known microbreweries in the United States (to the point where the "micro" prefix almost no longer applies), the Sierra Nevada Brewing Company's headquarters in Chico is a must-visit for beer aficionados. A free tour takes visitors from the brewhouse through the bottling plant, showcasing the brewery's time-honed European methods that utilize only four ingredients: water, hops, yeast, and barley malts. While the tour does not include complimentary samples, there is a retail store and a taproom/restaurant where patrons can enjoy a varied menu of steaks, seafood, pizzas, and pub fare. But many come just for the wide variety of tasty brews, including the renowned Sierra Nevada Pale Ale as well as some Sierra Nevada brews available only on draft. A music venue called the Big Room hosts a full calendar of rock and blues concerts. (Self-guided tours: daily 10 am-6 pm; guided tours: Mon-Fri, Sun 2:30 pm, Sat noon-3 pm) **FREE**

Spring Blossom Tour. Forty-mile tour allows participants to view the wealth of blooming orchards and wildflowers in Butte County. Blossoms include almond, prune, kiwi, pear, and iris. (Mid-Feb-June) **FREE**

Winter Migratory Waterfowl Tour. This 100-mile tour provides insight into the importance of farmlands and wildlife preserves to migrating waterfowl in Butte County. Approximately 150 bird species migrate here in winter. (Sept-Mar) **FREE**

Special Events

Bidwell Classic Marathon. *Bidwell Park, Chico. www.chicorunningclub.org/bidwell_classic.* Features a half-marathon walk, 3-mile and half-marathon runs, and a Kids Fun Run/Walk. First Sat in Mar.

Silver Dollar Fair. *2357 Fair St, Chico (95928). Phone 530/895-4666.* Family Fun Circus, Pro Rodeo, and Puppets and Players Little Theater are the highlights of this annual springtime fair. Late May. **$$**

Limited-Service Hotels

★ BEST WESTERN HERITAGE INN. *25 Heritage Ln, Chico (95926). Phone 530/894-8600; toll-free 800/446-4291; fax 530/894-8600. www.bestwestern.com.* 101 rooms, 3 story. Complimentary continental breakfast. Check-in 3 pm, check-out 11 am. High-speed Internet access. Outdoor pool, whirlpool. **$**

★ ★ HOLIDAY INN. *685 Manzanita Ct, Chico (95926). Phone 530/345-2491; toll-free 800/310-2491; fax 530/893-3040. www.holiday-inn.com.* 172 rooms, 5 story. Pets accepted; fee. Check-in 4 pm, check-out 11 am. High-speed Internet access. Restaurant, bar. Fitness room. Outdoor pool, whirlpool. Airport transportation available. **$**

Clear Lake Area (Lake County) (C-2)

See also Healdsburg, Ukiah

Web Site www.lakecounty.com

This is a popular recreation area for fishing, hunting, swimming, boating, golfing, and other sports.

What to See and Do

Clear Lake State Park. *5300 Soda Bay Rd, Clear Lake Area. 3 miles NE of Kelseyville on Soda Bay Rd. Phone 707/279-4293. www.parks.ca.gov.* Pomo Native Americans once occupied this area. Swimming, water-skiing, fishing, boating (ramp); nature and hiking trails; picnicking, camping (no hook-ups, dump station). Visitor center with wildlife dioramas, aquarium; nature films. **$**

Crazy Creek Soaring. *18896 Grange Rd, Middletown (95461). Phone 707/987-9112. www.crazycreekgliders.com.* In the land of outdoor adventure, Crazy Creek Soaring (formerly Calistoga Soaring Center) offers high-end thrills. Not only can participants take glider rides with the company over the Napa Valley and other parts of northern California, but they can sign up for lessons as well. The center is located off of Highway 29 in the eastern foothills of the Mayacamus Mountains, which creates optimal soaring conditions for these lightweight gliders. (Thurs-Mon; closed holidays) **$$$$**

Konocti Harbor Resort. *8727 Soda Bay Rd, Kelseyville (95451). Phone toll-free 800/660-5253. www.konoctiharbor.com.* Located on the south shore of Clear Lake, this lakeside resort specializes in family getaways and water sports. However, lately it has developed a reputation as a music venue, hosting both smaller indoor concerts and outdoor performances in the amphitheater. Some of the bigger names that Konocti has attracted include Tony Bennett; Crosby, Stills, & Nash; the B-52s; Robert Kray; and Randy Travis. The resort often offers special packages and theme parties on concert weekends.

Special Events

Lake County Fair and Horse Show. *Lake County Fairgrounds, 401 Martin St, Lakeport (95453). Phone 707/263-6181. www.lakecountyfair.com.* Horse shows for several different categories, talent competitions, and live music mark this annual festival. Late Aug-early Sept.

Lake County Rodeo. *Lakeport Fairgrounds, 404 Martin St, Lakeport (95453). Phone 707/995-3508. www.lakecounty.com.* In addition to the excitement of this Pro Rodeo, visitors will also enjoy a festive barbecue. July.

Limited-Service Hotel

★★ BEST WESTERN EL GRANDE INN. *15135 Lakeshore Dr, Clear Lake (95422). Phone 707/994-2000; toll-free 800/528-1234; fax 707/994-2042. www.bestwestern.com.* Spanish-style lobby. 68 rooms, 4 story. Check-in 3 pm, check-out 11 am. Restaurant, bar. Indoor pool, whirlpool. **$**

Concord (E-2)

See also Antioch, Martinez, Oakland, Vallejo, Walnut Creek

Population 121,780
Elevation 70 ft
Area Code 925
Information Concord Chamber of Commerce, 2280 Diamond Blvd, Suite 200, 94520; phone 925/685-1181
Web Site www.concordchamber.com

What to See and Do

Chronicle Pavilion at Concord. *2000 Kirker Pass Rd, Concord. Phone 925/363-5701. www.chroniclepavilion.com.* Roofed, open-air performance and assembly facility, with lawn and reserved pavilion seating for 12,500; popular entertainment performances, sports, and special events. (Apr-Oct)

Waterworld USA. *1950 Waterworld Pkwy, Concord (94520). Phone 925/609-1364. www.sixflags.com.* Twenty-acre park includes attractions such as Breaker Beach Wavepool; Treasure Island kids' area; Lazy River; and The Big Kahuna, a six-story raft adventure. The park also includes a multilevel activity pool and water slides. (Late May-early Sept: daily, call for hours) **$$$$**

Limited-Service Hotel

★★ CROWNE PLAZA CONCORD. *45 John Glenn Dr, Concord (94520). Phone 925/825-7700; fax 925/674-9567. www.crowneplaza.com.* 324 rooms, 3 story. Check-in 3 pm, check-out noon. High-speed Internet access. Restaurant, bar. Fitness room. Indoor pool, whirlpool. Business center. **$**

Full-Service Hotel

★★★ HILTON CONCORD. *1970 Diamond Blvd,*

Concord (94520). Phone 925/827-2000; toll-free 800/ 445-8667; fax 925/671-0984. www.concordhilton.com. One mile west of downtown Concord, in the East bay area, is this hotel. It caters to both business and leisure travelers, groups and individuals. It is equipped with meeting and banquet areas, restaurants, an outdoor pool, and more. 329 rooms, 11 story. Check-in 3 pm, check-out noon. High-speed Internet access. Restaurant, two bars. Fitness room. Outdoor pool, whirlpool. **$$**

Corte Madera

See also Muir Woods National Monument, San Francisco, San Rafael

Population 9,100
Elevation 27 ft
Area Code 415
Zip 94925
Web Site www.cortemadera.org

Limited-Service Hotel

★ BEST WESTERN CORTE MADERA INN. *56 Madera Blvd, Corte Madera (94925). Phone 415/924-1502; toll-free 800/777-9670; fax 415/924-5419. www.bestwestern.com.* 110 rooms, 2 story. Complimentary continental breakfast. Check-in 3 pm, check-out noon. Restaurant, bar. Children's activity center. Fitness room, spa. Outdoor pool, whirlpool. Business center. **$**

Restaurant

★★ IL FORNAIO. *223 Corte Madera Town Ctr, Corte Madera (94925). Phone 415/927-4400; toll-free 888/482-5426; fax 415/924-0906. www.ilfornaio.com.* Italian menu. Breakfast Sat-Sun, lunch, dinner, Sun brunch. Closed Thanksgiving, Dec 25. Bar. Children's menu. Reservations recommended. Outdoor seating. **$$**

Crescent City (A-1)

See also Redwood Highway

Founded 1852
Population 4,006
Elevation 44 ft
Information Chamber of Commerce, Visitor Information Center, 1001 Front St; phone 707/464-3174 or toll-free 800/343-8300.
Web Site www.northerncalifornia.net

The crescent-shaped beach that gives the city its name outlines a busy harbor. A party of treasure seekers discovered the harbor, and the city was laid out a year later.

What to See and Do

Battery Point Lighthouse. *577 H St, Crescent City (95531). Phone 707/464-3089.* (1856) On Battery Point, at the end of A St; accessible only at low tide; museum. (Apr-Sept, Wed-Sun, call for times) **$**

Del Norte County Historical Society Main Museum. *577 H St, Crescent City (95531). Phone 707/464-3922. www.delnortehistory.org.* Research center for local history; two-story lighthouse lens (1892), Native American and pioneer exhibits housed in former county jail. (May-Sept, Mon-Sat 10 am-4 pm) **$**

Elk Valley Casino. *2500 Howland Hill Rd, Crescent City (95531). Phone 707/464-1020. www.elkvalleycasino.com.* Just south of the Oregon-California border in Crescent City, the Tolowa Tribe's Elk Valley Casino features blackjack and poker tables, a bingo gallery, and 275 gambling machines. Poker tournaments are held every night and a prime rib buffet is available on Wednesdays. There is a 24-hour restaurant, but no hotel rooms on-site.

Ocean World. *304 Hwy 101 S, Crescent City (95531). Phone 707/464-4900. www.oceanworldonline.com.* Aquarium, shark-petting tank, sea lion show. Gift shop. (Daily) **$$**

Point St. George. *N of beach.* The *Brother Jonathan*, a side-wheeler, was wrecked here in 1865. Of 232 persons aboard, 203 died; they are buried in Brother Jonathan Cemetery, Pebble Beach Dr and 9th St.

Redwood National and State Parks. *1111 2nd St, Crescent City (95531). S of town. Phone 707/464-6101. www.nps.gov/redw.* The venerable redwoods that dominate the northwestern-most corner of California are some of the tallest and oldest trees in the world—topping out at about 350 feet in height and 2,000 years in age. To protect the redwoods from decimation by logging, the federal and California state governments created a checkerboard of four parks—three state and one national—containing more than 100,000 acres of redwood forest. Hiking and backpacking are the most popular out-of-the-car pursuits here, in part because of the sheer scale of the trees and other super-sized flora; boaters, bikers, equestrians, and fishermen are also frequent visitors. A number of long backcountry trails, including the 37-mile Coastal Trail connecting the parks along the coast, make for great multiday backpacking routes. There are also several beaches—great spots for watching the gray whale migration in winter and spring, but quite cold for swimming year-round. A large herd of elk also calls the parks home. **FREE** The three state parks located within the national park boundaries are

Del Norte Coast Redwoods State Park. *1111 2nd St, Crescent City. 7 miles S on Hwy 101. Phone 707/464-6101; toll-free 800/444-7275 (reservations).* Redwood trees grow on steep slopes just above the surf. Rhododendrons blanket the slopes, blooming in May and June. Nature, hiking trails; picnicking, camping (dump station). **$**

Jedediah Smith Redwoods State Park. *1111 2nd St, Carlsbad. 9 miles NE off Hwy 101 on Hwy 199. Phone 707/464-6101; toll-free 800/444-7275 (reservations).* Stout Memorial Grove, at the center of Mill Creek Flat, is about 4 miles from the park entrance. Swimming, fishing; nature and hiking trails, picnicking, camping (dump station). **$**

Prairie Creek Redwoods State Park. *1111 2nd St, Crescent City. 33 miles S on Hwy 101. Phone 707/464-6101; toll-free 800/444-7275 (reservations).* These 14,000 acres are adorned by magnificent groves of coast redwoods. Gold Bluffs Beach was worked for gold in 1851, but most of it remained hopelessly mixed in vast amounts of sand and rock. Lush ferns cover the 50-foot walls of Fern Canyon and moss carpets the fallen tree trunks. Fishing; hiking on 75 miles of nature trails, picnicking. Educational displays in visitor center. Frequent campfire programs and ranger-conducted hikes in summer. Two campgrounds: **Elk Prairie,** tent and trailer (reservations recommended); **Gold Bluffs Beach,** approximately 3 1/2 miles S via Hwy 101 to Davison Rd (unpaved road; vehicle size and weight restriction). **$**

Trees of Mystery. *15500 Hwy 101 N, Klamath (95548). Phone toll-free 800/638-3389. www.treesofmystery.net.* A giant Paul Bunyan and Babe the Blue Ox greet visitors to this tacky-but-fun landmark south of Klamath on Highway 101. The touristy complex includes a trail that runs through thick redwood forest, with more than a few trees carved into the form of Paul Bunyan's legendary cohorts, as well as a "SkyTrail" gondola that takes riders to an observation platform. A motel, restaurant, and kitschy souvenir shop round out the ever-expanding facilities. Museum (June-Aug: daily 8 am-7:30 pm; Sept-May: daily 9:30 am-4:30 pm). **$$$**

Special Event

World Championship Crab Races. *Del Norte County Fairgrounds, 1001 Front St, Crescent City (95531). Phone 707/464-3174; toll-free 800/343-8300.* In addition to watching the Dungeness crab races, visitors to this unique event can also peruse the art fair and children's games. Sun before President's Day.

Limited-Service Hotels

★ ★ BEST WESTERN NORTHWOODS INN. *655 Hwy 101 S, Crescent City (95531). Phone 707/464-9771; toll-free 800/557-3396; fax 707/464-9461. www.bestwestern.com.* 89 rooms, 2 story. Complimentary full breakfast. Check-in 3 pm, check-out 11 am. Restaurant, bar. Fitness room. Indoor pool, whirlpool. **$**

★ COMFORT INN & SUITES REDWOOD COAST. *100 Walton St, Crescent City (95531). Phone 707/464-3885; toll-free 800/228-5160; fax 707/464-5311. www.choicehotels.com.* 46 rooms, 2 story. Complimentary continental breakfast. Check-in 3 pm, check-out 11 am. **$**

Restaurant

★ ★ HARBOR VIEW GROTTO. *150 Starfish Way, Crescent City (95531). Phone 707/464-3815; fax 707/464-3875.* American, seafood menu. Lunch, dinner. Closed Jan 1, Thanksgiving, Dec 24-25. Bar. **$$**

Davis (D-2)

See also Napa, Sacramento, Vacaville

Settled 1868
Population 60,308
Elevation 50 ft
Area Code 530
Zip 95616
Information Chamber of Commerce and Visitor Center, 130 G St, Suite B; phone 530/756-5160
Web Site www.davischamber.com

The pioneer settler Jerome C. Davis planted 400 acres of wheat, barley, orchards, and vineyards and pastured great herds of livestock here. Since then, Davis has remained the center of a rich agricultural area. The city is also known for its energy conservation programs and projects. A prime example is Village Homes Solar Village. Obtain a self-guided tour brochure at City Hall, 23 Russell Blvd.

What to See and Do

University of California, Davis. *1 Shields Ave, Davis (95616). Between Hwy 113 and I-80. Phone 530/752-8111. www.ucdavis.edu.* (1905) (29,000 students) Nearly 5,200 acres with College of Agricultural and Environmental Sciences, College of Engineering, College of Letters and Science, School of Veterinary Medicine, School of Law, Graduate School of Management, and School of Medicine. Art exhibits are displayed in the Nelson and Union Memorial galleries and in the C. N. Gorman Museum. Tours.

Special Event

Picnic Day. *University of California, Davis, 2205 Haring, Davis (95616). picnicday.ucdavis.edu.* Sponsored by Associated Students of University of California at Davis. Includes parade, floats, exhibits, aquacade, dachshund races, concerts, horse show, rodeo, sheepdog trials. Mid-Apr.

Limited-Service Hotel

★ BEST WESTERN UNIVERSITY LODGE. *123 B St, Davis (95616). Phone 530/756-7890; toll-free 800/528-1234; fax 530/756-0245. www.universitylodgeucd.com.* The University of California is one block away. 52 rooms, 2 story. Pets accepted. Complimentary continental breakfast. Check-in 3 pm, check-out 11 am. Fitness room. Whirlpool. **$**

Restaurants

★ CAFE BERNARDO. *234 D St, Davis (95616). Phone 530/750-5101. www.cafebernardo.com.* California menu. Breakfast, lunch, dinner. Bar. Children's menu. Casual attire. Outdoor seating. **$**

★ ★ SOGA'S. *217 E St, Davis (95616). Phone 530/757-1733; fax 530/757-1846. www.sogasrestaurant.com.* California, fusion menu. Lunch, dinner. Closed Sun; Thanksgiving, Dec 25. Bar. Business casual attire. Reservations recommended. Outdoor seating. **$$$**

Death Valley National Park (G-5)

70 miles E of Lone Pine on Hwy 190.

Information PO Box 579, Death Valley, CA 92328; phone 760/786-3200

Web Site www.nps.gov/deva

Here, approximately 300 miles northeast of Los Angeles, are more than 5,200 square miles of rugged desert, peaks, and depressions—an unusual and colorful geography. The park is one vast geological museum, revealing secrets of ages gone by. Millions of years ago, this was part of the Pacific Ocean; then violent uplifts of the earth occurred, creating mountain ranges and draining water to the west. Today, 200 square miles of the valley are at or below sea level. The lowest point on the continent (282 feet below sea level) is here; Telescope Peak, at 11,049 feet, towers directly above it. The valley itself is about 140 miles long and 4-16 miles wide. The average rainfall is less than two inches a year. From October to May, the climate is very pleasant. In summer, it's extremely hot; a maximum temperature of 134° F in the shade has been recorded. If considered all together, this is the lowest, hottest, and driest area in North America.

Death Valley was named in 1849 when a party of gold hunters took a shortcut here and were stranded for several weeks awaiting help. The discovery and subsequent mining of borax, hauled out by the famous 20-mule teams, led to development of the valley as a tourist attraction.

The visitor center at Furnace Creek is open daily, and offers guided walks, evening programs, and talks (Nov-Apr). Golden Age, Golden Eagle, Golden A ccess passports (see MAKING THE MOST OF YOUR TRIP) are accepted. Per vehicle $$.

Note: venturing off paved roads in this area in the summer months can be very dangerous. Carefully obey all National Park Service signs and regulations. Make sure that your vehicle has plenty of gas and oil.

Carry water when you explore this park, especially in hot weather.

What to See and Do

20-Mule-Team Canyon. *Lone Pine. Phone 760/786-2331.* Viewed from a twisting road on which RVs and trailers are not allowed. (This is an unpaved, one-way road; watch carefully for the entrance sign.)

Artist's Palette. A particularly scenic auto drive (9 miles one way), with spectacular colors. Because of difficult roads, RVs and trailers are advised not to drive here.

Badwater. *Lone Pine. Phone 760/786-2331.* At 279 feet below sea level, near the lowest spot on the North American continent; look for the sea level sign.

Camping. *Phone 760/786-2331.* Developed and primitive camping in the area; limited hook-ups. It is suggested that campers check with the visitor center for important information on camping facilities and road conditions. (Daily) **FREE**

Charcoal kilns. *Phone 760/786-2331.* Beehive-shaped stone structures, formerly used to make charcoal for nearby mines. *Note:* the last mile of the access road is unpaved.

Dante's View. *Phone 760/786-2331.* (5,475 feet) View of Death Valley with a steep drop to 279 feet below sea level at Badwater.

Devil's Golf Course. *Phone 760/786-2331.* Vast beds of rugged salt crystals.

Golden Canyon. *Phone 760/786-2331.* Offers a display of color ranging from deep red to rich gold. A 1-mile trail provides access.

Natural Bridge. *Phone 760/786-2331.* A bridge spanning a rugged canyon in the Black Mountains; 1-mile walking trail.

Rhyolite Ghost Town. *Phone 760/786-2331. www.nps.gov/deva/rhyolite.htm.* This was the largest town in the mining history of Death Valley in the early 1900s; 5,000-10,000 people lived here then. The town bloomed from 1905 to 1910; by 1911, it was a ghost town. One structure still left standing from that era is the "bottle house," constructed of 12,000-50,000 beer and liquor bottles (depending on who does the estimating).

Sand dunes. *Phone 760/786-2331.* Sand blown by the wind into dunes 5 to 100 feet high.

Scotty's Castle. *Phone 760/786-2392.* A desert mansion (circa 1922-1931), designed and built to be viewed as a work of art, as well as a house. The furnishings are typical of the period; many were especially designed and hand crafted for this house. Living history tours are led by costumed interpreters. (Daily 8:30 am-6 pm) **FREE**

Telescope Peak. *Phone 760/786-2331.* Highest point in the Panamint Range (11,049 feet). Although there is a 14-mile round-trip hiking trail, it is inaccessible in the winter months.

Ubehebe Crater. *Phone 760/786-2331.* Colorful crater left by a volcanic steam explosion.

Visitor center. *Hwy 190, Death Valley (92328). At Furnace Creek. Phone 760/786-3200.* Before continuing on, we recommend that visitors stop here for an orientation film, day-trip suggestions, help in organizing sightseeing routes, and important information on camping areas and road conditions. (Daily 8 am-5 pm)

Zabriskie Point. *Phone 760/786-2331.* View of Death Valley and the Panamint Range from the rugged badlands of the Black Mountains.

Limited-Service Hotels

★★ CARRIAGE INN. *901 N China Lake Blvd, Ridgecrest (93555). Phone 760/446-7910; toll-free 800/772-8527; fax 760/446-6408. www.carriageinn.biz.* This family-run hotel offers a mix of luxury suites and poolside cabanas. 160 rooms, 1 story. Outdoor pool. **$$**

★★ HERITAGE INN AND SUITES. *1050 N Norma St, Ridgecrest (93555). Phone 760/446-6543; toll-free 800/843-0693; fax 760/446-3139.* 169 rooms, 2 story, all suites. Restaurant. **$**

★★ STOVEPIPE WELLS VILLAGE. *Hwy 190, Death Valley (92328). Phone 760/786-2387; fax 760/786-2389. www.stovepipewells.com.* Landing strip. Panoramic view of the mountains, desert, and dunes. 83 rooms. Pets accepted; fee. Check-in 2 pm, check-out noon. High-speed Internet access. Restaurant, bar. Outdoor pool. **$**

Restaurants

★ THE 19TH HOLE. *Hwy 190, Furnace Creek*

(92328). Phone 760/786-2345. www.furnacecreekresort.com. Located on a site overlooking the world's lowest golf course (214 feet below sea level), this establishment also offers drive-through service for golf carts. American menu. Breakfast, lunch. Closed June-Sept. **$**

★ CHARLIE'S PUB & GRILL. *901 N China Lake Blvd, Ridgecrest (93555). Phone 760/446-7910; toll-free 800/772-8527. www.carriageinn.biz.* Serves family-style food in a unique environment of aircrew memorabilia donated from squadrons around the world. American menu. Dinner. **$**

★ FARRIS RESTAURANT. *1050 N Norma St, Ridgecrest (93555). Phone toll-free 800/843-0693.* A favorite dining spot for locals, the Farris Restaurant offers regional American cuisine in a comfortable atmosphere. American menu. Lunch, dinner. **$**

★ ★ ★ FURNACE CREEK INN DINING ROOM. *Hwy 190, Death Valley (92328). Phone 760/786-2345; toll-free 800/236-7916; fax 760/786-2423. www.furnacecreekresort.com.* When you are in Death Valley, visit this inn for delicious food. Try their steak while enjoying the 1930s décor under beamed ceilings. American menu. Breakfast, lunch, dinner, brunch. Closed mid-May-mid-Oct. Bar. Children's menu. Business casual attire. Reservations recommended. Valet parking. **$$**

Devils Postpile National Monument (E-3)

See also Mammoth Lakes

56 miles NW of Bishop, off Hwy 395.

Web Site www.nps.gov/dep

Just southeast of Yosemite National Park (see) and surrounded by Inyo National Forest (see) is Devils Postpile National Monument. The monument is among the finest examples of columnar basalt in the world, formed approximately 100,000 years ago when basalt lava erupted in the area. These columns, standing 40 to 60 feet high, are protected by the National Park Service. The formation is a 1/2-mile hike from the ranger station. A short, steep trail leads to the top of the formation for a view of the ends of the columns, which have been polished by glaciers and resemble tilelike inlays. Pumice, a porous lava, and a nearby bubbling soda spring are evidence of recent volcanic activity.

Rainbow Falls is approximately 2 miles down the river trail from the Postpile. Here the San Joaquin River drops 101 feet—the foam-white water starkly contrasting with the dark cliffs. Its name was suggested by the rainbows that play across the falls in the afternoon. Fishing is permitted with a license; hunting is prohibited. There is a picnic area on the grounds. A campground is maintained in the northeast section. Park (mid-June-mid-Oct, daily; closed rest of year). Ranger station (daily; hours vary). Campfire programs and guided walks available; call for schedule. For further information contact PO Box 501, Mammoth Lakes 93546; 760/934-2289 (June-Oct) or 760/872-4881 (Nov-May). Camping per day **$$$$**

Dunsmuir (B-2)

See also Mount Shasta

Population 1,923
Elevation 2,289 ft
Area Code 530
Zip 96025
Information Chamber of Commerce, 4118 Pine St, PO Box 17; phone 530/235-2177 or toll-free 800/386-7684
Web Site www.dunsmuir.com

What to See and Do

Castle Crags State Park. *20022 Castle Creek Rd, Castella (96017). 6 miles S of Dunsmuir off I-5. Phone 530/235-2684.* On 4,250 acres. Named for nearby granite peaks up to 6,600 feet high. Fishing (except in the Sacramento River and its tributaries). Picnicking, camping. **$$$$**

Special Event

River Festival. *5819 Sacramento Ave, Dunsmuir (96025). Phone 530/235-2012. www.riverexchange.org.* Celebration of watershed stewardship. Exhibits, fishing clinics, demonstrations; art shows. Late Apr.

Limited-Service Hotel

★ ★ RAILROAD PARK RESORT. *100 Railroad Park Rd, Dunsmuir (96025). Phone 530/235-4440; toll-free 800/974-7245. www.rrpark.com.* Rooms in authentic railroad cars; 1/4 mile from Sacramento River. 27 rooms. Pets accepted; fee. Check-in 2 pm, check-out 11 am. Restaurant, bar. Outdoor pool, whirlpool. **$**

Restaurant

★ ★ ★ CAFE MADDALENA. *5801 Sacramento Ave, Dunsmuir (96025). Phone 530/235-2725. www.cafemaddalena.com.* Innovative menu featuring Spanish, Italian, and Provençal cuisine. Mediterranean menu. Dinner. Closed Mon-Wed; Jan-mid Mar. **$$**

Eureka (B-1)

See also Redwood Highway, Trinidad

Founded 1850
Population 26,128
Elevation 44 ft
Area Code 707
Zip 95501
Information Chamber of Commerce, 2112 Broadway; phone 707/442-3738 or toll-free 800/356-6381
Web Site www.eurekachamber.com

The largest fishing fleet north of the San Francisco Bay makes the city of Eureka its main port. Lumbering is the city's major industry.

What to See and Do

Arcata Architectural Tour. *Arcata Chamber of Commerce, 1635 Heindon Rd, Eureka (95521). Phone 707/822-3619.* Self-guided walking or driving tour to many Victorian structures, covering 35 city blocks. Obtain map at Chamber of Commerce.

Clarke Historical Museum. *240 E St, Eureka (95501). Phone 707/443-1947.* Regional history, collection of Karuk, Hupa, Wiyot, and Yurok basketry and ceremonial regalia; firearms, Victorian furniture and decorative art. Guided tours by appointment. (Tues-Sat 11 am-4 pm; closed holidays, also Jan) **FREE**

Ferndale Museum. *515 Shaw Ave, Ferndale (95536). 12 miles S on Hwy 101, then 5 miles W. Phone 707/786-4466. www.ferndale-museum.org.* Local history displays of "Cream City." (Feb-Dec: Wed-Sat 11 am-4 pm, Sun from 1 pm; June-Sept: Tues-Sat 11 am-4 pm, Sun from 1 pm; closed Jan) **$**

Fort Humboldt State Historic Park. *3431 Fort Ave, Eureka (95503). Phone 707/445-6567. www.parks.ca.gov.* Ulysses S. Grant was stationed at Fort Humboldt in 1854. Logging and military exhibits. Tours. Picnicking. (Daily 8 am-5 pm; closed Jan 1, Thanksgiving, Dec 25) **FREE**

Fortuna Depot Museum. *4 Park St, Fortuna (95540). 18 miles S on Hwy 101, in Rohner Park. Phone 707/725-7645. www.sunnyfortuna.com/departments/museum.* Train memorabilia, barbed wire collection, fishing and logging displays. In 1893 train depot. (June-Aug: daily noon-4:30 pm; Sept-May: Thurs-Sun noon-4:30 pm; closed Dec 25) **FREE**

Humboldt Bay Harbor Cruise. *1 C St, Eureka (95501). Phone 707/445-1910.* 1 1/4-hour trips. (May-Sept, Sun-Tues: two cruises offered; Wed-Sat: four cruises offered) Special charter rest of year. **$$$**

Humboldt Bay Maritime Museum. *423 1st St, Eureka (95501). Phone 707/444-9440.* Pacific and northcoast maritime heritage displays; marine artifacts. (Tues-Sat noon-4 pm; closed holidays) **DONATION**

Lost Coast Brewery. *617 4th St, Eureka (95501). Phone 707/445-4480. www.lostcoast.com.* A bustling bar and grill in Old Town Eureka, the Lost Coast Brewery attracts a diverse mix of patrons with its rich atmosphere (the place is laden with dark wood and local art) and even richer brews. Modeled after English and Welsh pubs, the brewery makes its home in an 1892 structure and serves pizza, burgers, and other pub standbys for lunch and dinner. The Great White Beer and 8-Ball Stout are among Lost Coast's signature beers. (Daily)

Old Town. *1st and C sts, Eureka (95501).* Designated a National Historic District, this section of town, situated on the waterfront of Humboldt Bay, has original buildings of early Eureka. Also here are a gazebo, a cascading water fountain, sculptured benches, and commercial and residential Victorian buildings; antiques and specialty shops; horse and buggy rides (fee); and restaurants. Cruises of the bay are available.

Romano Gabriel Wooden Sculpture Garden. *315 2nd St, Eureka (95501). www.eurekaheritage.org.* A colorful collection of folk art, constructed of wood in the mid-1900s. (Daily) **FREE**

Sequoia Park Zoo. *3414 W St, Eureka (95503). Phone 707/442-6552. www.sequoiaparkzoo.com.* Area surrounded by 46 acres of redwoods; duck pond, gardens, picnic facilities, snack bar, children's

Eureka's Victorian Architecture

The old-time lumber town of Eureka, situated along the coast in redwood country 270 miles north of San Francisco, displays its heritage in striking renovated Victorian homes and commercial buildings near the waterfront. Eureka has more Victorians per capita—over 10,000—than any other California city. This walking tour can take anywhere from one hour to several, depending on your pace. Along the way, you'll encounter a number of gaudily decorated gingerbread Victorians, including a lumber baron's mansion reputed to be the most photographed Victorian house in the world. To get an overview of the area's cultural history, start your walk in Old Town Eureka at the compact but excellent Clarke Historical Museum (240 E St); the lumberjacks, seafarers, pioneers, and Native Americans from Eureka's past are all represented here. Now walk two blocks west to C Street and turn south. Over the next 14 or so blocks you'll encounter some of Eureka's finest examples of Victorian architecture, including the Moorish arches at 1228 C Street, the columns at 1461 C Street, and the Eastlake-style ornamentation and gardens at 1406 C Street, now a bed-and-breakfast inn. After viewing the Victorians along the 1600 block of C Street, backtrack a few blocks to Hillsdale Street; turn right (east) and note the Eastlake, Queen Anne, and Carpenter Gothic styles at 216, 220, 233, 258, 261, and 303 Hillsdale. Turn left (north) on E Street, walk to 9th Street, and turn right two blocks to G Street. The Queen Anne at 904 G Street and the Italianate Victorian at 828 G Street are worth special attention. Continue north to 3rd Street and head right (east) on 3rd until you reach M Street. The famous Carson Mansion, at 143 M Street, is an incredibly ostentatious three-story, green Victorian that dates to 1884. Lumber baron William Carson employed 100 men for two years to build it. The mansion is built of redwood and combines elements of Queen Anne, Eastlake, and Italianate styles; few visitors can resist photographing it. Though not open to the public, it's perfectly acceptable to gawk out front. Across the street, at 202 M Street, is a combination Queen Anne-Eastlake Victorian known as the "Pink Lady," which Carson built for his son as a wedding present in 1889. To conclude the tour, walk back west down 2nd Street to take advantage of Old Town's shops, restaurants, and galleries.

playground. (Oct-Apr: Tues-Sun 10 am-5 pm; May-Sept: daily 10 am-7 pm) **DONATION**

Six Rivers National Forest. *1330 Bay Shore Way, Eureka (95501). Reached via Hwys 101, 199, 36, 96, 299. Phone 707/442-1721. www.fs.fed.us/r5/sixrivers.* On 1,111,726 acres. The Klamath, Eel, Trinity, Van Duzen, and Mad rivers provide excellent fishing. Hunting, camping, and picnicking. Resorts and lodges are located in and near the forest. Located within the forest is

> **Smith River National Recreation Area.** *10600 Hwy 199, Gasquet (95543). Phone 707/457-3131.* (305,337 acres) This is the heart of one of the largest Wild and Scenic River systems (315 miles) in the United States. The area offers whitewater rafting, wilderness hiking, bird-watching, nature study, world-class steelhead fishing, hunting, and camping.

Sjaak's Fine Chocolates. *Old Town Gazebo, 425 Snug Alley, Suite B, Eureka (95501). www.sjaakschocolate.com.* Using only Belgian chocolate—and following the Belgian code of no waxes, fillers, or preservatives, Sjaak's is a chocoholic's dream, where visitors can see traditional candy-making in action at the Old Town Gazebo in Eureka. The shop's namesake, founder Sjaak Holten, is a Dutch native who trained in some of Europe's finest culinary institutes and chocolate houses.

Victorian Village Self-Guided Tours. *580 Main St, Eureka (95501). 20 miles S. Phone 707/786-4477.* Ferndale's Victorian architecture is superior; the entire village has been declared a State Historic Landmark. Pick up walking and driving tour maps from Ferndale shops. **FREE**

Woodley Island Marina. *601 Startare Dr, Eureka (95501). 1 mile W via Hwy 101, Samoa Bridge exit (Hwy 255).* Mooring for commercial fishing boats and recreational craft; café and shops; site of *The Fisherman* memorial statue and Table Bluff Lighthouse.

Special Events

Cross-Country Kinetic Sculpture Race. *Phone 707/786-4477.* A three-day, 35-mile cross-country race over land, water, beaches, and highways. Participants race on their self-powered, artistically sculptured vehicles. Memorial Day weekend.

Redwood Coast Jazz Festival. *523 5th St, Eureka (95501). Various locations in town. Phone 707/445-3378. www.redwoodjazz.org.* Take your pick of musical styles—from Dixieland to blues to zydeco—grab a snack, take a seat, and enjoy a beautiful outdoor concert or two. Late Mar-early Apr. **$$$$**

Rhododendron Festival. *Phone 707/443-6580.* Varied events throughout Humboldt County include parades, races, art exhibits, contests, entertainment. Usually last weekend in Apr.

Limited-Service Hotel

★ ★ RED LION. *1929 Fourth St, Eureka (95501). Phone 707/445-0844; toll-free 800/733-5466; fax 707/445-2752. www.redlion.com.* This hotel is just 15 minutes from the Eureka/Arcata Municipal Airport. Golf, whitewater rafting, and charter fishing are nearby. 175 rooms, 4 story. Pets accepted; fee. Check-in 3 pm, check-out noon. High-speed Internet access, wireless Internet access. Restaurant, bar. Fitness room. Outdoor pool, whirlpool. Airport transportation available. **$**

Specialty Lodgings

The following lodging establishments are approved by Mobil Travel Guide, but due to their unique and individualized nature have not been given a traditional Mobil Star rating. Included in this listing you may find bed-and-breakfasts, limited-service inns, guest ranches, and other unique hotel properties.

ABIGAIL'S ELEGANT VICTORIAN MANSION. *1406 C St, Eureka (95501). Phone 707/444-3144. www.eureka-california.com.* This meticulously restored Victorian is a State Historic Site, offering elegance and luxury. Located in the heart of the north coastline amid California's impressive redwoods, this inn offers guests the opportunity to step back in time. 4 rooms, 2 story. Complimentary full breakfast. Check-in 3-6 pm, check-out 11 am. **$$**

CARTER HOUSE INN. *301 L St, Eureka (95501). Phone 707/444-8062; toll-free 800/404-1390; fax 707/444-8067. www.carterhouse.com.* Located alongside Humboldt Bay in Old Town, this bed-and-breakfast, a re-created 1884 San Francisco Victorian house, has access to the giant redwood forests, rugged Pacific beaches, and all the other wonders of northern California's Redwood Coast. 32 rooms, 4 story. Pets accepted; restrictions, fee. Complimentary full breakfast. Check-in 3-6 pm, check-out 11 am. **$**

GINGERBREAD MANSION. *400 Berding St, Ferndale (95536). Phone 707/786-4000; toll-free 800/952-4136; fax 707/786-4381. www.gingerbread-mansion.com.* This Victorian inn is surrounded by a formal Victorian garden and is one of northern California's most photographed inns. 11 rooms, 3 story. Complimentary full breakfast. Check-in 3 pm, check-out 11 am. **$$**

OLD TOWN BED AND BREAKFAST INN. *1521 3rd St, Eureka (95501). Phone 707/443-5235; toll-free 888/508-5235; fax 707/442-4390. www.oldtownbnb.com.* This Greek Revival Victorian home, built in 1871, is the oldest lodging in town and is only one and a half blocks from the bay. 4 rooms, 2 story. Pets accepted, some restrictions; fee. Complimentary full breakfast. Check-in 4-6 pm, check-out 11 am. **$$**

Restaurants

★ ★ ★ RESTAURANT 301. *301 L St, Eureka (95501). Phone 707/444-8062; toll-free 800/404-1390; fax 707/444-8067. www.carterhouse.com.* Located in the Victorian Carter House, Restaurant 301 offers a menu that changes with the seasons and features Redwood Coast's freshest produce. The chef uses a "garden to table" philosophy in his creative presentations. American menu. Dinner. Children's menu. **$$**

★ ★ SEA GRILL. *316 E St, Eureka (95501). Phone 707/443-7187.* Restored Victorian building (circa 1870). Seafood, steak menu. Lunch, dinner. Closed Sun; holidays; also two weeks in early Nov. Bar. Children's menu. **$$**

Fairfield (D-2)

See also Vacaville, Vallejo

Population 96,178
Elevation 15 ft
Area Code 707
Zip 94533

Web Site www.ffsc-chamber.com

This is the home of Travis Air Force Base and the seat of Solano County.

What to See and Do

Jelly Belly factory tours. *One Jelly Belly Ln, Fairfield (94533). Phone toll-free 800/953-5592. www.jellybelly.com.* The home of "the original gourmet jelly bean," the Jelly Belly factory is a can't-miss diversion for those with a sweet tooth. Made famous when President Ronald Reagan kept a jar on his Oval Office desk, the Jelly Belly catalog now consists of more than 150 flavors, including unusual ones like buttered popcorn, root beer, and piña colada. Located 20 miles northeast of the Bay Area in Fairfield, the factory is accessible via guided tours that lead visitors through the Jelly Belly-making process. (It takes more than a week to make each bean.) The 40-minute tour also includes stops at other candy-making kitchens, an art gallery (with works made entirely of Jelly Bellies!), a Jelly Belly sampling bar, and a gift shop. It's best to go on a weekday—videos replace the busy candy-making scene when the workers are at home on Saturday and Sunday. There is a restaurant on-site. (Daily 9 am-5 pm; closed holidays) **FREE**

Western Railway Museum. *5848 Hwy 12, Suisun. 12 miles E on Hwy 12. Phone 707/374-2978. www.wrm.org.* Take a 2-mile ride on electric streetcars and interurbans, with occasional steam and diesel operation. The museum collection includes 100 vintage railroad cars and trains operating on a demonstration railroad; bookstore, gift shop; picnic area. Museum admission includes unlimited rides. (Sat-Sun 10:30 am-5 pm; also Wed-Sun 10:30 am-5 pm from Memorial Day-Labor Day; closed Jan 1, Thanksgiving, Dec 25) **$$**

Limited-Service Hotels

★ HAMPTON INN. *4441 Central Pl, Fairfield (94534). Phone 707/864-1446; toll-free 800/426-7866; fax 707/864-4288. www.hamptoninn.com.* 57 rooms, 3 story. Complimentary continental breakfast. Check-in 4 pm, check-out noon. Wireless Internet access. Fitness room. Outdoor pool. **$**

★★ HOLIDAY INN. *1350 Holiday Ln, Fairfield (94533). Phone 707/422-4111; toll-free 800/465-4329; fax 707/428-3452. www.hiselect.com/fairfieldca.* 142 rooms, 4 story. Check-in 3 pm, check-out noon. High-speed Internet access. Restaurant, bar. Fitness room. Outdoor pool. Business center. **$**

Fort Bragg (C-1)

See also Mendocino, Ukiah, Willits

Founded 1884
Population 7,026
Elevation 75 ft
Area Code 707
Zip 95437
Information Fort Bragg-Mendocino Coast Chamber of Commerce, 332 N Main St, PO Box 1141; phone 707/961-6300 or toll-free 800/726-2780
Web Site www.mendocinocoast.com

The town is a lumber, agricultural, recreational, and fishing center that stands on the edge of the rocky coastline where the military post of Fort Bragg was set up in 1857. When the fort was abandoned in 1867, the land was opened for purchase, and a lumber town sprang up. It was rebuilt after the earthquake of 1906. Driftwood and shell hunting are popular on nearby beaches.

What to See and Do

Jughandle Ecological Staircase. *Hwy 1, Mendocino. Phone 707/937-5804. www.jughandle.creek.org.* Nature trail climbs from sea level to pygmy forest; 500,000 years of geological history.

MacKerricher State Park. *Hwy 1, Mendocino. 3 miles N on Hwy 1. Phone 707/937-5804. www.parks.ca.gov.* Approximately 10 miles of beach and ocean access. Fishing (nonmotorized boat launching); nature, hiking trails; picnicking, camping (dump station; fee). **$$$$**

Mendocino Coast Botanical Gardens. *18220 N Hwy 1, Fort Bragg (95437). 2 miles S on Hwy 1. Phone 707/964-4352. www.gardenbythesea.org.* Approximately 47 acres of rhododendrons, heathers, perennials, fuchsias, coastal pine forest, and ocean bluffs. Café; gift shop, nursery; picnic areas; self-guided tours. (Mar-Oct: daily 9 am-5 pm; Nov-Feb: daily 9 am-4 pm; closed the Saturday following Labor Day, Thanksgiving, Dec 25) **$$**

Noyo. *19101 S Harbor Dr, Fort Bragg (95437). 1/2 mile S on Hwy 1 at mouth of Noyo River. Phone 707/964-*

4719. www.fortbragg.com/noyo_harbor.html. Fishing village with picturesque harbor; public boat launching; charter boats available.

Skunk Train. *Laurel St, Fort Bragg (95437). Foot of Laurel St. Phone toll-free 800/866-1690. www.skunktrain.com.* Originally a logging railroad, the California Western Railroad train, affectionately known as "the Skunk," runs 40 miles through redwoods along the Noyo River and over the Coastal Range to Willits (see). Full-day round-trips available aboard either diesel-powered motor cars or a diesel-pulled train (all year). Half-day round-trips available from Fort Bragg (Mar-Nov, daily; rest of year, weekends). Half-day and full-day trips available from Willits (Memorial Day-Oct; inquire for schedule). **$$$$**

Special Events

Paul Bunyan Days. *Phone 707/961-6300. www.paulbunyandays.com.* Logging competition, gem and mineral show; parade (Mon); fuchsia show, arts and crafts. Labor Day weekend.

Rhododendron Show. *1197 Chestnut St, Fort Bragg (95437). Phone 707/964-3282. www.savorwinecountry.com/seasonal/spring04/68rhodie2.html.* More varieties of rhododendrons are grown here than anywhere else in the world. Early May.

Whale Festival. *Phone 707/961-6300. www.mendocinocoast.com.* Whale-watching cruises and walks; whale run; beerfest; chowder tasting. Mar.

Whale Watch. *18200 Old Coast Hwy, Fort Bragg. Phone toll-free 888/942-8284. www.fortbragg.org.* Nov-Mar.

Winesong. *Mendocino Coast Botanical Gardens, 18220 N Hwy 1, Fort Bragg (95437). Phone 707/961-4688. www.winesong.org.* More than 20 vintners pour for wine tasting, food tasting, music, wine auction. Sat after Labor Day. **$$$$**

World's Largest Salmon Barbecue. *Noyo Harbor, 19101 S Harbor Dr, Fort Bragg (95437). Phone 707/964-2781. www.salmonrestoration.org.* This annual old-fashioned barbecue raises money to support the Salmon Restoration Association. The fare includes grilled salmon, salad, corn on the cob, and garlic bread. Sat nearest July 4. **$$$$**

Limited-Service Hotels

★ HARBOR LITE LODGE. *120 N Harbor Dr, Fort Bragg (95437). Phone 707/964-0221; toll-free 800/643-2700; fax 707/964-8748. www.harborlitelodge.com.* Most rooms with harbor view. Footpath to beach. 79 rooms, 3 story. Complimentary continental breakfast. Check-in 3 pm, check-out noon. Business center. **$**

★★ PINE BEACH INN & SUITES. *16801 N Hwy 1, Fort Bragg (95437). Phone 707/964-5603; toll-free 888/987-8388; fax 707/964-8381. www.pinebeachinn.com.* 50 rooms, 2 story. Pets accepted; fee. Check-in 3 pm, check-out 11:30 am. Restaurant, two bars. Children's activity center. Tennis. **$**

Specialty Lodgings

The following lodging establishments are approved by Mobil Travel Guide, but due to their unique and individualized nature have not been given a traditional Mobil Star rating. Included in this listing you may find bed-and-breakfasts, limited-service inns, guest ranches, and other unique hotel properties.

GREY WHALE INN BED AND BREAKFAST. *615 N Main St, Fort Bragg (95437). Phone 707/964-0640; toll-free 800/382-7244; fax 707/964-4408. www.greywhaleinn.com.* Enjoy ocean beaches, tide pools, whale watching, hiking trails, and botanical gardens at this inn located on the Mendocino Coast. 14 rooms, 4 story. Complimentary full breakfast. Check-in 2 pm, check-out noon. **$**

LODGE AT NOYO RIVER. *500 Casa Del Noyo Dr, Fort Bragg (95437). Phone 707/964-8045; toll-free 800/628-1126; fax 707/964-9366. www.noyolodge.com.* This bed-and-breakfast, surrounded by the Noyo River, was built in 1868 and gives guests a great view of the ocean. 17 rooms, 2 story. Complimentary continental breakfast. Check-in 3 pm, check-out 11 am. **$**

Restaurants

★★★ RENDEZVOUS. *647 N Main St, Fort Bragg (95437). Phone 707/964-8142. www.rendezvousinn.com.* Located in a historic 1908 redwood home, this bed-and-breakfast restaurant is found along the beautiful Mendocino Coast, 10 miles from the village of Mendocino. The chef demonstrates his French training in many of his seasonal dishes. French menu. Dinner. Closed Mon-Tues; Dec 25. **$$**

★★★ **THE RESTAURANT.** *418 N Main St, Fort Bragg (95437). Phone 707/964-9800. www.therestaurantfortbragg.com.* Located in a historic building filled with original art, this restaurant has been a favorite of locals and guests since 1973. California menu. Dinner. Closed Tues-Wed; Dec 25. Children's menu. **$$**

Fort Ross State Historic Park

See also Bodega Bay, Guerneville, Healdsburg

Web Site www.parks.ca.gov

12 miles N of Jenner on Hwy 1.

This was once an outpost of the Russian empire. For nearly three decades, the post and fort set up by the Russian-American Company of Alaska was an important center for the Russian sea otter trade. The entire "Colony Ross of California" was purchased by Captain John A. Sutter in 1841. Here are reconstructions of the Russian Orthodox chapel (circa 1825), the original seven-sided and eight-sided blockhouses, the Commandant's house, officers' barracks, and stockade walls. Interpretive exhibits at Fort and visitor center. (Daily; closed Jan 1, Thanksgiving, Dec 25) Phone 707/865-2391 or 707/847-3286. Per vehicle **$$$**

What to See and Do

Salt Point State Park. *25050 Coast Hwy 1, Cazadero (95421). 18 miles N of Jenner. www.parks.ca.gov.* Located here are Pygmy forest, Gerstle Cove marine reserve. Hiking, riding trails; picnicking, camping. Visitor center (Apr-Oct: Sat-Sun 10 am-3 pm). (Daily, sunrise-sunset) Nearby is

> **Kruse Rhododendron State Reserve.** *Jenner. 2 miles N of park entrance. Phone 707/847-3221.* Here are 317 acres of coastal vegetation. Trails. Rhododendrons bloom Apr-May.

Sonoma Coast State Beach. *25381 Steelhead Blvd, Fort Ross State Historic Park. 12 miles S, between Jenner and Bodega Bay. www.parks.ca.gov.* On 4,200 acres along coastline. Sandy beaches, rocky headlands, sand dunes. Diving, fishing; hiking, picnicking, camping. (Daily) **$$$$**

Full-Service Inn

★★★ **TIMBER COVE INN.** *21780 N Coast Hwy 1, Jenner (95450). Phone 707/847-3231; fax 707/847-3704. www.timbercoveinn.com.* 50 rooms, 2 story. Check-out 11 am. Restaurant, bar. **$$**

Fremont (E-2)

See also Hayward, Livermore, Mount Diablo State Park, Newark, Oakland, Palo Alto, Pleasanton, San Jose, Santa Clara

Population 203,413
Elevation 53 ft
Area Code 510
Information Chamber of Commerce, 39488 Stevenson Pl #100, 94538; phone 510/795-2244
Web Site www.fremontbusiness.com

At the southeast end of San Francisco Bay, this young town was created in 1956 from five Alameda County communities whose origins go back to the days of the Ohlone.

What to See and Do

Don Edwards San Francisco Bay National Wildlife Refuge. *1 Marshlands Rd, Fremont. Phone 510/792-0222. desfbay.fws.gov.* Offers 25 miles of shoreline, boardwalks, and hiking trails. This was the nation's first urban wildlife refuge and is still its most popular. Houses more than a million birds during spring and fall migrations, also home to harbor seals. Exhibits and family programs. Visitor center (Tues-Sun 10 am-5 pm). (Daily) **FREE**

Mission San Jose. *43300 Mission Blvd, Fremont. Phone 510/657-1797. www.msjchamber.org/about_msj.html.* (1797) The reconstructed adobe church was originally built in 1809 and destroyed by an earthquake in 1868. A portion of the padres' living quarters that survived holds a museum. Found here are an original baptismal font, historic vestments, and mission-era artifacts. (Daily; closed holidays) **DONATION**

Regional parks. *East Bay Regional Parks District, 2950 Peralta Oaks Ct, Oakland (94605). Phone 510/562-7275. www.ebparks.org.*

Ardenwood Regional Preserve and Historic Farm. *34600 Ardenwood Blvd, Fremont (94555). I-880, Hwy 84 Decoto exit, right on Ardenwood Blvd to park entrance. Phone 510/796-0663. www.ebparks.org/parks/arden.htm.* A 208-acre 1890s working farm. Here are the Patterson House (tours), a horse-drawn wagon, haywagon rides, farming demonstrations, and rail car tour. Picnic area. (Tues-Sun 10 am-4 pm) **$**

Coyote Hills. *8000 Patterson Ranch Rd, Fremont (94555). Phone 510/795-9385. www.ebparks.org/parks/coyote.htm.* Wetlands preserved on 966 acres. Hiking, bicycle trails; picnicking. Guided tours of 2,000-year-old Native American shell mounds (Sun); freshwater marsh; nature programs; access to Alameda Creek Trail, San Francisco Bay National Wildlife Refuge. (Apr-Oct: daily 8 am-8 pm; rest of year: to 6 pm) **$**

Sunol Regional Wilderness. *Geary Rd, Sunol. NE on I-680 to Calaveras Rd, then S to Geary Rd. Phone 510/636-1684. www.ebparks.org/parks/sunol.htm.* Hiking trails, picnicking, camping ($). Nature center and program; backpack area by reservation. Rugged terrain includes Maguire Peaks (1,688 feet), Flag Hill (1,360 feet). Connects with Ohlone Wilderness Trail (permit required). (Daily 7 am-dusk) **$$**

Special Event

Fremont Festival of the Arts. *Walnut and Paseo Padre Pkwy, Fremont. Phone 510/795-2244. www.fremontfestival.net.* Arts and crafts, music, children's attractions and activities, food, and wine garden. Early August.

Limited-Service Hotel

★ BEST WESTERN GARDEN COURT INN. *5400 Mowry Ave, Fremont (94538). Phone 510/792-4300; toll-free 800/780-7234; fax 510/792-2643. www.bestwestern.com.* 122 rooms, 3 story. Pets accepted; fee. Complimentary continental breakfast. Check-in 3 pm, check-out noon. Outdoor pool, whirlpool. **$**

Full-Service Hotels

★ ★ ★ HILTON NEWARK/FREMONT. *39900 Balentine Dr, Newark (94560). Phone 510/490-8390; toll-free 800/774-1500; fax 510/651-7828. www.hilton.com.* This hotel is centrally located around San Jose's, San Francisco's, and Oakland's international airports. Guests staying here will find movie theaters and shopping just steps away. 315 rooms, 7 story. Pets accepted; restrictions, fee. Check-in 3 pm, check-out noon. Restaurant, bar. Fitness room. Outdoor pool. Business center. **$**

★ ★ ★ MARRIOTT FREMONT. *46100 Landing Pkwy, Fremont (94538). Phone 510/413-3700; fax 510/413-3710. www.marriott.com.* 357 rooms, 10 story. Pets accepted, some restrictions; fee. Check-in 3 pm, check-out 11 am. Restaurant, bar. Fitness room. Indoor pool. Business center. **$$**

Fresno (F-3)

See also Madera

Founded 1874
Population 427,652
Elevation 296 ft
Area Code 559
Information Convention & Visitors Bureau, 848 M St, 93721; phone 559/233-0836 or toll-free 800/788-0836
Web Site www.fresnocvb.org

Fresno was founded when the population of Millerton moved from that town to the railroad line. In the geographic center of the state and the heart of the San Joaquin Valley—the great central California "Garden of the Sun"—Fresno and Fresno County are enjoying tremendous growth. The county claims the greatest agricultural production of any in the United States, handling more than $3 billion annually. The world's largest dried fruit packing plant, Sun-Maid, is here.

What to See and Do

California State University, Fresno. *5241 N Maple Ave, Fresno (93740). Phone 559/278-4240. www.csufresno.edu.* (1911) (20,000 students) Includes a farm, arboretum, and California wildlife habitat exhibits. Tours available.

Discovery Center. *1937 N Winery Ave, Fresno (93703). Phone 559/251-5533. www.thediscoverycenter.net.* Participatory natural and physical science exhibits for families; outdoor exhibits, cactus garden; picnicking; Native American room. (Tues-Fri 9 am-4 pm) **DONATION**

Forestiere Underground Gardens. *5021 W Shaw, Fresno (93722). Phone 559/271-0734. www.undergroundgardens.com.* This former home of Italian immigrant Baldasare Forestiere has 10 acres of underground tunnels filled with citrus plants, grape vines, rose bushes, and other flora. (Apr-Sept, Wed-Sun) **$$**

Fresno Art Museum. *2233 N First St, Fresno (93703). Phone 559/441-4221. www.fresnoartmuseum.org.* The only modern art museum between Los Angeles and San Francisco, the Fresno Art Museum has been the centerpiece of Radio Park since it opened in the 1950s. The museum's exhibits display works from an international group of contemporary artists, as well as an impressive collection of Mexican art, dating to the pre-Columbian era to present day. The museum also plays host to a series of performances, lectures, and films. (Tues-Wed, Fri-Sun 11 am-5 pm; Thurs to 8 pm; closed Jan 1, Thanksgiving, Dec 25) **$**

Fresno Metropolitan Museum. *1515 Van Ness Ave, Fresno (93721). Phone 559/441-1444. www.fresnomet.org.* Displays on the heritage and culture of the San Joaquin Valley; hands-on science exhibits; touring exhibits. (Tues-Wed, Fri-Sun 11 am-5 pm, Thurs to 8 pm; closed holidays) **$$**

Kearney Mansion Museum. *7160 W Kearney Blvd, Fresno (93706). Phone 559/441-0862. www.valleyhistory.org.* (1900-1903) Historic mansion has been restored; contains many original furnishings, including European wallpapers and Art Nouveau light fixtures. Adjacent servants' quarters house ranch kitchen and museum gift shop. Narrated 45-minute tour of mansion. (Fri-Sun 1 pm, 2 pm, and 3 pm; closed Jan 1, Easter, Dec 25) **$**

Kingsburg. *Chamber of Commerce, 1475 Draper St, Fresno. 18 miles S via Hwy 99. Phone 559/897-1111.* Settled by Swedes, their colorful influence remains in this town. Swedish architectural design on buildings; dala horses and flags decorate streets. **Historical Society Museum** is at 2321 Sierra St.

Millerton Lake State Recreation Area. *5290 Millerton Rd, Fresno. 21 miles NE via Hwy 41, Friant Rd. Phone 559/822-2332. www.parks.ca.gov.* 14,107 acres. Swimming, water-skiing (lifeguards), fishing, boat launching; hiking and riding trails; picnicking, concession, store nearby; camping (dump station). **$$$**

Roeding Park. *890 W Belmont Ave, Fresno (93728). Phone 559/621-2900. www.fresno.gov/parks-rec/roeding.* Variety of trees and shrubs, ranging from high mountain to tropical species, on 157 acres. Boating (rentals). Tennis. Camellia garden, picnic areas; children's storyland (fee), playland (fee/ride), amphitheater. (Daily) In the park is

Chaffee Zoological Gardens. *894 W Belmont, Fresno (93728). At the S end of the park, near Olive Ave. Phone 559/498-2671. www.chaffeezoo.org.* This 18-acre zoo has more than 650 animals representing 200 species. Includes a reptile house, elephant exhibit, sunda forest; also tropical rain forest exhibit containing plants and animals found primarily in South American regions. (Feb-Oct: daily 9 am-4 pm; Nov-Jan: daily 10 am-3 pm) **$$**

★ **Sierra National Forest.** *1600 Tollhouse Rd, Clovis (93611). Sections NE and E reached via Hwy 41, 99, 168. Phone 559/297-0706; toll-free 877/444-6777 (reservations). www.fs.fed.us/r5/sierra.* Nearly 1.3 million acres ranging from rolling foothills to rugged, snow-capped mountains; two groves of giant sequoias, hundreds of natural lakes, 11 major reservoirs, and unique geological formations. The topography can be rough and precipitous in higher elevations, with deep canyons and many beautiful meadows along streams and lakes; five wilderness areas. Rafting, boating, sailing, fishing; hunting, downhill and cross-country skiing, picnicking, camping.

Sierra Summit Ski Area. *59265 Hwy 168, Huntington Lake. 65 miles NE on Hwy 168, in Sierra National Forest. Phone 559/233-2500. www.sierrasummit.com.* Three triple, two double chairlifts, four surface lifts; patrol, school, rentals; snowmaking; snack bar, cafeteria, restaurant, bar; lodge. Twenty-five runs; longest run 2 1/4 miles; vertical drop 1,600 feet. Half-day rates (weekends and holidays). (Mid-Nov-mid-Apr, daily) **$$$$**

Wild Water Adventures. *11413 E Shaw Ave, Clovis (93611). Phone 559/299-9453; toll-free 800/564-9453. www.wildwater1.com.* This water park with rides, slides, and picnicking has one of the West's largest wave pools, plus water slides for teens and a water play area for children. (June-mid-Aug, daily) **$$$$**

Woodward Park. *7150 N Abby St, Fresno (93720). Phone 559/621-2900. www.fresno.gov/parks-rec/woodward.* Approximately 300 acres. Authentic Japanese garden (weekends only; summer weekday evenings, fee); fishing ponds for children under 16; jogging course; picnic area; bird sanctuary. (Daily)

Special Events

Big Fresno Fair. *1121 S Chance Ave, Fresno (93702). Phone 559/650-3247. www.fresnofair.com.* Carnival, horse racing, livestock exhibits, and arts and crafts. Oct. **$$**

Clovis Rodeo. *Clovis Arena, Clovis. Phone 559/299-5203. www.clovisrodeo.com.* First a venue for local cowboys to compete, the Clovis Rodeo has evolved into a four-day festival featuring a parade, kids' rodeo, and competition categories that include bull riding, team roping, barrel racing, bareback riding, and saddle bronc riding. Late Apr. **$$$**

Fresno County Blossom Trail. *2629 S Clovis Ave, Fresno (92725). Phone 559/495-4800. www.co.fresno.ca.us/4510/tourism/agtrails.aspx.* This 62-mile self-guided driving tour features the beauty of California agriculture during peak season (weather permitting). Highlights of the trail are fruit orchards, citrus groves, vineyards, and historical points of interest. The visitors bureau has maps and information. Peak season is late Feb-mid-Mar.

Highland Gathering and Games. *Coombs Ranch, Fresno. Phone 559/265-6507.* Scottish athletics, dancing contests, bagpipe competition. Mid-Sept.

Swedish Festival. *1475 Draper St, Kingsburg (93631). Phone 559/897-1111.* Celebrate everything Swedish at this three-day festival. After a traditional Svenska pancake breakfast, stick around for a parade, entertainment, arts and crafts, carnival, Maypole, folk dancing, and more Swedish food. Third weekend in May.

Limited-Service Hotels

★ ★ FOUR POINTS BY SHERATON. *3737 N Blackstone Ave, Fresno (93726). Phone 559/226-2200; toll-free 800/742-1911; fax 559/222-7147. www.fourpoints.com.* 204 rooms, 2 story. Check-in 3 pm, check-out noon. High-speed Internet access. Restaurant, bar. Fitness room. Outdoor pool, whirlpool. Airport transportation available. Business center. **$$**

★ PICCADILLY INN-UNIVERSITY. *4961 N Cedar Ave, Fresno (93726). Phone 559/224-4200; toll-free 800/468-3587; fax 559/227-2382. www.piccadillyinn.com.* In the center of the financial district, this inn is conveniently located near Fresno State University. 90 rooms, 3 story. Complimentary continental breakfast. Check-in 3 pm, check-out noon. Fitness room. Outdoor pool, whirlpool. Airport transportation available. **$$**

★ ★ RADISSON HOTEL & CONFERENCE CENTER FRESNO. *2233 Ventura St, Fresno (93721). Phone 559/268-1000; toll-free 800/333-3333; fax 559/441-2954. www.radisson.com.* This hotel is situated adjacent to the Fresno Convention Center. Yosemite National Park and Sequoia and Kings Canyon National Parks are within driving distance. 321 rooms, 8 story. Check-in 3:30 pm, check-out noon. Restaurant, bar. Fitness room. Indoor pool, outdoor pool, whirlpool. Airport transportation available. Business center. **$**

Restaurant

★ ★ RIPE TOMATO. *5064 N Palm Ave, Fresno (93704). Phone 559/225-1850.* French menu. Lunch, dinner. Closed Sun-Mon. Business casual attire. Reservations recommended. Outdoor seating. **$$$**

Garberville

See also Humboldt Redwoods State Park, Richardson Grove State Park

Population 900
Elevation 533 ft
Area Code 707
Zip 95440
Web Site www.garberville.org

What to See and Do

Avenue of the Giants. *From Phillipsville N to Pepperwood. Phone 800/923-2613. www.avenueofthegiants.net.* Once a major hub for the timber industry, this 31-mile stretch of California State Highway 254 winds through some of the oldest growth forests in the United States, including a jaunt through Humboldt Redwoods State Park. Lined by towering redwoods, the Avenue of the Giants is a fun alternative to the busier Highway 101 as it runs through a number of quaint towns now dependent on tourism instead of logging. The road makes for a nice diversion off the beaten path with good access to both the park and Eel River. For fans of bizarre Americana, a number of kitschy roadside attractions are on and near the highway, including the J. R. R. Tolkien-inspired Hobbiton USA, several drive-through trees, and a house carved from a single 80,000-pound log. **FREE**

King Range National Conservation Area. *1695 Heindon Rd, Garberville (95521). 15 miles W off I-101. Phone 707/825-2300. www.ca.blm.gov.* Approximately 60,000 acres on the coast includes King Peak (4,087 feet). Saltwater fishing on 26 miles of coastline, inland stream fishing (subject to state regulations); hunting, hiking, picnicking, improved camping (fee/car/night).

Full-Service Inn

★★★ **BENBOW INN.** *445 Lake Benbow Dr, Garberville (95542). Phone 707/923-2124; toll-free 800/355-3301; fax 707/923-2897. www.benbowinn.com.* This 1926 Tudor-style mansion resort offers pleasantries such as complimentary English tea and scones served daily in the lobby to a basket of mysteries and poetry in each room. 55 rooms, 4 story. Closed early Jan-early Apr. Check-in 3 pm, check-out noon. Restaurant, bar. Outdoor pool. **$$**

Restaurant

★★ **BENBOW INN.** *445 Lake Benbow Dr, Garberville (95542). Phone 707/923-2124; toll-free 800/355-3301; fax 707/923-2897. www.benbowinn.com.* Overlooking the south fork of the Eel River, this English Tudor-style building was constructed in 1926 and boasts wonderful old-world charm. California menu. Breakfast, dinner. Closed Jan-early Apr. Bar. Children's menu. Business casual attire. Reservations recommended. Outdoor seating. **$$$**

Gilroy (E-2)

See also Salinas, San Jose, San Juan Bautista

Population 41,464
Elevation 200 ft
Information Gilroy Chamber of Commerce, 7471 Monterey St, 95020; phone 408/842-6437
Web Site www.gilroy.org

What to See and Do

Fortino Winery. *4525 Hecker Pass Hwy, Gilroy (95020). 5 miles W via Hwy 152. Phone 408/842-3305. www.fortinowinery.com.* Small family winery. Tours, wine tasting room, picnic area. (Tues-Sat 10 am-5 pm, Sun from 11 am; closed Easter, Thanksgiving, Dec 25) **FREE**

Gilroy Premium Outlets. *681 Leavesley Rd, Gilroy (95020). Phone 408/842-3729. www.premiumoutlets.com/gilroy.* Approximately 150 outlet stores. (Mon-Sat 10 am-9 pm, Sun to 6 pm)

Henry W. Coe State Park. *E Dunne Ave, Morgan Hill (95037). 9 miles N on Hwy 101, then 13 miles E of Morgan Hill on E Dunne Ave. Phone 408/779-2728. www.coepark.org.* Approximately 86,000 acres. Highlights include unusually large manzanita shrubs and a botanical island formed of ponderosa pines. Hiking, backpacking, horseback riding, and mountain biking. Primitive drive-in campsites (no electric). Pine Ridge Museum displays ranch life in the late 1880s (Sat, Sun). Guided walks and evening programs (Mar-June, weekends). (Daily, 24 hours) **$**

Special Event

Gilroy Garlic Festival. *Christmas Hill Park, 7050 Miller Ave, Gilroy (95020). Phone 408/842-1625. www.gilroygarlicfestival.com.* Features Gourmet Alley, a giant open-air kitchen; cooking demonstrations and contests; food and beverage booths; arts and crafts; entertainment. Last full weekend in July. **$$$**

Restaurant

★ **THE WHOLE ENCHILADA.** *Hwy 1, Moss Landing (95039). Phone 831/633-3038. www.wenchilada.com.* Mexican menu. Lunch, dinner. Bar. Casual attire. Outdoor seating. **$$**

Glen Ellen (D-2)

See also Calistoga, Napa, Petaluma, St. Helena, Santa Rosa, Sonoma

Web Site www.sonomavalley.com

Special Event

Wine Country Film Festival. *1200 Henno Rd, Glen Ellen (95442). Phone 707/935-3456. www.winecountryfilmfest.com.* Film festivals always seem to have an aura of glamour and extravagance around them, and that's especially true in the case of the Wine Country Festival. Not only does its proximity to Los Angeles enable it to attract more big stars than other regional film festivals, but the settings themselves look like they've been taken right out of a Hollywood soundstage. All the screenings are outdoors at wineries and parks, so the backdrops are breathtaking. Food and wine also take center stage, and there's plenty of celebratory bubbly on hand. Although the festival doesn't usually announce its schedule until two weeks before it begins, the screenings and other events often sell out well in advance. For out-of-towners, the festival offers special travel packages as well as all-inclusive passes. July-Aug. **$$**

Specialty Lodging

The following lodging establishment is approved by Mobil Travel Guide, but due to its unique and individualized nature has not been given a traditional Mobil Star rating. Included in this listing you may find bed-and-breakfasts, limited-service inns, guest ranches, and other unique hotel properties.

GAIGE HOUSE INN. *13540 Arnold Dr, Glen Ellen (95442). Phone 707/935-0237; toll-free 800/935-0237; fax 707/935-6411. www.gaige.com.* The only distractions that will intrude upon guests of the Gaige House Inn are the crackle of the fireplace, the gurgle of the Calabazas Creek, and the sizzle of the skillet. This paradise for wine lovers is nestled in the woods of picturesque Glen Ellen in the Sonoma Valley of California's wine country. The inn shares a blissful quietude with visitors, from the peaceful garden setting of the pool to hammocks gently swaying in the breeze. Airy and stylish, the guest rooms give the impression of outdoor living, with large windows showcasing views of the tranquil countryside. An Asian aesthetic creates a Zen-like ambience throughout the highly individualized accommodations. Several rooms feature fireplaces, while others enjoy private Japanese gardens. Four off-site cottages are even more secluded and are ideal for longer visits. The chef concocts sensational breakfasts, persuading late sleepers to rise early for memorable morning feasts. 15 rooms, 3 story. Children over 12 years only. Complimentary full breakfast. Check-in 3 pm, check-out 11 am. Outdoor pool, whirlpool. **$$$$**

Restaurants

★ ★ GLEN ELLEN INN. *13670 Arnold Dr, Glen Ellen (95442). Phone 707/996-6409; fax 707/996-1634. www.glenelleninn.com.* California menu. Lunch, dinner. Outdoor seating. **$$$**

★ ★ SAFFRON. *13648 Arnold Dr, Glen Ellen (95442). Phone 707/938-4844; fax 707/938-0298. www.saffronrestaurant.com.* Eclectic California menu. Lunch, dinner. Closed Sun-Mon; Thanksgiving, Dec 25. Reservations recommended. Outdoor seating. **$$**

Grass Valley (D-3)

See also Auburn, Mother Lode Country, Nevada City,

Settled 1849
Population 10,922
Elevation 2,411 ft
Information Chamber of Commerce, 248 Mill St, 95945-6783; phone 530/273-4667 or toll-free 800/655-4667 (CA)
Web Site www.grassvalleychamber.com

Immigrants followed their half-starved cattle to this spot, not knowing that under the thick grass were rich quartz deposits that were to make the Grass Valley area the richest gold mining region in California—the Mother Lode country. The stamp mills, cyanide tanks, and shafts are no longer in operation. Located on the edge of the Tahoe National Forest, Grass Valley has become a recreation center and retirement haven.

A Ranger District office of the Tahoe National Forest is located here.

What to See and Do

Empire Mine State Historic Park. *10791 E Empire St, Grass Valley (95945). Phone 530/273-8522. www.parks.ca.gov.* At one time, this historic hard rock gold mine was the largest and richest in California. The park features a baronial cottage with formal gardens among 850 acres, as well as a visitor center, mining exhibits, and opportunities for hiking and picnicking. Tours. (Jan-Apr: daily 10 am-5 pm; May-Aug: daily 9 am-6 pm: Sept-Dec: daily 10 am-5 pm; closed Dec 25) **$**

Lola Montez House. *248 Mill St, Grass Valley (95945). Phone 530/273-4667. www.grassvalleychamber.com.* Facsimile of 1851 Grass Valley house once owned by Lola Montez; singer, dancer, and *paramour* of the rich and famous. Now houses Grass Valley/Nevada County Chamber of Commerce.

North Star Power House and Pelton Wheel Mining Exhibit. *Mill St and McCourtney Rd, Grass Valley (95949). Phone 530/273-4255.* Hard rock mining display and artifacts; 30-foot Pelton water wheel; stamp mill; largest operational Cornish pump in the United States. (Daily 10 am-5 pm, May-Oct) **DONATION**

Rough and Ready Town. *Hwy 20, Grass Valley. 4 miles W on Hwy 20. Phone 530/272-4320.* Gold strike named after General Zachary Taylor, "Old Rough and Ready." At one time the miners tried to secede from the Union and form the independent Republic of Rough and Ready.

Special Events

Cornish Christmas. *Old Town, Grass Valley. Phone 530/272-8315. www.ncgold.com/Events/Winter/Cornish.html.* Street fair. Cornish treats, musicians, entertainment, vendors. Fridays, late Nov-early Dec. **FREE**

Father's Day Bluegrass Festival. *Nevada County Fairgrounds, 11228 McCourtney Rd, Grass Valley (95949). Phone 209/293-1559. www.cbaontheweb.org.* The largest bluegrass festival on the West Coast, this annual extravanganza features some of the best bluegrass music in the world as well as workshops and children's programs. Camping is available at the fairgrounds. Father's Day weekend. **$$$$**

Nevada County Fair. *Nevada County Fairgrounds, 11228 McCourtney Rd, Grass Valley (95949). Phone 530/273-6217. www.nevadacountyfair.com.* This popular fair is ranked as one of the top five county fairs in the western United States. And it's no wonder. Not only does the fair offer carnival rides, a rodeo, live entertainment, a petting zoo, and horse show (and that's only a few of the events), but it is held at one of the most beautiful fairgrounds in the state. Four days mid-Aug. **$**

Limited-Service Hotel

★ ★ HOLBROOKE HOTEL. *212 W Main St, Grass Valley (95945). Phone 530/273-1353; toll-free 800/933-7077; fax 530/273-0434. www.holbrooke.com.* This historic hotel harkens back to California's gold rush days. Established in 1851, the Holbrooke has hosted such luminaries as Mark Twain, Ulysses S. Grant, and Grover Cleveland. Modern-day guests enjoy quaint touches like brass canopy beds, exposed-brick walls, and clawfoot tubs. The Golden Gate Saloon, one of the longest in continuous operation west of the Mississippi, serves wines and spirits, while the 212 Bistro at the Holbrooke offers elegant meals at brunch, lunch, and dinner. 28 rooms, 2 story. Complimentary continental breakfast. Check-in 3 pm, check-out noon. Restaurant, bar. **$**

Restaurant

★ ★ ★ SWISS HOUSE RESTAURANT. *535 Mill St, Grass Valley (95945). Phone 530/273-8272; fax 530/273-0345. www.swisschef.com.* Swiss, German menu. Dinner. Closed Mon-Tues; also one-two weeks in June. Bar. Casual attire. **$$**

Gualala (D-1)

Population 1,200
Elevation 67 ft
Area Code 707
Zip 95445
Information Redwood Coast Chamber of Commerce, PO Box 199; phone toll-free 800/778-5252
Web Site www.gualala.com

Because of its relative isolation and quiet atmosphere, the area attracts many visitors. Favorite local activities include steelhead, abalone, and silver salmon fishing; canoeing and swimming in the Gualala River; and camping. A debate on the origin of the name "Gualala" has persisted for more than 100 years. Some say it derived from the native Pomo word *qhawala-li*, meaning "water coming down place," while others maintain that it is a Spanish rendering of Valhalla.

What to See and Do

Point Arena Lighthouse and Museum. *45500 Lighthouse Rd, Point Arena (95468). 15 miles N on Hwy 1. Phone 707/882-2777. www.pointarenalighthouse.com.* This 115-foot-tall lighthouse (1908) and Fog Signal Building (1869) houses historical artifacts and photographs. Viewing at top of lighthouse through a two-ton lens. (Apr-Sept: daily 10 am-4:30 pm; Oct-Mar: daily 10 am-3:30 pm; closed Thanksgiving, Dec 25; also weekdays in Dec and Jan) **$**

Limited-Service Hotel

★ ★ SEA RANCH LODGE. *60 Sea Walk Dr, Gualala (95497). Phone 707/785-2371; toll-free 800/732-7262; fax 707/785-2917. www.searanchlodge.com.* On bluff overlooking ocean; 5,500 acres in historic Sea Ranch. 20 rooms, 2 story. Check-in 4 pm, check-out 1 pm. Restaurant, bar. Golf. **$$**

Full-Service Inn

★★★ **ST. ORRES.** *36601 Coast Hwy 1 S, Gualala (95445). Phone 707/884-3303; fax 707/884-1840. www.saintorres.com.* This inn and restaurant are found three hours north of San Francisco on 42 acres of coastal sanctuary. Built by local craftsmen with local materials, the house is similar to a Russian dacha, with onion-domed towers, stained glass, and woodwork. Most rooms provide an ocean view, and the restaurant offers a wonderful menu with fine food. 21 rooms. Complimentary full breakfast. Check-in 3-7 pm, check-out noon. Restaurant. **$**

Specialty Lodgings

The following lodging establishments are approved by Mobil Travel Guide, but due to their unique and individualized nature have not been given a traditional Mobil Star rating. Included in this listing you may find bed-and-breakfasts, limited-service inns, guest ranches, and other unique hotel properties.

BREAKERS INN. *39300 S Hwy 1, Gualala (95445). Phone 707/884-3200; toll-free 800/273-2537; fax 707/884-3400. www.breakersinn.com.* With its panoramic views and ambience throughout, Breakers Inn is the perfect romantic getaway. While there, enjoy the abalone and scuba diving, kayaking, and whale-watching. 27 rooms, 3 story. Complimentary continental breakfast. Check-in 3 pm, check-out 11 am. Restaurant. **$**

NORTH COAST COUNTRY INN. *34591 S Hwy 1, Gualala (95445). Phone 707/884-4537; toll-free 800/959-4537; fax 707/884-1833. www.northcoastcountryinn.com.* Forested setting overlooking Mendocino coast. 6 rooms. Pets accepted, fee. Complimentary full breakfast. Check-in 2-8 pm, check-out 11 am. Whirlpool. **$$**

WHALE WATCH INN BY THE SEA. *35100 S Hwy 1, Gualala (95445). Phone 707/884-3667; toll-free 800/942-5342; fax 707/884-4815. www.whalewatchinn.com.* Situated on the rugged north coast, this inn offers a spectacular view from every room. Enjoy whale watching or use the private entrance to the beach for a romantic walk. 18 rooms, 2 story. Complimentary full breakfast. Check-in 3 pm, check-out 11 am. **$$**

Restaurant

★★★ **ST. ORRES.** *36601 Coast Hwy 1 S, Gualala (95445). Phone 707/884-3335; fax 707/884-1840. www.saintorres.com.* Drive three hours north from San Francisco and you will find a European inn set on 42 acres that is simply astonishing. In the dining room, Rosemary Campiformio's innovative menu changes often to reflect the changes in the North Coast seasons. California, seafood menu. Dinner. Closed Tues-Wed in Jan-May; also three weeks in Dec. Reservations recommended. Natural wood, stained glass. **$$$**

Guerneville

See also Bodega Bay, Fort Ross State Historic Park, Healdsburg, Petaluma, Santa Rosa

Population 2,441
Elevation 56 ft
Information Russian River Region Visitors Bureau, 16209 First St, 95446; phone 707/869-9000 or toll-free 888/644-9001
Web Site www.guerneville-online.com

With swimming, golfing, fishing, canoeing, and hiking nearby, this scenic area is popular for recreational vacations.

What to See and Do

Armstrong Redwoods State Reserve. *25381 Steelhead Blvd, Guerneville. 2 miles N off Hwy 116. Phone 707/865-2391. www.parks.ca.gov.* Named for Colonel James Boydston Armstrong of Ohio, who settled here with his family in 1874. Nature, hiking, riding trails; picnicking. **$**

Korbel Champagne Cellars. *13250 River Rd, Guerneville (95446). Phone 707/824-7000. www.korbel.com.* Produces wine, champagne, and brandy. Guided tours; century-old cellars; champagne, wine tasting and tours daily; garden tours in summer (one in morning, one in afternoon). (Daily; closed holidays) **FREE**

Special Events

Jazz on the River. *Russian River Resort Area, Guerneville (95446). Johnson's Beach. Phone 510/655-9471; toll-free 800/253-8800. www.russianriverbluesfest.com/jazz.* Grab a lawn chair or blanket—maybe even pack a swim suit—and enjoy a day of fun, sun, and some of the nation's best jazz artists. Weekend after Labor Day. **$$$$**

Russian River Blues Festival. *Johnson's Beach, Guerneville (95446). Phone 510/655-9471; toll-free 800/253-8800. www.russianriverbluesfest.com.* Wine tasting, food, arts and crafts, and, of course, world-class blues music featuring some of the most famous blues entertainers around. Mid June. **$$$$**

Full-Service Inn

★ ★ ★ APPLEWOOD INN & RESTAURANT. *13555 Hwy 116, Guerneville (95446). Phone 707/869-9093; toll-free 800/555-8509; fax 707/869-9170. www.applewoodinn.com.* With such activities as hot air balloon rides, hiking beneath the ancient redwoods, canoeing or kayaking the Russian River, the Applewood Inn allows you to truly get away. If you enjoy history, try visiting Fort Ross, an Imperial Russian settlement. 19 rooms, 3 story. Complimentary full breakfast. Check-in 3-8 pm, check-out noon. Restaurant. Outdoor pool, whirlpool. **$$**

Specialty Lodging

The following lodging establishment is approved by Mobil Travel Guide, but due to its unique and i ndividualized nature have not been given a traditional Mobil Star rating. Included in this listing you may find bed-and-breakfasts, limited-service inns, guest ranches, and other unique hotel properties.

RIDENHOUR RANCH HOUSE INN. *12850 River Rd, Guerneville (95446). Phone 707/887-1033; toll-free 888/877-4466; fax 707/869-2967. www.ridenhourinn.com.* 8 rooms, 3 story. Pets accepted, some restrictions; fee. Complimentary full breakfast. Check-in 3-8 pm, check-out 11 am. Whirlpool. **$**

Restaurant

★ ★ APPLEWOOD. *13555 Hwy 116, Guerneville (95446). Phone 707/869-9093; fax 707/869-9170. www.applewoodinn.com.* In Mediterranean-style, historic inn; own vegetable and herb garden. California menu. Dinner. **$$$**

Half Moon Bay (E-1)

See also San Mateo

Population 11,842
Elevation 69 ft
Area Code 650
Zip 94019
Web Site www.halfmoonbaychamber.org

What to See and Do

Half Moon Bay Golf Club. *2 Miramontes Point Rd, Half Moon Bay (94019). Phone 650/726-4438.* Half Moon bay is located just off historic Highway 1, right on the Pacific Ocean. The golf club's two courses, the Old Course and the Ocean Course, vary slightly in their makeup. The Old Course resembles Pebble Beach with its traditional American design, while the Ocean course lets wild grasses overtake the rough and looks more like a links layout. The average round is a little pricey, but you can keep the cost down if you don't lose too many balls in the salty brine that borders several holes. A cart is included in the price, as walking is not permitted. **$$$$**

Limited-Service Hotels

★ ★ BEST WESTERN HALF MOON BAY LODGE. *2400 S Cabrillo Hwy, Half Moon Bay (94019). Phone 650/726-9000; toll-free 800/710-0778; fax 650/726-7951. www.halfmoonbaylodge.com.* Overlooking the Arnold Palmer-designed Half Moon Bay Golf Links and 36 holes of oceanfront golf, this is truly a golfer's paradise. Other activities include whale-watching and the Purisima Creek Redwoods. 80 rooms, 2 story. Complimentary continental breakfast. Check-in 4 pm, check-out 11 am. Fitness room. Outdoor pool, whirlpool. **$$**

★ HOLIDAY INN EXPRESS. *230 S Cabrillo Hwy, Half Moon Bay (94019). Phone 650/726-3400; toll-free 800/465-4329; fax 650/726-1256. www.holiday-inn.com.* 52 rooms, 2 story. Pets accepted; fee. Complimentary continental breakfast. Check-in 3 pm, check-out noon. **$**

Full-Service Resort

★ ★ ★ ★ THE RITZ-CARLTON, HALF MOON BAY. *One Miramontes Point Rd, Half Moon Bay*

(94019). Phone 650/712-7000; fax 650/712-7070. www.ritzcarlton.com. From its craggy clifftop setting to its shingled architecture, The Ritz-Carlton, Half Moon Bay looks like a slice of Scotland on the northern California coast. While the windswept dunes and emerald links hint of a foreign land, this exquisite resort—only 30 miles from San Francisco—has a decidedly West Coast flavor. The public and private rooms are injected with a 21st-century interpretation of 19th-century grand seaside estates. The guest rooms and suites are the essence of relaxed sophistication and high style, with soft colors, floral or striped patterns, and nautical artwork. Golfers develop a soft spot for the resort's 36 oceanfront holes, while others enjoy the thrill of horseback riding on the secluded beach. Two dining venues celebrate traditions while creating their own culinary history. From the oceanfront yoga studio and candlelit Roman mineral bath to the tranquility fountains discovered throughout the facility, the spa delights the senses. Furry friends are welcome in the resort's guest houses. 261 rooms, 5 story. Pets accepted, some restrictions; fee. Check-in 4 pm, check-out noon. High-speed Internet access. Two restaurants, two bars. Children's activity center. Fitness room, fitness classes available, spa. Indoor pool, children's pool, whirlpool. Golf, 36 holes. Tennis. Airport transportation available. Business center. **$$$**

Specialty Lodgings

The following lodging establishments are approved by Mobil Travel Guide, but due to their unique and individualized nature have not been given a traditional Mobil Star rating. Included in this listing you may find bed-and-breakfasts, limited-service inns, guest ranches, and other unique hotel properties.

CYPRESS INN. *407 Mirada Rd, Half Moon Bay (94019). Phone 650/726-6002; toll-free 800/832-3224; fax 650/712-0380. www.cypressinn.com.* Located on Miromar Beach, this inn offers many amenities for their guests to enjoy. 12 rooms, 3 story. Complimentary full breakfast. Check-in 3 pm, check-out noon. Beach. **$$**

MILL ROSE INN. *615 Mill St, Half Moon Bay (94019). Phone 650/726-8750; toll-free 800/900-7673; fax 650/726-3031. www.millroseinn.com.* The well-manicured grounds and beautiful gardens are truly a pleasure to witness. 4 rooms, 2 story. Complimentary full breakfast. Check-in 3-9 pm, check-out 11 am. Fitness room. Whirlpool. **$$**

OLD THYME INN. *779 Main St, Half Moon Bay (94019). Phone 650/726-1616; toll-free 800/720-4277; fax 650/726-6394. www.oldthymeinn.com.* This romantic getaway, a Princess Anne Victorian home built in 1898, sits on a lovely street lined with galleries, antique shops, and restaurants. The inn has seven large, comfortable guest rooms with names like Rosemary, Chamomile, Oregano, and, of course, Thyme. The rooms have enticing featherbeds, fresh-cut flowers, and original artwork; several have Jacuzzis and fireplaces. An English-style herb and flower garden lures guests to the backyard and gives the inn its name. 7 rooms, 2 story. Complimentary continental breakfast. Check-in 3 pm, check-out 11 am. **$$**

SEAL COVE INN. *221 Cypress Ave, Moss Beach (94038). Phone 650/728-4114; toll-free 800/995-9987; fax 650/728-4116. www.sealcoveinn.com.* This bed-and-breakfast overlooks beautiful gardens. A ten-minute walk will take guests to the beach, and a short half-mile drive will take them to San Francisco. All rooms have a small fridge that is filled with complimentary beverages. 8 rooms, 2 story. Complimentary full breakfast. Check-in 3-8 pm, check-out 11 am. **$$**

Spa

★★★★ THE RITZ-CARLTON SPA, HALF MOON BAY. *1 Miramontes Point Rd, Half Moon Bay (94019). Phone 650/712-7040; toll-free 800/241-3333. www.ritzcarlton.com.* Anyone with a penchant for fresh ocean breezes and the feel of sand between their toes will relish time spent here, but this Ritz-Carlton is a true paradise for golfers and spa lovers. Marrying good looks with serious competition, 36 holes of oceanfront golf are sure to delight any player, while the 16,000-square-foot spa is a temple of tranquility for world-weary souls. Everything sparkles at this spa, where fountains enhance the peaceful atmosphere and highlight the facility's spiritual connection to water. Wind down with a co-ed, candlelit Roman mineral bath, or lounge in the oceanfront Jacuzzi. Exercise enthusiasts appreciate the well-equipped fitness center overlooking the ocean and the gazebo lawn. In addition to cardiovascular equipment and weights, the center has a heated yoga studio. Whether you book a soothing lavender facial especially for sensitive skin, pamper yourself with a therapeutic manicure or pedicure, or unwind to the soothing sounds of the sea piped into the room in which you receive a rejuvenating Half Moon Bay facial, these signature treatments are not to be missed. The signature pumpkin body peel is a unique spa experience delivering the nourishing benefits of this local treat. With water therapies, massages, facials, and body treatments, this spa takes care of your every need.

Restaurant

★ ★ PASTA MOON. *315 Main St, Half Moon Bay (94019). Phone 650/726-5125; fax 650/726-7631. www.pastamoon.com.* Italian menu. Lunch, dinner. Closed Thanksgiving, Dec 25. Bar. Reservations recommended. Outdoor seating. **$$**

Hanford

Population 41,686
Elevation 246 ft
Information Hanford Visitor Agency, 200 Santa Fe Ave, Suite D; phone 559/582-0483
Web Site www.hanfordchamber.com

China Alley, the century-old Chinatown, has been saved by Chef Wing's family. Two outstanding restaurants were the reason that presidents Eisenhower and Truman, Mao Tse-tung, and Chiang Kai-shek suggested that others eat in this historic town. One of these restaurants, Imperial Dynasty, remains open.

Full-Service Inn

★ ★ ★ INN AT HARRIS RANCH. *Rte 1, Coalinga (93210). Phone 559/935-0717; toll-free 800/942-2333; fax 559/935-5061. www.harrisranch.com.* Stay in a room with a private patio amid fresh flowers and archways of columns at this hacienda. Take advantage of a flight that lands on the hotel's 2,800-foot private airstrip. 153 rooms, 3 story. Pets accepted, some restrictions; fee. Check-in 3 pm, check-out noon. Restaurant, bar. Fitness room. Outdoor pool, whirlpool. **$**

Specialty Lodging

The following lodging establishment is approved by Mobil Travel Guide, but due to its unique and individualized nature has not been given a traditional Mobil Star rating. Included in this listing you may find bed-and-breakfasts, limited-service inns, guest ranches, and other unique hotel properties.

IRWIN STREET INN. *522 N Irwin St, Hanford (93230). Phone 559/583-8000; toll-free 866/583-7378; fax 559/583-8793. www.irwinstreetinn.com.* Historic buildings (late 1800s), restored; many antiques. 30 rooms, 2 story. Pets accepted; fee. Complimentary continental breakfast. Check-in 3 pm, check-out 11 am. Restaurant. Children's pool. **$**

Hayward

See also Fremont, Oakland, Pleasanton, San Francisco International Airport Area

Population 140,030
Elevation 111 ft
Area Code 510
Web Site www.ci.hayward.ca.us

What to See and Do

Garin Regional Park. *1320 Garin Ave, Hayward (94544). Phone 510/562-7275. www.ebparks.org.* Secluded 1,520 acres in the Hayward hills with vistas of south Bay Area. Fishing at Jordan Pond; bird-watching, hiking, riding trails, picnicking. Interpretive programs at visitor center; historic farm equipment (weekends). **$** Also here is

> **Dry Creek Pioneer Regional Park.** *1320 Garin Ave, Hayward (94544). Enter via Garin Regional Park. Phone 510/562-7275. www.ebparks.org/parks/garin.htm.* On 1,563 acres. Bird-watching, hiking, riding trails, picnicking. Interpretive programs. **$**

Hayward Area Historical Society Museum. *22701 Main St, Hayward (94541). Phone 510/581-0223. www.haywardareahistory.org.* Local history exhibits, library and archives, and corner store. Changing exhibits. (Tues-Sat 11 am-4 pm; closed holidays) **$**

McConaghy Estate. *18701 Hesperian Blvd, Hayward (94541). Phone 510/276-3010; toll-free www.haywardareahistory.org/mcconaghy.html.* (1886) Twelve-room Victorian farmhouse with period furnishings; carriage house, tank house. During December, the farmhouse is decorated for Christmas in 1886. Picnic and play areas are found in adjacent Kennedy Park. (Fri-Sun 1-4 pm; closed holidays, also Jan) **$**

Restaurant

★ ★ RUE DE MAIN. *22622 Main St, Hayward (94541). Phone 510/537-0812; fax 510/537-5587.*

www.ruedemain.com. French, Asian menu. Lunch. Closed holidays. **$$**

Healdsburg (D-1)

See also Bodega Bay, Clear Lake Area, Fort Ross State Historic Park, Guerneville, Santa Rosa

Population 10,722
Elevation 106 ft
Area Code 707
Zip 95448
Information Chamber of Commerce & Visitors Bureau, 217 Healdsburg Ave; phone 707/433-6935 or toll-free 800/648-9922 (CA)
Web Site www.healdsburg.org

What to See and Do

Canoe trips. *Trowbridge Canoe Trips, 13840 Old Redwood Hwy, Healdsburg. Phone 707/433-7247; toll-free 800/640-1386. www.trowbridgecanoe.com.* One-day or two-day trips on Russian River. Equipment and transportation provided. (Apr-Oct) **$$$$**

★ **Healdsburg area wineries.** *Phone 707/433-6935.* More than 60 wineries are located in the northern Sonoma County region; most are open to the public for wine tasting. A map listing the wineries and other area attractions is available from the Chamber of Commerce & Visitors Bureau. Among them are

Chateau Souverain. *400 Souverain Rd, Geyserville (95441). 5 miles N on Hwy 101, Independence Ln exit. Phone toll-free 888/809-4637. www.chateau souverain.com.* Wine tasting, restaurant (lunch daily, dinner Fri-Sun). **FREE**

Simi Winery. *16275 Healdsburg Ave, Healdsburg. Phone toll-free 800/746-4880. www.simiwinery.com.* Winery dates from the turn of the century. Two guided tours every day; wine tasting. (Daily 10 am-5 pm; closed holidays) **FREE**

Warm Springs Dam/Lake Sonoma. *3333 Skaggs Springs Rd, Geyserville (95441). 11 miles W via Hwy 101, exit on Dry Creek Rd. Phone 707/433-9483. www.spn.usace.army.mil/lakesonoma.* Earth-filled dam, anadromous fish hatchery operated by California Department of Fish and Game and the Army Corps of Engineers. Park overlook provides scenic views of lake and nearby wine country. Swimming, fishing, boating (marina); hiking and bridle trails; picnic facilities at marina, at Yorty Creek, and near visitor center; primitive and improved camping. Visitor center. (Wed-Sun; closed holidays) **FREE**

Special Event

Healdsburg Harvest Century Bicycle Tour. *217 Healdsburg Ave, Healdsburg (95448). Phone 707/433-6935. www.healdsburg.org.* Road and mountain bikes tour through Alexander, Russian River, and Dry Creek valleys. Mid-July.

Full-Service Hotels

★ BEST WESTERN DRY CREEK INN. *198 Dry Creek Rd, Healdsburg (95448). Phone 707/433-0300; toll-free 800/222-5784; fax 707/433-1129. www.drycreekinn.com.* If you'd prefer to spend the bulk of your wine country vacation budget on your favorite vintages or some of the area's plentiful antiques, consider the Dry Creek Inn, which puts you within 15 minutes of more than 50 wineries. The well-maintained property includes spacious rooms and a nice pool area. All guests receive a complimentary bottle of Sonoma County wine. 103 rooms, 3 story. Pets accepted; fee. Complimentary continental breakfast. Check-in 3 pm, check-out noon. High-speed Internet access, wireless Internet access. Restaurant. Fitness room. Outdoor pool, whirlpool. **$**

★★★ HOTEL HEALDSBURG. *25 Matheson St, Healdsburg (95448). Phone 707/431-2800; toll-free 800/889-7188; fax 707/431-0414. www.hotelhealdsburg.com.* The Hotel Healdsburg is a hip oenophile's dream. This striking, contemporary hotel right on the historic Town Plaza in northern Sonoma County's charming Healdsburg is a showpiece of minimalist design. The clean lines and uncluttered décor create a serene ambience throughout the public spaces, and the guest rooms and suites echo this sentiment. Windows look out over the plaza or toward the hotel's garden. All of wine country is easily explored from here, but this hotel is a culinary destination of its own, with noted chef Charlie Palmer's lauded Dry Creek Kitchen (see). 55 rooms, 3 story. Pets accepted, some restrictions; fee. Complimentary continental breakfast. Check-in 3 pm, check-out noon. High-speed Internet access. Restaurant, two bars. Fitness room, spa. Outdoor pool, whirlpool. Business center. **$$$$**

Full-Service Inn

★★★ **MADRONA MANOR.** *1001 Westside Rd, Healdsburg (95448). Phone 707/433-4231; toll-free 800/258-4003; fax 707/433-0703. www.madronamanor.com.* This lovely Victorian estate (1881), nestled in the hills above the Dry Creek Valley, has been accommodating guests since 1981. Enjoy quiet conversation with drinks on the veranda or relax by the cozy fire. 22 rooms, 3 story. Children over 12 years only. Complimentary full breakfast. Check-in 3 pm, check-out 11 am. Restaurant. Outdoor pool. **$$$**

Specialty Lodgings

The following lodging establishments are approved by Mobil Travel Guide, but due to their unique and individualized nature have not been given a traditional Mobil Star rating. Included in this listing you may find bed-and-breakfasts, limited-service inns, guest ranches, and other unique hotel properties.

BELLE DE JOUR INN. *16276 Healdsburg Ave, Healdsburg (95448). Phone 707/431-9777; fax 707/431-7412. www.belledejourinn.com.* Beautifully manicured grounds and rolling hills accentuate the peaceful and relaxing atmosphere at this inn. Enjoy a stroll along the footpaths or relax in the hammocks. Try kayaking, canoeing and, of course, wine tasting. 5 rooms. Closed Dec 25. Complimentary full breakfast. Check-in 4-7 pm, check-out 11 am. **$$$**

CALDERWOOD INN. *25 W Grant St, Healdsburg (95448). Phone 707/431-1110; toll-free 800/600-5444. www.calderwoodinn.com.* 6 rooms. Complimentary full breakfast. Check-in 4-6 pm, check-out 11 am. **$$**

CAMELLIA INN. *211 North St, Healdsburg (95448). Phone 707/433-8182; toll-free 800/727-8182; fax 707/433-8130. www.camelliainn.com.* Victorian house; antique furnishings. 9 rooms, 2 story. Complimentary full breakfast. Check-in 3:30-6 pm, check-out 11 am. Outdoor pool. **$$**

DUCHAMP HOTEL. *421 Foss St, Healdsburg (95448). Phone 707/431-1300; toll-free 800/431-9341; fax 707/491-1333. www.duchamphotel.com.* 6 rooms. Pets accepted; some restrictions, fee. Check-in 4-7 pm, check-out 11 am. Outdoor pool, whirlpool. **$$$$**

GEYSERVILLE INN. *21714 Geyserville Ave, Geyserville (95441). Phone 707/857-4343; toll-free 877/857-4343; fax 707/857-4411. www.geyservilleinn.com.* 38 rooms, 2 story. Complimentary continental breakfast. Check-in 3 pm, check-out 11 am. Restaurant. Outdoor pool, whirlpool. **$$**

GRAPE LEAF INN. *539 Johnson St, Healdsburg (95448). Phone 707/433-8140; toll-free 866/433-8140; fax 707/433-3140. www.grapeleafinn.com.* Victorian house (1900). 12 rooms, 2 story. Complimentary full breakfast. Check-in 4-6 pm, check-out 11 am. **$$**

HAYDON STREET INN. *321 Haydon St, Healdsburg (95448). Phone 707/433-5228; toll-free 800/528-3703; fax 707/433-6637. www.haydon.com.* Located in a quiet residential neighborhood at the south end of Healdsburg, this robin's-egg-blue Queen Anne/Victorian house (circa 1912) and cottage (added later) is within walking distance of Healdsburg Plaza shopping and restaurants. A wide veranda and comfortable lawn furnishings provide shady and sunny outdoor seating, while indoor common areas include a parlor, dining room, and breakfast area. Guest rooms are unique in décor and feature antiques, clawfoot tubs, canopy beds, Jacuzzi tubs, and fireplaces. 8 rooms, 2 story. Children over 12 years only. Complimentary full breakfast. Check-in 4-6:30 pm, check-out 11 am. **$$**

HONOR MANSION A RESORT INN. *14891 Grove St, Healdsburg (95448). Phone 707/433-4277; toll-free 800/554-4667; fax 707/431-7173. www.honormansion.com.* An Italianate Victorian house built in 1883, this inn is settled among century-old trees, including the landmark magnolia. For the wine lover, you might consider a local wine tour; for the adventurer, a canoe ride down the Russian River. 13 rooms, 2 story. Complimentary full breakfast. Check-in 4-6 pm, check-out 11 am. Outdoor pool, whirlpool. Tennis. **$$$**

HOPE BOSWORTH. *21253 Geyserville Ave, Geyserville (95411). Phone 707/857-3356; toll-free 800/825-4233; fax 707/857-4673. www.hope-inns.com.* 4 rooms. Complimentary full breakfast. Check-in 3-8 pm, check-out 11 am. **$$**

HOPE MERRILL HOUSE. *21253 Geyserville Ave, Geyserville (95441). Phone 707/857-3356; toll-free 800/825-4233; fax 707/857-4673. www.hope-inns.com.*

8 rooms. Complimentary full breakfast. Check-in 3-8 pm, check-out 11 am. **$$**

Restaurants

★★ **BISTRO RALPH.** *109 Plaza St, Healdsburg (95448). Phone 707/433-1380.* French bistro menu. Lunch, dinner. Closed Sun. Bar. Business casual attire. Reservations recommended. Outdoor seating. **$$**

★★★ **CHATEAU SOUVERAIN.** *400 Souverain Rd, Geyserville (95441). Phone 707/433-3141; fax 707/857-4656. www.chateausouverain.com.* Located in Sonoma County's beautiful Alexander Valley, this restaurant has beautiful views of the hills and vineyard. Chef Martin Courtman focuses on simple yet elegantly prepared meals. The combination is superb. Mediterranean menu. Lunch, dinner, Sun brunch. Closed Jan 1, Dec 25; also Jan-early Feb. Outdoor seating. **$$$**

★★ **DRY CREEK KITCHEN.** *317 Healdsburg Ave, Healdsburg (95448). Phone 707/431-0330; fax 707/431-8990. www.charliepalmer.com.* American menu. Dinner. Bar. Business casual attire. Reservations recommended. Outdoor seating. **$$$**

★ **LOTUS THAI.** *109-A Plaza St, Healdsburg (95448). Phone 707/433-5282. www.lotusthai restaurant.com.* Thai menu. Lunch, dinner. Closed holidays. Casual attire. Reservations recommended. Outdoor seating. **$**

★★★ **MADRONA MANOR.** *1001 Westside Rd, Healdsburg (95448). Phone 707/433-4231; toll-free 800/258-4003; fax 707/433-0703. www.madronamanor.com.* Formal dining in Victorian mansion. California, French menu. Dinner. Closed Mon-Tues in Jan-Apr. Reservations recommended. Outdoor seating. **$$$**

★★ **MANZANITA.** *336 Healdsburg Ave, Healdsburg (95448). Phone 707/433-8111.* Mediterranean menu. Dinner. Closed Mon-Tues; holidays. **$$**

★★ **RAVENOUS.** *420 Center St, Healdsburg (95448). Phone 707/431-1302.* California menu. Lunch, dinner. Closed Mon-Tues; Easter, Thanksgiving, Dec 25. Bar. Outdoor seating. **$$**

Humboldt Redwoods State Park

See also Garberville, Redwood Highway

45 miles S of Eureka via Hwy 101.

Web Site www.parks.ca.gov

This majestic park encompasses more than 52,000 acres, including 17,000 acres of old-growth coastal redwoods. The Avenue of the Giants, home to redwoods that are more than 300 feet tall, parallels Highway 101 and passes through the park. The South Fork of the Eel River follows the Avenue through the park. Recreational opportunities include swimming, fishing, hiking, mountain biking, and camping. Humboldt Redwoods State Park has a visitor center located next to the park headquarters at Burlington, 2 miles south of Weott on the Avenue. Campfire and nature programs are offered in summer. For more information, contact PO Box 100, Weott 95571; phone 707/946-2409. (Daily, dawn-dusk)

What to See and Do

Pacific Lumber Company. *Scotia. www.palco.com.* A cooperative agreement in the late 1920s between the Pacific Lumber Company and the Save-the-Redwoods League led to the establishment of Humboldt Redwoods State Park. Nearly 20,000 acres of magnificent groves once owned by Pacific Lumber are now permanently protected in parks. In Scotia, you can tour Pacific Lumber's mill, said to be the world's largest redwood operation. A museum, open in the summer months, features historic photographs and memorabilia from days gone by. (Mon-Fri; phone 707/764-2222 for tour schedule)

Inverness (D-1)

See also Bodega Bay, San Rafael

Population 1,421
Elevation 20 ft
Area Code 415
Zip 94937
Web Site www.pointreyes.org

What to See and Do

Hog Island Oyster Company. *20215 Hwy 1, Marshall (94940). Phone 415/663-9218. www.hogislandoysters.com.* Located just outside the boundaries of Point Reyes National Seashore in the tiny community of Marshall, the Hog Island Oyster Company has been farming top-notch West Coast oysters in the National Marine Sanctuary of Tomales Bay since 1982. Thanks to the bay's plankton-rich seawater, their beds produce more than 3 million oysters annually, including premium breeds that have been named the "Best American Oyster" in blind taste tests. The farm is also a leading advocate of sustainable and responsible aquaculture. Beyond getting a glimpse of a working oyster farm, visitors can buy fresh oysters to go or to shuck and slurp on-site—the farm provides waterfront picnic tables, shucking knives, and barbecue grills for a small fee. One of Marshall's oldest buildings, an 1860 redwood structure that first served as a general store, is also on the property. (Tues-Sun 9 am-5 pm) **$$**

★ **Point Reyes National Seashore.** *1 Bear Valley Rd, Point Reyes (94956). Phone 415/464-5137. www.nps.gov/pore.* A 20-mile long peninsula of pastoral beachfront jutting into the Pacific, Point Reyes National Seashore is a hodgepodge of active ranchland, dramatic sea cliffs, dense forests, and pristine beaches. It's also on a different tectonic plate than the rest of California and is slowly grinding northward along the infamous San Andreas Fault. Beyond the numerous recreational opportunities here—hiking, backpacking, sea kayaking, and biking are all popular—the seashore is a great spot for wildlife lovers: whale-watching is very popular in the winter and spring, and more than 45 percent of all bird species in North America have been sighted here at one time or another. But the manmade elements are also worth a look: a lighthouse at the peninsula's northernmost point, Johnson's Oyster Farm (where you can buy fresh oysters to cook on your campfire), and a re-creation of a onetime Point Reyes mainstay: a Miwok Indian community. **FREE**

Samuel P. Taylor State Park. *8889 Sir Francis Drake Blvd, Inverness. 2 miles S on Hwy 1 to Olema, then 6 miles E on Sir Francis Drake Blvd. Phone 415/488-9897. www.parks.ca.gov.* On 2,800 acres of wooded countryside with many groves of coastal redwoods. Historic paper mill site. Hiking and bridle trails, mountain biking, horseback riding, picnicking, camping (year-round, by reservations only, fee). **$**

Tomales Bay State Park. *Sir Francis Drake Blvd and Pierce Point Rd, Inverness (94937). 3 miles NW on Sir Francis Drake Blvd, 2 miles N on Pierce Point Rd. Phone 415/669-1140. www.parks.ca.gov.* Virgin groves of Bishop pine and more than 300 species of plants grow on 1,018 acres. Swimming, sand beach, fishing; hiking, biking, picnicking.

Full-Service Inn

★★★ MANKA'S INVERNESS LODGE. *30 Callendar Way, Inverness (94937). Phone 415/669-1034; fax 415/669-1598. www.mankas.com.* This old-time lodge and restaurant is situated in a small coastal village surrounded by national park land. 18 rooms, 2 story. Pets accepted; restrictions, fee. Check-in 4-6 pm, check-out 11 am. Restaurant. **$$$**

Specialty Lodgings

The following lodging establishments are approved by Mobil Travel Guide, but due to their unique and individualized nature have not been given a traditional Mobil Star rating. Included in this listing you may find bed-and-breakfasts, limited-service inns, guest ranches, and other unique hotel properties.

BLACKTHORNE INN. *266 Vallejo Ave, Inverness (94937). Phone 415/663-8621; fax 415/663-8635. www.blackthorneinn.com.* Located in a wooded canyon setting, this rustic structure resembles a treehouse and features decks on four levels. 5 rooms, 4 story. Complimentary full breakfast. Check-in 4-7 pm, check-out 11 am. Whirlpool. **$$$**

OLEMA INN. *10000 Sir Francis Drake Blvd, Olema (94950). Phone 415/663-9559; fax 415/663-8783. www.theolemainn.com.* This country inn was built in 1876. 6 rooms, 2 story. Pets accepted. Complimentary continental breakfast. Check-in 3 pm, check-out 11 am. Restaurant, bar. **$$**

POINT REYES SEASHORE LODGE. *10021 Hwy 1, Olema (94950). Phone 415/663-9000; toll-free 800/404-5634; fax 415/663-9030. www.pointreyesseashore.com.* Rustic; resembles turn-of-the-century lodge. 21 rooms. Fee for children under 12. Complimentary continental breakfast. Check-in 3-6 pm, check-out noon. **$**

TEN INVERNESS WAY. *10 Inverness Way, Inverness (94937). Phone 415/669-1648; fax 415/669-7403. www.teninvernessway.com.* This inn was built in 1904. 5 rooms, 3 story. Complimentary full breakfast. Check-in 3-6 pm, check-out 11 am. **$$**

Restaurants

★ ★ ★ **MANKA'S INVERNESS LODGE.** *30 Callendar Way, Inverness (94937). Phone 415/669-1034; fax 415/669-1598. www.mankas.com.* Built as a hunting lodge (1917). Dinner. Closed Tues-Wed; also first six weeks of the year. **$$$**

★ ★ **OLEMA INN.** *10000 Sir Francis Drake Blvd, Olema (94950). Phone 415/663-9559; fax 415/663-8783. www.theolemainn.com.* French menu. Dinner, brunch. Closed Tues. Outdoor seating. **$$$**

★ **STATION HOUSE CAFE.** *11180 Hwy 1, Point Reyes Station (94956). Phone 415/663-1515; fax 415/663-9443. www.stationhousecafe.com.* American menu. Breakfast, lunch, dinner. Closed Wed; Thanksgiving, Dec 25. Bar. Children's menu. Outdoor seating. **$$**

Inyo National Forest (F-4)

See also Bishop

In this 2,000,000-acre area are seven wilderness areas—John Muir, Golden Trout, Ansel Adams, Boundary Peak, South Sierra, Inyo Mountains, and Hoover—with hundreds of lakes and streams. Impressive peaks include Mount Whitney (14,496 feet) and the famous Minarets, a series of jagged, uniquely weathered peaks in the Sierra Nevada. Devils Postpile National Monument (see) is also within the boundaries of the forest. The Ancient Bristlecone Pine Forest (4,600 years old), 600-million-year-old fossils, views of one of the world's great fault scarps (the eastern Sierra Nevada), and a unique high-elevation alpine desert (10,000-14,000 feet) are all east of Highway 395 in the White Mountains. Palisade Glacier (the southernmost glacier in the United States) is west of Highway 395 (west of the town of Big Pine), on the boundary of John Muir Wilderness and Kings Canyon National Park. There are 83 campgrounds; many of them are accessible to the disabled (inquire for details).

The Mammoth Lakes Area (see MAMMOTH LAKES) includes Mammoth Lakes Basin, Inyo Craters, Earthquake Fault, Hot Creek, and many historic and archaeological features. Ranger naturalists conduct guided tours during the summer and offer ski tours during the winter; evening programs take place in the visitor center all year.

Deer; bear; tule elk; bighorn sheep; rainbow, brown, and golden trout; and a variety of birds abound in the forest. Swimming, fishing, hunting, boating, riding, picnicking, hiking, camping, and pack trips are available. Winter sports include nordic skiing, snow play areas, snowmobiling, and downhill skiing on Mammoth Mountain (see MAMMOTH LAKES) and June Mountain (see JUNE LAKE). For further information, contact the White Mountain Ranger Station, 798 N Main St, Bishop 93514; phone 760/873-2500.

Jackson (D-3)

See also Lodi, Mother Lode Country, Sacramento

Population 3,989
Elevation 1,235 ft
Area Code 209
Zip 95642
Web Site www.ci.jackson.ca.us

A Ranger District office of the El Dorado National Forest (see PLACERVILLE) is located in Jackson.

What to See and Do

Amador County Museum. *225 Church St, Jackson. Phone 209/223-6386.* Exhibits pertaining to gold country displayed in 1859 house; tours of Kennedy Mine model exhibit (fee). (Wed-Sun 10 am-4 pm; closed holidays) **DONATION**

Indian Grinding Rock State Historic Park. *14881 Pine Grove Volcano Rd, Jackson (95665). 11 1/2 miles NE via Hwy 88. Phone 209/296-7488. www.parks.ca.gov.* Site of reconstructed Miwok village with Native American petroglyphs, bedrock mortars. Interpretive trail, picnicking, camping. Regional museum. **$**

Limited-Service Hotels

★ **BEST WESTERN AMADOR INN.** *200 S Hwy*

49, Jackson (95642). Phone 209/223-0211; toll-free 800/543-5221; fax 209/223-4836. www.bestwestern.com. 118 rooms, 2 story. Pets accepted, fee. Check-in 3 pm, check-out noon. Bar. Outdoor pool. **$**

★ **JACKSON GOLD LODGE.** *850 N Hwy 49, Jackson (95642). Phone 209/223-0486; toll-free 888/777-0380; fax 209/223-2905.* 36 rooms, 2 story. Pets accepted, some restrictions; fee. Complimentary continental breakfast. Check-in 3 pm, check-out 11 am. Outdoor pool, children's pool. **$**

Specialty Lodgings

The following lodging establishments are approved by Mobil Travel Guide, but due to their unique and individualized nature have not been given a traditional Mobil Star rating. Included in this listing you may find bed-and-breakfasts, limited-service inns, guest ranches, and other unique hotel properties.

FOXES INN OF SUTTER CREEK. *77 Main St, Sutter Creek (95685). Phone 209/267-5882; toll-free 800/987-3344; fax 209/267-0712. www.foxesinn.com.* Nestled in the Mother Lode country, experience silver service at this idyllic hideaway in your beautifully appointed, Victorian-style room filled with period antiques and exquisite furnishings. The inn is the former Brinn House, built during the gold rush in 1857. 7 rooms, 2 story. Complimentary full breakfast. Check-in 3-6 pm, check-out 11 am. **$$**

GATE HOUSE INN. *1330 Jackson Gate Rd, Jackson (95642). Phone 209/223-3500; toll-free 800/841-1072; fax 209/223-1299. www.gatehouseinn.com.* Landscaped grounds and gardens are what you will find at this beautiful historic Victorian mansion, built in 1902. Just miles from downtown Jackson, enjoy the pleasures of relaxing on the expansive porches or sunbathing by the secluded pool. 6 rooms, 2 story. Children over 12 years only. Complimentary full breakfast. Check-in 3-6:30 pm, check-out 11 am. Outdoor pool. **$**

GREY GABLES BED AND BREAKFAST INN. *161 Hanford St, Sutter Creek (95685). Phone 209/267-1039; toll-free 800/473-9422; fax 209/267-0940. www.greygables.com.* Built in 1897; renovated in 1994. 8 rooms, 3 story. Complimentary full breakfast. Check-in 3-7 pm, check-out 11 am. **$$**

THE HANFORD HOUSE B&B INN. *61 Hanford St, Sutter Creek (95685). Phone 209/267-0747; toll-free 800/871-5839; fax 209/267-1825. www.hanfordhouse.com.* 10 rooms, 2 story. Complimentary full breakfast. Check-in 3-8 pm, check-out 11 am. High-speed Internet access. Business center. **$**

IMPERIAL HOTEL. *14202 Hwy 49, Amador City (95601). Phone 209/267-9172; fax 209/267-9249. www.imperialamador.com.* Built in 1879 (gold rush era). 6 rooms, 2 story. Children over 5 years only. Complimentary full breakfast. Check-in 3 pm, check-out noon. Restaurant. **$**

SUTTER CREEK INN. *75 Main St, Sutter Creek (95685). Phone 209/267-5606; fax 209/267-9287. www.suttercreekinn.com.* Pre-Civil War house. 17 rooms, 2 story. Complimentary full breakfast. Check-in 2:30 pm, check-out 11 am. **$$**

WEDGEWOOD INN. *11941 Narcissus Rd, Jackson (95642). Phone 209/296-4300; toll-free 800/933-4393; fax 209/296-4301. www.wedgewoodinn.com.* Total relaxation is the atmosphere here. Enjoy a nice stroll through the rose arbor that leads to the Victorian gazebo or just relax on the porch swing. If more excitement is what you want, try a game of croquet or horseshoes. 5 rooms, 2 story. Complimentary full breakfast. Check-in 3 pm, check-out 11 am. **$$**

Restaurant

★ **ROSEBUD'S CLASSIC CAFE.** *26 Main St, Jackson (95642). Phone 209/223-1035.* American menu. Breakfast, lunch. Closed Dec 25. Closed Tues. Children's menu. **$**

June Lake (E-4)

See also Lee Vining, Mammoth Lakes

Population 425
Elevation 7,600 ft
Area Code 760
Zip 93529
Web Site www.junemountain.com

What to See and Do

June Mountain Ski Area. *85 Boulder Dr, June Lake. W of Hwy 395. Phone toll-free 800/626-6684. www.junemountain.com.* Two detachable quad, five double chairlifts; patrol, school, rentals; snowboarding; cafeteria, bar, day care center. Longest run 2 1/2 miles; vertical drop 2,590 feet. Half-day rates. (Mid-Nov-Apr, daily) **$$$$**

Lake recreation. *June Lake. I-395 N from Mammoth Lakes, then Hwy 158 W.* Fishing, sailing, windsurfing, swimming; hiking, scenic drives. (Daily)

Limited-Service Hotel

★ BOULDER LODGE MOTEL. *2282 Hwy 158, June Lake (93529). Phone 760/648-7533; toll-free 800/458-6355; fax 760/648-7330. www.boulderlodge.net.* 60 rooms, 2 story. Check-in 4 pm, check-out 11 am. Children's activity center. Indoor pool, children's pool, whirlpool. Tennis. Overlooking June Lake. **$**

Restaurant

★ ★ SIERRA INN. *US 395 and Hwy 158, June Lake (93529). Phone 760/648-7774; fax 760/648-7990. www.sierrainnrestaurant.com.* American menu. Breakfast, lunch, dinner. Closed Oct. Bar. Children's menu. Casual attire. Reservations recommended. Valet parking. **$$**

Lake Tahoe Area (D-3)

Web Site www.visitinglaketahoe.com

Lake Tahoe is one of the most magnificent mountain lakes in the world, with an area of about 200 square miles, an altitude of approximately 6,230 feet, and a maximum depth of more than 1,600 feet. Mostly in California, partly in Nevada, it is circled by paved highways edged with campgrounds, lodges, motels, and resorts. The lake, with some fine beaches, is surrounded by forests of ponderosa, Jeffrey and sugar pine, white fir, juniper, cedar, aspen, dogwood, and cottonwood, as well as a splendid assortment of wildflowers.

The Sierra Nevada, here composed mostly of hard granite, is a range built by a series of roughly parallel block faults along its eastern side, which have tipped the mountainous area to the west, with the eastern side much steeper than the western. Lake Tahoe lies in a trough between the Sierra proper and the Carson Range, similarly formed and generally regarded as a part of the Sierra, to its east.

There are spectacular views of the lake from many points on the surrounding highways. Eagle Creek, one of the thousands of mountain streams that feed the lake, cascades 1,500 feet over Eagle Falls into Emerald Bay at the southwestern part of the lake. Smaller mountain lakes are scattered around the Tahoe area; accessibility varies. Tahoe and El Dorado National Forests stretch north and west of the lake, offering many recreational facilities.

Public and commercial swimming (there are 29 public beaches), boating, and fishing facilities are plentiful. In winter, the area is a mecca for skiers. There is legalized gambling on the Nevada side.

Note: accommodations around Lake Tahoe are listed under South Lake Tahoe, Tahoe City, and Tahoe Vista. In this area, many motels have higher rates in summer and during special events and holidays. Reservations are recommended.

What to See and Do

Alpine Meadows Ski Area. *2600 Alpine Meadows Rd, Lake Tahoe Area (96145). 6 miles NW of Tahoe City off Hwy 89. Phone 530/583-4232. www.skialpine.com.* Best known for its varied terrain—*Skiing* magazine labeled it a mountain with "a mild side and a wild side"—Alpine Meadows consists of 2,000 acres split between six bowls, steep chutes, and wide-open glades (25 percent beginner, 40 percent intermediate, and 35 percent advanced). The resort—13 miles south of I-80 at Truckee—features 14 lifts, a pair of snowboarding-oriented terrain parks, and a 600-foot superpipe for serious carvers. The nearest accommodations are in Tahoe City. (Mid-Nov-late May, daily) **$$$$**

D. L. Bliss State Park. *Hwy 89, Tahoma. 17 miles S of Tahoe City on Hwy 89. Phone 530/525-7277. www.parks.ca.gov.* Named for a local lumber and railroad baron of the early 1900s, D. L. Bliss State Park is on the western shore of Lake Tahoe and is home to a popular campground, a few trails, and good water access for swimmers and anglers. The park also boasts one of the lake's most sublime vistas: Rubicon Point affords views 100 feet down into Tahoe's blue depths. Also noteworthy is Balancing Rock Nature Trail, a half-mile jaunt to a 130-ton granite monolith positioned atop a much thinner pedestal. **$**

Desolation Wilderness Area. *Eldorado National Forest, 100 Forni Rd, Placerville (95667). Phone 530/622-5061. www.fs.fed.us/r5/eldorado/wild/deso.* Once known as Devil's Valley, Desolation is known for a natural beauty that rivals Yosemite's, but without the roads and, by extension, traffic. The granite peaks and 130 alpine lakes in this 64,000-acre wilderness southwest of Lake Tahoe still attract their fair share of backpackers and anglers, but the fact that travel is limited to horseback or foot helps keep the volume down. Glaciers were responsible for carving and polishing the rock here—1,000-foot-thick sheets of ice covered the entire area 200,000 years ago. The rocky ground supports limited tree cover and vegetation, but the animal life—including mule deer, black bears, porcupines, badgers, and coyotes—is diverse. The lakes and streams have sustaining populations of rainbow and brook trout, making fishing a big draw. Backpackers and hikers operate under daily quotas; reservations are required.

Emerald Bay State Park. *Hwy 89, Tahoe City. 22 miles S of Tahoe City on Hwy 89. Phone 530/525-7232. www.parks.ca.gov.* Home to the Scandinavian-style castle known as Vikingsholm (see), Emerald Bay State Park is, true to its name, one of the crown jewels of California's state park system. Centered on the glacially carved inlet of its name, the park is surrounded by granite peaks and cliffs on the west side of Lake Tahoe. The park is home to the only island in the entire lake, Fanette Island, a lone chunk of granite that survived the glacial period. Below the lake's surface is another noteworthy aspect: Underwater Park, a scuba-diving hotspot, thanks to the presence of numerous shipwrecks dating to the late 1800s, the heyday of the long-gone Emerald Bay Resort. There are also several nature trails, a 70-site campground, and a beach with swimming access. **$**

Grover Hot Springs State Park. *3415 Hot Springs Rd, Lake Tahoe Area. 29 miles S of South Lake Tahoe on Hwy 89. Phone 530/694-2248. www.parks.ca.gov.* This California state park sits where the Sierra Nevada and the Great Basin meet, a pine-clad valley surrounded on three sides by majestic peaks. Six mineral springs feed a concrete pool with a water temperature in excess of 100° F. The hot springs are hot year-round, soothing hikers, anglers, and campers in the summer and cross-country skiers and snowshoers in the winter. (Daily; closed Jan 1, Thanksgiving, Dec 25)

Heavenly Ski Resort. *3860 Saddle Rd, South Lake Tahoe (96150). 1 mile E of Hwy 50. Phone 775/586-7000; toll-free 800/243-2836. www.skiheavenly.com.* One of the crown jewels of Vail Resorts' portfolio of ski meccas, Heavenly straddles the Nevada-California border just south of Lake Tahoe and has a distinct ski area on each side of the line. In California, Heavenly West offers 18 lifts that take skiers and snowboarders to trails that have the state's longest vertical drop—3,500 feet—and a snowboarding half pipe. On the Nevada side of the mountain, Heavenly North has 11 lifts, a snowboard cross-trail, and a terrain park. In both states, the snow is revered and plentiful: 300 inches is the average annual snowfall, bolstered by one of the biggest snowmaking operations in the world. A redeveloped village opened in 2002, featuring a bevy of eateries, nightspots, shops, and hotel rooms, not to mention a movie multiplex and an ice-skating rink. **$$$$**

Kirkwood Mountain Resort. *1501 Kirkwood Meadows Dr, Lake Tahoe Area. 30 miles S off Hwy 88. Phone 209/258-6000; toll-free 877/547-5966 (snow conditions). www.kirkwood.com.* This beautiful resort is less crowded than some of the slopes closer in and has a nice variety of terrain among its 2,300 acres (15 percent beginner, 50 percent intermediate, and 35 percent advanced). It's also quite high, with a base of 7,800 feet and a vertical rise that adds another 2,000. There are 12 lifts in all, plus a halfpipe and a snowboard park that blasts loud music. Kirkwood also has about 12 miles of groomed cross-country trails, a 15-mile snowshoe trail system, and a wide range of on-mountain accommodations. (Mid-Nov-mid-May, daily) **$$$$**

Lake Tahoe Cruises. *900 Ski Run Blvd, Lake Tahoe Area (96150). Phone 775/589-4906. www.laketahoecruises.com.* This long-standing operation offers a full slate of cruises—breakfast, brunch, lunch, dinner/dance, and sightseeing. The fleet includes a pair of Mississippi River-style paddlewheelers used for the scheduled cruises: the 151-foot MS *Dixie II,* ported in Zephyr Cove, and the *Tahoe Queen,* based out of South Lake Tahoe. The former offers lake cruises year-round; the latter becomes a ski shuttle/charter vessel during winter. Cruises depart daily, and reservations are required. **$$$$**

Lake Tahoe Historical Society Museum. *3058 Lake Tahoe Blvd (Hwy 50), Lake Tahoe Area (95705). Phone 530/541-5458.* The highlights at this South Lake Tahoe museum are a scale model of the SS *Tahoe*—

a legendary steamship that was intentionally sunk in 1940—and the Lake Tahoe Basin's oldest building (1859). Among the black-and-white photos and rusty pioneer implements, you'll also find a fine collection of Washoe basketry. A few blocks west in Bijou Community Park is the museum's narrow-gauge railroad exhibit. (Late June-Labor Day: Tues-Sat afternoons; rest of year: weekends) **$**

Riding. *Camp Richardson Corral, 4 Emerald Bay Rd, Lake Tahoe Area. Phone 530/541-3113.* One- and two-hour rides, breakfast and steak rides (May-Oct, daily); sleigh rides (Dec-Mar). Contact PO Box 8335, South Lake Tahoe 96158. **$$$$**

Sierra at Tahoe. *1111 Sierra at Tahoe Rd, Twin Bridges (95735). 12 miles W of South Lake Tahoe on Hwy 50. Phone 530/659-7453. www.sierraattahoe.com.* Founded in 1968, Sierra at Tahoe is a big but low-key resort. Its 2,000 acres are set against a 2,212-foot rise, with 25 percent beginner, 50 percent intermediate, and 25 percent expert slopes. A favorite of snowboarders, the resort features two terrain parks, two halfpipes, and a superpipe. There is also a popular tubing hill, but no on-mountain lodging. Shuttle bus service is available. (Nov-Apr, daily) **$$$$**

Squaw Valley USA. *1960 Squaw Valley Rd, Olympic Valley (96146). 7 miles NW of Tahoe City off Hwy 89. Phone 530/583-6985. www.squaw.com.* Five high-speed quads, eight triple, eight double chairlifts, aerial cable car, gondola, five surface lifts; patrol, school, rentals; snack bars, cafeterias, restaurants, bars. Longest run 3.2 miles; vertical drop 2,850 feet. (Mid-Nov-mid-May, daily) Cross-country skiing (25 miles); rentals (Mid-Nov-late-May, daily). Aerial cable car also operates year-round (daily and evenings). **$$$$**

Tahoe State Recreation Area. *Hwy 28, Tahoe City. Phone 530/583-3074 (general information). www.parks.ca.gov.* **Sugar Pine Point State Park.** Cross-country skiing. Camping (fee). Pine Lodge is refurbished turn-of-century summer home (Ehrman Mansion), tours (July-Labor Day). Pier, picnicking, camping. (Late May-late Sept, daily 8 am-9 pm)

Tallac Historic Site. *Emerald Bay Rd at Fallen Leaf Rd, South Lake Tahoe (96150). Hwy 89, 3 miles NW of South Lake Tahoe. Phone 530/541-5227.* "Old Tahoe" is preserved in the form of this National Forest Service site, comprising three grand estates that give a good sense of what a Lake Tahoe getaway was like a century ago. Two of the estates date from the Roaring Twenties. Today, the Baldwin estate houses a museum, and the Heller estate, also known as Valhalla, serves as a community center and performing arts venue. The Tevis-Pope estate, which is the oldest of the three (1894), offers tours and living history presentations. All three properties sit on a quarter-mile of lakefront near Emerald Bay and the ruins of the long-abandoned Tallac Resort, once known as the "greatest casino in America." The site is also the former domain of the native Washoe people, and trails and exhibits examine their lifestyle. Visitor center (daily 8 am-5:30 pm, Fri until 7 pm). Museum (Wed-Mon 11 am-3 pm). **$**

US Forest Service Visitor Center. *870 Emerald Bay Rd, South Lake Tahoe (96150). On Hwy 89, 3 miles NW of South Lake Tahoe. Phone 530/573-2600.* Information, campfire programs, guided nature walks and self-guided trails. Visitors look into Taylor Creek from the Stream Profile Chamber; exhibits explain role of stream to Lake Clarity. (Memorial Day-Oct) **FREE**

Valhalla Boathouse Theatre. *Tallac Historic Site, Hwys 50 and 89, Lake Tahoe Area (96150). Phone 530/541-4975.* Dating to the 1880s, this former boathouse predates the neighboring historic structures at the Tallac Historic Site. After a long period of neglect, it was restored and converted into a charming 200-seat theatre that now serves as a cultural focal point for South Lake Tahoe. During the summer, plays, concerts, and films take place here nearly every night.

Vikingsholm. *Emerald Bay State Park, Lake Tahoe Area. 10 miles S of Tahoe City on Hwy 89. Phone 530/525-7277. www.vikingsholm.com.* Nestled amidst the cedars at the base of granite cliffs in Emerald Bay State Park is "Lake Tahoe's Hidden Castle," Vikingsholm. The surrounding land was the site of one of the lake's first summer homes (1863), but the Scandinavian-style castle dates to 1929. Then-landowner Lorna Knight commissioned her nephew, a Swedish architect, to design the place, taking cues from Norwegian churches, Swedish castles, and more common wooden homes in both countries. Note that visitors must hike a steep 1-mile trail from the parking lot to get to Vikingsholm's doors. Parking is limited. (Mid-June-late Sept: daily 10 am-4 pm) **$**

Special Events

American Century Investments Celebrity Golf Championship. *Edgewood Tahoe Golf Course, Lake Pkwy and Stateline Ave, Lake Tahoe Area (96150). Phone 530/544-5050.* More than 70 sports and entertainment celebrities compete for a $500,000 purse. Mid-July.

Great Gatsby Festival. *Tallac Historic Site, Hwys 50 and 89, Lake Tahoe Area (96150). Phone 530/544-5227.* The Tallac Historic Site turns back the clock to the roaring twenties for a weekend every August with this living history event; period costumes (flapper dresses, boiler hats) are encouraged. The atmosphere matches the F. Scott Fitzgerald classic for which the event is named, with an array of old-fashioned events: an antique car show, a croquet competition, big band concerts, and even a pie-eating contest. Mid-Aug.

Lake Tahoe Music Festival. *Throughout the city. Contact PO Box 62, Tahoe City (96145). Phone 530/583-3101. www.tahoemusic.org.* This highly regarded concert series has been a Lake Tahoe tradition since 1982. The festival tends to focus on classical and choral music-a 2003 highlight was a performance by the Vienna Boys Choir—but the calendar doesn't begin and end with symphonies and waltzes: It also includes an eclectic slate of performers, practitioners of everything from bluegrass to jazz to poetry. Special events include opening and closing galas, as well as an art auction. The performances take place during July and August at multiple venues in the Tahoe area (including Squaw Valley, Donner Lake, and the campus of Sierra Nevada College). The festival also has an educational component called the Academy Program, by which professional performers-in-residence tutor young artists. Late July-mid-Aug.

Larkspur

See also Corte Madera

Population 12,014
Elevation 43 ft
Area Code 415
Web Site www.ci.larkspur.ca.us

Restaurant

★ ★ ★ **LARK CREEK INN.** *234 Magnolia Ave, Larkspur (94939). Phone 415/924-7766; fax 415/924-7117. www.larkcreek.com.* Celebrity chef Bradley Ogden prepares a tantalizing California country cuisine menu that changes daily. Situated in a cozy 1888 Victorian, the property is surrounded by redwood trees and magnolias and gives the feeling of being in an ideal California country home. American menu. Lunch, dinner, Sun brunch. Bar. Children's menu. Outdoor seating. **$$**

Lassen Volcanic National Park (B-3)

See also Chester, Red Bluff, Redding

44 miles E of Redding via Hwy 44; 51 miles E of Red Bluff via Hwy 36, 89.

Web Site www.nps.gov/lavo

This 165-square-mile park was created to preserve the area including 10,457-foot Lassen Peak, a volcano last active in 1921. Lassen Park, in the southernmost part of the Cascade Range, contains glacial lakes, virgin forests, mountain meadows, and snow-fed streams. Hydrothermal features, the Devastated Area, and Chaos Jumbles can be seen from Lassen Park Road. Boiling mud pots and fumaroles (steam vents) can be seen a short distance off the road at Sulphur Works. At Butte Lake, colorful masses of lava and volcanic ash blend with the forests, meadows, and streams. The peak is named for Peter Lassen, a Danish pioneer who used it as a landmark in guiding immigrant trains into the northern Sacramento Valley.

After being denuded in 1915 by a mudflow and a hot blast, The Devastated Area is slowly being reclaimed by small trees and flowers. The Chaos Crags, a group of lava plugs, were formed some 1,100 years ago. Bumpass Hell, a colorful area of mud pots, boiling pools, and steam vents, is a 3-mile round-trip hike from Lassen Park Road. Clouds of steam and sulfurous gases pour from vents in the thermal areas. Nearby is Lake Helen, named for Helen Tanner Brodt, the first woman to climb Lassen Pea in 1864. At the northwest entrance is a visitor center (late June-Labor Day, daily) where you can find information about the park's human, natural, and geological history. There are guided walks during the summer; self-guided nature trails; and evening talks at some campgrounds. Camping (fee) is available at eight campgrounds; there's a two-week limit, except at Lost Creek and Summit Lake campgrounds, which impose a seven-day limit; check at a ranger station for regulations.

Lassen Park Road is usually open mid-June-mid-October, weather permitting. The Sulphur Works entrance to the south and the Manzanita Lake entrance to the northwest are open during the winter months for winter sports.

There are facilities for the disabled, including the visitor center, comfort station, and amphitheater at Manzanita Lake.

Lava Beds National Monument

Web site www.nps.gov/labe

Seventy-two square miles of volcanic formations are preserved here in the extreme northeastern part of the state. Centuries ago, rivers of molten lava flowed here. In cooling, they formed a strange and fantastic region. Cinder cones dot the landscape, one rising 476 feet from its base. Winding trenches mark the collapsed roofs of lava tubes, an indicator of the 380 caves beneath the surface. Throughout the area are masses of lava hardened into weird shapes. Spatter cones may be seen where vents in the lava formed vertical tubelike channels, some only 3 feet in diameter but reaching downward 100 feet.

Outstanding caves include Sentinel Cave, named for a lava formation in its passageway; Catacombs Cave, with passageways resembling Rome's catacombs; and Skull Cave, with a broad entry cavern reaching approximately 80 feet in diameter. (The name comes from the many skulls of mountain sheep that were found here.) The National Park Service provides ladders and trails in the 24 caves that are easily accessible to the public.

One of the most costly Native American campaigns in history took place in this rugged, otherworldly setting. The Modoc War of 1872-1873 saw a small band of Native Americans revolt against reservation life and fight a series of battles with US troops. Although they were obliged to care for their families and live off the country, the Modocs held off an army almost ten times their number for more than five months.

There is a campground at Indian Well (fee, water available mid-May-Labor Day), and there are picnic areas at Fleener Chimneys and Captain Jacks Stronghold (no water). Guided walks, audiovisual programs, cave trips, and campfire programs are held daily, mid-June-Labor Day. Park headquarters has a visitor center (daily). No gasoline is available in the park, so fill your gas tank before entering. Golden Eagle, Golden Age, and Golden Access passports accepted (see MAKING THE MOST OF YOUR TRIP). Per vehicle **$.**

Lee Vining (E-4)

See also Bridgeport, June Lake, Yosemite National Park

Settled 1923
Population 600
Elevation 6,781 ft
Area Code 760
Zip 93541
Web Site www.leevining.com

A Ranger District office of the Inyo National Forest (see) is located here.

What to See and Do

Mono Lake. *Hwy 395 and 3rd St, Lee Vining. Phone 760/647-6595. www.monolake.org.* Located in the Mono Basin National Forest Scenic Area, Mono Lake is one of North America's oldest lakes. It contains 250 percent more salt than the Pacific ocean, and millions of migratory waterfowl feed on brine shrimp and brine flies. Stratified limestone rock formations, or tufa, surround the lake. Samuel Clemens (aka Mark Twain) wrote about the lake and its islands, volcanoes, and gulls in *Roughing It.* (Daily) Forest Service Visitor Center offers exhibits, movie; guided tours of lake area (June-Sept, daily; fee). Summer interpretive programs (July and Aug). NE of town. Lake access on W side. **$$**

Limited-Service Hotel

★ YOSEMITE GATEWAY MOTEL. *51340 Hwy 395, Lee Vining (93541). Phone 760/647-6467; toll-free 800/282-3929; fax 760/647-1046. www.yosemitegatewaymotel.com.* View of Mono Lake. 16 rooms, 2 story. Check-in 2 pm, check-out 11 am. **$**

Restaurant

★ ★ WHOA NELLIE DELI. *22 Vista Point Rd, Lee Vining (93541). Phone 760/647-1088; fax 760/647-6019. www.thesierraweb.com/tiogagasmart.* Located in the Tioga Gas Mart is this shockingly gourmet restaurant where chef Matt Toomey serves unique, progressive California cuisine. Eclectic menu. Breakfast, lunch, dinner. **$**

Livermore

See also Fremont, Mount Diablo State Park, Oakland, Pleasanton, San Jose, Santa Clara

Population 73,345
Elevation 486 ft
Area Code 925
Zip 94550
Information Chamber of Commerce, 2157 First St; phone 925/447-1606
Web Site www.livermorechamber.org

What to See and Do

Concannon Vineyard. *4590 Tesla Rd, Livermore (94550). 3 miles S of I-580 via N Livermore Ave. Phone 925/456-2500. www.concannonvineyard.com.* (1883) Picnic facilities. Tours (by appointment); wine tasting (daily 11 am-4:30 pm). **FREE**

Course at Wente Vineyards. *5050 Arroyo Rd, Livermore (94550). Phone 925/456-2475. www.wentegolf.com.* Designed by PGA Tour pro Greg Norman, the course makes use of some of California's vaunted wine country, about 45 minutes east of San Francisco. The course is built into a lot of hillsides, so elevation changes are common. The first hole features a tee box some 100 feet higher than the green, so big hitters can have a short second shot to the green even from the 429-yard black tees. Greens fees include a cart, practice balls, a divot tool, and a yardage guide. No matter how the round goes, be sure to have some Napa Valley wine after the round. **$$$$**

Del Valle Regional Park. *7000 Del Valle Rd, Livermore (94550). From I-580, S on N Livermore, E on Tesla Rd, right on Mines Rd, S on Del Valle Rd to park entrance. Phone 925/373-0332. www.ebparks.org/parks/delval.htm.* Centerpiece of these 3,997 acres is a 5-mile-long lake. Swimming, windsurfing, lifeguards in summer, fishing, boating (launch, rentals; 10 mph limit); nature trails, picnicking, camping (all year, fee; 150 sites; dump station, showers, 20 water/sewage hookups). Visitor center. **$$**

Lawrence Livermore National Laboratory's Visitor Center. *7000 East Ave, Livermore (94550). Phone 925/422-4599. www.llnl.gov.* Research center operated by the University of California for the US Department of Energy. Features multimedia presentation of the laboratory's major programs; interactive and audio displays and computers allow for hands-on activities. (Mon-Fri, afternoons; closed holidays) **FREE**

Poppy Ridge Golf Course. *4280 Greenville Rd, Livermore (94550). Phone 925/447-6779. www.poppyridgegolf.com/livermore.* Similar to Pebble Beach's partner course, Poppy Hills, this facility has 27 holes, but only one tree original to the landscape before the course was built. The three courses are named Merlot, Zinfandel, and Chardonnay, mirroring the types of wine available in the surrounding Napa Valley. So take a day to enjoy the views, the wine, and the golf. **$$$$**

Shadow Cliffs Regional Park. *Between Livermore and Pleasanton; from I-580, S on Santa Rita Rd, left onto Valley Ave, then left onto Stanley Blvd to park entrance. Phone 925/846-3000. www.ebparks.org/parks/shadow.htm.* Formerly a gravel quarry on 255 acres. Swimming, bathhouse, fishing, boating (rentals); hiking and riding trails, picnicking. Giant water slide (Apr-Labor Day; fee). **$$**

Wente Brothers Winery. *5565 Tesla Rd, Livermore (94550). 2 1/2 miles SE via S Livermore Ave. Phone 925/456-2405. www.wentevineyards.com.* Guided tours, tasting. Café. (Daily 11 am-6:30 pm; closed holidays) **FREE**

Special Events

Livermore Rodeo. *Robertson Park, 3200 Robertson Park Rd, Livermore (94550). Phone 925/447-3008. www.livermorerodeo.org.* This PRCA sanctioned rodeo bills itself as the "World's Fastest Rodeo." Second weekend in June.

Livermore Wine Country Festival. *Phone 925/373-1795. www.livermoredowntown.com.* Taste wines from local vineyards, enjoy live entertainment, and browse arts and crafts booths at this event for the whole family. Early May.

Restaurant

★ ★ ★ **WENTE VINEYARDS.** *5050 Arroyo Rd, Livermore (94550). Phone 925/456-2450; fax 925/456-2401. www.wentevineyards.com.* Wente Vineyards' comfortably elegant restaurant is set amidst beautiful gardens and lush vineyards. The creativity and innovation of the dishes along with the warmth of the hospitality makes it a feast for all the senses. International/Fusion menu. Lunch, dinner, Sun brunch. Bar. Valet parking. Outdoor seating. **$$**

Lodi (D-2)

See also Jackson, Sacramento, Stockton

Population 56,999
Elevation 51 ft
Area Code 209
Information Lodi District Chamber of Commerce, 35 S School St, PO Box 386, 95240; phone 209/367-7840
Web Site www.lodichamber.com

Located in the northernmost county in the San Joaquin Valley, Lodi is surrounded by vineyards and a rich agricultural area. Lodi is home to the flame Tokay grape and more than 50 wineries.

What to See and Do

Camanche Recreation Area, South Shore. *11700 Wade Ln, Wallace (95254). 24 miles E off Hwy 12. Phone 209/763-5178.* Swimming, water-skiing, fishing, boating (rentals, marina); tennis, picnic facilities, concession, groceries, camping (fee; hook-ups); cottages. **$$$$**

Lodi Lake Park. *125 N Stockton St, Lodi. 1 mile W of Hwy 99 on Turner Rd. Phone 209/333-6742.* Major recreational facility for a wide area. Swimming beach, boating (rentals, ramp); nature area, discovery center, picnicking. (Daily) **$**

Micke Grove Park & Zoo. *11793 N Micke Grove Rd, Lodi (95240). Off Hwy 99, Armstrong Rd exit (from Stockton). Phone 209/953-8800. www.mgzoo.com.* Japanese garden, camellia and rose gardens; picnicking; historical museum. Zoo and park (daily; closed Dec 25). **$**

Special Events

Lodi Grape Festival and Harvest Fair. *Lodi Grape Festival Grounds, 413 E Lockeford St, Lodi (95240). Phone 209/369-2771. www.grapefestival.com.* A 60-year tradition during the September grape harvest, the Lodi Grape Festival celebrates the season with food, wine, live music, dancing, and—for those who don't mind the mess—a grape-stomping contest. The event's home base, the Lodi Grape Festival Fairgrounds, is a 20-acre facility with an RV campground, a 1,500-seat outdoor theatre, and a number of dining halls. **$$**

Lodi Spring Wine Show. *Lodi Grape Festival Grounds, 413 E Lockeford St, Lodi (95240). Phone 209/369-2771.* Wine from California wineries. Hors d'oeuvres served. Late Mar.

Limited-Service Hotel

★ HOLIDAY INN EXPRESS. *1140 S Cherokee Ln, Lodi (95240). Phone 209/334-6422; toll-free 800/432-7613; fax 209/368-7967. www.holiday-inn.com.* 95 rooms, 2 story. Complimentary continental breakfast. Check-in 3 pm, check-out 11 am. Fitness room. Outdoor pool, whirlpool. **$**

Full-Service Inn

★ ★ ★ WINE AND ROSES HOTEL. *2505 W Turner Rd, Lodi (95242). Phone 209/334-6988; toll-free 877/310-3358; fax 209/334-6570. www.winerose.com.* Historic inn, built in 1902; individually decorated rooms; fireplace in sitting room. 36 rooms, 2 story. Pets accepted; fee. Check-in 3 pm, check-out 11 am. Restaurant, bar. Fitness room, spa. **$$**

Restaurant

★ ★ WINE AND ROSES. *2505 W Turner Rd, Lodi (95242). Phone 209/334-6988; toll-free 877/310-3358; fax 209/334-6570. www.winerose.com.* California menu. Lunch, dinner, brunch. Closed Dec 25. Children's menu. Casual attire. Outdoor seating. **$$$**

Los Gatos

See also San Jose, Santa Cruz, Saratoga

Founded circa 1870
Population 28,592
Elevation 385 ft
Area Code 408
Zip 95030
Information Town of Los Gatos Chamber of Commerce, 349 N Santa Cruz Ave; phone 408/354-9300
Web Site www.losgatosweb.com

Free-roaming wildcats inspired the name "La Rinconada de Los Gatos," the corner of the cats. Today, two sculptured cats, Leo and Leona, guard the town entrance at Poets Canyon.

What to See and Do

The Art Museum of Los Gatos. *4 Tait Ave, Los Gatos (95031). Tait and Main. Phone 408/354-2646. www.losgatosmuseum.org.* Art displays, art history. In restored firehouse. (Wed-Sun afternoons; closed holidays) **DONATION**

Forbes Mill Museum of Regional History. *75 Church St, Los Gatos (95030). Phone 408/395-7375. www.losgatos.org.* Historic landmark; former grain mill. (Wed-Sun noon-4 pm) **DONATION**

Old Town. *50 University Ave, Los Gatos (95030).* Shops, restaurants, art galleries, flowered garden walkways, housed in what was once an elementary school (1921).

Youth Science Institute. *296 Garden Hill Dr, Los Gatos (95032). Phone 408/356-4945. www.ysi-ca.org.* Located in Vasona Lake County Park, this Junior Museum houses aquaria with local and native fish, reptiles, and amphibians. Native plant trail. Museum (Mon-Fri); park (daily). Parking fee. **DONATION**

Limited-Service Hotels

★ ★ LA HACIENDA INN. *18840 Los Gatos-Saratoga Rd, Los Gatos (95030). Phone 408/354-9230; toll-free 800/235-4570; fax 408/354-7590. www.lahaciendainn.com.* 20 rooms. Complimentary continental breakfast. Check-in 2 pm , check-out noon. Restaurant. Outdoor pool, whirlpool. **$$**

★ LOS GATOS LODGE. *50 Los Gatos-Saratoga Rd, Los Gatos (95032). Phone 408/354-3300; toll-free 800/231-8676; fax 408/354-5451. www.losgatoslodge.com.* 129 rooms, 2 story. Pets accepted. Complimentary continental breakfast. Check-in 10 am, check-out noon. Bar. Fitness room. Outdoor pool. **$**

★ ★ ★ TOLL HOUSE HOTEL. *140 S Santa Cruz Ave, Los Gatos (95030). Phone 408/395-7070; toll-free 800/238-6111; fax 408/395-3730. www.tollhousehotel.com.* Surrounded by picturesque low hills, this European-decorated hotel provides a relaxing atmosphere for all. Fine dining can be found within walking distance, and there is plenty of history in the area. 115 rooms, 3 story. Pets accepted: fee. Check-in 3 pm, check-out noon. High-speed Internet access. Restaurant, bar. Fitness room. Whirlpool. Business center. **$$**

Restaurant

★ C. B. HANNEGAN'S. *208 Bachman Ave, Los Gatos (95030). Phone 408/395-1233; fax 408/395-2584. www.cbhannegans.com.* International menu. Lunch, dinner, late-night. Closed July 4, Dec 25. Bar. Casual attire. Outdoor seating. **$$**

Madera (F-3)

See also Fresno

Population 43,207
Elevation 270 ft
Area Code 559
Zip 93637
Web Site www.cityofmadera.org

Limited-Service Hotel

★ ★ BEST WESTERN MADERA VALLEY INN. *317 N G St, Madera (93637). Phone 559/664-0100; fax 559/664-0200. www.maderavalleyinn.com.* 93 rooms, 5 story. Pets accepted; fee. Complimentary continental breakfast. Check-in 4 pm, check-out noon. Restaurant, bar. Fitness room. Outdoor pool. **$**

Mammoth Lakes (E-4)

See also Bishop, Devils Postpile National Monument, June Lake

Population 7,093
Elevation 7,800 ft
Area Code 760
Zip 93546
Information Mammoth Lakes Visitor Bureau, Hwy 203, PO Box 48; phone 760/934-2712 or toll-free 888/466-2666
Web Site www.visitmammoth.com

Spectacular scenery and a variety of recreational opportunities are found in this region of rugged peaks, numerous lakes, streams, and waterfalls, alpine meadows, and extensive forests. Much of the outstanding scenery was created by volcanos or carved by glaciers.

What to See and Do

Fishing, boating, rentals. *Hwy 203, Mammoth Lakes. Phone 760/924-5500. www.fs.fed.us/r5/inyo/about/*

#mammothrd. **Crowley Lake**, *6 miles S on I-395.* **Sherwin Creek** (fishing, camping), *3 miles SE of ranger station.* **Convict Lake**, *4 miles SE of Mammoth Junction, 2 miles W of I-395. SW on Lake Mary Rd* are **Twin Lakes** (camping), **Lake Mary** (camping), **Coldwater** (camping), **Lake George** (camping), **Pine City** (camping). Fees charged at recreation sites. All campgrounds first-come, first-served basis (self-registration). For further details and information on other areas contact the Mammoth Ranger District, Box 148, Mammoth Lakes, 93546. **$$$**

Hot Creek Fish Hatchery. *85 Old School Rd, Mammoth Lakes (93546). S on I-395 to Hot Creek Fish Hatchery exit, then Owens River Rd. Phone 760/934-2664. www.visitmammoth.com.* Most of the 5 million fish planted in eastern Sierra lakes and rivers are bred here. (Daily) **FREE**

Hot Creek Geological Site. *Hwy 203, Mammoth Lakes. S on I-395 to Hot Creek Fish Hatchery exit, then Owens River Rd. Phone 760/924-5500. www.visitmammoth.com.* Hot springs and fumaroles in a river setting surrounded by mountains. Boardwalks lead through a steep canyon for viewing volcanic features. Fly-fishing for trout is popular upstream from the hot springs. **FREE**

John Muir/Ansel Adams Wilderness Areas. *Phone toll-free 877/444-6777.* The 581,000-acre John Muir Wilderness Area is the largest and most-visited wilderness area in California. Marked by majestic mountains, an abundance of crystal-clear lakes and streams, and precipitous river gorges, this rugged, roadless expanse is the heart of the High Sierra, with an elevation that starts at about 4,000 feet and rises to snowcapped summits that top 14,000 feet. In tandem with the adjacent Ansel Adams Wilderness Area, the John Muir Wilderness Area attracts hikers, climbers, and fishermen, but backpacking is the true religion in these parts. A pair of trails that traverse both wilderness areas—the John Muir and the Pacific Crest—are prime routes for multiday backpacking excursions. For campers, reservations are key, as the forest service enforces quotas regarding the number of overnight visitors during the peak summer season.

Mammoth Mountain Ski Area. *1 Minaret Rd, Mammoth Lakes (93546). In Inyo National Forest. Phone 760/934-0745. www.manmothmountain.com.* Just 20 miles southeast of the confines of Yosemite National Park on the eastern fringe of the Sierras, the Mammoth Mountain ski area is a winter sports paradise, culminating in the 11,053 peak of the mountain itself. Blanketed by nearly 400 inches of snow each year, Mammoth's 3,500 skiable acres are served by 27 lifts and include three terrain parks and three halfpipes popular with the snowboarders. But that's not all: The comprehensive resort also encompasses a bevy of lodging and dining options, a golf course, a cross-country ski area, and a summertime mountain biking park. Beyond the hikers and bikers who come in the summer, fly-fishermen flock to the area's snowmelt-fed streams and lakes. The operating company is also behind June Mountain, a smaller, quieter ski area about 20 miles north of Mammoth Mountain. **$$$$**

Mammoth Visitor Center Ranger Station. *Hwy 203, Mammoth Lakes (93546). At the edge of town, surrounded by Inyo National Forest. Phone 760/924-5500. www.visitmammoth.com.* Visitor summer activities (July 4-Labor Day weekend) include interpretive tours, evening programs, and Jr.-Ranger programs (6-12 years). Visitor center (year-round). All family campgrounds (except half of Sherwin Creek, which requires reservations) on first-come, first-served basis; group camping and Sherwin Creek camping reservable through National Forest recreation reservations (800/280-2267). Shady Rest campground open in winter (tent camping only). Self-registration for backpackers during nonquota season; wilderness permits required all year. Quota season is the last Friday in June-mid-Sept. Reservations may be made six months to two days in advance by contacting Wilderness Reservations, PO Box 430, Big Pine 93513. Phone 888/374-3773. **$$$**

Pack trips. For wilderness camping.

Mammoth Lakes Pack Outfit. *Lake Mary Rd, Mammoth Lakes. 4 miles SW on Lake Mary Rd near Lake Mary. Phone 760/934-2434; toll-free 888/475-8747. www.mammothpack.com.*

McGee Creek Pack Station. *1 McGee Creek Rd, Mammoth Lakes (93546). 12 miles SW. Phone 760/878-2207; toll-free 800/854-7404. www.mcgeecreekpackstation.com.*

Red's Meadow Pack Station and Resort. *Red Meadow Rd and Hwy 203, Mammoth Lakes (93546). 15 miles W on Minaret Hwy. Phone 760/934-2345; toll-free 800/292-7758. www.redsmeadow.com.*

Limited-Service Hotel

★ QUALITY INN. *3637 Main St, Mammoth Lakes (93546). Phone 760/934-5114; toll-free 877/424-6423; fax 760/934-5165. www.qualityinn.com.* This well-maintained hotel is conveniently located on the way to the ski slopes, yet close to the center of town. The large indoor whirlpool eases the tired muscles of weary skiers, and the underground garage parking protects against winter's chill. Rooms have refrigerators and microwaves. 61 rooms, 2 story, all suites. Complimentary continental breakfast. Check-in 2 pm, check-out 11 am. Children's activity center. Whirlpool. **$**

Full-Service Inn

★★★ MAMMOTH MOUNTAIN INN. *1 Minaret Rd, Mammoth Lakes (93546). Phone 760/934-2581; toll-free 800/626-6684; fax 760/934-0701. www.mammothmountain.com.* Amenities include mountain bike park, rock climbing, scenic chairlift rides, and more. 211 rooms, 3 story. Check-in 4 pm, check-out 11 am. Two restaurants, two bars. Children's activity center. Outdoor pool, whirlpool. **$$**

Martinez (D-2)

See also Antioch, Concord, Oakland, Vallejo

Population 35,866
Elevation 23 ft
Area Code 510
Zip 94553
Web Site www.cityofmartinez.org

What to See and Do

Briones Regional Park. *5363 Alhambra Valley Rd, Lafayette (94553). N entrance 2 miles S of Arnold Industrial Hwy (Hwy 4) via Alhambra Valley Rd. Phone 510/635-0135.* Covers 5,484 acres of rolling hills and wooded ravines. John Muir Nature Area at north end. Hiking on many trails including two self-guided nature trails. Picnicking. Archery range. Connects with Briones to Mount Diablo Trail. (Daily) **$**

John Muir National Historic Site. *4202 Alhambra Ave, Martinez (94553). Phone 925/228-8860. www.nps.gov/jomu.* House built in 1882 was the home of the conservationist, author, and advocate of the National Park system. Visitor center, film, self-guided tours (Wed-Sun; closed Jan 1, Thanksgiving, Dec 25). Guided tour (Wed-Sun). Martinez Adobe (1849) is also on the grounds. **$**

Marysville (D-2)

See also Nevada City, Oroville

Settled 1842
Population 12,268
Elevation 63 ft
Area Code 530
Zip 95901
Information Yuba-Sutter Chamber of Commerce, 429 10th St, PO Box 1429; phone 530/743-6501

Marysville is at the confluence of the Yuba and Feather rivers. The river town was once the third-largest community in the state. Hydraulic mining has raised the Yuba River bed so that it is above, rather than below, the city. The river is contained by huge levees. Named for a survivor of the Donner Party, the town was the head of river navigation—the point where miners continued upriver by foot to the gold diggings.

Special Events

Bok Kai Festival. *Downtown, 100 C St, Marysville (95901). Phone 530/674-3413. www.bokkaifestival.com.* Parade, street entertainment, Lion Dances, martial arts demonstrations; 5K run/walk; climaxed by firing of the "Lucky Bombs." Late Feb-early Mar.

California Dried Plum Festival. *Yuba-Sutter Fairgrounds, 442 Franklin Ave, Yuba City (95991).* To celebrate California's dried plum industry, this weekend festival features live music, wine tasting, celebrity chefs, art displays, children's activities, and, of course, culinary creations with prunes as the main ingredient. First weekend after Labor Day.

Stampede Days. *Riverfront Park, 500 Bizz Johnson Dr, Marysville (95901). Phone 530/695-2727.* Stampede and rodeo sponsored by the Flying U Rodeo; parade, activities. Memorial Day weekend.

Limited-Service Hotel

★★ BEST WESTERN BONANZA INN. *1001 Clark Ave, Yuba City (95991). Phone 530/674-8824; toll-free 800/562-5706; fax 530/674-0563. www.bwbonanzainn.com.* 123 rooms, 3 story. Check-in 3 pm, check-out noon. High-speed Internet access. Restaurant, bar. Outdoor pool, whirlpool. **$**

Mendocino (C-1)

See also Fort Bragg, Ukiah, Willits

Founded 1852
Population 824
Elevation 125 ft
Area Code 707
Zip 95460
Information Fort Bragg-Mendocino Coast Chamber of Commerce, 332 N Main St, PO Box 1141, Fort Bragg 95437; phone 707/961-6300 or toll-free 800/726-2780
Web Site www.mendocinocoast.com

Once a remote lumber port, Mendocino has evolved into a cultural center and popular vacation spot. The town's 19th-century legacy is reflected in its Cape Cod/New England architecture.

What to See and Do

Apple Farm. *18501 Greenwood Rd, Philo (95466). Phone 707/895-2461. www.philoapplefarm.com.* This 2,000-tree orchard about 120 miles north of San Francisco grows more than 80 varieties of apple trees, and invites guests to pick fresh apples themselves. The peak season is September and October, and the apple stock is entirely sold out before it gets mushy, usually by mid-November. At the height of the season, visitors can get a glimpse at the active kitchen, where apples are made into preserves, butters, syrups, and cider.

Fetzer Vineyards. *13601 Eastside Rd, Hopland (95449). Phone 707/744-7600. www.fetzer.com.* The well-known wine makes its home in vineyards near Hopland, about 100 miles north of San Francisco. The tasting room offers free samples and also sells Fetzer clothing and souvenirs. Other notable amenities include a 10-room bed-and-breakfast, a professional teaching kitchen, deli, and organic gardens. The winery also has a tasting room in Mendocino.

Kelley House Museum & Library. *45007 Albion St, Mendocino (95460). Phone 707/937-5791. www.mendocinohistory.org.* (1861) Displays feature antique photographs, exhibits of local artifacts, and private collections. (Oct-May: Fri-Mon 1-4 pm; June-Sept: daily 1-4 pm) **FREE**

Mendocino Art Center. *45200 Little Lake St, Mendocino (95460). Phone 707/937-5818. www.mendocinoartcenter.org.* With an idyllic location overlooking the Pacific Ocean, the Mendocino Art Center (MAC) opened in 1959 and was the focal point for Mendocino's revitalization as an artistic community after its logging economy faltered a few years earlier. For the time since, MAC has been a haven for artists in all media looking for relief from the urban bustle. The facility, which sits on a location used in the James Dean movie *East of Eden*, features a main gallery where the exhibits change monthly and a pair of rental galleries generally occupied by month-long, one-artist shows. (For all three, the focus is squarely on the working artist.) There are a number of artists-in-residence who open their studios to the public on a regular basis, and a full slate of workshops in disciplines ranging from jewelry-making to drama. A community theatre group, the Mendocino Theatre Company, also makes its home here. (Daily; closed Jan 1, Dec 25) **FREE**

Mendocino Headlands. *735 Main St, Mendocino. Phone 707/937-5397. www.parks.ca.gov.* Includes an 1850s building (Ford House Visitor Center) containing exhibits on town and local history (daily). **FREE**

Onion Patch Country Market. *8000 Hwy 29, Kelseyville (95451).* A rural counterpoint to the Bay Area's urban shopping meccas, the Onion Patch Country Market offers a wide variety of art, crafts, and collectibles from local artisans. The stock on hand usually includes a good deal of sculptures as well as paintings, glass art, and woodwork, ranging in tone from clean and simple to whimsical and bizarre. The market is held on summer Saturdays in Kelseyville outside the Onion Patch, and offers a local visitor center and gift shop. (May-Sept, Sat 7 am-noon)

Russian Gulch. *Hwy 1, Mendocino. 2 miles N via Hwy 1. Phone 707/937-5804. www.parks.ca.gov.* Swimming beach, entry point for skin divers, fishing; hiking and bicycle trails, picnicking, camping (Apr-mid-Oct).

Van Damme. *Hwy 1, Little River. 3 miles S via Hwy 1. Phone 707/937-5804. www.parks.ca.gov.* In the southeast portion of this 2,190-acre park is Pygmy Forest, where poor soil conditions inhibit tree growth. Some trees, nearly 200 years old, have trunks only 1/4 inch in diameter. Fishing, beach with access for divers and boaters; nature and hiking trails, picnicking, camping.

Special Events

Crab and Wine Days Festival. *Phone 707/961-6300; toll-free 866/466-3636. www.gomendo.com.* Docks lined with crab traps, crab-clad banners waving in the seaside breeze, and oodles of fresh crab and great

Mendocino

A thriving lumber town way back in the 1850s, a quiet backwater a century after that, and now a popular artists' colony and resort town, the entire village of Mendocino is listed on the National Historic Register. It's a great place for strolling, with wide, quiet streets leading past old water towers, sea captains' homes, inns, galleries, shops, and restaurants. Much of the town is surrounded by Mendocino Headlands State Park, where cliffs overlooking the ocean are honeycombed by some 3 miles of trails. During the November to March migration season, you might spot California grey whales off the coast. The village itself is small enough that you could wander almost all of its streets in an hour or two, or make a day of it by browsing through the small museums and shops. Start your walk on Main Street at the corner of Evergreen, on the eastern edge of town not far from Highway 1. Stroll west along Main Street, where you'll pass the Sweetwater Inn, which incorporates one of Mendocino's remaining water towers that provided fresh water to settlers' homes here nearly 150 years ago. (Of the town's 80-plus 19th-century water towers, only a dozen survive today.) Look for another tower just beyond, at the corner of Main and Howard streets. Continuing along Main, stop into the Ford House, an 1854 home that serves as the interpretive center for the Mendocino Headlands State Park; a small museum with local artifacts and nature displays is inside. Walk the rest of Main Street, which is lined with inns, restaurants, and galleries, and turn right at Woodward Street to Albion Street. Turn right again on Albion and walk east. About halfway down the first block on the northern side of the road is the Kwan Tai Temple, the oldest Chinese temple along the north coast. In the next block, between Kasten and Lansing streets, look for the MacCallum House Inn (45020 Albion St), which combines Victorian architecture with rooms located in a converted water tower. On the other side of Albion Street (45007) is the Kelley House Museum, where old photos reveal more Mendocino history. At the end of the block, turn left up Lansing Street, then right on Ukiah Road past Howard Street. On the south side of Ukiah on the block between Howard and Evergreen streets is the Sweetwater Gardens (955 Ukiah Rd), another inn that incorporates a water tower. Nearby, the well-known Café Beaujolais (961 Ukiah Rd) serves candlelight dinners that rank with the best along the entire north coast. Backtrack along Ukiah to Lansing Street, and go right up to Little Lake Street. Turn left and go one block west to the corner of Ford Street. There you'll find Blair House, an inn better known as Jessica Fletcher's house in the fictitious Cabot Cove, Maine, on the long-running television series *Murder, She Wrote,* starring Angela Lansbury. Mendocino's weather-beaten architecture, often compared to that of New England, managed to fool millions of viewers. From here, if you still have energy, walk west along just about any street to pick up a trail leading out to the Mendocino Headlands and enjoy the sea views and salt air.

wine—all signs that Mendocino's Crab and Wine Days are in effect. Held annually since 2000 in late January and early February (the height of crabbing season), the week-long event is a Dungeness crab lover's dream. Dozens of local businesses, including charter boats, restaurants, wineries, galleries, and breweries, team up to offer a full and varied slate of activities that includes harbor cruises and fishing trips, cooking classes, crab cake cook-offs, concerts, and, of course, crab dinners and wine-tasting events. The festival draws dozens of top-name chefs, authors, and winemakers every year, and many of the bed-and-breakfasts in the area offer packages that include tickets and other perks, but rooms usually sell out well in advance. **$$$$**

Mendocino Christmas Festival. *Main and Franklin sts, Mendocino (95437).* Tour of inns; events. First two weeks in Dec.

Mendocino Music Festival. *735 Main St, Mendocino (95460). Phone 707/937-2044. www.mendocinomusic.com.* Chamber, symphonic, choral, opera, and jazz concerts. Twelve days in July. **$$$$**

Whale Festival. *Phone 707/961-6303. www.mendocinocoast.com.* Whale-watching walks, wine tasting, chowder tasting. Early Mar.

Full-Service Inns

★★★ **ALBION RIVER INN.** *3790 N Hwy 1,*

Albion (95460). Phone 707/937-1919; toll-free 800/479-7944; fax 707/937-2604. www.albionriverinn.com. Set in a historic town on 10 secluded acres, this elegant inn offers many complimentary treats including breakfast, wine, robes, and binoculars. You can even enjoy the breathtaking views of the ocean bluffs and rugged north coast from your bathtub. 20 rooms. Complimentary full breakfast. Check-in 3 pm, check-out noon. Restaurant. **$$**

★ ★ ★ **HARBOR HOUSE INN.** *5600 S Hwy 1, Elk (95432). Phone 707/877-3203; toll-free 800/720-7474; fax 707/877-3452. www.theharborhouseinn.com.* The elegant rooms and social areas of this refurbished 1916 bed-and-breakfast are surrounded by serene gardens. The dining room presents a stunning view of the ocean and Greenwood Cove. 10 rooms, 2 story. Children over 16 years only. Complimentary full breakfast. Check-in 3 pm, check-out noon. Restaurant. **$$$**

★ ★ ★ **HERITAGE HOUSE.** *5200 N Hwy 1, Little River (95456). Phone 707/937-5885; toll-free 800/235-5885; fax 707/937-0318. www.heritagehouseinn.com.* Guests may stay in one of the blufftop cottages found scattered over the 37 acres of green grass and gardens stretched along the Pacific coastline. 66 rooms, 2 story. Check-in 3 pm, check-out noon. Restaurant. **$$$**

★ ★ ★ **THE HILL HOUSE INN MENDOCINO.** *10701 Palette Dr, Mendocino (95460). Phone 707/937-0554; toll-free 800/422-0554; fax 707/937-1123. www.hillhouseinn.com.* This inn was the setting for the televison show, *Murder, She Wrote.* Rooms offer views of the ocean or garden, while every table in the dining room faces the ocean. 44 rooms, 2 story. Check-in 3 pm, check-out noon. Restaurant, bar. **$**

★ ★ ★ **MENDOCINO HOTEL AND GARDEN SUITES.** *45080 Main St, Mendocino (95460). Phone 707/937-0511; toll-free 800/548-0513; fax 707/937-0513. www.mendocinohotel.com.* Stay in Victorian elegance at this hotel situated on the northern California coastline. 51 rooms, 3 story. Check-in 4 pm, check-out noon. Restaurant, bar. **$$**

★ ★ ★ **MACCALLUM HOUSE INN.** *45020 Albion St, Mendocino (95460). Phone 707/937-0289; toll-free 800/609-0492; fax 707/937-2243. www.maccallumhouse.com.* 32 rooms. Pets accepted, some restrictions. Complimentary full breakfast. Check-in 4 pm, check-out 11 am. High-speed Internet access. Restaurant. Beach. **$$**

★ ★ ★ **THE STANFORD INN BY THE SEA.** *Hwy 1 at Comptche Ukiah Rd, Mendocino (95460). Phone 707/937-5615; toll-free 800/331-8884; fax 707/937-0305. www.stanfordinn.com.* Come feel at home at this inn situated on organic gardens and a farm located on the rugged Mendocino coast. Take in the panoramic view of the gardens and ocean while enjoying fine artwork and a wood-burning stove in the rooms. 41 rooms, 3 story. Pets accepted, some restrictions; fee. Complimentary full breakfast. Check-in 4-9 pm, check-out noon. Restaurant. Fitness room. Indoor pool, whirlpool. Airport transportation available. Business center. **$$$$**

Specialty Lodgings

The following lodging establishments are approved by Mobil Travel Guide, but due to their unique and individualized nature have not been given a traditional Mobil Star rating. Included in this listing you may find bed-and-breakfasts, limited-service inns, guest ranches, and other unique hotel properties.

AUBERGE MENDOCINO. *8200 N Hwy 1, Mendocino (95460). Phone 707/937-0088; toll-free 800/347-9252; fax 707/937-3620. www.rachelsinn.com.* 9 rooms. Pets accepted, restrictions, fee. Complimentary full breakfast. Check-in 3 pm, check-out 11 am. **$$**

BLACKBERRY INN. *44951 Larkin Rd, Mendocino (95460). Phone 707/937-5281; toll-free 800/950-7806. www.blackberryinn.biz.* Guests can stay in one of the theme rooms, each offering a unique stay, modeled after a Western movie set. Each room may be different, but the service remains consistent. 16 rooms. Pets accepted, some restrictions; fee. Complimentary continental breakfast. Check-in 2-8 pm, check-out 11 am. **$$**

BREWERY GULCH INN. *9401 N Coast Hwy 1, Mendocino (95460). Phone 707/937-4752; toll-free 800/578-4454; fax 707/937-1279. www.brewerygulchinn.com.* 10 rooms. Children over 12 years only. Complimentary full breakfast. Check-in 3-7 pm, check-out noon. **$$**

DENNEN'S VICTORIAN FARMHOUSE. *7001 N Hwy 1, Mendocino (95460). Phone 707/937-0697; toll-free 800/264-4723; fax 707/937-5238. www.victorianfarmhouse.com.* 12 rooms. Complimentary full breakfast. Check-in 3 pm, check-out 11 am. **$$**

ELK COVE INN. *6300 S Hwy 1, Elk (95432). Phone 707/877-3321; toll-free 800/275-2967; fax 707/877-1808. www.elkcoveinn.com.* This romantic bed-and-breakfast, with its stunning ocean views, serenely overlooks the shore. Relax on the roof deck or in the charming garden gazebo. 15 rooms. Complimentary full breakfast. Check-in 3-8 pm, check-out noon. Bar. **$$**

GLENDEVEN INN. *8205 N Hwy One, Little River (95456). Phone 707/937-0083; toll-free 800/822-4536; fax 707/937-6108. www.glendeven.com.* 10 rooms. Complimentary full breakfast. Check-in 3-7 pm, check-out 11 am. **$$**

HEADLANDS INN. *Albron and Howard sts, Mendocino (95460). Phone 707/937-4431; toll-free 800/354-4431; fax 707/937-0412. www.headlandsinn.com.* Enjoy breakfast in bed, afternoon tea and cookies, and peace and quiet at this 1868 Victorian house that was built as the town barber shop. Art galleries, small shops, superb restaurants, golf, and biking will keep guests busy. 7 rooms, 3 story. Complimentary full breakfast. Check-in 3-7 pm, check-out 11 am. **$$**

INN AT SCHOOLHOUSE CREEK. *7051 N Hwy 1, Little River (95460). Phone 707/937-5525; toll-free 800/731-5525; fax 707/937-2012. www.schoolhouse creek.com.* Built in 1862; on 8 1/2 acres; gardens, meadows, forests. 13 rooms. Pets accepted, some restrictions; fee. Complimentary continental breakfast. Check-in 3 pm, check-out 11 am. **$$**

JOSHUA GRINDLE INN. *44800 Little Lake Rd, Mendocino (95460). Phone 707/937-4143; toll-free 800/474-6353. www.joshgrin.com.* Guests at this historic 1879 inn may enjoy the rugged coastline and rising redwoods on horseback or by hiking or may visit the many surrounding shops. 10 rooms, 2 story. Complimentary full breakfast. Check-in 1 pm, check-out 11 am. Airport transportation available. **$**

STEVENSWOOD LODGE. *8211 Shoreline Hwy, Mendocino (95460). Phone 707/937-2810; toll-free 800/421-2810; fax 707/937-1237. www.stevenswood.com.* 10 rooms. Check-in 3 pm, check-out noon. Restaurant. **$$**

WHITEGATE INN. *499 Howard St, Mendocino (95460). Phone 707/937-4892; fax 707/937-1131. www.whitegateinn.com.* Restored using Victorian architecture, this inn treats guests to charming décor, fine antiques, and fresh-cut flowers. Enjoy the ocean view from the comfort of your room. 7 rooms, 2 story. Children over 10 years only (in inn). Complimentary full breakfast. Check-in 3-6 pm, check-out 11 am. **$$**

Restaurants

★★★ **ALBION RIVER INN.** *3790 N Hwy 1, Albion (95410). Phone 707/937-1919; toll-free 800/479-7944; fax 707/937-2604. www.albionriverinn.com.* Dine in the charm and breathtaking beauty of the north coast of California on a menu of international flavors and Mendocino's local produce. The view here is simply magnificent. Coastal country menu. Dinner. Bar. **$$$**

★★★ **CAFE BEAUJOLAIS.** *961 Ukiah St, Mendocino (95460). Phone 707/937-5614; fax 707/937-3656. www.cafebeaujolais.com.* Surrounded by a large and beautiful garden filled with antique roses, edible flowers, and unusual plants, this café features cuisine that uses locally grown organic produce and freshly baked goods from their on-site bakery, "The Brickery." French, California menu. Dinner. Closed Dec 25. **$$$**

Menlo Park

See also Palo Alto, Redwood City, San Francisco, Santa Clara, Saratoga

Founded 1854
Population 30,785
Elevation 70 ft
Area Code 650
Zip 94025
Web Site www.ci.menlo-park.ca.us

What to See and Do

Filoli House and Gardens. *86 Cañada Rd, Woodside (94062). N on El Camino Real to Woodside Rd (Hwy 84), then 4 miles W to Cañada Rd, then 5 miles N. Phone 650/364-8300. www.filoli.org.* (1917) This 654-acre estate contains the Georgian-style residence built for William B. Bourn II and 16-acre formal gardens. The gardens are an Italian Renaissance-style of parterres, terraces, lawns, and pools. The house was featured in the television series, *Dynasty*. House and garden: guided tours (mid-Feb-Oct: Tues-Sat 10 am-3:30 pm), reservations required; self-guided tours, no reservations required. Three-mile guided nature hike (Sat), reservations required. **$$**

Stanford Linear Accelerator Center (SLAC). *2575 Sand Hill Rd, Menlo Park (94025). E of I-280. Phone 650/926-2204. www.slac.stanford.edu.* This 426-acre national facility houses a 2-mile-long linear accelerator that generates the highest energy electron beams in the world. The 2 1/2-hour tour consists of orientation, slide show, and bus tour. (Limited hours; reservations required) **FREE**

Sunset Magazine Gardens. *80 Willow Rd, Menlo Park (94025). Phone 650/321-3600. www.sunset.com.* Publishers of *Sunset* magazine and books. Self-guided tour of gardens. (Mon-Fri; closed holidays) **FREE**

Limited-Service Hotel

★ MENLO PARK INN. *1315 El Camino Real, Menlo Park (94025). Phone 650/326-7530; toll-free 800/327-1315; fax 650/328-7539. www.menloparkinn.com.* 30 rooms, 2 story. Complimentary continental breakfast. Check-in 2 pm, check-out 11 am. High-speed Internet access. Business center. **$**

Full-Service Hotel

★ ★ ★ STANFORD PARK HOTEL. *100 El Camino Real, Menlo Park (94025). Phone 650/322-1234; toll-free 800/368-2468; fax 650/322-0975. www.stanfordparkhotel.com.* The hotel is located across from the Stanford Park Shopping Center, providing guests with plenty of shopping opportunities. 155 rooms, 4 story. Check-in 2 pm, check-out noon. Restaurant, bar. Children's activity center. Fitness room. Outdoor pool, whirlpool. Airport transportation available. Business center. **$$**

Restaurants

★ ★ DUCK CLUB. *100 El Camino Real, Menlo Park (94025). Phone 650/322-1234; fax 650/322-0975. www.stanfordparkhotel.com.* American menu. Breakfast, lunch, dinner, Sun brunch. Bar. Children's menu. Valet parking. **$$$**

★ ★ LEFT BANK. *635 Santa Cruz Ave, Menlo Park (94025). Phone 650/473-6543; fax 650/473-6536. www.leftbank.com.* French menu. Lunch, dinner, Sun brunch. Children's menu. **$$**

★ ★ ★ ★ THE VILLAGE PUB. *2967 Woodside Rd, Woodside (94062). Phone 650/851-9888; fax 650/851-6827. www.thevillagepub.net.* About half an hour from both San Francisco and San Jose, this upscale pub emphasizes the use of local artisanal and organic ingredients, including produce cultivated and harvested especially for the restaurant at its partner farm in the nearby Santa Cruz Mountains. The understated dining room is a clubby setting of dark woods, deep red upholstery, and black-and-white photographs evoking a bygone era. Seasonal menus feature contemporary dishes like duck leg confit with turnips, cabbage, and quince and cauliflower and Meyer lemon risotto with crispy pancetta and capers, although diners craving more traditional pub fare will find burgers, steaks, and fries as well. The ample wine list includes a number of reasonably priced selections along with half-bottles and a variety of options by the glass. American menu. Lunch, dinner. Bar. Casual attire. Reservations recommended. **$$$**

Merced (E-3)

Population 63,893
Elevation 172 ft
Area Code 209
Zip 95340
Information Conference & Visitors Bureau, 690 W 16th St; phone 209/384-7092 or toll-free 800/446-5353
Web Site www.yosemite-gateway.org

The Gateway to Yosemite National Park (see), Merced is the center of a rich agricultural area with dairy and beef production as well as peach, almond, tomato, and alfalfa crops. Publishing, canneries, and metal and plastic manufacturers contribute to its economic base.

What to See and Do

Castle Air Museum. *5050 Santa Fe Dr, Atwater (94530). 8 miles N, adjacent to Castle aviation park at Sante Fe Dr and Buhach Rd. Phone 209/723-2178. www.elite.net/castle-air.* Displays 45 vintage military aircraft; indoor military museum; inquire for guided tours. Restaurant. (May-late Sept: daily 9 am-5 pm; Oct-Apr: daily 10 am-4 pm; closed holidays) **$$**

Lake Yosemite Park. *5714 N Lake Rd, Merced (95340). 5 miles NE on G St, 2 miles E on Bellvue Rd, then 1/2 mile N on N Lake Rd to park entrance. Phone 209/372-0200. www.nps.gov.* Swimming, sailing, water-skiing, fishing, boating; picnicking. (Daily for sightseeing and fishing) Fee for group facility use and boat launching. **$$**

Merced County Courthouse Museum. *N and 21st sts, Merced (95340). Phone 209/723-2401. www.mercedmuseum.org.* Restored courthouse with collection of antique dolls, quilts, historical exhibits. (Wed-Sun 1-4 pm; closed holidays) **FREE**

Merced Multicultural Arts Center. *645 W Main St, Merced (95340). Phone 209/388-1090. www.artsmerced.org.* Three-story building contains theater, lobby, retail galleries, photo gallery, traveling exhibits, and six visual and performing arts studios. (Mon-Fri; weekends by appointment; closed holidays) **FREE**

Merced River Development Project. *9090 Lake McClure Rd, Snelling (95369). S of Hwy 132. Phone 209/378-2520.* Exchequer Dam rises 490 feet to impound Lake McClure (82-mile shoreline). McClure Point, Barrett Cove, Horseshoe Bend, and Bagby Recreation Areas. McSwain Dam stands 80 feet high; impounds Lake McSwain (12 1/2-mile shoreline). All areas offer swimming, showers, water-skiing, fishing, boating (launching facilities; fee), and marinas; picnicking, restrooms, concessions, and camping (fee; electricity additional).

Special Events

Central California Band Review. *Madera. Phone 559/673-3563. www.maderachamber.com.* High school and junior high school band competitions. Nov.

Merced County Fair. *County Fairgrounds, 900 Martin Luther King Jr. Way, Merced (95340). Phone 209/772-1506. www.mercedcountyfair.com.* A destruction derby, bull riding, and live entertainment draw crowds to this fair, which has been providing summer family fun for more than 100 years. Mid-July. **$$$**

West Coast Antique Fly-in. *Phone toll-free 800/446-5353. www.antiqueflyin.com.* Each year, thousands of people come to this event in Merced to view more than 1,000 antique airplanes on display. In addition to awards for youngest and oldest pilots and farthest distance flown, there are helicopter and airplane rides, activities, and food vendors. First full weekend in June. **$$**

Mill Valley

See also San Francisco, Muir Woods National Monument, San Rafael, Tiburon

Population 13,600
Elevation 80 ft
Area Code 415
Zip 94941
Information Mill Valley Chamber of Commerce, 85 Throckmorton Ave; phone 415/388-9700
Web Site www.millvalley.org

What to See and Do

Mount Tamalpais State Park. *801 Panoramic Hwy, Mill Valley (94941). 6 miles W on Panoramic Hwy. Phone 415/388-2070. www.parks.ca.gov.* This park is one of the favorite retreats of San Franciscans. The mountain rises 2,571 feet above sea level and provides a spectacular view of the entire Bay Area. A winding road climbs to a spot near the summit. Trails and bridle paths wind through the woods to attractive picnic areas; walk-in camping (fee; no vehicles). Muir Woods National Monument (see) is at the foot of the mountain. The Mountain Theatre in the park presents plays in a natural amphitheater (May-Sept). **$$**

Limited-Service Hotel

★ ★ ACQUA HOTEL - MILL VALLEY. *555 Redwood Hwy, Mill Valley (94941). Phone 415/380-0400; toll-free 888/662-9555; fax 415/380-9696. www.marinhotels.com.* 50 rooms. Complimentary continental breakfast. Check-in 3 pm, check-out noon. Fitness room. **$$**

Full-Service Inns

★ ★ ★ MOUNTAIN HOME INN. *810 Panoramic Hwy, Mill Valley (94941). Phone 415/381-9000; fax 415/381-3615. www.mtnhomeinn.com.* 10 rooms, 3 story. Complimentary continental breakfast. Check-in 3-9 pm, check-out 11 am. Restaurant, bar. **$$**

★ ★ ★ THE PELICAN INN. *10 Pacific Way, Muir Beach (94965). Phone 415/383-6000; fax 415/383-3424. www.pelicaninn.com.* 7 rooms. Complimentary full breakfast. Check-in 3 pm, check-out noon. Restaurant. **$$$**

Specialty Lodging

The following lodging establishment is approved by Mobil Travel Guide, but due to its unique and individualized nature has not been given a traditional Mobil Star rating. Included in this listing you may find bed-and-breakfasts, limited-service inns, guest ranches, and other unique hotel properties.

MILL VALLEY INN. *165 Throckmorton Ave, Mill Valley (94941). Phone 415/389-6608; toll-free 800/595-2100; fax 415/389-5051. www.jdvhospitality.com.* This inn, set in a cozy California mill town, offers European style with California charm. Rooms feature original pieces by North Bay craftspeople. 25 rooms, 3 story. Complimentary continental breakfast. Check-in 4 pm, check-out noon. **$$**

Restaurants

★★ **BUCKEYE ROADHOUSE.** *15 Shoreline Hwy, Mill Valley (94941). Phone 415/331-2600; fax 415/331-6067. www.buckeyeroadhouse.com.* Roadhouse first opened in 1937. American, California menu. Lunch, dinner, Sun brunch. Closed Dec 25. Bar. Children's menu. Valet parking. Outdoor seating. **$$**

★★ **FRANTOIO.** *152 Shoreline Hwy, Mill Valley (94941). Phone 415/289-5777; fax 415/289-5775. www.frantoio.com.* Italian menu. Dinner. Closed July 4, Thanksgiving, Dec 25. Bar. Outdoor seating. **$$**

★★ **MOUNTAIN HOME INN.** *810 Panoramic Way, Mill Valley (94941). Phone 415/381-9000; fax 415/381-3615. www.mtnhomeinn.com.* American menu. Breakfast, lunch Wed-Sun, dinner Wed-Sun. Closed Dec 25. Bar. Outdoor seating. **$$**

★★ **ROBATA GRILL AND SUSHI.** *591 Redwood Hwy, Mill Valley (94941). Phone 415/381-8400; fax 415/381-2942. www.robatagrill.com.* Japanese, sushi menu. Lunch, dinner. Closed holidays. **$$**

Modesto (E-2)

See also Oakdale, Sonora, Stockton

Founded 1870
Population 188,856
Elevation 91 ft
Area Code 209
Zip 95353
Information Convention & Visitors Bureau, 1114 J Street, PO Box 844; phone 209/571-6480 or toll-free 800/266-4282
Web Site www.modestocvb.org

A processing, shipping, and marketing center for the rich farmlands of the central San Joaquin Valley and Stanislaus County, Modesto was named for a San Francisco banker who was too modest to publicize his own name. Nearby Don Pedro Dam provides the irrigation and power that is the key to the area's prosperity. Modesto is a gateway to Yosemite National Park (see) and the Gold Country.

What to See and Do

Caswell Memorial State Park. *28000 S Austin Rd, Modesto (95366). 15 miles N via Hwy 99, S on Austin Rd. Phone 209/599-3810.* On 260 acres. Swimming, fishing; nature and hiking trails, picnicking, camping (no hook-ups).

Great Valley Museum of Natural History. *1100 Stoddard Ave, Modesto (95350). Phone 209/575-6196. www.gomjc.org/greatvalley.* Exhibits of natural plant and animal habitats and complete ecosystems. Also children's discovery room. (Tues-Fri 9 am-4:30 pm, Sat 10 am-4 pm; closed in Aug) **$**

McHenry Museum. *1402 I St, Modesto (95354). Phone 209/577-5366. www.mchenrymuseum.org.* Historical exhibits in period rooms; schoolroom, doctor's office, blacksmith shop. (Tues-Sun noon-4 pm) **FREE** One block NE is the

> **McHenry Mansion.** *906 15th St, Modesto (95354). Phone 209/577-5344. www.mchenrymuseum.org.* (1883) Restored Victorian mansion built for one of Modesto's first families. Period furnishings. (Mon-Thurs, Sun 1-4 pm, Fri noon-3 pm; closed holidays) **FREE**

Turlock Lake State Recreation Area. *22600 Lake Rd, Modesto. 23 miles E on Hwy 132. Phone 209/874-2008; toll-free 800/894-2267.* On 3,000 acres. Swimming, water-skiing, fishing, boating; picnicking, camping.

Special Events

International Festival. *Graceada Park, 401 Needham St, Modesto (95353). Phone 209/521-3852. www.internationalfestivalmodesto.com.* The International Festival brings together and celebrates the blend of diverse cultures in the Central Valley through exploration of dance, music, crafts, and customs at the fest's Global Village. Oct. **FREE**

Riverbank Cheese & Wine Exposition. *6709 2nd St, Riverbank (95367). 6 miles E on Hwy 108.* Street festival with food booths, arts and crafts, antiques, entertainment. Tasting of local wines and cheeses. Oct.

Limited-Service Hotels

★ ★ **DOUBLETREE HOTEL.** *1150 9th St, Modesto (95354). Phone 209/526-6000; toll-free 800/222-8733; fax 209/526-6096. www.modesto.doubletree.com.* This hotel meets all the needs of its visitors with two restaurants, an outdoor heated pool, Jacuzzi and sauna, as well as fax and data ports for business travelers. Many area attractions, as well as tennis and golf, are found near this downtown hotel. 258 rooms, 10 story. Pets accepted; fee. Check-in 3 pm, check-out noon. Restaurant, bar. Fitness room. Outdoor pool, whirlpool. Airport transportation available. Business center. **$**

★ ★ **RED LION.** *1612 Sisk Rd, Modesto (95350). Phone 209/521-1612; toll-free 800/733-5466; fax 209/527-5074. www.redlion.com.* 186 rooms, 2 story. Pets accepted; fee. Check-in 3 pm, check-out noon. Restaurant, bar. Fitness room. Indoor pool, outdoor pool, whirlpool. Business center. **$**

Monterey (F-2)

See also Big Sur, Carmel, Carmel Valley, Pacific Grove, Pebble Beach, Salinas

Founded 1770
Population 29,674
Elevation 40 ft
Area Code 831
Zip 93940
Information Monterey Peninsula Visitors & Convention Bureau, 401 Camino El Estero, PO Box 1770; phone 831/649-1770
Web Site www.montereyinfo.org

The calm harbor, red-roofed white stucco houses, white sand beach, Monterey cypress, and Monterey pine all existed in the days when Monterey was the Spanish heart of California. A mélange of Mexican, New England, sea, mission, and ranch makes Monterey uniquely Californian in its culture and history. The Spanish explorer Sebastian Vizcaino sailed into the bay in 1602 and named it for the Count of Monte-Rey, Viceroy of Mexico. The spot was rediscovered in 1770 when Fray Crespi, Fray Junipero Serra, and Gaspar de Portola took possession, founding the Presidio and the Mission San Carlos Borromeo de Rio Carmelo (see CARMEL). The King of Spain recognized it as the capital of California in 1775, but in 1822, it became part of the Mexican Republic. Soon after, American whalers and traders began to arrive. Commodore Sloat raised the American flag in 1846, ending years of opposition to Mexican rule. Delegates to a constitutional convention in 1849 met in Monterey and drew up California's first constitution. The city became a whaling center; fisheries, canneries, and specialized agriculture developed. The sardine fisheries and canneries, in particular, inspired the novels *Cannery Row* and *Sweet Thursday* by John Steinbeck. Now, with the sardines gone and the canneries silent, the row has been taken over by an aquarium, gourmet restaurants, and art galleries, while Fisherman's Wharf offers fishing and sightseeing trips and the bay's famous sea otters; nearby is the Maritime Museum of Monterey.

What to See and Do

Cannery Row. *Cannery Row, Monterey (93940). Phone 831/373-1902. www.canneryrow.com.* Immortalized in John Steinbeck's 1945 novel of the same name, Cannery Row grew around the Asian and American companies that established canning and fishing operations in the Monterey area at the turn of the 20th century. Development boomed during World War I, and the city became known as the "Sardine Capital of the World," at least until the Monterey Bay sardine population collapsed in the face of over-fishing. The Cannery Row described by Steinbeck followed in its wake, a haven for bums, prostitutes, and eccentrics. Locals pushed to revitalize the decaying strip in the 1950s, an initiative that culminated in 1984 when the Monterey Bay Aquarium opened in the former Hovden Cannery. Today, Cannery Row is again the vibrant heart of Monterey, complete with lavish waterfront hotels, nearly 100 shops, and a dizzying array of seafood restaurants and other eateries.

Colton Hall Museum. *Civic Center, second floor, Pacific and Madison sts, Monterey (93940). Phone 831/646-5640. www.monterey.org/museum.* (1849) and **Old Monterey Jail** (1854). Built as a town hall and public school by the Reverend Walter Colton, alcalde (mayor or judge) of Monterey District during the American occupation of California, 1846-1848. Classic Revival design of stone and adobe mortar. The first constitution of California (in Spanish and English) was writ-

In the Footsteps of Steinbeck: Monterey's Cannery Row

In 1945, John Steinbeck published one of his best-loved novels, *Cannery Row,* which chronicled the lives and fortunes of characters in the rough-and-tumble neighborhood encompassing the sardine factories along the Monterey shoreline. Steinbeck, born in nearby Salinas but living in Monterey, described the area then as "a poem, a stink, a grating noise, a quality of light, a tone, a habit, a nostalgia, a dream." On this walking tour, you'll find a new Cannery Row, but one that retains some of its old flavor (minus the stink and noise, unless you happen to stand too close to a sea lion). When the sardines were fished out by the late 1940s, the area fell into decay. However, the old canneries and warehouses were subsequently renovated and transformed into shops, restaurants, hotels, and attractions. If you start at the far end of the Row, near the boundary with the town of Pacific Grove, you can visit the Monterey Bay Aquarium (886 Cannery Row), itself fashioned from what was once the largest sardine factory along the Row. The aquarium's indoor-outdoor design is a perfect setting for its displays of sea otters, sharks, and jellyfish. Continue down Cannery Row past sites Steinbeck celebrated in his book: La Ida's Café (once a house of ill repute) at 851 Cannery Row; Wing Chong's Heavenly Flower Grocery (once a general store, bank, and gambling hall) at 835 Cannery Row; and Ed "Doc" Ricketts's lab at 800 Cannery Row, where the Steinbeck hero collected sea specimens. (None of the original business remains, however.) Proceed down Cannery Row to Steinbeck's Spirit of Monterey Wax Museum (at 700 Cannery Row), which features wax figures and scenes and narration by "Steinbeck" and is a fun way to absorb some of the area's history. Cannery Row extends for about a mile in all. Farther along, you'll pass several restaurants and cafés where you can have lunch or a drink. Cannery Row ends at Coast Guard pier, but continue the pretty seaside walk along the Monterey Peninsula Recreation Trail to Fisherman's Wharf, where boats once unloaded tons of sardines. The Wharf now caters mainly to tourists, but there are several good seafood restaurants and places to pick up snacks and watch sea lions. Leaving the Wharf, walk south a short distance to Custom House Plaza; there you'll find the Maritime Museum of Monterey, which contains exhibits on Monterey's seafaring past, from early explorers up to the sardine-fishing days of Steinbeck's time.

ten here. Changing exhibits. The jail, a single-story addition of granite, was added to the building in 1854 at which time Colton Hall served as the Monterey County Courthouse. (Daily 10 am-4 pm; closed Jan 1, Thanksgiving, Dec 25) **FREE**

Fisherman's Wharf. *99 Pacific St #100 H, Monterey (93940). On Monterey Harbor. www.montereywharf.com.* Restaurants, shops, tour boat departure area.

Gray Line bus tours. *Pier 43 1/2, San Francisco (94103). Phone 415/558-9400; toll-free 888/428-6937. www.grayline.com.* Tours to Santa Cruz and along the coast of Monterey Bay. **$$$$**

La Mirada. *720 Via Mirada, Monterey (93940). Phone 831/372-3689. www.montereyart.org.* Original residence of Jose Castro, prominent Californian during the Mexican period, and later Frank Work, who added a collection of art and antiques to the 2 1/2-acre estate. Garden and house tours (Wed-Sat 11 am-5 pm, Sun 1-4 pm). **$**

Marina. *351 Madison St, Monterey (93940). Foot of Figueroa St. Phone 831/646-3950.* Berths for 420 vessels up to 50 feet long; two launching ramps. Municipally owned. (Office closed Jan 1, Thanksgiving, Dec 25)

Maritime Museum of Monterey. *Stanton Center, 5 Custom House Plaza, Monterey (93940). Adjacent to Fisherman's Wharf. Phone 831/372-2608. www.montereyhistory.org.* Seven major theme areas provide exhibits on maritime and naval history of the area, including the sailing ship era and whaling industry; ship models, maritime artifacts, interactive exhibits; paintings; research library. The jewel of the museum collection is the 16-foot-tall intricately crafted first order Fresnel Lens from the old lighthouse at Point Sur. Also here is a 100-seat theater featuring an orientation film and reenactments. (Thurs-Tues 10 am-5 pm; closed Jan 1, Thanksgiving, Dec 25) **$**

Monterey Bay Aquarium. *886 Cannery Row, Monterey (93940). Phone 831/648-4888. www.mbayaq.org.*

The preeminent aquarium in the United States, the Monterey Bay Aquarium attracts more than a million visitors a year, and it's easy to see why. Located in the converted former Hovden Cannery (which canned squid and sardines until the early 1970s) on Monterey's legendary Cannery Row, the facility is now the home of 300,000 plants and animals representing some 550 species, with a specific focus on local sea life. Visitors can explore a number of impressive exhibits, such as a three-story kelp forest; Outer Bay, a million-gallon indoor ocean with sharks, barracuda, tuna, and sea turtles; and a walk-through shorebird aviary. A surefire hit for kids, the aquarium also features Splash Zone, an educational play area with tunnels, clam-shaped chairs, "petting pools" with bat rays and starfish, and a penguin habitat. There is also a pair of restaurants and a lounge with great bay views on-site. (Daily 10 am-6 pm; opens at 9:30 am in summer and on holiday weekends; closed Dec 25) **$$$$**

Monterey Museum of Art. *559 Pacific St, Monterey (93940). Phone 831/372-5477. www.montereyart.org.* Displays early California and American art, folk, ethnic and tribal art, and Asian art. Photography exhibits; changing exhibitions of major American artists. Docent-guided tour available. (Wed-Sat 11 am-5 pm, Sun 1-4 pm; closed Jan 1, Thanksgiving, Dec 25) **$**

Monterey State Historic Park. *20 Custom House Plz, Monterey (93940). Polk, Munras, and Alvarado sts. Phone 831/649-7118. www.parks.ca.gov.* Day ticket valid in all historic buildings in state historic park. (Park and building hours may vary) **FREE**

Boston Store. *Scott and Olivier sts, Monterey (93940). Phone 831/649-3364. www.parks.ca.gov.* (1845) Restored general store built by Thomas Larkin and operated by Joseph Boston & Company. Houses a general merchandise store operated by the Monterey History and Art Association. (Thurs-Sun, 11 am-2 pm; closed Jan 1, Thanksgiving, Dec 25) **FREE**

Casa Soberanes. *336 Pacific St, Monterey (93940). Phone 831/649-7118. www.parks.ca.gov.* (1842) Adobe house containing displays of Monterey history from 1840 to 1970. Excellent example of adobe construction; walls are 38 inches thick. Local art collection. (Daily; closed Jan 1, Thanksgiving, Dec 25) Guided tours (Mon, Fri-Sun 11:30 am). **FREE**

Cooper-Molera Adobe. *Polk and Munras, Monterey (93940). Phone 831/649-7118. www.parks.ca.gov.* (1827) Largest complex in the park. Built by John Rogers Cooper, half-brother of Thomas Larkin. Tours (Wed 2:30 pm, Fri-Mon 3 pm; closed Jan 1, Thanksgiving, Dec 25). **FREE**

Custom House. *Custom House Plaza, Del Monte Ave and Alvarado St, Monterey (93940). Phone 831/649-7118. www.parks.ca.gov.* (1827) Old Mexican custom house exhibit re-creates a cargo of the 1840s. Commodore Sloat raised the American flag over this adobe building in 1846, bringing 600,000 square miles into the Union. (Thurs-Mon 10 am-3 pm; closed Jan 1, Thanksgiving, Dec 25) **FREE**

Larkin House. *510 Calle Principal, Monterey (93940). At Jefferson St. Phone 831/649-7118. www.parks.ca.gov.* (1830s) Consulate for Thomas Larkin, the first and only US consul to Mexican California (1843-1846). Large collection of antiques. (Daily; closed Jan 1, Thanksgiving, Dec 25) Guided tours (Wed 1:30 pm, Sat-Sun 2 pm). **FREE**

Pacific House. *Custom House Plaza, Del Monte Ave and Alvarado St, Monterey (93940). Phone 831/649-7118. www.parks.ca.gov.* (1847) A museum of California history and the Holman Native American artifact collection. (Fri-Mon, Wed 10 am-3 pm; closed Jan 1, Thanksgiving, Dec 25) **FREE**

Robert Louis Stevenson House. *530 Houston St, Monterey (93940). Phone 831/649-7118. www.parks.ca.gov.* Preserved as a state historic monument with large collection of Stevenson memorabilia. Stevenson lived here for four months while visiting his future wife. (Daily; closed Jan 1, Thanksgiving, Dec 25) Guided tours (hours vary, inquire for schedule).

"Path of History" tour. *Phone 831/649-7118. www.parks.ca.gov.* Leads to many old buildings of distinction. These are marked with a plaque explaining the history and architecture. Several buildings are open to the public. Some of these buildings and a number of others are part of the Monterey State Historic Park. Obtain a map at the Monterey Peninsula Visitor and Convention Bureau, Camino El Estero and Franklin streets.

Presidio of Monterey. *360 Patton Ave, Monterey (93944). Pacific St, N of Scott St. Phone 831/242-5104. pom-www.army.mil.* Home of the Defense Language

Institute. Developed in 1902 as a cantonment for troops returning from the Philippine Insurrection. Monument to John Drake Sloat, commander of the American troops that captured Monterey (1846); statue in honor of Fray Junipero Serra. There are 12 historic sites and monuments on Presidio Hill; a brochure and map are available. Hours vary. **FREE**

Royal Presidio Chapel. *500 Church St, Monterey (93940). San Carlos Cathedral, between Camino El Estero and Figueroa St. Phone 831/373-2628. www.dioceseofmonterey.org/parishes/sancarlos.htm.* Founded June 3, 1770, the only presidio chapel remaining in California; in continuous use since 1795. Façade is considered the most ornate of all the California missions. (Daily) **FREE**

★ **Seventeen-Mile Drive.** A famous scenic drive between Monterey and Carmel (see) along the Pacific Coast past Seal Rock, Lone Cypress, Cypress Point, and Spyglass Hill and Pebble Beach golf courses. This private community in Del Monte Forest is known around the world for its natural beauty. The road may be entered at several points; follow the red-and-yellow center lines and the Seventeen-Mile Drive signs.

Special Events

AT&T-Pebble Beach National Pro-Am Golf Championship. *Phone toll-free 800/541-9091. www.attpbgolf.com.* Takes place on Pebble Beach, Cypress, and Spyglass courses. Late Jan or early Feb.

Monterey County Fair. *Fairgrounds and Exposition Park, 2004 Fairground Rd, Monterey (93940). Phone 831/372-5863. www.montereycountyfair.com.* Kids will love the carnival and pony rides, mom and dad will like the wine tasting and cooking demonstrations, and the entire family will enjoy the three stages of entertainment and food from around the world. Aug. **$$**

Monterey Jazz Festival. *County Fairgrounds, 2000 Fairground Rd, Monterey (93940). Phone 925/275-9255. www.montereyjazzfestival.org.* Started in 1958, the Monterey Jazz festival has been entertaining crowds with all types of jazz music, and the event now also includes several workshops and panel discussions. Third weekend of Sept. **$$$$**

Limited-Service Hotels

★★ BEST WESTERN THE BEACH RESORT. *2600 Sand Dunes Dr, Monterey (93940). Phone 831/394-3321; toll-free 800/242-8627; fax 831/393-1912. www.bestwestern.com.* Built in the late 1960s as a beachfront motel, The Beach Resort predates the subsequent restrictions on beach development in the area (it's the only resort in Monterey that's located right on the beach). It has a beautiful panorama of the bay and is easily accessible from Highway 1. While the exterior still resembles a motel, lots of potted plants, artwork, antiques, and comfortable furnishings give the place a resort sensibility, although the pounding surf can shake the whole building. 196 rooms, 4 story. Pets accepted; fee. Check-in 4 pm, check-out noon. Restaurant, bar. Fitness room. Beach. Outdoor pool. Business center. **$$**

★ BEST WESTERN VICTORIAN INN. *487 Foam St, Monterey (93940). Phone 831/373-8000; toll-free 800/232-4141; fax 831/373-4815. www.victorianinn.com.* Victorian furnishings. Two blocks from the bay. 68 rooms, 3 story. Pets accepted; fee. Complimentary continental breakfast. Check-in 4 pm, check-out noon. Whirlpool. **$$**

★ HOLIDAY INN EXPRESS. *443 Wave St, Monterey (93940). Phone 831/372-1800; toll-free 800/248-8442; fax 831/372-1969. www.hiexpress.com/montereyca.* 43 rooms, 3 story. Complimentary continental breakfast. Check-in 3 pm, check-out noon. Whirlpool. **$$**

★★ PORTOLA PLAZA HOTEL AT MONTEREY BAY. *2 Portola Plz, Monterey (93940). Phone 831/649-4511; toll-free 888/222-5851; fax 831/649-3109. www.portolaplazahotel.com.* This hotel is a short drive from Pebble Beach, great golf courses, fine restaurants, and many shops and galleries. 380 rooms, 7 story. Check-in 3 pm, check-out noon. Restaurant, bar. Fitness room, spa. Outdoor pool, whirlpool. Business center. **$$**

★ SAND DOLLAR INN. *755 Abrego St, Monterey (93940). Phone 831/372-7551; toll-free 800/982-1986; fax 831/372-0916. www.sanddollarinn.com.* The adobe-style Sand Dollar is more a motel than an inn, but it's spotlessly clean and well maintained, and it has improved dramatically over the years. While the inn is not in an upscale neighborhood, it's convenient to many Monterey attractions. The standard guest rooms are pleasant, and deluxe rooms and suites have a fireplace, a balcony or patio, and a sitting area; the heated outdoor pool is also inviting. 63 rooms, 3 story.

Complimentary continental breakfast. Check-in 3 pm, check-out noon. Outdoor pool, whirlpool. **$**

Full-Service Hotels

★ ★ ★ **HILTON MONTEREY.** *1000 Aguajito Rd, Monterey (93940). Phone 831/373-6141; toll-free 800/234-5697; fax 831/655-8608. www.monterey.hilton.com.* This hotel offers 204 rooms, each with its own private patio or balcony, all set in a wonderful garden landscape. 204 rooms, 3 story. Pets accepted; restrictions, fee. Check-in 4 pm, check-out noon. Restaurant, bar. Fitness room. Outdoor pool, whirlpool. Tennis. Business center. **$**

★ ★ ★ **HOTEL PACIFIC.** *300 Pacific St, Monterey (93940). Phone 831/373-5700; toll-free 800/554-5542; fax 831/373-6921. www.hotelpacific.com.* Located a block from Fisherman's Wharf in downtown Monterey, the adobe-style Hotel Pacific boasts an exceptional attention to detail, with few missteps. It has lush patios with potted plants, fountains, Mexican patio furniture, and colorful umbrellas. The welcoming lobby emphasizes the area's Spanish-California heritage. Guest rooms, all of which are suites, include a fireplace, goose-down feather beds, hardwood floors, original artwork, and private balconies; baths feature Aveda products and separate tub and shower. Although the hotel is located on a busy street, it is quiet and tranquil. 105 rooms, 3 story, all suites. Complimentary continental breakfast. Check-in 4 pm, check-out noon. Whirlpool. **$$**

★ ★ ★ **HYATT REGENCY MONTEREY.** *1 Old Golf Course Rd, Monterey (93940). Phone 831/372-1234; fax 831/375-3960. www.monterey.hyatt.com.* This hotel is situated on 23 landscaped acres and is adjacent to the Del Monte Golf Course. 575 rooms, 4 story. Pets accepted, some restrictions; fee. Check-in 3 pm, check-out noon. Restaurant, bar. Fitness room. Outdoor pool, whirlpool. Tennis. Airport transportation available. Business center. **$$**

★ ★ ★ **MARINA DUNES RESORT.** *3295 Dunes Dr, Marina (93933). Phone 831/883-9478; toll-free 877/944-3863; fax 831/883-9477. www.marinadunes.com.* 60 rooms, 2 story. Complimentary continental breakfast. Check-in 4 pm, check-out noon. Restaurant. Spa. Beach. Indoor pool, outdoor pool, children's pool, whirlpool. **$$$**

★ ★ ★ **MONTEREY PLAZA HOTEL AND SPA.** *400 Cannery Row, Monterey (93940). Phone 831/646-1700; toll-free 800/334-3999; fax 831/646-0285. www.montereyplazahotel.com.* Situated right on Monterey Bay on Cannery Row and within walking distance to the area's major sights, the Monterey Plaza Hotel and Spa is a natural choice when visiting this scenic resort town. Luxuriously appointed rooms and suites are complemented by large windows focusing attention on the sparkling water views. Many of the rooms give guests the impression of being on a ship with their ocean-view balconies. European elegance defines this hotel, from the gracious lobby to the luxuriously appointed accommodations. Two restaurants provide culinary diversions, while a host of recreational activities entertain guests both on and off the property. The landscaped pool deck right on the water is definitely the place to be at this coastal retreat. 290 rooms, 4 story. Check-in 4 pm, check-out noon. Restaurant, bar. Fitness room, spa. Beach. Whirlpool. Business center. **$$**

★ ★ ★ **SPINDRIFT INN.** *652 Cannery Row, Monterey (93940). Phone 831/646-8900; toll-free 800/841-1879; fax 831/646-5342. www.spindriftinn.com.* At high tide, guests of the Spindrift Inn stand directly over the ocean, enjoying great views of the bay, sailboats, fishing boats, and kayaks. The inn, which is intimate and luxurious, provides an oasis in the hurly-burly of raucous Cannery Row. It's a top-quality hotel that pays attention to detail. The atrium lobby has hand-tiled floors, antiques, and a wood-burning fireplace; guest rooms have window seats, plush carpeting, marble vanities, and canopy beds, and some offer views of the ocean. The on-site restaurant specializes in pan-Asian cuisine. 42 rooms, 4 story. Complimentary continental breakfast. Check-in 4 pm, check-out noon. Restaurant. Beach. **$$$**

Specialty Lodgings

The following lodging establishments are approved by Mobil Travel Guide, but due to their unique and individualized nature have not been given a traditional Mobil Star rating. Included in this listing you may find bed-and-breakfasts, limited-service inns, guest ranches, and other unique hotel properties.

JABBERWOCK BED AND BREAKFAST. *598 Laine St, Monterey (93940). Phone 831/372-4777; toll-free 888/428-7253; fax 831/655-2946. www.jabberwockinn.com.* Built in 1911 as a private home, this vintage Craftsman building opened as an inn in 1982. It is situated in a residential neighborhood, high enough for superb views of Monterey Bay. There is an English garden, an enclosed porch with a piano, and a parlor with books, cozy seating, and a readied chess game. Rooms are comfortable but not overly decorated, with featherbeds and large whirlpools (no phones or TVs, but plentiful books and games). A Lewis Carroll poem gave the inn its name, and the *Alice in Wonderland* theme is evident throughout. 7 rooms, 3 story. Closed Dec 24-25. Complimentary full breakfast. Check-in 3 pm, check-out noon. Whirlpool. **$$**

MONTEREY BAY INN. *242 Cannery Row, Monterey (93940). Phone 831/373-6242; toll-free 800/424-6242; fax 831/373-7603. www.montereybayinn.com.* Although its exterior is rather industrial looking, this inn has an excellent location overlooking the bay and Fisherman's Wharf, and the rooms are comfortable, clean, and well maintained. Nearly every room has a view, and they all have balconies equipped with a table, two chairs, and a flowering geranium. All rooms have binoculars, CDs, and local photography books as well—personal touches that you're unlikely to find in a larger hotel. Pampering options include a continental breakfast delivered to the room and a massage or facial at the hotel spa. 47 rooms, 4 story. Complimentary continental breakfast. Check-in 4 pm, check-out noon. Whirlpool. **$$**

THE MONTEREY HOTEL. *406 Alvarado St, Monterey (93940). Phone 831/375-3184; toll-free 800/727-0960; fax 831/373-2899. www.montereyhotel.com.* Marking its centennial in 2004, this restored hotel, located in the heart of Monterey, is close to shops, restaurants, nightlife, and Fisherman's Wharf, perfect for travelers who like a lively environment. The lovely lobby features Waterford crystal lamps, crown moldings, carved Victorian furniture, a grand stone fireplace, and marble floors. The guest rooms have elegant, hand-carved furniture, along with ceiling fans and plantation shutters; master suites have fireplaces. Since the antique elevator cannot be fixed, the hotel is not handicapped accessible. 45 rooms, 4 story. Complimentary continental breakfast. Check-in 3 pm, check-out 11 am. **$**

OLD MONTEREY INN. *500 Martin St, Monterey (93940). Phone 831/375-8284; toll-free 800/350-2344; fax 831/375-6730. www.oldmontereyinn.com.* The breathtaking views on the drive south from San Francisco are only the beginning. Perfect for golfers visiting nearby courses or those wanting a romantic escape, this historic inn is set amidst striking gardens. Extra in-room comforts abound with feather beds, down comforters, terrycloth robes, and candles. A pleasant breakfast and a sunset wine hour make this a first-rate escape. 10 rooms. Complimentary continental breakfast. Check-in 3-7 pm, check-out noon. **$$$**

Restaurants

★ **ABALONETTI SEAFOOD TRATTORIA.** *57 Fisherman's Wharf, Monterey (93940). Phone 831/373-1851; toll-free 800/457-4786; fax 831/373-2058. www.restauranteur.com/abalonetti.* Exhibition kitchen. Seafood menu. Lunch, dinner. Closed Dec 25. Bar. Children's menu. Casual attire. Outdoor seating. **$$**

★★ **CAFE FINA.** *47 Fisherman's Wharf, Monterey (93940). Phone 831/372-5200; toll-free 800/843-3462; fax 831/372-5209. www.cafefina.com.* Collection of family photos displayed. Italian, seafood menu. Lunch, dinner. Closed Thanksgiving, Dec 25. Bar. Casual attire. **$$$**

★★ **CHART HOUSE.** *444 Cannery Row, Monterey (93940). Phone 831/372-3362; fax 831/372-1277. www.chart-house.com.* Seafood menu. Lunch (Sat-Sun), dinner. Bar. Children's menu. Casual attire. **$$**

★★★ **CIBO RISTORANTE ITALIANO.** *301 Alvarado St, Monterey (93940). Phone 831/649-8151; fax 831/649-5042. www.cibo.com.* This simple yet elegant California-style restaurant offers a perfect setting for innovative interpretations of classic Sicilian cooking. Considered one of the best places for live jazz on the Monterey Bay, Cibo is located in the heart of the historic downtown area. Italian menu. Dinner. Closed Thanksgiving, Dec 25. Bar. Children's menu. Casual attire. **$$$**

★★ **DOMENICO'S.** *50 Fisherman's Wharf, Monterey (93940). Phone 831/372-3655; fax 831/372-2073. www.restauranteur.com/domenicos.* Seafood menu. Lunch, dinner. Closed Dec 25. Bar. Children's menu. Casual attire. **$$**

★ ★ ★ **THE DUCK CLUB.** *400 Cannery Row, Monterey (93940). Phone 831/646-1700; toll-free 800/334-3999; fax 831/646-5937. www.woodsidehotels.com.* Acclaimed for its innovative cuisine, this elegant restaurant tucked away in the Monterey Plaza Hotel features a seasonal menu and wood-roasted dishes prepared in an exhibition-style kitchen. As the name suggests, duck is a specialty. Visit this popular spot to celebrate a special occasion or simply to enjoy spectacular views of the bay. California menu. Breakfast, dinner. Closed Mon. Bar. Children's menu. Casual attire. Valet parking. **$$$**

★ ★ ★ **FRESH CREAM.** *99 Pacific St, Building 100 C, Monterey (93940). Phone 831/375-9798; fax 831/375-2283. www.freshcream.com.* Lauded by local and national publications, Fresh Cream serves California-French fare in a beautiful setting overlooking Fisherman's Wharf and Monterey Bay. Though it's in the heart of the tourist area, the restaurant has a sophisticated look, both inside and out. The building was created in the historic manner, and the interior incorporates soft colors of gray and mauve, etched glass dividers, and California artwork. Entrée selections include grilled Holland Dover sole, pan-seared ahi tuna, and pan-roasted chicken with truffle-whipped potatoes. French menu. Dinner. Closed Dec 24. Bar. Casual attire. **$$$**

★ **INDIAN SUMMER.** *220 Olivier St, Monterey (93940). Phone 831/372-4744; fax 831/372-5008. www.indiansummerca.com.* Indian menu. Lunch, dinner. Closed Mon. Bar. Casual attire. Outdoor seating. **$$**

★ ★ ★ **JOHN PISTO'S WHALING STATION PRIME STEAKS AND SEAFOOD.** *763 Wave St, Monterey (93940). Phone 831/373-3778; fax 831/373-2460. www.restauranteur.com/whalingstation.* Just two blocks from Cannery Row and Monterey Bay, John Pisto's is a destination restaurant, with a handsome, horseshoe-shaped bar, copper walls, alabaster lamps, beveled glass windows, and large French posters. Pick your lobster out of the tank, or opt for a tasty steak or quality cut of prime rib, and remember to come hungry: the portions are generous. Chef and restaurateur John Pisto hosts a cooking show on TV and has four restaurants in his empire. American, steak menu. Dinner. Closed Dec 25. Bar. Children's menu. Casual attire. **$$$**

★ ★ ★ **MONTRIO BISTRO.** *414 Calle Principal, Monterey (93940). Phone 831/648-8880; fax 831/648-8241. www.montrio.com.* Housed in a historical firehouse, Montrio is located in downtown Monterey near the convention center. Visually atractive with a sense of whimsy, the restaurant has soft sculptures suspended from the ceiling to muffle sound and track lighting made from fine metalwork twisted into the shape of grapevines. Leather-covered bar stools enhance the bar area. A professional staff serves the food, which is influenced by American, French, and Italian cuisine. House specialties include crab cakes with spicy remoulade, rotisserie chicken over whipped potatoes, and oven-roasted portabella mushroom. American, Mediterranean menu. Dinner. Closed July 4, Thanksgiving, Dec 25. Bar. Children's menu. Casual attire. **$$**

★ ★ **RAPPA'S SEAFOOD.** *101 Fisherman's Wharf, Monterey (93940). Phone 831/372-7562; fax 831/372-1932. www.rappas.com.* This family-owned spot offers scenic views of the bay. Seafood menu. Lunch, dinner. Closed Thanksgiving, Dec 25. Bar. Children's menu. Casual attire. **$$$**

★ ★ ★ **SARDINE FACTORY.** *701 Wave St, Monterey (93940). Phone 831/373-3775; fax 831/373-4241. www.sardinefactory.com.* Often called the flagship of Cannery Row, this restaurant features New American cuisine served in one of several elegant dining rooms, including The Captain's Room, with beautiful striped silk wallpaper, and The Conservatory, a glassed-in space with lots of plants. A Monterey icon, it is a popular place among celebrities, sports figures, and industry leaders. The historic building was originally built as a canteen for sardine workers. Seafood menu. Dinner. Closed the week of Dec 25. Bar. Children's menu. Casual attire. **$$$**

★ ★ **STOKES RESTAURANT & BAR.** *500 Hartnell St, Monterey (93940). Phone 831/373-1110. www.stokesrestaurant.com.* Historic 1833 adobe. California menu. Lunch, dinner. Closed Memorial Day, Dec 25. Bar. Children's menu. Casual attire. **$$**

★ ★ ★ **TARPY'S ROADHOUSE.** *2999 Monterey-Salinas Hwy, Monterey (93940). Phone 831/647-1444; fax 831/647-1103. www.tarpys.com.* Housed in a historic 1917 hacienda on Salinas Highway, Tarpy's serves innovative American country fare—steaks, wild game, and seafood—on five charming landscaped acres of land. Lovely gardens surround an attractive stone building, and the restaurant maintains a down-home ranch look, aided by the cowboy signage and interior cowboy art. American menu. Lunch, dinner, Sun brunch. Closed July 4, Thanksgiving, Dec 25. Bar. Children's menu. Casual attire. Outdoor seating. **$$$**

Mother Lode Country (D-3)

See also Auburn, Grass Valley, Jackson, Nevada City, Placerville, Sonora, Truckee

Information El Dorado Chamber of Commerce, 542 Main St, Placerville, 95667; phone 530/621-5885
Web Site www.yosemitegate.com/motherlode.htm

Three hundred eighteen miles long and only a few miles wide, this strip of land stretching through nine counties from the Sierra foothills was the scene of the gold rush of the mid-19th century. Discovery of gold at Coloma in 1848 touched off a wave of migration to the West that accelerated the development and population of all the western states by several decades. The enormous gold-bearing quartz vein was surface-mined until the end of the century; a few mines still exist, but it is now necessary to penetrate deep into the earth. In this narrow stretch of country, frontier and mining camp legends that are part of the warp and woof of the American West have developed.

Today, the scenic Mother Lode country is dotted with ghost towns, old mine shafts, rusting machinery, and ancient buildings. Recreational gold panning is a favorite pastime. Highway 49, a delightful but not high-speed highway, connects many of the towns where the 49ers panned for gold. Many picnic and camping areas can be found here. A map is available from Chamber of Commerce offices throughout Mother Lode Country.

Mount Diablo State Park

See also Fremont, Livermore, Pleasanton, Santa Clara

5 miles E of I-680 on Diablo Rd

Web Site www.parks.ca.gov

A spiraling road leads to the summit of Mount Diablo (3,849 feet), the highest peak in the San Francisco Bay Area. From here, on a clear day, one can see 200 miles in each direction. The mountain is dotted with rock formations containing fossilized shells. Hiking trails wind from ridge to ridge throughout the more than 19,000 acres of the park. Near the south entrance are unusual rock formations known as the Devil's Slide and the Wind Caves. There are more than 100 miles of unpaved roads and 68 miles of trails available to hikers and horseback riders. Also available are picnic and camping facilities.

Mount Shasta (A-2)

See also Burney, Dunsmuir, Redding, Yreka

Population 3,621
Elevation 3,554 ft
Area Code 530
Zip 96067
Information Chamber of Commerce or the Visitors Bureau, 300 Pine St; phone 530/926-4865 or toll-free 800/926-4865
Web Site www.mtshastachamber.com

Set in Strawberry Valley, Mount Shasta offers a central location to fishing in nearby lakes and streams and year-round outdoor activities in the surrounding area. City water from a nearby spring is so pure that it is untreated.

A Ranger District office of the Shasta-Trinity National Forest (see REDDING) is located in Mount Shasta.

What to See and Do

Campgrounds. *204 Alma St, Mount Shasta (96067).* The US Forest Service maintains the following:

> **Castle Lake.** *Castle Lake Rd and W. A. Barr, Mount Shasta (96067). Phone 530/926-4511.* Six units. Swimming, fishing; picnicking. No trailers. 12 miles SW, 1/2 mile from Castle Lake. Sims Flat. Fishing. 20 miles S, 1 mile E of I-5. 19 units. McBride Springs. Nine units. 5 miles E of Mount Shasta. All closed in winter. Fee at Sims and McBride. For additional information on these and other campgrounds, contact the Shasta-Trinity National Forest, 204 Alma St.

Lake Siskiyou. *4239 W. A. Barr Rd, Mount Shasta (96067). 2 1/2 miles SW, off I-5.* Box Canyon Dam impounds the Sacramento River, creating a 430-acre lake for fishing and swimming. On west shore of lake is

> **Lake Siskiyou Camp-Resort.** *4239 W A Barr Rd, Mount Shasta (96067). Phone toll-free 888/926-2618. www.lakesis.com.* Swimming beach, fishing,

boating (rentals, ramp, marina); hiking, picnicking, snack bar, store, camping (tent and RV sites; hook-ups, rentals; dump station). Contact PO Box 276. **$$$$**

Mount Shasta. *E of I-5, in Shasta-Trinity National Forest (see REDDING). www.shastahome.com.* Perpetually snow-covered double peak volcano towering to 14,162 feet. Five glaciers persist on the slopes, feeding the McCloud and Sacramento rivers. A scenic drive on the Everitt Memorial Highway climbs from the city of Mount Shasta up the slope to 7,840 feet for a magnificent view. White pine, the famous Shasta lily, and majestic stands of red fir are found at various elevations.

Mount Shasta Ski and Board Park. *Hwy 89, Mount Shasta. 10 miles E of I-5 via Hwy 89. Phone 530/926-8610; toll-free 800/754-7427. www.skipark.com.* Three triple chairlifts, one surface lift; patrol, school, rentals; cafeteria, bar. Thirty-one runs; longest run 1.75 miles; vertical drop 1,400 feet. Night skiing (Wed-Sat 4-10 pm), snowboarding. Park open for mountain biking, chairlift rides, climbing tower, and volcanic exhibit (Wed-Sat 9 am-10 pm, Sun-Tues to 4 pm).

Shasta Sunset Dinner Train. *328 Main St, McCloud (96057). Phone 530/964-2142; toll-free 800/733-2141. www.shastasunset.com.* The Shasta Sunset Dinner Train takes the same route that the lumber-heavy McCloud Railway did in the late 19th century, departing from the historic station in McCloud and soaring over the southern foothills of 14,162-foot Mount Shasta, and then coming back again. The three-hour ride is filled with breathtaking views as the vintage gold-finished cars (which were originally built in 1916 for the Illinois Central Railroad and are now lavish inside and out) climb inclines and switchbacks and cross trestles and bridges. The dinner menu changes monthly, but would be best described as continental with a regional spin, and such entrées as salmon, roasted rack of lamb, and beef Wellington are often available; the extensive wine list emphasizes California labels. There are also sightseeing excursions on open-air railcars and luncheon trips. **$$$$**

State Fish Hatchery. *3 N Old Stage Rd, Mount Shasta (96067). 1/2 mile W off I-5, Central Mount Shasta exit. Phone 530/926-2240. www.mountshastasissonmuseum .org.* Raises trout; in continuous operation since 1888. Self-guided tour of trout ponds. Picnic tables, restrooms. (Daily) **FREE** Adjacent is

Sisson Museum. *1 N Old Stage Rd, Mount Shasta (96067). Phone 530/926-5508. www.mountshasta sissonmuseum.org.* Features exhibits on area history, mountain climbing, fish hatchery, and local Native American culture. (Summer: Mon-Sat 10 am-4 pm, Sun 1-4 pm; winter 1-4 pm; closed Easter) Also annual quilt show (late-June-early-July). **DONATION**

Limited-Service Hotels

★ ★ BEST WESTERN TREE HOUSE MOTOR INN. *111 Morgan Way, Mount Shasta (96067). Phone 530/926-3101; toll-free 800/545-7164; fax 530/926-3542. www.bestwestern.com.* View of Mount Shasta. 98 rooms, 3 story. Pets accepted; fee. Complimentary full breakfast. Check-in 3 pm, check-out noon. Restaurant, bar. Indoor pool, whirlpool. **$**

★ ★ MOUNT SHASTA RESORT. *1000 Siskiyou Lake Blvd, Mount Shasta (96067). Phone 530/926-3030; toll-free 800/958-3363; fax 530/926-0333. www. mountshastaresort.com.* 65 rooms, 2 story. Check-in 4 pm, check-out 11 am. Restaurant, bar. Spa. Beach. Whirlpool. Golf, 18 holes. Tennis. **$$**

Specialty Lodging

The following lodging establishment is approved by Mobil Travel Guide, but due to its unique and individualized nature has not been given a traditional Mobil Star rating. Included in this listing you may find bed-and-breakfasts, limited-service inns, guest ranches, and other unique hotel properties.

MCCLOUD HOTEL BED AND BREAKFAST. *408 Main St, McCloud (96057). Phone 530/964-2822; toll-free 800/964-2823; fax 530/964-2844. www.mccloudhotel.com.* Built in 1915. 16 rooms, 2 story. Complimentary full breakfast. Check-in 3-7 pm, check-out 11 am. **$**

Restaurants

★ ★ THE HIGHLAND HOUSE. *1000 Siskiyou Lake Blvd, Mount Shasta (96067). Phone 800/958-3363; fax 530/926-0333. www.mountshastaresort.com.* Upscale white tablecloth dining room featuring modern American cuisine and outdoor dining with views of Mount Shasta. American menu. Breakfast, lunch, dinner, Sun brunch. **$$$**

★ ★ **SERGE'S RESTAURANT.** *531 Chestnut St, Mount Shasta (96067). Phone 530/926-1276. www.shastaspirit.com/Serge.* Intimate country restaurant with outdoor dining available. French menu. Dinner. Closed Mon-Tues. **$$**

Mountain View

See also Palo Alto, Santa Clara

Population 70,708
Elevation 97 ft
Area Code 650
Web Site www.ci.mtnview.ca.us

Limited-Service Hotel

★ **BEST WESTERN MOUNTAIN VIEW INN.** *2300 W El Camino Real, Mountain View (94040). Phone 650/962-9912; toll-free 800/785-0005; fax 650/962-9011. www.bestwestern.com/mountainviewinn.* 71 rooms, 3 story. Complimentary continental breakfast. Check-in 2 pm, check-out 11 am. High-speed Internet access. Fitness room. Outdoor pool, whirlpool. Business center. **$**

Restaurants

★ ★ **AMBER INDIA.** *2290 El Camino Real, #9, Mountain View (94040). Phone 650/968-7511; fax 650/968-1820. www.amber-india.com.* Indian menu. Lunch, dinner. Closed Thanksgiving, Dec 25. Bar. Casual attire. Reservations recommended. **$$**

★ ★ ★ **CHEZ T. J..** *938 Villa St, Mountain View (94041). Phone 650/964-7466; fax 650/964-9647. www.cheztj.com.* Intimate dining in Victorian house; original art, wood-burning fireplace. French menu. Dinner. Closed Sun-Mon; Thanksgiving, Dec 25. Business casual attire. Reservations recommended. **$$$**

Muir Woods National Monument (D-1)

See also Corte Madera, Mill Valley, San Francisco, Sausalito

Web site www.nps.gov/muwo

12 miles N of the golden Gate Bridge. Take Hwy 101 to the Hwy 1/Muir Woods exit.

Part of the Golden Gate National Recreation Area, this was the first area in the national park system to preserve an old-growth stand of redwoods (Sequoia sempervirens), the tallest species of tree on Earth. Every effort has been made to keep this area as close as possible to the way it was when the first European settlers glimpsed it in 1850. For this reason, pets, picnicking, fishing, camping, and hunting are not allowed in the park. However, you may explore the woods on trails designated for hiking and nature walks and take in the breathtaking sight of these majestic giants on foot. There are 1 1/2 miles of flat, asphalt trail suitable for wheelchairs and strollers. Because the area is so popular, during the summer months it's best to arrive before 11 am or after 5 pm. (Daily)

What to See and Do

Slide Ranch. *2025 Shoreline Hwy, Muir Beach (94965). Phone 415/381-6155. www.slideranch.org.* A dairy farm since the 19th century (and home to the Miwok Indians long before that), the Slide Ranch shifted its mission from agriculture to education and preservation in 1970, when the Nature Conservancy bought it to stave off development. Located near Muir Beach just north of San Francisco, the ranch is now dedicated to teaching visitors about sustainable agriculture and the balance of man and nature. Visitors can take a short tour or enroll in a class.

Napa (D-2)

See also Calistoga, Davis, Petaluma, Rutherford, Sonoma, St. Helena, Yountville

Population 72,585
Elevation 17 ft

Area Code 707
Information Chamber of Commerce, 1556 First St, 94559; phone 707/226-7455. Conference & Visitors Bureau, 1310 Napa Town Center, 94559; phone 707/226-7459
Web Site www.napavalley.com/napa

The city of Napa, situated 50 miles north of San Francisco along Highway 29, serves as the gateway to Napa Valley. With approximately 70,000 residents, it's the most populous city in all of California's wine country. Correspondingly, Napa is the most commercially developed, if not the most pastoral, city in the region. Napa offers considerably more accommodation options than neighboring cities to the north, and the breadth of options means heightened competition and, in turn, the most affordable rates in Napa Valley. Wine tasters will be kept busy at the many vintners in Napa. There are more than 240 wineries in the Napa Valley area, and most of them are open to the public.

What to See and Do

Bothe-Napa Valley State Park. *Calistoga. Located 5 miles N of St. Helena and 4 miles S of Calistoga on Hwy 29/128. Phone 707/942-4575. www.parks.ca.gov.* Showcasing the natural beauty of Napa Valley, this 1,800-acre state park sports pine and redwood groves and offers camping, picnicking, swimming, and more than 10 miles of hiking and horseback riding trails. There's even a horseshoe pit. Mostly, however, the park is rugged; some areas up in the canyons reach elevations as high as 2,000 feet. Near the day-use picnic area is the Pioneer Cemetery, where some of Napa Valley's original settlers are buried. (Daily) **$**

Copia: The American Center for Wine, Food, and the Arts. *500 First St, Napa (94559). Phone 707/259-1600; toll-free 888/512-6742. www.copia.org.* Named after the goddess of abundance, Copia bills itself as a cultural museum and education center dedicated to the American contribution to food, wine, the arts, and humanities. A rather ambitious undertaking, but this 80,000-square-foot building (opened in fall 2001) couldn't be located in a better place than Napa Valley, where food and wine are regarded as arts. The center offers a fascinating mix, from cooking demonstrations and programs on building a wine cellar to gardening, feng shui, artist lectures, and exhibits—even an installation of Julia Child's cookware. Admission allows you access to the gardens, tours, exhibitions, and short programs; long programs may cost extra. The center also offers a gift shop and several restaurants, including the *Wine Spectator* Tasting Table and Julia's Kitchen. (Wed-Mon 10 am-5 pm; closed Jan 1, Thanksgiving, Dec 25) **$$$**

di Rosa Preserve. *5200 Carneros Hwy, Napa (94559). Phone 707/266-5991. www.dirosapreserve.org.* The di Rosa Preserve houses the largest collection of contemporary California Bay Area art in the world, including nearly 2,000 works by approximately 750 artists. What makes this collection unique, however, is the peaceful, natural setting—250 acres with a 35-acre lake—which transforms an ordinary art viewing experience into an extraordinary one. On the grounds are four gallery buildings, a sculpture meadow, gardens, and a meditation chapel. Reservations are required; tours last two and a half hours. (Tues-Fri 9:30 am-3 pm; tour times vary, call or visit Web site for schedule) **$**

Downtown Napa. *Between Soscol Ave and Jefferson St and Division and Clinton sts.* Since man and woman cannot live by wine alone, be sure to take some time to explore the city of Napa, which has more pre-1906 (the year of the big earthquake) Victorian residences still standing than anywhere else in northern California. Many of them are clustered in the Fuller Park neighborhood and the Napa Abajo District. If you have less time, stick to downtown, where you can see the Italianate Opera House and the Art Deco-style post office or visit the Napa Firefighter's Museum or the Historical Society. If you want a little help, Napa County Landmarks periodically conducts 90-minute guided tours May through October. (Call either the landmarks organization at 707/255-1836 or the Napa Conference and Visitors Bureau at 707/226-7459 for more information.) There's also a free downtown trolley that goes through several Victorian neighborhoods and makes stops at Copia and Napa Premium Outlets (see).

Dreamweavers Theatre. *River Park Shopping Center, 1637 Imola Ave, Napa (94559). Phone 707/255-5483. www.dreamweaverstheatre.org.* Napa Valley's only nonprofit theater, Dreamweavers was started in 1978 by two friends who wrote screenplays for silent movies and then casually produced and viewed them with their friends and families. A decade later, the group incorporated as a theater troupe and began regular performances of established material. Today, the troupe is a regular fixture in the region and can be counted on for quality productions and crowd-pleasing selections. **$$$$**

Getaway Adventures. *Calistoga (94515). Phone toll-free 800/499-2453. www.getawayadventures.com.* A fantastic way to tour the Napa Valley area is by bicycle. If you want to plan your own itinerary, there are several bike rental shops in the neighboring towns; however, more and more people are opting for an all-out luxury tour, either through a national company like Backroads or with a regional purveyor like Getaway Adventures. Getaway offers the advantage of being based locally, which means that the company knows the terrain well and can stay up-to-date on events and changes in the valley. Typical "Best of Napa and Sonoma" weekend tours span two days and two nights, covering bikes and equipment, gourmet meals, stays in small luxury hotels or bed-and-breakfasts, a support van, tours of wineries, and elegant picnic lunches. The groups are small—generally six to eight people—and the itinerary often uncovers off-the-beaten-track restaurants and inns. Longer tours are available, as are specialty trips like spa and holiday weekend packages. **$$$$**

Hot air ballooning. *5091 Solano Ave, Napa (94558). Phone 707/253-2222. www.balloonrides.com.* Hot air balloon trips (approximately an hour in the air) above the Napa Valley vineyards. Contact Balloons Above the Valley. **$$$$**

John F. Kennedy Park. *Hwy 221, Napa (94559). Phone 707/257-9529. www.cityofnapa.org.* An inviting and accessible place for children and families, this city park provides tables and barbecue pits for picnicking; softball, baseball, and soccer fields; a volleyball court; a boat launch; a children's playground; and a public golf course. Those more interested in nature can hike the trails, scout birds at the duck pond, and relax in the formal gardens. Several areas of the park can be reserved for private parties. (Daily)

Lake Berryessa. *5520 Knoxville Rd, Napa (94558). Phone 707/966-2111. www.recreation.gov.* Created in 1957, Lake Berryessa is one of the largest bodies of fresh water in California. With 165 miles of shoreline, it has become a year-round recreation favorite of locals, offering opportunities to boat, swim, fish, hike, hunt, camp, bike, and picnic. The lake has seven resorts, popular with boaters, and offers abundant birdwatching opportunities for eagles, hawks, songbirds, great blue herons, pelicans, ducks, and geese. (Daily)

Napa Chef's Market. *First St and Napa Town Center, Napa (94599). Phone 707/253-9282. www.napadowntown.com.* Few things are more appealing when traveling than the local farmers' markets, and the Napa Chef's Market is truly a delight. Not only does it have outstanding farm-fresh produce and gourmet specialty items, but it also features artisans, cooking demonstrations, beer and wine gardens, and live entertainment. The market is a Friday night favorite with locals and visitors alike. If you're in town during a summer weekend, make sure to stop by. (May-July, Fri 5-9 pm)

Napa Premium Outlets. *629 Factory Stores Dr, Napa (94558). Phone 707/226-9876. www.premiumoutlets.com.* Surprisingly, the Napa Valley is a great place to pick up bargains on brand-name and designer merchandise. At the Napa Premium Outlets, you can save 25 to 65 percent on direct-from-the-factory clothes, shoes, and home furnishings. Among the more than 50 stores, you'll find Barney's New York, Kenneth Cole, Max Studio, J. Crew, Ellen Tracy, Calvin Klein, DKNY Jeans, Timberland, Tommy Hilfiger, Ann Taylor, and more. (Mon-Thurs 10 am-8 pm, Fri-Sat to 9 pm, Sun to 6 pm; closed Jan 1, Thanksgiving, Dec 25)

Napa Valley Opera House. *1030 Main St, Napa (94559). Phone 707/226-7372. www.napavalleyopera house.org.* The name is a bit misleading, because the Napa Valley Opera House is actually a venue for all the performing arts, including jazz, classical, and world music; dance; comedy; and theater. Built in 1879, the Opera House is not only one of Napa's most significant historic landmarks, but also one of only two remaining historic second-story theaters in California. Closed for almost a century, it reopened following a partial restoration; performances are being staged only in the first floor Café Theatre. Hours and ticket prices vary with performance.

★ **Napa Valley Wine Train.** *1275 McKinstry St, Napa (94559). Phone 707/253-2111; toll-free 800/427-4124. www.winetrain.com.* One way to sample the Napa Valley's food and wine without the worries of appointing a designated driver is to reserve a spot on the wine train. Take a scenic trip aboard a turn-of-the-century Pullman or a 1950s diesel Steamliner. Typically a three-hour ride, the train travels a 36-mile route from Napa through St. Helena, passing by dozens of vineyards. Though a tad touristy, the train combines the comfort and elegance of years past with the sophisticated palate that today's foodies demand. A wide variety of packages are available—standard lunch and dinner rides, which can include wine tastings (in the wine tasting car) and stops at various vineyards, as well as gourmet and champagne meals, a Sunday dinner and concert series, a murder mystery dinner theater, and family fun nights. (Daily) **$$$$**

Oakville Grocery. *7856 St. Helena Hwy, Oakville (94562). Phone 707/944-8802. www.oakvillegrocery.com.* How many grocery stores make it onto the National Registry of Historic Places? In 1993, this longtime Napa favorite did. And though it may look like a quaint, old-time country store, don't let that fool you: inside, you'll find an astonishing array of gourmet foods, cheeses, northern California wines, fresh produce, pastries, breads, and local specialty items—perfect for gifts, picnics, and cooking. For early risers, the espresso bar opens at 8 am daily. (Daily 9 am-6 pm; closed holidays)

Silverado Trail. *Take Hwy 29 through the city of Napa to Trancas St. Turn right, drive approximately 2 miles, and then turn left onto the Silverado Trail. Phone 707/257-0130. www.silveradotrail.com.* This 29-mile drive, the first permanent road to be built between Napa and Calistoga in 1852, was once a major trade route. Today, it is the link between many of Napa Valley's smaller wineries (the majority of the major ones are located on the more congested Hwy 29). The quieter Silverado Trail is said to afford travelers a glimpse of the nation's foremost wine region as it looked 30 years ago. Whether or not that's true, it makes for a leisurely drive and offers an excellent view of the vineyards and mountains. As you drive, be sure to stop at some of the more than 30 wineries along the way; many of them sell wines only available directly from the winery, so you're in for a treat. Although it takes less than an hour to follow the trail, you can easily turn it into a full day's exploration. (Daily)

Skyline Wilderness Park. *2201 Imola Ave, Napa (94559). Phone 707/252-0481. www.ncfaa.com/skyline/skyline_park.* Some of the best hiking in the area can be found at the Skyline Wilderness Park, which has dedicated trails just for hikers in addition to trails for horseback riding and mountain biking. The well-maintained park also has several camping areas—including some for horse camping and RVs—as well as picnic grounds, gardens, and an archery range. A favorite day hike leads to an overlook above Lake Marie, which is also a good spot for bird- and wildlife-watchers. (Daily; closed holidays) **$**

Sonoma Cattle Company and Napa Valley Trail Rides. *Napa (94559). Phone 707/255-2900. www.napasonomatrailrides.com.* For those who prefer to see the Napa Valley at a slower pace and from a different perspective, the Sonoma Cattle Company and Napa Valley Trail Rides offers several options: year-round rides through Sugarloaf Ridge State Park, including sunset, full-moon, and wildflower tours; April-November explorations of the Bothe-Napa Valley State Park, in the heart of Napa Valley just 4 miles south of Calistoga; and trips through the vineyards and redwood groves in Jack London State Historic Park, also April-November. Rides range from several hours to overnight camping; and half-day trips include a box lunch. A popular outing is the sunset ride at Sugarloaf Ridge, when the valley is bathed in golden light. *Note:* riders must be over age 8 and weigh less than 240 pounds. (Year-round; closed major holidays) **$$$$**

Wineries. Among these are

Artesa Winery. *1345 Henry Rd, Napa (94559). Phone 707/224-1668. www.artesawinery.com.* Unlike the restored historic vineyards that define the Napa Valley, Artesa is defined by its sleek modernist architecture, more museum than vineyard. In fact, with its own artist-in-residence, the winery places as much emphasis on art as it does on wine. Built by the old Codorniu family, Spain's largest makers of sparkling wine, Artesa (which means "handcrafted" in Catalan) started with "method champenoise" but has since expanded to quality still wines. Go for the wine, go for the art, and go for the view—one of the most spectacular in the region, overlooking the entire Carneros Valley and the San Francisco Bay. (Daily 10 am-5 pm; closed holidays) **$$**

Bouchaine Vineyards. *1075 Buchli Station Rd, Napa (94559). Phone 707/252-9065; toll-free 800/654-9463. www.bouchaine.com.* Best known for its pinot noir, a grape that thrives in the cool Carneros Valley, Bouchaine is the oldest continually operating winery in the Carneros region. The winery was renovated extensively in 1995, receiving numerous local architectural and historic awards, due in part to its use of recycled materials. The end result is a fireplace-warmed tasting room, as well as a deck and terrace with views of the Carneros hills, which makes for cozy, friendly wine tastings. Tours by appointment. (Daily 10:30 am-4 pm; closed holidays) **FREE**

Carneros Creek Winery. *1285 Dealy Ln, Napa (94559). Phone 707/253-9463. www.carneroscreek.com.* Founded in 1972, this winery is known for pinot noir and its stock of rare older wines. (Daily 10 am-5 pm) **$$**

Domaine Carneros by Taittinger. *1240 Duhig Rd, Napa (94559). Phone 707/257-0101.*

www.domainecarneros.com. The majestic hilltop chateau makes this one of the most spectacular to view. The house specialty is sparkling wine. (Daily 10:15 am-4 pm) **FREE**

Hess Collection Winery. *4411 Redwood Rd, Napa (94558). Phone 707/255-1144; toll-free 877/707-4377. www.hesscollection.com.* The "Collection" part of this vineyard's name refers as much to art as it does to wine. Owner Donald Hess found a way to merge his two passions—traditional winemaking and contemporary art—in one place. You can experience both on the premises; the tasting room and the gallery are both open to the public. The wine has a reputation for being high quality and good value and is available for purchase at the vineyard store. (Daily 10 am-4 pm; closed holidays) **$$**

Luna Vineyards. *2921 Silverado Trail, Napa (94558). Phone 707/255-5862. www.lunavineyards.com.* Luna Vineyards has the feel of an Italian villa from centuries past. With its lovely covered porch on which to relax while sipping wine, you might just be transported back to the old country for a few moments. Luna specializes in Italian varietals: pinot grigio, sangiovese, merlot, and their proprietary wine, Canto. Tours and tastings are by appointment. (Daily 10 am-5 pm; closed holidays) **FREE**

Pine Ridge Winery. *5901 Silverado Trail, Napa (94558). Phone 707/253-7500; toll-free 800/575-9777. www.pineridgewinery.com.* Chosen by the *Wall Street Journal* as one of the top five wineries to visit in the area, this elegant winery was also rated as the regional winery of 2002 by *Wine & Spirits* magazine. With an array of award-winning wines, Pine Ridge attracts serious oenophiles, who especially appreciate the new reserve tasting room. Visitors can also wander estate gardens, tour the vast cabernet caves 100 feet underground, and participate in barrel tastings (special tastings by appointment only). (Daily 10:30 am-4:30 pm; closed holidays). Guided tours by appointment only (10 am, noon, 2 pm) **$$$$**

William Hill Winery. *1761 Atlas Peak Rd, Napa (94558). Phone 707/224-4477. www.williamhill.com.* Specializing in cabernet sauvignon, William Hill is a small, elegant winery in southern Napa. Reserve a spot in the "Aura Experience Tasting," in which visitors can share in the staff's favorite pairings and learn how to deconstruct wine flavors using all the senses. Seating is limited and dates and times vary, so call ahead. (Daily 10:30 am-4 pm; closed holidays) **$**

Special Event

Music in the Vineyards: Napa Valley Chamber Music Festival. *Phone 707/258-5559. www.napavalleymusic.org. At various venues in Napa Valley.* An absolutely lovely way to experience the Napa Valley ambience, the Napa Valley Chamber Music Festival presents musical performances at various vineyards and holds wine tastings during intermission. The intimacy of the settings makes them ideal for chamber music, and the festival is a favorite with locals. Performances are presented on Saturdays and Sundays during August; midweek events include concerts, recitals, lecture demonstrations, and open rehearsals that are free to the public. Early-mid-Aug. **$$$$**

Limited-Service Hotels

★ BEST WESTERN ELM HOUSE INN. *800 California Blvd, Napa (94559). Phone 707/255-1831; toll-free 888/849-1997; fax 707/255-8609. www.bestwestern.com.* 22 rooms, 3 story. Complimentary full breakfast. Check-in 3 pm, check-out noon. High-speed Internet access. Outdoor pool. **$**

★ ★ EMBASSY SUITES. *1075 California Blvd, Napa (94559). Phone 707/253-9540; fax 707/253-9202. www.embassynapa.com.* An all-suites property, this lodging is located just off Highway 29, the main highway through the Napa Valley. It has an attractive and distinctive Mediterranean décor, featuring a high-ceilinged, terra-cotta-tiled lobby, an inner courtyard with a mill pond (complete with swans), gardens, old winery equipment, and a large dining atrium. The guest rooms are spacious, comfortable, and well equipped for travelers, with a full sitting section, a kitchenette, and a separate sleeping area. A complimentary cooked-to-order breakfast, as well as an on-site restaurant and lounge, are available. There is also an afternoon manager's reception highlighting Napa Valley wines. 205 rooms, 3 story. Complimentary full breakfast. Check-in 4 pm, check-out noon. Restaurant, bar. Indoor pool, whirlpool. **$$**

★ ★ HILTON GARDEN INN NAPA. *3585 Solano Ave, Napa (94558). Phone 707/252-0444; toll-free 800/782-9444; fax 707/252-0244. www.hiltongardeninn.com.*

80 rooms. Check-in 3 pm, check-out noon. Restaurant, bar. Outdoor pool, whirlpool. Airport transportation available. **$$**

★ JOHN MUIR INN. *1998 Trower Ave, Napa (94558). Phone 707/257-7220; toll-free 800/522-8999; fax 707/258-0943. www.johnmuirnapa.com.* This property is conveniently located just off Highway 29, on the north end of Napa. It is a nicely maintained motor lodge, with an attractive entry pergola, courtyard pool, hot tub, and small but comfortable lobby with fireside seating. The guest rooms are reasonably priced, a positive feature in the pricey Napa Valley. A complimentary continental breakfast is provided, and a family restaurant is nearby. 56 rooms, 3 story. Complimentary continental breakfast. Check-in 3 pm, check-out 11 am. Outdoor pool, whirlpool. **$**

★ ★ NAPA RIVER INN. *500 Main St, Napa (94558). Phone 707/251-8500; toll-free 877/251-8500; fax 707/251-8504. www.napariverinn.com.* 66 rooms. Complimentary continental breakfast. Check-in 3 pm, check-out noon. Restaurant, bar. **$$**

Full-Service Hotel

★ ★ ★ MARRIOTT NAPA VALLEY HOTEL AND SPA. *3425 Solano Ave, Napa (94558). Phone 707/253-8600; toll-free 800/228-9290; fax 707/258-1320. www.napavalleymarriott.com.* The largest hotel in the Napa Valley, the Marriott is located on the north end of the city of Napa, facing onto Highway 29, which runs up the length of the valley though the wine country. Renovation and expansion have made this sprawling complex of two story, beige stucco wings a full-service property, meeting all the needs of guests. There is a central courtyard with a large pool, and a spa, salon, and fitness facility on the south side of the hotel. There are also two restaurants and a sports bar. The guest rooms are quite handsome and feature pillow-top mattresses, down duvet bed covers, high-speed Internet access, and large practical work desks. 272 rooms, 2 story. Check-in 4 pm, check-out noon. High-speed Internet access. Restaurant, bar. Fitness room, spa. Outdoor pool, whirlpool. Business center. **$$**

Full-Service Resorts

★ ★ ★ THE CARNEROS INN. *4048 Sonoma Hwy, Napa (94559). Phone 707/299-4900; toll-free 888/400-9000; fax 707/299-4950. www.thecarnerosinn.com.* Tucked between Napa and Sonoma and surrounded by vineyards, the Carneros Inn is an inviting spot to take in the beauty of the wine country. This intimate property instantly soothes guests with its monochromatic, contemporary styling, and this all-cottage hotel offers spacious accommodations with high-tech amenities. From heated slate floors in the bathrooms to flat-screen televisions, this hotel knows how to pamper the modern traveler. The spa looks to the region for its inspiration, and most of the treatments use local herbs, fruits, and other ingredients harvested from the land. Fine dining is just a few steps away at the Hilltop Dining Room, while the Boon Fly Café is just the place to celebrate morning, grab lunch to go, or taste local wines. 86 rooms. Check-in 4 pm, check-out noon. Restaurant, bar. **$$$$**

★ ★ ★ SILVERADO RESORT. *1600 Atlas Peak Rd, Napa (94558). Phone 707/257-0200; toll-free 800/532-0500; fax 707/257-2867. www.silveradoresort.com.* With two 18-hole, Robert Trent Jones-designed courses and 17 tennis courts, the Silverado Resort attracts sports enthusiasts from across northern California. Although most come to play, and to use the state-of-the-art spa—many come to shop. 280 rooms, 2 story. Check-in 4 pm, check-out noon. Restaurant, bar. Fitness room, spa. Outdoor pool, children's pool, whirlpool. Golf. Tennis. Business center. **$$**

Full-Service Inns

★ ★ ★ LA RESIDENCE. *4066 Howard Ln, Napa (94558). Phone 707/253-0337; toll-free 800/253-9203; fax 707/253-0382. www.laresidence.com.* La Résidence combines the charms of Napa Valley with the style of the French countryside. This gracious 1870 Gothic Revival mansion feels tucked away, yet it remains convenient to the region's world-renowned vineyards. This delightful inn is the perfect place to unwind after a day of wine tasting or biking. Leafy trees shade guests relaxing by the pool, while the gentle trickle of the fountains soothes visitors. Wonderful buffet breakfasts are available each morning, and in the evenings, wine and hors d'oeuvres are served by the fire or outside on the terrace. 25 rooms, 3 story. Complimentary full breakfast. Check-in 2 pm, check-out 11 am. Outdoor pool, whirlpool. **$$$**

★★★ **MILLIKEN CREEK INN.** *1815 Silverado Trail, Napa (94558). Phone 707/255-1197; toll-free 888/622-5775; fax 707/255-3112. www.millikencreekinn.com.* Napa Valley's Milliken Creek Inn is tranquility defined. This posh hideaway lulls visitors into a Zen-like state on its 3 acres resting alongside the Napa River. Located on the Silverado Trail, the inn is minutes from the valley's acclaimed wineries, yet its gentle pace and beautiful setting often convince guests to remain here. With riverside massages and dining on the scenic terrace, there is no reason to leave. Luxury is in the details, and warm touches abound at this property. Beds are fitted with exclusive linens, piled high for extra comfort, and fresh flowers and candles fill the guest rooms. Cosmopolitan elegance is the mantra here, where Asian furnishings add an exotic appeal to the stylish accommodations. 12 rooms, 2 story. Children over 16 years only. Complimentary full breakfast. Check-in 4 pm, check-out 11 am. Spa. **$$$$**

Specialty Lodgings

The following lodging establishments are approved by Mobil Travel Guide, but due to their unique and individualized nature have not been given a traditional Mobil Star rating. Included in this listing you may find bed-and-breakfasts, limited-service inns, guest ranches, and other unique hotel properties.

THE BEAZLEY HOUSE. *1910 1st St, Napa (94559). Phone 707/257-1649; toll-free 800/559-1649; fax 707/257-1518. www.beazleyhouse.com.* Located in a quiet residential area, this is the oldest bed-and-breakfast in the city of Napa. The 1902 Colonial Revival building has a five-room carriage house at the rear and an all-suite addition two doors away in a 19th-century mansion. A charming blend of modern comforts and amenities with Victorian décor, the property is well situated at the entrance to the Napa Valley wine country. Lodging features include off-street parking, a full hot breakfast, rear lawn and gardens, and many rooms with fireplaces and spa tubs. 11 rooms, 2 story. Pets accepted. Complimentary full breakfast. Check-in 3:30-6:30 pm, check-out noon. **$$**

BLACKBIRD INN. *1755 First St, Napa (94559). Phone 707/226-2450; toll-free 888/567-9811; fax 707/258-6391. www.foursisters.com.* A quality bed-and-breakfast, this lodging is one of the ten upscale Four Sisters small inn properties located in California and Washington State. The property is on a busy corner in the historic residential area of downtown Napa and occupies a circa-1900 Craftsman-style former residence. Close to Highway 29 and the Napa Valley wine country, the totally nonsmoking inn has eight eclectically furnished and decorated guest rooms, which are packed with amenities (all have CD players, bathrobes, automatic turndown, and duvet bed covers, and most have fireplaces and Jacuzzi tubs). A full breakfast, afternoon wine and hors d'oeuvres, and complimentary soft drinks and cookies are featured. 8 rooms. Complimentary full breakfast. Check-in 3 pm, check-out noon. **$$**

BLUE VIOLET MANSION. *443 Brown St, Napa (94559). Phone 707/253-2583; toll-free 800/959-2583; fax 707/257-8205. www.bluevioletmansion.com.* 17 rooms. Complimentary full breakfast. Check-in 3:30-6 pm, check-out 11 am. Outdoor pool, whirlpool. **$$$**

HENNESSEY HOUSE B&B. *1727 Main St, Napa (94559). Phone 707/226-3774; fax 707/226-2975. www.hennesseyhouse.com.* 10 rooms. Complimentary full breakfast. Check-in 3:30-8 pm, check-out 11 am. **$$**

LA BELLE EPOQUE. *1386 Calistoga Ave, Napa (94559). Phone 707/257-2161; toll-free 800/238-8070; fax 707/226-6314. www.labelleepoque.com.* 6 rooms. Complimentary full breakfast. Check-in 3-5 pm, check-out 11 am. **$$$**

THE OLD WORLD INN. *1301 Jefferson St, Napa (94559). Phone 707/257-0112; toll-free 800/966-6624; fax 707/257-0118. www.oldworldinn.com.* This 1906 Victorian, a former residence, houses furnishings and décor from a bygone era. There is a Scandinavian influence in the décor and fabrics, and pastel shades predominate in the guest room color schemes. The property is located on a busy street in the center of residential Napa and not far from Highway 29 and access to the Napa Valley Wine Country. There is off-street parking, a backyard hot tub and patio, a full breakfast, afternoon refreshments, and evening desserts. 10 rooms, 2 story. Complimentary full breakfast. Check-in 3:30-6 pm, check-out 11 am. **$**

Spa

★★★★ THE CARNEROS INN SPA. *4048 Sonoma Hwy, Napa (94559).* Napa Valley's Carneros Inn takes the country farmhouse and turns it on its head with clean lines and simple sophistication. The sun-filled, mood-lifting spa perfectly complements this resort's laid-back attitude with its uncluttered, chic décor. This inviting space pampers guests with a theme-oriented treatment menu, which includes regional inspiration from the harvests, farms, cellars, minerals, and creeks of the Carneros Valley. Therapies include tantalizing selections such as honeydew exfoliations, paprika facials, goat butter massages, grape seed and guava body scrubs, and lemongrass and ginger sea mineral body wraps. The massage treatment menu caters to everyone, including pregnant and sports-minded guests, with customized therapies. For those guests who prefer to remain within the confines of their private cottages, the spa presents a "to go" menu of in-room treatments, including organic garden wraps and couples massages.

Restaurants

★★ BISTRO DON GIOVANNI. *4110 Howard Ln, Napa (94558). Phone 707/224-3300; fax 707/224-3395. www.bistrodongiovanni.com.* The décor and landscaping of this quaint mauve-colored stucco bistro will make you feel like you're dining in the Tuscan countryside. The heated outdoor terrace looks out over beautifully manicured gardens that showcase modern sculptures and the centerpiece fountain. The ambience inside is equally inviting, with colorful tiles and artwork and an open kitchen with a wood-burning oven. California, Italian menu. Lunch, dinner. Closed Thanksgiving, Dec 25. Bar. Reservations recommended. Outdoor seating. **$$**

★★ CELADON. *500 Main St, Suite G, Napa (94559). Phone 707/254-9690; fax 707/254-9692. www.celadonnapa.com.* On a creek. International menu. Lunch, dinner. Closed holidays. Outdoor seating. **$$$**

★ JONESY'S FAMOUS STEAK HOUSE. *2044 Airport Rd, Napa (94558). Phone 707/255-2003; fax 707/255-2008. www.jonesysfamoussteakhouse.com.* There could be a few reasons this steakhouse is considered "famous." One could be that the restaurant is actually located inside the terminal at the Napa County Airport, providing for an interesting view of the comings and goings of the operations there. Another could be the method in which the steaks here are cooked—under seasoned rocks from the Sacramento River, allowing the natural juices to be seared inside. Either way, diners are sure to enjoy their experience here. Seafood, steak menu. Lunch, dinner. Closed Mon; Dec 25. Bar. Children's menu. **$$**

★★ JULIA'S KITCHEN. *500 First St, Napa (94559). Phone 707/265-5700. www.copia.org.* California menu. Lunch, dinner. Closed Tues; holidays. Casual attire. Reservations recommended. **$$**

★★ LA BOUCANE. *1778 2nd St, Napa (94559). Phone 707/253-1177; fax 707/253-1190.* House built in 1885. French menu. Dinner. Closed Sun; holidays; also two weeks in Jan. Reservations recommended. **$$**

★★★ NAPA VALLEY WINE TRAIN. *1275 McKinstry St, Napa (94559). Phone 707/253-2111; toll-free 800/427-4124; fax 707/253-9264. www.winetrain.com.* Offering a threefold adventure returning to the days of elegant rail travel, this restaurant offers a deliciously crafted culinary and wine experience, a relaxing tour through the heart of the Napa Valley in meticulously restored Pullman dining cars, and pampering service. The 36-mile trip takes diners through vineyards to St. Helena and back to Napa. California menu. Lunch, dinner, brunch. Closed Jan 1, Dec 25. Bar. Children's menu. Reservations recommended. **$$$$**

Nevada City (D-3)

See also Auburn, Grass Valley, Marysville, Mother Lode Country, Oroville

Settled 1849
Population 3,001
Elevation 2,525 ft
Area Code 530
Zip 95959
Information Nevada City Chamber of Commerce, 132 Main St; phone 530/265-2692 or toll-free 800/655-6569 (CA & NV)
Web Site www.ncgold.com

Two years after gold was discovered here, 10,000 miners were working every foot of ground within a radius of 3 miles. The gravel banks are said to have yielded $8 million in gold dust and nuggets in two years. Of the major gold rush towns, Nevada City remains one of the most picturesque, its residential areas dotted with multigabled frame houses. Principal occupations are lumbering, tourism, government, electronics, and craft shops. The gold mines were closed in 1956.

A Ranger District office of the Tahoe National Forest is located here.

What to See and Do

Firehouse No. 1 Museum. *214 Main St, Nevada City (95959). Phone 530/265-5468.* (1861) On display are Donner Party relics, Joss House altar, Quan Yin alton Maidu artifacts, clothing and photos of early settlers. (Fri-Sat noon-3 pm) **DONATION**

Historic Miners Foundry. *325 Spring St, Nevada City (95959). Phone 530/265-5383.* (1856) Group of stone, brick, and frame buildings. The Pelton Wheel was originally tested and manufactured here (1878). Special events, theater, and concerts are held here.

Malakoff Diggins State Historic Park. *23729 N Bloomfield Rd, Nevada City (95959). 15 miles NE off Hwy 49 at Tyler-Foote Crossing. Phone 530/265-2740. www.parks.ca.gov.* Gold mining town on 3,000 acres. Museum with hydraulic mining exhibits (May-Oct: daily; rest of year: weekends). Swimming, fishing; hiking and bridle trails, picnicking, camping, cabins. **$**

National Hotel. *211 Broad St, Nevada City (95959). Phone 530/265-4551. www.thenationalhotel.com.* Three stories, with balconies and balustrades reaching over the sidewalks. Victorian furnishings. Conducted a prosperous bar business during 1860s and 1870s. Still operates dining room (see RESTAURANTS) and saloon.

Nevada Theatre. *401 Broad St, Nevada City (95959). Phone 530/265-6161. www.nevadatheatre.com.* (1865) The Foothill Theatre Company performs several productions in this historic theater. (Mar-Dec)

Walking tours. *Phone toll-free 800/655-6569. www.nevadacitychamber.com.* Booklets describing historic buildings and sites may be obtained at the Chamber of Commerce.

Special Events

Constitution Day Parade and Celebration. *132 Main St, Nevada City (95959). Phone 530/265-2692 (Chamber of Commerce); toll-free 800/655-6569. www.nevadacitychamber.com/events_constitution.htm.* Floats, marching bands, and local favorites like the Marching Presidents of Nevada City parade through the historic downtown district. Other annual activities include a duck race and battle reenactments. Second weekend in Sept. **FREE**

Fall Color Spectacular. *132 Main St, Nevada City (95959). Phone 530/265-2692 (Chamber of Commerce).* Colorful maples, aspens, fruit trees, poplars, firs, cedars, and pines. Mid-Oct-mid-Nov.

International Teddy Bear Convention. *Miners Foundry, 325 Spring St, Nevada City (95959). At Bridge St. Phone 530/265-5804. www.teddybearcastle.com.* Teddies and "Bearaphermalia"—from jewelry to costumes to furniture—are available for purchase. Be sure to also check out the Flying Teddy Bear Circus in the Big Bear Top. First weekend in Apr. **$**

Nevada City Classic Bicycle Tour. *132 Main St, Nevada City (95959). Phone 530/265-2692 (Chamber of Commerce).* Every Father's Day, both amateur and professional cyclists flock to Nevada City to take part in this competition, the second-oldest bike race in the country. As cyclists speed around the city's hilly streets, they are cheered on by thousands of enthusiastic spectators. The day's events include a 40-mile senior race and a 20-mile junior race. June.

Victorian Christmas. *132 Main St, Nevada City (95959). Phone 530/265-2692 (Chamber of Commerce). www.nevadacitychamber.com/events_victorian.htm.* Take a step back in time to a Christmas from years past, complete with Victorian singers, strolling minstrels, chestnuts roasting over an open fire, and a living nativity scene. Three Wed nights and Sun preceding Christmas. **FREE**

Specialty Lodgings

The following lodging establishments are approved by Mobil Travel Guide, but due to their unique and individualized nature have not been given a traditional Mobil Star rating. Included in this listing you may find bed-and-breakfasts, limited-service inns, guest ranches, and other unique hotel properties.

EMMA NEVADA HOUSE. *528 E Broad St, Nevada City (95959). Phone 530/265-4415; toll-free 800/916-3662; fax 530/265-4416. www.emmanevadahouse.com.* Built in 1856; antiques. 6 rooms, 2 story. Children over 10 years only. Complimentary full breakfast. Check-in 3-6 pm, check-out 11 am. **$**

FLUME'S END BED AND BREAKFAST. *317 S Pine St, Nevada City (95959). Phone 530/265-9665; toll-free 800/991-8118. www.flumesend.com.* Victorian inn built 1861. On stream; historic water flume on property. 6 rooms, 2 story. Complimentary full breakfast. Check-in 3:30-6 pm, check-out 11 am. **$**

RED CASTLE. *109 Prospect St, Nevada City (95959). Phone 530/265-5135. www.redcastleinn.com.* Built in 1860, this historic inn is a fine example of domestic Gothic architecture. Antiques and period pieces artfully decorate each room. 7 rooms, 4 story. Complimentary full breakfast. Check-in Sun-Thurs 4 pm, Fri-Sat 2 pm; check-out 11 am. **$**

Restaurants

★ BELLAVISTA CREEKSIDE. *101 Broad St, Nevada City (95959). Phone 530/265-3445; fax 530/265-8110.* On the creek. Italian menu. Lunch, dinner, Sun brunch. Closed Mon; Jan 1, Dec 25. Bar. Children's menu. Outdoor seating. **$$$**

★ ★ NATIONAL HOTEL VICTORIAN DINING ROOM. *211 Broad St, Nevada City (95959). Phone 530/265-4551. www.thenationalhotel.com.* Victorian décor. In historic hotel (1852). American menu. Breakfast, lunch, dinner, Sun brunch. Bar. **$$**

Newark

See also Fremont

Web Site www.ci.newark.ca.us

Limited-Service Hotel

★ ★ COURTYARD BY MARRIOTT. *34905 Newark Blvd, Newark (94560). Phone 510/792-5200; fax 510/792-5255. www.courtyard.com.* Designed for both business and pleasure travelers alike, this property is conveniently located near restaurants, shopping, and major corporations. 181 rooms, 6 story. Check-in 3 pm, check-out noon. Bar. Fitness room. Outdoor pool. **$**

Full-Service Hotel

★ ★ ★ W SILICON VALLEY. *8200 Gateway Blvd, Newark (94560). Phone 510/494-8800; fax 510/794-3001. www.whotels.com.* 174 rooms, 10 story, all suites. Pets accepted; fee. Check-in 3 pm, check-out noon. High-speed Internet access. Restaurant, bar. Fitness room, spa. Outdoor pool, whirlpool. Business center. **$$**

Novato

See also San Rafael

Web Site www.tourism.novato.org

What to See and Do

Olompali State Historic Park. *Hwy 101, Novato. 3 miles N of Novato on Hwy 101. Entrance is accessible only to southbound traffic on Hwy 101. Phone 415/892-3383. www.parks.ca.gov.* Inhabited by the Coastal Miwok peoples from 6,000 BC to the 1850s, this site near the base of Mount Burdell looks out over the Pelaluma River and San Pablo Bay. Today, the Olompali State Historic Park (named for the Miwok word for "southern village') consists of several archaeological relics of the area's former residents, as well as horseback and hiking trails. A project to build a replica of a Miwok village is underway.

Limited-Service Hotel

★ ★ BEST WESTERN NOVATO OAKS INN. *215 Alameda Del Prado, Novato (94949). Phone 415/883-4400; toll-free 800/625-7466; fax 415/883-4128. www.renesonhotels.com.* 107 rooms, 3 story. Complimentary continental breakfast. Check-in 3 pm, check-out noon. Restaurant, bar. Children's activity center. Fitness room. Outdoor pool, whirlpool. Business center. **$**

Restaurant

★ ★ CACTI. *1200 Grant Ave, Novato (94948). Phone 415/898-2234; fax 415/898-4313. www.cactigrill.com.* What makes this Marin County restaurant particularly intriguing is the fact that it is set in what used to be a church, complete with high, open-beamed ceilings and hardwood floors. Out on the patio, where customers can dine under the stars, a unique Mexican tile fountain makes a beautiful focal point. The menu is Southwestern with a distinctly Californian twist. Southwestern menu. Lunch, dinner. Closed Jan 1, Thanksgiving, Dec 25. Bar. Children's menu. Outdoor seating. **$$**

Oakdale (E-3)

See also Modesto, Sonora

Population 15,503
Area Code 209
Zip 95361
Information Chamber of Commerce, 590 S Yosemite Ave; phone 209/847-2244
Web Site www.yosemite-gateway.net

Oakdale's birth is linked to gold and the railroad. An important town along the freight lines to the Mother Lode towns, it was founded by the Stockton & Visalia Railroad Company in 1871. Beef and dairy cattle and a variety of produce support the area now, as do major industries such as Hershey Chocolate and Hunt-Wesson Foods.

What to See and Do

Oakdale Cowboy Museum. *355 E F St, Oakdale. Phone 209/847-7049. www.oakdalecowboymuseum.org.* Pays tribute to local rodeo champions, farmers, ranchers, and working cowboys. Housed in historic Depot Building. Tours. (Mon-Fri 10 am-2 pm) **$**

Woodward Reservoir. *14528 26-Mile Rd, Oakdale. 5 miles N. Phone 209/847-3304.* Swimming, water-skiing, fishing, boating (moorings, marina); duck hunting, picnicking, concession (Apr-mid-Sept), camping, showers. (Daily) **$$$$**

Special Events

California Dally Team Roping Championships. *Oakdale Saddle Club Rodeo, 1624 E F St, Oakdale (95361). Phone 209/847-1641.* The public is welcome to come watch this annual event in which two-person teams compete in team roping: whoever gets a calf roped and tied in the shortest amount of time wins a cash prize. Labor Day weekend. **FREE**

Chocolate Festival. *Wood Park, Hwy 120 and 108, Oakdale (95361). Phone 209/847-2244.* Entertainment, arts and crafts, classic car show, food booths, games, and Chocolate Avenue. Third weekend in May. **$**

PRCA Rodeo. *1624 E F St, Oakdale (95361). Phone 209/847-2244.* The self-proclaimed "Cowboy Capital of the World," Oakdale hosts one of the most authentic Old West rodeos. Everyone in town gets in on the action from the parade to the rodeo itself to the dance that follows. Second weekend of Apr.

Limited-Service Hotel

★ ★ RAMADA. *825 E F St, Oakdale (95361). Phone 209/847-8181; toll-free 800/272-6232; fax 209/847-9546. www.ramada.com.* 70 rooms, 2 story. Complimentary continental breakfast. Check-out noon. Restaurant, bar. Outdoor pool, whirlpool. **$**

Oakhurst (E-3)

See also Yosemite National Park

Population 2,868
Elevation 2,300 ft
Area Code 559
Zip 93644
Information Yosemite-Sierra Visitors Bureau, 40637 Hwy 41; phone 559/683-4636
Web Site www.go2yosemite.net

Limited-Service Hotel

★ ★ BEST WESTERN YOSEMITE GATEWAY INN. *40530 Hwy 41, Oakhurst (93644). Phone 559/683-2378; fax 559/683-3813. www.bestwestern.com.* 123 rooms, 2 story. Pets accepted, some restrictions. Check-in 1 pm, check-out 11 am. Restaurant, bar. Fitness room. Indoor pool, outdoor pool, whirlpool. **$**

Full-Service Inn

★ ★ ★ ★ ★ CHATEAU DU SUREAU. *48688 Victoria Ln, Oakhurst (93644). Phone 559/683-6860; fax 559/683-0800. www.chateausureau.com.* Located in the middle of the California woods, not far from Yosemite National Park, is a lovely hideaway known as Chateau du Sureau. This magical estate is set on 9 acres of rolling fields filled with elderberry bushes and wildflowers. The Chateau seems like it is scripted straight from a fairy tale, with shuttered windows and an ivy-covered turret, while the interiors reflect French Provençal influences. This is a place where visitors come to leave the modern world behind. Sunny Provençal fabrics and patterns come alive in the ten highly unique bedrooms, nearly all of which have fireplaces. Canopy and sleigh beds, cathedral ceilings, and stunning views of the Sierra Nevada Mountains add to the romance of this secluded spot.

Erna's Elderberry House (see) attracts gourmets from long distances who savor the sublime meals artfully prepared by the Austrian proprietor. 10 rooms, 2 story. Complimentary full breakfast. Check-in 3 pm, check-out noon. High-speed Internet access. Restaurant, bar. Outdoor pool, whirlpool. **$$$$**

Specialty Lodging

The following lodging establishment is approved by Mobil Travel Guide, but due to its unique and individualized nature has not been given a traditional Mobil Star rating. Included in this listing you may find bed-and-breakfasts, limited-service inns, guest ranches, and other unique hotel properties.

HOUNDS TOOTH INN. *42071 Hwy 41, Oakhurst (93644). Phone 559/642-6600; toll-free 888/642-6610; fax 559/658-2946. www.houndstoothinn.com.* 13 rooms, 2 story. Complimentary full breakfast. Check-in 3 pm, check-out noon. **$$**

Restaurant

★★★★ ERNA'S ELDERBERRY HOUSE. *48688 Victoria Ln, Oakhurst (93644). Phone 559/683-6800; fax 559/683-0800. www.chateausureau.com.* Surrounded by the majesty of the Sierra Nevada Mountains, just miles from Yosemite National Park, Erna's Elderberry House is a romantic, enchanted hideaway. The restaurant is divided into three precious dining areas, each richly appointed with antique French Provençal furnishings, brocade tapestries, and original oil paintings. Erna Kubin-Clanin opened this fairy tale restaurant in 1984 and has been the guiding force in the kitchen ever since, turning out exquisite California cuisine that respects the seasons and features farm-raised meats and local produce. To complement the daily changing prix fixe menu consisting of six courses, the sommelier and chef pair each course with three or four wines from California and around the world. The 725-bottle wine list is overseen by Erna's daughter Renée and includes several rare, "cult" California wines as well as many Austrian selections in honor of Erna's birthplace. After dinner, you can relax in the estate's lush flower gardens with a fine cigar, a cognac, or both. California, French menu. Dinner, Sun brunch. Closed first two weeks in Jan. Bar. Business casual attire. Reservations recommended. Valet parking. Outdoor seating. **$$$**

Oakland (E-2)

See also Antioch, Berkeley, Concord, Fremont, Hayward, Livermore, Martinez, Pleasanton, San Francisco, San Francisco International Airport Area, San Mateo, Sausalito, Vallejo, Walnut Creek

Founded 1850
Population 399,484
Elevation 42 ft
Area Code 510
Zip 94612
Information Oakland Chamber of Commerce, 475 14th St, Suite 120; phone 510/874-4800 or toll-free 800/262-5526
Web Site www.oaklandnet.com

Oakland lies just across the bay from San Francisco. The port of Oakland has excellent facilities and caters to heavy Pacific trade. More than 1,500 factories help make Alameda County a leading manufacturing center. The Bay Area Rapid Transit system (BART) links suburban areas and Oakland with San Francisco. Once part of the Rancho San Antonio, a 48,000-acre domain of former Spanish cavalry sergeant Luis Maria Peralta, it was acquired as a townsite by Horace W. Carpentier, who named it for the evergreen oaks that marked the landscape.

What to See and Do

Camron-Stanford House. *1418 Lakeside Dr, Oakland (94612). Phone 510/874-7802. www.cshouse.org.* (1876) Once the home of the Camron family and later the Stanford family, this building served as the Oakland Public Museum from 1910 to 1967. Today, the house operates as a resource center and museum with authentic period furnishings, sculpture, and paintings. Slide program; library. Guided tours. (Wed 11 am and 4 pm, Sun 1-5 pm twice a month, also by appointment) **$**

Chabot Observatory and Science Center. *10000 Skyline Blvd, Oakland (94612). Phone 510/336-7300. www.chabotspace.org.* This 70,000-square-foot complex includes the nation's largest public telescope, a state-of-the-art planetarium, an Omnimax theater, and hands-on science exhibits. It also includes a 6-acre environmental education area, nature trail, and education facilities. (Tues-Thurs 10 am-5 pm, Fri-Sat 10 am-10 pm, Sun 11 am-5 pm; call or visit the Web site for telescope viewing and holiday hours) **$$$**

Dunsmuir House and Gardens. *2960 Peralta Oaks Ct, Oakland (94605). Phone 510/615-5555. www.dunsmuir.org.* (1899) A 37-room neoclassical maison; 50 acres of trees, lawns, shrubs, and gardens; special events. Guided (Apr-Sept, $) and self-guided tours. (Tues-Fri 10 am-4 pm) **FREE**

East Bay Regional Park District. *2950 Peralta Oaks Ct, Oakland (94605). Phone 510/562-7275. www.ebparks.org.* This organization maintains more than 75,000 acres in 50 parks and recreation areas in Alameda and Contra Costa counties. Facilities include swimming, fishing, boating; archery, riding, picnic grounds, campgrounds, and other pastimes. Most parks are open daily. The park system includes

Anthony Chabot Regional Park & Lake Chabot. *Redwood Rd, Oakland (94605). Park entrances along Skyline Blvd, between Redwood and Golf Links rds and along Redwood Rd E of Skyline Blvd; stables and hiking along Skyline Blvd. At Lake Chabot there are fishing and boating facilities (rentals); bicycle trails and picnic areas. Park: E and S via 35th Ave and Redwood Rd; Lake Chabot: S on I-580 to Fairmont Ave, then E to Lake Chabot Rd and left to parking area. Phone 510/562-2267.* Park offers 4,927 acres for hiking and riding, horse rentals; marksmanship range for rifle, pistol, and trapshooting; 18-hole golf course. Camping: motor home and tent camping (fee). (Daily 7 am-10 pm) **$$**

Martin Luther King Jr. Regional Shoreline. *Doolittle Dr and Swan Way, Oakland (94621). S on I-880 to Hegenberger exit, then NW on Doolittle Dr. Phone 510/635-0135.* On 1,219 acres, near Oakland International Airport. Sunning beach, fishing, boating (two-lane launching ramp); hiking trails, birdwatching, picnicking, children's playfields, beach café. Nature study. (Daily 5 am-10 pm) **FREE**

Redwood Regional Park. *7867 Redwood Rd, Oakland (94619). E of Skyline Blvd on Redwood Rd. Phone 510/562-7275.* Redwood groves, evergreens, chaparral, and grassland on 1,830 acres. Hiking; nature study. Picnicking, playfields, children's playground. Creek with native rainbow trout. **$**

Golden Gate Fields. *1100 Eastshore Hwy, Albany (94710). Phone 510/559-7345. www.goldengatefields.com.* An East Bay institution since it opened in 1941, Golden Gate Fields is one of the top horse racing venues in northern California. The 1-mile oval track is in view of nearly 15,000 seats, between the grandstand, clubhouse, and private Turf Club. The racing schedule consists of 105 days from November to March. (Oct-Jan: daily; gates open 9:30 am; Club House and Turf Club, 11 am) **$**

Golden State Warriors (NBA). *The Arena at Oakland, 7000 Coliseum Way, Oakland (94607). Phone 510/986-2200. www.nba.com/warriors.* Professional basketball team.

Heinhold's First and Last Chance Saloon. *56 Jack London Square, Oakland (94607).* Writer Jack London's favorite watering hole during his tenure in the East Bay, Heinhold's First and Last Chance Saloon opened in 1883 and is still pouring drinks today. A National Historic Landmark and a veritable museum of Oakland history, Heinhold's still retains the ambience immortalized in London's autobiographical *John Barleycorn*, and is the true heart of the square that now bears the writer's name. While the place is the very definition of weathered, the bar looks pretty much like it did when Johnny Heinhold founded it, aside from a tilted (read: earthquake-ravaged) floor and a ceiling plastered with grimy paper money left by several different generations of war-bound American soldiers. (And, yes, the gas lamps and pot-bellied stove are the bar's 1883 originals.) The beer menu might be sparse, but the atmosphere is as thick as a brick wall.

★ **Jack London Square.** *311 Broadway, Oakland (94607). Formed by Clay, Franklin, Embarcadero, and the Oakland Estuary. www.jacklondonsquare.com.* This colorful waterfront area is where the author Jack London worked. Heinold's First and Last Chance Saloon (see) at the foot of Webster Street, is where London spent much of his time and wrote his most famous novels. Several restaurants and the reconstructed cabin in which the author weathered the Klondike winter of 1898 reflect characters and situations from his life and books. Adjacent is Jack London Village, at the foot of Alice Street, which features shops, restaurants, and a marina area. (Daily)

Joaquin Miller Park. *Joaquin Miller Rd, Oakland (94602). Phone 510/238-3187. www.oaklandparks.com.* Here is the site of the "Hights," the former house of Joaquin Miller, "Poet of the Sierras." Four monuments erected by Miller to Moses, General Frémont, Robert and Elizabeth Browning are found here, as is a funeral pyre for himself, and a fountain and statuary from the 1939 World's Fair. The park is also the site of Woodminster Amphitheater, scene of Woodminster Summer Musicals (see SPECIAL EVENT). Hiking and picnic areas. (Daily) **FREE**

Kaiser Center. *300 Lakeside Dr, Oakland (94601). Phone 510/271-6146.* This complex was founded by industrialist Henry J. Kaiser and remains the home of Kaiser Aluminum & Chemical Corporation. The Kaiser Building is of aluminum and glass construction. Changing art exhibits on mezzanine; remarkable 3 1/2-acre rooftop garden with trees, shrubs, flowers, a pool, and fountains. Restaurants. (Mon-Fri; closed holidays) **FREE**

Lake Merritt. *568 Bellevue, Oakland (94613). In the heart of downtown Oakland. Phone 510/238-2196.* At 155 acres, it's the largest natural body of saltwater in the world completely within a city, surrounded by drives and handsome buildings. Boat rentals (daily; fee), sightseeing launch (weekends, some holidays). Sailing lessons, day camps. Special events include sailing regattas. Adjacent to the lake is

Children's Fairyland. *699 Bellevue Ave, Oakland (94610). Phone 510/452-2259. www.fairyland.org.* Everything child-size, with tiny buildings depicting fairyland tales. Many contain live animals and birds. Carousel, Ferris wheel, train and trolley rides, children's bumper boats, and puppet theater (fee for some activities). (Nov-mid-Apr: Fri-Sun 10 am-4 pm; mid-Apr-mid-June, Wed-Sun 10 am-4 pm; mid-June-Sept: daily 10 am-4 pm; Sept-Oct: Wed-Sun 10 am-4 pm; closed Jan 1, Thanksgiving, Dec 25) **$$**

Lake Merritt Wildlife Refuge and Rotary Nature Center. *552 Bellevue Ave, Oakland (94610). Phone 510/238-3739.* North America's oldest wildlife refuge (1870); nature and conservation exhibits; native birds; illustrated lectures, and walks (weekends); animal feeding area. (Daily) **FREE**

Lakeside Park. *Bellevue and Grand aves, Oakland (94610). Phone 510/238-3187.* Approximately 120 acres. Picnic areas, free children's play area; lawn bowling, putting greens; trail and show gardens, duck-feeding area; bandstand concerts (summer, Sun and holidays).

Trial and Show Gardens. *666 Bellevue Ave, Oakland (94610).* Demonstration Gardens; includes cactus, fuchsia, dahlia, chrysanthemum, Polynesian, palm, herb, and Japanese gardens. (Daily; closed Jan 1, Thanksgiving, Dec 25) **FREE**

Oakland Athletics (MLB). *Oakland Coliseum, 7000 Coliseum Way, Oakland (94621). Phone 510/638-4900. oakland.athletics.mlb.com.* Professional baseball team.

Oakland Museum of California. *1000 Oak St, Oakland (94607). Near Lake Merritt. Phone 510/238-2200. www.museumca.org.* The only museum dedicated exclusively to California's history, art, and natural sciences, the Oakland Museum of California is a gem of a museum for more reasons than one. The building itself is a three-tiered, multi-terraced structure built in 1969 and integrated with lush outdoor gardens and ponds. In terms of subject matter, it covers each of its three disciplines with aplomb in its own tier and permanent gallery. "The Gallery of California Art" traces the work of California artists from the 1800s to today; "California: A Place, A People, A Dream" illuminates the state's cultural history; and the "Walk Across California" exhibit presents visitors with an in-depth look at the diverse past and present ecosystems within the boundaries of the Golden State. The museum also hosts several excellent temporary exhibitions every year, ranging in subject matter from fashion to photography to archaeology. (Wed-Sat 10 am-5 pm, Sun noon-5 pm; closed Mon, Tues; holidays) **$$**

Oakland Raiders (NFL). *Network Associates Coliseum, 7000 Coliseum Way, Oakland (94621). Phone 510/864-5000. www.raiders.com.* Professional football team.

Oakland Zoo. *9777 Golf Links Rd, Oakland (94605). Phone 510/632-9523. www.oaklandzoo.org.* Situated on 525 acres, the zoo houses 330 native and exotic animals, a children's petting zoo, and "Simba Pori," a 1 1/2-acre habitat with a pride of six lions, and Siamang Island. Also here are children's rides and picnic areas. Free parking the first Monday of each month except holidays. (Daily 10 am-4 pm; closed Thanksgiving, Dec 25) **$$**

Paramount Theatre. *2025 Broadway, Oakland (94612). Phone 510/465-6400. www.paramounttheatre.com.* Impressive, restored 1931 Art Deco movie palace, home of the Oakland Ballet. Hosts organ pops series and a variety of musical performances. Ninety-minute tours start from the box office (first and third Sat of each month; no tours on holidays). **$**

Skyline Boulevard. On top of Berkeley-Oakland Hills; superb views of the entire East Bay area.

USS *Potomac*. *Franklin D. Roosevelt Pier, Jack London Sq, 530 Water St, Oakland (94607). Phone 510/627-1215. www.usspotomac.org.* Originally built in 1934 as the Coast Guard cutter *Electra*, this was Franklin D. Roosevelt's beloved "Floating White House." The fully restored, 165-foot steel vessel is now owned and operated as a floating museum by the Potomac

Association; it is a National Historic Landmark. Dockside tours (Wed, Fri, Sun; groups by appointment only). Narrated two-hour educational cruises around Treasure Island and San Francisco Bay (Apr-Nov, departures first and third Thurs and second and fourth Sun of each month). Reservations required for cruises. **$$$$**

Western Aerospace Museum. *Building 621, 8250 Earhart Rd, Oakland (94614). Phone 510/638-7100. www.cyberair.com/musuems/usa/va/wam.html.* This museum is housed in a 1940 military-type hanger at Oakland International Airport; many of the first flights across the Pacific Ocean took off here. Collections include 1920s and 1930s civilian aircraft, military jets, and a plane used in the film *Raiders of the Lost Ark.* (Wed-Sun 10 am-4 pm; closed Jan 1, Dec 25) **$$**

Special Event

Woodminster Summer Musicals. *Joaquin Miller Park, 3300 Joaquin Miller Rd, Oakland (94602). Phone 510/531-9597. www.woodminster.com.* Pack a picnic and enjoy an evening under the stars watching a Broadway musical. This unique treasure is beloved to the people of Oakland, many of whom make the event a family tradition, returning year after year. July-Sept. **$$$$**

Limited-Service Hotels

★ ★ BEST WESTERN INN AT THE SQUARE. *233 Broadway, Oakland (94607). Phone 510/452-4565; toll-free 800/938-4774; fax 510/452-4634. www.innatthesquare.com.* 100 rooms, 3 story. Pets accepted; fee. Complimentary continental breakfast. Check-in 2 pm, check-out 11 am. Restaurant. Fitness room. Outdoor pool. **$**

★ MARINA VILLAGE INN. *1151 Pacific Marina, Alameda (94501). Phone 510/523-9450; toll-free 800/345-0304; fax 510/523-6315. www.marinavillageinn.com.* 51 rooms, 2 story. Complimentary continental breakfast. Check-in 3 pm, check-out noon. Outdoor pool. **$**

Full-Service Hotel

★ ★ ★ WATERFRONT PLAZA HOTEL. *10 Washington St, Oakland (94607). Phone 510/836-3800; toll-free 800/729-3638; fax 510/832-5695. www.waterfrontplaza.com.* The Waterfront Plaza Hotel calls Jack London Square home. This casually elegant hotel sits right on the Oakland Harbor, affording fantastic views of San Francisco. Just a short ferry ride from the city, this hotel is conveniently located near Oakland's own attractions, including many shopping and entertainment options. The rooms have a breezy, coastal décor, with sunny colors and an upbeat ambience, while the suites feature floor-to-ceiling windows with balconies from which guests can further enjoy the water views. The hotel's convivial atmosphere extends to its restaurant, Jack's Bistro (see), where a large menu and a laid-back spirit make everyone feel welcome. 145 rooms, 5 story. Check-in 3 pm, check-out noon. Restaurant, bar. Fitness room. Outdoor pool. Business center. **$$**

Restaurants

★ ★ ★ BAY WOLF. *3853 Piedmont Ave, Oakland (94611). Phone 510/655-6004. www.baywolf.com.* Thriving since 1975 in an early 1900s Victorian on a chic street in Oakland, Bay Wolf serves food influenced by the cuisines of Tuscany, Provence, and the Basque country, but with a California twist. Diners can eat on the veranda, or in one of the two small dining rooms. Wherever you sit, the feeling here is warm, friendly, and inviting. The menu changes regularly, but may include duck leg confit, baked lasagna al forno, or pan-seared local sardines, along with an enticing dessert list. California, Mediterranean menu. Lunch, dinner. Closed holidays. Casual attire. Reservations recommended. Outdoor seating. **$$**

★ ★ CHEF PAUL'S. *4179 Piedmont Ave, Oakland (94611). ; fax 415/388-5019.* French menu. Dinner. Closed Mon. Jacket required. Reservations recommended. Outdoor seating. **$$$**

★ ★ IL PESCATORE. *57 Jack London Sq, Oakland (94607). Phone 510/465-2188; fax 510/465-0238. www.ilpescatoreristorante.com.* Italian, Seafood menu. Dinner, brunch. Closed Jan 1, Thanksgiving, Dec 25. Bar. Casual attire. Reservations recommended. Outdoor seating. **$$$**

★ ★ JACK'S BISTRO. *1 Broadway, Oakland (94607). Phone 510/444-7171; fax 510/891-9058. www.jacksbistro.com.* California, Mediterranean menu. Breakfast, lunch, dinner, late-night, Sun brunch. Bar. Casual attire. Valet parking. Outdoor seating. **$$$**

★ QUINN'S LIGHTHOUSE. *1951 Embarcadero Cove, Oakland (94606). Phone 510/536-2050; fax*

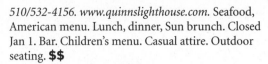

510/532-4156. www.quinnslighthouse.com. Seafood, American menu. Lunch, dinner, Sun brunch. Closed Jan 1. Bar. Children's menu. Casual attire. Outdoor seating. **$$**

★ ★ **SCOTT'S SEAFOOD.** *2 Broadway, Oakland (94607). Phone 510/444-3456; fax 510/444-6917. www.scottseastbay.com.* Seafood menu. Lunch, dinner, Sun brunch. Closed Dec 25. Bar. Children's menu. Casual attire. Valet parking. Outdoor seating. **$$**

★ **SILVER DRAGON.** *835 Webster St, Oakland (94607). Phone 510/893-3748; fax 510/893-4918.* Chinese menu. Lunch, dinner. Closed Thanksgiving, Dec 25. Bar. **$$**

★ ★ **SOIZIC.** *300 Broadway, Oakland (94607). Phone 510/251-8100; fax 510/251-8722. www.soizicbistro.com.* Bistro-style atmosphere in a former warehouse building; eclectic art collection. California bistro menu. Lunch, dinner. Closed Mon; holidays. Bar. Casual attire. Reservations recommended. **$$**

★ ★ ★ **TRADER VIC'S.** *9 Anchor Dr, Emeryville (94608). Phone 510/653-3400; toll-free 877/762-4824; fax 510/653-9384. www.tradervics.com.* Famous for introducing the original Mai Tai to the world in 1944, this restaurant is located on the water, offering views of the bay. American, Polynesian menu. Lunch, dinner, Sun brunch. Closed holidays. Bar. Valet parking. **$$$**

Oroville (C-2)

See also Chico, Marysville, Nevada City

Settled 1850
Population 13,004
Elevation 174 ft
Area Code 530
Zip 95965
Information Chamber of Commerce, 1789 Montgomery St; phone 530/538-2542 or toll-free 800/655-4653
Web Site www.oroville-ca.com

Water-oriented recreation, tourism, and hunting predominate in Oroville—where the lure of gold once held sway and "too many gambling houses to count" catered to the wants of miners. Miners' Alley is a historic remnant of those days when Oroville was the second-largest city in California.

Oroville, in addition to being the portal to the Sierra's great watershed, the Feather River, also has orange and olive groves, which thrive in the area's thermal belt. Fruit and olive processing, as well as lumber, contribute much to the community's economy.

A Ranger District office of the Plumas National Forest (see QUINCY) is located in Oroville.

What to See and Do

Chinese Temple. *1500 Broderick St, Oroville (95965). At Elma. Phone 530/538-2496.* (1863) The "Temple Beside the River," largest of the authentic temples in California, has a tapestry hall and display room. It is all that remains of a Chinatown that was second in size only to San Francisco's. (Daily noon-4 pm; closed mid-Dec-Jan) **$**

Feather Falls. *875 Mitchell Ave, Oroville (95965). 25 miles NE in Plumas National Forest (see QUINCY). Phone 530/534-6500.* Sixth-highest in United States. A 3 1/2-mile trail leads to a 640-foot drop of the Fall River into the canyon just above the Middle Fork of the Feather River in Feather Falls Scenic Area. Allow 4-6 hours for round-trip and carry drinking water.

Feather River Fish Hatchery. *5 Table Mountain Blvd, Oroville (95965). Phone 530/538-2222.* Raises salmon and steelhead. Underwater viewing chamber (Sept-June); hatchery (daily). **FREE**

Historic Judge C. F. Lott House. *Lott-Sank Park, 1067 Montgomery St, Oroville (95965). Phone 530/538-2497.* (1856) Authentically restored; period furnishings. Picnic area. (Sun-Mon, Fri 11:30 am-3:30 pm; closed mid-Dec-Jan) **$**

Lake Oroville State Recreation Area. *Hwy 70 and Grand Ave, Oroville. 3 miles W, Hwy 70 Grand Ave exit.* Forebay-North. *1 mile W, Hwy 70 Garden Dr exit.* Loafer Creek Campground. *9 miles E via Hwy 162.* Spillway. *7 miles E via Hwy 162, N via Canyon Dr, 3 miles W across dam. Phone 530/538-2200 (swimming and launching status); toll-free 800/444-7275. www.parks.ca.gov.* In several sections. Forebay-South. Powerboats allowed (fee for boat launch); no camping. (Daily; fees) Forebay-North. Swimming, bathhouse; no powerboats. (Daily; fees) Loafer Creek Campground. Swimming; camping (fee). (Daily, Apr-Oct) All three recreation areas have fishing, boat ramps; hiking trails, picnicking. Two marinas: Lime Saddle and Bidwell Canyon. Also camping facilities at Bidwell Canyon (campground all year; full RV hook-up; fees). Spillway. Wayside camping; launch ramp. (Daily; fees)

Oroville Dam & Reservoir. *7 miles E on Hwy 162, then 3 miles N on Canyon Dr. Phone 530/538-2219.* This 770-foot-high earth-filled dam impounds Lake Oroville with a 167-mile shoreline. The dam is a vital part of the $3.2 billion California State Water Project. **FREE**

Visitor Center & Overlook. *917 Kelly Ridge Rd, Oroville (95966). 9 miles E on Hwy 162, 2 1/2 miles N on Kelly Ridge Rd. Phone 530/538-2219.* Exhibits, slide shows, films; observation tower. (Daily; closed Jan 1, Thanksgiving, Dec 25) **FREE**

Special Events

Bidwell Bar Days. *Phone 530/538-2219.* Gold panning, pioneer arts and crafts. First Sat in May.

Feather Fiesta Days. *Downtown, Oroville. Phone 530/534-7690.* This ten-day event features parades, a car show, craft fair, and a firefighters chili cook-off. Early May. **FREE**

Old Time Fiddlers' Contest. *1220 Myers St, Oroville (95965). Phone 530/589-4844.* Northern California Regional Championship. Usually late Apr.

Limited-Service Hotel

★ COMFORT INN. *1470 Feather River Blvd, Oroville (95965). Phone 530/533-9673; toll-free 800/626-1900; fax 530/533-5862. www.choicehotels.com.* 54 rooms, 3 story. Pets accepted, some restrictions; fee. Complimentary continental breakfast. Check-in 2 pm, check-out 11 am. Fitness room. Outdoor pool, whirlpool. **$**

Specialty Lodging

The following lodging establishment is approved by Mobil Travel Guide, but due to its unique and individualized nature have not been given a traditional Mobil Star rating. Included in this listing you may find bed-and-breakfasts, limited-service inns, guest ranches, and other unique hotel properties.

LAKE OROVILLE BED AND BREAKFAST. *240 Sunday Dr, Berry Creek (95916). Phone 530/589-0700; fax 530/589-3800. www.lakeorovillebedandbreakfast.com.* Eat a hearty breakfast and stroll 40 acres of rolling hills at this relaxing escape. The guest rooms are quaintly decorated, and the quiet sunroom is great for watching sunsets. 6 rooms. Pets accepted; fee. Complimentary full breakfast. Check-in 3-6 pm, check-out 11:30 am. **$**

Restaurant

★★ THE DEPOT. *2191 High St, Oroville (95965). Phone 530/534-9101. www.oroville-city.com/depot.* In 1908 Western Pacific railroad depot. Seafood, steak menu. Lunch, dinner. Closed Dec 25. Bar. Children's menu. Outdoor seating. **$$$**

Pacific Grove (F-2)

See also Big Sur, Carmel, Carmel Valley, Monterey, Pebble Beach, Salinas

Population 15,522
Elevation 0-300 ft
Area Code 831
Zip 93950
Information Chamber of Commerce, Central and Forest aves, PO Box 167; phone 831/373-3304 or toll-free 800/656-6650
Web Site www.pacificgrove.org

What to See and Do

Asilomar Conference Grounds. *800 Asilomar Blvd, Pacific Grove (93950). Phone 831/372-8016. www.asilomarcenter.com.* A 105-acre beachfront conference center, historical landmark, and park. Recreational facilities, meeting rooms, accommodations. (Daily)

Monarch Grove Sanctuary. *1205 Jewell Ave, Pacific Grove (93950). Enter from Ridge Rd off Lighthouse Ave. Phone 831/375-0982.* Grove of Monterey pines where Monarch butterflies typically migrate each year to spend the winter. Monarchs are typically visible Oct-mid-Feb; best chance to see them flying around is when temperatures warm up by mid-morning (otherwise, they cluster in the trees). (Daily) **FREE**

Ocean View Boulevard. Five-mile scenic road along rocky, flower-bordered shoreline.

Pacific Grove Museum of Natural History. *165 Forest Ave, Pacific Grove (93950). Phone 831/648-5716. www.pgmuseum.org.* Natural history of Monterey County, including birds, shells, mammals, Native American exhibits; native plants garden. (Tues-Sat

10 am-5 pm; closed holidays) (See SPECIAL EVENTS) **FREE**

Point Pinos Lighthouse. *Asilomar and Lighthouse aves, Pacific Grove (93950). Phone 831/648-3116. www.pgmuseum.org.* (1855) Oldest continuously operating lighthouse on Pacific Coast. (summer: daily, 11:30 am-5 pm; rest of year: Thurs-Mon 1-4 pm) **DONATION**

Special Events

Butterfly Parade. *485 Pine Ave, Pacific Grove (93950). Phone 831/646-6540.* Celebrates arrival of thousands of Monarch butterflies. Oct.

Christmas at the Inns. *Chamber of Commerce, Central and Forest aves, Pacific Grove (93950). Phone 831/373-3304.* Tour of old Victorian inns decorated for the holidays. Usually second Tues in Dec. **$$$**

Feast of Lanterns. *Various locations. www.feast-of-lanterns.org.* Lantern-lit processions on land and sea, barbecue; pageant. Late July.

Good Old Days. *Pacific Grove Lighthouse Ave, Pacific Grove (93950). Downtown. Phone 831/373-3304.* Parade, fair, entertainment, quilt show, contests. Apr.

Marching Band Festival. *Phone 831/373-3304.* Parade, field show; competition of statewide high school championship bands. Early Nov. **$$**

Wildflower Show. *Pacific Grove Museum of Natural History, 165 Forest Ave, Pacific Grove (93950). Phone 831/648-3116.* More than 600 species and varieties of Montery County wildflowers are displayed. Mid-Apr. **FREE**

Specialty Lodgings

The following lodging establishments are approved by Mobil Travel Guide, but due to their unique and individualized nature have not been given a traditional Mobil Star rating. Included in this listing you may find bed-and-breakfasts, limited-service inns, guest ranches, and other unique hotel properties.

CENTRELLA INN. *612 Central Ave, Pacific Grove (93950). Phone 831/372-3372; toll-free 800/233-3372; fax 831/372-2036. www.centrellainn.com.* 16 rooms, 3 story. Children over 10 years only in main house. Complimentary full breakfast. Check-in 3 pm, check-out noon. **$$**

GOSBY HOUSE INN. *643 Lighthouse Ave, Pacific Grove (93950). Phone 831/375-1287; toll-free 800/527-8828; fax 831/655-8621. www.gosbyhouseinn.com.* Queen Anne/Victorian mansion built in 1887 by cobbler from Nova Scotia. Wine cellar. 22 rooms, 2 story. Complimentary full breakfast. Check-in 3 pm, check-out noon. **$**

GRAND VIEW INN. *557 Ocean View Blvd, Pacific Grove (93950). Phone 831/372-4341. www.pginns.com.* Victorian mansion (1886) with antiques. 10 rooms, 3 story. Children over 12 years only. Complimentary full breakfast. Check-in 2:30-10 pm, check-out noon. Oceanfront **$$$**

GREEN GABLES INN. *301 Ocean View Blvd, Pacific Grove (93950). Phone 831/375-2095; toll-free 800/722-1774; fax 206/748-0533. www.foursisters.com.* Victorian mansion (1888); on Monterey Bay. 11 rooms, 3 story. Complimentary full breakfast. Check-in 3 pm, check-out noon. **$$**

THE INN AT 213 SEVENTEEN MILE DRIVE. *213 Seventeen Mile Dr, Pacific Grove (93950). Phone 831/642-9514; toll-free 800/526-5666; fax 831/642-9546. www.innat17.com.* 14 rooms, 2 story. Check-in 3 pm, check-out 11:30 am. Whirlpool. **$$**

THE MARTINE INN. *255 Ocean View Blvd, Pacific Grove (93950). Phone 831/373-3388; toll-free 800/852-5588; fax 831/373-3896. www.martineinn.com.* Victorian, Mediterranean-style home built 1899. On Monterey Bay. 24 rooms, 3 story. Complimentary full breakfast. Check-in 3-9 pm, check-out noon. **$**

ROSEDALE INN. *775 Asilomar Blvd, Pacific Grove (93950). Phone 831/655-1000; toll-free 800/822-5606; fax 831/655-0691. www.rosedaleinn.com.* 19 rooms. Complimentary continental breakfast. Check-in 3 pm, check-out 11 am. **$$**

SEVEN GABLES INN. *555 Ocean View Blvd, Pacific Grove (93950). Phone 831/372-4341. www.pginns.com.* Privately owned and operated, The Seven Gables Inn welcomes visitors as though they were family. This gracious bed-and-breakfast occupies a glorious spot on the edge of Monterey Bay, overlooking Lover's Point Beach, where guests can watch sea otters and whales at play in the crashing surf. This seaside estate dates to 1886, and its Victorian-style buildings, priceless European antiques, and elegant furnishings are the picture of refinement. The grand accommodations are scattered among the abundant gardens, and the ocean views are exceptional. Afternoon tea is celebrated daily here, and the gourmet breakfasts, served in the formal dining room, are certainly worth the early rising. 13 rooms, 3 story. Children over 12 years only. Complimentary full breakfast. Check-in 2:30-10 pm, check-out noon. **$$**

Restaurants

★★★ **FANDANGO.** *223 17th St, Pacific Grove (93950). Phone 831/372-3456; fax 831/372-2673. www.fandangorestaurant.com.* Mediterranean menu. Lunch, dinner, Sun brunch. Bar. Casual attire. **$$$**

★ **FISHWIFE.** *1996 1/2 Sunset Dr, Pacific Grove (93950). Phone 831/375-7107. www.fishwife.com.* Caribbean menu. Lunch, dinner, Sun brunch. Closed Thanksgiving, Dec 25. Bar. Children's menu. Casual attire. **$$**

★★★ **OLD BATH HOUSE.** *620 Ocean View Blvd, Pacific Grove (93950). Phone 831/375-5195; fax 831/375-5379. www.oldbathhouse.com.* In 1930s Victorian-style building overlooking Lovers' Point. California menu. Dinner. Bar. Casual attire. **$$$**

★★ **PASSIONFISH.** *701 Lighthouse Ave, Pacific Grove (93950). Phone 831/655-3311. www.passionfish.net.* Seafood menu. Dinner. Closed Thanksgiving, Dec 25. Children's menu. Casual attire. **$$**

★ **PEPPERS MEXICALI CAFE.** *170 Forest Ave, Pacific Grove (93950). Phone 831/373-6892; fax 831/373-5467. www.peppersmexicalicafe.com.* Own tamales, chips, salsa. Mexican menu. Lunch, dinner. Closed Tues; holidays. Bar. Children's menu. Casual attire. **$$**

★★ **TASTE CAFE AND BISTRO.** *1199 Forest Ave, Pacific Grove (93950). Phone 831/655-0324; fax 831/655-0325. www.tastecafebistro.com.* American menu. Lunch, dinner. Closed Mon. Bar. **$$**

★★ **VITO'S.** *1180 Forest Ave, Pacific Grove (93940). Phone 831/375-3070; fax 831/375-5623. www.restauranteur.com/vitos.* Italian menu. Dinner. Closed Easter, Thanksgiving, Dec 25. Casual attire. **$$**

Palo Alto (E-2)

See also Fremont, Menlo Park, Mountain View, Redwood City, Santa Clara, Saratoga

Founded 1889
Population 58,598
Elevation 23 ft
Area Code 650
Information Chamber of Commerce, 325 Forest Ave, 94301; phone 650/324-3121
Web Site www.paloaltoonline.com

A tall and ancient redwood tree stands at the northwest entrance to the city. Nearly two centuries ago, Spanish explorers used it as a landmark, calling it El Palo Alto ("tall tree"). Stanford University is a major economic factor. The city is also one of the nation's most important electronics development and research centers.

What to See and Do

Junior Museum & Zoo. *1451 Middlefield Rd, Palo Alto (94301). Phone 650/329-2111. www.pajmzfriends.org.* Displays introduce children to art, science, history, and anthropology through a variety of media; hands-on exhibits, workshops. Zoo on grounds. (Tues-Sat 10 am-5 pm, Sun 1-4 pm; closed holidays) **FREE**

Palo Alto Baylands Nature Interpretive Center. *2775 Embarcadero Rd, Palo Alto (94303). Phone 650/329-2506.* Nature preserve at edge of salt marsh. Naturalist-guided walking tours; slide shows; bicycling; bird-watching. (Tues-Fri 2-5 pm, Sat-Sun 1-5 pm; closed Thanksgiving, Dec 25) **FREE**

Stanford Shopping Center. *680 Stanford Shopping Center, Palo Alto (94304). Phone 650/617-8585; toll-free 800/772-9332. www.stanfordshop.com.* Adjacent to—and named for—Stanford University in the San Francisco suburb of Palo Alto, the Stanford Shopping Center is one of the largest and most posh malls in all of northern California. With storefronts intermingling with lush, meticulously manicured gardens, the open-air facility is home to more than 140 tenants, including such top-tier department store anchors as Bloomingdale's, Nordstrom, and Macy's alongside a nice variety of specialty stores and restaurants. Among the shopping center's over-and-above perks are a concierge and a summer jazz concert series on Thursday evenings. In addition to the national and local retailers and restaurants, there is also a pair of markets—an

upscale supermarket and an open-air farmers' market—and a European-style block lined with coffees houses, bakeries, and flower shops. (Mon-Fri 10 am-
9 pm, Sat to 7 pm, Sun 11 am-6 pm)

Stanford University. *1 Stanford University, Palo Alto. Near El Camino Real (Hwy 82). Phone 650/723-2300. www.stanford.edu.* (1891) (14,173 students) Founded by Senator and Mrs. Leland Stanford in memory of their only son, it has become one of the great universities of the world. Features of the campus include

Hoover Tower. *Serra and Galvez sts, Stanford (94305). Phone 650/723-2053.* Library houses collection begun by President Herbert Hoover during World War I. At 250 feet high, the carillon platform on the 14th floor offers panoramic view of campus and peninsula (daily; closed school holidays). Information desk (daily; closed school holidays). **$**

Stanford Guide Service. *Serra and Galvez sts, Stanford (94305). Phone 650/723-2560.* Located in Memorial Hall and in Hoover Tower (daily; closed school holidays). Free one-hour campus tours leave information booth (twice daily; closed school holidays). Maps and brochures are at both locations.

Stanford Medical Center. *300 Pasteur Dr, Palo Alto (94304). Phone 650/725-2408.* A $21 million cluster of buildings on a 56-acre site, designed by internationally famous architect Edward Durell Stone. Tours by appointment.

Stanford Stadium. *625 Nelson, Palo Alto (94305).* Home of the Stanford Cardinal football team.

Thomas Welton Stanford Art Gallery. *419 Lasuan Mall, Palo Alto (94305). Phone 650/723-3404. www.stanford.edu/dept/art/gallery.* Changing exhibits. (Tues-Fri 10 am-5 pm, Sat-Sun 1-5 pm; closed summer, holidays) **FREE**

Trees. *300 Pasteur Dr, Palo Alto (94304).* Palo Alto is famous for its trees. El Palo Alto, "The Tall Tree" that gives the city its name, is located at Palo Alto Ave near Alma St. Also, 60 varieties are found along Hamilton Ave, blocks between 100 and 1500.

Winter Lodge. *3009 Middlefield Rd, Palo Alto (94306). Phone 650/493-4566. www.winterlodge.com.* The only outdoor ice rink in the United States west of the Sierra Nevada Mountains. Skate rentals. (Late Sept-mid-Apr, daily 3-5 pm; also 8-10 am Tues-Fri, 8-10 pm Wed and Fri-Sat, 5:30-7:30 pm Sun) **$$**

Limited-Service Hotel

★ STANFORD TERRACE INN. *531 Stanford Ave, Palo Alto (94306). Phone 650/857-0333; toll-free 800/729-0332; fax 650/857-0343. www.stanfordterraceinn.com.* Stanford University is opposite. 80 rooms, 3 story. Complimentary continental breakfast. Check-out noon. Fitness room. Outdoor pool. **$$**

Full-Service Hotels

★★ CREEKSIDE INN. *3400 El Camino Real, Palo Alto (94306). Phone 650/493-2411; toll-free 800/492-7335; fax 650/493-6787. www.creekside-inn.com.* Located in the heart of Silicon Valley, this inn is only 1 mile from Stanford University. Three and a half acres of landscaped land with oak trees and a creek provide the parklike setting. 136 rooms, 4 story. Complimentary continental breakfast. Check-in 3 pm, check-out noon. High-speed Internet access. Restaurant, bar. Fitness room. Outdoor pool. Airport transportation available. **$$**

★★★ DINAH'S GARDEN HOTEL. *4261 El Camino Real, Palo Alto (94306). Phone 650/493-2844; toll-free 800/227-8220; fax 650/856-4713. www.dinahshotel.com.* Described aptly as a tranquil oasis in the midst of Silicon Valley, this property is richly appointed with furniture of exotic woods. Each room has its own shower/steam room plus exercise bike and weights, complete kitchen with granite counter, dishwasher, ice machine, and dining area. The 10 acres of cultivated gardens are truly spectacular. 148 rooms, 3 story. Check-in 3 pm, check-out noon. Restaurant, bar. Fitness room. Two outdoor pools. **$**

★★★ GARDEN COURT HOTEL. *520 Cowper St, Palo Alto (94301). Phone 650/322-9000; toll-free 800/824-9028; fax 650/324-3609. www.gardencourt.com.* Located downtown, this hotel is in the heart of Silicon Valley near Stanford University, shopping, and restaurants. Rooms overlook the courtyard of flowers and feature four-poster beds, down comforters, and plush terry robes. 62 rooms, 4 story. Pets accepted, some restrictions; fee. Check-in 2 pm, check-out noon. Restaurant, bar. Fitness room. **$$$**

★★★ SHERATON PALO ALTO HOTEL. *625 El Camino Real, Palo Alto (94301). Phone 650/328-2800; toll-free 888/625-5144; fax 650/327-7362.*

www.sheraton.com. This resort hotel is surrounded by flower gardens, ponds, and fountains. The property is located at the entrance to Stanford University and near the Stanford Shopping Center. Guest rooms offer generous work stations for the business traveler. 346 rooms, 4 story. Pets accepted, some restrictions; fee. Check-in 3 pm, check-out noon. Restaurant, bar. Fitness room. Outdoor pool. Business center. **$$**

★ ★ ★ **THE WESTIN PALO ALTO.** *675 El Camino Real, Palo Alto (94301). Phone 650/321-4422; toll-free 800/937-8461; fax 650/321-5522. www.westin.com/paloalto.* 163 rooms, 5 story. Check-in 3 pm, check-out noon. Restaurant. Fitness room. Outdoor pool, whirlpool. Business center. **$$**

Restaurants

★ **BLUE CHALK CAFE.** *630 Ramona St, Palo Alto (94301). Phone 650/326-1020; fax 650/326-1022. www.ispot.com/bluechalk.* Southern regional menu. Lunch, dinner. Closed Sun; Jan 1, Thanksgiving, Dec 25. Bar. Children's menu. Casual attire. Outdoor seating. **$$**

★ ★ ★ **EVVIA.** *420 Emerson St., Palo Alto (94301). Phone 650/326-0983; fax 650/326-9552. www.evvia.net.* This warm and rustic restaurant features an open kitchen that provides entertainment for guests while they dine. Greek menu. Lunch, dinner. Closed holidays. Bar. Valet parking. **$$**

★ ★ **SCOTT'S SEAFOOD.** *1 Town and Country Village, Palo Alto (94301). Phone 650/323-1555; fax 650/323-1553. www.scottsseafood.com.* Seafood, steak menu. Breakfast, lunch, dinner, brunch. Closed holidays. Bar. Outdoor seating. **$$$**

★ ★ ★ **SPAGO.** *265 Lytton Ave, Palo Alto (94301). Phone 650/833-1000; fax 650/325-9586. www.wolfgangpuck.com.* Spago, slang for *string* in Italian, serves creative cuisine, influenced by Asia and Mediterranean regions. Guests enter through a garden courtyard and have a choice of dining in the main dining room, outdoor pavilion, or private dining rooms. Reservations can be hard to get due to the restaurant's continuing popularity. American, Mediterranean menu. Lunch, dinner. Closed Sun; Easter. Bar. Valet parking. Outdoor seating. **$$$**

★ ★ ★ **TAMARINE.** *546 University Ave, Palo Alto (94301). Phone 650/325-8500; fax 650/325-8504. www.tamarinerestaurant.com.* This contemporary, vegetarian-friendly Vietnamese restaurant creates meals out of small plates, encouraging lots of sharing. Entrees like tri-squash scallop curry and lemongrass bass are mixed and matched with six different types of rice, from plain to coconut to "festive" (flavored with turmeric, ginger, and cinnamon). Specialty cocktails, including lychee and gingermint martinis, win raves. The graceful, minimalist dining room is lined with original works of Vietnamese art, available for purchase at a semiannual auction. Vietnamese menu. Lunch, dinner. Bar. Business casual attire. Reservations recommended. **$$**

★ ★ **ZIBIBBO.** *430 Kipling St, Palo Alto (94301). Phone 650/328-6722; fax 650/328-6700. www.restaurantlulu.com.* Mediterranean menu. Lunch, dinner, brunch. Closed holidays. Bar. Valet parking. Outdoor seating. **$$**

Pebble Beach

See also Carmel, Monterey, Pacific Grove

Population 5,000
Elevation 0-37 ft
Area Code 831
Zip 93953
Web Site www.pebblebeach.com

Pebble Beach is noted for its scenic beauty, the palatial houses of its residents, and its golf courses, where the annual National Pro-Amateur Golf Championship and other prestigous tournatments are held.

What to See and Do

Pebble Beach Golf Links. *1700 Seventeen Mile Dr, Pebble Beach (93953). Phone 831/625-8518; fax 831/622-8795. www.pebblebeach.com.* You can't talk about California golf without mentioning Pebble Beach. Although it's quite a drive from San Francisco, any opportunity to play on one of the nation's most exclusive courses is not to be missed. To get a tee time, call well in advance (at least a month is a good idea) and be prepared to spend well in excess of $400 per person. The course goes over the Pacific Ocean at times, and the sounds and views of the waves lapping at the edges of the course are what make the trip worthwhile, as is the thought that you're playing in the footsteps of many of golf's elite. **$$$$**

Full-Service Resorts

★★★★ CASA PALMERO AT PEBBLE BEACH. *1518 Cypress Drive, Pebble Beach (93953). Phone 831/622-6650; toll-free 800/654-9300; fax 831/622-6655. www.pebblebeach.com.* The path to Casa Palmero may be lined with verdant fairways, but it is certainly a gilded route. With its villa-style architecture and gentle intimacy, Casa Palmero feels like a grand European estate. This gracious hideaway overlooks the first and second fairways of Pebble Beach, one of the most lauded golf courses in the world. Old-world charm and first-class service make this hotel a favorite of luxury-loving golfers. With overstuffed furniture and neutral tones interspersed with soft plaids, the guest rooms echo the resort's sophistication. Visitors are invited to enjoy the serene pool area or venture beyond to take advantage of the larger Pebble Beach complex's four restaurants, shops, private Oceanside Beach & Tennis Club, spa, and, of course, world-renowned golf. Offering the best of all worlds, this quietly romantic hotel brings many guests back for repeat visits. 24 rooms, 2 story. Complimentary continental breakfast. Check-in 3 pm, check-out noon. High-speed Internet access. Bar. Fitness room, spa. Outdoor pool. Golf, 18 holes. Airport transportation available. **$$$$**

★★★★ THE INN AT SPANISH BAY. *2700 Seventeen Mile Dr, Pebble Beach (93953). Phone 831/647-7500; toll-free 800/654-9300; fax 831/622-3603. www.pebblebeach.com.* The Inn at Spanish Bay is the essence of contemporary elegance at Pebble Beach. Direct access to the revered links makes it popular with golfers, while the splendid natural setting overlooking the Pacific Ocean and Spanish Bay has a universal appeal. Views of the Del Monte Forest, golf course, and ocean are striking, especially when enjoyed from the privacy of a splendid guest room or suite. A gallery of shops showcases fine sportswear and resort apparel along with tennis and golf equipment. From an expertly staffed tennis and fitness facility to the wonderful outdoor pool, the amenities are top notch. Massages are offered, and self-guided tours through the windswept dunes prove therapeutic. Four distinctive dining establishments tease taste buds with an array of offerings. All diners will find something here, from comfort food and Tuscan dishes to casual American fare and exuberant Hawaiian fusion cuisine. 269 rooms, 4 story. Check-in 4 pm, check-out noon. High-speed Internet access. Three restaurants, three bars. Fitness room, fitness classes available, spa. Beach. Outdoor pool, whirlpool. Golf, 18 holes. Tennis. Airport transportation available. Business center. **$$$$**

★★★★ THE LODGE AT PEBBLE BEACH. *1700 Seventeen Mile Dr, Pebble Beach (93953). Phone 831/624-3811; toll-free 800/654-9300; fax 831/625-8598. www.pebblebeach.com.* Distinguished by its impressive architecture and spectacular oceanside setting, The Lodge at Pebble Beach is the jewel in the crown of the world-class Pebble Beach resort. Exclusive and refined, the fashionably appointed rooms and suites are supremely comfortable. All feature balconies, and the spa rooms even feature private gardens with outdoor whirlpools. In addition to its famous golf, the Lodge encourages its guests to unwind by the pool, enjoy a vigorous workout in the fitness center, or play a tennis match in its state-of-the-art facility. Its four restaurants offer a variety of casually elegant settings and run the gamut from casual American fare and succulent seafood to updated, lightened versions of French classics. The Lodge's spa celebrates the diversity of natural resources indigenous to the Monterey Peninsula in its treatments and therapies, and the shops tantalize visitors with an array of apparel, jewelry, and art. 161 rooms, 3 story. Pets accepted, restrictions. Check-in 4 pm, check-out noon. High-speed Internet access. Four restaurants, four bars. Fitness room. Beach. Outdoor pool, whirlpool. Golf, 18 holes. Airport transportation available. Business center. **$$$$**

Spa

★★★★ THE SPA AT PEBBLE BEACH RESORTS. *1700 Seventeen Mile Dr, Pebble Beach (93953). Phone 831/624-3811.* The Spa at Pebble Beach goes far beyond simple body treatments and massage therapies to offer a well-rounded therapeutic experience. From water therapies and signature services to the renowned Keller Skin Institute, this spa covers all the bases. Relaxation is paramount at this spa, where water rituals revive, replenish, and restore energy with seaweed and rose petals, and body treatments nourish and polish the skin with grapeseeds, chai soy mud, and sea salt. The massage menu is particularly thorough, offering everything from classic, light touch massages and Eastern-inspired Shiatsu and Thai therapies to massages designed specifically with the golfer in mind. The spa's signature treatments are worth noticing, from wild strawberry body scrubs to seductive milk baths a la Cleopatra. The Keller Skin Institute is a full-service facility within the spa, where Botox injections, laser hair removal, photo facelifts, microdermabrasion, and vascular laser therapy are among the available beautification procedures.

Restaurant

★★★ CLUB XIX. *1700 Seventeen Mile Dr, Pebble Beach (93953). Phone 831/625-8519; toll-free 800/644-9300; fax 831/644-7960. www.pebblebeach.com.* Located in The Lodge at Pebble Beach (see), just off the famous 18th green of the championship Pebble Beach Golf Links, Club XIX is a luxurious restaurant with glorious views of the Carmel Bay. Featuring the clean flavors of the season and accented with California style, the food here is prepared with refined French technique. Even the most addicted golfers slow down for a lavish meal at Club XIX. The indoor dining room is small and intimate, while the cozy, outdoor brick patio is warmed by the glow of a blazing fireplace, making either choice ideal for romance. The only problem is that seasoned golfers may find it difficult to focus on romance or food, because the mind tends to wander to the next morning's tee time. It is Pebble Beach, after all. California menu, French menu. Dinner. Bar. Reservations recommended. Valet parking. Outdoor seating. **$$$$**

Petaluma (D-2)

See also Calistoga, Guerneville, Napa, Santa Rosa, Sonoma

Population 54,548
Elevation 12 ft
Area Code 707
Zip 94952
Information Petaluma Visitors Program, 800 Baywood Dr, 94954; phone 707/769-0429
Web Site www.petalumaonline.com

What to See and Do

Great Petaluma Mill. *6 Petaluma Blvd N, Petaluma (94952).* Refurbished historic grain mill housing shops intermingled with remnants of the riverboat era of the building. (Daily; closed Dec 25) **FREE**

Marin French Cheese Company. *7500 Red Hill Rd, Petaluma (94952). 1/4 mile S of junction Novato Blvd and Petaluma-Point Reyes Rd. Phone 707/762-6001; toll-free 800/292-6001; fax 707/762-0430. www.marinfrenchcheese.com.* Stop in to taste a variety of soft cheeses (the Brie is fabulous), tour the small operation, and enjoy the grassy picnic area. Guided tours (daily 10 am-4 pm). **FREE**

Mrs. Grossman's Paper Company. *3810 Cypress Dr, Petaluma (94954). Phone 707/763-1700; toll-free 800/429-4549; fax 707/763-7121. www.mrsgrossmans.com.* Mrs. Grossman's makes stickers—millions of them. After a video introduction, tour guides take visitors directly onto the factory floor to see the printing presses in action. Following the tour—liberally peppered with sticker giveaways—try your hand at sticker art in the art room. (Mon-Fri 9 am-5:30 pm; reservations required) **FREE**

Petaluma Adobe State Historic Park. *3325 Adobe Rd, Petaluma (94954). 3 miles E of Hwy 101 on Hwy 116. Phone 707/762-4871. www.parks.ca.gov.* Restored adobe cattle ranch headquarters, built 1834-1846 for General M. G. Vallejo, combines Monterey Colonial style with the traditional Spanish-Mexican plan. (Daily; closed Jan 1, Thanksgiving, Dec 25) **$**

Petaluma Historical Museum and Library. *20 Fourth St, Petaluma (94952). Phone 707/778-4398; fax 707/762-3923. www.petalumamuseum.com.* Built with a grant from Andrew Carnegie in 1906, the museum contains one of California's only free-standing glass domes. Permanent and changing exhibits of Petaluma history. (Wed-Sat 10 am-4 pm, Sun noon-3 pm; closed holidays) **FREE**

Petaluma Village Premium Outlets. *2200 Petaluma Blvd N, Petaluma (94952). Phone 707/778-9300. www.premiumoutlets.com.* Forty-three name-brand outlet stores in village-style setting. (Mon-Thurs 10 am-8 pm, Fri-Sat 10 am-9 pm, Sun to 6 pm)

Special Event

Sonoma-Marin Fair. *175 Fairgrounds Dr, Petaluma (94952). Phone 707/283-3247; fax 707/283-3250. www.sonoma-marinfair.org.* The five days of the Sonoma-Marin Fair are jam-packed with fun. From live music, jugglers, and musicians to chef demonstrations, community exhibits, and a destruction derby, there's definitely no shortage of things to see and do. Five days in mid-June. **$$$**

Limited-Service Hotel

★★ SHERATON SONOMA COUNTY. *745 Baywood Dr, Petaluma (94954). Phone 707/283-*

2888; toll-free 888/627-8458; fax 707/283-2828. www.sheraton.com. 183 rooms, 4 story. Pets accepted, some restrictions. Check-in 3 pm, check-out noon. High-speed Internet access. Restaurant, bar. Fitness room, spa. Outdoor pool, whirlpool. Business center. **$$**

Restaurants

★ **DE SCHMIRE.** *304 Bodega Ave, Petaluma (94952). Phone 707/762-1901.* At first glance, one might underestimate this little bistro on Petaluma's central west end, with its small sign and tucked-away location. However, step inside and you'll realize you've found a local gem that has been serving fine California fare to local devotees for several years. The two dining rooms feature local art and an open kitchen that turns out great slow-cooked steaks. California, French menu. Dinner. Closed July 4, Dec 24-25. **$$**

★ **GRAZIANO'S.** *170 Petaluma Blvd N, Petaluma (94952). Phone 707/762-5997; fax 707/762-3507. www.grazianosristorante.com.* In historic downtown Petaluma, this northern Italian restaurant has been a local favorite for years. With a wine list that includes both California and Italian wines, the menu features an array of pasta, seafood, and steak dishes, as well as decadent desserts. Enjoy your meal amid modern art from the chef/owner's personal collection. Italian menu. Dinner. Closed Mon; holidays. Bar. **$$**

Placerville (D-3)

See also Auburn, Mother Lode Country, Sacramento

Founded 1848
Population 9,610
Elevation 1,866 ft
Area Code 530
Zip 95667
Information El Dorado County Chamber of Commerce, 542 Main St; phone 530/621-5885 or toll-free 800/457-6279
Web Site www.placerville-downtown.org

This one-time rough-and-tough gold town was first known as Dry Diggins (because the gravel had to be carried to water to be washed for gold) and later as Hangtown (because of the number of hangings necessary to keep law and order). At one time, the town rivaled San Francisco and nurtured three notables: Mark Hopkins, railroad magnate; Philip D. Armour, meatpacking magnate; and John Studebaker, automobile magnate. A few mines still function, but lumbering, agriculture, and recreation are the main industries.

What to See and Do

El Dorado County Historical Museum. *104 Placerville Dr, Placerville (95667). Phone 530/621-5865; fax 530/621-6644. www.co-el-dorado.ca.us/museum.* Displays and exhibits of early gold rush days, when Miwok, Maidu, and Washoe inhabited the area. (Wed-Sat 10 am-4 pm, Sun noon-4 pm; closed holidays) **FREE**

El Dorado National Forest. *100 Forni Rd, Placerville (95667). 25 miles E via I-50. Phone 530/622-5061. www.fs.fed.us/r5/eldorado.* This forest of approximately 786,000 acres includes the 105,364-acre Mokelumne Wilderness, located between Hwy 4 and Hwy 88, and the popular 63,475-acre Desolation Wilderness, located immediately west of Lake Tahoe (see LAKE TAHOE AREA). There are more than 70 developed campgrounds, which have varying fees and facilities; all are closed in winter.

Gold Bug Mine. *Gold Bug Park, 2635 Gold Bug Ln, Placerville (95667). Phone 530/642-5207; fax 530/642-5238. www.goldbugpark.org.* Municipally owned double-shaft gold mine with exposed vein; restored gold stampmill. Picnic area. Guided tours available (reservations required, fee). (Mid-Apr-Oct: daily 10 am-4 pm; Nov-Mar: Sat-Sun noon-4 pm) **$**

Marshall Gold Discovery State Historic Park. *Hwy 49, Coloma. 8 miles NW on Hwy 49. Phone 530/622-3470. www.parks.ca.gov.* The park marks the place where James Marshall found flecks of gold in tailrace of Sutter's Mill in January of 1848. By the next year, more than $10 million in gold had been taken from the American River's South Fork. Park includes Gold Discovery Museum (daily 10 am-4:30 pm; closed Jan 1, Thanksgiving, Dec 25), Marshall's cabin and monument where he is buried, Thomas House Museum, operating replica of Sutter's mill, blacksmith shop, and several other buildings. Fishing; nature and hiking trails, picnicking, concession. Park (daily 8 am-sunset). **$**

Special Events

El Dorado County Fair. *Fairgrounds, 100 Placerville Dr, Placerville (95667). SW on Hwy 50. Phone 530/621-5860; fax 530/295-2566. www.eldoradocountyfair.org.* Battle of the Bands, livestock shows, bull riding, and wine tasting are just some of the reasons people flock to this popular fair every year. There are special surprises for dads on Sunday! Father's Day weekend. **$$**

Wagon Train Week. *Phone 530/621-5885.* Celebrations each night along wagon train trek (I-50) from Nevada to Placerville. Sat celebrations at fairgrounds; parade on Sun. Early June.

Limited-Service Hotels

★ BEST WESTERN PLACERVILLE INN.
6850 Greenleaf Dr, Placerville (95667). Phone 530/622-9100; toll-free 800/854-9100; fax 530/622-9376. www.bestwestern.com. 105 rooms, 3 story. Pets accepted; fee. Check-out 11 am. Outdoor pool, whirlpool. **$**

★ CAMERON PARK INN SUITES. *3361 Coach Ln, Cameron Park (95682). Phone 530/677-2203; toll-free 800/601-1234; fax 530/676-1422. www.bestwestern.com.* 62 rooms, 2 story. Pets accepted; fee. Complimentary continental breakfast. Check-in 3 pm, check-out noon. Outdoor pool. Business center. **$**

Specialty Lodging

The following lodging establishment is approved by Mobil Travel Guide, but due to its unique and individualized nature has not been given a traditional Mobil Star rating. Included in this listing you may find bed-and-breakfasts, limited-service inns, guest ranches, and other unique hotel properties.

COLOMA COUNTRY INN. *345 High St, Coloma (95613). Phone 530/622-6919. www.colomacountry inn.com.* Built in 1852. 5 rooms. Complimentary full breakfast. Check-in 4-7 pm, check-out 11 am. **$**

Pleasanton

See also Fremont, Hayward, Livermore, Mount Diablo State Park, Oakland

Settled 1851
Population 63,654
Elevation 352 ft
Area Code 925
Zip 94566
Information Tri-Valley Convention & Visitors Bureau, 260 Main St; phone 925/846-8910 or toll-free 888/874-9253
Web Site www.ci.pleasanton.ca.us

Named for the friend of an early settler, Pleasanton was once called "the most desperate town in the West," for its many bandits and desperados. Phoebe Apperson Hearst founded the PTA in Pleasanton.

What to See and Do

Alameda County Fairgrounds. *4501 Pleasanton Ave, Pleasanton (94566). I-680 at Bernal Ave. Phone 925/426-7600; fax 925/426-7599.* Exhibit area; 9-hole golf course. Events and activities. Oldest racetrack west of the Mississippi River. Thoroughbred racing during county fair (see SPECIAL EVENT); satellite-broadcast races year-round.

Blackhawk Auto Museum. *3700 Blackhawk Plaza Cir, Danville (94506). 7 miles N on I-680 to Crow Canyon Rd in San Ramon, then 4 miles E to Camino Tassajara, then 1 block E, turn left on Blackhawk Plaza Dr. Phone 925/736-2280; fax 925/736-4818. www.blackhawkmuseum.org.* Display of 110 classic and rare automobiles, many custom-built. Modern sculpture building; library. (Wed-Sun 10 am-5 pm; closed Jan 1, Thanksgiving, Dec 25) **$$**

Eugene O'Neill National Historic Site. *7 miles W of I-680, near Danville. Phone 925/838-0249. www.nps.gov/euon.* Winner of the Nobel Prize and four Pulitzer Prizes, O'Neill wrote some of his finest works at Tao House, including the autobiographical *Long Day's Journey Into Night* and *A Moon For the Misbegotten.* A blend of Chinese philosophy and Spanish-style architecture, Tao House was to be O'Neill's "final home and harbor." The house commands a spectacular view of the hills and orchards of the San Ramon Valley and Mt. Diablo. Tours (Wed-Sun, 10 am and 12:30 pm; by reservations only; closed Jan 1, Thanksgiving, Dec 25). Shuttle service provided from Danville. **FREE**

Special Event

Alameda County Fair. *Fairgrounds, 4501 Pleasanton Ave, Pleasanton (94566). Junction I-680 and I-580, Bernal Ave exit. Phone 925/426-7600; fax 925/426-7599. www.alamedacountyfair.com.* Horse racing, exhibitions, carnival, concert headliners. Late June-mid-July. **$**

Limited-Service Hotels

★ **CANDLEWOOD SUITES.** *5535 Johnson Dr, Pleasanton (94588). Phone 925/463-1212; fax 925/463-6080. www.larkspurlanding.com.* 126 rooms, 4 story, all suites. Pets accepted, some restrictions; fee. Check-in 3 pm, check-out noon. Fitness room. Whirlpool. **$**

★ ★ **WYNDHAM PLEASANTON GARDEN.** *5990 Stoneridge Mall Rd, Pleasanton (94588). Phone 510/463-3330; toll-free 800/996-3426; fax 510/463-3315. www.wyndham.com.* 171 rooms, 6 story. Check-out noon. Restaurant, bar. Fitness room. Outdoor pool. **$**

Full-Service Hotel

★ ★ ★ **HILTON PLEASANTON AT THE CLUB.** *7050 Johnson Dr, Pleasanton (94588). Phone 925/463-8000; toll-free 800/774-1500; fax 925/463-3801. www.pleasantonhilton.com.* This property is located close to Oakland and San Jose airports as well as BART for easy transportation to San Francisco. 290 rooms, 5 story. Check-in 3 pm, check-out noon. Restaurant, bar. Children's activity center. Fitness room. Outdoor pool, children's pool, whirlpool. Tennis. Business center. **$$**

Specialty Lodging

The following lodging establishment is approved by Mobil Travel Guide, but due to its unique and individualized nature has not been given a traditional Mobil Star rating. Included in this listing you may find bed-and-breakfasts, limited-service inns, guest ranches, and other unique hotel properties.

THE ROSE HOTEL. *807 Main St, Pleasanton (94566). Phone 925/846-8802; toll-free 800/843-9540; fax 925/846-2272. www.rosehotel.net.* The Rose Hotel is a distinguished getaway for discriminating travelers. No detail has been overlooked here, where polished woods, marble, granite, and mosaic-tile floors capture guests' attention. Eclectic European design influences this sophisticated property, where the rooms and suites are spacious and plush. Romantic in spirit, this hotel is also appropriate for business travelers. Breakfast is served daily in the lobby, and tea service is available nightly. Pleasanton's old-town charms enchant visitors, and The Rose Hotel's location right on Main Street makes it a terrific choice for those who want to enjoy the many fairs and festivals of this picture-perfect American town. 38 rooms, 3 story. Complimentary continental breakfast. Check-in 3 pm, check-out noon. Fitness room. **$$**

Restaurant

★ ★ **GIRASOLE.** *3180 Santa Rita Rd, Pleasanton (94566). Phone 925/484-1001; fax 925/484-3505. www.girasolegrill.com.* Italian, steak menu. Lunch, dinner. Closed holidays. Children's menu. Casual attire. Outdoor seating. **$$**

Quincy (C-3)

See also Chester

Population 1,879
Elevation 3,432 ft
Area Code 530
Zip 95971
Information Plumas County Visitors Bureau, PO Box 4120; phone toll-free 800/326-2247
Web Site www.plumascounty.org

What to See and Do

Plumas County Museum. *500 Jackson St, Quincy (95971). Phone 530/283-6320. www.plumascountymuseum.org.* Period rooms, changing historical displays, artifacts, and photographs featured in main gallery; permanent exhibit of baskets woven by area's native Maidu. Mezzanine gallery features contemporary cultural displays by county artisans, historical exhibits, and Western Pacific and local railroad collections. Archival collection of Plumas County documents. (Tues-Sat 8 am-5 pm) **$**

Plumas National Forest. *159 Lawrence St, Quincy (95971). Phone 530/283-2050; toll-free 877/444-6777. www.fs.fed.us/r5/plumas.* A beautiful 1 1/2 million-acre forest in Feather River Country. Feather Falls (640-foot drop), the sixth-highest waterfall in the United States, is accessible by a 3.5-mile trail (see OROVILLE). Highway 70, which runs approximately 150 miles through the forest, is a designated National Scenic Byway. Groomed cross-country skiing, snowmobile trails. Interpretive trails; hiking, backpacking. Fishing, boating; hunting (deer, bear, game birds), picnicking, camping (Apr-Oct, fee).

Special Event

Plumas Sierra County Fair. *Plumas County Fairgrounds, 204 Fairground Rd, Quincy (95971). Phone 530/283-6272; toll-free www.countyofplumas.com/fair.* Held annually since 1859. Horse shows, stock car races, country/western entertainment, parade, 4-H livestock auction. Second week in Aug.

Restaurants

★★ MOON'S. *501 Cresent St, Quincy (95971). Phone 530/283-0765.* Restored early 1900s building. Italian, American menu. Dinner. Closed Mon; holidays. Outdoor seating. **$$**

★★★ OLSEN'S CABIN. *589 Johnsville Rd, Gray Eagle (96103). Phone 530/836-2801.* Situated back in the trees, this restaurant not only has a beautiful setting but also an inviting interior. American menu. Dinner. Closed Sun-Wed. Bar. Children's menu. **$$**

Rancho Cordova

See also Roseville, Sacramento

Population 55,060
Elevation 126 ft
Area Code 916
Information Cordova Chamber of Commerce, 3328 Mather Field Rd, 95670; phone 916/361-8700
Web Site www.ranchocordova.org

Limited-Service Hotel

★ INNS OF AMERICA - SACRAMENTO/ RANCHO CORDOVA. *12249 Folsom Blvd, Rancho Cordova (95742). Phone 916/351-1213; toll-free 800/ 826-0778; fax 916/351-1817. www.innsofamerica.com.* 122 rooms, 3 story. Pets accepted. Complimentary continental breakfast. Check-in 3 pm, check-out 11 am. Outdoor pool. **$**

Full-Service Hotel

★★★ MARRIOTT SACRAMENTO RANCHO CORDOVA. *10683 White Rock Rd, Rancho Cordova (95670). Phone 916/638-3800; fax 916/638-6776. www.marriott.com.* This Rancho Cordova hotel is just 12 miles from Sacramento, the capital of the state. 262 rooms, 11 story. Check-in 3 pm, check-out noon. High-speed Internet access, wireless Internet access. Restaurant, bar. Fitness room. Outdoor pool, whirlpool. Airport transportation available. Business center. **$**

Restaurant

★★★ SLOCUM HOUSE. *7992 California Ave, Fair Oaks (95628). Phone 916/961-7211; fax 916/967-3035. www.slocum-house.com.* Guests will delight in this charming restaurant situated on a majestic hilltop surrounded by lush gardens and 100-year-old maple trees. This historic 1920s house features Art Deco décor and cozy fireside dining. American, Asian menu. Lunch, dinner, Sun brunch. Closed Mon; Jan 1, July 4. Bar. Outdoor seating. **$$$**

Red Bluff (C-2)

See also Lassen Volcanic National Park, Redding

Population 13,147
Elevation 340 ft
Area Code 530
Zip 96080
Information Red Bluff-Tehama County Chamber of Commerce, 100 Main St, PO Box 850; phone 530/527-6220
Web Site www.redbluffchamberofcommerce.com

A marketing center for the products of the upper Sacramento Valley, the town is named for the reddish sand and gravel cliffs in the vicinity. The first settlers came for gold but found wealth in wheat fields and orchards instead. As river steamers discharged passengers and freight, the city also became a transportation center for the mines around it. Now, lumbering, agriculture, and wood products are important industries. One notable pioneer of Red Bluff, William Ide, led the Bear Flag Revolt against Mexico.

What to See and Do

City River Park. *100 Main St, Red Bluff (96080). On the Sacramento River, between Reeds Creek Bridge and Sycamore St. Phone 530/527-8177.* Swimming pool (June-Aug, daily; fee), boat ramp; picnic areas, playgrounds. Band concerts (summer, Mon). **FREE**

Fishing. *1500 S Jackson St, Red Bluff (96080). Phone 530/527-1196. In Sacramento River.* Steelhead, salmon, trout. Sam Ayer Park and Dog Island Fishing Access, 1 mile N on Sacramento River. Footbridge to 11-acre island; nature trails, picnicking. Permit required. **FREE**

Kelly-Griggs House Museum. *311 Washington St, Red Bluff (96080). Phone 530/527-1129.* (1880s) Renovated Victorian house with period furnishings; Pendleton Gallery of Art; Chinese and Native American artifacts; historical exhibits. Map of auto tours of Victorian Red Bluff available (fee). (Thurs-Sun, afternoons; closed holidays) **FREE**

William B. Ide Adobe State Historic Park. *21659 Adobe Rd, Red Bluff (96080). Phone 530/529-8599. www.parks.ca.gov.* This 1850s adobe house commemorates William B. Ide, the only president of the California Republic. Includes a collection of household artifacts, a picnicking area, and demonstrations on the process of adobe brickmaking and pioneer crafts in summer. (Daily 8 am-4 pm; closed Jan 1, Thanksgiving, Dec 25) **$**

Special Events

Red Bluff Roundup. *Tehama County Fairgrounds, 650 Antelope Blvd, Red Bluff (96080). Phone 530/527-8700. www.redbluffroundup.com.* PRCA approved. One of the biggest three-day rodeos in the West. Three days in mid-Apr.

Tehama District Fair. *650 Antelope Blvd, Red Bluff (96080). Phone 530/527-5920. www.tehamadistrictfair.com.* Includes livestock shows, food and arts and crafts competitions, a destruction derby, and "Battle of the Bands." Four days in late Sept.

Limited-Service Hotel

★ COMFORT INN. *90 Sale Ln, Red Bluff (96080). Phone 530/529-7060; fax 530/529-7077. www.comfortinn.com.* 67 rooms, 3 story. Complimentary continental breakfast. Check-in 2 pm, check-out 11 am. Fitness room. Outdoor pool, whirlpool. **$**

Restaurant

★ PEKING CHINESE RESTAURANT. *860 Main St, Red Bluff (96080). Phone 530/527-0523; fax 530/527-0536.* American, Chinese menu. Lunch, dinner. Closed Thanksgiving, Dec 25. Bar. **$**

Redding (B-2)

See also Burney, Lassen Volcanic National Park, Mount Shasta, Red Bluff, Weaverville

Founded 1872
Population 80,865
Elevation 557 ft
Area Code 530
Information Convention and Visitors Bureau, 777 Auditorium Dr, 96001; phone 530/225-4100 or toll-free 800/874-7562
Web Site www.visitredding.org

The hub city of northern California's vast scenic Shasta-Cascade Region is located at the top of the Sacramento Valley, in the shadow of Mount Shasta—with the rugged Coast Range on the west, the Cascades on the north and east, and the Sierra Nevada to the southeast. The city was founded when the California and Oregon Railroad chose the site as its northern terminus; it became the county seat in 1888. Lumber and tourism are its principal industries. The Sacramento River flows directly through the city, providing popular pastimes such as fishing, rafting, and canoeing.

What to See and Do

Coleman National Fish Hatchery. *24411 Coleman Fish Hatchery, Anderson (96007). S on I-5 to Cottonwood, 5 miles E on Balls Ferry Rd to Ash Creek Rd, 1 mile to Gover Rd, 2 1/2 miles to Coleman Fish Hatchery Rd. Phone 530/365-8622.* Chinook (king) salmon and steelhead trout are raised here to help mitigate the loss of spawning area due to construction of Shasta Dam. (Daily 7:30 am-4 pm) **FREE**

Lake Redding-Caldwell Park. *1250 Parkview Ave, Redding (96001). Rio Dr, N on Market St, on N shore of Sacramento River. Phone 530/225-4095.* An 85-acre park; boat ramp, swimming pool. Picnic facilities. Falls of the lake are lighted in summer. **FREE** In Caldwell Park is the

★ Lake Shasta Caverns. *20359 Shasta Caverns Rd, Redding (96070). 16 miles N on I-5, then 1 1/2 miles E on Shasta Cavern Rd. Phone 530/238-2341; toll-free 800/795-2283. www.lakeshastacaverns.com.* Stalactites, stalagmites, flowstone deposits; 58° F. Guided tour includes boat ride across McCloud Arm of Lake Shasta and bus ride up mountain to cavern entrance. Tours (Apr-May, Sept: daily every hour from 9 am-3 pm; summer: daily every 30 minutes 9 am-4 pm; winter: daily 10 am, noon, 2 pm; closed Thanksgiving, Dec 25). **$$$$**

Paul Bunyan's Forest Camp. *800 Auditorium Dr, Redding (96001). Phone 530/243-8960.* Forestry and ecology exhibits. Also hosts a popular summer butterfly house. (Memorial Day-Labor Day: daily 9 am-5 pm; Sept-May: Wed-Mon 9 am-5 pm; closed holidays) **$$$**

Shasta State Historic Park. *Hwy 299 W, Shasta. 6 miles W on Hwy 299. Phone 530/243-8194. www.parks.ca.gov.* Remains of gold rush town with several well-preserved original buildings; historical museum; art gallery. Picnicking. (Wed-Sun; closed Jan 1, Thanksgiving, Dec 25) **$**

Shasta-Trinity National Forest. *2400 Washington Ave, Redding (96001). N, E, and W via Hwy 299, I-5. Phone 530/226-2500. www.fs.fed.us/r5/shastatrinity.* More than 2 million acres contain portions of the Trinity Alps Wilderness, Mount Shasta Wilderness, Castle Crags Wilderness, Chanchelulla Wilderness, and the Yolla Bolly-Middle Eel Wilderness. Picnicking, camping (fee). **FREE**

Turtle Bay. *800 Auditorium Dr, Redding (96099). Phone 530/243-8850. www.turtlebay.org.* A developing museum-arboretum complex along the Sacramento River. Live wildlife exhibits, aquariums, cultivated gardens, and a pedestrian bridge over the Sacramento River. (Memorial Day-Labor Day: daily 9 am-5 pm; rest of year: Wed-Mon 9 am-5 pm) **$$$**

Waterworks Park. *151 N Boulder Dr, Redding (96003). Jct I-5 and Hwy 299 E. Phone 530/246-9550. www.waterworkspark.com.* Water theme park with three giant serpentine slides, Raging River inner tube ride, activity pool, kiddie water playground. (Memorial Day-Labor Day, daily, hours vary; call or visit Web site for schedule) **$$$$**

Whiskeytown-Shasta-Trinity National Recreation Area, Whiskeytown Unit. *8 miles W via Hwy 299. Phone 530/242-3400. www.nps.gov/whis.* Water sports, fishing, boating (marinas); picnicking, snack bars, camping (fee), campfire programs. Visitor center (Memorial Day-Labor Day: daily 9 am-6 pm; winter: daily 10 am-4 pm; closed Jan 1, Thanksgiving, Dec 25). (Daily 24 hours) **$$** Contains areas surrounding

Lewiston Dam and Lake. *17 miles NW on Hwy 299, then 6 miles N on unnumbered roads.* Regulator and diversion point for water to Whiskeytown Dam near Shasta.

Shasta Dam and Power Plant. *5 miles W of I-5. Schedule may vary. Phone 530/275-4463.* Three times as high as Niagara Falls: 602 feet high, 3,460 feet long. Visitor center. Waters of three rivers back up to form Shasta Lake, 35 miles long with a 365-mile shoreline. Houseboating is popular here; boats are available for rent at several local marinas. Guided tours daily; schedule may vary. (Daily) **FREE**

Trinity Dam and Lake. *22 miles NW via Hwy 299 W. Phone 530/623-2121.* Large earthfill dam (465 feet high) creates lake, known locally as Trinity Lake, 20 miles long with 145-mile shoreline.

Whiskeytown Dam and Lake. *17 miles NW on Hwy 299, then 6 miles N on unnumbered roads. Phone 530/246-1225.* Part of the Central Valley Project; forms lake with a 36-mile shoreline. Camping (fee). Information center NE of dam at junction Hwy 299 and Kennedy Memorial Dr. Contact Box 188, Whiskeytown 96095.

Special Events

Rodeo Week. *715 Auditorium Dr, Redding (96001). Phone 530/241-5731. www.reddingrodeo.com.* In addition to the rodeo itself, Redding's Rodeo Week includes a kick-off dinner and dance, a horseback basketball game, and a pancake breakfast. Mid-May.

Shasta District Fair. *Shasta District Fairgrounds, Hwy 273 and Briggs St, Anderson (96007). 11 miles S on Hwy 99, I-5. Phone 530/378-6789. www.shastadistrictfair.com.* The fact that there is something for everyone—arts and crafts, a carnival, national and local musical entertainment, and auto races—makes this the largest annual event in Shasta County with attendance hitting more than 100,000. Third week of June. **$$**

Shasta Highlands Renaissance and Celtic Faire. *Anderson River Park, Dodson Rd, Anderson. I-5 to Riverside Ave exit and E to Airport Rd. Right on Airport Rd, proceed two blocks, turn left, and left on Stingy Ln. Proceed 1 1/2 miles to Dodson Rd. www.shastahighlands.org.* You'll travel back in time to the 1500s at this fair and see Mary, Queen of Scots; jousting; parades; plays; and a fire-breathing dragon. First weekend in May.

Limited-Service Hotels

★ ★ BEST WESTERN HILLTOP INN. *2300 Hilltop Dr, Redding (96002). Phone 530/221-6100; toll-free 800/336-4880; fax 530/221-2867. www.thehilltopinn.com.* 115 rooms, 2 story. Complimentary full breakfast. Check-in 2 pm, check-out noon. High-speed Internet access. Restaurant, bar. Outdoor pool, children's pool, whirlpool. Business center. **$**

★ ★ RED LION. *1830 Hilltop Dr, Redding (96002). Phone 530/221-8700; toll-free 800/733-5466; fax 530/221-0324. www.redlion.com.* This hotel is located in the northern end of the Sacramento Valley, an area known for its scenic beauty and quaint mining towns. 192 rooms, 2 story. Pets accepted; fee. Check-in 3 pm, check-out noon. High-speed Internet access, wireless Internet access. Two restaurants, bar. Fitness room. Outdoor pool, whirlpool. Airport transportation available. Business center. **$**

Specialty Lodging

The following lodging establishment is approved by Mobil Travel Guide, but due to its unique and individualized nature has not been given a traditional Mobil Star rating. Included in this listing you may find bed-and-breakfasts, limited-service inns, guest ranches, and other unique hotel properties.

O'BRIEN MOUNTAIN INN. *18026 O'Brien Inlet Rd, O'Brien (96070). Phone 530/238-8026; toll-free 888/799-8026; fax 530/238-2027. www.obrienmountain inn.com.* This unique mountain getaway offers rooms decorated according to its musical theme, including Jazz, World Beat, and Folk. Area activities include mountain biking, tandem hang gliding, and more. 7 rooms. Complimentary full breakfast. Check-in 4-6 pm, check-out 11 am. **$$**

Redwood City (E-2)

See also Menlo Park, Palo Alto, San Francisco International Airport Area, San Mateo, Saratoga

Settled 1854
Population 75,402
Elevation 15 ft
Area Code 650
Information Redwood City San Mateo County Chamber of Commerce, 1675 Broadway, 94063; phone 650/364-1722
Web Site www.ci.redwood-city.ca.us

In the center of the booming commercial and industrial peninsula area, Redwood City has the only deepwater bay port south of San Francisco on the peninsula. Once a Spanish ranch, it was settled by S. M. Mezes, who called it Mezesville; lumbermen who cut the nearby virgin redwoods renamed it Redwood City. It was incorporated in 1867 and is the seat of San Mateo County.

What to See and Do

Lathrop House. *627 Hamilton St, Redwood City (94063). Phone 650/365-5564. lathrophouse.org.* Victorian house and furnishings. (Tues-Thurs; closed holidays; also Aug, late Dec) **FREE**

Marinas. Port of Redwood City Yacht Harbor. *675 Seaport Blvd, Redwood City (94063). Phone 650/365-3258.* Docktown Marina, foot of Maple St; Pete's Harbor, Uccelli Blvd, at foot of Whipple Ave.

Methuselah Redwood. *Junipero Serra Frwy via Woodside Rd exit, W on Hwy 84 to Skyline Blvd, 4 miles N.* Tree more than 1,500 years old, measures 55 feet in circumference. Trunk has been blackened by repeated fires.

Special Event

San Mateo County Fair. *2495 S Delaware St, Redwood City (94403). Phone 650/574-3247. www.sanmateo countyfair.com.* Features a carnival with rides, live musical entertainment, food booths, art and floral exhibits, and contests, including a chili cook-off. Mid-Aug. **$$**

Limited-Service Hotel

★ BEST WESTERN EXECUTIVE SUITES. *25 Fifth Ave, Redwood City (94063). Phone 650/366-5794; toll-free 800/366-7377; fax 650/365-1429. www.bestwestern.com.* 29 rooms, 2 story. Check-in 3 pm, check-out 11 am. High-speed Internet access. Fitness room. Whirlpool. **$**

Full-Service Hotel

★ ★ ★ SOFITEL SAN FRANCISCO BAY. *223*

Twin Dolphin Dr, Redwood City (94065). Phone 650/598-9000; toll-free 800/763-4835; fax 650/598-0459. www.sofitel.com. Located in the San Francisco Bay area, this hotel is within five minutes of the airport. 42 rooms, 9 story. Pets accepted. Check-in 3 pm, check-out noon. Restaurant, bar. Fitness room. Airport transportation available. Business center. **$**

Redwood Highway

See also Crescent City, Eureka, Humboldt Redwoods State Park

Web Site www.redwoodempire.com

Highway 101 runs for 387 miles from San Francisco to the wine country of Sonoma and Mendocino counties, through scenic countryside where 97 percent of the world's coastal redwoods grow. Redwoods can be seen in Marin County at Muir Woods National Monument (see), which has 6 miles of hiking trails and no vehicle access. The bulk of the giant redwood trees, *Sequoia sempervirens,* are from Leggett north to the Oregon state line. The Humboldt Redwoods State Park (see) runs on both sides of the highway; many of the major groves are here, including the spectacular Avenue of the Giants north of Phillipsville, south of Pepperwood. A guidebook with maps is available from the Redwood Empire/North Coast Visitors Services (fee). Other concentrations of redwoods are at Grizzly Creek Redwoods State Park, 18 miles east of Highway 101 on Highway 36, with camping (fees), picnicking, swimming, and fishing; and at Redwood National and State Parks (see CRESCENT CITY), which takes in Prairie Creek Redwoods State Park, 6 miles north of Orick on Highway 101, Del Norte Coast Redwoods State Park, 7 miles south of Crescent City, and Jedediah Smith Redwoods State Park, 9 miles northeast of Crescent City. The highway has several spectacular overlooks of the Pacific Ocean and the north coast of California.

The Redwood Highway, a major thoroughfare from the Golden Gate Bridge north, has four lanes for more than 260 miles and two lanes with many turnabouts for the remainder. Lodging is usually available, but heavy summer traffic makes it wise to plan ahead.

Richardson Grove State Park (B-1)

See also Garberville

8 miles south of Garberville on Hwy 101.

Web Site www.parks.ca.gov

One of California's beautiful redwood parks, Richardson Grove covers a 1,000-acre tract along the south fork of the Eel River. Swimming, fishing (October-January); hiking trails, picnicking, camping. Visitor center. Nature programs offered daily in summer. Standard fees. Phone 707/247-3318.

Roseville (D-2)

See also Rancho Cordova, Sacramento

Population 79,921
Elevation 160 ft
Area Code 916
Zip 95678
Web Site www.roseville.ca.us

What to See and Do

Folsom Premium Outlets. *13000 Folsom Blvd, Folsom (95630). E of Sacramento on Hwy 50. Phone 916/985-0312. www.premiumoutlets.com.* More than 70 outlet stores, including Kenneth Cole, Bebe, London Fog, and the Nike Factory Store. (Mon-Sat 10 am-9 pm, Sun to 6 pm)

Full-Service Hotel

★ ★ ★ BEST WESTERN ROCKLIN PARK HOTEL. *5450 China Garden Rd, Rocklin (95677). Phone 916/630-9400; toll-free 888/630-9400; fax 916/630-9448. www.bestwestern.com.* This European-inspired hotel offers 67 guest rooms with views of the surrounding foothills. The Rose Garden and Terrace features a granite staircase which leads to an open patio surrounded by rose bushes, a redwood arbor, and a fountain. It is an ideal location for weddings and social functions. The main ballroom showcases the views of the arbor through expansive windows, perfect for both business meetings or social events. 67 rooms, 2 story. Pets accepted, fee. Check-in 3 pm, check-out noon. Restaurant, bar. Fitness room. Outdoor pool, whirlpool. Airport transportation available. **$**

Restaurant

★ **ROSY'S.** *3950 Pacific St, Rocklin (95677). Phone 916/624-1920; fax 916/624-4677.* American menu. Breakfast, lunch, dinner. Children's menu. Casual attire. Outdoor seating. Football memorabilia. **$**

Rutherford

See also Calistoga, Napa, Santa Rosa, St. Helena, Yountville

What to See and Do

Lake Hennessey Recreational Area. *Take Silverado Trail to Hwy 128 W (also known as Sage Canyon Rd). Phone 707/226-7455.* With its proximity to so many wineries and tourist attractions, Lake Hennessey Recreational Area offers a soothing counterpoint to the bacchanalia of gourmet food and fine wines for visitors. It is also a prime destination for area anglers, who fish the waters for large- and smallmouth bass, trout, and crappies. No motor boats are allowed on the lake, which makes it especially peaceful. (Daily)

St. Supéry Wine Discovery Center. *8440 St. Helena Hwy, Rutherford (94573). Phone 707/963-4507. www.stsupery.com.* If you're curious about the winemaking process, the Wine Discovery Center is an excellent starting place. Located at the St. Supéry Winery, the center offers visitors a hands-on lesson in grape-growing and winemaking, from planting through bottling. For those who are lost when it comes to describing wine (is it oaky or does it have just a hint of berry and pepper?), there's SmellaVision, which enables you to deconstruct a wine's bouquet and recognize the various elements that contribute to its uniqueness—and perhaps impress your friends back home later. You can take a free self-guided tour or sign up for a one-hour guided tour (held daily at 1 pm, and 3 pm), as well as participate in tastings and sample the small production wines in the reserve tasting library. (Daily; closed Jan 1, Thanksgiving, Dec 25) **$$**

Full-Service Resort

★★★ **AUBERGE DU SOLEIL.** *180 Rutherford Hill Rd, Rutherford (94573). Phone 707/963-1211; toll-free 800/348-5406; fax 707/963-8764. www.aubergedusoleil.com.* Auberge du Soleil basks in a golden glow on its perch along the slopes of the Napa Valley's Rutherford Hill. Mediterranean in spirit and appearance, this wine country retreat offers adults a sophisticated and romantic country escape. Opened in 1981 as a restaurant alone, the name Auberge du Soleil has become synonymous with fine dining—even in a region noted for its gourmet cuisine. Today, the kitchen continues to win praise from critics and patrons for its inventive wine country dishes. The accommodations feel every bit the Provençal farmhouse, and balconies open out to enchanting views of the vine-filled countryside. Between the tranquil setting, the shimmering pool, and the sensational spa, which uses grape seeds in many of its treatments, total relaxation is guaranteed. 52 rooms, 2 story. Children over 16 years only. Check-in 3 pm, check-out noon. Restaurant, bar. Fitness room. Outdoor pool, two whirlpools. Tennis. **$$$$**

Full-Service Inn

★★★ **RANCHO CAYMUS.** *1140 Rutherford Rd, Rutherford (94573). Phone 707/963-1777; toll-free 800/845-1777; fax 707/963-5387. www.ranchocaymus.com.* Spanish-style architecture. 26 rooms, 2 story. Complimentary continental breakfast. Check-in 3 pm, check-out noon. Restaurant. **$$**

Spa

★★★★ **SPA DU SOLEIL.** *180 Rutherford Hill Rd, Rutherford (94573). Phone 707/963-1211.* Auberge du Soleil brings a bit of Provence to the California wine country with its sunny, Mediterranean style and warm spirit. Terraced along a hillside overlooking the lush Napa Valley, this inviting inn and accompanying spa are a true haven for the world-weary. The glorious surroundings have inspired the spa's philosophy, with vineyard, garden, and valley themes dominating the treatment menu. While nutrient-rich grapeseeds are the foundation for the vineyard's massages, body treatments, and facials, locally grown herbs and flowers and regional muds and minerals are the basis for the garden and valley menus. Seasonal treatments are also a highlight of a visit to this spa, where guests can see the arrival of spring with a rosemary renewal massage, celebrate summer with a luscious peaches and cream body mask, look forward to fall with a harvest-inspired cleanse or body glaze, or welcome winter with a peppermint and eucalyptus body treatment.

Restaurant

★★★★ AUBERGE DU SOLEIL. *180 Rutherford Hill Rd, Rutherford (94573). Phone 707/963-1211; toll-free 800/348-5406; fax 707/963-8764. www.aubergedusoleil.com.* French-born, San Francisco restaurateur Claude Rouas set out to create a Province-like destination restaurant in northern California with his 1981 fine dining room Auberge du Soleil. In a mere four years he would respond to clamor for overnight accommodations. But born a restaurant, Auberge keeps its culinary promise today, still among the hottest restaurants in Napa Valley. Whether indoors in the sunny, light-filled room or outdoors on the umbrella-shaded terrace, well-appointed tables frame inspiring views over the valley, creating a casually elegant ambience. French-California menus change seasonally, touting artisanal sources and local farms in dishes such as heirloom melon and duck prosciutto salad, artichoke soup with truffled gnocchi, and wild boar filet with carrot juice. Don't miss the area cheese selections for dessert. The six-course tasting menu comes with wines to match from the large, locally strong list. If you're touring the valley by car, consider a lunch stop; midday fare is similar to the evening's selections. California, Mediterranean menu. Breakfast, lunch, dinner. Bar. Business casual attire. Reservations recommended. Valet parking. Outdoor seating. **$$$$**

Sacramento (D-2)

See also Auburn, Davis, Jackson, Lodi, Placerville, Rancho Cordova, Roseville,

Settled 1839
Population 407,018
Elevation 25 ft
Area Code 916
Information Convention and Visitors Bureau, 1303 J Street, Suite 600, 95814; phone 916/264-7777.
Web Site www.sacramentocvb.org

Capital of the state since 1854, Sacramento is known to flower lovers as the Camellia capital of the world. It is the marketing center for 11 counties in the Sacramento Valley, producing a cash farm income approaching 11 percent of the state's income.

Modern Sacramento started when Captain John A. Sutter established New Helvetia, a colony for his Swiss compatriots. Sutter built a fort here and immigrants came. He prospered in wheat raising, flour milling, distilling, and in a passenger and freight boat service to San Francisco. The discovery of gold at Coloma in 1848 (see PLACERVILLE) brought ruin to Sutter. Workers deserted to hunt gold, and he soon lost possession of the fort. The next year his son, who had been deeded family property near the boat line terminus, laid out a town there, naming it Sacramento City. At the entrance to the gold rush country, its population rocketed to 10,000 within seven months. Chosen as California's capital in 1854, the new capitol building was constructed at a cost of more than $2.6 million over a 20-year period.

Transportation facilities were important in the city's growth. In 1860, the Pony Express made Sacramento its western terminus. Later, Sacramento's "Big Four"—Mark Hopkins, Charles Crocker, Collis P. Huntington, and Leland Stanford—financed the building of the Central Pacific Railroad over the Sierras. Deepwater ships reach the city via a 43-mile-long channel from Suisun Bay. Sacramento's new port facilities handle an average of 20 ships a month carrying import and export cargo from major ports around the world.

What to See and Do

Blue Cue. *1004 28th St, Sacramento (95816). Phone 916/442-7208. www.paragarys.com/bluecue.* A favorite hangout in Sacramento's eclectic Midtown neighborhood, the Blue Cue is one of a rare breed: an upscale pool hall. Housed in a historic redbrick, the place is packed with pool tables (with blue felt, of course) and other drinking diversions, and has one of the deepest selections of beer, wine, and liquor in the city. The menu consists of sandwiches, pizza, and a page full of potent specialty drinks. (Mon-Wed 5 pm-midnight, Thurs-Sat to 2 am)

Blue Diamond Growers Visitors Center & Retail Store. *1701 C St, Sacramento (95814). Phone 916/446-8438. www.bluediamond.com.* Headquarters of one of the world's leading almond producers. Features a 20-minute video (Mon-Fri 9:30 am-5 pm, Sat to 4 pm). **FREE**

Cal Expo. *1600 Exposition Blvd, Sacramento (95815). Phone 916/263-3000; toll-free 877/225-3976. www.calexpo.com.* Multipurpose facility for a variety of activities, including various consumer shows, auto racing, and concerts. (See SPECIAL EVENTS)

California Museum for History, Women, & the Arts. *1020 O St, Sacramento (95814). Phone 916/653-7524. www.californiamuseum.org.* Museum about California's past, present, and future; exhibits look at "Place," "People," "Promise," and "Politics." (Mon-Sat 10 am-5 pm, Sun noon-5 pm; closed holidays) **$**

California State Capitol and Museum. *10th and L sts, Sacramento (95814). Phone 916/324-0333. www.capitolmuseum.ca.gov.* The stately California State Capitol has been the heart of Sacramento since its construction concluded in 1874. Now a "working museum" and a fixture in California's state park system, the lavish Roman-inspired structure is surrounded by Capitol Park, 40 lush acres with flora from all corners of the globe, including such California natives as redwoods and fan palms, and memorials to veterans of the Vietnam War and other conflicts. The building's domed rotunda straddles the two houses of the Legislature, with many of the meticulously restored rooms—including the former governor's office, decorated to match its 1906 appearance—accessible to the public. In-depth guided tours cover the law making process (with stops on balconies that overlook the Assembly and the Senate chambers) and California's often-turbulent political history. (Tours daily 9 am-4 pm; closed Jan 1, Thanksgiving, Dec 25) **FREE**

California State University, Sacramento. *6000 J St, Sacramento (95819). On the banks of the American River on the E side of campus. Take Hwy 50 to exit Power Inn and follow the signs. Phone 916/278-6156. www.csus.edu.* (1947) (27,000 students) A replica of the Golden Gate Bridge serves as a footbridge across the river.

Crocker Art Museum. *216 O St, Sacramento (95814). Phone 916/264-5423. www.crockerartmuseum.org.* In 1868, Judge Edwin Crocker bought a lavish Victorian mansion in what is now the heart of downtown Sacramento. Within five years, he had added an elaborate gallery structure to house his family's extensive collection of European artworks. Then, in 1885, Edwin's wife, Margaret, set the stage for the modern Crocker Art Museum when she donated the family's gallery and its resident collection to the city. More than a century (and several expansions and renovations) later, the museum is the foremost arts institution in the Sacramento Valley, an ornate showcase for the original Crocker collection as well as impressive forays into contemporary regional work, East Asian paintings, and ceramics. The museum's seasonal exhibits are an eclectic lot, spanning time and place with emphasis on past and present California artists. The museum hosts art classes for all ages and there is a gift shop on-site. (Tues-Sun 10 am-5 pm, Thurs to 9 pm; closed Jan 1, Thanksgiving, Dec 25) **$$**

Discovery Museum Science & Space Center. *3615 Auburn Blvd, Sacramento (95821). Phone 916/575-3941. www.thediscovery.org.* The Discovery Museum in Old Sacramento presents engaging exhibits on history, science, space, and technology that are geared toward young minds, but also fun for mom and dad. Artifacts from the city's history are enshrined in a replica of the 1854 City Hall, but the broader historical focus is on the California gold rush, depicted through such displays as a re-created mineshaft. Other highlights are a planetarium, a space shuttle simulation, and an outdoor nature trail. (Tues-Fri noon-5 pm, Sat-Sun and July-Aug from 10 am; closed Mon; holidays) **$**

Downtown Plaza. *547 L St, Sacramento (95814). Phone 916/442-4000. www.westfield.com.* A block off the Capitol Mall in downtown Sacramento, the Downtown Plaza is a sprawling retail and entertainment complex. The enclosed, 1.2 million-square-foot facility presents a who's who of national retailers and restaurants—the more than 100 establishments include Hard Rock Cafe, Macy's, Gap, and Carl's Jr.—as well as a movie theater. (Daily 10 am-9 pm, Sun to 6 pm)

Fairytale Town. *3901 Land Park Dr, Sacramento (95822). Phone 916/264-5233. www.fairytaletown.org.* A city-owned, nonprofit kids' park that has been a local institution since 1959, Fairytale Town livens up a number of favorite children's stories and rhymes with 25 fantastic play-sets. Beginning with the entrance gate that Humpty Dumpty sits atop, the 2 1/2-acre park is a launching pad for the young mind, as the perfect setting for make-believe, with opportunities for exercise and education also on hand. Don't expect big-budget, Disney-style rides, but rather a fun, low-tech experience that allows kids to climb up (and tumble down) Jack and Jill's hill, jump Jack-be-Nimble's candlestick, and play on the Beanstalk Giant's foot in the span of an afternoon. Located adjacent to the Sacramento Zoo, Fairytale Town also has a puppet theater, snack bars, and a petting zoo. Unless accompanied by a child, adults are not permitted. (Nov-Feb:

Thurs-Sun 10 am-4 pm; March-Nov: daily 9 am-4 pm; closed Jan 1, Thanksgiving, Dec 25) **$**

Fanny Ann's Saloon. *1023 2nd St, Sacramento (95814). Phone 916/441-0505.* Amusingly disorderly with a Wild West theme, Fanny Ann's Saloon is five levels of knickknacks and bric-a-brac in Old Sacramento. Everything from old street signs to wagon wheels to vintage toys hangs in the towering space, many of the items balanced in seemingly precarious ways. It's fun to look at, but the joint also offers something for the sense of taste as well, serving what many locals consider the best hamburger in town. Watch out for the signs on the bathrooms—the genders are intentionally reversed. (Thurs-Sat 11-2 am, Sun-Wed 11:30 am-midnight)

Gold Rush District State Parks. *Adjacent to the Central Business District between I-5 and the I St bridge. Phone 916/324-0539.* (Circa 1850-1870) This 28-acre area of historic buildings along the banks of the Sacramento River, known as the Old Sacramento Historic District, has been restored to its 1850-1870 period of the Pony Express, the arrival of the Central Pacific Railroad, and the gold rush. Special events are held throughout the year. The area also has shops and restaurants. Most buildings are closed Jan 1, Thanksgiving, and Dec 25. Phone for recorded information, including the Governor's Mansion and Sutter's Fort State Historic Park, State Indian Museum, State Railroad Museum, the Leland Stanford Mansion, and Woodland Upper House State Park. **FREE** Includes

California State Railroad Museum and Railtown State Historic Park. *125 I St, Sacramento (95814). Phone 916/445-6645. www.californiastaterailroadmuseum.org.* The largest part of this complex is the Museum of Railroad History, which houses 21 pieces of rolling stock and a total of 40 exhibits covering all aspects of railroading. (Daily 10 am-5 pm; closed Jan 1, Thanksgiving, Dec 25) **$$**

Central Pacific Passenger Depot. *930 Front St, Sacramento (95814).* (Same days as railroad museum)

Governor's Mansion State Historic Site. *1526 H St, Sacramento (95814). Phone 916/323-3047. www.parks.ca.gov.* Built by a hardware tycoon in 1877, this majestic Second Empire-Italianate mansion in downtown Sacramento served as California's executive mansion from 1903 to 1967. The lavish house is now a historic museum, with guided tours on the hour. Former California Governor and US President Ronald Reagan was its last full-time resident, and the interior décor remains pretty much what it was when the Reagans left in 1967: a melting pot of the tastes of 13 governors and first ladies, with Victorian, French, Italian, and Persian furnishings and details. (Daily 10 am-4 pm; closed Jan 1, Thanksgiving, Dec 25) **$**

Hastings Building. *2nd and J sts, Sacramento (95814).* Western terminus of the Pony Express and original home of the California Supreme Court.

Old Eagle Theatre. *925 Front St, Sacramento (95814). Phone 916/323-6343.* Docent-led programs on Sacramento history.

State Indian Museum. *2618 K St, Sacramento (95816). K St at 26th St. Phone 916/324-0971. www.parks.ca.gov.* Displays include dugout canoes, weapons, pottery, and basketry. Films. (Daily 10 am-5 pm; closed Jan 1, Thanksgiving, Dec 25) **$**

★ **Sutter's Fort State Historic Park.** *2701 L St, Sacramento (95816). Phone 916/445-4422. www.parks.ca.gov.* In 1839, a Swiss immigrant by the name of John Sutter landed on the shore near the confluence of the American and Sacramento rivers. Thanks to a 48,000-acre land grant from the Mexican government, Sutter established a fort as the center of a settlement called New Switzerland that was overrun in 1849 by gold-seekers from the East. Today, the fort is all that remains of Sutter's community, located in what is now Sacramento's hip Midtown neighborhood and restored to its 1840s appearance. Volunteer actors in period costumes help re-create the ways of life in the days before the California gold rush, and visitors can embark on either a guided or self-guided tour. The store here is a treasure trove for anyone with an interest in California history. (Daily 10 am-5 pm; closed Jan 1, Thanksgiving, Dec 25) **$**

Midtown Sacramento Shopping District. *Alhambra Blvd and C St, Sacramento (95816).* As its name implies, Sacramento's Midtown neighborhood is in the heart of the city, just east of downtown and partitioned by 15th Street and Alhambra Boulevard on the west and east, and C and W streets on the north and south. Reminiscent of the funkier shopping districts in San Francisco and Seattle, Midtown's J and K streets bustle with sidewalk cafés, coffee shops, hip clothiers, art galleries, and interesting home and garden merchants—the best description of the shops here is eclectic. Most of the neighborhood's retailers are independent and owner-operated, in contrast to the chain-heavy downtown area. Among the area's stalwarts are Mixed Bag (2404 K St), jam-packed with a diverse inventory of jewelry, kitchenware, and gifts, and Tasha's: The Uncommon Shop (1005 22nd St at J), specializing in imports ranging from batik dresses to Middle Eastern décor.

Old Sacramento. *3rd and J sts, Sacramento (95814). Downtown. I-5 to J St exit. www.oldsacramento.com.* After the establishment of Sutter's Fort in 1839, savvy entrepreneurs looked to capitalize on the new settlement's rapid growth. Storefronts went up alongside the Sacramento River and a city was born, but floods devastated it three times between 1850 and 1862. As a result, a project to raise the riverfront came to pass, and the fledgling city rebuilt itself atop 12 feet of relocated earth. As the years passed, the area steadily went downhill, and by the 1960s, it was a slum. Locals hatched a plan to simultaneously preserve and revive the district, and it soon became a National Landmark and a State Historic Park, full of shops, eateries, nightclubs, and museums (including a railroad museum and the Discovery Museum History Center), many of them housed in historic buildings. Old Sacramento also hosts numerous special events, including the renowned Jazz Jubilee music festival and Gold Rush Days, where the entire district dresses up as its 1850s self.

Public Market Bar. *1230 J St, Sacramento (95814). Phone 916/447-1700. www.starwoodhotels.com/sheraton.* A sleek urban lounge on the ground floor of the Sheraton Grand in downtown Sacramento, the Public Market Bar opened in 1923 and underwent a 21st-century makeover in 2001. The remodeling instantly established it as the top after-work drinking spot in the Capitol Park area, and a favorite of local fat cats and politicos. The sumptuous décor is a perfect match for the PMB's house specialties: martinis and Manhattans. (Sun-Thurs 11 am-midnight, Fri-Sat to 1:30 am)

Sacramento Kings (NBA). *ARCO Arena, One Sports Pkwy, Sacramento (95834). Phone 916/928-0000. www.nba.com/kings.* Professional basketball team. **$$**

Sacramento Monarchs (WNBA). *ARCO Arena, One Sports Pkwy, Sacramento (95834). Phone 916/419-9622. www.wnba.com/monarchs.* Professional basketball team. **$$**

Sacramento Zoo. *3930 W Land Park Dr, Sacramento (95822). Phone 916/264-5888. www.saczoo.com.* While this zoo first opened its gates in William Land Park in 1927, the facility has undergone an impressive transformation since 1980: In place of cages and concrete enclosures are expanses that re-create natural habitats and fully realized ecosystems. Among the dozens of endangered denizens are orangutans, chimpanzees, tigers, and cheetahs. Of special note is the Claire Mower Red Panda Forest, a mixed-species environment with a breeding pair of endangered red pandas living alongside Asian birds, fish, and reptiles. (Feb-Oct: daily 9 am-4 pm; Nov-Jan: daily 10 am-4 pm; closed Thanksgiving, Dec 25) **$$**

Six Flags Waterworld USA. *1600 Exposition Blvd, Sacramento (95815). Phone 916/924-3747. www.sixflags.com.* The largest water park in the Sacramento Valley, the sprawling Six Flags Waterworld USA is a magnet for those looking to neutralize the area's infamous summer sizzle. The attractions within the park range from the fairly tame (the kiddie-oriented Hook's Lagoon and a slow-moving tubing river) to the extreme (the six-story Cliffhanger speed slide and Shark Attack, five "thrill slides" named for a creatures of the deep, and anchored by Great White, the fastest, longest water luge in the state). (Mid-May-Sept, hours vary; call or visit Web site for schedule) **$$$$**

Towe Auto Museum. *2200 Front St, Sacramento (95818). Phone 916/442-6802. www.toweautomuseum.org.* E xtensive collection of American automobiles. (Daily 10 am-6 pm; closed Jan 1, Thanksgiving, Dec 25) **$$**

Whitewater rafting on the American River System. The American River—which run runs through the heart of Sacramento—and its tributaries are one of California's premiere staging grounds for whitewater adventures, with rapids that range from Class III to Class V. For a guided trip, W. E. T. River Trips (www.raftwet.com) takes customers on raft trips ranging in duration from one to five days. The rafting season usually runs from March to June.

William Land Park. *3930 W Land Park Dr, Sacramento (95822). Phone 916/277-6060.* Wading pool (summer, daily); fishing (children under 16 only). Nine-hole golf course. Picnic facilities, playground, ballfields. The amusement area near the zoo has pony and amusement rides (summer, daily). **$$**

Special Events

Bockbierfest. *3349 J St, Sacramento (95816).* Held annually at the downtown Turner Hall in early April, the Sacramento Turn Verein's Bockbierfest is a one-night celebration of German dance, music, food, and, of course, beer. Expect plenty of sausages, polka bands, folk dancing, and bockbier, the dark, rich, and potent Bavarian brew after which the festival is named. **$$**

California State Fair. *California Exposition Grounds, 1600 Exposition Blvd, Sacramento (95815). Phone 916/263-3247. www.bigfun.org.* Includes traditional state fair activities; exhibits, livestock, carnival food, and entertainment on ten stages, thoroughbred racing and 1-mile monorail. Mid Aug-early Sept. **$$**

Festival de la Familia. *Cal Expo, 1600 Exposition Rd, Sacramento (95815). Old Sacramento.Phone 916/422-2700. www.festivaldelafamilia.com.* The "Festival of the Family" celebrates Latino culture with music, entertainment, food, arts and crafts, and children's activities. Last Sun in Apr. **$$**

Music Circus. *Wells Fargo Pavilion, 1419 H St, Sacramento (95814). Phone 916/557-1999. www.californiamusicaltheatre.com.* Summer professional musical theater. July-Sept. **$$$$**

Sacramento Jazz Jubilee. *Old Sacramento. Phone 916/372-5277. www.sacjazz.com.* Every Labor Day weekend since 1974, Old Sacramento and other downtown venues have drawn a bee-bop-loving horde to the Jazz Jubilee, the top jazz festival in the West. Sponsored by the Sacramento Traditional Jazz Society, the event features a lineup that includes more than 100 bands from all over the country—and all over the stylistic map: Beyond the traditional jazz, there's blues, Western swing, ragtime, salsa, zydeco, barbershop, and just about every other jazz-influenced music genre imaginable. The event kicks off with a parade on Friday morning and runs through Monday, propelled by a number of unique shows along the way: children's concerts, a Sunday morning "Celebration of Faith" with upbeat gospel, swing and salsa dancing classes, and the ever-popular washboard concert on Sunday afternoon, performed by an unusual orchestra of more than 20 washboards, two banjos, a tuba, a piano, and a duck call. Free shuttles transport concert-goers between the event's myriad venues. **$$$$**

Limited-Service Hotels

★ BEST WESTERN HARBOR INN AND SUITES. *1250 Halyard Dr, West Sacramento (95691). Phone 916/371-2100; toll-free 800/937-8376; fax 916/373-1507. www.bestwestern.com.* 138 rooms, 4 story. Pets accepted; fee. Complimentary full breakfast. Check-in 3 pm, check-out 11 am. High-speed Internet access. Fitness room. Outdoor pool, whirlpool. Airport transportation available. **$**

★ ★ CLARION HOTEL. *700 16th St, Sacramento (95814). Phone 916/444-8000; toll-free 800/443-0880; fax 916/442-8129. www.sacramentoclarion.com.* 106 rooms, 4 story. Pets accepted; fee. Check-in 3 pm, check-out noon. High-speed Internet access. Restaurant, bar. Outdoor pool. Business center. **$**

★ ★ DOUBLETREE HOTEL. *2001 Point West Way, Sacramento (95815). Phone 916/929-8855; toll-free 800/222-8733; fax 916/924-4913. www.doubletree.com.* The comfortable guest rooms and suites are conveniently located just 6 miles from the California State Capitol. Across the street, the Arden Fair Mall features 160 stores. 448 rooms, 4 story. Pets accepted, some restrictions; fee. Check-in 3 pm, check-out noon. High-speed Internet access. Restaurant, bar. Fitness room. Outdoor pool, whirlpool. Airport transportation available. Business center. **$$**

★ GOVERNORS INN. *210 Richards Blvd, Sacramento (95814). Phone 916/448-7224; toll-free 800/999-6689; fax 916/448-7382. www.governorsinn.net.* 133 rooms, 3 story. Complimentary continental breakfast. Check-in 3 pm, check-out 11 am. Fitness room. Outdoor pool, whirlpool. Airport transportation available. **$**

★ ★ HAWTHORN SUITES. *321 Bercut Dr, Sacramento (95814). Phone 916/441-1200; toll-free 800/767-1777; fax 916/444-2347. www.hawthorn.com.* 272 rooms, 3 story, all suites. Pets accepted, some restrictions; fee. Complimentary full breakfast. Check-in 3 pm, check-out noon. Restaurant, bar. Fitness room. Outdoor pool, whirlpool. **$$**

★ LA QUINTA INN. *4604 Madison Ave, Sacramento (95841). Phone 916/348-0900; toll-free 800/687-6667; fax 916/331-7160. www.laquinta.com.* 122 rooms, 3 story. Pets accepted, some restrictions. Complimentary continental breakfast. Check-in 3 pm, check-out noon. Restaurant. Outdoor pool, whirlpool. **$**

★ LA QUINTA INN. *200 Jibboom St, Sacramento (95814). Phone 916/448-8100; toll-free 800/531-5900;*

fax 916/447-3621. www.laquinta.com. On the Sacramento River. 165 rooms, 3 story. Pets accepted. Complimentary continental breakfast. Check-in 3 pm, check-out noon. Fitness room. Whirlpool. Airport transportation available. **$**

★ ★ RADISSON HOTEL SACRAMENTO. *500 Leisure Ln, Sacramento (95815). Phone 916/922-2020; toll-free 800/333-3333; fax 916/920-7310. www.radisson.com.* This hotel's unique resort surroundings offer guests a varied choice of diversions: a lakeside pool and spa, rental paddleboats for the lake, a 35-mile trail for jogging or bicycling along the American River, and a scenic "par" course, complete with a complimentary health drink. A courtesy shuttle service is available to surrounding areas. Their 21,000-square-foot trade show area includes a 16,000-square-foot ballroom, the largest hotel ballroom in Sacramento. 307 rooms, 2 story. Pets accepted, restrictions, fee. Check-in 3 pm, check-out noon. High-speed Internet access. Two restaurants, bar. Fitness room. Outdoor pool, whirlpool. Airport transportation available. **$**

★ ★ RED LION. *1401 Arden Way, Sacramento (95815). Phone 916/922-8041; toll-free 800/733-5466; fax 916/922-0386. www.redlion.com.* 376 rooms, 3 story. Pets accepted; fee. Check-in 4 pm, check-out noon. High-speed Internet access. Restaurant, bar. Fitness room. Three outdoor pools, whirlpool. Business center. **$**

★ ★ VAGABOND INN. *909 3rd St, Sacramento (95814). Phone 916/446-1481; toll-free 800/522-1555; fax 916/448-0364. www.vagabondinn.com.* Only a couple of blocks from Old Town, just off I-5/Hwy 99, the Vagabond Inn combines good rates with a good location. The Capital Plaza mall is across the street. 108 rooms, 3 story. Pets accepted; fee. Complimentary continental breakfast. Check-in 1 pm, check-out noon. High-speed Internet access. Restaurant. Fitness room. Outdoor pool, whirlpool. Airport transportation available. Business center. **$**

Full-Service Hotels

★ ★ ★ HILTON SACRAMENTO ARDEN WEST. *2200 Harvard St, Sacramento (95815). Phone 916/922-4700; fax 916/922-8418. www.hilton.com.* Located in Sacramento's Point West area, 1.5 miles from the Cal Expo state fairgrounds, and minutes from the Capitol Rotunda. 331 rooms, 12 story. Check-in 3 pm, check-out noon. High-speed Internet access. Restaurant, bar. Fitness room. Outdoor pool, whirlpool. Airport transportation available. Business center. **$$**

★ ★ HOLIDAY INN. *300 J St, Sacramento (95814). Phone 916/446-0100; toll-free 800/465-4329; fax 916/446-0117. www.holidayinnsacramento.com.* 362 rooms, 16 story. Check-in 3 pm, check-out noon. High-speed Internet access. Restaurant, bar. Fitness room. Outdoor pool. Airport transportation available. Business center. **$$**

★ ★ ★ HYATT REGENCY. *1209 L St, Sacramento (95814). Phone 916/443-1234; toll-free 800/633-7313; fax 916/321-3099. www.sacramento.hyatt.com.* Directly across from the State Capitol and Capitol Park, this hotel is adjacent to the Sacramento Convention Center and Community Theater. 503 rooms, 15 story. Check-in 3 pm, check-out noon. Two restaurants, two bars. Fitness room. Outdoor pool, whirlpool. Airport transportation available. Business center. **$$**

★ ★ ★ SHERATON GRAND. *1230 J St, Sacramento (95814). Phone 916/447-1700; toll-free 800/325-3535; fax 916/447-1701. www.sheraton.com/sacramento.* The Sheraton Grand breathes new life into Sacramento's historic Public Market Building. Located in the center of downtown, this hotel has a sunny disposition thanks to its light-filled atriums. The guest rooms and suites are simply furnished, creating a pleasant environment to conduct business or relax after a long day of sightseeing. All of the amenities associated with Sheraton are available, including whimsical touches, such as special dog beds for those traveling with four-legged friends. From the all-you-can-eat breakfast buffet to the sensational lunch and dinner menus, Morgan's Central Valley Bistro is sure to please. Glide's Market is a nice spot for coffee or snacks, while the Public Market Bar encourages patrons to kick back and relax in the heart of the city. 503 rooms. Pets accepted, some restrictions. Check-in 3 pm, check-out noon. High-speed Internet access. Two restaurants, two bars. Fitness room. Outdoor pool. Business center. **$$**

Full-Service Inn

★ ★ ★ **THE STERLING HOTEL.** *1300 H St, Sacramento (95814). Phone 916/448-1300; toll-free 800/365-7660; fax 916/448-8066. www.sterlinghotel.com.* The Sterling Hotel offers guests the best of both worlds in the center of Sacramento. This charming Victorian mansion set on beautifully landscaped gardens feels like a countryside retreat, yet it is only several blocks from the city's downtown shopping plaza, the State Capitol, and the convention center. Just 17 rooms are available here, and the accommodations reflect the hotel's dedication to detail with fresh flowers and elegant furnishings. Italian marble bathrooms with Jacuzzi tubs add a luxurious element to the accommodations. A continental breakfast is included in the room rate, and the hotel's Chanterelle restaurant (see) is a lovely spot for gourmet lunches and dinners. 17 rooms, 3 story. Complimentary continental breakfast. Check-in 3 pm, check-out 11 am. Restaurant. **$$**

Specialty Lodgings

The following lodging establishments are approved by Mobil Travel Guide, but due to their unique and individualized nature have not been given a traditional Mobil Star rating. Included in this listing you may find bed-and-breakfasts, limited-service inns, guest ranches, and other unique hotel properties.

AMBER HOUSE BED AND BREAKFAST INN. *1315 22nd St, Sacramento (95816). Phone 916/444-8085; toll-free 800/755-6526; fax 916/552-6529. www.amberhouse.com.* The rooms of this inn are scattered between three beautifully restored historic homes, all situated adjacent to or on the opposite side of this quiet street of turn-of-the-century homes. In the evening, beverages and fresh-baked cookies are delivered. 14 rooms, 2 story. Complimentary full breakfast. Check-in 4 pm, check-out noon. **$$**

INN AT PARKSIDE. *2116 6th St, Sacramento (95818). Phone 916/658-1818; toll-free 800/995-7275; fax 916/658-1809. www.innatparkside.com.* Built in 1936 by Chinese ambassador and used as cultural center. 7 rooms, 3 story. Complimentary full breakfast. Check-in 3-8 pm, check-out noon. **$$**

VIZCAYA. *2019 21st St, Sacramento (95814). Phone 916/455-5243; toll-free 800/456-2019; fax 916/455-6102. www.sterlinghotel.com.* Landscaped gardens, Victorian gazebo. Built in 1899; Italian marble in bathrooms. 9 rooms, 3 story. Complimentary full breakfast. Check-in 3 pm, check-out 11 am. **$**

Restaurants

★ ★ ★ **BIBA.** *2801 Capitol Ave, Sacramento (95816). Phone 916/455-2422; fax 916/455-0542. www.biba-restaurant.com.* With its open atmosphere and abstract painting-lined walls, this restaurant offers a relaxed yet elegant experience. Italian menu. Lunch, dinner. Closed Sun; holidays; also first week of July. Bar. Business casual attire. Reservations recommended. Outdoor seating. **$$**

★ ★ ★ **CHANTERELLE.** *1300 H St, Sacramento (95814). Phone 916/442-0451; fax 916/449-6811. www.sterlinghotel.com.* International menu. Lunch, dinner. Casual attire. Reservations recommended. Outdoor seating. **$$$**

★ ★ ★ **FIREHOUSE.** *1112 2nd St, Sacramento (95814). Phone 916/442-4772; fax 916/442-6617. www.firehouseoldsac.com.* With old-fashioned, sophisticated décor, this restaurant, a restored 1853 firehouse, is a good choice for an intimate dining experience. American, California menu. Lunch, dinner. Closed Sun; holidays. Bar. Children's menu. Casual attire. Outdoor seating. **$$$**

★ ★ **FRANK FAT'S.** *806 L St, Sacramento (95814). Phone 916/442-7092; fax 916/442-0115. www.fatsrestaurants.com.* Serving the finest Chinese cuisine from four provinces of Peking, Szechuan, Canton, and Shanghai in a superbly decorated surrounding. Located one block west of the State Capitol, it is known to be the second home to governors, legislators, lobbyists, and all kinds of celebrities since 1939. Chinese menu. Lunch, dinner. Closed July 4, Thanksgiving, Dec 25. Bar. Casual attire. Valet parking. **$$$**

★ ★ ★ **LEMON GRASS.** *601 Munroe St, Sacramento (95825). Phone 916/486-4891; fax 916/486-1627. www.lemongrassrestaurant.com.* Thai, Vietnamese menu. Lunch, dinner. Closed Sun; holidays. Bar. Children's menu. Business casual attire. Reservations recommended. Outdoor seating. **$$**

★ ★ ★ **MORTON'S, THE STEAKHOUSE.** *521 L St, Sacramento (95814). Phone 916/442-5091; fax 916/442-7877. www.mortons.com.* This steakhouse chain, which originated in Chicago in 1978, appeals to the serious meat lover. With a selection of belt-busting carnivorous delights (like the house specialty, a 24-ounce porterhouse), as well as fresh fish, lobster, and chicken entrées, Morton's rarely disappoints. When you're just not sure what you're in the mood for, the tableside menu presentation may help you decide. Here, main course selections are placed upon a cart that is rolled to your table, where servers describe each item in detail. Steak menu. Dinner. Closed holidays. Bar. Business casual attire. Reservations recommended. Valet parking. **$$$**

★ ★ PILOTHOUSE. *1000 Front St, Sacramento (95814). Phone 916/441-4440; toll-free 800/825-5464; fax 916/444-5314.* Seafood menu. Lunch, dinner, Sun brunch. Bar. Children's menu. Casual attire. Valet parking. **$$**

★ RICK'S DESSERT DINER. *2322 K St, Sacramento (95816). Phone 916/444-0969.* Dessert diner. Lunch, dinner, late-night. Closed holidays. Casual attire. **$**

★ ★ RISTORANTE PIATTI. *571 Pavilions Ln, Sacramento (95825). Phone 916/649-8885; fax 916/649-8907. www.piatti.com.* Italian menu. Lunch, dinner. Closed Dec 25. Bar. Children's menu. Business casual attire. Reservations recommended. Valet parking. Outdoor seating. **$$**

★ ★ RUSTY DUCK. *500 Bercut Dr, Sacramento (95814). Phone 916/441-1191; fax 916/441-7087.* Seafood menu. Lunch, dinner. Bar. Children's menu. Casual attire. **$$$**

★ ★ SILVA'S SHELDON INN. *9000 Grant Line Rd, Elk Grove (95624). Phone 916/686-8330; fax 916/686-8331. www.silvassheldoninn.com.* In turn-of-the-century building. American, Mediterranean menu. Dinner. Closed Mon; holidays; also week of Jan 1 and week of July 4. Bar. Children's menu. Outdoor seating. **$$**

Salinas

See also Big Sur, Carmel, Gilroy, Monterey, Pacific Grove, San Juan Bautista

Population 151,060
Elevation 53 ft
Area Code 831
Information Salinas Valley Chamber of Commerce, 119 E Alisal St, PO Box 1170, 93901; phone 831/424-7611
Web Site www.salinaschamber.com

Salinas is best known as the birthplace of novelist John Steinbeck, many of whose works, including *East of Eden* (1952), *Tortilla Flat* (1935), and *Of Mice and Men* (1937), are set in the Salinas Valley area.

What to See and Do

Hat in Three Stages of Landing. *Sherwood Park Community Center, 940 N Main St, Salinas.* Sculpture by Claes Oldenburg. Concept of a straw hat tossed out of the rodeo grounds (adjacent) in three stages of landing on the field.

National Steinbeck Center Museum. *1 Main St, Salinas (93901). Phone 831/796-3833. www.steinbeck.org.* Interactive exhibits, artifacts, and displays hightlight the life and works of John Steinbeck. (Daily 10 am-5 pm; closed Jan 1, Easter, Thanksgiving, Dec 25) **$$$**

Steinbeck House. *132 Central Ave, Salinas (93901). Phone 831/424-2735. www.steinbeckhouse.com.* Former home of famous Salinas native John Steinbeck. Gift shop. Lunch served 11:30 am-2 pm. (Tues-Sat; closed three weeks in late Dec-early Jan). Guided tours (Sun, June-Sept) **$**

Special Events

California International Airshow. *Salinas Municipal Airport, 30 Mortensen Ave, Salinas (93905). Airport Blvd exit off Hwy 101, at airport.Phone 831/754-1983; toll-free 888/845-7469. www.salinasairshow.com.* Aerobatic displays, formation parachute jumping, precision close-formation flying by top US and international performers, including the US Navy's Blue Angels. Oct. **$$$**

California Rodeo. *California Rodeo Grounds, 1034 N Main St, Salinas (93906). 1/4 mile N off Hwy 101. Phone 831/775-3100; toll-free 800/771-8807. www.carodeo.com.* Parades, dancing, entertainment, competitions, barbecue. Third week in July. **$$$**

Steinbeck Festival. *National Steinbeck Center, 1 Main St, Salinas (93901). Phone 831/775-4721. www.steinbeck.org.* The National Steinbeck Center Foundation sponsors this annual event in honor one of the America's greatest writers. Held in Steinbeck's hometown of Salinas, the festival features bus and walking tours of Steinbeck country, films, plays, readings, and lectures about the author. Early Aug. **$$$**

Limited-Service Hotels

★ COMFORT INN. *144 Kern St, Salinas (93905). Phone 831/758-8850; toll-free 800/888-3839; fax 831/758-3611. www.choicehotels.com.* 32 rooms, 3 story.

Complimentary continental breakfast. Check-in 2 pm, check-out 11 am. **$**

★★ **LAUREL INN MOTEL.** *801 W Laurel Dr, Salinas (93906). Phone 831/449-2474; toll-free 800/ 354-9831; fax 831/449-2476. www.laurelinnmotel.com.* 148 rooms, 2 story. Check-in 2 pm, check-out 11 am. Restaurant. Outdoor pool, whirlpool. Business center. **$**

Restaurant

★ **SMALLEY'S ROUNDUP.** *700 W Market St, Salinas (93901). Phone 831/758-0511. www.smalleysroundup.com.* Barbecue menu. Lunch, dinner. Closed Mon; also Easter and Thanksgiving; weeks of July 4 and Dec 25. Children's menu. Casual attire. **$$**

San Francisco (E-2)

See also Berkeley, Corte Madera, Menlo Park, Mill Valley, Oakland, San Francisco International Airport Area, San Rafael, Sausalito, Tiburon

Founded 1776
Population 776,733
Elevation 63 ft
Area Code 415
Information Convention & Visitors Bureau, 900 Market St, 94103-2804; phone 415/391-2000
Web Site www.sfvisitor.org

Suburbs Berkeley, Corte Madera, Hayward, Mill Valley, Oakland, San Mateo, San Rafael, Sausalito, Tiburon. (See individual alphabetical listings.)

Nearly everyone who comes to San Francisco falls in love with it. A city of hills, parks, cable cars, a bustling waterfront, and bridges that span mighty spaces—all freshened by clean Pacific breezes and warmed by a cooperative sun and a romantic fog—San Francisco is alive and lovely. The heart of a great Pacific empire, it is the true capital of the West.

This city of precipitous hills stretches 7 miles across in each direction, rimmed on three sides by water. Its awe-inspiring bay, 500 square miles, constitutes one of the most nearly perfect natural harbors on Earth. Rome has its seven hills; San Francisco was built on 43 hills. The city encompasses a total of 129.4 square miles, of which only 46.6 square miles are land. Within its boundaries are islands—Yerba Buena, Treasure Island, and Alcatraz—plus the Farallon group 32 miles west, part of the city since 1872.

San Francisco is one of nature's few "air-conditioned cities"—relatively warm in winter and cool in summer. Weather Bureau statistics show sunshine on 66 of every 100 possible hours. The average mean temperatures for San Francisco are 50° F in winter, 55° F in spring, 62° F in summer, and 60° F in fall.

Gateway to the Orient, San Francisco is a melting pot of cultures. Its population descends from peoples of almost every nation of the world and every state of the Union. The leading national groups are Italian, German, Irish, Chinese, English, Russian, Latin American, Japanese, Korean, and Filipino. More than 500 churches, temples, and meeting houses conduct services in 23 different tongues. Fifty periodicals are published in 13 languages.

San Francisco is an important financial center and the headquarters of Bank of America, one of the largest banks in the world. Although no longer considered the air hub of the West (Los Angeles now holds that title), the city still plays a major role in the nation's air travel: San Francisco International Airport, a $250 million air gateway to the world, is located 14 1/2 miles south off Bayshore Freeway and Highway 101. The San Francisco Bay Area ranks second on the West Coast in waterborne commerce. The Port of San Francisco is a $100 million public utility with a 7 1/2-mile stretch of ship-berthing space, 229 acres of covered and open wharf area, and a total of 43 piers. More than 1,500 San Francisco firms engage in international trade.

Hellenic in its setting and climate, European in its intellectual and cultural scope, American in its vigor and informality, and Asian in its tranquility, San Francisco is indeed an exciting city. Author and raconteur Gene Fowler said, "Every man should be allowed to love two cities—his own and San Francisco."

San Francisco's lusty history began with early Portuguese, English, and Spanish explorers penetrating the Bay. In 1775, the Spanish ship *San Carlos* sailed through the Golden Gate to drop the first anchor off San Francisco. On March 28, 1776, a mission site was selected and dedicated to St. Francis of Assisi. The little village of Yerba Buena developed

Chinatown and North Beach

This tour covers two of the most walkable neighborhoods in San Francisco—Chinatown and North Beach—places where it's much easier to enjoy the sights if you're on foot. Begin at Chinatown gate—topped with dragons—at Bush Street and Grant Avenue, where you'll wind past Chinatown's exotic herb and tea shops, Buddhist temples, neon-lit cafés, colorful produce markets, and dim sum restaurants. Walk north for four blocks past the curio shops along commercially oriented Grant Avenue, the gaudiest (and least authentic) stretch of Chinatown. At Clay Street, turn left. Walk a short block to Waverly Place and turn right. The Tin How Temple, located at 125 Waverly, is the oldest Buddhist temple in the country; climb to the third floor to smell the incense and see the lanterns and carved deities. At the end of Waverly Place, cross Washington Street and jog left into narrow Ross Alley, where the tiny Golden Gate Fortune Cookie Factory (number 56) sits near the end of the block. You can watch fortune cookies being made, and then choose between regular fortunes and X-rated ones.

Turn left on Jackson Street until you reach Stockton Street, and then go right. You'll pass a series of colorful markets stocked with exotic produce and fresh fish. Walk north on Stockton to Broadway, which forms a rough boundary between Chinatown and North Beach, the Italian-flavored district known for its many cafés, bakeries, family-style restaurants, and night spots. Walk east on Broadway to Columbus Avenue, North Beach's main thoroughfare. Turn right on Columbus to City Lights Books (261 Columbus), San Francisco's most famous bookstore. Founded by poet Lawrence Ferlinghetti, City Lights was the center of Beat life in the 1950s, nurturing authors such as Jack Kerouac and Allen Ginsberg. Just down the block at 255 Columbus is Vesuvio, an atmospheric café of the Beat era.

Now turn around and walk back up Columbus, heading northwest, where you'll pass many of the area's best-known cafés and restaurants. Mario's Bohemian Cigar Store, a tiny café and bar at the corner of Columbus and Union Street, offers a pleasant stop for lunch or cappuccino. Across the street is Washington Square, North Beach's main plaza, where grasses attract sunbathers and Frisbee tossers. On the north side of the square (666 Filbert St) is the twin-spire Italianate Saints Peter and Paul Church, one of the area's foremost landmarks. The square is lined with restaurants, bakeries, and cafés.

Those looking for further exercise can climb Telegraph Hill for great views from Coit Tower (you can follow the path from Greenwich St off Grant Ave, one block north of Filbert). After riding the elevator to the top of the tower, walk down the other side of Telegraph Hill via the Filbert or Greenwich stairways that descend steeply through hidden gardens and offer stunning views of the bay. The steps will bring you to the Embarcadero, where streetcars run north toward Fisherman's Wharf or south toward the Ferry Building.

near the mission but slumbered until 1836, when the port grew into an important trading post.

In 1846, the USS *Portsmouth* dropped anchor in the cove; Captain John B. Montgomery and 70 men came ashore and hoisted the Stars and Stripes, marking the end of Mexican rule. The next year, the village changed its name to San Francisco, taking its cue from the mission.

A year later, gold was discovered in Sutter's millrace on the American River at Coloma. This discovery had a tremendous impact on San Francisco; few of the inhabitants remained, and, as the news spread around the world, a torrent of people and ships descended on the city. A year later, 6,000 miners were digging, and San Francisco was a wild tent city of 20,000 rough, tough transients. An average of 50 sailing ships a month anchored in San Francisco Bay; many were deserted by crews eager for gold.

A few farsighted men realized that fortunes could be made in San Francisco as well as in the gold camps. Their foresight is reflected today in many of the city's distinguished stores.

Meanwhile, thirsty for gold, Easterners were migrating to California. With the aid of imported Chinese

Reliving the Gold Rush Days

This walking tour takes you down streets that gave birth to the city of San Francisco back in the gold rush days. It's an easy walk that starts at the center of the shopping district, passes through parts of the Financial District and Chinatown, and ends in the historic Barbary Coast areas near North Beach.

Start at Union Square, the heart of downtown San Francisco, which dates to the 1850s and bounded by Geary, Post, Powell, and Stockton streets. On the east (Stockton) side of the square, walk down little Maiden Lane, the ironically named former "red light" district of the gold rush era. Maiden Lane is closed to cars, so its two blocks are a pleasant place to stroll amid the shops and cafés where brothels once stood. At the end of Maiden Lane, go left up Kearny Street and then right on Bush Street, where Sam's Grill (374 Bush St) offers excellent seafood and classic San Francisco atmosphere. Or check out the outdoor tables along Belden Place (turn left just before Sam's Grill), which is lined with Mediterranean-style restaurants. At the end of Belden Place, turn right down Pine Street to Montgomery Street. You'll find the Wells Fargo History Museum, open weekdays only, at 420 Montgomery between California and Pine streets. This excellent museum paints a fascinating portrait of gold rush San Francisco, with a re-created Wells Fargo office (complete with telegraph machine) and a century-old stagecoach. Walk back north on Montgomery to Commercial Street, and go left. Now on the fringes of Chinatown, Commercial Street was once a haven of gold rush-era merchants. Note the plaque at 608 Commercial Street, marking the site of the first US Branch Mint in 1854; it's also the location of the Pacific Heritage Museum. Continue on Commercial to Kearny, and turn right; after a short block you'll see Portsmouth Square, the oldest section of San Francisco, on your left. Now the central square of Chinatown, it blossomed from a sleepy plaza to the dynamic center of the city during the gold rush of the late 1840s and early 1850s. Turn right again on Clay Street (walking east back to Montgomery); the intersection of Clay and Montgomery marks the spot where the Pony Express ended its route during its fabled 2,000-mile runs of 1860-1861. Continue north on Montgomery past the gold rush-era Belli Building (722 Montgomery St), and turn right on Jackson Street, lined with ornately decorated gold rush buildings, many of which are now antique shops. Note little Hotaling Place, where San Francisco Bay once lapped the shoreline before landfill extended the city borders. At Balance Street, go left into narrow Gold Street, site of San Francisco's first gold assaying office. Explore Gold Street, then continue east to Sansome Street, and take a left to Pacific Avenue. You'll pass rows of brick buildings that were built following the earthquake of 1906; these once served as Barbary Coast-era dancehalls, theaters, and saloons. You can now return to Union Square via Chinatown if you wish, or walk to adjoining North Beach.

labor, 2,000 miles of railroad track crossed the nation's two greatest mountain ranges to join East and West. Shipping to Asia flourished, and small industries prospered.

Young and raw, San Francisco spent the last half of the 19th century as an exciting mix of growing metropolis, frontier, and boomtown. Then, on April 18, 1906, came the great earthquake (8.6 on the Richter scale) and ensuing fire. Raging unchecked for three days, the fire wiped out the entire business area and burned out 497 blocks of buildings in the heart of the city. Losses amounted to some 2,500 lives and nearly $350 million. With the ashes still warm, the city started rebuilding; it was largely completed by 1915, when the city celebrated the opening of the Panama Canal with the Panama Pacific International Exposition.

The opening of the San Francisco-Oakland Bay Bridge in 1936, followed by the Golden Gate Bridge in 1937 and the completion of the Bay Area Rapid Transit System (BART), have tied the cities of the Bay Area together.

A significant historical event took place between April 25 and June 26, 1945, when delegates from the nations of the world assembled here to found the United Nations. San Francisco became the birthplace of the UN—another facet of its cosmopolitan personality.

Waterfront Walk

While most visitors to San Francisco make their way to the city's waterfront, many confine their walking to the few blocks along Jefferson Street comprising Fisherman's Wharf, culminating at Pier 39. This tour will also take you to that area; however, the focus is on often-missed attractions along the way. Start just to the east of Presidio National Park at the corner of Baker Street and Marina Boulevard. The neoclassical domed and pillared structure here is the Palace of Fine Arts; it was built for an exposition in 1915 and now houses the Exploratorium, one of the country's top science museums. An adjacent tree-shaded lagoon harbors ducks and swans. Cross Marina Boulevard and go north to the end of Baker Street, turning right on Yacht Road. As you follow the path past the St. Francis Yacht Club, you'll have prime views of the Marina Small Craft Harbor, where dozens of yachts bob in the water. Continue out to the end of the breakwater, where there are exceptional views of the Golden Gate Bridge to the west and Alcatraz Island ahead. You'll also find one of San Francisco's lesser-known delights—the Wave Organ. The tides make "natural music" as they filter through stone pipes here. You can relax on the steps while you enjoy the "concert" and the bay views. To continue on, retrace your steps back to Marina Boulevard and turn left (east) along the pedestrian walkway that leads past the southern edge of the yacht harbor and the Marina Green. One of San Francisco's prettiest parks, the Marina Green is a favorite of kite-flyers. Note the well-kept houses of the Marina District on the opposite side of Marina Boulevard, then try to picture the rubble that marked this area following the devastating 1989 earthquake. It is amazing that no evidence of this disaster remains. Follow the walkway past another yacht harbor to Fort Mason Center. This former military outpost is now a cultural center and includes several small museums, as well as the excellent Greens Restaurant (at the end of Building A), the city's longtime favorite for vegetarian food. Greens has a take-out stand where you can pick up a delicious sandwich for a picnic lunch. Climb the steps that lead up the hillside(across from Building E) to the park, where you'll find rolling hills of green grass, paved pathways, and benches to relax on. From here, follow the concrete walkway that leads up the hill (northeast) at the rear of the park; as you come over the crest of the hill, you'll be treated to one of the best views of the western edges of Fisherman's Wharf. Ahead lays Aquatic Park, with a small beach and fishing pier. The surf here is usually calm enough for swimming, though the water is too chilly for most. The Ghirardelli Square shopping complex hovers on a hillside above it. The cable car turnaround boards passengers for the Powell-Hyde Street line, which climbs up steep Hyde Street. At the foot of Hyde Street stands the Hyde Street Pier, home to the world's largest fleet of historic ships. You can tour the ships, including the *Balclutha*, a magnificent 1886 square-rigged sailing ship. Then, if you wish, you can continue walking into the always-crowded Fisherman's Wharf area along Jefferson Street.

In sightseeing, dining, nightlife, shopping, and all other tourist adventures, San Francisco is rivaled—and perhaps not exceeded—only by New York City.

From the Twin Peaks area, the center of the city, Market Street bisects the eastern segment of San Francisco, ending at the Ferry Building and the Embarcadero. The business section, the "Wall Street of the West," is a cluster of skyscrapers extending from Kearny Street to the waterfront and south of Market Street from New Montgomery Street north to Jackson Street. Chinatown, Nob Hill, Telegraph Hill, and Fisherman's Wharf fan out north of Market Street. Russian Hill gives a panoramic view of San Francisco Bay. Here is Lombard Street, known as "the crookedest street in the world"—lined by hydrangea gardens and handsome residences, it makes nine hairpin turns in a single block. The Presidio, several museums, and the Golden Gate Bridge are on the northwest side of the peninsula.

One formula for a systematic exploration is to start with a guided three-and-a-half-hour "Around San Francisco" sightseeing tour. (You can book these bus tours through your hotel.) Note the places you want to visit at greater length, and then explore in detail later. Use your own car or rent one to reach outlying areas and explore across the bridges. The San

Francisco hills are not for fainthearted drivers, but they're not as bad as they look. Be sure to turn your wheels toward the curb and set your brake when parking.

San Francisco also has its scenic "49-Mile Drive," marked with blue and white seagull signs. This drive begins at City Hall in the Civic Center (Van Ness Avenue and McAllister Street), twisting around the entire city and leading to most of the spectacular sights. You can pick up this route and follow its signs at any point, or obtain a map of the drive from the San Francisco Visitor Information Center, lower level of Hallidie Plaza, Powell and Market streets.

San Francisco's famous cable cars, designated a National Historic Landmark, were the brainchild of Andrew Hallidie. The inaugural run was made down Clay from Jones Street on August 2, 1873. The century-old cable car system was temporarily shut down in 1982 for renovations. The $60 million project was completed in June 1984.

These cable cars offer a thrilling roller coaster experience (**$**). The natives hop on and off with abandon, but visitors are advised to be more cautious. Also, avoid rush hours. There are three lines: Powell-Mason and Market streets goes up Powell, over Nob Hill, along Columbus Avenue to Taylor, and down to Bay Street at Fisherman's Wharf; the Powell-Hyde cable runs from Powell and Market streets, up Powell to Jackson Street, west on Jackson to Hyde, north on Hyde over Russian Hill to Beach Street at Aquatic Park; and the California cable runs from California and Market streets to Van Ness Avenue, through the financial district, past Chinatown, and over Nob Hill.

The city's diverse restaurants number nearly 3,300. The gold of the mining camps attracted some of the finest chefs in the world to San Francisco, and this heritage persists today. Chinatown features the exotic cuisines of Asia; Fisherman's Wharf is famous for seafood. Mexican, Italian, French, Armenian, Russian, Japanese, Vietnamese, East Indian, and American are all here—you can make a culinary trip around the world without leaving San Francisco.

Nightlife in San Francisco is only partly carried on in the tradition of the "Barbary Coast" days. One of the most famous cocktail lounges in the world is "The Top of the Mark" in the Mark Hopkins Inter Continental Hotel. The Fairmont, across the street, offers an equally fine view of the city, as do several other high-rise hotels and office buildings. The theaters have long, successful seasons. In sports, baseball's San Francisco Giants play in spring and summer, and the 49ers pick up in fall for professional football.

San Francisco Fun Facts

- San Francisco Bay is not really a bay at all–it's an estuary. A bay is filled with ocean water, while an estuary is filled with a combination of salt water and fresh water.
- The San Francisco Ballet is the oldest ballet company in America. Founded in 1933, it was the first American ballet company to perform *The Nutcracker and Swan Lake.*
- Covering 47 square miles, Walt Disney World is about the size of San Francisco.
- In 1850, California became the 31st state in the union, and by 1854 the booming gold-rush town had more than 500 saloons and 20 theaters to entertain the miners.

Additional Visitor Information

San Francisco Magazine, available at newsstands, has up-to-date information about cultural events and articles of interest to visitors.

The San Francisco Convention & Visitors Bureau handles written inquiries. Tourist guides may be obtained by mail (postage and handling fee) or at the San Francisco Visitor Information Center, Hallidie Plaza, Powell and Market streets on the lower plaza level. Phone 415/391-2001 for a daily recording of events.

Public Transportation

In San Francisco: cable cars, streetcars, subway trains, buses (San Francisco Municipal Railway), phone 415/673-6864. From San Francisco across the bay: ferries (Golden Gate Bus Transit), phone 415/923-2000. From San Francisco to Bay Area towns: buses (AC Transit), phone 510/839-2882.

Airport Information. For additional accommodations, see SAN FRANCISCO AIRPORT AREA, which follows SAN FRANCISCO.

What to See and Do

Acres of Orchids (Rod McLellan Company). *1450 El Camino Real, South San Francisco (94080). Phone 415/362-1520.* Largest orchid and gardenia nursery in the world; scientific laboratories show cloning. Guided tours (twice daily: mid-morning and early afternoon). Visitor center (daily; closed holidays). **FREE**

Alcatraz Island. *Golden Gate National Recreation Area, San Francisco (94113). In San Francisco Bay, 1 1/4 miles from shore. Phone 415/705-5555. www.nps.gov/alcatraz.* From 1934 to 1963, "The Rock" was a maximum-security federal penitentiary famous for making escapes next to impossible. It was also the site of the first permanent US fortress on the West Coast. Visit the cells of Al Capone; "Machine Gun" Kelly; public enemy #1 Al Karpis; and Robert Stroud, the "Birdman of Alcatraz," while listening to the stories of former inmates and correctional officers on a 35-minute self-guided audio tour. A wide range of interpretive programs led by rangers and volunteers are available as well. Be advised: the tour of the Cell House includes a long, uphill walk. Want to see Alcatraz at your own pace? Take a self-guided tour with a map and written guide, available for $1. Blue & Gold fleet boats leave Pier 41 in Fisherman's Wharf every half hour beginning at 9:30 am, with the last run at 4:30 pm (6:30 pm in summer). Be sure to book your tickets in advance, as this is one of the most popular sights in the city. (Closed Dec 25, Jan 1, and in extreme weather) **$$$$**

American Conservatory Theatre. *415 Geary St, San Francisco (94109). Phone 415/749-2228. act-sf.org.* Theatergoers will appreciate the rich history of this conservatory. In its star-studded past, Sarah Bernhardt, Isadora Duncan, Ethel Barrymore, and Basil Rathbone performed on this stage. In 1967, the Victorian Geary Theater became the permanent home of the American Conservatory Theater (ACT), and soon after, it made its way onto the National Register of Historic Places. The theater is nationally recognized for classical as well as contemporary works in an exquisitely renovated space built for comfort and easy accessibility. (Performances are at 8 pm, with some 2 pm matinees; no performances Mon) **$$$$**

Angel Island State Park. *Island accessible only by ferry (or private boat) from San Francisco (Fisherman's Wharf) and Tiburon. Phone 415/435-5390. www.angelisland.org.* This beautiful, 740-acre woodsy park occupying San Francisco Bay's largest island was once known as the "Ellis Island of the West." Although it did process immigrants from Asia, it was used primarily to detain Chinese immigrants and stem the flow of immigration. During World War II, German and Japanese prisoners of war were kept here. Visitors can tour the old barracks, which were saved from demolition in 1970. Despite the island's bittersweet history, Angel Island today is a destination for visitors who not only want to learn its history but also seek to partake in a number of recreational activities, such as biking, hiking, camping, and kayaking. Motorized tram tours of the island are available on weekends in March and November and daily from April to October. Docent-led tours that explore the nature, history, and culture of the island are offered on weekends during the peak season. (Daily 8 am-sunset)

Aquarium of the Bay. *Pier 39, Embarcadero at Beach St, San Francisco (94103). Phone 415/623-5300; toll-free 888/732-3483. www.aquariumofthebay.com.* In an area that has a few outstanding aquariums to offer, the Aquarium of the Bay finds its niche by focusing its exhibits on the aquatic life of the nearby waters. It's divided into four areas: Discover the Bay, an introduction to the creatures that inhabit the Bay; Under the Bay, a more in-depth look at rarer creatures; Touch the Bay, with tide pools and hands-on exhibits; and Save the Bay, which focuses on conservation of sharks, jellyfish, and other marine life in the area. (Mon-Thurs 10 am-6 pm, Fri-Sun 10 am-7 pm; open later in summer; closed Dec 25) **$$$**

Asian Art Museum. *200 Larkin St, San Francisco (94102). Phone 415/581-3500. www.asianart.org.* Art and culture lovers will find an unequaled collection of ancient Asian treasures in this Beaux Arts space devoted to masterworks from Southeast Asia, the Himalayas, China, Korea, and Japan. Hundreds of shades of jade are housed here, as are sensuous bodhisattvas, a 1,500-year-old earthenware warrior, a massive dancing Indian elephant-god, life-size Tang Dynasty tomb guardian figures, and more than 15,000 ornamental objects. An entire wing is devoted to Chinese Buddhist art, and a glass-enclosed escalator ride takes visitors to a gallery dedicated to Indian art. (Tues-Wed, Fri-Sun 10 am-5 pm, Thurs to 9 pm; closed holidays) **$$**

Barbary Coast Trail. *Mission and Fifth sts, San Francisco (94142). Phone 415/775-1111.* History mavens and travelers itching for exercise will want to put on dependable walking shoes for this 3.8-mile self-guided historic trail through more than 20 of the city's most historic sites. See the birthplace of the gold rush, the oldest Asian temple in North America, and the largest collection of ships in the United States while you meander old streets, squares, parks, hills, wharves, piers, and business districts. When you get to the end at Aquatic Park, you can hop onto the Powell-Hyde cable car line and get a ride back to the end at which you started to rest your tired feet. Trail guides are available for purchase at the Visitor Information Center at Hallidie Plaza (Powell and Market sts), as well as at various bookstores.

Basic Brown Bear Factory. *2801 Leavenworth St, San Francisco (94133). Phone toll-free 866/522-2327. www.basicbrownbear.com.* Kids will love touring this factory, which has been in operation since 1976. The 30-minute tours run daily, on the hour, and conclude by giving children the opportunity to stuff, sew, and groom their own bears. **FREE**

Cable Car Museum. *1201 Mason St, San Francisco (94108). Phone 415/474-1887. www.cablecarmuseum.com.* Gain insight into how San Francisco's most famous people-movers work! Displayed here are three antique cable cars (including the world's first), vintage photographs, historic displays, a collection of model cable cars, and a real cable car bell that you can ring. In the underground viewing area, observe a part of the network of tunnels, cables, and sheaves that guide the cable car system from under the streets. You can also view a video presentation highlighting the history of the cable car system (shown every 17 minutes) while sitting in a cable car, and browse the bookstore for cable car- and San Francisco-related items. (Apr-Sept: daily 10 am-6 pm; Oct-Mar: daily 10 am-5 pm; closed holidays) **FREE**

California Academy of Sciences, Natural History Museum and Aquarium. *875 Howard St, San Francisco (94103). Phone 415/750-7145.* Where in San Francisco can you study the stars, see the first signs of life on Earth, and come face-to-face with underwater creatures, all in one day? The California Academy of Sciences, of course! Visitors can amuse and educate themselves as they explore the hands-on displays and interactive exhibits in the three museums housed in this massive structure. The Steinhart Aquarium is home to nearly 600 species of fish, large invertebrates, reptiles, and amphibians and includes a Touch Tidepool; at the Natural History Museum, you can experience a simulated earthquake or go on a safari in the African Hall; and inside the Morrison Planetarium, northern California's largest "indoor universe," you can view a variety of shows relating to everything from astronomy to life on other planets. (Daily 10 am-5 pm) Admission free the first Wed of the month. **$$**

Cannery. *2801 Leavenworth St, San Francisco (94133). At Beach St. www.thecannery.com.* A complex of shops, restaurants, and markets housed in an old fruit-processing factory; informal entertainment on the mall.

Cartoon Art Museum. *655 Mission St, San Francisco (94105). Phone 415/227-8666. www.cartoonart.org.* With a generous donation in 1987 from *Peanuts* creator Charles Schultz, the Cartoon Art Museum was able to establish a permanent residence (before that, shows were set up as temporary exhibits wherever space was available) and become the only museum in the United States devoted to preserving cartoon art. In addition to displaying close to 6,000 original pieces—some dating to the 18th century—the museum showcases seven major exhibits each year. Past exhibits have included "Comic Book Superheroes," "Comic Strip Controversies," and "A Tribute to Charles Schultz." (Tues-Sun 11 am-5 pm; closed holidays) **$$**

CCInc Auto Tape Tours. *San Francisco. Phone 201/236-1666. www.autotapetours.com.* These 90-minute cassettes offer mile-by-mile self-guided tours to Monterey (139 miles) along Skyline Blvd, atop the Santa Cruz Mountains, to Henry Cowell Redwoods, Monterey's Fisherman's Wharf, and Cannery; to Sacramento (166 miles) with a visit to Sausalito, Muir Woods, wineries in the Napa Valley, the historic State Capitol; to the wine country (160 miles) through Sausalito, Muir Woods, a winery tour, dramatic re-creation of the great San Francisco earthquake. Fourteen different tour tapes of California are available. Tapes may be purchased directly from CCInc. **$$$**

Chinatown. *Bush and Grant sts, San Francisco (94108).* The entrance to this vibrant neighborhood at Bush and Grant streets is marked by a gateway topped with dragons—a gift from the Republic of China. Past these gates is a community with more than 90,000 residents, and jammed with a number of exotic herb and tea shops, bustling markets, Buddhist temples, and dim sum restaurants. Grant Street, Chinatown's main thoroughfare, has been called the "Street of 25,000 Lanterns," and is known for its many shops that sell kitschy items loved by tourists. Points of interest include St. Mary's Square, home to Beniamino Bufano's 12-foot, stainless steel statue of Sun Yat Sen, founder of the Republic of China, as well as a plaque dedicated to the Americans of Chinese ancestry who gave their lives for America in World Wars I and II. Also visit the Chinese Culture Center (750 Kearny St), which features art exhibitions, Chinese cultural performances, and a gift shop, and offers docent-guided walks through the community (fee, 24-hour advance reservation required). **FREE**

City Lights Bookstore. *261 Columbus Ave, San Francisco (94133). Phone 415/362-8193. www.citylights.com.* Considered a literary landmark, City Lights was founded—and is still owned by—beat poet Lawrence Ferlinghetti. One of the country's earliest bookstores, it was frequented by other beat writers such as Allen Ginsberg and Jack Kerouac. It was also the publisher of Ginsberg's 1956 book, *Howl.* Today, the store retains a uniquely intimate and *independent* (it calls itself *anarchistic*) feel in an era of mega-bookstores. (Daily 10 am-midnight)

Civic Center. *Intersections of Franklin, 7th, Golden Gate, and Hayes sts, San Francisco.* Eleven-square-block cluster of buildings includes

Bill Graham Civic Auditorium. *99 Grove St, San Francisco (94102). Phone 415/974-4060. www.billgrahamcivic.com.* Venue for many expositions, trade shows, concerts, and sporting events. Seats 7,000.

Brooks Hall. *99 Grove St, San Francisco (94102). Phone 415/974-4060.* Under Civic Center Plaza; connected to Civic Auditorium by ramp and escalators; 90,000 square feet of exhibit space.

City Hall. *1 Dr. Carlton B. Goodlett Pl, San Francisco (94102). Phone 415/554-4000. www.sfgov.org.* Classic building with a dome more than 13 feet taller than that of the Capitol in Washington, DC. Tours (Mon-Fri at 10 am, noon, and 2 pm, Sat at 12:30 and 2 pm). (Mon-Fri 7:30 am-8 pm, Sat noon-4 pm; closed holidays)

Federal and State Buildings. *880 Front St, San Francisco (94111).* Also part of the Civic Center group.

Louise M. Davies Symphony Hall. *Van Ness Ave and Grove St, San Francisco (94102). Phone 415/864-6000. www.sfsymphony.org.* This $30 million concert hall opened in 1980; capacity of 2,743. (See SPECIAL EVENTS)

Performing Arts Center. *401 Van Ness Ave, San Francisco (94102). Phone 415/621-6600. www.sfwmpac.org.* Second-largest performing arts center in United States, with a total seating capacity of 7,233. Tours (Mon 10 am-3 pm; closed holidays).

San Francisco Public Library. *100 Larkin St, San Francisco (94102). Phone 415/557-4400. sfpl.lib.ca.us.* In April 1996, the library opened its expanded seven-story facility across the street from its previous location. Special Collections Department features rare books and many volumes on California and San Francisco (tours daily). (Mon, Sat 10 am-6 pm, Tues-Thurs 9 am-8 pm, Fri noon-6 pm, Sun noon-5 pm; closed holidays)

War Memorial Opera House. *301 Van Ness Ave, San Francisco (94102). Phone 510/524-5220. www.sfwmpac.org.* Opened in 1932, it was here that the UN was established in 1945 and the Japanese Peace Treaty Conference was held in 1951. First civic-owned opera house in the country. Tours. (See SPECIAL EVENTS)

Cow Hollow. *Union St and Van Ness Ave, San Francisco (94109).* Originally the location of a milk-producing area populated mostly by cows, this has been developed into an area of specialty shops, art galleries, and bookshops. Many shops are in restored Victorian houses. Numerous restaurants are also in the area.

Cow Palace. *2600 Geneva Ave, San Francisco (94014). 1 mile W off Bayshore Blvd. Phone 415/404-4111. www.cowpalace.com.* World famous exhibit center and arena, seating 14,700. Used for sports events, exhibits, and concerts. (See SPECIAL EVENTS)

Embarcadero Center. *1 Embarcadero Center, San Francisco (94111). Phone 415/772-0700. www.embarcaderocenter.com.* Embarcadero Center has been called a city within a city. It spans six blocks—from Clay and Sacramento streets between Drumm and Battery streets in the heart of San Francisco's prime Commercial District. A former shipping dock, it was nicknamed the Barbary Coast and was known as a raucous district of saloons, prostitution, and thievery in the 1840s. It has since evolved into five office towers with three interconnected shopping levels, four in the historic former Federal Reserve Bank Building Center. The center offers more than 125 retail shops and restaurants and a five-screen cinema featuring first-run independent and foreign-language films. Choose from a vast array of dining choices, wine and music festivals, concerts, and garden shows. There's even a chance for some holiday ice skating. The center is considered one of the most accessible spots in the city by train, bus, or cable car and provides ample parking. (Mon-Fri 10 am-8 pm, Sat 10 am-6 pm, Sun noon-6 pm)

Ferry Building. *One Ferry Building, San Francisco (94111). Located at the Embarcadero at the foot of Market St.* Ferries to Sausalito and Larkspur leave from the Ferry Plaza end of the building (Pier 1/2); ferries to Oakland, Alameda, Vallejo, and Tiburon leave from the terminal at the north end ($$). Also here are a waterfront promenade and many shops and restaurants (most open Mon-Fri 10 am-6 pm, Sat 9 am-6 pm, Sun 11 am-5 pm; closed Jan 1, Thanksgiving, Dec 25). Tours (Sat, Sun, Tues at noon).

Ferry Plaza Farmers' Market. *The Embarcadero at Market St, San Francisco (94111). Phone 415/291-3276. www.ferryplazafarmersmarket.com.* This is truly a farmers' market with a mission. At its home in the restored Ferry Building on the San Francisco waterfront, facing the Embarcadero, this mostly open-air market is a permanent market and education center dedicated to regional produce. The markets feature seasonal farm products from area organic farmers, specialty food producers, exhibits, classes, and workshops and conferences on local agriculture issues, rain or shine. Pull up a chair and sit down on a Saturday morning with a wild mushroom omelet, crab cake with mixed greens, and a cappuccino, and take in the enticing aromas and the beautiful water's edge view. (Sun 10 am-2 pm, Tues 10 am-2 pm, Thurs 4-8 pm, Sat 8 am-2 pm)

Fillmore. *1805 Geary Blvd, San Francisco (94115). Phone 415/346-6000. www.thefillmore.com.* This Italian-style dance hall was the home of Wednesday night socials and masquerade balls in the early 1900s. It became well known again in the 1960s, when legendary concert promoter Bill Graham took over the management of the Fillmore and bands like The Grateful Dead and Jefferson Airplane hit the stage. After a stint in the 1970s and 1980s as a private club, and almost a century after its doors first opened, the Fillmore is once again a thriving rock-and-roll venue, hosting well-known acts and up-and-comers.

★ **Fisherman's Wharf.** *Embarcadero and Jefferson St, San Francisco (94133). Foot of Taylor St. Phone 415/705-5500. www.fishermanswharf.org.* Center of multimillion-dollar commercial fishing industry and location of many seafood restaurants.

Fort Mason Center. *Marina Blvd and Buchanan St, San Francisco (94123). Phone 415/441-3400. www.fortmason.org.* Multicultural complex for all ages located in what was once the Army's western headquarters and port of embarkation. Includes four theaters and a gourmet vegetarian restaurant. A National Historic Landmark, Fort Mason Center boasts spectacular views of the Golden Gate Bridge and the hills of Marin. Located here is

Museo ItaloAmericano. *Fort Mason Center, Building C, San Francisco (94123). Phone 415/673-2200. www.museoitaloamericano.org.* Dedicated to researching, collecting, and displaying the works of Italian and Italian-American artists. Promotes educational programs for the apprecation of Italian art and culture. Gift shop. (Wed-Sun noon-4 pm; closed holidays) Free admission the first Wed of the month. **$**

San Francisco Museum of Modern Art Artists Gallery. *Fort Mason Building A, San Francisco (94123). Phone 415/441-4777. www.sfmoma.org/museumstore/artists_overview.html.* Exhibition program of 11 shows each year that feature the works of California artists. The works of more than 1,300 northern California artists are also available for rental and sale. (Tues-Sat 11:30 am-5:30 pm; closed Aug) **FREE**

Whale-watching. *Fort Mason Center, Building E, San Francisco (94123). Phone 415/474-3385; toll-free 800/326-7491. www.oceanic-society.org.* Water wildlife fans can explore one of the most unspoiled places in the Bay Area and, if they are lucky, lay their eyes on gray or humpback whales, dolphins, sea birds, or sea lions. Expertly guided boating tours leave from the coast for daylong journeys to the Farallon Islands 26 miles out to sea. Some trips are as long as eight hours (though half-day tours are available to Half Moon or Bodega Bay during the winter). The Oceanic Society sponsors these expeditions from Fort Mason in the Marina-Presidio area all year long, rain or shine, for naturalists ages 10 and up. **$$$$**

Ghirardelli Square. *900 North Point St, San Francisco (94109). North Point, Beach, and Larkin sts, W of Fisherman's Wharf. Phone 415/775-5500. www.ghirardellisq.com.* This charming complex of shops and restaurants is on the site of the Ghirardelli Chocolate factory. Go on a shopping spree in the numerous clothing stores, galleries, jewelry and gift shops; satisfy your sweet tooth at the Ghirardelli Chocolate Chocolaterie & Café; or take part in one of the many celebrations held here, including a St. Patrick's Day celebration in March and the Ghirardelli

Square Chocolate Festival in September. On weekends from July to September, you can gain insight into the history of the Ghirardelli Chocolate Company and its founder, Domingo Ghirardelli, through 20-minute docent-led tours of the Square. Or get a free walking tour map at the Information Booth to take a tour at your own pace.

★ **Golden Gate Bridge.** *Hwy 101, San Francisco (94129). Phone 415/921-5858. www.goldengate.org.* The Golden Gate Bridge stands as one of America's most recognized and beloved landmarks, its bold and beautiful design capturing the spirit and style of the West Coast. Stretching across the chilly, choppy waters of the Golden Gate Strait, the bridge links San Francisco to the south and Marin County to the north. The engineer Joseph Strauss envisioned and oversaw the building of the bridge. A $35 million bond issue was appropriated in 1930 for its construction, although many skeptics believed that the bridge either would never be completed or would be unable to withstand the fierce winds generated by the Pacific Ocean to its immediate west. With the help of architects Irving and Gertrude Morrow, Strauss employed subtle Art Deco elements in the bridge's timeless design, the most prominent attributes being the two towers linked by a pair of sweeping cables. Irving Morrow chose to paint the bridge "international orange," a striking hue that blends remarkably well with the scenic natural surroundings. Franklin D. Roosevelt used a telegraph key to announce the bridge's opening to vehicular traffic in 1937, completed under budget and ahead of schedule. Strauss died a year later, but his legacy lives on in the form of the Golden Gate Bridge, universally regarded as one of the greatest architectural achievements of the 20th century. The bridge's main span extends 4,200 feet, a record at the time of its construction. Each of its towers weighs 44,400 tons and stretches 746 feet above sea level. The best way to view the bridge may be on foot; the bridge's sidewalks—situated on either side of the 1.7-mile-long structure—are open to walkers and bicyclists. Vehicles crossing the bridge from the north must pay a toll of $5.

★ **Golden Gate National Recreation Area.** *204 Bay St, San Francisco (94123). Phone 415/561-4700. www.nps.gov/goga.* Within the 75,000 acres of the recreation area are most of the shoreline of San Francisco, and the countryside that extends 20 miles north in Marin County and covers a 1,047-acre area in San Mateo County to the south. The Golden Gate Bridge connects the two segments of the park. The most popular visitor areas are the former penitentiary on Alcatraz Island (see), the historic Cliff House, Fort Point National Historic Site, Muir Woods National Monument (see), and the cultural-entertainment center, Fort Mason Center. The area has 28 miles of shoreline with many beaches, lagoons, rugged headlands, meadows, fortifications, valleys, hillsides, picnic facilities, and 100 miles of trails within the area Congress designated in 1972 as one of the first urban national parks. Hours vary, but most areas are always open during the day.

Baker Beach. *Gibson Rd, San Francisco (94129). Phone 415/561-4700. www.nps.gov/prsf/places/bakerbch.htm.* A sandy beach on the western shore of the Presidio.

China Beach. *Sea Cliff Ave, San Francisco (94121). Phone 415/556-8371.* A wind-protected cove with a swimming beach.

Fort Point National Historic Site. *Long Ave and Marine Dr, San Francisco (94129). Under the S end of the Golden Gate Bridge in the Presidio. www.nps.gov/fopo.* This restored Civil War-era fort houses an exhibit explaining the story of the fort; there is also a museum with military artifacts. Guided tours. (Daily; closed Jan 1, Thanksgiving, Dec 25) **FREE**

Golden Gate Promenade. *Fort Point and Fort Mason, San Francisco.* Bay shoreline between Fort Point and Fort Mason provides an area to walk, run, and observe; also off-leash dog walking permitted.

Marin Headlands. *Marin Headlands Visitor Center, San Francisco (94965). Phone 415/331-1540. www.nps.gov/goga.* Children as young as 5 will delight in catching a glimpse of rabbits, deer, or bobcats in the beautiful headlands in the Golden Gate National Recreation Area in Marin County. If quickly moving furry creatures don't do the trick, the bugs, flowers, lizards, and other living things might. Grown-ups will enjoy the area's beautiful, sweeping vistas. For the best entry point for families with small children, try the Tennessee Valley Trail which is mostly flat and short (1.3 miles from the parking lot to the ocean) and provides a lovely picnic spot. For more challenging trails, try Rodeo Beach/Fort Cronkhite, and Muir Beach.

Muir Beach. *Hwy 1 and Pacific Way, Muir Beach (94965). Marin County. Phone 415/388-2596. www.muirbeach.com.* An idyllic ribbon of shoreline just northwest of the Golden Gate Bridge, Muir Beach is where Redwood Creek flows into the Pacific Ocean. The beach is a favorite for picnicking and beachcombing, and fires are permitted in certain spots. Swimming is also allowed, but not all that popular, thanks to the cold water and occasional shark sighting. Behind the beach, wetlands and a lagoon are protected wildlife habitats. On an adjacent bluff, the Muir Beach Overlook is a great perch for gazing in every direction.

Ocean Beach. *Hwy 1, San Francisco (94121).* 3 1/2 miles of beach on San Francisco's Pacific shore.

Seal Rocks & Cliff House. *1090 Point Lobos, San Francisco (94121).* Restaurants at the Cliff House (1909) overlook the ocean, the Marin Coast to the north, and the Seal Rocks habitat of sea lions. Visitor information center (limited hours). **FREE**

Stinson Beach. *Hwy 1 at Arenal Ave, San Francisco (94970). Phone 415/868-0942.* A popular surfing, swimming, and sunbathing spot, Stinson Beach abuts a quiet town of the same name and is the most trafficked beach between San Francisco and Point Reyes. Lifeguards man the 3 1/2-mile beach between May and October, and there is a 51-acre park with picnic tables immediately behind it, as well as a seasonal snack bar.

Tennessee Valley and Beach and Bonita Cove. *San Francisco. Exit Tennessee Valley Rd off Hwy 101 and drive to the end. Phone 415/331-1540.* Secluded, protected beach on the ocean. Approximately a 1 1/2-mile walk from parking. (Daily)

Golden Gate Park. *101 California St, San Francisco (94111). Bounded by Lincoln Way, Stanyan and Fulton sts, and Great Hwy. Phone 415/831-2700.* Once a 1,017-acre sand waste, from 1887 the area was developed by John McLaren, master botanist and landscaper, into one of the most beautiful parks in the world. The park contains more than 10,000 trees and shrubs, a restored Dutch windmill, statues and monuments, 11 gardens, 2 waterfalls, 11 lakes, and 40 picnic areas. You'll also find the McLaren Rhododendron Dell, a conservatory on Kennedy Drive near Arguello Boulevard, a music concourse near the Fulton Street and 8th Avenue entrance (band concerts on Sundays and holidays, weather permitting), and the Strybing Arboretum and Botanical Garden at King Drive and 9th Avenue. Sporting activities abound, with a nine-hole golf course, 3 lawn bowling greens, 21 tennis courts, 3 fly and plug casting pools, 2 indoor and 2 outdoor handball courts, an archery field, horseshoe courts, a trotting track, a bicycle track, running trails, and baseball diamonds. Other park attractions include

Buffalo paddock. *Lincoln Way and Great Hwy, San Francisco (94121).* A 10-acre enclosure with bison.

Japanese Tea Garden. *Tea Garden Dr, San Francisco (94122). Phone 415/752-1171.* Oriental landscaping; includes a teahouse, gift shop, pagoda, Buddha, several ponds, streams, and footbridges. In spring, cherry blossoms, azaleas, and flowering shrubs are in bloom. (Daily 9 am-6 pm) **$**

Mary Connolly Children's Playground. *King Dr and 3rd Ave, San Francisco (94107). Phone 415/831-2700.* The nation's oldest public park playground, it features innovative play equipment and a Herschel Spillman Carousel (1912-1914; fee); picnic area. **$**

Prayerbook Cross. *Kennedy Dr, San Francisco (94111).* (1894) Commemorates the first prayer service held in the English language on the Pacific Coast, conducted by Sir Francis Drake's chaplain.

Spreckels Lake. *36th Ave and Spreckles Lake Dr, San Francisco (94121).* Used primarily for sailing model boats.

Stow Lake. *50 Stow Lake Dr, San Francisco (94118). Off Kennedy Dr, near 16th Ave. Phone 415/752-0347.* Surrounds Strawberry Hill. View of the park and the city. One-hour boat rentals (fee): electric motorboat, rowboat, pedal boat.

Gray Line bus tours. *Embarcadero Center, Pier 34 1/2, San Francisco (94133). Phone 415/434-8687; toll-free 888/428-6937. www.grayline.com.* Offers a variety of tours ranging from one hour to one day, including Muir Woods/Sausalito, Yosemite by train, Chinatown walking tour, and Napa Valley Wine Train. (Daily) **$$$$**

Haas-Lilienthal House. *2007 Franklin St, San Francisco (94109). Between Washington and Jackson sts. Phone 415/441-3004 (recording). www.sfheritage.org/house.html.* (1886) Queen Anne-style Victorian house. One-hour guided tour (Wed and Sat noon-3 pm, Sun 11 am-4 pm). **$$**

Haight-Ashbury. *Haight and Ashbury sts, San Francisco (94117). District runs from Stanyan St to about Lyon St, and from Oak St up to Ashbury Heights.* Intersection made famous by the "Flower Power/Summer of Love" days in the late 1960s; actually the name of the entire district just east of Golden Gate Park. Offers many second-hand clothing stores and shops specializing in retro fashions and items.

Hang gliding, paragliding, aquagliding. *San Francisco. www.sfhanggliding.com.* It is an awe-inspiring sight to see a human being flying overhead in a hang glider, paraglider, or aquaglider in the San Francisco Bay Area. Airsports such as these are very popular for observers, as well as doers. Just 10 miles north of the city, mere humans (ages 8 to 80) can glide through the air hanging from a suspended kitelike harness (hang gliding) or paraglide from a high point (a ram aircraft controlled with risers like a parachute). These flights often leave Mount Tamalpais in Marin County and land on Stinson Beach. Aquagliders stay closer to the water using an ultralight hang glider equipped with pontoons and a power system for taking off and landing. Check area listings for lessons and rentals.

Harding Park Golf Course. *99 Harding Rd, San Francisco (94132). Phone 415/664-4690. www.harding-park.com.* Harding Park was put in the capable hands of Arnold Palmer Golf Management in 2002 to redesign, manage, and operate for 35 years. This change coincided with the announcement that the PGA will bring back a tournament, the season-ending World Golf Championships, to the course every three years. The course is adjacent to Lake Merced, and the 11th hole goes right along the water for 185 yards (a medium-length par-three). Even after the redesign, the rates should remain reasonable, but call ahead to get a tee time, because San Fran residents are allotted some 65 percent of the slots. **$$$$**

Harry Denton's Starlight Room. *450 Powell St, 21st Fl, San Francisco (94102). Phone 415/395-8595. www.harrydenton.com.* As you walk, no, make that saunter into Harry Denton's Starlight Room, you may feel as if you have entered Maxim's in Paris or an opulent Vienna opera house. This historic nightclub is a "see-and-be-seen" nightspot with an emphasis on glamour in which nothing is free except the fabulous 300-degree view of the city. Nine glimmering chandeliers, velvety red booths, beveled mirrors, silk draperies with fringes and tassels, Art Deco door handles, walnut paneled elevators, and lavish carpeting offer up luxurious details at every eye level. Come for cocktails—the Cable Car Martini is a local favorite—look for celebrities and enjoy a trip to one of the plushest ladies' rooms you'll ever see. (Daily from 6 pm)

Hayes Street. *Hayes and Octavia sts, San Francisco (94102).* In these four blocks on Hayes Street just behind the San Francisco Opera House, shoppers will find urban home furnishings and offbeat apparel in what locals call San Francisco-style, or, one-of-a-kind items. Among the cozy cafés and artistically appointed restaurants, there isn't a chain store in sight. Visitors can easily make a day of shopping here, with perhaps a side trip to the Asian Art Museum, which is just a block from this shopping district.

Jackson Square. *Washington, Jackson, and Pacific sts from Montgomery to Battery sts, San Francisco.* Historic district; many buildings date to the mid-1800s. Includes One Jackson Place (formerly a paper warehouse), a compound of shops, showrooms, and gaslit courtyards.

Japan Center. *1625 Post St, San Francisco (94115). Between Fillmore, Geary, and Laguna sts, 1 mile W of Union Square. Phone 415/922-6776.* An authentic Japanese bathhouse and twin origami-style fountains leveled for sitting and cooling your feet punctuate this traffic-free, open-air mall containing everything Japanese. The wooden drum tower, the five-tiered Peace Pagoda, and copper-roofed Peace Walkway are architecturally interesting, but don't let some of the less visually exciting buildings such as the Nihonmachi keep you from going inside for some truly amazing finds. Witness taiko drumming and martial arts demonstrations. Taste Asian street barbecue. These three blocks also host such annual events as the Nihonmachi Street Fair, the International Asian American Film Festival, and Cherry Blossom Festival. (Daily; most businesses closed Jan 1-3, Thanksgiving, Dec 25)

Kristi Yamaguchi Holiday Ice Rink. *Justin Herman Plaza, Market and Embarcadero, San Francisco (94111). Phone 415/772-0700.* From November through January, this ice-skating arena at the foot of the Embarcadero Center in Justin Herman Plaza is perfectly positioned for a great view of the tall buildings that surround it, and if the light is just right, for a beautiful reflection from the ice. Open skate sessions take place every even hour starting at 10 am for 90 minutes, and lessons are also available by reservation. Kristi Yamaguchi is apt to show up for a surprise visit from time to time. A note for beginners: weekend afternoons can be quite crowded. (Nov-Jan, Sun-Thurs 10 am-10 pm; Fri-Sat 10 am-11:30 pm) **$$$**

Legion of Honor. *100 34th Ave, San Francisco (94121). Phone 415/863-3330. www.thinker.org.* Making its home in a magnificent Beaux Arts building that was constructed to commemorate Californian soldiers who died in World War II, this museum houses a vast collection of ancient and European art. Among the furniture, tapestries, illustrated books, prints, paintings, and drawings displayed here are works by many well-known artists, including El Greco, Rembrandt, Monet, Matisse, and Picasso. Come here to see a bronze cast of one of the world's most famous sculptures, Rodin's *The Thinker,* which sits in the Court of Honor. View these objects at your leisure, or drop in for one of the scheduled tours given Tuesday through Sunday. (Tues-Sun 9:30 am-5 pm) **$$**

Lincoln Park Golf Course. *300 34th Ave, San Francisco (94121). Phone 415/221-9911.* This San Francisco course was built just after the turn of the 20th century and redesigned in the 1960s. It's less than 5,500 yards long, so the par measures out to only 68, but this makes for a fast 18 holes at a reasonable price during the week and on weekends. The course is notable for its views of the Golden Gate Bridge and the Legion of Honor, as well as for its 17th hole, which parallels San Francisco Bay for about 240 yards. **$$$$**

Little Italy. *Broadway and Columbus Ave, San Francisco (94133). Phone 415/974-6900.* Originally settled by Italians, this community in the North Beach neighborhood still evokes a feeling of romantic Italy, with its old-world delis, cafés, gelato parlors, and Italian restaurants. But for many, it is best known as the home of the Beat Generation. The Beats, a group of young writers and poets that included Jack Kerouac and Allen Ginsberg, made their home here, and the area became the center of bohemian life in the 1950s. The neighborhood is also home to the City Lights Bookstore—owned by Beat poet Lawrence Ferlinghetti—which published Ginsberg's *Howl.*

Lombard Street. *1000 block of Lombard St, San Francisco (94109). Lombard St between Hyde and Leavenworth sts. Phone 415/391-2000.* The "crookedest street in the world" curves several times while snaking its way down one steep block from Russian Hill.

Lotta's Fountain. *Dolores Park, 20th and Church sts, San Francisco (94102).* This ornate fountain—the oldest surviving monument in San Francisco—was a gift to the city from vaudeville star Lotta Crabtree in 1875. During the 1906 earthquake, it was the central meeting place for families who were separated. Today, renovated to a spectacular gold, it is the spot where the earthquake is commemorated each year.

Marina Green. *Marina Blvd, San Francisco (94123). Marina Blvd between Baker and Buchanan sts. Phone 415/831-2700.* An eight-block-long stretch of greenery running from Fort Mason past the Marina Small Craft Harbor. Offers views of the Bay, Alcatraz, and the Golden Gate Bridge. Activities here include kite flying, skating, jogging, and volleyball.

Market Street. San Francisco's best-known street, lined with business establishments and a center for municipal transportation. It runs from the Ferry Building to the base of Twin Peaks.

Metreon. *101 Fourth St, San Francisco (94103). Phone 415/369-6000; toll-free 800/638-7366. www.metreon.com.* A futuristic Sony Entertainment Complex. Includes 15 movie screens ($$), IMAX theater ($$$), shops, restaurants, and family attractions. (Daily 10 am-10 pm)

Mission District Murals. *2981 24th St, San Francisco (94114). Balmy Alley in the Mission District, and nearby area. Phone 415/285-2287. www.sfmission.com/galleries.* Hundreds of murals painted on walls around the Mission District. Self-guided tours (daily); guided tours (weekends). **$$$**

Mission Dolores. *3321 16th St, San Francisco (94114). Phone 415/621-8203. www.missiondolores.citysearch.com.* (1776) Fountainhead from which the city grew. Mission San Francisco de Asís was the sixth in a chain of missions established by Franciscan fathers under the direction of Junipero Serra. (It is now known as Mission Dolores, the name being taken from nearby Laguna de Nuestra Señora de los Dolores.) The cornerstone of the present mission building was laid in 1782. Many pioneers are buried in the ancient emetery beside the church. (Daily 9 am-5 pm; closed Jan 1, Thanksgiving, Dec 25) **$**

Montgomery Street. Called the "Wall Street of the West," it's the West's financial hub. Tall buildings form a canyon beginning at Market Street and extending to within a block of the Embarcadero.

Musee Mecanique. *Pier 45 at end of Taylor St, Fisherman's Wharf, San Francisco (94133). Phone 415/346-2000. www.museemechanique.org.* Visitors to the Musée Mécanique will get lost in the world of simple machines—the kind that entertain. But be sure to bring plenty of quarters: most of the attractions here are coin-operated. You'll find player-pianos, dancing human and animal figurines, and machines that can tell your fortune. (Mon-Fri 11 am-7 pm, Sat-Sun, holidays 10 am-8 pm) **FREE**

Museum of Craft & Folk Art. *Fort Mason Center, Building A, Buchanan St and Marina Blvd, San Francisco (94123). Phone 415/775-0991. www.sfcraftandfolk.org.* Promotes the understanding and appreciation of human expression, ranging from utilitarian objects to contemporary art, through innovative exhibits of craft and folk art from cultures past and present. Gift shop. Free admission the first Wed of the month. (Tues-Fri and Sun 11 am-5 pm, Sat 10 am-5 pm; closed holidays) **$**

Nob Hill. *Sacramento and Jones sts, San Francisco (94108).* Home to Grace Cathedral (replica of Notre Dame in Paris) and Huntington Park (site of many art shows, also features a replica of a 16th-century Roman fountain).

Painted Ladies/Alamo Square. *Hayes and Pierce sts, San Francisco (94117).* These six beautifully restored Victorian houses set against the San Francisco skyline have become one of the classic images of the city. They've been called Postcard Row and are the often photographed scenic transition in more than a few films. Architecture and photography buffs can get up close by way of several walking tours in the area. Flower Power Haight-Ashbury Walking Tours (fee) leads two-hour tours on Tuesdays and Saturdays at 9:30 am. (Call 415/221-8442 for reservations.) One-hour docent-led tours start at Haas-Lilienthal House on Wednesdays from noon to 3 pm and on Sundays from 11 am to 4 pm. Tours are $5 for adults and $3 for seniors and children under 12. (Call 415/441-3004.)

Palace of Fine Arts. *3301 Lyon St, San Francisco (94123). Phone 415/561-0360. www.palaceoffinearts.org.* Monumental Greco-Romanesque rotunda with Corinthian colonnades; built for the 1915 Panama-Pacific International Exposition; has been restored. Surrounded by a duck lagoon and park. **FREE** Housed here is the

Exploratorium. *3601 Lyon St, San Francisco (94123). Phone 415/563-7337. www.exploratorium.edu.* Discover the science behind sports, learn how we see, and explore the structure of the nature of life at this hands-on museum dedicated to providing insights into scientific and natural phenomena. The more than 650 interactive exhibits on science, art, and human perception are both educational and entertaining for everyone from toddlers to adults. In one of the most popular exhibits in the museum, the Tactile Dome (fee, reservations required), you are guided only by your sense of touch in a pitch-black, geodesic structure. Free admission first Wed of month. (Tues-Sun 10 am-5 pm, some Mon holidays; closed Thanksgiving, Dec 25) **$$$**

Pier 39. *Beach St and the Embarcadero, San Francisco (94133). E edge of Fisherman's Wharf. Phone 415/981-7437. www.pier39.com.* Pier 39 is the kind of noisy and eye-popping shop hub on Fisherman's Wharf that will appeal to everyone, but especially children. There are 100 shops filled with San Francisco-oriented souvenirs, numerous fast-food stands, street entertainers, and an antique Venetian carousel. Season and weather depending, visitors to the pier may be lucky to see the sea lions. Parking is expensive and hard to find, so consider taking public transportation.

Presidio. *102 Montgomery St, San Francisco (94123). Phone 415/561-4323. www.nps.gov/prsf.* Wooded tract of 1,450 acres, fortified since 1776 and now a national park. The present Officer's Club contains sections of the first building to be erected in San Francisco. Markers indicate points of historical interest; hiking. **FREE**

Presidio Golf Course. *300 Finley Rd, San Francisco (94129). Phone 415/561-4661. www.presidiogolf.com.* Presidio was once an exclusive private club that hosted dignitaries like Teddy Roosevelt and Dwight Eisenhower for rounds of golf. Today, it is part of Golden Gate National Park and is open to the public. Only ten minutes from downtown, the course is lined with eucalyptus and pine trees hundreds of years old. The hardest hole is probably number 12, a 453-yard-long par-four with bunkers in the left middle of the fairway and surrounding the green. The price is reasonable, and the layout a fan favorite. **$$$$**

Randall Museum. *199 Museum Way, San Francisco (94114). Phone 415/554-9600. www.randallmuseum.org.* The museum offers science, art, and interactive exhibits. It also includes a live animal room with more than 100 animals that can no longer survive in the wild. (Tues-Sat 10 am-5 pm) **FREE**

Ripley's Believe It or Not Museum. *175 Jefferson St, San Francisco (94133). Phone 415/771-6188. www.ripleysf.com.* If you have a penchant for the strange and unusual, this museum is for you. Robert Ripley's collection of oddities from around the world was first seen at the 1933 World's Fair in Chicago and became so popular that he began to open "Odditoriums" around the country. Today, there are 25 Ripley's Believe It or Not Museums throughout the world. Housed in this museum are many odd—and sometimes shocking—displays, which include a two-headed calf, a cable car made out of more than 270,000 matchsticks, and a shrunken torso once owned by Ernest Hemingway. (Sun-Thurs 9 am-11 pm, Fri-Sat to midnight) **$$$**

San Francisco 49ers (NFL). *3Com Park, 4949 Centennial Blvd (Business Office), San Francisco (94124). Phone 415/656-4949. www.49ers.com.* The San Francisco 49ers were the first major league professional sports franchise on the West Coast. The team formed in 1946 and was granted a National League franchise in 1950. They take their name from the wave of gold miners that came to the area in 1849.

San Francisco Architectural Heritage. *2007 Franklin St, San Francisco (94109). Phone 415/441-3000. www.sfheritage.org.* This preservation group offers various tours, lectures, and other events related to the architectural heritage of one of America's most beautiful cities. Regular tours include the Haas-Lilienthal House (see) and a two-hour walking tour of the eastern part of the Pacific Heights neighborhood. **$$**

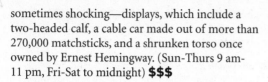

San Francisco Ballet. *War Memorial Opera House, 301 Van Ness Ave, San Francisco (94102). Phone 415/865-2000. www.sfballet.org.* Repertory season early Feb-early May; *Nutcracker,* Dec.

San Francisco Bay cruises. *Phone 415/447-0597.* Red & White Fleet. Bay cruises. (Daily) Fisherman's Wharf, at Pier 43 1/2. Phone toll-free 877/855-5506. Blue & Gold Fleet. Offers 1 1/4-hour cruise. (Daily) Adjacent to Fisherman's Wharf. Pier 41. Phone 415/705-5555. Hornblower Dining Yachts. Luxury dining yachts cruise San Francisco Bay. The flagship is the *California Hornblower,* a 183-foot, 1,000-passenger vessel with three decks. Luncheon, dinner/dance, weekend champagne brunch, and special event cruises available. Reservations required. Pier 33, along the Embarcadero. Phone 415/788-8866, ext 6, or toll-free 800/668-4322. **$$$$**

San Francisco Fire Engine Tours. *Columbus Ave and Beach St, San Francisco (94109). Phone 415/333-7077. www.fireenginetours.com.* For anyone who ever craved seeing the sights of San Francisco from the top of a fire truck, this is the tour for you. A 75-minute trip on a big, red, shiny Mack fire engine includes authentic fireproof garb and room for thirteen. Leave from Fisherman's Wharf and travel through the Presidio to Fort Point at the base of the bridge to Sausalito and return through the Union Street neighborhood back to the Cannery. Advance reservations are necessary. Passengers travel in comfort and safety; the seats are upholstered and the truck is equipped with seatbelts. **$$$$**

San Francisco Giants (MLB). *SBC Park, 24 Willie Mays Plz, San Francisco (94107). Phone 415/972-2000. www.sfgiants.com.* The Giants have drawn regular sellout crowds since the record-setting home run season Barry Bonds had in 2001 (he eventually hit 73 round-trippers). Outside the park is a 9-foot statue of baseball great Willie Mays, as well as an illuminated, 80-foot Coca-Cola bottle with playground slides and a mini-SBC park.

San Francisco Maritime National Historical Park. *2905 Hyde St Pier, San Francisco (94123). Adjacent to Fort Mason, at the W end of Fisherman's Wharf. Phone 415/561-7100. www.nps.gov/safr.* Visitor center (Memorial Day-Oct 1: daily 9:30 am-7 pm; rest of year: to 5 pm). Includes

Aquatic Park. *Beach St, Fisherman's Wharf and Fort Mason, San Francisco (94123). Phone 415/561-7100.* Cove contains a swimming beach and a municipal pier for fishing.

Hyde Street Pier Historic Ships. *900 Beach St, San Francisco (94109). Phone 415/447-5000.* A collection of six historic merchant ships, including SV *Balclutha,* a sailing ship built in 1886 and restored as a Cape Horn trader, and several smaller ships. (Daily 9:30 am-5:30 pm; closed Jan 1, Dec 25) **$**

National Maritime Museum. *900 Beach St, San Francisco (94109). At Polk St. Phone 415/561-7100. www.maritime.org.* Situated on San Francisco Bay across from Ghirardelli Square, this museum offers a peek into the history of West Coast vessels. Don't miss the hands-on radio room where you can explore communication technology, from signal flags to Morse Code. The sandy beach at Aquatic Park is right outside the back door. (Daily 10 am-5 pm; closed Jan 1, Thanksgiving, Dec 25) **FREE**

San Francisco Museum of Modern Art. *151 Third St, San Francisco (94103). Phone 415/357-4000. www.sfmoma.org.* The museum displays 20th-century art on permanent exhibit, also traveling exhibitions; concerts, lectures, and special events. Gift shop, café. (Summer: Fri-Tues 10 am-6 pm, Thurs to 9 pm; winter: Fri-Tues 11 am-6 pm, Thurs to 9 pm; closed holidays). Free admission on the first Tuesday of every month. **$$**

San Francisco-Oakland Bay Bridge. Stretches 8 1/2 miles to the East Bay cities. Double-decked, with five lanes on each deck; the upper deck is one-way westbound, the lower deck one-way eastbound. Tunnels through Yerba Buena Island in midbay. Auto toll collected on the westbound side only.

San Francisco Shopping Centre. *865 Market St, San Francisco (94103). Phone 415/512-6776. www.westfield.com.* A multistory mall with stores like Ann Taylor, Coach, Kenneth Cole, L'occitane, and Nordstrom. (Mon-Sat 9:30 am-8 pm, Sun 11 am-6 pm; closed Thanksgiving, Dec 25)

San Francisco Zoo. *1 Zoo Rd, San Francisco (94132). Sloat Blvd at 45th Ave. Phone 415/753-7080. www.sfzoo.org.* A favorite among children and the young-at-heart, the San Francisco Zoo houses a collection of more than 1,000 animals. See 14 species of rare and exotic monkeys in the Primate Discovery Center; visit red kangaroos, grey kangaroos, and wallabies in the Australian Walkabout; and view gorillas up close as they play and interact with each other in Gorilla World. Kids will love the restored 1921 Dentzel Carousel at the zoo's entrance and will surely beg to climb aboard the Little Puffer for a ride on an old-fashioned miniature steam train ($). (Daily 10 am-5 pm) **$$$**

Sigmund Stern Memorial Grove. *Sloat Blvd and 19th Ave, San Francisco.* Natural amphitheater enclosed by eucalyptus trees. Free outdoor concerts in the summer (see SPECIAL EVENTS). Picnic tables and barbecue pits nearby.

SS *Jeremiah O'Brien* at Fisherman's Wharf. *Pier 45, Fisherman's Wharf, San Francisco (94133). Phone 415/441-5969. www.ssjeremiahobrien.com.* The last surviving intact Liberty ship. (Daily 10 am-4:30 pm; closed Jan 1, Thanksgiving, Dec 25) **$$**

Surfing. *San Francisco Bay, San Francisco.* Visitors to San Francisco would be remiss if they did not make a stop south of the city at some of the beaches and bay area to take in the surf. Whether you choose to watch from a safe, sandy footing or to jump on in, there is a wave for every size rider—with or without experience—be it on a surfboard, boogie board, snowboard, kite board, or using one's own body. At Linda Mar Beach in Pacifica, children—and their parents—can take lessons in many of these surfing styles. The surf is also up in nearby San Jose, Santa Cruz, and Monterey. Wet suits, boards, and booties are often provided for rental; just come wearing a bathing suit and be sure to bring along sunscreen, lip balm, a hat, towel, water, and a set of dry clothes.

Telegraph Hill. *Lombard and Kearny sts, San Francisco (94111).* (284 feet) Topped by the 210-foot Coit Memorial Tower, a monument to volunteer firefighters of the 1850s and 1860s. Murals decorating the first and second floors can also be seen from the outside. Elevator to the top. (Daily; closed Thanksgiving, Dec 25) The hill itself is occupied by artists' studios and expensive homes.

Coit Tower. *1 Telegraph Hill Blvd, San Francisco (94133). Phone 415/362-0808. www.coittower.org.* (1933) Upon her death in 1904, heiress Lilly Coit donated money to the city of San Francisco for the construction of a monument to honor firefighters. The result was Coit Tower, a 210-foot, fire-nozzle-shaped tower, built in 1933. From the top, the tower offers spectacular views of the Embarcadero, Pier 39, the Golden Gate Bridge, and the financial district. Inside, there is a mural gallery with frescoes inspired by Diego Rivera. (Daily 10 am-6:30 pm) **$**

Twin Peaks. *Twin Peaks Blvd, San Francisco (94131). Near center of city. Phone 415/391-2000.* The thrilling experience it provides comes not only from the breathtaking panorama, but also from the breezes that whip the hilltops. The north peak is 903 feet, and the south peak is 910 feet. Many apartment buildings and homes dot the hillsides.

Union Square. *Bounded by Geary, Powell, Post, and Stockton sts.* Union Square is a colorful, flower shop-dotted, block-long park blessed with goodies for the serious shopper in the heart of San Francisco. International boutiques, unique gift shops and galleries, plus major retailers make it some of the best shopping in the city. Facing the square are anchors Tiffany's, Macy's, Neiman-Marcus, and Saks Fifth Avenue. On Stockton Street between Post and Sutter, you will find high-end art galleries. The city's only Frank Lloyd Wright building—a gallery of tribal art—is located on Maiden Lane. Follow Maiden to Grant Street to find upscale retailers such as Gump's, nationally known for its abundance of silver, china, antiques, and crafts. A four-level parking garage beneath the square is the first underground garage in the United States. On Post Street is Crocker Galleria, featuring apparel, accessories, gift shops, and home furnishings as well as a selection of cafés under a glass dome. A few blocks to the south is the nine-story San Francisco Shopping Centre, home of the only curving escalator of its kind in the world and the nation's biggest Nordstrom's, as well as 65 other retailers.

Washington Square. *Bounded by Powell, Union, Stockton, and Filbert sts, San Francisco (94133).* Plaza in the heart of North Beach, San Francisco's Italian district and one of its restaurant/nightlife capitals. Surrounded by cafés, restaurants, bakeries, and Italian businesses. A popular spot for sunbathing and art shows. The Church of Saints Peter and Paul borders one end of the square. Close to Telegraph Hill.

Wax Museum at Fisherman's Wharf. *145 Jefferson St, San Francisco (94133). Phone 415/885-4834; toll-free 800/439-4305. www.waxmuseum.com.* This 100,000-square-foot museum contains wax reproductions of celebrities and famous artistic masterpieces. (Mon-Fri 10 am-9 pm, Sat-Sun 9 am-9 pm) **$$$**

Wells Fargo Bank History Museum. *420 Montgomery St, San Francisco (94104). Phone 415/396-2619. www.wellsfargo.com/about/about.jhtml.* Artifacts and displays dating from the gold rush to the 1906 earthquake to present-day banking; Concord stagecoach. (Mon-Fri 9 am-5 pm; closed holidays) **FREE**

Windsurfing. *Mason and Halleck sts (Crissy Park), and throughout the Bay Area, San Francisco (94101).* From mid-March through September, San Francisco's gusty winds can be ideal for windsurfing. Crissy Field is one of the most popular spots because of its spectacular views of the Golden Gate Bridge, but locals say this spot is best left for the intermediate and advanced surfers. Beginners might want to start with a lesson at Shoreline Park, Foster City Lagoon, the Delta, or Lake del Valle. In addition to riding the waves and steering that sail, if you are very lucky, you might even catch a glimpse of a great white whale. Other good surf spots within driving distance are Coyote Point at 3rd Avenue, Candlestick, and Waddell Creek. A number of shops that rent equipment, as well as give lessons, including Advanced Surf Design, 650/348-8485; California Windsurfing, 650/594-0335; Marin Boardsports, 415/258-9283; Shoreline Aquatic Center, 650/965-7474; and Windsurf Del Valle, 925/455-4008.

Yerba Buena Center for the Arts. *701 Mission St, San Francisco (94103). Phone 415/978-2787. www.yerbabuenaarts.org.* Visitors to this contemporary arts hub will be stimulated by fresh multidisciplinary works and programs by young and emerging local artists in the visual, performing, film, and video arts. The multipurpose Forum provides space for experimental performances, special events, and meetings. Ticket prices and performance times vary; call or visit the Web site for more information.

Yerba Buena Gardens. *221 4th St, San Francisco (94103). Bounded by Mission, 3rd, 4th, and Folsom sts. Phone 415/247-6500. www.yerbabuenagardens.com.* This parklike complex contains museums, gardens, cafés, the Martin Luther King Jr, Memorial Fountain, and the Rooftop at Yerba Buena Gardens, a children's center with ice rink, carousel, and high-tech arts studio (Zeum). (Daily) Located here is

Zeum. *221 Fourth St, San Francisco (94103). Phone 415/777-2800. www.zeum.org.* Zeum is a fascinating interactive museum situated on the roof of Yerba Buena Gardens designed to bridge the technical with the artistic. Budding animators can try their hands at animation; curious videographers can produce a multimedia show; and those handy with an iMac can experiment with illustration, video editing, 3-D modeling, or Web page design. There's lots to see even if you don't feel like doing the creating. Also on the premises are youth conservatory presentations, ice skating, a bowling center, and beautiful gardens. (Summer: Tues-Sun 11 am-5 pm; winter: Wed-Sun 11 am-5 pm) **$$**

Special Events

Ala Carte, Ala Park. *Bowling Green Dr and Middle Dr S, San Francisco (94142). Phone 415/458-1988.* Whether you enjoy Italian, Indian, Mexican, or American cuisine, this three-day food festival has something to please your palate. Thousands of food lovers flock to this end-of-summer festival to taste what nearly 40 of San Franciso's best-loved restaurants have to offer as well as to enjoy a great selection of wines, cocktails, and microbrews. Make sure to bring a blanket so you can sit and take in the live music and San Francisco sunshine while you eat. Labor Day weekend.

Bay to Breakers Footrace. *1 The Embarcadero, San Francisco (94105). From S of Market St through Golden Gate Park to Ocean Beach. Phone 415/359-2800. www.baytobreakers.com.* Some 100,000 people run, walk, jog, or ride in strollers from San Francisco Bay to Ocean Beach, about 7 1/2 miles. Many participants run in colorful costumes; some, in just their birthday suits. Sun morning mid-May.

Carnaval. *Harrison and 17th sts, San Francisco (94110). Mission District. Phone 415/920-0125. www.carnavalsf.com.* Colorful floats in the grand parade, costumed dancers, and the beats of samba music set the mood for this lively, multi-ethnic festival that features food, live music, and art. Memorial Day weekend.

Castro Street Fair. *Castro and Market sts, San Francisco (94114). www.castrostreetfair.org.* This street festival in the Castro District, the heart of the city's gay community—at the intersection of Market and Castro streets—has been drawing lively crowds on the first Sunday in October for more than 30 years. While most visitors come to chow down, drink beer, bargain shop, and take in some entertainment, the most popular aspect of the fair is watching, or becoming a part of, the nonstop dancing in the outdoor pavilions. **FREE**

Cherry Blossom Festival. *Japan Center, 1625 Post St, San Francisco (94115). Phone 415/563-2313.* Japanese music, dancing, flower arranging, doll and sword exhibits, bonsai show, martial arts, calligraphy, origami, Akita dog exhibit, tea ceremony, children's village, arts and crafts, films, food bazaar, and a parade. Two weekends in Apr.

Chinese New Year. *Chinatown, 233 Sansome St, San Francisco (94104). Phone 415/391-9680. www.chineseparade.com.* The largest and most colorful celebration of this occasion held in the United States. The weeklong festival's activities include the Golden Dragon Parade, lion dancing, a carnival, and cultural exhibits. The parade begins at Market and Second streets. Feb.

Cinco de Mayo. *24th and Bryant sts, San Francisco (94110).* Although Mexico's actual victory over the French soldiers occurred in September, this annual celebration is held in early May and has come to represent Mexico's national pride and identity. This is a full five-senses affair—traditional costumes are shown off, mariachis sing, folk dancers twirl, authentic Mexican dishes beckon, and Latin, salsa, and hip-hop music draws all ages, making this a family-friendly experience in the name of Mexican heritage. **FREE**

Comedy Celebration Day. *Sharon Meadow, Golden Gate Park, Kezar Dr and Waller St, San Francisco (94117). www.comedyday.com.* Imagine a Sunday afternoon of outdoor comedy in Golden Gate Park. Sound good? Well it's not just a good idea—it's a reality. More than a dozen well-known comics gather here each summer for this free outdoor celebration of comedy. Though it is free, donations are accepted for different causes every year. All you need is a couple of hours, a blanket and a picnic basket, or a credit card, as food and drink vendors are on hand and many take plastic. Mid Sept-Oct. **FREE**

Grand National Rodeo, Horse & Stock Show. *San Francisco Cow Palace, 2600 Geneva Ave, San Francisco (94014). Phone 415/404-4111. www.grandnational rodeo.com.* This week of entertainment includes a PRCA rodeo, free concerts, an art sale, and wine tasting. Apr.

Italian Heritage Parade. *Powell and Jefferson sts, San Francisco (94133). www.sfcolumbusday.org.* The largest Columbus Day party in the West parades appropriately down Columbus Avenue every October celebrating Italian heritage and lovers of Italy from Fisherman's Wharf to North Beach. Watch the festivities from a sidewalk table where you can enjoy Italian delicacies, or walk the length of the parade along with the floats. But get your spot early, as this gathering draws quite the crowd in one of the city's most temperate months.

Leap Sand Castle Classic. *Great Hwy and Fulton St, San Francisco (94121). Phone 415/512-1899. www.leap4kids.org.* Appreciators of art—and sand—will get an eyeful from the imaginative architectural beach creations built by designers and developers at Ocean Beach. This innovative fund-raising event, held on the last weekend in September, is designed to promote creativity among young people, but has, during the last two decades, become a popular visual and performing arts event. **$**

Opera in the Park. *Golden Gate Park, Sharon Meadow, Kezar and John F. Kennedy drs, San Francisco (94117). Phone 415/777-7770.* Designed to excite opera novices and provide pleasure for longtime buffs, Opera in the Park is a perfect place to enjoy a picnic while you revel in the beautiful music. Each September, the San Francisco Opera and Orchestra hosts this free afternoon of opera's greatest hits in the Sharon Meadow in Golden Gate Park, at Kezar and John F. Kennedy drives. Limited special seating is available for seniors and the disabled. (No lawn chairs or umbrellas, please.) **FREE**

San Francisco Blues Festival. *Marina Blvd and Laguna St, Great Meadow, San Francisco (94123). Phone 415/979-5588. www.sfblues.com.* Headliner musicians as well as regional acoustic acts have drawn blues lovers to this exquisite location every year for more than 30 years. It offers a unique combination of music for the ears as well as the eyes by the San Francisco Bay. Highlighting Mississippi Delta, Chicago Electric, Memphis

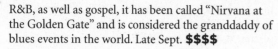

R&B, as well as gospel, it has been called "Nirvana at the Golden Gate" and is considered the granddaddy of blues events in the world. Late Sept. **$$$$**

San Francisco International Film Festival. *Presidio, 39 Mesa St, San Francisco (94129). www.sffs.org.* The San Francisco International Film Festival has been a showcase every spring for new feature, documentary, and short films for more than 45 years at various locations around town. Film fanatics who just can't get enough can see documentaries, shorts, animation, experimental and television production; edgy films; world cinema; animation as well as video presentations and interactive seminars for two weeks straight. Apr-May.

San Francisco Marathon. *The Embarcadero at Market St, San Francisco (94111). Phone 415/284-9653. www.runsfm.com.* Consider seeing this scenic city while running a full or half marathon, relay, or 5K race along the waterfront with spectacular views of the bay at its start from the Ferry Building on the Embarcadero at Market Street. Or, consider watching others do it instead! The marathon takes place in July when the San Francisco weather can be an ideal 60 degrees. Entertainment and 60 vendors dot the race route with sounds, sights, and marathon merchandise, and the finish line at Justin Herman Plaza offers participants bananas, oranges, water, massages, and other goodies. **$$$$**

San Francisco Opera. *War Memorial Opera House, 301 Van Ness Ave, San Francisco (94102). At Grove St. Phone 415/861-4008. www.sfopera.org.* Founded in 1923, the San Francisco Opera has a long and celebrated history that includes presenting debut performances of several well-known artists and conductors. The Opera also holds one free concert in Golden Gate Park each fall. June-July and Sept-Dec. **$$$$**

San Francisco Symphony's Black and White Ball. *201 Van Ness Ave, San Francisco (94102). Phone 415/864-6000. www.bwball.org.* For partygoers and ball revelers, this is the event of the year. The biggest black-tie fundraiser in the country, it is held every other May in historic buildings around the city, including Davies Symphony Hall, City Hall, War Memorial Veterans Building, and the War Memorial Opera House. It begins with a lavish cocktail reception with hors d'oeuvres from many of the city's finest restaurants and hotels and continues with dancing and entertainment in various venues, with symphonic, rock, swing, jazz, Latin, big band, and country music available all night long. Tickets are pricey at $200 per person or more, but this popular event is a lot of fun. **$$$$**

San Francisco Symphony Orchestra. *Louise M. Davies Symphony Hall, 201 Van Ness Ave, San Francisco (94102). Phone 415/552-8000. www.sfsymphony.org.* The San Francisco Symphony Orchestra prides itself on the fact that each and every one of its musicians has great passion and aptitude for music, which makes each performance a powerful and unsurpassable expression of emotion and talent. Sept-July. **$$$$**

Shakespeare at Stinson. *Stinson Beach, State Hwy 101 and Calle Del Mar, Stinson Beach. Phone 415/868-1115. www.shakespeareatstinson.org.* Two of the Bard's works come to life annually at a 155-seat outdoor theater a stone's throw from the tide coming in on Marin County's popular Stinson Beach. (A third classic play by a different master playwright rounds out the annual calendar.) The Shakespeare at Stinson season runs from mid-spring through mid-fall, with many family-friendly ticket deals (including free kids' nights). May-Oct. **$$$$**

Stern Grove Midsummer Music Festival. *Sigmund Stern Memorial Grove, 2750 19th Ave, San Francisco (94110). At Sloat Blvd. Phone 415/252-6252. www.sterngrove.org.* Pack a picnic, grab a blanket, and enjoy a casual afternoon at one of these weekly Sunday concerts in the relaxing and beautiful Stern Grove. Mid-June-mid-Aug. **FREE**

Limited-Service Hotels

★ BEST WESTERN AMERICANIA. *121 Seventh St, San Francisco (94103). Phone 415/626-0200; toll-free 800/444-5816; fax 415/863-2529. www.renesonhotels.com.* 43 rooms, 4 story. Check-out noon. Bar. Fitness room. Outdoor pool. **$**

★ ★ CARLTON HOTEL. *1075 Sutter St, San Francisco (94109). Phone 415/673-0242; toll-free 800/922-7586; fax 415/673-4904. www.carltonhotel.com.* Located two blocks from Van Ness Avenue, a main artery through the city, this boutique hotel, built circa 1928, features a spacious marble-floored lobby, complete with traditional furnishings, fireplace, library, and computer station. It is also the site of a free wine reception in the evening. The guest rooms are comfortably dated, with lots of floral patterns, two large plaid wingback chairs, a writing desk, and an armoire. The hotel offers complimentary limo service to the Financial District, Civic Center, and Moscone Center. 165 rooms, 9 story. Check-in 3 pm, check-out 1 pm. Restaurant. **$$**

★★ COURTYARD BY MARRIOTT. *299 Second St, San Francisco (94105). Phone 415/947-0700; toll-free 800/321-2211; fax 415/947-0800. www.courtyard.com.* Situated in the heart of the South of Market business district, guests will find this property convenient to SBC Park, Union Square, and other area attractions. 405 rooms, 18 story. Check-in 3 pm, check-out noon. High-speed Internet access. Restaurant, bar. Fitness room. Indoor pool. **$$**

★★ EXECUTIVE HOTEL VINTAGE COURT. *650 Bush St, San Francisco (94108). Phone 415/392-4666; toll-free 800/654-1100; fax 415/433-4065. www.vintagecourt.com.* Situated between Nob Hill and Union Square, this historic 1912 hotel makes much of its wine theme, from the evening wine reception in the lobby to guest rooms named after California wineries (the Niebaum-Coppola penthouse suite features a wood-burning fireplace). The décor is soothing, with dark woods and green, beige, and cream bedding and draperies. Many rooms have bay windows, and all are nonsmoking. Prices are reasonable given the hotel's comfort and location. 107 rooms, 8 story. Pets accepted. Complimentary continental breakfast. Check-in 3 pm, check-out noon. Restaurant. **$$**

★★ HARBOR COURT HOTEL. *165 Stuart St, San Francisco (94105). Phone 415/882-1300; toll-free 800/346-0555; fax 415/882-1313. www.harborcourthotel.com.* Because of its perch along the Embarcadero, rear rooms at the Harbor Court provide fabulous views of the Bay Bridge and Treasure Island. The rooms are small but inviting, with minimal furnishings, canopied beds, and shades of avocado, lime, gold, and purple. The large, stylish upper lobby hosts an evening wine reception; Ozumo, the hotel's Japanese restaurant, serves sushi, sashimi, sake, and more. The hotel is affiliated with the attached YMCA, which has an indoor pool. 131 rooms, 8 story. Pets accepted. Check-in 3 pm, check-out noon. Restaurant. Fitness room. Indoor pool, whirlpool. **$$**

★★ HOTEL GRIFFON - A SUMMIT HOTEL. *155 Steuart St, San Francisco (94105). Phone 415/495-2100; toll-free 800/321-2201; fax 415/495-3522. www.hotelgriffon.com.* Situated in the Embarcadero section of the Financial District, the Hotel Griffon is a charming boutique hotel with a European flair. Guest rooms are sophisticated, with white down duvets and pillows, plush robes, CD players, and umbrellas, should you need one. The lobby opens onto Red Herring restaurant (from which the full menu is available for room service). The location is great and the rooms are comfortable, and even better if you nab one with a bay view. 62 rooms, 5 story. Complimentary continental breakfast. Check-in 3 pm, check-out noon. High-speed Internet access. Restaurant. Fitness room. Indoor pool, whirlpool. **$$$**

★★ RADISSON MIYAKO HOTEL. *1625 Post St, San Francisco (94115). Phone 415/922-3200; toll-free 800/333-3333; fax 415/921-0417. www.radisson.com.* This hotel features a blend of Eastern and Western influences that mix with Japanese style, resulting in a gracious ambience. With handsomely appointed guest rooms and superb service, your stay is guaranteed to be one of pleasure and relaxation. 418 rooms, 16 story. Check-in 3 pm, check-out noon. High-speed Internet access. Restaurant, bar. Fitness room. Business center. **$$**

★★ SAVOY HOTEL. *580 Geary St, San Francisco (94102). Phone 415/441-2700; toll-free 800/227-4223; fax 415/441-0124. www.thesavoyhotel.com.* This small Theater District hotel a few blocks from Union Square was built in the early 1900s for the Panama-Pacific Exposition. A boutique hotel with a lobby of marble columns, a black-and-white marble floor, and velvet armchairs, the Savoy exudes Parisian atmosphere. Comfortable rooms feature goose-down pillows, feather beds, and soundproof windows; the color scheme tends toward shades of red, taupe, and cream. Guests can mingle and enjoy complimentary wine and cheese in the afternoon, or visit Millennium, a gourmet, environmentally friendly vegetarian restaurant, for dinner. 96 rooms, 7 story. Check-in 3 pm, check-out noon. Restaurant, bar. Business center. **$$**

★★ TUSCAN INN. *425 Northpoint St, San Francisco (94133). Phone 415/561-1100; fax 415/561-1199.* Several blocks from Fisherman's Wharf and Ghirardelli Square, this three-story European-style boutique hotel breaks the "corporate chain" mold. The lobby has a warm, colorful feel, and guest room décor includes upholstered furnishings and a palette of green, burgundy, and gold. The hotel also houses Café Pescatore, a casual trattoria serving pizzas, pastas, and grilled meats. Although it lacks the amenities of larger hotels, the Tuscan Inn is comfortable and conveniently situated. 221 rooms, 4 story. Pets accepted, some restrictions; fee. Complimentary continental breakfast. Check-in 3 pm, check-out noon. Restaurant, bar. **$$**

★ ★ **VILLA FLORENCE.** *225 Powell St, San Francisco (94102). Phone 800/553-4411; fax 415/397-1006.* Oozing Italian style, this boutique hotel, just a few paces from Union Square, has an Italian Renaissance-style lobby, with columns, a large mural of 16th-century Florence, and a wishing fountain. The comfortable guest rooms feature high ceilings, plantation shutters (with windows that actually open), writing desks, and brightly colored bedspreads. Guest services include a complimentary shuttle and wine tasting. The hotel is also home to Kuleto's, a "designer" Italian restaurant and wine bar. 183 rooms, 7 story. Check-in 3 pm, check-out noon. Restaurant, bar. **$$**

Full-Service Hotels

★ ★ ★ **ARGENT HOTEL.** *50 Third St, San Francisco (94103). Phone 415/974-6400; toll-free 877/222-6699; fax 415/348-8207. www.argenthotel.com.* Located south of Market, this 36-story hotel offers easy access to SoMa attractions like the Yerba Buena Gardens and San Francisco Museum of Modern Art and is well suited for both business and leisure travelers. The elegant lobby is decorated with marble and mahogany woodwork, and guest rooms have floor-to-ceiling windows, feather bedding, large writing desks, and three phones. Other hotel amenities include a fitness center, a sauna, a business center, an early-morning guided city jog, and a complimentary town car shuttle. An R&B band plays in the hotel lounge every Friday night. 667 rooms, 36 story. Check-in 3 pm, check-out noon. Restaurant, bar. Fitness room, spa. Business center. **$$$$**

★ ★ ★ **CAMPTON PLACE HOTEL.** *340 Stockton St, San Francisco (94108). Phone 415/781-5555; toll-free 800/235-4300; fax 415/955-5536. www.camptonplace.com.* Campton Place is a haven of serenity right on San Francisco's energetic Union Square. Just steps from the shops and restaurants that define this neighborhood, guests feel an immediate hush when entering this sophisticated boutique hotel. Thoughtful service makes everyone feel at home here. The rooms and suites have a modern, fresh look, with pear wood paneling, unique photography, and simple furnishings. Most rooms have window seats with a view of the city—perfect for daydreaming—and the hotel's rooftop fitness center boasts terrific skyline vistas. City residents and hotel guests compete for reservations at the Campton Place Restaurant (see), praised for its triumphant New American cuisine. 110 rooms, 17 story. Pets accepted; fee. Check-in 3 pm, check-out noon. High-speed Internet access. Restaurant, bar. Fitness room. **$$$$**

★ ★ ★ **CLIFT - AN IAN SCHRAGER HOTEL.** *495 Geary St, San Francisco (94102). Phone 415/775-4700; toll-free 800/606-6090; fax 415/441-4621. www.clifthotel.com.* Creatively updated and modernized by hotel guru Ian Schrager and French designer Philippe Starck, the Clift reopened in the summer of 2001 in its historic Theater District location. The so-called lobby living room is your first clue that this hotel defies tradition, with its oversized "chair art" pieces and rich dark woods. The more understated guest rooms are still luxurious, with lavender and ivory color schemes, orange Lucite end tables, 400-thread-count sheets, wheelbarrow chairs, and cordless phones. A well-heeled crowd would feel comfortable in these trendy, hip, and luxe environs. The Clift also houses the restaurant Asia de Cuba, which has branches in several cities, and the see-and-be-seen Redwood Room. The landmark Art Deco bar on the first floor blends old and new (for example, digital portraits are displayed on plasma television screens on walls that retain their original redwood paneling). 374 rooms, 17 story. Check-in 3 pm, check-out 1 pm. High-speed Internet access. Restaurant, bar. Fitness room. Business center. **$$$$**

★ ★ ★ **CROWNE PLAZA UNION SQUARE.** *480 Sutter St, San Francisco (94108). Phone 415/398-8900; toll-free 866/652-3705; fax 415/989-8823. www.crowneplaza.com.* Well situated for tourists and business travelers alike, this Crowne Plaza is one block from Union Square. The Powell Street cable car conveniently stops at the hotel's corner. 403 rooms, 30 story. Pets accepted, some restrictions. Check-in 3 pm, check-out noon. High-speed Internet access. Two restaurants, bar. Fitness room. Business center. **$$**

★ ★ ★ **DONATELLO HOTEL.** *501 Post St, San Francisco (94102). Phone 415/441-7100; toll-free 800/227-3184; fax 415/885-8891.* This European-style hotel, named for the 15th-century Italian sculptor, boasts modern Italian décor and some of the largest guest rooms in the city (425 square feet). Each room has a wet bar and kitchenette equipped with a microwave, toaster, and refrigerator. Extra seating, which includes a loveseat and a chaise, is ample. The hotel, one block from Union Square, also has a private rooftop garden. Guests can enjoy live jazz four nights a week at Zingari, the hotel's restaurant. 94 rooms, 14 story. Check-in 3 pm, check-out noon. Restaurant, bar. Fitness room. Whirlpool. **$$**

★ ★ ★ THE FAIRMONT SAN FRANCISCO. *950 Mason St, San Francisco (94108). Phone 415/772-5000; toll-free 800/441-1414; fax 415/772-5013. www.fairmont.com.* Majestically resting atop one of San Francisco's famous hills, The Fairmont is a true legend. Since the early 1900s, this palatial hotel has enjoyed an illustrious history filled with glittering balls, lavish parties, glamorous debutantes, and quirky characters. From its sweeping staircase to its impressive columns, this classic hotel's lobby is the very definition of a grand entrance. The guest rooms are traditional in style, yet all rooms incorporate modern conveniences and thoughtful touches. The hotel's convenient location in the exclusive Nob Hill neighborhood places it near Fisherman's Wharf and the Financial District, and the rooms afford views of the city and the bay. (Be aware, though, that Nob Hill is a *big* hill, and the walk home from the nearby Union Square, with plentiful shopping and dining options, means a very steep climb.) Both corporate and leisure travelers are well cared for here, where business and fitness facilities cater to specific needs. Exotic Asian dishes and popular mai tai cocktails are sampled at the Tonga Room and Hurricane Bar, while the Laurel Court pays tribute to the refinement of the hotel's early days. 591 rooms, 24 story. Pets accepted, some restrictions; fee. Check-in 3 pm, check-out noon. High-speed Internet access. Restaurant, bar. Fitness room (fee). Whirlpool. Business center. **$$**

★ ★ ★ ★ ★ FOUR SEASONS HOTEL SAN FRANCISCO. *757 Market St, San Francisco (94103). Phone 415/633-3000; toll-free 800/332-3442; fax 415/633-3001. www.fourseasons.com.* Occupying 12 levels of a residential tower, it's no wonder that the Four Seasons Hotel San Francisco feels so much like home. The hotel sparkles, from its floor-to-ceiling windows to its impressive art and sculpture collection. This showpiece of contemporary design is in a perfect location, with the shopping of Union Square only two blocks away and the Museum of Modern Art just around the bend. The guest rooms and suites are a wonderful blend of sophisticated city living and extra-luxurious amenities. Every detail has been considered in this stunning environment, even the strategically placed lights highlighting elegantly appointed floral arrangements throughout the lobby. In the guest rooms, large windows frame unparalleled views of San Francisco's lively streets or its glittering bay. A refined elegance pervades the Four Seasons, whether in the stunning lobby or the restaurant. The Sports Club/LA, adjacent to the hotel, takes a comprehensive approach to fitness with state-of-the-art equipment and cutting-edge classes. The center's Splash is the city's premier day spa, attracting hotel guests and city dwellers alike. 277 rooms, 10 story. Pets accepted. Check-in 3 pm, check-out noon. High-speed Internet access, wireless Internet access. Restaurant, bar. Fitness room, fitness classes available, spa. Indoor pool, whirlpool. Airport transportation available. Business center. **$$$$**

★ ★ ★ GRAND HYATT SAN FRANCISCO. *345 Stockton St, San Francisco (94108). Phone 415/398-1234; fax 415/391-1780. grandsanfrancisco.hyatt.com.* A few steps away from Union Square and the Chinatown gate, the 36-story Grand Hyatt is in the heart of the San Francisco shopping and dining action, with many of its rooms overlooking Union Square. Room décor is typical of the large chain, with bronze and navy bedding and TVs tucked away in armoires (small TVs are also in the bathrooms). The hotel also offers complimentary transportation to the Financial District, access to the health club, and dining at Grandviews, the aptly named rooftop restaurant. 685 rooms, 36 story. Check-in 3 pm, check-out noon. High-speed Internet access. Restaurant, bar. Fitness room. Business center. **$$**

★ ★ ★ HILTON FISHERMAN'S WHARF. *2620 Jones St, San Francisco (94133). Phone 415/885-4700; toll-free 800/445-8667; fax 415/771-8945. www.hilton.com.* Located at a busy intersection in Fisherman's Wharf, this chain establishment is a fairly short walk to North Beach, Ghirardelli Square, and the Embarcadero, making it a convenient choice for leisure travelers. The pleasant hotel is nicely maintained and offers spacious guest rooms decorated in shades of burgundy, plum, and gold. 234 rooms, 3 story. Check-in 3 pm, check-out noon. High-speed Internet access. Restaurant, bar. Fitness room. Business center. **$$**

★ ★ ★ **HOTEL ADAGIO.** *550 Geary St, San Francisco (94102). Phone 415/775-5000; toll-free 800/228-8830; fax 415/775-9388. www.thehoteladagio.com.* Located in Union Square, the Hotel Adagio (formerly the Shannon Court) celebrates its Spanish Colonial architecture while bringing in the essentials of modern design. The guest rooms are done in rich tones of chocolate, charcoal, and brick red, with modern-style furnishings throughout the hotel. The on-site restaurant serves small plates of Mediterranean cuisine; private rooms are available for events. Morning Town Car service to the Financial District is a nice extra for business travelers. 171 rooms. Check-in 3 pm, check-out noon. High-speed Internet access. Restaurant, bar. Fitness room. Business center. **$$$**

★ ★ ★ **HOTEL MONACO.** *501 Geary St, San Francisco (94102). Phone 415/292-0100; toll-free 866/622-5284; fax 415/292-0111. www.monaco-sf.com.* Bright colors, cheerful ambience, and a whimsical style greet visitors of this luxury hotel, housed in a remodeled Beaux Arts building that showcases a fanciful mural in the lobby. Guest rooms continue the theme of patterns and colors, from the walls to the canopied beds, with multi-hued headboards and bedding (courtesy of Frette). Complimentary amenities include morning coffee, afternoon tea, an evening wine reception, and a shoe shine. The Grand Café (see) next door is worth a visit, as is the on-site, full-service spa. 235 rooms, 7 story. Pets accepted. Check-in 3 pm, check-out noon. Restaurant, bar. Fitness room, spa. Business center. **$$$**

★ ★ ★ **HOTEL NIKKO.** *222 Mason St, San Francisco (94102). Phone 415/394-1111; toll-free 800/645-5687; fax 415/394-1106. www.nikkohotels.com.* Situated between Union Square, the Theater District, and SoMa, this high-end hotel caters to international and business travelers. Despite its imposing size, the hotel achieves an understated harmony and serenity, in keeping with its Japanese influence. Notable features include the striking two-story lobby, which visitors enter via stairs, escalator, or elevator, and the 8-foot, hand-blown glass orange lamps. Extensive amenities include a fully staffed fitness center and spa; an indoor, atrium-style swimming pool; and a tanning cabana. The hotel's Anzu restaurant (see) serves fabulous sushi and sake martinis. 532 rooms, 25 story. Pets accepted, some restrictions. Check-in 3 pm, check-out noon. High-speed Internet access. Restaurant, bar. Fitness room, spa. Indoor pool, whirlpool. Business center. **$$$**

★ ★ ★ **HOTEL PALOMAR.** *12 Fourth St, San Francisco (94103). Phone 415/348-1111; toll-free 866/373-4941; fax 415/348-0302. www.hotelpalomar.com.* Hotel Palomar personifies sophisticated exuberance. Occupying the fifth through ninth floors of a historic building just off Union Square, this hotel captures the imagination of its guests with its eclectic style. Full of character, the hotel's playful décor is most evident in the guest rooms, where leopard-print carpets reside alongside cool furnishings and contemporary artwork. Residents of the one-of-a-kind Renée Magritte Suite sleep under a ceiling of blue sky and white clouds while enjoying prints of this modern master's work. Guests are properly cosseted in this joyous hotel, from business services and complimentary car service to pet-friendly policies and in-room spa services. Fifth Floor (see), with its modern French cuisine and dazzling décor and convivial scene, is one of downtown San Francisco's hippest dining establishments. 198 rooms, 5 story. Pets accepted. Check-in 3 pm, check-out noon. High-speed Internet access. Restaurant, bar. Children's activity center. Fitness room. **$$$**

★ ★ ★ **HOTEL REX.** *562 Sutter St, San Francisco (94102). Phone 415/433-4434; toll-free 800/433-4434; fax 415/433-3695. www.thehotelrex.com.* Hotel Rex, a sophisticated boutique hotel embracing a Jazz Age theme, takes its cue from the art and literary salons of the 1920s and '30s. Despite its nondescript exterior, the hotel is surprisingly upscale inside. The lobby has a suave, clublike atmosphere and décor, with dark wood, book-lined walls, original paintings and murals, muted lighting, a traditional bar and lounge (which hosts literary events), and soft jazz music. Guest rooms feature a Provençal color scheme, and are packed with amenities, including CD players, cordless phones, candy jars, original artwork, and hand-painted lamps. En route to the rooms, notice the pages from the San Francisco Social Registry decorating the elevator doors. An evening wine reception and morning newspaper are complimentary. 94 rooms, 7 story. Check-in 3 pm, check-out noon. High-speed Internet access. Restaurant, bar. **$$**

★ ★ ★ THE HUNTINGTON HOTEL. *1075 California St, San Francisco (94108). Phone 415/ 474-5400; toll-free 800/227-4683; fax 415/474-6227. www.huntingtonhotel.com.* Reigning over the city from its Nob Hill perch, The Huntington Hotel & Spa is one of San Francisco's gems. This refined hotel has been catering to discriminating travelers since 1924. Its hilltop location affords some of the best panoramas in the city, while its quiet elegance and historic charm make for an inviting stay. Warm touches, such as customary tea or sherry service upon arrival and complimentary chauffeur service, create special memories. The rich wood paneling and emerald green seating at the Big 4 Restaurant (see) recall a distinguished gentleman's club, while the Nob Hill Spa embraces the present with its elegant styling and innovative treatments. 135 rooms, 12 story. Check-in 3 pm, check-out noon. High-speed Internet access. Restaurant, bar. Fitness room, spa. Indoor pool, whirlpool. **$$$**

★ ★ ★ HYATT AT FISHERMAN'S WHARF. *555 North Point St, San Francisco (94133). Phone 415/ 563-1234; toll-free 888/591-1234; fax 415/749-6122. www.hyatt.com.* One of the best choices in the Fisherman's Wharf area, this Hyatt is a few blocks from Ghirardelli Square and the Hyde Street cable car line, which chugs past the crooked part of Lombard Street. The hotel is built in a U shape around a brick driveway and central fountain. Public areas are spacious, conference facilities are extensive, and the outdoor pool is a rarity in this city. Catch Giants and 49ers action at Knuckles, the hotel's sports bar. 313 rooms, 5 story. Check-in 3 pm, check-out noon. Restaurant, bar. Children's activity center. Fitness room. Outdoor pool, whirlpool. Business center. **$$**

★ ★ ★ HYATT REGENCY SAN FRANCISCO. *5 Embarcadero Center, San Francisco (94111). Phone 415/788-1234; toll-free 800/233-1234; fax 415/398-2567. www.hyatt.com.* This large, convention-style hotel is situated in the Embarcadero Center, a movie, shopping, and office space complex at the foot of Market Street in San Francisco's Financial District. The wildly popular Ferry Building, with its gourmet food center, restaurants, and farmers' market, is a short walk from the hotel's atrium-style lobby, which is 17 stories high and surrounds a giant globe sculpture constructed of metal. Guest rooms are spacious, comfortable, and tastefully decorated, and many have views of the water. 805 rooms, 15 story. Check-in 3 pm, check-out noon. Wireless Internet access. Restaurant, bar. Fitness room. Business center. **$$**

★ ★ ★ INN AT THE OPERA. *333 Fulton St, San Francisco (94102). Phone 415/863-8400; toll-free 800/ 590-0157; fax 415/861-0821. www.innattheopera.com.* Intimate and upscale, this boutique hotel was built to accommodate visiting opera stars at the nearby War Memorial Opera House. The small, graceful lobby welcomes guests with marble accents, wood furnishings, original artwork, and antiques. Rose and green dominate the comfortable guest rooms, which also feature queen-size beds, wet bars with refrigerators, and armoires with televisions. Civic Center cultural activities and Hayes Street dining and shopping are within walking distance. Ovation at the Opera serves traditional French fare in an elegant setting. 47 rooms, 7 story. Complimentary full breakfast. Check-in 3 pm, check-out 11 am. Restaurant, bar. **$$**

★ ★ ★ ★ MANDARIN ORIENTAL, SAN FRANCISCO. *222 Sansome St, San Francisco (94104). Phone 415/276-9888; toll-free 800/622-0404; fax 415/433-0289. www.mandarinoriental.com.* Savvy travelers in search of the ultimate in skyscraper style head for the Mandarin Oriental, San Francisco. Occupying the top levels of the city's third-tallest building, the Mandarin Oriental offers unsurpassed views of the lovely city by the bay. Situated in the heart of the downtown business district, the hotel is also a convenient base for exploring major attractions and sites. The guest rooms and suites are spacious and incorporate Asian decorative objects and furnishings, although it is the jaw-dropping views that attract most of the attention. All accommodations feature dazzling city or bay views, and binoculars are provided for better viewing opportunities. Guests are invited to dine on Pacific Rim cuisine at Silks or enjoy continental dishes at the Mandarin Lounge. 158 rooms, 13 story. Pets accepted; fee. Check-in 3 pm, check-out noon. High-speed Internet access. Two restaurants, bar. Fitness room, fitness classes available. Airport transportation available. Business center. **$$$$**

★ ★ ★ MARK HOPKINS INTERCONTINENTAL. *999 California St, San Francisco (94108). Phone 415/392-3434; toll-free 800/ 662-4455; fax 415/421-3302. www.markhopkins.net.* Impressive and stately, the Mark Hopkins Inter-Continental is a San Francisco treasure. Resembling a French château, this lovely hotel is within close proximity to nearly all of the city's attractions. Reigning over Nob Hill, it has some of the best views in the city. The dashing lobby greets guests with warm spice tones, while handsome appointments create an enticing ambience in the guest rooms. Guests dashing off to important meetings are delighted to discover the complimentary town car service, as well as the multilingual business center. When hunger strikes, visitors head to the Nob Hill restaurant for regional dishes or the Lobby Lounge for light meals. Of course, no visit to San Francisco is complete without a trip to the Top of the Mark, where diners marvel at unmatched panoramas of the city. 380 rooms, 19 story. Check-in 3 pm, check-out noon. High-speed Internet access. Restaurant, bar. Fitness room. Business center. **$$$**

★ ★ ★ MARRIOTT FISHERMAN'S WHARF. *1250 Columbus Ave, San Francisco (94133). Phone 415/775-7555; toll-free 800/228-9290; fax 415/474-2099. www.marriott.com.* 285 rooms, 5 story. Pets accepted, some restrictions; fee. Check-in 4 pm, check-out noon. High-speed Internet access. Restaurant, bar. Fitness room. Business center. **$$**

★ ★ ★ OMNI HOTEL. *500 California St, San Francisco (94104). Phone 415/677-9494; toll-free 800/843-6664; fax 415/273-3038. www.omnisanfrancisco.com.* This former bank building was gutted and transformed into the Omni, a top-notch San Francisco hotel. Guest rooms are spacious, elegant, and well appointed, featuring 330-thread-count bed lines, cordless phones, and large working desks. The lobby is decorated in a Florentine Renaissance style, with Italian marble and intricate woodwork. Located in the heart of the Financial District, the hotel is a short walk to the Embarcadero and North Beach. Bob's Steak and Chop House, which opened in 2002, is on the premises. 362 rooms, 17 story. Pets accepted, some restrictions; fee. Check-in 3 pm, check-out noon. High-speed Internet access. Restaurant, bar. Fitness room. Business center. **$$**

★ ★ ★ PALACE HOTEL. *2 New Montgomery St, San Francisco (94105). Phone 415/512-1111; toll-free 888/627-7196; fax 415/243-8062. www.sfpalace.com.* The Palace Hotel is a San Francisco landmark. Opened in 1875 and designed to rival the best in Europe, this hotel has enjoyed a storied past filled with illustrious guests and exciting events. After a devastating fire, the hotel was rebuilt to exacting standards and continues to dazzle guests with its stunning architecture and luxurious details. Located downtown in the Financial District, its central location makes it ideal for business or leisure visitors. The princely accommodations are fit for modern-day kings and queens with stately furnishings and 21st-century technology. Fine dining is a signature touch, from the extraordinary, sun-filled Garden Court and the clubby Maxfield's to the serene Kyo-Ya (see). 553 rooms, 8 story. Pets accepted, some restrictions; fee. Check-in 3 pm, check-out noon. High-speed Internet access. Restaurant, bar. Fitness room, spa. Indoor pool, whirlpool. Business center. **$$$$**

★ ★ ★ PAN PACIFIC. *500 Post St, San Francisco (94102). Phone 415/771-8600; toll-free 800/533-6465; fax 415/398-0267. sanfrancisco.panpacific.com.* Located on fashionable Post Street in Union Square, this hotel is one of only two US outposts of its luxury Pacific Rim chain. The architecture and design of the public spaces and the guest rooms are Asian-inspired. The penthouse-level terrace is the highlight of the 14,000 square feet of meeting space with its panoramic views of the Bay. 329 rooms, 21 story. Pets accepted, some restrictions; fee. Check-in 3 pm, check-out noon. Restaurant, bar. Fitness room. Business center. **$$$**

★ ★ ★ ★ PARK HYATT SAN FRANCISCO. *333 Battery St, San Francisco (94111). Phone 415/392-1234; toll-free 800/233-1234; fax 415/421-2433. www.parkhyatt.com.* The Park Hyatt is a delightful hotel in the heart of San Francisco's Financial District. It is located at Embarcadero Center, where sidewalk cafés, galleries, and shops are de rigueur. Tastefully designed, the hotel is a serene haven from a hectic pace. Le Courbusier chairs add a modern flair to the lobby, while Biedermeir furnishings enhance the sophistication of the lounge. The guest rooms, done in rich shades of black and brown, emphasize comfort with goose-down duvets, plush furniture, and luxurious amenities. The on-site fitness center is convenient and fully equipped, but if you're looking for a more comprehensive choice, guests are offered admission to the adjacent Club One, one of the city's best health clubs. Two lounges offer light fare and piano entertainment, but the Park Grill, with its lovely setting and delicious continental cuisine, is a standout. 360 rooms, 24 story. Check-in 3 pm, check-out noon. High-speed Internet access. Restaurant, two bars. Fitness room. Airport transportation available. Business center. **$$**

★ ★ ★ **PRESCOTT.** *545 Post St, San Francisco (94102). Phone 415/563-0303; toll-free 866/271-3832; fax 415/563-6831. www.prescotthotel.com.* Smack in the middle of Union Square shopping is the Prescott Hotel. Guest rooms are not large, but they are comfortable, with hardwood floors and Ralph Lauren décor of coordinating fabrics; baths come stocked with Aveda shampoos and other amenities. The private, inviting club-level lounge comes equipped with a personal concierge, an evening bar service, and other extras. The adjoining Postrio restaurant (see) is part of the famed, though no longer quite as trendy, Wolfgang Puck empire. 164 rooms, 7 story. Pets accepted. Complimentary full breakfast. Check-in 3 pm, check-out noon. Restaurant, bar. Fitness room. **$$$**

★ ★ ★ **RENAISSANCE PARC 55 HOTEL.** *55 Cyril Magnin St, San Francisco (94102). Phone 415/392-8000; toll-free 800/650-7272; fax 415/403-6602. www.renaissancehotels.com.* Filling a city block with its 1,000+ guest rooms, this sand-colored high-rise is located downtown, just a half block from Market Street, one of the city's main arteries. The huge hotel offers all the guest services you would expect from an establishment of its size, with a focus on the business traveler's needs (including a free shuttle service to the Financial District). The guest rooms are handsomely finished and decorated, with gold and mauve duvets, granite-top vanities, and bay windows. 1,010 rooms, 32 story. Check-in 3 pm, check-out 1 pm. High-speed Internet access. Restaurant, bar. Fitness room. Business center. **$$**

★ ★ ★ **RENAISSANCE STANFORD COURT HOTEL.** *905 California St, San Francisco (94108). Phone 415/989-3500; toll-free 800/227-9290; fax 415/391-0513. www.renaissancehotels.com.* Located on San Francisco's esteemed Nob Hill, this grand hotel pampers its guests with elegance and superb service. From the amazing lobby dome of Tiffany-style stained glass to the Beaux Arts fountain, there is elegance and a quality of service that makes this hotel truly extraordinary. 393 rooms, 8 story. Pets accepted, some restrictions. Check-in 3 pm, check-out noon. High-speed Internet access. Restaurant, bar. Fitness room. Business center. **$$**

★ ★ ★ ★ ★ **THE RITZ-CARLTON, SAN FRANCISCO.** *600 Stockton St, San Francisco (94108). Phone 415/296-7465; toll-free 800/241-3333; fax 415/291-0288. www.ritzcarlton.com.* Housed within a majestic 1909 historic landmark, The Ritz-Carlton treats its guests to the most classically elegant accommodations available in San Francisco. This refined hotel presides over Nob Hill on a lovely tree-lined street, yet the attractions of Union Square and Chinatown are only a short distance away. Aubusson tapestries, Persian carpets, and Georgian and Regency antiques lend an aristocratic air to the public spaces, while the museum-quality collection of European and American artwork can be enjoyed throughout the hotel. The guest rooms and suites are sumptuous, defined by rich fabrics and bold colors. Club level accommodations include separate concierge service and lovely food and beverage displays five times daily. The award-winning Dining Room (see) is ideal for special occasions with its distinguished setting and artful cuisine. Other venues include The Terrace for Mediterranean specialties and the Lobby Lounge and Bar, home to the largest single malt scotch collection in the United States. 336 rooms, 9 story. Pets accepted, some restrictions; fee. Check-in 3 pm, check-out noon. High-speed Internet access, wireless Internet access. Two restaurants, three bars. Fitness room, spa. Indoor pool, whirlpool. Airport transportation available. Business center. **$$$**

★ ★ ★ **SERRANO.** *405 Taylor St, San Francisco (94102). Phone 415/885-2500; toll-free 866/289-6561; fax 415/474-4879. www.serranohotel.com.* A boutique hotel in the Theater District, the Serrano has a relatively small street entrance that belies the elaborate Spanish Revival lobby, ornate with Moorish/Spanish pillars and an intricately decorated ceiling. Inviting guest rooms boast stylish décor and a great many amenities (such as an umbrella, robes, pre-arrival turndown, high-speed Internet access, and cordless phones). The extensive guest services include a fitness center, sauna, afternoon wine tasting with complimentary shoulder massage, and tarot reading. 236 rooms. Pets accepted. Check-in 3 pm, check-out noon. High-speed Internet access. Restaurant, bar. Fitness room, spa. Business center. **$$**

★ ★ ★ **SHERATON FISHERMAN'S WHARF.** *2500 Mason St, San Francisco (94133). Phone 415/362-5500; toll-free 800/325-3535; fax 415/956-5275. www.sheratonatthewharf.com.* One block from the waterfront and close to prime touristy areas like Pier 39 and Ghirardelli Square, this hotel has four floors with six interconnected buildings. A nautical theme, in keeping with the waterfront location, pervades the public areas, both inside and out. With an attractive and relaxed atmosphere, the hotel is also attentively landscaped, with many colorful flowerbeds. Comfortable guest rooms accommodate both tourists and business travelers. Other notables include a heated outdoor pool, a large fitness center, and a manned business center. 529 rooms, 4 story. Pets accepted, some restrictions. Check-in 3 pm, check-out noon. High-speed Internet access. Restaurant, bar. Fitness room, spa. Outdoor pool. Business center. **$$**

★ ★ ★ THE WESTIN ST. FRANCIS. *335 Powell St, San Francisco (94102). Phone 415/397-7000; toll-free 800/228-3000; fax 415/774-0124. www.westin.com.* The Westin St. Francis is classic elegance defined. Opened in 1904, this hotel has played a part in much of San Francisco's history and remains one of its treasures today. Facing Union Square, this conveniently located hotel effortlessly blends the traditional with the contemporary. Rooms in the historic building are tastefully appointed with Empire-style furnishings, while the tower building's accommodations show off a modern style. Westin's signature beds and baths ensure the ultimate in comfort in both buildings. Body treatments, massages, and facials are among the offerings at the spa, and three restaurants continue the hotel's tradition of great dining. 1,195 rooms, 32 story. Pets accepted, some restrictions. Check-in 3 pm, check-out noon. High-speed Internet access. Restaurant, bar. Fitness room, spa. Business center. **$$**

★ ★ ★ W SAN FRANCISCO. *181 Third St, San Francisco (94103). Phone 415/777-5300; fax 415/817-7823. www.whotels.com.* Another chic spot in this national chain's list of hotels geared to meet the ever-increasing demands of tech-savvy business clientele. In the South of Market district and adjacent to the Museum of Modern Art, the stylishly modern rooms all contain a signature "heavenly bed." The eclectic and aptly named restaurant, XYZ (see), finishes off the dramatic three-story lobby. 423 rooms, 31 story. Pets accepted, some restrictions; fee. Check-in 3 pm, check-out noon. High-speed Internet access. Restaurant, bar. Fitness room. Indoor pool, whirlpool. Business center. **$$$$**

Specialty Lodgings

The following lodging establishments are approved by Mobil Travel Guide, but due to their unique and individualized nature have not been given a traditional Mobil Star rating. Included in this listing you may find bed-and-breakfasts, limited-service inns, guest ranches, and other unique hotel properties.

ALAMO SQUARE INN. *719 Scott St, San Francisco (94117). Phone 415/315-0123; toll-free 866/515-0123; fax 415/315-0108. www.alamoinn.com.* In an area celebrated for its historic residences, this inn (midway between Golden Gate Park and the Civic Center) comprises two restored Victorian mansions: a three-story 1895 Queen Anne and an 1896 two-story Tudor Revival. The family-owned bed-and-breakfast has several public parlors and a large dining room where guests dine on a complimentary full breakfast. Period pieces appear throughout the common areas and in the guest rooms, which range from small studio rooms to suites with Asian appointments. 15 rooms, 3 story. Complimentary full breakfast. Check-in 1 pm, check-out 11 am. **$**

ALBION HOUSE INN BED AND BREAKFAST. *135 Gough St, San Francisco (94102). Phone 415/621-0896; toll-free 800/400-8295; fax 415/621-3811. www.albionhouseinn.com.* Built in the Edwardian style in 1907, this Civic Center inn occupies the top two floors of a building once made entirely of redwood (every door still is). The inn has the look and feel of a small European lodge. While it lacks some standard amenities, like an elevator and TVs, it's big on charm and attention to detail: robes, nature "noises," earplugs, rotating original artwork, and triple sheeting. Guests can enjoy complimentary afternoon tea and evening wine and cheese. 9 rooms, 2 story. Complimentary full breakfast. Check-in 11 am, check-out 11 am. **$**

ARCHBISHOP'S MANSION. *1000 Fulton St, San Francisco (94117). Phone 415/563-7872; toll-free 800/543-5820; fax 415/885-3193. www.jdvhospitality.com.* This elegant old mansion—the former residence of the Archbishop—dating to 1904 is a beautifully maintained property with country inn charm. Located on Alamo Square near the city's famous Victorians, the hotel is an official landmark, restored in the 1980s. Common areas downstairs include a large foyer, parlor, and dining room; most of the second-floor guest rooms, each named for a famous opera, pair fireplaces and canopied beds with modern amenities. 15 rooms, 3 story. Complimentary continental breakfast. Check-in 3 pm, check-out 11:30 am. **$$**

HOTEL BOHEME. *444 Columbus Ave, San Francisco (94133). Phone 415/433-9111; fax 415/362-6292. www.hotelboheme.com.* This European-style boutique hotel is situated on the upper two floors of a midblock property on busy Columbus Avenue. The lobby is reached by a steep, narrow staircase leading from a green-canopied entry; there is no elevator. With Beat Generation heroes Allen Ginsburg and Jack Kerouac having once been residents, the hotel is a throwback to the San Francisco of the 1940s and 1950s. The small, colorful guest rooms are uniquely decorated, with armoires, sheer canopies over the beds, and coral-colored walls. 16 rooms, 3 story. Check-in 2 pm, check-out noon. **$$**

HOTEL DRISCO. *2901 Pacific Ave, San Francisco (94115). Phone 415/346-2880; toll-free 800/634-7277; fax 415/567-5537. www.hoteldrisco.com.* Visitors seeking residential-style accommodations away from the hustle and bustle book rooms at the Hotel Drisco. This century-old hotel in the exclusive residential neighborhood of Pacific Heights is sheltered from the city's frenetic pace, allowing guests to enjoy the city as if they were residents. The rooms and suites are elegantly appointed and provide luxurious amenities for business travelers and vacationers alike. Sophisticated, with a slightly romantic look, the accommodations exude relaxation. A gourmet breakfast buffet is served daily, along with afternoon tea and evening wine aperitif service. 48 rooms, 6 story. Complimentary full breakfast. Check-in 4 pm, check-out noon. Fitness room. Airport transportation available. Business center. **$$$**

HOTEL MAJESTIC. *1500 Sutter St, San Francisco (94109). Phone 415/441-1100; toll-free 800/869-8966; fax 415/673-7331. www.thehotelmajestic.com.* Sitting on the outskirts of Pacific Heights, this gracious, intimate hotel spells romance. Constructed as a private residence in 1902, the exterior's elegant Edwardian architecture complements the guest rooms, which feature canopied beds with silk spreads and fine linens; many rooms have fireplaces, too. French and English antiques are scattered throughout public spaces and guest rooms. Stop by the hotel's Avalon Bar for a cocktail, a glass of local wine, or a peek at the large butterfly collection; for a more wholesome evening, nibble on the cookie that's included in your nightly turndown service. 58 rooms, 5 story. Complimentary continental breakfast. Check-in 3 pm, check-out noon. Wireless Internet access. Bar. **$**

INN AT UNION SQUARE. *440 Post St, San Francisco (94102). Phone 415/397-3510; toll-free 800/288-4346; fax 415/989-0529. www.unionsquare.com.* This small inn on the northwest corner of Union Square offers a cozy atmosphere in an ideal San Francisco location. The lobby is small and simple, guest rooms have traditional décor in greens and muted pastels, and every room has fresh seasonal flowers. Each floor has a small sitting area where guests can enjoy continental breakfast and the complimentary morning newspaper. In an unusual twist, the staff does not accept tips. 30 rooms, 6 story. Complimentary continental breakfast. Check-in 3 pm, check-out noon. Bar. **$$**

INN SAN FRANCISCO. *943 S Van Ness Ave, San Francisco (94110). Phone 415/641-0188; toll-free 800/359-0913; fax 415/641-1701. www.innsf.com.* Occupying two Victorian-era mansions, one an Italianate-style built in 1872 and the other built in 1905, this Mission District bed-and-breakfast inn offers an intimate stay in an urban setting. The elegant guest rooms, each one unique in size, shape, and décor, are lovingly appointed with fresh flowers, antique furnishings, and feather beds; some with fireplaces and canopied beds. Outside, you'll find an English garden and a gazebo complete with a hot tub; on the top floor is a sundeck. 21 rooms, 3 story. Complimentary full breakfast. Check-in 2 pm, check-out noon. Whirlpool. **$$**

JACKSON COURT. *2198 Jackson St, San Francisco (94115). Phone 415/929-7670; fax 415/929-1405. www.jacksoncourt.com.* A former residence that was built in 1900, Jackson Court is a three-story red brick building in tony Pacific Heights, with an arched entrance and an attractive, flower-filled courtyard. The inn's ten guest rooms vary in size, furnishings, and décor. Four of the rooms have working fireplaces, and many have sitting areas, bookshelves, and private decks. Breakfast is served in a kitchen nook on the second floor, and there are two sitting rooms on the ground floor. 10 rooms, 3 story. Complimentary continental breakfast. Check-in 2 pm, check-out 11 am. **$$**

MARINA INN. *3110 Octavia St, San Francisco (94123). Phone 415/928-1000; toll-free 800/274-1420; fax 415/928-5909. www.marinainn.com.* Staking out a corner spot on busy Lombard Street in the Marina District in a restored 1928 building, the Marina Inn provides good value and a convenient location for a no-nonsense clientele. Relatively simple rooms have a pleasant English country décor, with pine poster beds and floral bedspreads; be warned that the bathrooms are tiny. A complimentary continental breakfast is served in the sitting area on the second floor. Chestnut and Union streets shopping is close by, as is the lush and scenic Marina Green. 40 rooms, 4 story. Complimentary continental breakfast. Check-in 2 pm, check-out noon. **$**

NOB HILL LAMBOURNE. *725 Pine St, San Francisco (94108). Phone 415/433-2287; toll-free 800/274-8466; fax 415/433-0975. www.nobhilllambourne.com.* In a residential section of Nob Hill, this European-style boutique hotel is a short walk from Union Square and Chinatown. It's a chic, intimate three-story hotel with an emphasis on healthful living: the contents of the minibar are organic, the continental breakfast is healthy, the housekeeping staff uses chemical-free cleaning products, and vitamins accompany the nightly turndown service. Guest rooms have a contemporary look; offer plenty of space and comfort for work or relaxation; and feature CD players, down comforters, kitchenettes, fax machines, and two-line phones. Other enticements include a spa treatment room and a free wine and cheese reception. 20 rooms, 3 story. Complimentary continental breakfast. Check-in 3 pm, check-out noon. High-speed Internet access. Spa. **$$**

UNION STREET INN. *2229 Union St, San Francisco (94123). Phone 415/346-0424; fax 415/922-8046. www.unionstreetinn.com.* 6 rooms. Complimentary full breakfast. Check-in 2 pm, check-out noon. **$$**

WASHINGTON SQUARE INN. *1660 Stockton St, San Francisco (94133). Phone 415/981-4220; toll-free 800/388-0220; fax 415/397-7242.* In the heart of North Beach facing Washington Square Park, this intimate inn is a breath of fresh air compared to mammoth downtown hotels, yet it is also well situated for strolling and people-watching. The inn has a lobby with polished hardwood floors, a fireplace, and antique furniture. Guest rooms are individually decorated and furnished with French and English antiques, along with down bedding and abundant fresh flowers. Breakfast is served in your room, and in the afternoon the inn hosts a wine and hors d'oeuvres reception. 15 rooms, 2 story. Complimentary continental breakfast. Check-in 2 pm, check-out 11 am. **$$**

WHITE SWAN INN. *845 Bush St, San Francisco (94108). Phone 415/775-1755; toll-free 800/999-9510; fax 415/775-5717. www.whiteswaninnsf.com.* 26 rooms. Complimentary full breakfast. Check-in 3 pm, check-out noon. Fitness room. **$$**

Restaurants

★ ★ A. SABELLA'S. *2766 Taylor St, San Francisco (94133). Phone 415/771-6775; fax 415/771-6777. www.asabellas.com.* The Fisherman's Wharf location of this restaurant offers sweeping views of the bay through arched windows. Fresh local seafood and Dungeness crab go "from tank to table," and the restaurant offers new twists on the traditional seafood offerings of the area. Seafood menu. Dinner. Closed Thanksgiving, Dec 25. Bar. Children's menu. **$$$**

★ ACE WASABI'S ROCK AND ROLL SUSHI. *3339 Steiner St, San Francisco (94123). Phone 415/567-4903; fax 415/749-1873.* Japanese menu. Dinner. Closed holidays. Bar. **$$**

★ ★ ★ ACQUERELLO. *1722 Sacramento St, San Francisco (94109). Phone 415/567-5432; fax 415/567-6432. www.acquerello.com.* Consistently garnering high points for its northern Italian cuisine, Acquerello, which means "watercolor" in Italian, does much for the palate. The restaurant is housed in a former chapel, and it has maintained its high-arched ceiling with exposed wood beams. Suzette Gresham's rustic cuisine, along with an extensive and carefully selected wine list, launched Acquerello onto *Wine Spectator's* top 10 list for America's best Italian restaurants. Specialties include house-made pasta with foie gras and black truffles. Italian menu. Dinner. Closed Sun-Mon; holidays. **$$$**

★ ALEGRIA'S FOODS FROM SPAIN. *2018 Lombard St, San Francisco (94123). Phone 415/929-8888; fax 415/929-9215. www.alegrias.citysearch.com.* Spanish menu. Dinner. Closed holidays. Bar. Children's menu. **$$**

★ ★ **ANJOU.** *44 Campton Pl, San Francisco (94108). Phone 415/392-5373.* French menu. Lunch, dinner. Closed Sun-Mon; holidays. Bar. **$$**

★ ★ **ANNABELLE'S BAR AND BISTRO.** *68 Fourth St, San Francisco (94103). Phone 415/777-1200; fax 415/357-6238. www.annabelles.net.* A block south of Market Street, this bistro is located near Yerba Buena Gardens and the Sony Metreon. Two small dining rooms have been serving American cuisine like classic Caesar salads, rotisserie chicken, steaks, burgers, and pasta dishes for many years. California menu. Lunch, dinner. Closed holidays. Bar. Reservations recommended. **$$**

★ **ANTICA TRATTORIA.** *2400 Polk St, San Francisco (94109). Phone 415/928-5797; fax 415/928-2828.* Italian menu. Dinner. Closed Mon; holidays. Children's menu. **$$**

★ ★ ★ **ANZU.** *222 Mason St, San Francisco (94102). Phone 415/394-1100; fax 415/394-1179. www.restaurantanzu.com.* An elegant addition to the Hotel Nikko (see), Anzu blends East and West with house specialties of fine sushi and prime cuts of beef, with a Tokyo-trained master sushi chef steering the full-service sushi bar. The restaurant perches on a balcony overlooking the hotel's unusual lobby, and showcases works by local artists. Like the hotel, the crowd is a mix of international travelers and domestic visitors. Anzu also has a cocktail lounge and bar seating where visitors can try an array of sake cocktails. International, sushi menu. Breakfast, lunch, dinner, Sun brunch. Bar. Children's menu. **$$$**

★ ★ ★ ★ **AQUA.** *252 California St, San Francisco (94111). Phone 415/956-9662; fax 415/956-5229. www.aqua-sf.com.* Power brokers, deal makers, deal breakers and their lawyers, and assorted well-dressed media moguls frequent Aqua, a sophisticated, sleek, "it" spot for contemporary seafood. The spare, modern, ochre-toned dining room is decorated with towering floral arrangements and large mirrors that reflect the high-powered crowd. Luxurious ingredients like caviar, oysters, foie gras, and ahi tuna mingle with rarer creatures of the sea, such as Japanese hamachi and Alaskan black cod. But Aqua isn't all glitz and glamour. Diners also find modern comfort food on the menu; the kitchen's signature is a bubbly potpie made from a 1 1/2-pound Maine lobster. Indeed, there is a dish for every culinary temperament at Aqua. Using a blend of classic European cooking techniques, the chef is a master of perfect-pitch cooking, bringing the riches of the ocean together in striking harmony on the plate. Seafood menu. Lunch, dinner. Bar. Business casual attire. Reservations recommended. Valet parking. **$$$**

★ ★ **ASIA SF.** *201 Ninth St, San Francisco (94103). Phone 415/255-2742; fax 415/255-8887. www.asiasf.com.* Everything at this loud SoMa spot plays second fiddle to the show, which consists of dancing and entertainment—by men dressed as women—in the downstairs lounge. Asia SF is more of a bar with food than an actual restaurant, with gender-bending waiters in heels navigating around the red-tile bar in the center of the room that takes up much of the floor space. California, Pan-Asian menu. Dinner. Bar. **$$**

★ ★ ★ **AZIE.** *826 Folsom St, San Francisco (94107). Phone 415/538-0918. www.restaurantlulu.com.* This SoMa spot, a sister restaurant to nearby Lulu, has lowered its prices since the dot-com crash, but certainly not its high standards. The renovated warehouse now has dark wood and a dramatic, intimate interior; some booths have their own curtains. Dishes, served on unusual, colorful glass plates, range from an extensive appetizer list of iron skillet spicy prawns and moules frites to entrées like miso monkfish and tandoori steak. The concept of exotic Asian flavors with a classic French influence is executed well. French, Asian menu. Dinner. Closed July 4, Dec 25. Bar. Valet parking. **$$$**

★ ★ ★ **BACAR RESTAURANT AND WINE SALON.** *448 Brannan St, San Francisco (94107). Phone 415/904-4100; fax 415/904-4113. www.bacarsf.com.* South of Market district's stylish Bacar spreads out in one vast loft to combine a stylish wine bar/lounge and an upscale restaurant under one roof without shortchanging either. The cozy confines of the lower level house the bar, a great spot to sip a pinot noir from a leather armchair before dinner. Then proceed upstairs to a booth in the vast dining room of soaring ceilings and exposed-brick walls. The exhibition kitchen provides a focal point, issuing such wine-friendly food as duck and foie gras sausage, wok-roasted mussels, roast rack of lamb, and honey-cured king salmon. Plenty of appetizers, by-the-glass pours, and wine flights encourage sampling. The convivial setting makes for good group gatherings. American, California menu. Lunch Fri, dinner daily. Casual attire. Reservations recommended. **$$$**

★ **BAKER STREET BISTRO.** *2953 Baker St, San Francisco (94123). Phone 415/931-1475; fax 415/931-7489. bakerstbistro.citysearch.com.* Near the Presidio in Cow Hollow, this tiny but popular neighborhood French bistro draws customers from all over the city. With only about 15 tables and basic furnishings and décor, the restaurant relies on its excellent "bang-for-the-buck" factor. The menu, which changes daily, comprises a handful of entrées and a solid wine list. French bistro menu. Lunch, dinner, brunch. Reservations recommended. Outdoor seating. **$$**

★ ★ BALBOA CAFE. *3199 Fillmore St, San Francisco (94123). Phone 415/921-3944; fax 415/921-3957. www.plumpjack.com.* This American bistro in Cow Hollow has a lively lunch crowd and after-work clientele. A traditional long bar meanders along one wall of the long, narrow space, which also boasts brass rails, wood paneling, old-style hanging light fixtures, and eclectic artwork. It's a popular gathering place for reasonably priced drinks and comfort food. American menu. Lunch, dinner, brunch. Bar. Children's menu. **$$$**

★ ★ BASIL. *1175 Folsom St, San Francisco (94103). Phone 415/552-8999; fax 415/552-8889. www.basilthai.com.* Located in a commercial, not-super-attractive part of SoMa, this small, hip Thai restaurant is off the beaten path and home to great cuisine that changes seasonally. The narrow dining room has contemporary décor and furnishings with Asian touches: hardwood floors, bamboo plants, framed cartoon art, a small Asian fountain, and pale yellow walls. Thai menu. Lunch, dinner. Bar. **$$**

★ ★ BETELNUT PEJIU WU. *2030 Union St, San Francisco (94123). Phone 415/929-8855; fax 414/929-8894. www.betelnutrestaurant.com.* Exotic drinks, a hopping bar and lounge scene, and delicious pan-Asian cuisine reel in 20- and 30-somethings in a steady stream. The red lacquer bar, Chinese lanterns, and muted lighting set the right tone at this ever-popular Cow Hollow destination. If you don't make reservations, prepare for a long wait. Pan-Asian menu. Lunch, dinner, late-night. Closed Thanksgiving, Dec 25. Bar. Outdoor seating. **$$**

★ ★ ★ BIG 4. *1075 California St, San Francisco (94108). Phone 415/771-1140; fax 415/474-6227. www.huntingtonhotel.com.* Part of the elegant Huntington Hotel (see), this bar/restaurant caters to an upscale, upper-crust crowd; the name itself is a reference to Nob Hill's four favorite tycoons. Sink into a green leather armchair and dive into American cuisine with a chicken potpie or a Cobb salad, or choose from spa menu items like fish tacos and mixed field greens with roasted soy nuts and feta. Dark wood, historic prints, and etched glass tables fill the bar area, along with a grand piano; most nights feature a pianist tickling the ivories. American menu. Breakfast, lunch, dinner, Sun brunch. Bar. Valet parking. **$$$**

★ BISCUITS AND BLUES. *401 Mason St, San Francisco (94102). Phone 415/292-2583; fax 415/292-4701. www.biscuitsandbluessf.com.* Billed as the first blues club in the United States, this lively spot in downtown San Francisco serves food in its quarters below street level. Nightly live blues entertainment takes place in a dark, unadorned room. The music complements the Southern cuisine—catfish, fried chicken, and jambalaya. Sip a New Orleans iced tea or a Southern punch and let the music take you on a journey below the Mason-Dixon line. Southern menu. Dinner, late-night. Closed Thanksgiving, Dec 25. Bar. Casual attire. **$$**

★ ★ BISTRO AIX. *3340 Steiner St, San Francisco (94123). Phone 415/202-0100; fax 415/202-0153. www.bistroaix.com.* French menu. Dinner. Children's menu. **$$$**

★ ★ ★ BIX. *56 Gold St, San Francisco (94133). Phone 415/433-6300; fax 415/433-4574. www.bixrestaurant.com.* Tucked away on an alley in the Financial District, Bix is a throwback to an earlier era, with its speakeasy atmosphere and nightly jazz music setting the tone. A traditional mahogany bar runs the length of the restaurant, and it's typically packed with an older (translation: hipsters in their 30s and 40s) crowd. The main dining room is downstairs, though there's also balcony seating. The menu, which changes weekly, features classic American dishes like chicken hash and a fancy burger with frites; tuxedoed waiters do your bidding. American, California menu. Lunch Fri, dinner. Closed holidays. Bar. Valet parking. **$$$**

★ ★ ★ BOULEVARD. *1 Mission St, San Francisco (94105). Phone 415/543-6084; fax 415/495-2936. www.boulevardrestaurant.com.* Housed in the 1889 French-style Audiffred Building on San Francisco's waterfront, Boulevard has been a steady favorite for contemporary American cuisine since its doors opened in 1993. Created in partnership with designer Pat Kuleto, Boulevard is decorated in classic Belle Époque style, and the stunning room is warmed by the delicious aromas of chef Nancy Oakes' fabulous home cooking. Serving simple but inspired food that speaks directly to the heart and soul, Oakes is known for her innovative, earthy cooking style. The menu offers up-to-the-minute modern riffs on classic American plates alongside Mediterranean and Asian dishes accented with native Californian ingredients. Sporting glorious bay views and an open kitchen, Boulevard is a great choice for sophisticated yet comfortable San Francisco dining. American menu. Lunch, dinner, late-night. Closed holidays. Bar. Valet parking. **$$$**

★ **CAFE KATI.** *1963 Sutter St, San Francisco (94115). Phone 415/775-7313; fax 415/379-9952. www.cafekati.com.* Eclectic menu. Dinner. Closed Mon; holidays. Valet parking. **$$**

★ ★ **CAFE TIRAMISU.** *28 Belden Pl, San Francisco (94104). Phone 415/421-7044; fax 415/421-3009.* On pedestrian-only Belden Place in the Financial District, this café has a Tuscany-like taupe façade and numerous outdoor, European-style tables. Whether you're eating in the main dining room, the cozy downstairs space, or on the attractive alley, the place is always bustling, pleasing customers with northern Italian pastas, meat dishes, and seafood options. Italian menu. Lunch, dinner. Closed Sun; holidays. Outdoor seating. **$$**

★ ★ ★ ★ **CAMPTON PLACE DINING ROOM.** *340 Stockton St, San Francisco (94108). Phone 415/955-5555; toll-free 800/235-4300; fax 415/955-5559. www.camptonplace.com.* Elegance, luxury, and grace are the hallmarks of the Campton Place Dining Room, yet the restaurant remains warm and comfortable; any sense of pretension is left by the wayside. The contemporary, urban dining room is bathed in golden light and accented smartly with natural, earth-toned walls; wood floors; deep, soft, tan fabric-covered banquettes; and vaulted ceilings. You'll find an innovative menu that focuses on the robust cuisine of Gascony and the Basque country, created with the season's most pristine ingredients and with impeccable attention to detail. Dishes are light but full of flavor, complex but balanced, and each bite is a delicious adventure, making this restaurant a haven for discerning foodies as well as those who just love to eat. French, Mediterranean menu. Breakfast, lunch, dinner, Sun brunch. Bar. Children's menu. Business casual attire. Valet parking. **$$$**

★ ★ ★ **CARNELIAN ROOM.** *555 California St, San Francisco (94104). Phone 415/433-7500; fax 415/433-5827. www.carnelianroom.com.* Location, location, location. No matter what they serve here (and it happens to be contemporary American fare and expensive cocktails), it would be secondary to the view of the bay, the bridges, and the city. Located on the 52nd floor of downtown's Bank of America building, the Carnelian Room draws crowds for its compelling and spectacular vistas. The décor is formal—think wood, antiques, and old-world artwork—and the service is impeccable. American menu. Dinner, Sun brunch. Closed holidays. Bar. Children's menu. Jacket required. Reservations recommended. **$$$**

★ **CHA CHA CHA.** *1801 Haight St, San Francisco (94117). Phone 415/386-7670; fax 415/386-0417. www.cha3.com.* This popular Upper Haight restaurant packs 'em in—even during off-hours—for Caribbean- and Cuban-style tapas. The décor is festive and casual, with cement floors, bright vinyl tablecloths, and voodoo altars. Small plates include Jamaican jerk chicken, fried new potatoes, and Cajun shrimp. Don't expect many romantic moments here: Caribbean music plays at a lively volume. Caribbean, Cuban menu. Lunch, dinner, late-night. Closed Dec 25. Casual attire. **$$**

★ ★ ★ **CHAYA.** *132 The Embarcadero, San Francisco (94105). Phone 415/777-8688; fax 415/247-9952. www.thechaya.com.* French, Japanese fusion menu. Lunch, dinner. Closed holidays. Bar. Outdoor seating. **$$$**

★ ★ **CHIC'S SEAFOOD.** *Pier 39, San Francisco (94133). Phone 415/421-2442; fax 415/983-3764. www.chicsseafood.com.* This casual seafood restaurant catering to tourists takes advantage of its waterfront location on the second deck of Pier 39. Chic's maximizes its impressive vistas with large windows that provide a panoramic view of the San Francisco Bay, Alcatraz, and the Golden Gate Bridge. One menu highlight, as expected, is fresh mesquite-grilled fish. Sip a cocktail at the marble-topped bar if there's a wait. Seafood menu. Breakfast, lunch, dinner. Bar. Children's menu. **$$**

★ ★ **CHOW.** *215 Church St, San Francisco (94114). Phone 415/552-2469; fax 415/552-8629.* Serving casual, reasonably priced American fare on the edge of the Castro District, Chow swarms with impatient diners eager to sample the kitchen's dishes made with fresh, seasonal ingredients. A long bar/counter at the front of the restaurant adds to the hustle and bustle, as does the click-clack on wood floors and tables. A shady rear patio extends the seating options in fair weather. American menu. Lunch, dinner, brunch. Closed Thanksgiving, Dec 25. Children's menu. Casual attire. Outdoor seating. **$**

★ **DAVID'S.** *474 Geary St, San Francisco (94102). Phone 415/276-5950; fax 415/276-5953.* A longtime San Francisco institution just a few blocks from Union Square, this Jewish deli has been in its current location, and under the same ownership, for more than 50 years. Counter seating and unadorned tables also haven't changed much. The restaurant offers New York-style Jewish deli fare like knishes, kugel, and piled-high sandwiches on rye. Jewish deli menu. Breakfast, lunch, dinner. Closed Jewish high holidays. Casual attire. Outdoor seating. **$$**

★ ★ DELFINA. *3621 18th St, San Francisco (94110). Phone 415/552-4055; fax 415/552-4095. www.delfinasf.com.* More than a bustling neighborhood trattoria, chef-owned Delfina serves award-winning seasonal Italian fare with an emphasis on fresh-from-the-farmers'-market ingredients. The setting, in the increasingly gentrified Mission District, is modern, lively, and cheerful, with pale yellow walls, rotating local artwork, wood floors and chairs, and an open kitchen. Though the menu changes daily, the grilled fresh calamari with warm white bean salad is a house specialty. Other dishes may include gnocchi with morels and English peas or halibut with fennel, olives, and aioli. Italian menu. Dinner. Outdoor seating. **$$**

★ ★ ★ ★ ★ THE DINING ROOM. *600 Stockton St, San Francisco (94108). Phone 415/296-7465; toll-free 800/241-3333; fax 415/291-0288. www.ritzcarlton.com.* Located in a 1909 Nob Hill landmark, just minutes from Union Square shopping, The Dining Room at The Ritz-Carlton, San Francisco (see) sets the standard in elegant dining. Romance is the order of the day in this dining room set with floral accents, large murals, and widely spaced tables topped with polished silver, Frette linens, fresh flowers, and tall, slim candles. Adding to the ambience is a harpist who weaves romance in the form of song. Guests are greeted with a champagne cart to start the meal (this is so much fun that other restaurants might want to clone it), followed by a flawless meal of contemporary French fare—fresh fish, meats, game, and poultry are on hand. Guests have the option of ordering the tasting menu or their choice of three, four, or five courses from the regular menu, and the genial sommelier will skillfully present wines to pair with your selections if you like. If you still have room, you can indulge in a wonderful selection of farmhouse cheeses after dinner. French, American menu. Dinner. Closed Sun-Mon. Bar. Valet parking. **$$$$**

★ DOTTIE'S TRUE BLUE CAFE. *522 Jones St, San Francisco (94102). Phone 415/885-2767; fax 415/885-0834.* American menu. Breakfast, lunch. Closed Tues-Wed. **$**

★ ★ ★ EASTERN & ORIENT TRADING CO. *314 Sutter St, San Francisco (94108). Phone 415/693-0303; fax 415/693-9137. www.eotrading.com.* On the edge of the Financial District, conveniently located next to the large Stockton-Sutter parking garage, this sleek fusion restaurant specializes in Southeast Asian cuisine. The contemporary Asian motif plays out in the restaurant's décor—long bamboo-rimmed bar and artifacts such as face masks and lanterns—and on the menu, which includes dishes like Indonesian corn fritters, Malaysian lamb shank, and tiger prawns satay. The cellar brewery provides microbrew beer in addition to an extensive list of wine and cocktails; the after-work crowd often imbibes. Pan-Asian menu. Lunch, dinner. **$$**

★ EL TOREADOR. *50 W Portal, San Francisco (94127). Phone 415/566-2673; fax 415/566-1214.* In the quiet West Portal area, El Toreador livens things up with its festive atmosphere. This is a popular, inexpensive Mexican destination with cheerful décor—wood tables and chairs in a variety of colors and painted designs, and Mexican-themed knickknacks adorning the walls and hanging from the ceiling. Mexican music and funky mood lighting seal in the flavor. Mexican menu. Lunch, dinner. Closed Mon; Easter,Thanksgiving, Dec 25. Children's menu. Casual attire. **$$**

★ ELIZA'S. *1457 18th St, San Francisco (94107). Phone 415/648-9999.* This neighborhood Chinese restaurant in Potrero Hill features such Hunan and Mandarin specialties as spicy eggplant, Hunan salmon, and Peking duck. The décor mixes Asian artifacts, large potted palms, and pink tablecloths with blown-glass objects d'art and large modern paintings. Dishes are delightfully free of MSG and excessive oil. Chinese menu. Lunch, dinner. Closed Thanksgiving, Dec 25. Bar. **$$**

★ ★ EMPRESS OF CHINA. *838 Grant Ave, San Francisco (94108). Phone 415/434-1345; fax 415/986-1187. www.empressofchinasf.com.* Presiding over Grant Avenue in Chinatown for almost 40 years, this landmark has played host to a parade of politicians and celebrities. The restaurant, on the sixth floor of the China Trade Center, treats visitors to views of Coit Tower and the Bay Bridge. Elaborate decorations include a flower garden, ornately carved wooden screens, and Chinese artwork. Alas, the ambience surpasses the food. Chinese menu. Lunch, dinner. Bar. **$$$**

★★ ENRICO'S SIDEWALK CAFE. *504 Broadway, San Francisco (94133). Phone 415/982-6223; fax 415/397-7244. www.enricossidewalkcafe.com.* This supper club—in the heart North Beach's safe but seedy strip club row—has offered outdoor dining and nightly jazz entertainment since 1958. Inside, you'll find energy and contemporary décor, with a large bar stretching along one wall, and framed posters of international films elsewhere. The Mediterranean cuisine has Italian and Spanish influences, and the mojitos are delicious, but potent. California, Mediterranean menu. Lunch, dinner. Closed Thanksgiving, Dec 25. Bar. Outdoor seating. **$$$**

★★ EOS. *901 Cole St, San Francisco (94117). Phone 415/566-3063; fax 415/566-2663. www.eossf.com.* Eclectic, Asian menu. Dinner. Closed holidays. Bar. **$$**

★★★ FARALLON. *450 Post St, San Francisco (94102). Phone 415/956-6969; fax 415/834-1234. www.farallonrestaurant.com.* Dinner as theater is the name of the game in this upscale downtown restaurant, with both menu and atmosphere featuring an over-the-top "under the sea" theme. Pat Kuleto designed the unique space, with its porthole windows, nautical scenes, mosaic mural ceiling, shell-patterned chairs, and jellyfish chandeliers. The menu changes daily, with options like house-made caviar, pan-roasted king salmon, Rhode Island striped bass, and oysters on the half shell; grilled filet of beef and a few other nonseafood items are also available. Seafood menu. Lunch, dinner. Closed holidays. Bar. Valet parking. **$$$**

★ FATTOUSH. *1361 Church St, San Francisco (94114). Phone 415/641-0678; fax 415/641-0557. www.fattoush.com.* This Palestinian-owned neighborhood-style restaurant in a 1903 building cooks up Middle Eastern fare in a Noe Valley locale. Dine on dishes like sabanech (lamb shank with spinach and garbanzo beans) and mashwi (skewers of prawns and sea bass) at the colorful wood tables, which are enhanced by cushions and other Arabic touches. The ivy-covered rear patio is open when the weather permits. Middle Eastern menu. Lunch, dinner, brunch. Closed Dec 25. Outdoor seating. **$$**

★★★★ FIFTH FLOOR. *12 Fourth St, San Francisco (94103). Phone 415/348-1555; fax 415/348-1551. www.hotelpalomar.com.* Intimate and sleek, the Fifth Floor is a devilishly charming, urban dining room with deep burgundy curtains, camel-and-black zebra-printed carpets, and black leather chairs. The modern French menu, which changes with the seasons, is as sophisticated and seductive as the space. Cleverly divided between Ocean, Field and Forest, Farm, and Black Truffle (for spring), the kitchen delights in playing with the contrast between textures, temperatures, and spices, flirting with opposites until culinary balance is deliciously achieved. Dining here is an epic experience marked by extraordinary, artful cuisine; service that is in tune with your every need; and a wine list that spans the globe. French menu. Dinner. Closed Sun. Bar. Business casual attire. Reservations recommended. Valet parking. **$$$**

★★ FIGARO. *414 Columbus Ave, San Francisco (94133). Phone 415/398-1300; fax 415/398-8845. www.figaroristorante.com.* On the main artery in North Beach, Figaro has a lovely rear patio and contemporary Italian touches: large posterlike paintings on the walls, red tile flooring, faux marble tabletops, a long mahogany bar, and an eye-catching ceiling painting. The self-proclaimed "house of gnocchi" also whips up a tasty tiramisu. Italian menu. Lunch, dinner. Bar. Outdoor seating. **$$**

★★ FINO. *624 Post St, San Francisco (94109). Phone 415/928-2080; fax 415/928-6919. www.andrewshotel.com.* A contemporary Italian *ristorante* in downtown San Francisco, Fino is housed in the Andrews Hotel, a boutique hotel near Union Square. The dining room features a large traditional mahogany bar, modern artwork, and a fireplace in the back room. Classic Italian favorites appear on the appealing menu, including minestrone, carpaccio, and an array of veal and chicken dishes. Italian menu. Dinner. Closed holidays. Bar. **$$**

★ FIREFLY. *4288 24th St, San Francisco (94114). Phone 415/821-7652; fax 415/821-5812. www.fireflyrestaurant.com.* After more than a decade in business, this chef-owned restaurant in Noe Valley still pleases with its eclectic American fare. The imaginative menu may include such dishes as sautéed monkfish with saffron fennel broth or black lentil and kale soup. An artistically sculpted firefly greets patrons as they enter, but the furnishings and décor are simple. American menu. Dinner. Closed holidays. Casual attire. **$$**

★★ FIRST CRUSH. *101 Cyril Magnin St, San Francisco (94102). Phone 415/982-7874; fax 415/982-7800. www.firstcrush.com.* Serving a gourmet French-American menu downtown, First Crush is popular with the after-work crowd for its extensive

California-only wine list. Alas, the wine list and the remodeled interior win more raves than the menu, which includes everything from crab cakes and foie gras to pork tenderloin and rib eye steak. California, French menu. Dinner, late-night. Bar. **$$**

★ ★ ★ ★ **FLEUR DE LYS.** *777 Sutter St, San Francisco (94109). Phone 415/673-7779; fax 415/673-4619.* The dramatic tented main dining room is awash in saffron and black-cherry tones and decorated with magnificent floral creations. Chef/owner Hubert Keller is in the kitchen and thriving in his space. The art of food is taken seriously here, and the menu is haute gastronomy. Plates pop with flavor and tend to resemble curated works of art. The service is friendly, knowledgeable, and attentive to every last detail. French menu. Dinner. Closed Sun. Bar. Business casual attire. Reservations recommended. Valet parking. **$$$**

★ ★ **FOG CITY DINER.** *1300 Battery St, San Francisco (94111). Phone 415/982-2000; fax 415/982-3711. www.fogcitydiner.com.* Though it's situated along the Embarcadero, Fog City Diner is more reminiscent of a train than a boat, with its long interior space and chrome décor. Both locals and tourists hunker down in the inviting booths for the California fusion fare, which ranges from meat loaf and ribs to ethnic dishes like quesadillas and mu shu pork burritos. The raw oyster bar is also a popular draw. California menu. Lunch, dinner, brunch. Closed Thanksgiving, Dec 25. Bar. Children's menu. Outdoor seating. **$$**

★ **FOREIGN CINEMA.** *2534 Mission St, San Francisco (94110). Phone 415/648-7600; fax 415/648-7669. www.foreigncinema.com.* Walk down a candlelit corridor to reach the main dining area of this trendy Mission District restaurant and nightspot. The establishment earns its name for the nightly foreign films that are projected onto a white brick wall in the courtyard, which is covered and heated in winter. French, Mediterranean menu. Dinner, brunch. Closed holidays. **$$**

★ ★ **FRANCISCAN.** *Pier 43 1/2 Embarcadero, San Francisco (94133). Phone 415/362-7733; fax 415/362-0174. www.franciscanrestaurant.com.* Fresh fish and crab cakes are the draw at this restaurant in touristy Fisherman's Wharf serving contemporary California cuisine. Tables boast wide-angle views of San Francisco Bay, and the dining and bar areas offer tiered seating to provide patrons with unencumbered vistas. Soft jazz and old photographs of the waterfront accompany seafood standards like spicy calamari, cracked crab, snapper, and grilled salmon (the fish, they claim, is caught the day you eat it from boats based in the Wharf). Seafood menu. Lunch, dinner. Closed Thanksgiving, Dec 25. Bar. Children's menu. Outdoor seating. **$$$**

★ ★ **FRASCATI.** *1901 Hyde St, San Francisco (94109). Phone 415/928-1406; fax 415/928-1983. www.frascatisf.com.* A charming, intimate Russian Hill restaurant, Frascati serves regional Italian food with the occasional French flair to both neighborhood folks and more distant city dwellers. The menu features a wine of the day, the artisanal cheese course, and meat and fish dishes like pan-roasted Atlantic salmon with caramelized shallots or roasted pork tenderloin with bacon mashed potatoes. Friendly waiters easily navigate the two levels of dining. Cab here, if possible, as parking is terrible; request a window seat to watch the cable cars breeze by. Mediterranean menu. Dinner. Closed July 4, Thanksgiving, Dec 25. Valet parking. Outdoor seating. **$$**

★ ★ **FRINGALE.** *570 Fourth St, San Francisco (94107). Phone 415/543-0573; fax 415/905-0317. www.fringalerestaurant.com.* This romantic, intimate French bistro in SoMa has only 20 tables and a semi-circular bar squeezed into its small, attractive dining space, with freshly painted yellow walls decorated with modern art. Located near China Basin and Pac Bell Park, the chef-owned restaurant features French cuisine with a Basque influence, and an extensive dessert menu. French menu. Lunch, dinner. Closed Sun; holidays. Bar. Reservations recommended. **$$**

★ ★ ★ ★ ★ **GARY DANKO.** *800 North Point St, San Francisco (94109). Phone 415/749-2060; fax 415/775-1805. www.garydanko.com.* Bathed in blond wood, filled with artistic floral arrangements, and swathed in serene amber light, restaurant Gary Danko is a sophisticated and civilized culinary destination. From the minute you enter this stunning room, you will understand that dining here—a heavenly experience—is about elegance, luxury, and excessive comfort. Mr. Danko, the chef and owner of this distinctive restaurant, has the rare ability to make diners swoon with his refined menu of museum-worthy dishes, each one featuring pristine seasonal ingredients prepared with classic French technique. Signature dishes include roast lobster, foie gras, and lamb loin, each prepared with changing accompaniments as Mother Nature dictates. The 1,500-bottle wine cellar offers an exceptional selection of grand vintages as well as coveted wines from small producers. Gary

Danko is a mesmerizing wonderland for lovers of food, wine, and charming elegance. American menu. Dinner. Closed holidays. Bar. Reservations recommended. Valet parking. **$$$$**

★★ **GAYLORD INDIA.** *900 North Point St, San Francisco (94109). Phone 415/771-8822; fax 415/771-4980. www.gaylords.com.* On the third floor of Ghirardelli Square, the acclaimed Indian restaurant has expansive views of the Bay and the Marin Headlands. Distinct Indian influences show up in fabrics and artwork, and with the Indian music that plays in the background. Notice the tandoori oven behind glass near the front entrance; classic dishes like prawn vindaloo and chicken masala appear on the menu. Indian menu. Lunch, dinner. Closed Thanksgiving, Dec 25. **$$**

★★ **GLOBE.** *290 Pacific, San Francisco (94111). Phone 415/391-4132; fax 415/391-4198.* An energetic Financial District destination serving American-Italian fare, Globe stays open late, thus earning it a reputation as a favorite stop for chefs after they close their own restaurants. Two skylights add a bright, sunny glow to the restaurant's industrial décor: a zinc-topped bar and counter and exposed-brick walls with frequently changing artwork. California, Italian menu. Lunch, dinner, late-night. Closed Thanksgiving, Dec 24-25. Bar. Outdoor seating. **$$**

★★★ **GRAND CAFE.** *501 Geary St, San Francisco (94102). Phone 415/292-0101; fax 415/292-0150. www.grandcafe-sf.com.* Truly grand in both scale and style, this brasserie attracts a pre- and post-theater crowd in its corner Theater District location in the Hotel Monaco (see). High ceilings, ornate moldings, and large sculptures add to the fanciful and unique setting. The seasonal French bistro menu may include fresh oysters, oven-roasted half chicken, and bouillabaisse; the menu—and equally friendly service—is also available in the spacious bar area. French bistro menu. Breakfast, lunch, dinner, late-night, brunch. Closed July 4, Thanksgiving, Dec 25. Bar. Children's menu. Valet parking. **$$**

★ **GRANDEHO'S KAMEKYO.** *2721 Hyde St, San Francisco (94109). Phone 415/673-6828; fax 415/673-6863.* Japanese menu. Lunch, dinner. **$$**

★★ **GREENS.** *Fort Mason, Building A, San Francisco (94123). Phone 415/771-6222; fax 415/771-3472. greensrestaurant.com.* This contemporary vegetarian restaurant on a pier in Fort Mason boasts spectacular views of the marina, the Bay, and the Golden Gate Bridge. Established by Marin's Zen Center in 1979, Greens features organic produce courtesy of Green Gulch farms in Marin and Bolinas. The menu changes with the seasons. Vegetarian menu. Lunch, dinner, Sun brunch. Closed holidays. Children's menu. **$$$**

★★ **HARRIS'.** *2100 Van Ness Ave, San Francisco (94109). Phone 415/673-1888; fax 415/673-8817. www.harrisrestaurant.com.* On busy Van Ness Avenue in Pacific Heights, Harris' is a steakhouse with the feel of a men's club, with mahogany woods, dark carpet, and leather chairs and booths. The restaurant also has a large bar and lounge with live music (Thursday through Saturday). Large murals grace the walls, and large plants provide an extra wall of privacy between booths. Seafood, steak menu. Dinner. Closed holidays. Bar. Valet parking. **$$$**

★★★ **HAWTHORNE LANE.** *22 Hawthorne St, San Francisco (94105). Phone 415/777-9779; fax 415/777-9782. www.hawthornelane.com.* Located in the historic Crown Point Press building, a stone's throw from culture hotspots like the San Francisco Museum of Modern Art and the Yerba Buena Center for the Arts, Hawthorne Lane personifies sophisticated San Francisco dining. Furnished with cherry wood, rich floral arrangements, crisp white linen tablecloths, and modern art, this warm, stylish California bistro is a mecca for savvy San Francisco foodies. Crowds flock here for consistently delicious yet inventive seasonal New American fare that takes cues from Asia and the Pacific Northwest. Chinese-style roasted duck with steamed green onion buns and blood-orange licorice salad is a signature dish. A piano player comes in nightly, which is lovely, but entertainment just isn't necessary with all the fun to be had on the plate. California menu. Lunch, dinner. Closed holidays. Bar. Valet parking. **$$$**

★★ **HAYES STREET GRILL.** *320 Hayes St, San Francisco (94102). Phone 415/863-5545; fax 415/863-1873. www.hayesstreetgrill.com.* Convenient for a pre- or post-opera evening, Hayes Street Grill is in trendy Hayes Valley, which is host to popular but subdued restaurants and shops. The menu changes daily and emphasizes California cuisine and West Coast seafood. Décor includes framed, autographed photos of celebrities who have dined here. Local food critic Patricia Unterman is a co-owner. California, seafood menu. Lunch, dinner. Closed holidays. Bar. **$$$**

★★ **THE HELMAND.** *430 Broadway, San Francisco (94133). Phone 415/362-0641; fax 415/362-0862.*

www.helmandsf.com. Diners looking for something different should head to The Helmand, a restaurant on the outskirts of North Beach that features the ambience and cuisine of Afghanistan. The dining room has Afghan rugs, paintings, photos, and artifacts; dim lighting also adds to the milieu. The cuisine, which has Middle Eastern and Indian influences, provides an unusual culinary evening of a relatively unfamiliar cuisine. Afghan menu. Lunch, dinner. Closed Thanksgiving. Bar. **$$**

★ ★ THE HOUSE. *1230 Grant Ave, San Francisco (94133). Phone 415/986-8612; fax 415/682-3892. www.thehse.com.* This unobtrusive, tiny restaurant in North Beach offers a respite from the area's domineering Italian spots with its Asian-American fusion fare. Interior touches are simple but attractive, with lime- and grey-colored walls dotted with black-and-white framed photos. The menu emphasizes fish dishes like grilled Chilean sea bass with garlic ginger soy and blackened mahi mahi with couscous. Pan-Asian menu. Lunch, dinner. **$$**

★ HUNAN. *924 Sansome St, San Francisco (94111). Phone 415/956-7727; fax 415/959-5772.* This Financial District spot is large and somewhat plain, but is popular for its consistent and fast fare, generous portions, and reasonable prices. The dining room is large, with a long, open kitchen. Favorites include house-smoked duck and other smoked meats. Chinese menu. Lunch, dinner. Closed July 4, Thanksgiving, Dec 25. Bar. Casual attire. **$$**

★ ★ INDIGO. *687 McAllister St, San Francisco (94102). Phone 415/673-9353; fax 415/673-9369. www.indigorestaurant.com.* American menu. Dinner. Closed Mon; Jan 1, Thanksgiving, Dec 25. Children's menu. **$$**

★ ISOBUNE. *1737 Post St, San Francisco (94115). Phone 415/563-1030; fax 415/563-3337.* Located in a Japantown mall, this small, unique restaurant was the first of its kind in the United States, established in 1982. Isobune means "canal boat" in Japanese, and sure enough, sushi floats by in wooden boats on a small river of water. Diners sit at an oval counter; colorful Japanese lanterns and curios make up the décor. Japanese sushi menu. Lunch, dinner. Closed Jan 1, Thanksgiving, Dec 25. Casual attire. **$**

★ ★ ★ JARDINIERE. *300 Grove St, San Francisco (94102). Phone 415/861-5555; fax 415/861-5580. www.jardiniere.com.* Housed in a historic, exposed-brick landmark building in the Civic Center area (it's a perfect place to dine if you're attending the opera, ballet, or symphony), Jardiniere is one of the city's true culinary gems. Chef/owner Traci Des Jardins (formerly of Montrachet in New York) opened her ode to Californian-French fare with Pat Kuleto, and together they have created a restaurant that delights in both cuisine and design. An oval-shaped mahogany and marble bar; heavy velvet drapes; a sweeping staircase; and moody, bronze-hued lighting lend richness, warmth, and opulence to this dramatic two-tiered space. Des Jardins is a rare talent; not only does her daily changing seasonal menu surprise and thrill, but her commitment to local, organic, and sustainable foods shows her dedication to more than just satisfying taste buds. California, French menu. Dinner. Closed holidays. Bar. Valet parking. **$$$**

★ ★ ★ JEANTY AT JACK'S. *615 Sacramento St, San Francisco (94111). Phone 415/693-0941; fax 415/693-0947. www.jeantyatjacks.com.* Owned by Philippe Jeanty, Jeanty at Jack's is a delightful brasserie that has long been seducing guests with its delicious, authentic French fare and old-world Parisian elegance. The restaurant, set in a two-story redwood-paneled cottage, is something out of an old French movie, with lace curtains, vintage brass lighting, 14-foot sculpted relief ceilings and walls, and a black-and-white checkered tile floor. Aside from the charmed interior, diners come here because Jeanty captures the essence of French bistro dining, serving perfectly prepared standards like steamed mussels with fries, sole meuniere, grilled rib eye steak béarnaise, cassoulet with duck confit, and delicious last-course classic treats like crepes suzette and apple tarte tatin. French Bistro menu. Lunch, dinner, late-night. Bar. **$$**

★ ★ JULIUS' CASTLE. *1541 Montgomery St, San Francisco (94133). Phone 415/392-2222; fax 415/989-1544. www.juliuscastle.com.* A San Francisco landmark tucked into a residential neighborhood on the eastern slopes of Telegraph Hill, Julius' Castle was built in 1922. The light pink, three-story turreted structure is justifiably famous for its stunning, unobstructed views of Treasure Island, the Bay Bridge, and the city itself. The contemporary European fare includes dishes like braised Chilean sea bass and Colorado rack of lamb, which are paired with selections from a highly rated wine list. A winding stairway leads from the ground-floor bar and lounge to the dining room, with its exhibition kitchen, dark hardwoods, and lovely chandeliers. Contemporary European menu. Dinner. Bar. Valet parking. Outdoor seating. **$$$**

★★ **KABUTO SUSHI.** *5121 Geary Blvd, San Francisco (94118). Phone 415/752-5652; fax 415/386-0149. www.kabutosushi.com.* This chef-owned restaurant in the Outer Richmond District is a popular and inviting sushi bar. There is a Japanese-style garden inside, and the kitchen serves authentic but reasonably priced Japanese cuisine. Japanese, sushi menu. Dinner. Closed Sun-Mon. **$$**

★ **KATIA'S RUSSIAN TEA ROOM.** *600 5th Ave, San Francisco (94118). Phone 415/668-9292; fax 415/668-9298. www.katias.com.* Filling an Eastern European void in San Francisco, Katia's is a friendly Richmond District eatery that serves traditional Russian fare (think salmon caviar, beef stroganoff, piroshki, and vodka). Katia is the chef and owner, and her restaurant offers friendly service and reliable food. A guitarist-accordionist entertains patrons several nights each week. Russian menu. Lunch, dinner. Closed Mon-Tues; holidays. **$$**

★ **KHAN TOKE THAI HOUSE.** *5937 Geary Blvd, San Francisco (94121). Phone 415/668-6654.* Thai menu. Dinner. Closed holidays. **$$**

★★★ **KOKKARI.** *200 Jackson St, San Francisco (94111). Phone 415/981-0983; fax 415/982-0983. www.kokkari.com.* Power diners and sophisticated restaurant-goers come to downtown's Kokkari for delicious contemporary Greek and Mediterranean cuisine. The upscale taverna, named after a fishing village on an island in the Aegean Sea, spreads its old-world charm among several large rooms; the rustic front dining room has a large fireplace with wood-plank flooring and high ceilings. Greek classics like freshly baked pita bread, moussaka, grilled lamb chops, and baklava fill the menu, along with a varied selection of Greek brandy, ouzo, and grappa. Greek menu. Lunch, dinner, late-night. Closed Sun; holidays. Bar. Children's menu. Reservations recommended. Valet parking. **$$$**

★★★ **KYO-YA.** *2 New Montgomery St, San Francisco (94105). Phone 415/546-5090; fax 415/243-8062. www.kyo-ya-restaurant.com.* Spartan Asian ambience fills four interconnected dining rooms in this downtown sushi establishment in the Palace Hotel (see). Unobtrusive Japanese music is as understated as the décor, which includes original Asian art, green satin drapes, and a small vase of flowers on each table. In addition to an extensive sake list, the menu offers sushi, sashimi, tempura, noodle dishes, and traditional Japanese soups. Given the prices and the authenticity, Japanese businessmen are a large part of the clientele. Make reservations to dine at the eight-seat sushi bar. Japanese menu. Lunch, dinner. Closed Sun-Mon; also two weeks in early July. Bar. Valet parking. **$$$**

★★★★ **LA FOLIE.** *2316 Polk St, San Francisco (94109). Phone 415/776-5577; fax 415/776-3431. www.lafolie.com.* After dining at La Folie, you'll realize that haute cuisine can be lots of fun. As the restaurant's name suggests, chef/owner Roland Passot has a passion for food, folly, and adventure. The whimsical dining room is awash in blond wood and deep wine-toned carpet, with skylights above and cotton-candy clouds painted on sky-blue walls, creating a dreamy sense of wonder and charm. The ambience is perfect for Passot's magical Discovery Menu: a chef-led culinary journey that features innovative and impeccably prepared dishes of French-Californian descent. (A la carte and vegetarian menus are also available.) Citrus lobster salad with shaved fresh hearts of palm and a trio of rabbit are Passot's signature creations. The impressive wine list includes pricey French wines, a variety of California selections, and several wallet-friendly wines from lesser-known regions such as Australia and Chile. French menu. Dinner. Closed Sun; holidays. Bar. Reservations recommended. Valet parking. **$$$**

★ **LA VIE.** *5830 Geary Blvd, San Francisco (94121). Phone 415/668-8080; fax 415/668-9101.* Located in the ethnically diverse Richmond District, this small Vietnamese spot is more unassuming than its swankier Vietnamese brethren (San Francisco hotspots like Le Colonial and The Slanted Door). The décor complements the authentic cuisine, with photos, artifacts, and memorabilia from Vietnam, plus two tanks filled with fish and crustaceans. Vietnamese menu. Lunch, dinner. Closed Mon. **$$**

★★ **LE CHARM.** *315 Fifth St, San Francisco (94107). Phone 415/546-6128; fax 415/546-6712. www.lecharm.com.* A cozy, French-style bistro in SoMa, this small restaurant has an indoor dining room and an informal, seasonal courtyard. The gourmet menu is moderately priced and features prix fixe options; basically, it's a fantastic spot for quality, classic French cuisine at bargain prices. While the space is a bit noisy, it isn't a deterrent. French menu. Lunch, dinner. Closed holidays. Outdoor seating. **$$$**

★★ **MANDARIN.** *900 North Point St, San Francisco (94109). Phone 415/673-8812; fax 415/673-5480. www.themandarin.com.* Offering elegant dining in Ghirardelli Square, Mandarin serves cuisine from northern China in a prime tourist location. Carved wooden screens and an ornate turquoise-and-green tile floor divide the dining room into several sections, and the attractive ceiling has exposed beams with lanterns. Peking duck, smoked tea duck, and beggar's chicken are house specialties. Chinese menu. Lunch, dinner. Bar. **$$$**

★ ★ MARRAKECH MOROCCAN. *419 O'Farrell St, San Francisco (94102). Phone 415/776-6717; fax 415/776-1538. www.marrakechsf.com.* Located in downtown San Francisco, this exotic spot is uniquely Moroccan, from décor to furnishings to cuisine. Ornate features typical of Islamic North Africa include circular, etched brass tables; Oriental rugs over carpeting; hassocks; brass teapots and hookahs; a tiled fountain; and low cushioned seating. Dim lighting and nightly belly dancing add to the experience. Moroccan menu. Dinner. Bar. **$$$**

★ ★ ★ ★ MASA'S. *648 Bush St, San Francisco (94108). Phone 415/989-7154; fax 415/989-3141. www.masas.citysearch.com.* If you crave luxury of the over-the-top degree, Masa's is a place you must plant yourself for the night. Located in the Hotel Vintage Court (see), the opulent, freshly made-over dining room is dressed in rich garnet and espresso tones and has a sleek, sophisticated feel. The decadent atmosphere extends to the tabletop: the china is Bernardaud, the pearly white linens are Frette, the flatware is Cambonet, and the glassware is Reidel. As for the cuisine, it is modern and divine, a savvy blend of French technique with Asian innovation that pays loving attention to stunning ingredients. It's prix fixe only here, so be prepared to loosen your belt and enjoy signatures like Atlantic skate with braised butter lettuce, potato rosti, and truffle sauce (in season) and Niman Ranch lamb chops with fettuccine, ratatouille of Provençal-style vegetables, and thyme-infused lamb reduction. French menu. Dinner. Closed Sun-Mon; also first two weeks in Jan and first two weeks in July. Bar. Jacket required. Reservations recommended. Valet parking. **$$$$**

★ ★ ★ MAYA. *303 Second St, San Francisco (94107). Phone 415/543-2928; fax 415/543-6679. www.mayasf.com.* Divey burrito spots are ubiquitous in San Francisco, but this lively upscale Mexican restaurant South of Market fills a much-needed niche. At the long bar, sip a potent margarita while waiting for your table in one of two dining areas, with tables featuring white linens, fresh flowers, and Spanish-style chairs. The food has the stylish presentation of a fancy French restaurant, but instead of cassoulet, diners can savor mole dishes, gazpacho with crabmeat, and chayote relleno. There's patio dining at the front entrance. Mexican menu. Lunch, dinner. Bar. Outdoor seating. **$$**

★ ★ MCCORMICK AND KULETO'S. *900 North Point St, San Francisco (94109). Phone 415/929-1730; fax 415/567-2919. www.mccormickandkuletos.com.* This Ghirardelli Square restaurant is part of the McCormick and Schmick's dining empire operating in more than a dozen states. In this multilevel location, floor-to-ceiling windows afford diners anywhere in the restaurant excellent views of San Francisco Bay and Alcatraz. The menu changes daily according to the fresh catch; pastas, sirloin steak, and crab cakes are also reliable options. Seafood menu. Lunch, dinner. Bar. Children's menu. **$$**

★ ★ ★ MECCA. *2029 Market St, San Francisco (94114). Phone 415/621-7000; fax 415/621-7094. www.sfmecca.com.* A swanky supper club on busy Upper Market Street, Mecca has an unadorned concrete façade that masks a high-energy restaurant. A large, circular, full-service bar dominates the main dining room, serving fancy drinks and attracting a see-and-be-seen crowd. The feel is modern, with concrete floors, mirrors, and exposed ceiling ducts. The kitchen—partly revealed to patrons—whips up Asian-fusion fare with an emphasis on seafood. Don't come here expecting a quiet, romantic evening, especially on Wednesday, when the restaurant features live music. American menu. Dinner. Closed Mon; Thanksgiving, Dec 25. Bar. Valet parking. **$$**

★ MO'S GOURMET HAMBURGERS. *1322 Grant Ave, San Francisco (94133). Phone 415/788-3779; fax 415/885-5721. www.mosgrill.com.* North Beach takes a break from Italian fare at this hamburger joint, which beckons with its neon signage. Mo's is still willing to serve a "bloody," high-quality burger (if you want it that way), along with thick fries and milkshakes. Colorful folk-art murals and a large framed photo of the Three Stooges observe as you indulge. American menu. Breakfast, lunch, dinner. Closed Thanksgiving, Dec 25. Casual attire. **$**

★ ★ ★ MOOSE'S. *1652 Stockton St, San Francisco (94133). Phone 415/989-7800; fax 415/989-7838. www.mooses.com.* A grand piano, elegant floral arrangements, soft lighting, and the memory of late newspaper columnist Herb Caen sipping martinis contribute to Moose's sophisticated atmosphere. Located across from Washington Square Park, this

North Beach restaurant boasts large windows with views of the park and a dark wood bar equipped with television sets. The cuisine is American, with an emphasis on local, organic produce and naturally raised fish and meats; the mooseburger is a perennial favorite that's always on the menu. Enjoy jazz music nightly or if you visit for Sunday brunch. American menu. Lunch, dinner, Sun brunch. Closed holidays. Bar. Valet parking. **$$$**

★ ★ ★ **MORTON'S, THE STEAKHOUSE.** *400 Post St, San Francisco (94102). Phone 415/986-5830; fax 415/986-5829. www.mortons.com.* This steakhouse chain, which originated in Chicago in 1978, appeals to the serious meat lover. With a selection of belt-busting carnivorous delights (like the house specialty, a 24-ounce porterhouse), as well as fresh fish, lobster and chicken entrées, Morton's rarely disappoints. When you're just not sure what you're in the mood for, the tableside menu presentation may help you decide. Here, main course selections are placed upon a cart that is rolled to your table, where servers describe each item in detail. Steak menu. Dinner. Closed holidays. Bar. **$$$**

★ ★ ★ **NORTH BEACH.** *1512 Stockton St, San Francisco (94133). Phone 415/392-1700; fax 415/392-0230. www.northbeachrestaurant.com.* A sophisticated spot in the heart of North Beach, this Tuscan ristorante has thrived in the city's Italian district for more than 30 years (though it received a facelift in the 1990s). Waiters in tuxes complement the traditional fare, which features fresh fish, veal, and pasta. House specialties include spaghetti with vodka, sand dabs, and pasta with bay shrimp and cream sauce. Slide up to the granite bar and peruse the sizeable wine selection (nearly 600 vintages); the list also includes 75 types of grappa. Italian menu. Lunch, dinner. Closed holidays. Bar. Valet parking. **$$$**

★ **O'REILLY'S.** *622 Green St, San Francisco (94133). Phone 415/989-6222; fax 415/989-6228. www.oreillysirish.com.* This raucous watering hole and eatery serves Guinness and Irish fare on the outskirts of North Beach. Dine on dishes like the Irishman's quesadilla (with shredded corned beef), fish and chips, or chicken potpie while perusing Irish memorabilia, bric-a-brac, photos, and murals. Eat outside on the sidewalk if the sun is shining. Irish menu. Breakfast, lunch, dinner. Bar. Children's menu. Casual attire. Outdoor seating. **$$**

★ ★ ★ **ONE MARKET.** *1 Market St, San Francisco (94105). Phone 415/777-5577; fax 415/777-3366. www.onemarket.com.* Serving seasonal American cuisine in a prime location in the Embarcadero area, One Market has proven its staying power. The atmosphere is soothing, with wrought-iron chandeliers, mustard and terra-cotta walls, and floor-to-ceiling windows offering views of the cable cars and passersby. This restaurant also wins points for attentive service, a nice selection of wines by the glass, and a nightly jazz pianist. The crowd is part business, part tourist. Larger groups can request the chef's table in the kitchen for a memorable meal. American menu. Lunch, dinner. Closed Sun; holidays. Bar. Children's menu. **$$$**

★ ★ **PALIO D'ASTI.** *640 Sacramento St, San Francisco (94111). Phone 415/395-9800; fax 415/362-6002. www.paliodasti.com.* Named for the Palio, a medieval, bareback horse race in the Italian town of Asti, this spacious Financial District restaurant features a large mural depicting the event, which was reborn 35 years ago. Banners and flags representing the villages around Asti that participate in the Palio decorate the main dining room. The well-priced northern Italian cuisine has its roots in Piedmont and Tuscany. Italian menu. Lunch, dinner. Closed Sat-Sun; holidays. Bar. **$$$**

★ ★ **PANE E VINO.** *3011 Steiner St, San Francisco (94123). Phone 415/346-2111; fax 415/346-0741.* This intimate but bustling Cow Hollow restaurant is reminiscent of trattorias in Tuscany or Umbria, with traditional northern Italian fare that draws crowds. Stucco walls, a red-tile floor, and the waiters' lovely Italian lilt add to the authenticity, along with menu standards like rack of lamb and tiramisu. Nearby Via Vai is Pane e Vino's more casual "sister" restaurant. Italian menu. Lunch, dinner. Closed holidays. Reservations recommended. **$$$**

★ ★ **PARAGON.** *701 Second St, San Francisco (94107). Phone 415/537-9020; fax 415/537-9021. www.paragonrestaurant.com.* Just a block away from SBC Park, this brick-fronted brasserie serves American fare to casual business folks and an after-work drinking crowd, as well as baseball fans looking for a pre- or post-game meal. The large, contemporary space has a long bar (which serves more than 60 vodkas from all over the globe) backed by an enormous mirror. American menu. Lunch, dinner. Closed Sun. Bar. Outdoor seating. **$$**

★ **PARC HONG KONG.** *5322 Geary Blvd, San Francisco (94121). Phone 415/668-8998; fax 415/668-0318.* Chinatown hasn't cornered the market on Chinese fare. This Richmond District Cantonese restaurant serves excellent dim sum in three dining rooms decorated in shades of red, green, and gold. The main dining room also features a fish tank, as lobster and crab are prominent items on the dinner menu. Chinese menu. Lunch, dinner. Bar. **$$**

★ **PERRY'S.** *1944 Union St, San Francisco (94123). Phone 415/922-9022; fax 415/929-0843.* For 30-plus years, Perry's has been a popular standby for its weekend brunch and tasty burgers, salads, and chowder. The sidewalk tables on trendy Union Street offer prime people-watching, and the classic mahogany bar is perfect for a casual drink. There's an offshoot in the Galleria Park Hotel at 185 Sutter Street (phone 415/989-6895). American menu. Breakfast, lunch, dinner, late-night. Closed Thanksgiving, Dec 25. Bar. Children's menu. Outdoor seating. **$$**

★ ★ **PIPERADE.** *1015 Battery St, San Francisco (94111). Phone 415/391-2555; fax 415/391-1139. www.piperade.com.* This European-style bistro in the Financial District has charmed many diners since its opening. Formerly a warehouse, the dining room is contemporary yet warm and features exposed brick walls, a large central farm table, and a unique chandelier made from wine bottles. Serving Basque country fare with a California twist, this restaurant is all about fresh ingredients. French, Spanish menu. Lunch, dinner. Closed Sun; holidays. Bar. Outdoor seating. **$$**

★ ★ **PLOUF.** *40 Belden Pl, San Francisco (94104). Phone 415/986-6491; toll-free www.ploufsf.com; fax 415/986-6492.* Part of Belden Place's charming restaurant row, Plouf is a French-influenced seafood bistro. The waitstaff dresses like French seamen, and the cuisine has influences from across the pond. The heart of the seafood menu is mussels, a Plouf house specialty and a favorite in countries bordering the North Sea. In warm weather, dine outside at European-style tables. French, seafood menu. Lunch, dinner. Closed Sun. Bar. Outdoor seating. **$$**

★ ★ ★ **PLUMPJACK CAFE.** *3127 Fillmore St, San Francisco (94123). Phone 415/563-4755; fax 415/776-5808. www.plumpjack.com.* A few blocks off trendy Union Street, PlumpJack draws a sophisticated crowd for its California-Mediterranean fare, served in slightly cramped quarters. The award-winning chef frequently changes the menu, but the ahi tartare cones remain a house specialty; other dishes may include seared local halibut or duck confit risotto. Wine-lovers take note: the restaurant is famous for having a low markup on its extensive wine list. Handsome local politician Gavin Newsom is part owner of this Cow Hollow spot, which is part of an empire that includes the Matrix Fillmore bar (across the street) and a Lake Tahoe branch. California, Mediterranean menu. Lunch, dinner. Closed holidays. Reservations recommended. **$$$**

★ ★ ★ **POSTRIO.** *545 Post St, San Francisco (94102). Phone 415/776-8358; fax 415/776-6702. www.postrio.com.* Postrio, Wolfgang Puck's splashy, stylish, and sophisticated San Francisco restaurant, is a feast for the senses. Decorated with brightly colored ribbons and modern art by Rauschenberg and Rosenquist, the sleek, chic, tri-level space buzzes with a savvy crowd of well-heeled locals who gather in numbers nightly, in need of Puck's lavish brand of Californian-Asian-Mediterranean cuisine. The menu, which changes daily, features a top-notch selection of fish, meats, and produce from farms surrounding the Bay Area. The service here is attentive, leaving you feeling pampered and rested. If you crave Puck's signature wood-burning oven pizzas, you don't have to worry about missing out; they are on the menu. American menu. Lunch, dinner. Bar. Business casual attire. Reservations recommended. Valet parking. **$$$**

★ **POT STICKER.** *150 Waverly Pl, San Francisco (94108). Phone 415/397-9985; fax 415/397-3829.* Smack dab in the middle of Chinatown, Pot Sticker is a small, single-room restaurant serving Hunan-style cuisine. Wall paintings and prints make up the Chinese décor. While the kitchen creates satisfactory dishes (including, of course, an ample variety of pot stickers), there are many similar restaurants in the area. Chinese menu. Lunch, dinner. **$$**

★ ★ **PREGO.** *2000 Union St, San Francisco (94123). Phone 415/563-3305; fax 415/563-1561. www.pregoristorante.com.* Serving Italian food on fashionable Union Street in Cow Hollow, Prego has sidewalk tables that are perfect for people-watching, along with two main dining rooms—one with a large brick pizza oven. There is also a large bar and lounge area near the entrance. The vibe is fun and relaxed, with standard choices like pizzas, pastas, and grilled fish. Italian menu. Lunch, dinner, late-night. Closed Thanksgiving, Dec 25. Bar. Outdoor seating. **$$**

★★ **RESTAURANT LULU.** *816 Folsom St, San Francisco (94107). Phone 415/495-5775; fax 415/495-7810. www.restaurantlulu.com.* This dynamic SoMa-area restaurant serves a seasonal, rustic Provençal-style menu in a transformed 1910 warehouse. Architectural highlights include a main dining room with sunken tables; a large bar (with extensive wines by the glass); and high ceilings. The half-open kitchen showcases the large, wood-fired oven and rotisserie. Dining here is typically family-style at long wood tables. French menu. Lunch, dinner. Closed holidays. Bar. **$$**

★★ **RISTORANTE IDEALE.** *1309 Grant Ave, San Francisco (94133). Phone 415/391-4129.* Italian menu. Lunch, dinner. Closed Mon; holidays. Bar. Children's menu. **$$**

★★ **ROSE PISTOLA.** *532 Columbus Ave, San Francisco (94133). Phone 415/399-0499; fax 415/399-8758.* An active entry gives way to a more sedate atmosphere at this North Beach hotspot. Wandering waiters serve antipasti from trays, and the exhibition kitchen showcases Italian-style cuisine with wood-fire ovens. Italian menu. Lunch, dinner. Bar. Children's menu. Outdoor seating. **$$**

★★ **ROSE'S CAFE.** *2298 Union St, San Francisco (94123). Phone 415/775-2200; fax 415/775-9600.* On the cheerful corner of Fillmore and Union streets, Rose's Cafe serves California-Italian fare—think salads, thin-crust pizzas, grilled chicken—to a mostly local crowd. This casual off-shoot of Rose Pistola in North Beach has outdoor sidewalk seating protected by yellow awnings, and the inside space resembles an Italian trattoria, with multicolored floor tiles, Venetian chandeliers, and close quarters. Italian menu. Breakfast, lunch, dinner. Closed Jan 1, Thanksgiving, Dec 25. Bar. Outdoor seating. **$$**

★★★ **RUBICON.** *558 Sacramento, San Francisco (94111). Phone 415/434-4100; fax 415/421-7648. www.sfrubicon.com.* This two-story restaurant in the Financial District has an elegant, sophisticated atmosphere enhanced by its celebrity chic: Robert De Niro, Robin Williams, and Francis Ford Coppola are co-owners. The C-shaped bar offers an impressive—though expensive—wine list; the menu, California fare with French influences, may include dishes like John Dory, Rubicon tuna tartare, and braised veal cheek. Three- and four-course prix fixe options are available. Touches like exposed brick walls, glass sculptures, and abstract oil paintings give the place a jolt of personality. California, French menu. Lunch Wed, dinner. Closed Sun. Bar. **$$$**

★ **RUE LEPIC.** *900 Pine St, San Francisco (94108). Phone 415/474-6070; fax 415/474-6187. www.ruelepic.com.* French menu. Dinner. Closed holidays. Reservations recommended. **$$**

★★★ **RUTH'S CHRIS STEAK HOUSE.** *1601 Van Ness Ave, San Francisco (94109). Phone 415/673-0557; fax 415/673-5309. www.ruthschris.com.* A popular nationwide chain, this outpost serves an array of tasty steaks to the masses, accompanied by masculine steakhouse ambience. Don't come looking for a fashionable scene, but come for generous portions of corn-fed beef in all its incarnations: rib eye, T-bone, filet, and so on. Artery-clogging side dishes also appear on the menu, such as creamed spinach and potatoes au gratin. The busy strip of Van Ness defies the term neighborhood, though it hovers between Nob Hill and Pacific Heights. Seafood, steak menu. Dinner. Closed Thanksgiving, Dec 25. Bar. **$$$**

★ **SAM'S GRILL & SEAFOOD.** *374 Bush St, San Francisco (94104). Phone 415/421-0594; fax 415/421-2632. www.samsgrill.citysearch.com.* Originally an oyster bar and saloon established in 1867, this downtown seafood house retains much of its period décor. Fish artwork adorns the walls, and dishes like scallops, calamari, and crab legs dominate the menu. A few original wood booths with curtains, a linoleum floor, and gruff service are a welcome part of the package. American, seafood menu. Lunch, dinner. Closed Sat-Sun; holidays. Bar. **$$**

★★ **SCALA'S BISTRO.** *432 Powell St, San Francisco (94102). Phone 415/395-8555; fax 415/395-8549. www.scalasbistro.com.* In the Sir Francis Drake Hotel just off Union Square, this upscale Italian eatery draws both locals and tourists. The unique décor includes an ornate ceiling, original murals, and a partially open rear kitchen with dangling copper pots and plates. Salads, pizzas, pastas, and meat dishes are among the specialties. Country French, rustic Italian menu. Breakfast, lunch, dinner, late-night. Closed holidays. Bar. **$$**

★ **SCHROEDER'S.** *240 Front St, San Francisco (94111). Phone 415/421-4778; fax 415/421-2217. www.schroederssf.com.* Having first opened its doors in 1893, Schroeder's is an old-world German beer hall and restaurant located in the Financial District. The spacious, wood-paneled dining room features large murals of traditional scenes above the bar, along with a collection of beer steins on display. You may find that the German music is better than the cuisine.

German menu. Lunch, dinner. Closed Sun; Jan 1, July 4, Dec 25. Bar. Children's menu. **$$**

★ ★ **SCOMA'S.** *Pier 47 on Al Scoma Way, San Francisco (94133). Phone 415/771-4383; toll-free 800/644-5852; fax 415/775-2601. www.scomas.com.* Located in touristy Fisherman's Wharf, San Francisco's long-time seafood restaurant is almost an institution. The white-and-blue color scheme enhances the aquatic theme, and the dining room faces the fishing boat moorings. There is a large bar and adjacent lounge at the entry, with three smallish, separate dining areas to the rear of the restaurant. Seafood menu. Lunch, dinner. Closed Thanksgiving, Dec 24-25. Bar. Valet parking. **$$$**

★ **SEARS FINE FOODS.** *439 Powell St, San Francisco (94102). Phone 415/986-0700; fax 415/765-0957. www.searsfinefood.com.* Patrons flock to this San Francisco institution, established in 1938, for the "world-famous" Swedish pancakes. American menu. Breakfast, lunch, dinner. Closed Jan 1, Thanksgiving, Dec 25. Children's menu. **$**

★ ★ **SLANTED DOOR.** *1 Ferry Building #3, San Francisco (94111). Phone 415/861-8032; fax 415/861-8329. www.slanteddoor.com.* Eternally popular, this Vietnamese favorite has continued to thrive in its SoMa location (after a move from its Mission digs) with food that has garnered consistent raves. The atmosphere is light, airy, contemporary, and sleek, with an open chrome kitchen and leather banquettes. Favorite menu items include the famous shaking beef, stuffed Monterey squid, and vegetarian glass noodles. Vietnamese menu. Lunch, dinner. Closed holidays. Bar. **$$$**

★ **SWAN OYSTER DEPOT.** *1517 Polk St, San Francisco (94109). Phone 415/673-1101.* This counter-seating-only seafood establishment is a longtime, family-owned restaurant and market on Polk Street. The menu on the wall tempts patrons with clam chowder, shucked oysters, and a variety of other seafood options. The friendly brothers will serve you at the marble counter, or you can order your food to go. If you want to eat dinner here, go early: the restaurant closes at 5:30 pm. Seafood menu. Breakfast, lunch. Closed Sun; holidays. Casual attire. **$$**

★ ★ **TADICH GRILL.** *240 California St, San Francisco (94111). Phone 415/391-1849; fax 415/391-2373.* Opened in 1849 by three Croatian immigrants, this Financial District institution is a draw primarily for its expansive seafood menu, although pork chops, steaks, and other meat dishes are also available. Request an enclosed wood booth for an old school-atmosphere. Seafood menu. Lunch, dinner. Closed Sun; Thanksgiving, Dec 25. Bar. **$$$**

★ ★ ★ **TOMMY TOY'S.** *655 Montgomery St, San Francisco (94111). Phone 415/397-4888; fax 415/397-0469. www.tommytoys.com.* Chinese cuisine has been getting a French twist since 1985 at this downtown eatery, where Toy combines the taste and technique of China with French-influenced presentations (no chopsticks) and flair. Daily specials always appear at lunch and dinner; diners can also opt for the six-course signature dinner, which may include seafood bisque that is oven-baked and topped with a French puff pastry and Peking duck with lotus buns. Dress the part for the opulent setting: think old tapestries, silk draperies, and Toy's collection of original Chinese fans. Chinese menu. Lunch, dinner. Closed Jan 1, Dec 25. Bar. Jacket required. Reservations recommended. Valet parking. **$$$**

★ **UNIVERSAL CAFE.** *2814 19th St, San Francisco (94110). Phone 415/821-4608; fax 415/285-6760. www.universalcafe.net.* While this chef-owned restaurant highlights rustic Mediterranean fare, it also has muses all over the globe, as the name suggests. Located in the Mission District near Potrero Hill, the café showcases an industrial décor, with a cement floor and marble tables, espresso bar, and counter. When the weather permits, escape the tight quarters and dine outside. California, Mediterranean menu. Dinner, brunch. Closed Mon. Reservations r ecommended. Outdoor seating. **$$**

★ ★ **WATERFRONT.** *Pier 7, San Francisco (94111). Phone 415/391-2696; fax 415/391-7125. www.waterfrontsf.com.* This Embarcadero seafood restaurant incorporates its scenic views of the Bay Bridge, Treasure Island, and meandering tour boats into a romantic setting. The restaurant is split into two levels, with fine dining upstairs and a more laid-back atmosphere downstairs. On a sunny afternoon, opt for the covered terrace or a table shielded by umbrellas. Seafood menu. Lunch, dinner. Bar. Valet parking. Outdoor seating. **$$$**

★ ★ ★ **WOODWARD'S GARDEN.** *1700 Mission St, San Francisco (94103). Phone 415/621-7122.* Despite its location under a freeway overpass in the Mission District, Woodward's Garden remains a gem, with its intimate atmosphere and seasonally driven menu of New American food. The devoted chef-owners do not allow themes or pretensions to distract from the menu, which may feature grilled hangar steak and other Niman Ranch meats, local salmon, or sautéed sea bass. An extensive wine list complements the menu. Pots and pans hang over the counter of the open kitchen, and artwork and sconces adorn the walls. American menu. Dinner. Closed Sun-Mon; holidays. **$$$**

★ ★ ★ XYZ. *181 Third St, San Francisco (94103). Phone 415/817-7836; fax 415/817-7823. www.xyz-sf.com.* Expect excessively hip—though not relaxing—dining at this outpost in the W Hotel (see) serving self-described urban continental fare with a French influence (that's California cuisine to you and me). The house specialty is a black Angus filet with horseradish potato mousseline and burgundy reduction; just don't spill the sauce on the camel-colored suede chairs. Notable design elements include multicolored pseudo-portholes on one wall and floor-to-ceiling windows on the outer wall. The adjacent bar and café are also extremely popular. American, French menu. Breakfast, lunch, dinner. Children's menu. **$$$**

★ ★ YABBIE'S COASTAL KITCHEN. *2237 Polk St, San Francisco (94109). Phone 415/474-4088; fax 415/474-4962. www.yabbiesrestaurant.com.* Seafood menu. Dinner. Closed holidays. Bar. Casual attire. **$$**

★ ★ YANK SING. *101 Spear St, San Francisco (94105). Phone 415/957-9300; fax 415/957-9322. www.yanksing.com.* During the week, mostly business types sink into rattan chairs as carts of dim sum (Chinese "tapas") zoom around this always-busy restaurant near the Embarcadero. Banish thoughts of a menu: just signal for steamed pork buns, potstickers, seafood dumplings, and more as the waiters whoosh by. Overeaters beware: it's easy to overindulge. Chinese menu. Lunch. Bar. **$$**

★ ★ YOSHIDA-YA. *2909 Webster St, San Francisco (94123). Phone 415/346-3431; fax 415/346-0907. www.yoshida-ya-restaurant.com.* The décor of this two-story Cow Hollow Japanese restaurant blends East and West. Traditional Japanese low tables with seat cushions dominate the upstairs, while the street level has a sushi bar, an alcohol bar, and standard Western table seating. Japanese rice-paper lanterns and artwork complement the red interior. The food is agreeable, and the wait is rarely long. Japanese menu. Lunch, dinner. Closed holidays. Bar. Children's menu. **$$**

★ ZARZUELA. *2000 Hyde St, San Francisco (94109). Phone 415/346-0800; fax 415/346-0880.* Part of a mini-restaurant row on Russian Hill's Hyde Street, Zarzuela serves Spanish tapas, paella, sangria, and other traditional fare in a friendly neighborhood setting. The prices are reasonable, the staff is welcoming, and the Spanish décor is inviting, but other diners know this too, so be prepared for a long wait. Spanish menu. Dinner. Closed Sun-Mon; Thanksgiving. **$$**

★ ★ ZUNI CAFE. *1658 Market St, San Francisco (94102). Phone 415/552-2522; fax 415/552-9149.* Celebrity chef and cookbook author Judy Rodgers continues to steer her vibrant eatery to the head of the competitive San Francisco restaurant scene. Zuni's two-story brick building on Market Street is full of light, unusual angles, and large windows. Adding to the atmosphere are the long, copper-topped bar; a large wood-burning oven; colorful modern artwork;, a baby grand piano that's tickled nightly; and an array of flowers. The menu, which focuses on Mediterranean cuisine, changes daily, although the famous Caesar salad and roasted chicken are perennial favorites. French, Italian menu. Lunch, dinner, Sun brunch. Closed Mon; holidays. Bar. Outdoor seating. **$$$**

San Francisco International Airport Area

See also Hayward, Oakland, Redwood City, San Francisco, San Mateo

Web Site www.flysfo.com

Information phone 650/821-8211 or toll-free 800/897-1910

Lost and Found 650/821-7014.

Airlines Aeroflot, Air Canada, Air China, Air France, Alaska Airlines, America West Airlines, American Airlines, ANA (All Nippon Airways), Asiana, American Trans Air, British Airways, Cathay Pacific Airways, China Airlines, Continental Airlines, Delta Airlines, Eva Airways, Frontier Airlines, Hawaiian Airlines, Horizon Air, Japan Airlines, KLM Airlines, Korean Air, LACSA, Lufthansa, Mexicana, Midwest Airlines, Northwest Airlines, Philippine Airlines,

Singapore Airlines, TACA, United Airlines, United Express, US Airways, Virgin Atlantic

Limited-Service Hotel

★★ **DOUBLETREE HOTEL.** *835 Airport Blvd, Burlingame (94010). Phone 650/344-5500; toll-free 800/222-8733; fax 650/340-8851. www.doubletree.com.* 390 rooms, 8 story. Check-out noon. Restaurant, bar. Fitness room. Airport transportation available. Business center. **$**

Full-Service Hotels

★★★ **HYATT REGENCY SAN FRANCISCO AIRPORT.** *1333 Bayshore Hwy, Burlingame (94010). Phone 650/347-1234; toll-free 800/633-7313; fax 650/696-2669. www.hyatt.com.* 793 rooms, 9 story. Check-in 3 pm, check-out noon. Restaurant, bar. Fitness room. Outdoor pool, whirlpool. Airport transportation available. Business center. **$**

★★★ **MARRIOTT SAN FRANCISCO AIRPORT.** *1800 Old Bayshore Hwy, Burlingame (94010). Phone 650/692-9100; toll-free 800/228-9290; fax 650/692-8016. www.marriott.com.* Perched along the waterfront, this hotel is just 1 mile south of the airport and convenient to the city and Silicon Valley. There is a lounge with a great view of the bay and several dining options. 685 rooms, 11 story. Pets accepted; fee. Check-in 3 pm, check-out noon. Restaurant, bar. Fitness room. Indoor pool, whirlpool. Airport transportation available. **$**

★★★ **SHERATON GATEWAY SAN FRANCISCO AIRPORT HOTEL.** *600 Airport Blvd, Burlingame (94010). Phone 650/340-8500; fax 650/343-1546. www.sheratonsfo.com.* 404 rooms, 15 story. Pets accepted; restrictions. Check-in 3 pm, check-out noon. Restaurant, bar. Fitness room. Indoor pool, whirlpool. Airport transportation available. Business center. **$**

★★★ **THE WESTIN SAN FRANCISCO AIRPORT.** *1 Old Bayshore Hwy, Millbrae (94030). Phone 650/692-3500; fax 650/872-8111. www.westin.com.* 393 rooms, 7 story. Pets accepted; fee. Check-in 3 pm, check-out 1 pm. Restaurant, bar. Fitness room. Indoor pool, whirlpool. Airport transportation available. Business center. **$**

Restaurants

★★ **KULETO'S.** *1095 Rollins Rd, Burlingame (94010). Phone 650/342-4922; fax 650/344-3376. www.kimptongroup.com.* Italian menu. Lunch, dinner. Closed holidays. **$$**

★★★ **PISCES.** *1190 California Dr, Burlingame (94010). Phone 650/401-7500; fax 650/401-8321. www.piscesrestaurant.com.* This petite, small-town cousin of San Francisco's Aqua (see) may not be as slick and savvy as its big-city relative, but it shines in its own wonderful way. Located in a historic train station, Pisces is intimate and airy, awash in blond wood with shuttered windows, tall mirrors, and a slick marble bar. Seafood specialist chef Michael Mina consulted on this project, so it makes sense that the signatures focus on the wonders of the deep blue. A seasonal raw bar glistens with the briny waters of the ocean; foie gras is smartly paired with seared day boat scallops; and tuna tartare is infused with sesame and scotch bonnet chilies. Pisces has a great selection of inventive cocktails as well; make time to sample a few before dinner. Seafood menu. Dinner. Closed Sun-Mon. Bar. Children's menu. Casual attire. Reservations recommended. **$$$**

San Jose (E-2)

See also Fremont, Gilroy, Livermore, Los Gatos, Santa Clara, Santa Cruz, Saratoga

Founded 1777
Population 894,943
Elevation 87 ft
Area Code 408
Information Convention & Visitors Bureau, 333 W San Carlos St, Suite 1000, 95110; phone 408/295-2265 (24-hour recording)
Web Site www.sanjose.org

At the south end of San Francisco Bay, 50 miles from San Francisco, San Jose is known as the "Capital of Silicon Valley." San Jose was founded as Pueblo de San Jose de Guadalupe in the name of Charles III of Spain; the first American flag was raised above the town hall in 1846. The city was one of the first to be incorporated in California. Before California was even a state, San Jose became the first state capital; the first state legislature assembled here on December 15, 1849. In recent years, it has become an important electronic and aerospace center. It is also the home of San Jose State University.

What to See and Do

Alum Rock Park. *16240 Alum Rock Ave, San Jose (95127). Phone 408/259-5477. www.sanjoseca.gov/prns/regionalparks/arp/arpindex.htm.* These 720 acres are known as "Little Yosemite" because of the natural formations. Hiking, bicycle, bridle trails. Picnic grounds, playground. (Daily) **$$** Also in the park is

Youth Science Institute. *16260 Alum Rock Ave, San Jose (95127). Phone 408/258-4322. www.ysi.ca.org.* Natural science classes, exhibits, and nature trips. (Tues-Sun) **$**

Bay 101 Casino. *1801 Bering Dr, San Jose (95112). Phone 408/451-8888. www.bay101.com.* The premiere poker club in the Bay Area, San Jose's Bay 101 offers 40 tables of card games, with your options ranging from draw poker to California blackjack. The place has an elegant feel, with amenities that are expected (a sports bar) and unexpected (a beauty salon). There are daily tournaments, with the big annual event, the Bay 101 Open, taking place in late October.

Cardinal Coffee Shop. *3197 Meridian Ave, San Jose (95124). Phone 408/269-7891. www.cardinalcoffeeshop.com.* An establishment with a vibe straight out of the 1950s, the Cardinal Coffee Shop and Lounge is a San Jose institution. A combination full-service bar and 24-hour diner, the place serves breakfast around the clock and features live music (nostalgia acts and R&B) and dancing every night. The crowd is diverse, with a heavy concentration of baby boomers reliving their youth. (Daily, 24 hours)

Children's Discovery Museum. *Guadalupe River Park, 180 Woz Way, San Jose (95110). Phone 408/298-5437. www.cdm.org.* This museum's hand-on exhibits explore the relationships between the natural and the created worlds, and among people of different cultures and times. Exhibits include "Streets," a 5/8-scale replica of an actual city, with street lights, parking meters, and fire hydrants; and "Waterworks," which allows an operation of pumps and valves to move water through a reservoir system. (Tues-Sat 10 am-5 pm, Sun from noon; closed holidays) **$$**

J. Lohr Winery. *1000 Lenzen Ave, San Jose (95126). Phone 408/288-5057. www.jlohr.com.* Home of J. Lohr wines. Tasting room (daily 10 am-5 pm; closed holidays). **FREE**

Japantown Shopping District. *Jackson and 6th sts, San Jose.* After the internment of Japanese Americans during World War II, most Japanese-dominated neighborhoods in the United States faded and eventually disappeared. Bucking the trend, San Jose's Japantown is one of the few remaining urban districts of its kind, with a rich history that dates to the first Japanese immigrants who settled here circa 1900. Centered on the intersection of Sixth and Jackson streets, modern Japantown balances preservation and tradition with a vision for the future. The mix of businesses and merchants includes a plethora of Asian groceries and eateries, art galleries, martial arts studios, and gift shops, a number of which were first established in the early 1900s. On Sunday mornings, there is a farmers' market with an Asian bent on Jackson between 6th and 7th streets.

Jungle Fun and Adventure. *950 El Paseo De Saratoga, San Jose (95130). Phone 408/866-4386. www.junglefunandadventure.com.* Who says you can't find a jungle near the city? This massive four-story indoor play facility is perfect for children 12 and under and for rainy days. With two locations near San Francisco, in Concord and San Jose, and open every day except Thanksgiving and Christmas, what could be better than 20,000 square feet of room with towering giraffes and jungley-themed things for children to see and climb on and a place for lunch afterward? (Daily; closed Thanksgiving, Dec 25) **$$**

Kelley Park. *1300 Senter Rd, San Jose (95112). Phone 408/277-5561. www.sanjoseca.gov/prns/regionalparks/kp/.* The park includes

Happy Hollow Park and Zoo. *1300 Senter Rd, San Jose (95112). Phone 408/277-3000. www.happyhollowparkandzoo.org.* On 12 acres. Themed children's rides; creative play areas; zoo and contact area; special events. (Daily 10 am-5 pm; no admittance during last hour open; closed Dec 25) **$$**

History San Jose. *1650 Senter Rd, San Jose (95112). Phone 408/287-2290. www.historysanjose.org.* Original and replica structures have been placed on the grounds to re-create most elements of early San Jose. Outdoor exhibits include original pioneer houses, a doctor's office, print shop, fruit barn, and 1927 gas station; replicas of early landmarks, including a hotel, stables, a trolley barn, firehouse, bank, 117-foot electric light tower, an operating ice cream store, and 1880 Chinese Temple with original altar. Indoor hotel exhibits trace history of area's Native American, Spanish, Mexican, and Chinese background. Museum (Sat-Sun noon-4 pm; closed Jan 1, Thanksgiving, Dec 25). **$$**

Japanese Friendship Garden. *1300 Senter Rd, San Jose (95112).* A 6 1/2-acre Japanese Stroll Garden patterned after Korakuen Park in Okayama, Japan; on two levels with a waterfall dropping from a lake on the upper level into one of two lakes on the lower level; 22 symbolic features include bridges and lanterns; teahouse; 3/4-mile paved walkway trail. (Daily 10 am-4 pm) **FREE**

Municipal Rose Garden. *Naglee and Dana aves, San Jose (95112). Phone 408/277-5422. www.sanjoseca.gov/prns/regionalparks/rg.* Approximately 5,000 rose plants on 6 acres, peak blooming in late Apr-May. Picnicking. (Daily) **FREE**

Lick Observatory. *Hwy 130, Mount Hamilton (95140). 25 miles SE. Phone 408/274-5061. www.ucolick.org.* The main building has astronomical exhibits, guide lectures, and a 36-inch refracting telescope. At the 120-inch reflecting telescope, there is a Visitors Gallery with a self-guided tour. Maintained by the University of California at Santa Cruz. (Daily; closed holidays) **FREE**

Mirassou Winery. *3000 Aborn Rd, San Jose (95135). Phone 408/274-4000. www.mirassou.com.* Produces vintage wines. Wine tasting and tours. (Daily noon-5 pm; closed holidays) **FREE**

Overfelt Gardens. *2145 Mckee Rd, San Jose (95116). Educational Park Dr, W of Jackson Ave via Hwy 101 and I-680. Phone 408/251-3323. www.sanjoseca.gov/prns/regionalparks/og.* This 33-acre botanical preserve includes extensive natural areas, a formal botanic garden, and a wildlife sanctuary. Migratory waterfowl and other wildlife inhabit three lakes; wooded areas with wildflowers; the Chinese Cultural Garden has a bronze and marble statue of Confucius overlooking a reflecting pond, an ornate Chinese gate, and three Chinese pavilions—all a gift from the Chinese community. No pets, skates, skateboards, or bicycles. (Daily) **FREE**

Peralta Adobe and Fallon House. *175 W St. John St, San Jose (95110). Phone 408/993-8300. www.historysanjose.org/visiting_hsj/peralta_fallon.* Built in 1797, the Peralta adobe is the last remaining home of the first pueblo (city) in California. The Fallon house is a Victorian home built for a wealthy resident. Both homes are furnished in the period. (Sat-Sun noon-5 pm) **FREE**

Raging Waters San Jose. *Lake Cunningham Regional Park, 2333 S White Rd, San Jose (95148). Phone 408/238-9900. www.rwsplash.com.* Water-themed amusement park with 23 acres of slides and attractions, including Great White Shark, lazy river, Wacky Water Works, and a 350,000-gallon wave pool. (Mid-June-late Aug, daily; mid-May-mid-June and late Aug-Sept, Sat-Sun) **$$$$**

Rosicrucian Park. *1342 Naglee Ave, San Jose (95191). Phone 408/947-3600. www.rosicrucian.org/park.* Headquarters of the English Grand Lodge of the Rosicrucian Order, AMORC; worldwide philosophical fraternity. **$$** On the grounds are

Egyptian Museum. *1342 Naglee Ave, San Jose (95191). Phone 408/947-3635. www.egyptianmuseum.org.* One of the largest collections of Egyptian antiques west of the Mississippi resides at this museum. Here you'll find both human and animal mummies (including fish, cats, and a baboon); an exhibit on the Egyptian afterlife, which includes the treasures the dead had hoped would accompany them to the afterlife; and a full-scale replica of a nobleman's tomb with images of daily life in the Nile Valley. (Tues-Fri 10 am-5 pm, Sat-Sun 11 am-6 pm; closed Mon, holidays) **$$**

San Jose Earthquakes (MLS). *Spartan Stadium, 1257 S 10th St, San Jose (95112). Phone 408/985-4625. www.sjearthquakes.com.* Professional soccer team.

San Jose Farmers' Market. *San Pedro Square, San Pedro St, San Jose (95113). Between Santa Clara and St. John sts. Phone 408/279-1775.* From May to December, locals head to San Pedro Square in downtown San Jose on Friday to shop for local produce, fresh flowers, and gourmet foods. Beyond the fruit and vegetable carts, there are also such events as cooking demonstrations and musical performances. Among the special events is a twice monthly "Chef at the Market," where a local culinary luminary prepares a dish for all to sample. (May-mid-Dec, Fri 10 am-2 pm) **FREE**

San Jose Flea Market. *1590 Berryessa Rd, San Jose (95113). Phone 408/453-1110. www.sjfm.com.* Flying in the face of Silicon Valley's high-tech reputation, the San Jose Flea Market is a decidedly low-tech spectacle, as the largest open-air market in the United States, encompassing 120 acres and 8 miles of retail-laden pathways. Founded in 1960 by a landfill operator who saw too many good items going to waste, the market now attracts more than 4 million visitors a year to its myriad shops, carts, restaurants, and other attractions. Each week 6,000 vendors hawk everything from army surplus to wigs, and everything in between. But that's not all: the quarter-mile long "Produce Row" overflows with fresh fruits and vegetables of all descriptions, a carousel, arcade, and two playgrounds thrill the kids, and street musicians sing and strum in the background. (Wed-Sun, dawn-dusk)

San Jose Museum of Art. *110 S Market St, San Jose (91553). Phone 408/294-2787. www.sjmusart.org.* The only accredited museum in San Jose and the top museum in all of Silicon Valley, the San Jose Museum of Art (SJMA) has a totally free admission policy that helps it serve all segments of the population. The downtown facility is best known for its permanent collection of contemporary works from the 20th and 21st centuries, with the focus on those by West Coast artists. Often edgy and abstract, these pieces run the gamut from oil paintings to room-size installations and together comprise one of the top collections of modern art in the area, rivaling that of San Francisco's better-known MOMA. The SJMA's seasonal exhibitions are similar in focus and quality; showcases for regional contemporary artists and high-concept, themed exhibitions dominate the calendar. The last Sunday of every month is Kids ArtSunday, with workshops and other activities targeting the 15-and-under set. (Tues-Sun 11 am-5 pm, Fri to 10 pm; closed Jan 1, Thanksgiving, Dec 25) **FREE**

San Jose Museum of Quilts & Textiles. *110 Paseo de San Antonio, San Jose (95112). Phone 408/971-0323. www.sjquiltmuseum.org.* Regularly changing exhibits feature quilts and other textiles from around the world. The museum's collection includes quilts and coverlets from the 19th century. Explores the role of quilts in cultural traditions, the lives of their makers, and their significance as historical documents. (Tues-Wed, Fri-Sun 10 am-5 pm, Thurs to 8 pm; closed holidays) **$**

San Jose Sharks (NHL). *Compaq Center, 525 W Santa Clara St, San Jose (95113). Phone 408/287-7070; toll-free 800/225-2277. www.sj-sharks.com.* Professional hockey team.

Santana Row. *355 Santana Row, San Jose (95128). Phone 408/551-4600. www.santanarow.com.* This upscale shopping center adjacent to the Valencia Hotel features such favorite names as Diesel, Gucci, and Tod's, as well as mall staples like Crate & Barrel and Borders Books and Music. In keeping with the focus on making this a living space and not just a shopping space, you'll also find a fitness center, day spas, a movie theater, a number of restaurants, and an open-air café with ongoing entertainment that cater to the residents of Santana Row's lofts and townhomes.

The Tech Museum of Innovation. *201 S Market St, San Jose (95113). Phone 408/294-8324. www.thetech.org.* With more than 240 interactive exhibits, this 132,000-square-foot facility offers visitors four themed galleries: Innovation, Exploration, Communication, and Life Tech. See how a microchip is made, design a roller coaster, or make a movie in the Digital Studio. The Hackworth IMAX Theater (fee), whose dome has become a landmark in the San Jose skyline, presents shows on a larger-than-life screen with groundbreaking computer graphics and technology. (Daily 10 am-5 pm; closed Thanksgiving, Dec 25) **$$**

West San Carlos Street Antique Row. *W San Carlos St and Bascom Ave, San Jose.* The 15-block stretch of West San Carlos Street—bounded on the west by Bascom Avenue and the east by McEvoy Street—boasts one of the highest concentrations of antique shops on the Pacific Coast. The selection is unusually diverse, running the gamut from European crystal to African art to Western Americana. There are a number of multi-dealer collectives among the shops, including Antiques Village (1225 W San Carlos), Laurelwood Antiques (1824 W San Carlos), Briarwood Antiques & Collectibles (1885 W San Carlos), and Antiques Colony (1915 W San Carlos). Targeting a younger set, there are also a number of resale shops packed with vintage and almost-new clothing and décor, as well as a few standard thrift stores. In other words, if it's someone else's former possession, it's probably here.

Winchester Mystery House. *525 S Winchester Blvd, San Jose (95128). At I-280 and Hwy 17. Phone 408/247-2101. www.winchestermysteryhouse.com.* Construction began on this architectural oddity in 1884 at the behest of eccentric widow Sarah Winchester (of the Winchester Rifle Winchesters). And it went on and on and on—all the while without the guidance of blueprints—until Winchester died in 1922. (It seems a fortuneteller had told old Sarah that the only way to appease the spirits of those slain by the family's firearms was the continual pounding of hammers.) By the time she passed away, her home had grown to 160 rooms—and so many oddball features—that it became a tourist attraction. Within the four-story mansion are 17 chimneys, 47 fireplaces, 950 doors, and 40 bedrooms, as well as staircases that go nowhere and cabinets that are the sole entry to entire wings. Also here are two museums, one dedicated to the Winchester Rifle, and extensive gardens open for guests to explore. (Opens daily 9 am; hours vary according to season) **$$$$**

Special Events

Metro Fountain Blues Festival. *San Jose State University, Paseo de San Carlos, San Jose. Phone 408/924-6262.* Held in early May at San Carlos Plaza on the campus of San Jose State University, the Metro Fountain Blues Festival is the preeminent annual musical event in Silicon Valley. The free concert showcases a slate of about ten local and national blues talents every year, from Mississippi Delta and Chicago legends to up-and-coming guitar prodigies. **FREE**

Obon Festival. *640 N 5th St, San Jose (95112). Phone 408/293-9292. www.bca-ocbc.org.* Japanese-American outdoor celebration with hundreds of costumed dancers and Taiko drummers; games, food, crafts. Early or mid-July.

San Jose America Festival. *2011 Little Orchard St, San Jose (95125). Phone 408/294-2100.* This celebration of cultural diversity in San Jose features food booths, arts and crafts, rides, games, entertainment, and a breathtaking fireworks display. Early July.

Santa Clara County Fair. *Santa Clara County Fairgrounds, 344 Tully Rd, San Jose (95111). Phone 408/494-3247. www.thefair.org.* Children's stage acts, a Demolition Derby, concerts, and a fireworks show are just a few of the reasons crowds gather at this county fair year after year. Early Aug.

Tapestry Arts Festival. *255 N Market St, San Jose (95110). Phone 408/494-3590. www.tapestryarts.org.* More than 350 visual artists and craftspeople display works ranging from ceramics and paintings to jewelry, clothing, and woodwork at this three-day festival celebrating the arts and ethnic diversity. Music overs will enjoy the three entertainment stages, which feature performers of rock, blues, jazz, and classical music as well as dance and theater performances; foodies will revel in the choices from 40 food booths; and kids can explore their inner-artist through hands-on art activities. Labor Day weekend. **FREE**

Limited-Service Hotels

★ ★ BEST WESTERN GATEWAY INN. *2585 Seaboard Ave, San Jose (95131). Phone 408/435-8800; toll-free 800/437-8855; fax 408/435-8879. www.bestwestern.com.* 150 rooms, 2 story. Complimentary continental breakfast. Check-out noon. Outdoor pool, whirlpool. Airport transportation available. **$**

★ ★ COURTYARD BY MARRIOTT. *10605 N Wolfe Rd, Cupertino (95014). Phone 408/252-9100; toll-free 800/321-2211; fax 408/252-0632. www.marriott.com.* 149 rooms, 3 story. Check-in 3 pm, check-out noon. Fitness room. Outdoor pool, whirlpool. **$$**

★ ★ DOUBLETREE HOTEL. *2050 Gateway Pl, San Jose (95110). Phone 408/453-4000; toll-free 800/222-8733; fax 408/437-2898. www.doubletree.com.* Set in a contemporary architectural design featuring two high-rise towers, this hotel is located in the heart of the Silicon Valley with spacious guest rooms. 505 rooms, 10 story. Pets accepted, some restrictions; fee. Check-in 3 pm, check-out noon. Restaurant, bar. Fitness room. Outdoor pool. Airport transportation available. Business center. **$**

★ ★ EMBASSY SUITES. *901 E Calaveras Blvd, Milpitas (95035). Phone 408/942-0400; toll-free 800/362-2779; fax 408/262-8604. www.embassysuites.com.* 266 rooms, 9 story, all suites. Complimentary full breakfast. Check-out 1 pm. Restaurant, bar. Indoor pool, whirlpool. **$**

★ ★ RADISSON HOTEL SAN JOSE AIRPORT. *1471 N 4th St, San Jose (95112). Phone 408/452-0200; toll-free 800/333-3333; fax 408/437-8819. www.radisson.com.* 185 rooms, 5 story. Check-out noon. Restaurant, bar. Fitness room. Outdoor pool, whirlpool. Airport transportation available. **$$**

★ STAYBRIDGE SUITES. *1602 Crane Ct, San Jose (95112). Phone 408/436-1600; fax 408/436-1075. www.staybridge.com.* 98 rooms, 3 story, all suites. Pets accepted, some restrictions; fee. Complimentary continental breakfast. Check-in 3 pm, check-out noon. Fitness room. Outdoor pool, whirlpool. Airport transportation available. **$$**

Full-Service Hotels

★ ★ ★ CROWNE PLAZA. *282 Almaden Blvd, San Jose (95113). Phone 408/998-0400; fax 408/289-9081.*

www.crowneplaza.com. 231 rooms, 9 story. Pets accepted. Check-in 3 pm, check-out noon. Restaurant, bar. Fitness room. Airport transportation available. **$$**

★ ★ ★ CROWNE PLAZA. *777 Bellew Dr, Milpitas (95035). Phone 408/321-9500; fax 408/321-9599. www.crowneplaza.com.* 305 rooms, 12 story. Check-in 3 pm, check-out noon. Restaurant, bar. Fitness room. Outdoor pool, whirlpool. Airport transportation available. Business center. **$$**

★ ★ ★ THE FAIRMONT SAN JOSE. *170 S Market St, San Jose (95113). Phone 408/998-1900; toll-free 800/441-1414; fax 408/287-1648. www.fairmont.com.* The 20-story twin-tower complex of The Fairmont San Jose is a perfect match for its location in the heart of Silicon Valley, the nerve center of the computer industry. The hotel provides its guests with the best. Cream-and-pastel tones create a light, breezy décor synonymous with California's relaxed style. Spacious and comfortable, the accommodations are a welcome respite from the hustle and bustle of the city. Business travelers seek the services of the well-equipped business center, while others head for the fitness center and spa to work off the pressures of the day. From The Grill on the Alley's steaks and seafood and the Fountain Restaurant's traditional American menu to the sophisticated Chinese dishes of Pagoda, the hotel's three restaurants offer something for everyone. 808 rooms, 20 story. Pets accepted; fee. Check-in 3 pm, check-out noon. High-speed Internet access. Three restaurants, bar. Fitness room. Outdoor pool. Business center. **$$**

★ ★ ★ HILTON SAN JOSE AND TOWERS. *300 Almaden Blvd, San Jose (95110). Phone 408/287-2100; toll-free 800/774-1500; fax 408/947-4489. www.sanjose.hilton.com.* 354 rooms, 16 story. Pets accepted; restrictions fee. Check-in 4 pm, check-out 1 pm. High-speed Internet access. Restaurant, bar. Fitness room. Outdoor pool, whirlpool. Business center. **$$**

★ ★ ★ HOTEL DE ANZA. *233 W Santa Clara St, San Jose (95113). Phone 408/286-1000; toll-free 800/843-3700; fax 408/286-0500. www.hoteldeanza.com.* This classic Art Deco hotel provides a pleasant stay for business travelers and vacationers who are made to feel at home by being invited to "raid the pantry" and make themselves a snack at any time of the day or night. Guest rooms are decorated in a quirky, colorful style, and there is plenty of space available for meetings and special events. 100 rooms, 10 story. Pets accepted; fee. Check-in 3 pm, check-out noon. High-speed Internet access. Restaurant, bar. Fitness room. Business center. **$**

★ ★ ★ HOTEL VALENCIA SANTANA ROW. *355 Santana Row, San Jose (95128). Phone 408/551-0010; fax 408/551-0550. www.hotelvalencia.com.* An upscale, tech-savvy clientele frequents this hip hotel for its sleek style and state-of-the-art amenities. From the faux mink bed cover to the toiletries provided by California apothecary Lather, luxury is in the details here. Nestled within the tony shopping area of Santana Row, this hotel is a paradise for those seeking a little retail therapy. Carnivores head for the hotel's fantastic Citrus steakhouse, while the V bar and Cielo Wine Terrace & Bar are among the hottest night spots in town. The Valencia represents Silicon Valley at its best: not only does the hotel offer wireless Internet access throughout the property, including remote curbside check-in, but it also offers high-speed connections at the desk, bedside, and on TV. 120 rooms. Check-in 3 pm, check-out noon. High-speed Internet access, wireless Internet access. Restaurant, bar. Fitness room. Outdoor pool, whirlpool. Business center. **$$**

★ ★ ★ HYATT SAN JOSE. *1740 N 1st St, San Jose (95112). Phone 408/993-1234; toll-free 888/915-1234; fax 408/453-0259. www.hyattsanjose.hyatt.com.* 512 rooms, 3 story. Check-in 3 pm, check-out noon. Restaurant, bar. Fitness room. Outdoor pool, whirlpool. Airport transportation available. Business center. **$**

★ ★ ★ MARRIOTT SAN JOSE. *301 S Market St, San Jose (95113). Phone 408/280-1300; toll-free 800/314-0928; fax 408/278-4444. www.marriott.com.* 506 rooms. Check-in 3 pm, check-out noon. Restaurant, bar. **$$**

★ ★ ★ SAINTE CLAIRE HOTEL. *302 S Market St, San Jose (95113). Phone 408/295-2000; toll-free 800/238-6111; fax 408/977-0403. www.sainteclaire hotel.com.* This National Historic Landmark is centrally located in the beautiful area of downtown San Jose, and within walking distance of museums, theaters, and the San Jose McEnery Convention Center. 171

rooms, 6 story. Check-in 3 pm, check-out noon. High-speed Internet access, wireless Internet access. Two restaurants, bar. Fitness room. Airport transportation available. Business center. **$$**

★ ★ ★ SHERATON SAN JOSE HOTEL. *1801 Barber Ln, Milpitas (95035). Phone 408/943-0600; toll-free 800/325-3535; fax 408/943-0484. www.sheraton.com.* 229 rooms, 9 story. Check-in 3 pm, check-out 1 pm. Restaurant, bar. Fitness room. Outdoor pool, whirlpool. Airport transportation available. Business center. **$**

Specialty Lodging

The following lodging establishment is approved by Mobil Travel Guide, but due to its unique and individualized nature has not been given a traditional Mobil Star rating. Included in this listing you may find bed-and-breakfasts, limited-service inns, guest ranches, and other unique hotel properties.

PRUNEYARD INN. *1995 S Bascom Ave, Campbell (95008). Phone 408/559-4300; toll-free 800/559-4344; fax 408/559-9919. www.pruneyardinn.com.* 171 rooms, 3 story. Complimentary continental breakfast. Check-in 3 pm, check-out noon. High-speed Internet access, wireless Internet access. Fitness room. Outdoor pool, whirlpool. Airport transportation available. Business center. **$**

Restaurants

★ ★ ★ EMILE'S. *545 S 2nd St, San Jose (95112). Phone 408/289-1960; fax 408/998-1245. www.emiles.com.* Fresh flowers on every table, and hand-sculpted brass work lend an elegant touch to the décor. French menu. Dinner. Closed Sun-Mon; holidays. Bar. Valet parking. **$$**

★ ★ ★ LA PASTAIA. *233 W Santa Clara, San Jose (95113). Phone 408/286-8686; fax 408/286-8787. www.lapastaia.com.* Located in the gorgeous Hotel De Anza (see), the blue-tiled terrace, with its fountains and palm trees, provides an idyllic spot to enjoy the cuisine. Italian menu. Lunch, dinner. Closed holidays. Valet parking. Outdoor seating. **$$**

★ ★ ★ LOU'S VILLAGE. *1465 W San Carlos St, San Jose (95126). Phone 408/293-4570; fax 408/293-9424. www.lousvillage.com.* Photographs of entertainers who performed here in the '50s and '60s illustrate the long history of this restaurant. Seafood menu. Lunch, dinner. Closed Jan 1, Dec 25. Children's menu. **$$$**

★ O'FLAHERTY'S IRISH PUB. *25 N San Pedro St, San Jose (95110). Phone 408/947-8007; fax 408/947-7963. www.oflahertyspub.com.* Irish menu. Lunch, dinner. Bar. Casual attire. Outdoor seating. **$**

San Juan Bautista (F-2)

See also Gilroy, Salinas

Population 1,549
Elevation 150 ft
Area Code 831
Zip 95045
Information Chamber of Commerce, 1 Polk St, PO Box 1037, 95045-1037; phone 831/623-2454
Web Site www.san-juan-bautista.ca.us

The San Andreas Fault intersects this little town, providing residents with a few minor tremors and a topic of speculation, but little worry; most of the buildings have been standing more than 150 years. San Juan Bautista began in 1797 with the Spanish mission. The town that spread around the mission prospered as a center of cattle ranching and commerce from a nearby lode of quicksilver. However, in 1870 the Southern Pacific Railroad ran the region's first tracks through a nearby town and San Juan Bautista began to decline. Today, tourists and artists contribute to the economy of the town.

What to See and Do

San Juan Bautista State Historic Park. *19 Franklin St, San Juan Bautista. 3 miles E of Hwy 101. Phone 831/623-4881. www.parks.ca.gov.* Here are

Mission San Juan Bautista. *2nd and Mariposa sts, San Juan Bautista. Phone 831/623-2127.* (1797) Fifteenth and largest mission church built by the Franciscans. Church, finished in 1812 and still in use, contains many original items. The museum has old vestments, music books, barrel organ, relics, and original kitchen and dining room. Cemetery has graves of 4,300 Native Americans. (Daily; closed holidays) **DONATION**

Plaza Stable. (1861) Houses collection of restored horse-drawn carriages, blacksmith and wagon-wright equipment, and tools; **Castro-Breen House**

(1841) (self-guided tours); **Plaza Hall** (1868), used as a residence, assembly place, and dance hall; **Plaza Hotel**, restored. Picnicking. (Daily; closed Jan 1, Thanksgiving, Dec 25) All buildings **$**

Special Events

Early Days Celebration. *State Historic Park, 19 Franklin St, San Juan Bautista. Phone 831/623-4526.* Commemorates founding of mission; food, entertainment, history demonstrations. Father's Day weekend.

San Benito County Saddle Horse Show & Rodeo. *Bolado Park Fairgrounds, Hwy 25, Tres Pinos (95075). 8 miles W on Hwy 156 to Hollister, then 8 miles S on Hwy 25. Phone 831/628-3545. www.sanbenitocountyfair.com.* In addition to the horse and rodeo competitions, this annual event also holds a family barbecue, an art fair, and a kickoff parade downtown. Late June. **$$**

Restaurant

★★ JARDINES DE SAN JUAN. *115 3rd St, San Juan Bautista (95045). Phone 831/623-4466; fax 831/623-4340. www.jardinesrestaurant.com.* Mexican menu. Lunch, dinner. Closed Jan 1, Thanksgiving, Dec 25. Bar. Casual attire. Outdoor seating. **$**

San Martin

Full-Service Hotel

★★★★ THE LODGE AT CORDEVALLE. *One Cordevalle Club Dr, San Martin (95046). Phone 408/695-4500; toll-free 877/255-2626; fax 408/695-4578. www.cordevalle.com.* Sequestering, clubby, and out of the way are all attributes that give The Lodge at CordeValle cachet. Combining the sports amenities of a golf club with the service of a social club, CordeValle sprawls over 1,700 acres in the foothills between San Jose and Monterey, attracting small business groups as well as golfers and romantic weekend seekers. Run by the pampering, California-based Auberge du Soleil hotel group, the luxurious inn overlooks a rolling 18-hole Robert Trent Jones Jr. golf course from spacious, high-ceilinged bungalows trimmed in earthy woods and warm leather furnishings. The spa, also home to a fitness center and lap pool, capitalizes on the resort's outdoor splendor, planting a private garden accessible from each treatment room. Hike the property to fully appreciate how blest are the grounds. An on-site vineyard, for example, produces the wine left in the guest rooms, along with cheese and crackers, as a welcome gift. 45 rooms. Check-in 3 pm, check-out noon. Restaurant, bar. Fitness room. Outdoor pool, whirlpool. Golf. Tennis. **$$$$**

Spa

★★★★ THE SPA AT CORDEVALLE. *One Cordevalle Club Dr, San Martin (95046).* The Lodge at Cordevalle is a first-rate golf resort. Tucked away on an exclusive course designed by Robert Trent Jones Jr. this resort's world seems to revolve around golf, yet the world-class spa gives the greens a run for their money. This top-notch facility treats its guests to luxurious amenities, elegant interiors, and a full-service spa menu. Classic contemporary is the reigning style at this spa, where earth tones take precedence and sandstone fireplaces create a serene atmosphere. The services blend European traditions with modern philosophies for the ultimate in relaxation and rejuvenation, and most of the treatments use locally grown herbs, flowers, and even grapes from the hillsides just outside the window. Several treatments have been created specifically with the golfer's needs in mind. The restful pace and quietude found here is perhaps best enjoyed from the private gardens accompanying each treatment room.

San Mateo (E-2)

See also Half Moon Bay, Oakland, Redwood City, San Francisco International Airport Area

Settled 1851
Population 92,482
Elevation 28 ft
Area Code 650
Information San Mateo Area Chamber of Commerce, 1021 S El Camino Real, 94402; phone 650/341-5679
Web Site www.sanmateoca.org

Once a stop between the chain of missions established by Fray Junipero Serra, San Mateo is now a busy suburban area within easy access to both the coast and the bay.

What to See and Do

Bay Meadows Race Course. *2600 S Delaware St, San Mateo (94403). Phone 650/574-7223. www.baymeadows.com.* About an hour from the city of San

Francisco, horseracing fans can make their bets at California's oldest racetrack. Races continued here during World War II and continue to run even in inclement weather. Bay Meadows is home to well-known horses and trainers as well as jockeys such as Russell Base, who had an unprecedented 400-win streak. It was the first park of its kind to introduce the "photo finish." Races usually take place Wednesday through Sunday afternoons. **$**

Coyote Point Museum. *1651 Coyote Point Dr, San Mateo. Via Hwy 101, northbound exit Dore Ave; southbound exit Poplar Ave. Phone 650/342-7755. www.coyoteptmuseum.org.* Museum features four-level exhibition including ecological concepts, dioramas, computer games, live insect colonies, aquarium displays. Two-acre Wildlife Center features native bay-area animals, walk-through aviaries, and native plants. (Tues-Sat 10 am-5 pm, Sun from noon; closed holidays) Free admission first Wed of month. **$$**

Japanese Tea Garden. *5th and Laurel aves, San Mateo. Phone 650/522-7434.* Collection of koi (carp), bonsai specimens; pagoda from Toyonaka, Japan; teahouse. (Daily; closed Dec 25) **FREE**

Woodside Store. *3300 Tripp Rd, Woodside (94062). 10 miles SW via I-280 then E on Hwy 84 (Woodside Rd) to Kings Mountain and Tripp rds. Phone 650/851-7615.* (1854) First store between San Jose and San Francisco. The building, once used as a post office and general store, still contains original equipment and furnishings. Tours by appointment. (Tues, Thurs 10 am-4 pm, Sat-Sun from noon) **FREE** Also in Woodside is

Filoli Gardens. *86 Cañada Rd, Woodside (94062). Phone 650/364-8300. www.filoli.org.* This was a filming location for the *Dynasty* TV program. Georgian-style mansion and 16 acres of gardens. Guided tours of mansion require reservations. (Mid-Feb-late Oct, Tues-Sat 10 am-3:30 pm; closed holidays) **$$**

Special Event

San Mateo County Fair. *San Mateo County Expo Center, 2495 S Delaware, San Mateo (94403). Phone 650/574-3247. www.sanmateocountyfair.com.* Entertainment, food, music, carnival, and horse racing. Mid-Aug. **$$**

Full-Service Hotel

★★★ MARRIOTT SAN MATEO. *1770 S Amphlett Blvd, San Mateo (94402). Phone 650/653-6000; toll-free 800/228-9290; fax 650/573-0533. www.marriott.com.* 476 rooms, 6 story. Check-in 3 pm, check-out noon. Restaurant, bar. Fitness room. Outdoor pool. Business center. **$$**

Specialty Lodging

The following lodging establishment is approved by Mobil Travel Guide, but due to its unique and individualized nature has not been given a traditional Mobil Star rating. Included in this listing you may find bed-and-breakfasts, limited-service inns, guest ranches, and other unique hotel properties.

COXHEAD HOUSE B&B. *37 E Santa Inez Ave, San Mateo (94401). Phone 650/685-1600; fax 650/685-1684. www.coxhead.com.* 4 rooms, 2 story. Complimentary full breakfast. Check-in 4-6 pm, check-out 11 am. Beach access. Airport transportation available. Business center. **$$**

Restaurant

★★★ VIOGNIER. *222 E 4th Ave, San Mateo (94401). Phone 650/685-3727; fax 650/685-3723. www.viognierrestaurant.com.* This upscale, chic café caters to a range of regular customers, both to dine and to shop at Dreager's Gourmet Market. Seafood, steak menu. Lunch, dinner, brunch. **$$**

San Rafael (D-2)

See also Berkeley, Corte Madera, Inverness, Mill Valley, San Francisco, Tiburon

Founded 1817
Population 56,063
Elevation 34 ft
Area Code 415
Information Chamber of Commerce, 817 Mission Ave, 94901; phone 415/454-4163
Web Site www.sanrafael.org

Built around an early Spanish mission, San Rafael is a busy residential community across the Golden Gate Bridge, north of San Francisco. It is the commercial, cultural, and governmental hub of scenic Marin County.

What to See and Do

Marin County Civic Center. *3501 Civic Center Dr, San Rafael (94903). 2 miles N on N San Pedro Rd off Hwy 101. Phone 415/499-7407.* Complex designed by Frank Lloyd Wright; one of his last major projects. Tours (reservations required). (Mon-Fri; closed holidays) **FREE**

Mission San Rafael Arcangel. *1104 5th Ave A, San Rafael. 3 blocks W of Hwy 101. Phone 415/454-8141.* Originally established in 1817 as a sanitarium for Bay Area natives infected with white settlers' diseases, Mission San Rafael Arcángel is 20 miles north of San Francisco in present-day San Rafael. The original mission structures were replaced in 1870, but in 1949, a replica of the first church was erected. Displays detail the mission's history; a self-guided audio tour is available.

Panama Hotel. *4 Bayview St, San Rafael (94901). Phone 415/457-3993. www.panamahotel.com.* The restaurant in the stucco-clad Panama Hotel, a bed-and-breakfast in the quiet Marin County confines of San Rafael, transforms into a smooth jazz club on Tuesdays and Thursdays. Specializing in top-notch Italian and French fare, the place serves lunch and dinner at a swank but cozy corner bar. On Sundays, live music accompanies brunch.

San Quentin State Prison Museum. *Bldg #106, Dolores Way, San Quentin (94964). From the south, Hwy 101 to Sir Francis Drake Blvd exit to San Quentin, then Hwy 17 E to the next exit. From the north, Hwy 101 to Hwy 17, exit Main St. Follow Main St to the main gate. Phone 415/454-8808.* Established in the 1850s, the infamous San Quentin State Prison grew up with California from its Wild West infancy. The still-operational prison now has a museum just inside the front gate that offers a fascinating (and somewhat macabre) glimpse into the facility's past through historic displays, a replica of a prison cell, a diorama of a gas chamber, and artifacts from the original gallows. (Mon-Fri 10-am-4 pm, Sat 11:45-3:15) **$**

Limited-Service Hotel

★ ★ FOUR POINTS BY SHERATON. *1010 Northgate Dr, San Rafael (94903). Phone 415/479-8800; fax 415/479-2342. www.fourpoints.com/sanrafael.* 235 rooms, 4 story. Pets accepted. Check-in 3 pm, check-out noon. Restaurant, bar. Fitness room. Outdoor pool, whirlpool. **$$**

Specialty Lodging

The following lodging establishment is approved by Mobil Travel Guide, but due to its unique and individualized nature has not been given a traditional Mobil Star rating. Included in this listing you may find bed-and-breakfasts, limited-service inns, guest ranches, and other unique hotel properties.

GERSTLE PARK INN. *34 Grove St, San Rafael (94901). Phone 415/721-7611; toll-free 800/726-7611; fax 415/721-7600. www.gerstleparkinn.com.* This 1895 estate, nestled in the foothills of San Rafael, reopened in December 1995 as an elegant inn. 12 rooms. Pets accepted, some restrictions. Complimentary full breakfast. Check-in 3 pm, check-out noon. **$$**

San Ramon

Population 44,722
Area Code 925
Information City of San Ramon, 2222 Camino Ramon, 94583; phone 925/973-2500
Web Site www.ci.san-ramon.ca.us

Full-Service Hotel

★ ★ ★ MARRIOTT SAN RAMON. *2600 Bishop Dr, San Ramon (94583). Phone 925/867-9200; toll-free 800/228-9290; fax 925/830-9326. www.marriotthotels.com.* View of Mount Diablo. 368 rooms, 6 story. Pets accepted; fee. Check-in 3 pm, check-out noon. Restaurant, bar. Fitness room. Indoor pool, outdoor pool, whirlpool. Business center. **$$**

Santa Clara (E-1)

See also Fremont, Livermore, Menlo Park, Mount Diablo State Park, Mountain View, Palo Alto, San Jose, Santa Cruz, Saratoga, Sunnyvale

Founded 1777
Population 102,361
Elevation 88 ft
Area Code 408
Information Convention & Visitors Bureau, 1850 Warburton Ave, 95050; phone 408/244-9660 or toll-free 800/272-6822
Web Site www.santaclara.org

Santa Clara, the "Mission City," is in the heart of Silicon Valley, just 50 minutes south of San Francisco.

What to See and Do

Intel Museum. *2200 Mission College Blvd, Santa Clara (95054). Phone 408/765-0503. www.intel.com/go/museum.* Have you ever wondered how computer chips are made? Or how microprocessors work? If so, consider visiting this 10,000-square-foot museum located in the main lobby of Intel's corporate headquarters. As the inventor of the Pentium processor, Intel is an authority on these subjects. Interactive exhibits describe the differences between various types of chips, how they're constructed and how they're used, and provide insight into the history of this technology. Surf the Internet or play computer games in the Application Lab, where a huge microprocessor demonstrates the brain of a computer. (Mon-Fri 9 am-6 pm, Sat 10 am-5 pm; closed holidays) **FREE**

Paramount's Great America. *2401 Agnew Rd, Santa Clara (95054). Great America Pkwy, off Hwy 101. Phone 408/988-1776. www.pgathrills.com.* In this 100-acre park is a blend of movie magic and theme park thrills. It features an array of thrilling rides, live stage shows, and entertainment; among Paramount's Great America's premier attractions are "Top Gun," a mind-boggling inverted roller-coaster; and "Invertigo," a face-to-face roller coaster. Also featured are *Star Trek,* Nickelodeon, and Hanna-Barbera characters. Also spectacular are the IMAX theater and the world's tallest double-decker carousel, Carousel Columbia, which is near the park's entrance. There is a Nickelodeon area for children called "Splat City." Admission includes rides and attractions. (Apr-Oct, days and times vary; call or visit Web site for schedule) **$$$$**

Santa Clara University. *500 El Camino Real, Santa Clara (95053). Phone 408/554-4000. www.scu.edu.* (1851) (7,900 students) Oldest institution of higher learning in California. Self-guided tour of the Mission Gardens, which includes the Adobe Lodge and Wall (restored) from the 1822-1825 mission. Olive trees and grinding stones in the gardens also date to the early mission period. On campus are

> **De Saisset Museum.** *500 El Camino Real, Santa Clara (95050). Phone 408/554-4528. www.scu.edu/desaisset.* Rotating exhibits (all year); California Historical Collection focuses on precontact Native American period, Mission period, and early years of the university. (Tues-Sun 11 am-4 pm; closed Memorial Day, July 4, Thanksgiving weekend; also Aug-Sept, early Dec-mid-Jan) **FREE**
>
> **Mission Santa Clara de Asis.** *Santa Clara. Phone 408/554-4023. www.scu.edu/visitors/mission.* (1777) The modern mission, dedicated in 1928, is an enlarged and adapted replica of the original mission. The present roof contains 12,000 cover tiles salvaged from earlier missions. Of the four mission bells in the tower, one was a gift from Carlos IV of Spain in 1798 and survived the 1926 fire; another was a gift from Alfonso XIII of Spain in 1929. Surrounded by beautiful gardens and restored Adobe Lodge and Wall; part of the 1822 mission quadrangle. (Mon-Fri)

Triton Museum of Art. *1505 Warburton Ave, Santa Clara (95050). Phone 408/247-3754. www.tritonmuseum.org.* Permanent and changing exhibits of 19th- and 20th-century American and contemporary works; sculpture garden; landscaped grounds on 7 acres. (Daily 11 am-5 pm, Thurs to 9 pm; closed holidays) **FREE**

Special Event

Santa Clara Art & Wine Festival. *Central Park, 969 Kiely Blvd, Santa Clara (95051). Phone 408/615-3140. www.santaclaraartandwine.com.* Features works from local and regional artists; entertainment stages; international foods; and the "Kids' Kingdom." Sept.

Full-Service Hotels

★ ★ ★ MARRIOTT SANTA CLARA-SILICON VALLEY. *2700 Mission College Blvd, Santa Clara (95054). Phone 408/988-1500; toll-free 800/228-9290; fax 408/352-4353. www.marriott.com.* 759 rooms, 15 story. Pets accepted; fee. Check-in 3 pm, check-out 11 am. High-speed Internet access. Two restaurants, two bars. Fitness room. Outdoor pool, whirlpool. Tennis. Business center. **$$**

★ ★ ★ THE WESTIN SANTA CLARA. *5101 Great America Pkwy, Santa Clara (95054). Phone 408/986-0700; toll-free 800/937-8461; fax 408/980-3990. www.westin.com.* 505 rooms, 14 story. Pets accepted. Check-in 3 pm, check-out noon. High-speed Internet access. Two restaurants, bar. Fitness room. Outdoor pool, whirlpool. Business center. **$$**

Specialty Lodging

The following lodging establishment is approved by Mobil Travel Guide, but due to its unique and individualized nature has not been given a traditional Mobil Star rating. Included in this listing you may find bed-and-breakfasts, limited-service inns, guest ranches, and other unique hotel properties.

MADISON STREET INN. *1390 Madison St, Santa Clara (95050). Phone 408/249-5541; toll-free 800/491-5541; fax 408/249-6676. www.madisonstreetinn.com.* Victorian furnishings (1895); library, antiques, bearclaw tubs. 6 rooms. Complimentary full breakfast. Check-in 3-7 pm, check-out noon. Outdoor pool. **$**

Santa Cruz (D-2)

See also Big Basin Redwoods State Park, Los Gatos, San Jose, Santa Clara, Aptos, Watsonville,

Founded 1840
Population 54,543
Elevation 20 ft
Area Code 831
Information Santa Cruz County Conference & Visitors Council, 1211 Ocean St, 95060; phone 831/425-1234 or toll-free 800/833-3494
Web Site www.scccvc.org

Santa Cruz is a bustling seaside resort and arts and crafts center with 29 miles of public beaches. The county is home to a wide variety of agricultural products such as strawberries, apples, and begonias. The present town is predated by the village of Branciforte, which it has now assimilated. Branciforte was founded in 1797 as a colonial venture of the Spanish government. Lacking financial support, the village failed to develop, and its colonists made much trouble for the nearby mission. The Santa Cruz Valley was given its name, which means Holy Cross, by Don Gaspar de Portola and Father Crespi, who discovered it in 1769.

What to See and Do

Año Nuevo State Reserve. *New Year's Creek Rd, Hwy 1, Pescadero (94060). Take Hwy 1 about 22 miles N. Phone 650/879-0227; toll-free 800/444-4445. www.parks.ca.gov.* Wild, windswept coastal reserve where thousands of massive elephant seals come to mate and give birth each winter. (Daily; park accessible by guided walks only, mid-Dec-Mar)

Bargetto Winery. *3535 N Main St, Santa Cruz (95073). E on Hwy 1, exit Capitola/Soquel exit, right on Main St in Soquel. Phone 831/475-2258. www.bargetto.com.* Family winery with tours and tasting. (Daily noon-5 pm; closed holidays) **FREE**

Felton covered bridge. Built in 1892; spans San Lorenzo River 80 feet above the water.

Forest of Nisene Marks. *Aptos Creek Rd, Aptos. 6 miles SE on Hwy 1 to Aptos, then N on Aptos Creek Rd. Phone 831/763-7063. www.parks.ca.gov.* Seismologists identified the epicenter of the October 1989 earthquake (7.1 magnitude) in this 10,000-acre state park. Diagonal fault ridges are evident although the earthquake epicenter can barely be distinguished. Hiking, bicycling, picnicking, primitive camping (fee; 6-mile hike to campsite). (Daily, sunrise-sunset)

Henry Cowell Redwoods. *101 N Big Trees Park Rd, Santa Cruz (95018). 5 miles N on Hwy 9. Phone 831/335-4598. www.parks.ca.gov.* These 1,737 acres contain some of the finest specimens of coastal redwood in the world, including one tree that has a base large enough to shelter several people. Self-guided nature trail, hiking, bridle trails, picnicking, camping. Some campfire programs and guided walks conducted by rangers. (Daily, sunrise-sunset; Nature Center weekends, holidays, and summer: 10 am-4 pm, winter weekdays: 11 am-3 pm) **$$**

Municipal Wharf. *Pacific Ave and Beach St, Santa Cruz (95060). Phone 831/420-5250.* Extends 1/2 mile into Monterey Bay. One of few piers of this type to permit auto traffic. Restaurants, gift shops, fish markets, charter boats; free fishing area.

Mystery Spot. *465 Mystery Spot Rd, Santa Cruz (95065). Phone 831/423-8897. www.mysteryspot.com.* Area 150 feet in diameter that "defies" conventional laws of gravity, perspective; balls roll uphill, trees grow sideways. Discovered in 1939. Guided tours. (Memorial Day-Labor Day: daily 9 am-7 pm; rest of year: daily 9 am-5 pm) **$**

Natural Bridges Beach. *2531 W Cliff Dr, Santa Cruz (95060). Phone 831/423-4609. www.parks.ca.gov.* Ocean-formed sandstone arch; winter site for monarch butterflies. Fishing; nature trail, picnicking. Displays of local tidepool life. Day use only. (Daily 8 am-sunset) **$$**

Roaring Camp & Big Trees Narrow-Gauge Railroad. *Graham Hill Rd, Felton. 6 miles N on Graham Hill Rd. Phone 831/335-4484. www.roaringcamprr.com.*

Authentic 19th-century narrow-gauge steam locomotives carry passengers up North America's steepest railroad grades through groves of giant redwoods. Stopover at Bear Mountain for picnicking, hiking; round-trip 6 miles, 1 1/4 hours. Historic townsite with 1880s depot, old-time general store, covered bridge. Trains leave Roaring Camp depot, 1/2 mile SE of Felton at junction Graham Hill and Roaring Camp rds. (Schedule varies; additional trains weekends, holidays, and in summer) Chuckwagon barbecue (May-Oct, weekends). **$$$$** Also here is

Santa Cruz, Big Trees & Pacific Railway. *Graham Hill Rd, Felton (95018). Phone 831/335-4484. www.roaringcamp.com.* 1920s-era railroad operating vintage passenger coaches over spectacular rail route between redwoods at Roaring Camp and beach and boardwalk at Santa Cruz. A 2 1/2-hour round-trip excursion through tunnel, over trestles, and along rugged San Lorenzo River Canyon on its way to the beach at Santa Cruz. Historic railroad dates to 1875. (June-Sept: daily; rest of year: weekends and holidays) **$$$$**

Santa Cruz Beach Boardwalk. *400 Beach St, Santa Cruz (95060). Phone 831/423-5590. www.beachboardwalk.com.* Few amusement parks exude a more nostalgic vibe than the Santa Cruz Beach Boardwalk. Open since 1907, it is the oldest amusement park in California—making it a State Historical Landmark—and the only one that is smack-dab on the beach. Some of the antique rides are still fan favorites, including the Giant Dipper, a wood rail roller coaster that first scared riders in 1924, and a meticulously preserved carousel from 1911. Among the other attractions at the Boardwalk are many newer thrill rides (including modern coasters and a pair of interactive funhouses); a bowling alley; arcades; numerous restaurants and souvenir shops; and a concert venue, Cocoanut Grove, that has been a cornerstone of the park since it opened. A number of annual events are held here, including a clam chowder cook-off in February and free Friday concerts during the summer. (Memorial Day-Labor Day; closed Dec 24, 25). **$$$$**

Santa Cruz Mission State Historical Park. *144 School St, Santa Cruz (95060). Phone 831/425-5849. www.parks.ca.gov.* Casa Adobe (Neary-Rodriguez Adobe) is the only remaining building of the old Santa Cruz Mission; the date of construction is 1822-1824; displays. (Thurs-Sun 10 am-4 pm) **$**

Santa Cruz Surfing Museum. *1305 E Cliff Dr, Santa Cruz (95062). Phone 831/420-6289. www.santacruzmuseums.org/surfin.html.* Natural and cultural history of the northern Monterey Bay region. California Native American exhibits; tidepool aquarium. (Tues-Sun; closed holidays) **DONATION**

Seacliff Beach. *Santa Cruz. 5 miles S on Hwy 1. Phone 831/685-6500. www.parks.ca.gov.* Fishing pier leads to *"The Cement Ship,"* sunk here in 1929 to serve as an amusement center. Swimming beach, seasonal lifeguards, fishing; picnicking, campsites (full hook-ups, no tents). **$$**

University of California, Santa Cruz. *1156 High St, Santa Cruz (95064). NW section of town. Phone 831/459-0111. www.ucsc.edu.* (1965) (10,000 students) Made up of ten colleges on a 2,000-acre campus overlooking Monterey Bay. The Institute of Marine Sciences offers guided tours of the Long Marine Laboratory. Art galleries, astronomical exhibits, agroecology farm, and arboretum.

West Cliff Drive. *On N shoreline of Santa Cruz Beach.* One of the most renowned ocean drives in the state.

Wilder Ranch. *3 miles NW on Hwy 1. Phone 831/426-0505. www.parks.ca.gov.* Coastal terraces, pocket beaches, and historic farm on 3,000 acres. Nature, hiking, biking, and bridle trails. Interpretive displays. Farm and blacksmith demonstrations. Day use only. **$$**

Special Events

Monterey Bay Strawberry Festival. *Downtown Plaza, Watsonville. Phone 831/728-6183; fax 831/728-9036. www.mbsf.com.* In California's Pajaro Valley is some of the best strawberry-growing land in the country. Almost 50,000 people attend this festival every year, which offers such menu items as strawberry tamales. Like many food festivals, there are contests for eating the namesake fruit and its pie, as well as more traditional summertime fare like local pizzas and sausages. Enjoy the main crop from nearly 12,000 acres of lush California land to begin your August. First weekend in Aug.

Mountain Man Rendezvous. *Roaring Camp and Big Trees Railroad. Phone 831/335-4484.* Reenactment of an early-days rendezvous with participants authentically costumed as trappers and traders as they gather to exchange products, swap tales, and engage in old-time games. Thanksgiving weekend. **FREE**

Santa Cruz County Fair. *Santa Cruz County Fairgrounds, 2601 E Lake Ave, Watsonville (95076). Phone 831/724-5671. www.santacruzcountyfair.com.* The fair starts on Tuesday with a barbecue and band, and several concerts, games, and animal exhibitions are held throughout the week and weekend. Early-mid-Sept. **$$**

Shakespeare/Santa Cruz Festival. *UCSC Campus, 1156 High St, Santa Cruz (95064). Phone 831/459-2121.* Presentation of Shakespearean and contemporary plays by professional actors; indoor and outdoor performances. Mid-July-late Aug.

Limited-Service Hotels

★ ★ BEST WESTERN SEACLIFF INN. *7500 Old Dominion Ct, Aptos (95003). Phone 831/688-7300; toll-free 800/367-2003; fax 831/685-3603. www.seacliffinn.com.* 149 rooms, 2 story. Complimentary full breakfast. Check-in 3 pm, check-out noon. Restaurant, bar. Fitness room. Outdoor pool. **$**

★ ★ COAST SANTA CRUZ HOTEL. *175 W Cliff Dr, Santa Cruz (95060). Phone 831/426-4330; toll-free 800/663-1144; fax 831/427-2025. www.coasthotels.com.* 163 rooms, 10 story. Pets accepted, some restrictions; fee. Check-in 4 pm, check-out 11 am. High-speed Internet access. Restaurant, bar. Beach. Outdoor pool, whirlpool. Business center. **$$**

★ SEA AND SAND INN. *201 W Cliff Dr, Santa Cruz (95060). Phone 831/427-3400; fax 831/466-9882. www.santacruzmotels.com.* On cliffs overlooking Monterey Bay. 20 rooms, 2 story. Complimentary continental breakfast. Check-in 3 pm, check-out 11 am. Beach. **$$**

Full-Service Hotel

★ ★ ★ CHAMINADE. *One Chaminade Ln, Santa Cruz (95065). Phone 831/475-5600; toll-free 800/283-6569; fax 831/476-4798. www.chaminade.com.* 153 rooms. Check-in 4 pm, check-out noon. High-speed Internet access. Two restaurants, bar. Fitness room. Outdoor pool, whirlpool. **$$$**

Specialty Lodgings

The following lodging establishments are approved by Mobil Travel Guide, but due to their unique and individualized nature have not been given a traditional Mobil Star rating. Included in this listing you may find bed-and-breakfasts, limited-service inns, guest ranches, and other unique hotel properties.

BABBLING BROOK INN. *1025 Laurel St, Santa Cruz (95061). Phone 831/427-2437; toll-free 800/866-1131; fax 831/427-2457. www.babblingbrookinn.com.* Built on the foundation of an old tannery and mill, the Babbling Brook Inn fully embodies its name with cascading waterfalls and a meandering brook set amongst the thick trees at this secluded nook. A truly romantic inn, each room is themed after old-world artists and poets. 13 rooms. Complimentary full breakfast. Check-in 3 pm, check-out 11:30 am. **$$**

BAYVIEW HOTEL. *8041 Soquel Dr, Aptos (95003). Phone 831/688-8654; toll-free 800/422-9843; fax 831/688-5128. www.bayviewhotel.com.* Built in 1878; antiques. 12 rooms, 3 story. Pets accepted. Complimentary continental breakfast. Check-in 3 pm, check-out 11 am. **$$**

CHATEAU VICTORIAN. *118 1st St, Santa Cruz (95060). Phone 831/458-9458. www.chateauvictorian.com.* One block to beach. Victorian house; fireplaces. 7 rooms, 2 story. No children allowed. Complimentary full breakfast. Check-in 3:30-6:30 pm, check-out noon. **$**

Restaurants

★ ★ BITTERSWEET BISTRO. *787 Rio del Mar Blvd, Rio del Mar (95003). Phone 831/662-9799; fax 831/662-9779. www.bittersweetbistro.com.* American, Mediterranean menu. Dinner. Bar. Children's menu. Outdoor seating. **$$$**

★ ★ CAFE SPARROW. *8042 Soquel Dr, Aptos (95003). Phone 831/688-6238; fax 831/477-0732. www.cafesparrow.com.* French menu. Lunch, dinner, Sun brunch. Closed holidays; also Halloween. **$$$**

★ ★ CROW'S NEST. *2218 E Cliff Dr, Santa Cruz (95062). Phone 831/476-4560; fax 831/476-6085. www.crowsnest-santacruz.com.* Seafood, steak menu. Lunch, dinner. Closed Dec 25. Bar. Children's menu. Outdoor seating. **$$**

★ GILBERT'S SEAFOOD GRILL. *Municipal Wharf #25, Santa Cruz (95060). Phone 831/423-5200.* Seafood menu. Lunch, dinner. Bar. Children's menu. **$**

★ ★ **SANDERLINGS RESTAURANT.** *1 Seascape Resort Dr, Aptos (95003). Phone 831/688-6800; fax 831/685-0615. www.seascaperesort.com.* Crown jewel of Monterey Bay, on the ocean. American menu. Breakfast, lunch, dinner, brunch. Children's menu. **$$**

Santa Nella

Population 500
Area Code 209
Zip 95322

Limited-Service Hotel

★ **BEST WESTERN ANDERSEN'S INN.** *12367 S Hwy 33, Santa Nella (95322). Phone 209/826-5534; fax 209/826-4353. www.bestwestern.com.* 94 rooms, 2 story. Complimentary continental breakfast. Check-in 3 pm, check-out 11 am. Outdoor pool. **$**

Restaurant

★ **PEA SOUP ANDERSEN'S.** *12411 S Hwy 33, Santa Nella (95322). Phone 209/826-1685; fax 209/826-5996.* American menu. Breakfast, lunch, dinner. Bar. Children's menu. Casual attire. **$$**

Santa Rosa (D-2)

See also Bodega Bay, Calistoga, Guerneville, Healdsburg, Petaluma, Rutherford, Sonoma, St. Helena

Settled 1829
Population 147,595
Elevation 167 ft
Information Sonoma Valley Visitors Bureau, 453 First St, 95476; phone 707/996-1090
Web Site www.sonoma.com

Surrounded by vineyards and mountains, the county seat of Sonoma County is within minutes of more than 150 wineries. The rich soil and even climate of the Sonoma Valley lured famed horticulturist Luther Burbank here to develop innumerable new and better plants. Many farm and ranch products originate from the area today.

What to See and Do

Luther Burbank Home & Gardens. *Santa Rosa and Sonoma aves, Santa Rosa. Phone 707/524-5445. www.lutherburbank.org.* Features work of the famous horticulturist who lived and worked in Santa Rosa. Site includes greenhouse, gardens, carriage house exhibits. Gift shop. Home tours (Apr-Oct, Tues-Sun 10 am-3 pm). Gardens (year-round, daily 8 am-7 pm; free). **$**

Patrick Amiot's Art. *Florence St, Sebastopol (95472). www.patrickamiot-brigittelaurent.com.* Just blocks from Sebastopol's Main Street, turn-of-the-century homes mingle with sculptures such as a giant caveman and a replica of an old Oliver tractor. Made of what some of us might call junk, Amiot's art is on display in an unusual venue—his neighbors' yards. Walk the street to get an up-close look at the clever artwork. **FREE**

Redwood Empire Ice Arena. *1667 W Steele Ln, Santa Rosa (95403). Phone 707/546-7147. www.snoopyshomeice.com.* Built by Charles M. Schulz, the creator of the Peanuts comic strip, this ice arena, known as Snoopy's Home Ice, is a great place to cool off on a hot summer day. The rink offers skate rentals and has a restaurant on-site. Next door is the Charles M. Schulz Museum. It's great for comic aficionados, but young children may find it less than exciting. (Hours vary; call or visit Web site) **$$**

Safari West Wildlife Preserve. *3115 Porter Creek Rd, Santa Rosa (95404). Phone toll-free 800/616-2695. www.safariwest.com.* Board a safari vehicle and head into the hills in search of the more than 400 exotic mammals and birds that call this place home. Tours. (Spring-fall: daily 9 am, 1 pm, and 4 pm; winter: daily 10 am and 2 pm) **$$$$**

Snoopy's Gallery. *1665 W Steele Ln, Santa Rosa (95403). Phone 707/546-3385. www.snoopygift.com.* Houses a museum of Charles Schulz's original drawings of the *Peanuts* characters, as well as awards and trophies, and *Peanuts* memorabilia. (Daily 10 am-6 pm; closed holidays) **FREE**

Sonoma County Museum. *425 7th St, Santa Rosa (95402). Phone 707/579-1500. www.sonomacountymuseum.com.* Regional history and art museum of Sonoma County and northern California. Changing exhibits. Guided tours (by appointment). Special events throughout the year. (Wed-Sun 11 am-4 pm; closed holidays) **$**

Special Events

Luther Burbank Rose Festival. *Downtown, Santa Rosa. www.roseparadefestival.com.* Three days of art and flower shows, parade. Third Sat in May.

Sonoma County Fair. *1350 Bennett Valley Rd, Santa Rosa (95402). Phone 707/528-3247.* Join in the fun at this two-week fair, which features carnival rides, livestock shows, horse racing, a talent show, and competitions for budding magicians, scarecrow building, and bubblegum bubble blowing. A highlight of the fair each year is the Hall of Flowers exhibit, where participants incorporate a chosen theme into their floral displays. Late July-early Aug.

Limited-Service Hotels

★ ★ DOUBLETREE HOTEL SONOMA WINE COUNTRY. *1 Doubletree Dr, Rohnert Park (94928). Phone 707/584-5466; fax 707/586-9726. www.doubletree.com.* 245 rooms. Pets accepted, some restrictions; fee. Check-in 3 pm, check-out noon. Restaurant, bar. Fitness room. Outdoor pool, whirlpool. Business center. **$**

★ ★ FOUNTAINGROVE INN HOTEL AND CONFERENCE CENTER. *101 Fountain Grove Pkwy, Santa Rosa (95403). Phone 707/578-6101; toll-free 800/222-6101; fax 707/544-3126. www.fountaingroveinn.com.* Situated in the heart of wine country in Sonoma, this inn is surrounded by the landmark Round Barn and Fountaingrove Ranch. 124 rooms, 2 story. Pets accepted. Complimentary continental breakfast. Check-in 3 pm, check-out noon. Restaurant, bar. Outdoor pool, whirlpool. Airport transportation available. Business center. **$**

Full-Service Hotels

★ ★ ★ HILTON SONOMA COUNTY/SANTA ROSA. *3555 Round Barn Blvd, Santa Rosa (95403). Phone 707/523-7555; toll-free 800/445-8667; fax 707/569-5555. www.winecountryhilton.com.* Hilton Sonoma, situated on the crest of a hill, offers the perfect stay for any guest. It is centrally located to more than 140 world-class Sonoma County wineries and golf courses. Picturesque towns and state parks are close by, offering hiking, biking, and sailing. 246 rooms, 3 story. Check-in 3 pm, check-out noon. Restaurant, bar. Fitness room. Outdoor pool, whirlpool. Business center. **$$**

★ ★ ★ HOTEL LA ROSE. *308 Wilson St, Santa Rosa (95401). Phone 707/579-3200; toll-free 800/527-6738; fax 707/579-3247. www.hotellarose.com.* In historic Railroad Square. 49 rooms, 4 story. Complimentary continental breakfast. Check-in 3 pm, check-out noon. High-speed Internet access, wireless Internet access. Restaurant, bar. Whirlpool. Airport transportation available. Business center. **$$**

★ ★ ★ HYATT VINEYARD CREEK HOTEL & SPA. *170 Railroad St, Santa Rosa (95401). Phone 707/284-1234; toll-free 800/633-7313; fax 707/636-7130. www.hyatt.com.* The Vineyard Creek Hotel is at home in the picturesque countryside of Sonoma wine country. Conveniently located to the area's many wineries, this resort, conference center, and spa is an inspired choice for visitors to this fabled region. From the guest rooms and suites to the outdoor sculpture garden, an artistic flair sets this hotel apart from others. The spa features a full menu of treatments, including seven types of massage and six types of facials. Several treatments are influenced by the region, using crushed grape seeds and olive oil to soften and smooth skin. The hotel's restaurant, Seafood Brasserie, marries the taste of French country cooking with Sonoma county ingredients on its tempting menu. 155 rooms, 2 story. Check-in 3 pm, check-out noon. High-speed Internet access. Restaurant, bar. Fitness room, spa. Outdoor pool, whirlpool. Airport transportation available. Business center. **$$**

Full-Service Resort

★ ★ FLAMINGO RESORT HOTEL. *2777 4th St, Santa Rosa (95405). Phone 707/545-8530; toll-free 800/848-8300; fax 707/528-1404. www.flamingoresort.com.* 170 rooms, 2 story. Check-in 3 pm, check-out 11 am. Restaurant, bar. Fitness room, spa. Outdoor pool, children's pool, whirlpool. Tennis. **$**

Full-Service Inns

★ ★ ★ KENWOOD INN & SPA. *10400 Sonoma Hwy, Kenwood (95452). Phone 707/833-1293; toll-free 800/353-6966; fax 707/833-1247. www.kenwoodinn.com.* A magnificent Mediterranean villa transplanted to the heart of California wine country, the Kenwood Inn & Spa is an exceptional retreat. This magical place channels the warmth and charm of a Tuscan villa in its interiors. Striped fabric headboards, iron scrollwork, and terra-cotta tile floors exude the romance of the Italian countryside in the rooms and suites. Guests could certainly develop a lord- or lady-of-the-manor complex at this unusual hotel, where trickling fountains make music in intimate courtyards and 2,000 acres of vineyards are the backdrop. Two pools, a wine bar, and a full-service spa are among the amenities, but the Kenwood Inn's most precious amenity is that of peace and quiet in a stunning setting. 30 rooms, 2 story. No children allowed. Complimentary full breakfast. Check-in 3 pm, check-out 11 am-noon. Restaurant. Spa. Outdoor pool, whirlpools. **$$$$**

★ ★ ★ **SEBASTOPOL INN.** *6751 Sebastopol Ave, Sebastopol (95472). Phone 707/829-2500; toll-free 800/653-1082; fax 707/823-1535. www.sebastopolinn.com.* 31 rooms. Check-in 3 pm, check-out 11 am. Restaurant. Outdoor pool, whirlpool. **$$**

★ ★ ★ **VINTNERS INN.** *4350 Barnes Rd, Santa Rosa (95403). Phone 707/575-7350; toll-free 800/421-2584; fax 707/575-1426. www.vintnersinn.com.* Nestled in the heart of the Sonoma County wine country, this lodging is on the grounds of a 92-acre vineyard. It is located just north of Santa Rosa and close to Highway 101 and the Luther Burbank Center for the Performing Arts. There are three two-story guest room buildings arrayed around an attractive central courtyard with a fountain. Next door to the property is an excellent restaurant that faces onto the vineyard. Guest rooms are spacious and nicely appointed and include such amenities as turndown service, bathrobes, honor bars, decks or patios, and whirlpool tubs. A full complimentary breakfast is provided along with a welcoming bottle of wine. 44 rooms, 2 story. Complimentary full breakfast. Check-in 4 pm, check-out noon. Restaurant, bar. Outdoor pool. **$$$**

Specialty Lodgings

The following lodging establishments are approved by Mobil Travel Guide, but due to their unique and individualized nature have not been given a traditional Mobil Star rating. Included in this listing you may find bed-and-breakfasts, limited-service inns, guest ranches, and other unique hotel properties.

THE GABLES WINE COUNTRY INN. *4257 Petaluma Hill Rd, Santa Rosa (95404). Phone 707/585-7777; toll-free 800/422-5376; fax 707/584-5634. www.thegablesinn.com.* House of 15 gables in Gothic Revival style (1877) with unusual keyhole window in each gable. 7 rooms. Complimentary full breakfast. Check-in 3-6 pm, check-out 11 am. **$$**

VINE HILL INN. *3949 Vine Hill Rd, Sebastopol (95472). Phone 707/823-8832; fax 707/824-1045. www.vine-hill-inn.com.* 4 rooms. Complimentary full breakfast. Check-in 3-7 pm, check-out 11 am. **$$**

Restaurants

★ ★ **CA BIANCA ITALIAN RESTAURANT.** *835 2nd St, Santa Rosa (95404). Phone 707/542-5800; fax 707/542-2129. www.cabianca.com.* In Victorian house built in 1876. Italian menu. Lunch, dinner. Outdoor seating. **$$**

★ **CAFE CITTI.** *9049 Sonoma Hwy, Kenwood (95452). Phone 707/833-2690; fax 707/539-6255.* Locals have been flocking to this little cottage restaurant since it opened for business about six years ago. Nestled in Kenwood's Valley of the Moon, and known for its excellent chicken and super-friendly service, this is a fantastic place to stop for a quick bite between winery tours. Italian menu. Lunch, dinner. Closed Easter, Dec 25. Casual attire. Outdoor seating. **$$**

★ ★ ★ **EQUUS.** *101 Fountaingrove Pkwy, Santa Rosa (95403). Phone 707/578-0149; toll-free 800/222-6101; fax 707/544-3126. www.fountaingroveinn.com.* American menu. Lunch, dinner, late-night. Bar. **$$**

★ ★ **GARY CHU'S.** *611 5th St, Santa Rosa (95404). Phone 707/526-5840; fax 707/526-3102. www.garychus.com.* Chinese menu. Lunch, dinner. Closed Mon; July 4, Thanksgiving. **$$**

★ ★ ★ **JOHN ASH & CO.** *4350 Barnes Rd, Santa Rosa (95403). Phone 707/575-7350; fax 707/575-1426. www.johnashrestaurant.com.* California menu. Lunch, dinner, Sun brunch. Bar. Outdoor seating. **$$**

★ ★ **JOSEF'S.** *308 Wilson St, Santa Rosa (95401). Phone 707/571-8664; fax 707/571-8760. www.josefs restaurant.com.* Intimate, European-style restaurant with mahogany bar. Continental, French menu. Lunch, dinner. Closed holidays. Bar. **$$**

★ ★ ★ **KENWOOD.** *9900 Hwy 12, Kenwood (95452). Phone 707/833-6326; fax 707/833-2238. www.kenwoodrestaurant.com.* California menu. Lunch, dinner. Closed Mon-Tues; Jan 1, Thanksgiving, Dec 25; also first week in Jan. Bar. Outdoor seating. **$$$**

★ ★ **LA GARE.** *208 Wilson St, Santa Rosa (95401). Phone 707/528-4355; fax 707/528-2519.* French. Dinner. Closed Mon-Tues; Jan 1, Thanksgiving, Dec 25. Children's menu. **$$**

★ ★ **MIXX RESTAURANT.** *135 4th St, Santa Rosa (95401). Phone 707/573-1344; fax 707/573-0631. www.mixxrestaurant.com.* Italian menu. Lunch, dinner. Closed Sun; July 4, Thanksgiving, Dec 25. Bar. Children's menu. **$$$**

Saratoga

See also Los Gatos, Menlo Park, Palo Alto, Redwood City, San Jose, Santa Clara, Sunnyvale

Population 29,843
Elevation 455 ft
Area Code 408
Zip 95070
Information Chamber of Commerce, 20460 Saratoga-Los Gatos Rd; phone 408/867-0753
Web Site www.saratoga-ca.com

An early California lumber town nestled in the lush, redwood-covered foothills of the Santa Cruz Mountains, Saratoga was named after Saratoga, New York, when mineral springs were found nearby. Located just 26 miles east of the Pacific Coast, this quaint town offers many restaurants and cultural activities in the tranquillity of the romantic Santa Clara Valley. Visitors enjoy strolling through the village Main Street with its historic homes and intriguing shops.

What to See and Do

Hakone Gardens. *21000 Big Basin Way, Saratoga (95070). Phone 408/741-4994. www.hakone.com.* Japanese gardens, pond, bridge, Japanese-style houses, waterfall, picnic area. (Mon-Fri 10 am-5 pm, Sat-Sun from 11 am; closed Jan 1, Dec 25) **FREE**

Villa Montalvo. *15400 Montalvo Rd, Saratoga (95070). 1/2 mile S, just off Hwy 9. Phone 408/961-5800. www.villamontalvo.org.* (1912) Mediterranean-style summer house of Senator James D. Phelan. Now a cultural center with art galleries, concerts, plays, lectures, poetry readings, artists in residence. Formal gardens with hiking trails, arboretum, outdoor amphitheater, and Carriage House Theatre. Grounds (Mon-Thurs 8 am-5 pm, Fri-Sun and holidays from 9 am). Galleries (Wed-Sun 1-4 pm; closed Jan 1, Thanksgiving, Dec 25). **FREE**

Special Event

Villa Montalvo Performing Arts. *15400 Montalvo Rd, Saratoga (95070). Phone 408/961-5858. www.villamontalvo.com.* Montalvo, an organization dedicated to art education and creation, presents events highlighting the visual, performing, and literary arts.

Specialty Lodging

The following lodging establishment is approved by Mobil Travel Guide, but due to its unique and individualized nature has not been given a traditional Mobil Star rating. Included in this listing you may find bed-and-breakfasts, limited-service inns, guest ranches, and other unique hotel properties.

THE INN AT SARATOGA. *20645 Fourth St, Saratoga (95070). Phone 408/867-5020; toll-free 800/543-5020; fax 408/741-0981. www.innatsaratoga.com.* Surround yourself with culture and history at this beautiful inn located in the heart of the Santa Cruz Mountains. Stroll through the Hakone Gardens or visit the historic Mountain Winery. All rooms are oversized, each overlooking Saratoga Creek and a wooded park. 45 rooms, 5 story. Complimentary continental breakfast. Check-in 3 pm, check-out noon. **$$**

Restaurant

★ ★ ★ **SENT SOVI.** *14583 Big Basin Way, Saratoga (95070). Phone 408/867-3110; fax 408/705-2016. www.sentsovi.com.* Featuring good wines, this small restaurant offers a creative menu of New French food. David Kinch runs this elegant, quiet, and romantic restaurant that offers outdoor dining. While it is a little pricey, the experience is worth it. French menu. Dinner. Closed Mon; holidays. Outdoor seating. **$$$**

Sausalito

See also Berkeley, Muir Woods National Monument, Oakland, San Francisco, Tiburon

Settled 1800
Population 7,330
Elevation 14 ft
Area Code 415

Zip 94965
Information Chamber of Commerce, 29 Caledonia St, 94965; phone 415/332-0505 or 415/331-7262
Web Site www.sausalito.org

Sausalito, a picturesque town above San Francisco Bay, is an art colony and residential suburb in the shadow of the Golden Gate Bridge. Whalers first used the cove here. The town's name is a corruption of the Spanish for *willows*, which flourished here at one time. Sausalito's springs were San Francisco's major source of water for many years.

What to See and Do

Bridgeway Street. Known simply as "The Street" to locals, Sausalito's Bridgeway Street is a dream come true for window shoppers and people watchers. Bordering the downtown marina, Bridgeway has more than its fair share of high-end clothing shops and galleries, alongside souvenir shops and unique boutiques specializing in handcrafted goods of all kinds. Caledonia Street, one block to the west, is also home to many shops and restaurants.

Fort Baker. *557 McReynolds Rd, Sausalito (94965). www.nps.gov/goga/mahe/foba.* At the confluence of San Francisco Bay and the Pacific Ocean, Fort Baker sits on the edge of the Golden Gate National Recreation Area as a reminder to the area's frontier origins. Originally designated a military installation in the 1850s, the site was active in one capacity or another through the end of the Cold War. The buildings here—most of which date to the late 19th century—have been meticulously preserved and are now one of the best remaining examples of that era's seacoast fortification strategy. Located here is

> **Bay Area Discovery Museum.** *Fort Baker, 557 E McReynolds Rd, Sausalito (94965). Phone 415/339-3900. www.baykidsmuseum.org.* Museum filled with interactive exhibits for kids ages 1 to 10; special focus is on science and discovery. Includes a special area for toddlers and a play area with views of the bay and bridge. (Tues-Fri 9 am-4 pm, Sat-Sun 10 am-5 pm; closed holidays) **$$**

Marine Mammal Center. *1065 Fort Cronkhite, San Francisco (94965). Phone 415/289-7325. www.tmmc.org.* Founded in 1975, this center—the largest marine mammal facility in the world—rescues injured or sick animals from sites stretching along the West Coast and nurses them back to health. Come for a tour to learn how the hospital rescues, rehabilitates, and releases hundreds of dolphins, sea lions, and otters each year, and see these animals during the recovery process. Note that winter is usually the quietest time of year, sometimes with one or two animals on site, whereas spring is the busiest. (Daily 10 am-4 pm; closed Jan 1, Thanksgiving, Dec 25) **DONATION**

Munchies. *613 Bridgeway, Sausalito (94965). Phone 415/331-3863.* This neat little candy store has a huge selection of saltwater taffy, as well as old-fashioned taffy and licorice, and different flavors of Tootsie Rolls...just everything you'd think a candy store should have. Buckets of sweets line the entire room, and you are welcomed to taste anything before you buy. (Daily 10 am-6:30 pm)

San Francisco Bay & Delta Hydraulic Model. *2100 Bridgeway, Sausalito (94965). Model in operation only during testing. Phone 415/332-3870 (recording).* Hydraulic model reproduces tidal action, currents, and mixing of salt and fresh water and indicates trends in sediment deposition; the 850-square-mile bay-delta area is duplicated in a 3-acre building. Interactive exhibits, nine-minute orientation video, and 45-minute general information audio tour. Self-guided tour; audio tours available in six languages: English, French, German, Japanese, Spanish, and Russian. (Memorial Day-Labor Day: Tues-Fri 9 am-4 pm, Sat-Sun 10 am-5 pm; rest of year: Tues-Sun 9 am-4 pm) **FREE**

Venice Gourmet. *625 Bridgeway, Sausalito (94965). Phone 415/332-3544. www.venicegourmet.com.* In addition to a wide selection of made-to-order sandwiches, this deli also sells a variety of interesting wines, cheeses, sauces, oils, vinegars, teas, and kitchen accessories. (Daily 9 am-6 pm)

Village Fair. *777 Bridgeway, Sausalito (94965). Opposite Yacht Harbor.* Fascinating and colorful three-story complex of specialty shops selling unusual crafts, artifacts, and imports. The building was once a Chinese gambling hall, opium den, and distillery for bootleg whiskey. Cafeteria. (Daily; closed Thanksgiving, Dec 25)

Special Event

Sausalito Art Festival. *2100 Bridgeway, Sausalito (94965). Phone 415/332-3555. www.sausalitoartfestival.org.* Known as "the granddaddy" of outdoor fine art shows, the Sausalito Art Festival was born in 1952 and now attracts more than 50,000 people to the waterfront Manship Park every Labor Day weekend. More than 20,000 artworks have been on display at the festival in recent years, complemented by live music, a sculpture garden, and vendors selling local food, beer, and wine. **$$$$**

Full-Service Hotel

★ ★ ★ **CASA MADRONA HOTEL.** *801 Bridgeway, Sausalito (94965). Phone 415/332-0502; toll-free 800/288-0502; fax 415/332-2537. www.casamadrona.com.* High above in the hills of Sausalito, this enchanting inn offers views of the harbor and bay for romance and enchanted evenings. With its elegant blend of 19th-century Victorian and New England style, it is a place you will want to visit over and over again. 66 rooms, 4 story. Complimentary continental breakfast. Check-in 3 pm, check-out noon. Restaurant, bar. Spa. Whirlpool. **$$$**

Full-Service Inn

★ ★ ★ **THE INN ABOVE TIDE.** *30 El Portal, Sausalito (94965). Phone 415/332-9535; toll-free 800/893-8433; fax 415/332-6714. www.innabovetide.com.* Built over water, rooms provide view of bay and San Francisco. 30 rooms, 3 story. Complimentary continental breakfast. Check-in 3 pm, check-out noon. **$$$**

Specialty Lodging

The following lodging establishment is approved by Mobil Travel Guide, but due to its unique and individualized nature has not been given a traditional Mobil Star rating. Included in this listing you may find bed-and-breakfasts, limited-service inns, guest ranches, and other unique hotel properties.

HOTEL SAUSALITO. *16 El Portal, Sausalito (96965). Phone 415/332-0700; toll-free 888/442-0700; fax 415/332-8788. www.hotelsausalito.com.* 16 rooms. Complimentary continental breakfast. Check-in 3 pm, check-out 11 am. **$$**

Restaurants

★ ★ **HORIZONS.** *558 Bridgeway, Sausalito (94965). Phone 415/331-3232; fax 415/332-0400. www.horizonssausalito.com.* For the best view of the Bay Bridge outside of San Francisco, head to this casual bayside restaurant, which also offers full views of Tiburon and Angel Island. If you can take your eyes off the shimmering water, you'll notice the dining room's creative nautical theme with muraled ceilings. The food is also super, featuring fresh seafood and great burgers. California, seafood menu. Breakfast, lunch, dinner, brunch. Closed Dec 25. Bar. Children's menu. Valet parking. Outdoor seating. **$$**

★ ★ **SCOMA'S.** *588 Bridgeway, Sausalito (94965). Phone 415/332-9551; fax 415/332-0827. www.scomassausalito.com.* Housed in a blue Victorian building directly overlooking the water, one of this seafood restaurant's main draws is the incredible view of the city of San Francisco and the waters of the bay. The other highlight, of course, is the creative, fresh seafood dishes on the menu, in addition to pasta and steak dishes. Italian, seafood menu. Lunch, dinner. Closed Jan 1, Thanksgiving, Dec 25. Bar. Children's menu. Outdoor seating. **$$**

★ **SPINNAKER.** *100 Spinnaker Dr, Sausalito (94965). Phone 415/332-1500; fax 415/332-7062. www.thespinnaker.com.* Seafood menu. Lunch, dinner, Sun brunch. Closed Thanksgiving, Dec 24-25. Bar. Children's menu. Valet parking. **$$**

★ **WINSHIPS.** *670 Bridgeway, Sausalito (94965). Phone 415/332-1454. www.winships.com.* California menu. Breakfast, lunch. Closed Thanksgiving, Dec 25. Bar. Children's menu. Casual attire. Outdoor seating. **$**

Sequoia and Kings Canyon National Parks

See also Porterville, Three Rivers

55 miles E of Fresno on Hwy 180; 35 miles E of Visalia on Hwy 198.

Web Site www.nps.gov/seki

Although independently established, Sequoia and Kings Canyon National Parks are geographically and administratively one. Lying across the heart of the Sierra Nevada in eastern central California, they comprise more than 1,300 square miles and include more than 25 isolated groves of spectacular giant sequoias, towering granite peaks, deep canyons, and hundreds of alpine lakes. Giant sequoias reach their greatest size and are found in the largest numbers here. Mount Whitney, 14,495 feet, is the highest point in the lower 48 states. Some rocks of the foothill and summit area indicate that this whole region once lay under the ocean.

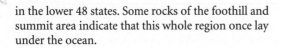

Allow plenty of driving time due to the gradient into and out of the mountains. Limited groceries are available all year in both parks. Gasoline may not be available; inquire before entering. Camping (no trailer hook-ups) is restricted to designated areas. Many of the campgrounds are closed by snow, October-late May. Winter visitors should carry tire chains. Entry fee valid for seven days. For information, contact Sequoia and Kings Canyon National Parks, Three Rivers 93271; phone 559/565-3134.

What to See and Do

Boyden Cavern. *74101 E Kings Canyon Rd, Kings Canyon National Park (95222). Located in Kings River Canyon in Sequoia National Forest between Grant Grove and Cedar Grove. Phone 209/736-2708. www.caverntours.com/boydenrt.htm.* A 45-minute tour on a lighted, handrail-equipped trail through ornate chambers with massive stalagmites, stalactites, and columns. (Summer: daily 10 am-5 pm; early Sept-Oct: daily 11 am-4 pm; early Oct to road closure: Sat-Sun 11 am-4 pm; closed mid-Nov-late Apr) **$$**

Cedar Grove. *Three Rivers. In canyon of South Fork of Kings River.* Towering peaks rise a mile high above the stream. Horses, pack animals. Hiking trails. Road closed Nov-Apr.

Fishing. *83918 Grant Grove Dr, Sequoia and Kings Canyon National Parks (93633).* Trout are abundant in a few lakes and streams; the most popular spots are along Kings River and the forks of the Kaweah River. Some stores in the park sell state fishing licenses.

Foothills, Lodgepole, and Grant Grove visitor centers. *Three Rivers. Foothills: located on the Generals Hwy, 1 mile from Sequoia Park entrance at Hwy 198. Lodgepole: located on Lodgepole Rd, 21 miles from the Sequoia Park entrance on Hwy 198. Grant Grove: located 3 miles E on Hwy 80 from the Big Stump Entrance Station. Phone 559/565-3134.* Exhibits, photos, data about the parks; expert advice on how to organize sightseeing. Schedules of campfire talks and guided trips are posted here. (Daily)

General Grant Grove. *83918 Grant Grove Dr, Sequoia and Kings Canyon National Parks (93633).* Includes the General Grant Tree, 267 feet tall with a circumference of 108 feet. Saddle rides. Hiking trails.

★ **Giant Forest.** *83918 Grant Grove Dr, Sequoia and Kings Canyon National Parks (93633).* One of the finest groves of giant sequoias. The General Sherman Tree is the largest living thing on Earth. At 275 feet high and 103 feet in circumference, it is estimated to be 2,300-2,700 years old. Moro Rock, Crescent Meadow, Crystal Cave, and Tokopah Valley are in this section of the park. Horses, pack animals available at Wolverton Pack Station. Hiking trails.

High Country. *83918 Grant Grove Dr, Sequoia and Kings Canyon National Parks (93633).* A vast region of wilderness, mountains, canyons, rivers, lakes, and meadows; accessible by trail. The Sierra Crest forms the eastern boundary.

Redwood Mountain Grove. *83918 Grant Grove Dr, Sequoia and Kings Canyon National Parks (93633).* Includes the Hart Tree, a large sequoia; accessible by trail.

Sequoia National Forest. *900 W Grand Ave, Porterville (93257). 20 miles E via Hwy 190. Phone 559/784-1500. www.r5.fs.fed.us/sequoia.* Precipitous canyons, spectacular views of the Sierra Nevada, and more than 30 groves of giant sequoias on 1,139,000 acres. Largest tree of any national forest is here; the Boole Tree stands 269 feet and is 90 feet in circumference. (The General Sherman Tree in Sequoia National Park is a few feet taller.) The forest contains the 303,290-acre Golden Trout, 130,995-acre Dome Land, 10,610-acre Jennie Lake, 63,000-acre South Sierra, 88,290-acre Kiavah, and the 45,000-acre Monarch wilderness areas. Activities include swimming, lake and stream fishing for trout, whitewater rafting in the Kern and Kings rivers; hunting; hiking, riding, and backpacking trails in wilderness areas (permit required). Cross-country skiing, snowshoeing, and snowmobiling in winter. Picnicking. Camping (for reservations, phone toll-free 877/444-6777) at 50 areas; 14-day/month limit, no electric hook-ups or other utility connections, campgrounds (fees vary).

Limited-Service Hotels

★ CEDAR GROVE LODGE. *Hwy 180, Kings Canyon National Park (93633). Phone 559/335-5507; fax 559/565-0101.* 21 rooms, 2 story. Closed Nov-Mar. Check-out 11 am. **$**

★ ★ GRANT GROVE VILLAGE. *5755 E Kings Canyon, Kings Canyon National Park (93633). Phone 559/335-5500; toll-free 866/522-6966; fax 559/335-5507. www.kcanyon.com.* 47 rooms. Check-in 4 pm, check-out 11 am. Restaurant. **$**

Sonoma (D-2)

See also Calistoga, Napa, Petaluma, Santa Rosa, St. Helena

Founded 1823
Population 9,128
Elevation 84 ft
Area Code 707
Zip 95476
Information Sonoma Valley Visitors Bureau, 453 First St E; phone 707/996-1090
Web Site www.sonomavalley.com

Accessed via Highway 12, a mere 45 miles from the hustle and bustle of San Francisco, the laid-back town of Sonoma anchors the Sonoma County wine region. Sonoma played a significant role in California's early history. In 1846, American settlers, or Anglos, revolted against Mexican control of California and declared Sonoma the capital of the "Bear Flag Republic," so named for the grizzly bear painted upon the flag that the settlers raised over Sonoma. The town's reign as capital of the Republic lasted only 25 days, ending when the United States military invaded California. The Bear Flag was replaced with the stars and stripes of the US flag, but California's current state flag, with a grizzly adorning its center, bears a resemblance to the one of the Republic.

Sonoma's 9,000+ residents enjoy pleasant weather and beautiful scenery, with the rugged Pacific coastline to the west and the Mayacamas Mountains to the east. Sonoma may not receive as much publicity as some of the cities in nearby Napa Valley, but it's not for a lack of wineries. Sonoma is home to many renowned vintners—including Buena Vista Winery, Fallenleaf Vineyards, and Moondance Cellars, to name a few—with dozens more wineries found in nearby Sonoma County communities such as Glen Ellen and Santa Rosa.

Sonoma Plaza

A walk around Sonoma Plaza—California's largest and prettiest town square—combines local history with opportunities to sample foods of the Wine Country and relax in a shady park. Begin at the corner of Spain Street and First Street East, where you'll find the Sonoma Mission (its formal name is Mission San Francisco de Solano). The mission, which is open daily for tours, dates to 1823. It is the last and farthest north of the 21 Franciscan missions that dot the state from San Diego to the northern San Francisco Bay Area. The Sonoma Cheese Factory is on Spain Street, just west of the mission. Stop in to watch the production of Sonoma Jack Cheese and perhaps pick up some picnic supplies. Continuing west on Spain Street, you'll pass the Sonoma Barracks, which were built in 1836 (when California was still a Mexican outpost) to quarter Mexican army troops. Walk another mile west on Spain Street (a 10- to 15-minute walk beyond the plaza) to reach Lachryma Montis. This splendidly furnished 1852 Gothic-Victorian home belonged to General Mariano Vallejo, the charismatic figure who commanded the aforementioned Mexican troops. California's last Mexican governor, General Vallejo laid out the original Sonoma Plaza in 1834. Guided tours of the house are available, and there are picnic facilities in the gardens where you can enjoy the supplies you picked up at Sonoma Jack Cheese. Continuing on, retrace your steps back to the northwest corner of the plaza (Spain St and First St W) to the Sonoma Hotel, a three-story 19th-century adobe whose furnishings reflect the era (step into the lobby for a look around). Across the intersection (heading south on First St W) is the El Dorado Hotel, an 1843 white-trimmed adobe built by Don Salvador Vallejo, brother of the general. Unlike the Sonoma Hotel, this hotel's interior has been modernized. Continue walking around the plaza counterclockwise until you return to the Sonoma Mission. Your stroll will take you past a variety of restaurants and shops, many located in restored adobes. Besides the Sonoma Cheese Factory, there are several places to buy picnic food and ice cream. If you like, you can carry your snacks to the park that occupies the center of the plaza, where you'll find plenty of green grass, shade trees, two children's playgrounds, and a duck pond. The Sonoma Valley Visitors Bureau has an office at 453 First Street East, on the eastern side of the plaza.

What to See and Do

★ **Buena Vista Winery.** *18000 Old Winery Rd, Sonoma (95476). Phone 707/938-1266; toll-free 800/926-1266. www.buenavistawinery.com.* Cellars built in 1857. Historical panels, tasting room, art gallery, picnic area. Concerts in summer; special events. Tours. (Daily 10 am-5 pm; closed Jan 1, Thanksgiving, Dec 25) **FREE**

Gloria Ferrer Champagne Caves. *23555 Hwy 121, Sonoma (95476). Phone 707/996-7256. www.gloriaferrer.com.* Guided tours through "champagne caves" (inquire for schedule); wine tasting. (Daily 10:30 am-5:30 pm; closed Jan 1, Thanksgiving, Dec 25, also early Jan) **FREE**

Haraszthy Villa. *1695 Castle Rd, Sonoma (95476). E via Napa St, then N on Old Winery Rd, in Bartholomew Memorial Park.* Villa built in 1861 by Count Agoston Haraszthy has been re-created; also vineyard and gazebo. Picnicking. (Wed, Sat, Sun) **FREE**

Infineon Raceway. *Hwys 37 and 121, Sonoma (95476). Phone toll-free 800/870-7223. www.searspoint.com.* Motor sports entertainment, including NASCAR Cup, NHRA drag racing, SCCA pro and amateur road races, AMA and AFM motorcycle events, vintage car races, amateur drag racing, and car clubs. Under 12 years with adult only. (Daily; closed Dec 25) **$$$$**

Jack London State Historic Park. *2400 London Ranch Rd, Glen Ellen (95442). 8 1/2 miles W on Hwy 12, then 1 1/2 miles W of Glen Ellen on London Ranch Rd. Phone 707/938-5216. www.jacklondonpark.com.* A memorial to author Jack London, the park is located in the Valley of the Moon. Just before its completion, fire consumed London's magnificent dream home. See the rock-wall ruins of the Wolf House, the Pig Palace, and the House of Happy Walls, now a museum. Hiking trails traverse the park. Museum (daily 10 am-5 pm; closed Jan 1, Thanksgiving, Dec 25). (Early Apr-Oct: daily 9:30 am-5 pm; rest of year: 10 am-5 pm) **$$**

Sebastiani Sonoma Cask Cellars. *389 4th St E, Sonoma (95476). Phone 707/938-5532; toll-free 800/888-5532. www.sebastiani.com.* Large collection of carved casks. Guided tours; tasting room and aging cellars may be visited. Free tram ride to the winery from Sonoma Plaza. (Daily 10 am-5 pm; closed holidays) **FREE**

Sonoma State Historic Park. *20 E Spain St, Sonoma (95476). Phone 707/938-1519. www.parks.ca.gov.* General Vallejo's house (1851-1880), *W Spain St and 3rd St W;* Mission San Francisco Solano (1823-1846), barracks (1840-1846), *E Spain St and 1st St E;* other buildings on and near Sonoma Plaza. Picnicking. (Daily 10 am-5 pm; closed Jan 1, Thanksgiving, Dec 25) **$**

Train Town. *20264 Broadway, Sonoma (95476). Phone 707/938-3912. www.traintown.com.* Young children will find Train Town enchanting. Miniature trains take visitors on a 20-minute ride through a landscaped park with animals, waterfalls, and historic replica structures. (June-Labor Day: daily 10 am-5 pm; rest of year: Fri-Sun 10 am-5 pm; closed Thanksgiving, Dec 25) **$**

Special Event

Valley of the Moon Vintage Festival. *Sonoma Plaza, Sonoma. Phone 707/996-2109. www.sonomavinfest.org.* The Valley of the Moon Vintage Festival, Sonoma's oldest wine festival, was first held in 1896 to celebrate the end of the grape-growing season and to give thanks for the harvest. Today, the tradition continues with a grape stomp, winemaking contest, parade, food, arts and crafts, and, of course, wine tastings. Sept.

Limited-Service Hotels

★ BEST WESTERN SONOMA VALLEY INN. *550 2nd St W, Sonoma (95476). Phone 707/938-9200; toll-free 800/334-5784; fax 707/938-0935. www.sonomavalleyinn.com.* This pleasant, inviting motor lodge is well situated for visiting Sonoma and the surrounding wine country. It is configured around a nicely landscaped and furnished central courtyard with a pool, hot tub, and steam room. The large guest rooms are comfortably furnished, and many offer gas fireplaces and balconies or decks. A gift bottle of Sonoma County wine is a nice touch. 80 rooms, 2 story. Pets accepted, some restrictions; fee. Complimentary continental breakfast. Check-in 3 pm, check-out noon. Fitness room. Outdoor pool, whirlpool. **$$**

★ ★ EL DORADO HOTEL. *405 First St W, Sonoma (95476). Phone 707/596-3030; toll-free 800/289-3031; fax 707/996-3148. www.hoteleldorado.com.* 26 rooms. Check-in 3 pm, check-out noon. Restaurant, bar. Outdoor pool. **$$**

★ EL PUEBLO INN. *896 W Napa St, Sonoma (95476). Phone 707/996-3651; toll-free 800/900-8844; fax 707/935-5988. www.elpuebloinn.com.* This renovated and expanded motor lodge is a good lower-rate alternative to Sonoma's higher-end properties. It is located on Highway 12 on the western approaches to the historic downtown plaza area. Although it's situated on a heavily traveled corner, the property is nicely shielded by a stand of trees, a landscaped lawn, and an attractive pool complex. 53 rooms, 2 story. Complimentary continental breakfast. Check-in 2 pm, check-out noon. Fitness room. Outdoor pool, whirlpool. **$**

Full-Service Hotel

★ ★ ★ MACARTHUR PLACE. *29 E MacArthur St, Sonoma (95476). Phone 707/938-2929; toll-free 800/722-1866; fax 707/933-9833. www.macarthurplace.com.* MacArthur Place is a lush country estate. Located just a few blocks from the town plaza, this magical inn is a pastoral paradise on 7 acres of fragrant, blooming gardens. The Victorian-style buildings house 64 guest rooms that bear a California country charm. Comfort is the highest priority here, and oversized bathrooms, fluffy beds, and fireplaces attest to that standard. A nightly wine and cheese reception whets the appetite, but those in the know are sure to save room for the juicy steaks and succulent seafood at Saddles (see), the hotel's steakhouse. Even in this tranquil setting, the Garden Spa stands out for its serenity. Bathed in glorious sunlight, this airy spa uses flowers, plants, and herbs found on the property in its many treatments. 64 rooms, 2 story. Complimentary continental breakfast. Check-in 4 pm, check-out noon. Restaurant. Fitness room. Outdoor pool, whirlpool. **$$$**

Full-Service Resorts

★ ★ ★ FAIRMONT SONOMA MISSION INN AND SPA. *100 Boyes Blvd, Sonoma (95476). Phone*

707/938-9000; toll-free 800/862-4945; fax 707/938-4250. www.sonomamissioninn.com. Built on a sacred healing ground for Native Americans, the Sonoma Mission Inn & Spa has been attracting visitors since the early 1920s. This idyllic country retreat, built over the Boyes Hot Springs, is nestled on 13 acres in the wine country's renowned Sonoma Valley. The region's famous vineyards lie just outside, although many guests are convinced to remain within this all-encompassing resort. The guest rooms blend country inn style with sophistication. The suites are especially romantic, with fireplaces and four-poster beds. Hearty American fare has been served for more than 50 years at the Big 3 Diner, while Santé (see) earns praise for its imaginative cuisine. Guests relax by the pool or play a round of golf on the historic 1927 course. Inspired by the thermal mineral springs that flow underneath the inn, the spa is a fantastic destination unto itself, wowing city slickers with its comprehensive treatment menu. 228 rooms, 3 story. Check-in 4 pm, check-out noon. Restaurant, bar. Fitness room, spa. Two outdoor pools, whirlpool. Golf. Business center. **$$$**

★ ★ ★ RENAISSANCE LODGE AT SONOMA RESORT AND SPA. *1325 Broadway, Sonoma (95476). Phone 707/935-6600; toll-free 800/468-3571; fax 707/935-6829. www.thelodgeatsonoma.com.* 182 rooms, 2 story. Pets accepted, fee. Check-in 4 pm, check-out noon. Restaurant, bar. Fitness room, spa. Outdoor pool, whirlpool. Business center. **$$$**

Specialty Lodgings

The following lodging establishments are approved by Mobil Travel Guide, but due to their unique and individualized nature have not been given a traditional Mobil Star rating. Included in this listing you may find bed-and-breakfasts, limited-service inns, guest ranches, and other unique hotel properties.

THE COTTAGE INN AND SPA - MISSION B&B. *310 First St E, Sonoma (95476). Phone 707/996-0719; toll-free 800/944-1490. www.cottageinnandspa.com.* 8 rooms. Complimentary full breakfast. Check-in 4 pm, check-out 11 am. **$$**

INN AT SONOMA. *630 Broadway, Sonoma (95476). Phone 707/939-1340; toll-free 888/568-9818; fax 707/939-8834. www.innatsonoma.com.* 19 rooms. Complimentary continental breakfast. Check-in 3 pm, check-out noon. **$$**

LEDSON HOTEL. *480 First St, Sonoma (95476). Phone 707/996-9779; fax 707/996-9776. www.ledsonhotel.com.* 6 rooms. Complimentary continental breakfast. Check-in 3 pm, check-out noon. Bar. **$$$**

SONOMA HOTEL. *110 W Spain St, Sonoma (95476). Phone 707/996-2996; toll-free 800/468-6016; fax 707/996-7014. www.sonomahotel.com.* 16 rooms. Complimentary continental breakfast. Check-in 2 pm, check-out 11 am. **$$**

THISTLE DEW. *171 W Spain St, Sonoma (95476). Phone 707/938-2909; toll-free 800/382-7895; fax 707/938-2129. www.thistledew.com.* A half-block walk from the historic Sonoma Plaza, this bed-and-breakfast is well situated for access to the shops, restaurants, and sights of this charming wine country town. It is also a close amble to General Vallejo's home in Sonoma State Historic Park. The inn encompasses two old structures (built in 1869 and 1910), closely set within a residential area. There are gardens around the property and some decks and private entrances; some rooms also have fireplaces and whirlpool tubs. A garden hot tub and loaner bicycles are available for guests. 6 rooms. Complimentary full breakfast. Check-in 3-7 pm, check-out noon. Whirlpool. **$$**

TROJAN HORSE INN. *19455 Sonoma Hwy, Sonoma (95476). Phone 707/996-2430; toll-free 800/899-1925; fax 707/996-9185. www.trojanhorseinn.com.* An early pioneer farmhouse built in 1887, this bed-and-breakfast is now an interesting reminder of a long-gone era. Furnished with 19th-century antiques, it has the relaxed ambience of a slower, less hectic time. The inn is located on an acre of land facing busy Highway 12 as it approaches historic Sonoma from the west. The sunken backyard, with gardens, large trees, and a hot tub, is away from traffic noise. Guest rooms are surprisingly large and have modern comforts to blend with the historic furnishings. A full breakfast, evening wine and hors d'oeuvres, and loaner bicycles are available for guests. 6 rooms. Children over 12 yrs only. Complimentary full breakfast. Check-in 4-6 pm, check-out 11 am. Whirlpool. **$$**

VICTORIAN GARDEN INN. *316 E Napa St, Sonoma (95476). Phone 707/996-5339; toll-free 800/543-5339; fax 707/996-1689. www.victoriangardeninn.com.* Located in a residential neighborhood a few block east of Sonoma's historic plaza and Spanish mission, this bed-and-breakfast evokes thoughts of a quieter time. The Greek Revival farmhouse was built in the 1870s and now is set amongst lovely Victorian-style gardens adjacent to Nathan Creek. This tranquil setting can be appreciated from a white wicker chair on the wraparound porch, on a colorful garden path, or while soaking in the property's hot tub or pool. You can also wind down from a day of sightseeing with a massage in a treatment room or in your own room. In addition to accommodations in the main house, there are guest rooms in an adjacent wooden water tower. 4 rooms, 2 story. Complimentary full breakfast. Check-in 10 am-5 pm, check-out 11 am. Outdoor pool, whirlpool. **$**

Restaurants

★ ★ **CAFE LAHAYE.** *140 E Napa St, Sonoma (95476). Phone 707/935-5994; fax 707/935-7747.* Artwork from a neighboring art gallery hangs all throughout this cozy restaurant, just off the main square in Sonoma. Diners rave about the upscale yet fun atmosphere, comparing the restaurant to a friend's dining room—a friend, that is, who also happens to be a phenomenal cook. The menu items are all made with locally grown and produced meats, cheeses, and fruits and vegetables, resulting in what the chef calls "homegrown cuisine." California menu. Dinner. Closed Sun-Mon; holidays. Reservations recommended. Outdoor seating. **$$**

★ ★ ★ **CARNEROS.** *1325 Broadway, Sonoma (95476). Phone 707/931-2042; fax 707/935-6829. www.carnerosrestaurant.com.* California, Mediterranean menu. Breakfast, lunch, dinner, Sun brunch. Bar. Children's menu. Outdoor seating. **$$$**

★ ★ **DELLA SANTINA'S.** *133 E Napa St, Sonoma (95476). Phone 707/935-0576; fax 707/935-7046. www.dellasantinas.com.* Fountain on patio. Italian menu. Lunch, dinner. Closed holidays. Outdoor seating. **$$**

★ ★ **THE DEPOT HOTEL CUCINA RUSTICA.** *241 1st St W, Sonoma (95476). Phone 707/938-2980; fax 707/938-5103. www.depothotel.com.* Historic stone building (1870); originally a hotel, later a saloon and private residence. Restored in 1962. Italian menu. Lunch, dinner. Closed Mon-Tues; Jan 1, Dec 25. Bar. Children's menu. Outdoor seating. **$$**

★ ★ **DEUCE.** *691 Broadway, Sonoma (95476). Phone 707/933-3823; fax 707/933-9002. www.dine-at-deuce.com.* The atmosphere and menu at this chef-owned restaurant are diverse: looking out onto an English garden, the dining room is lit by unique Italian lights, while guests peruse creative American cuisine options. With great outdoor dining, seasonal menus, and friendly and knowledgeable service, it's not surprising that both locals and tourists keep coming back. American menu. Lunch, dinner. Closed Dec 24-25. Bar. Children's menu. Outdoor seating. **$$**

★ ★ ★ **GENERAL'S DAUGHTER.** *400 W Spain St, Sonoma (95476). Phone 707/938-4004; fax 707/938-4099. www.thegeneralsdaughter.com.* This restaurant, inside an old Victorian home built in the 1800s, specializes in French, Italian, and Southwestern standards. Enjoy your meal outside on the rose-covered wraparound porches or indoors in the grand parlors. American, Mediterranean menu. Lunch, dinner. Closed Mon; Dec 25. Bar. Casual attire. Outdoor seating. **$$**

★ ★ **GIRL & THE FIG.** *110 W Spain St, Sonoma (95476). Phone 707/938-3634; fax 707/938-2064. www.thegirlandthefig.com.* French bistro menu. Lunch, dinner, Sun brunch. Closed Thanksgiving, Dec 25. Bar. Outdoor seating. **$$**

★ ★ **SADDLES.** *29 E MacArthur St, Sonoma (95476). Phone 707/933-3191; fax 707/933-9833. www.macarthurplace.com.* Magically managing to stay very much on the good side of the tasteful-to-tacky spectrum, this downright elegant Western-themed steakhouse at the MacArthur Place hotel sits among lush, peaceful gardens. The décor is decidedly "cowboy," with antique boots, saddles, and cowboy hats throughout the restaurant, but the food is decidedly delicious, featuring excellent steaks and seafood. Steak menu. Lunch, dinner. Bar. Children's menu. Outdoor seating. **$$$**

★ ★ ★ **SANTÉ.** *100 Boyes Blvd, Sonoma (95476). Phone 707/938-9000; toll-free 800/441-1414; fax 707/938-4250. www.fairmont.com.* California, eclectic menu. Breakfast, dinner. Bar. Outdoor seating. **$$$**

Sonora (E-3)

See also Modesto, Mother Lode Country, Oakdale

Settled 1848
Population 4,423
Elevation 1,825 ft
Area Code 209
Zip 95370
Information Tuolumne County Visitors Bureau, 222 S Shepherd St; phone 209/532-4212
Web Site www.tcchamber.com

Mexican miners named this the Sonoran Camp for their home state. Mexicans, Chileans, and Americans did not mix well and the camp became peaceful only after the varied groups dispersed. At the Big Bonanza, richest pocket mine in the Mother Lode, $160,000 in nearly pure gold was harvested in a single day. Stretching across seven hills, this colorful town, the seat of Tuolumne County, was the setting for several tales by Mark Twain and Bret Harte.

What to See and Do

Bear Valley. *1 Bear Valley Rd, Sonora (95223). 17 miles NW on Hwy 49, then 50 miles E on Hwy 4. Phone 209/753-2301. www.bearvalley.com.* Two triple, seven double chairlifts, two surface lifts; patrol, school, rentals; restaurant, cafeteria, concession area, bar; lodging. Longest run 3 miles; vertical drop 1,900 feet. (Nov-Apr, daily) **$$$$**

Calaveras Big Trees State Park. *1170 E Hwy 4, Arnold. Along Hwy 4, 4 miles NE of Arnold. Phone 209/795-2334. www.parks.ca.gov.* This 6,500-acre state park features groves of giant sequoias and mixed conifer forests, as well as opportunities for hiking, cross-country skiing, and camping. (Daily, sunrise-sunset) **$**

Columbia State Historic Park. *22708 Broadway St, Sonora (95310). 4 miles N via Hwy 49 and Parrotts Ferry Rd. Phone 209/532-0150. www.parks.ca.gov.* The 1850 gold town of Columbia has been restored to its early glory. The gold boom brought stages, freight wagons, brick stores, all the facilities of civilization, and thousands of gold-hungry miners. Operating gold mine tour; gold panning; stagecoach ride; concessions (fees). Free slide show in the museum. Most of the buildings are open daily from 10 am to 5 pm (closed Thanksgiving, Dec 25); some shops are closed weekdays in winter. **FREE** Among the 40 buildings on the self-guided tour are

City Hotel. *22768 Main St, Columbia (95310). Phone 209/532-1479.* Refitted as a period restaurant and hotel.

Eagle Cotage. *22708 Broadway, Columbia (95310). Phone 209/532-0150.* Reconstructed boardinghouse. Outside viewing only.

Firehouse. *22708 Broadway, Columbia (95310).* Tuolumne Engine Co #1 and pumper "Papeete."

Schoolhouse. *22708 Broadway, Columbia (95310). Phone 209/532-0150. www.columbiacalifornia.com.* (1860) One of the oldest of its kind in the state; in use until 1937; authentically refurnished.

Dodge Ridge. *Dodge Ridge Rd, Pinecrest (95364). 30 miles E on Hwy 108. Phone 209/965-3474; fax 209/965-4437. www.dodgeridge.com.* Two triple, five double chairlifts, four rope tows; patrol, school, rentals; cafeteria, bar, day-lodge, nursery. Twenty-eight runs; longest run 2 1/4 miles; vertical drop 1,600 feet. Snowboarding. (Mid-Nov-mid-Apr, Mon-Fri 9 am-4 pm, Sat-Sun, holidays 8:30 am-4 pm) **$$$$**

Don Pedro Lake Recreation Area. *31 Bonds Flat Rd, Sonora (95329). 13 miles S off Hwy 120. Phone 209/852-2396. www.donpedrolake.com.* A 26-mile-long lake impounded by a 580-foot dam. Swimming (fee), fishing, boat launching (marinas); picnicking, camping (fee; hook-ups). No pets. (Daily) Fee for activities. **$$**

Mercer Caverns. *1665 Sheep Ranch Rd, Sonora. 10 miles N on Hwy 49, then 5 miles NE on Hwy 4. Phone 209/728-2101. www.mercercavern.com.* Stalagmites, stalactites, aragonite, other formations in caves discovered in 1885. Ten rooms; lighted walkways; 55° F; 45-minute guided tours. Picnic area. (Memorial Day weekend-late Sept: Sun-Thurs 9 am-5 pm, Fri-Sat to 6 pm; Oct-Memorial Day weekend: daily 10 am-4:30 pm; closed Dec 25) **$$**

Moaning Cavern. *5350 Moaning Cave Rd, Vallecito. 12 miles N near Vallecito. Phone 209/736-2708. www.caverntours.com.* Discovered in 1851. View formations from 165-foot spiral staircase. Walking tour (45 minutes). Visitors may also descend into the cavern via 180-feet rope rappel, or take a three-hour tour into the undeveloped cavern depths (by appointment). Display of Native American and mining artifacts. (May-late Oct: daily 9 am-6 pm; Nov-late May: Mon-Fri 10 am-5 pm, Sat-Sun 9 am-5 pm) **$$$**

New Melones Lake Recreation Area. *6850 Studhorse Flat Rd, Sonora (95370). 10 miles N via Hwy 49, situated between Angels Camp, Sonora, and Columbia. Phone 209/536-9094. www.recreation.gov.* When full, the lake offers more than 100 miles of shoreline for water and fishing sports, as well as seven-lane launch ramps, fish-cleaning facilities, and a marina. During low lake levels, river rafting is popular on the Stanislaus River. Improved camping and day-use facilities available in the Glory Hole and Tuttletown recreation areas. (All year, daily; some sections of day-use areas and campgrounds may be closed during winter) **$$$**

Railtown 1897 State Historic Park. *5th Ave and Resevoir Rd, Jamestown. Phone 209/984-3953.*

www.parks.ca.gov. Steam passenger train rides (daytime, one hour; evening, two hours) over the Sierra foothills. Roundhouse tour. Park (daily). Rides (Mar-Nov, Sat-Sun, holidays). Reservations necessary for evening rides. Combination tickets available. (Daily 9:30 am-4:30 pm; closed Jan 1, Thanksgiving, Dec 25)

Stanislaus National Forest. *19777 Greenley Rd, Sonora (95370). NE and SE of town. Phone 209/532-3671.* More than 890,000 acres; contains Emigrant Wilderness, Carson-Iceberg Wilderness, and a portion (22,917 acres) of the Mokelumne Wilderness. The forest has many developed recreation sites with swimming, fishing, boating, rafting; hiking, bridle trails, picnicking, winter sports. More than 40 developed campgrounds (fee).

Special Events

Calaveras County Fair and Jumping Frog Jubilee. *101 Frogtown Rd, Angels Camp (95222). Phone 209/736-2561. www.frogtown.org.* Fair highlighted by frog-jumping contest, inspired by Mark Twain's short story. Mid-May.

Fireman's Muster. *Columbia State Historic Park, 22708 Broadway, Columbia (95310). Phone 209/536-1672.* Antique fire engines, parade, pumping contests. Early May.

Mother Lode Fair. *Mother Lode Fairgrounds, 220 Southgate Dr, Sonora (95370). Phone 209/532-7428. www.motherlodefair.com.* With everything from art exhibits and a demolition derby to live entertainment and baking and winemaking competitions, everyone of all ages will find something to interest them at this annual fair. Four days in mid-July. **$$$**

Mother Lode Roundup Parade and Rodeo. *Mother Lode Fairgrounds, 220 Southgate Dr, Sonora (95370). Phone toll-free 800/446-1333. www.mymotherlode.com/Round_Up.* Nearly 200 groups—from marching bands to motorcycles—parade down Washington Street, bull riders and steer wrestlers take part in rodeo action, and locals and visitors celebrate with a dance. Mother's Day weekend. **$$$**

Limited-Service Hotel

★ ★ MURPHYS HISTORIC HOTEL. *457 Main St, Murphys (95247). Phone 209/728-3444; toll-free 800/532-7684; fax 209/728-1590. www.murphyshotel.com.* 29 rooms, 1-2 story. Check-in 3 pm, check-out 11 am. Restaurant, bar. **$**

Full-Service Resort

★ ★ GREENHORN CREEK RESORT. *711 McCauley Ranch Rd, Angels Camp (95222). Phone 209/736-8120; toll-free 888/736-5900; fax 209/736-6210. www.greenhorncreek.com.* 55 rooms. Check-in 3 pm, check-out 11 am. Restaurant, bar. Fitness room, spa. Outdoor pool, children's pool. Golf. Tennis. **$$**

Specialty Lodgings

The following lodging establishments are approved by Mobil Travel Guide, but due to their unique and individualized nature have not been given a traditional Mobil Star rating. Included in this listing you may find bed-and-breakfasts, limited-service inns, guest ranches, and other unique hotel properties.

1859 HISTORIC NATIONAL HOTEL, A COUNTRY INN. *Po Box 502, Jamestown (95327). Phone 209/984-3446; toll-free 800/894-3446; fax 209/984-5620. www.national-hotel.com.* Continuously operated since 1859. 9 rooms, 2 story. Pets accepted, some restrictions; fee. Children over 10 years only. Complimentary full breakfast. Check-in 2 pm, check-out noon. Restaurant, bar. Whirlpool. **$**

BARRETTA GARDENS. *700 S Baretta St, Sonora (95370). Phone 209/532-6039; toll-free 800/206-3333; fax 209/532-8257. www.barrettagardens.com.* Victorian house (1903). 5 rooms, 2 story. Complimentary full breakfast. Check-in 3 pm, check-out 11 am. **$**

JAMESTOWN HOTEL. *18153 Main St, Jamestown (95327). Phone 209/984-3902; toll-free 800/205-4901; fax 209/984-4149. www.jamestownhotel.com.* 11 rooms, 2 story. Pets accepted, restrictions, fee. Complimentary full breakfast. Check-in 2-8 pm, check-out noon. Restaurant, bar. **$**

MCCAFFREY HOUSE BED & BREAKFAST INN. *23251 Hwy 108, Twain Harte (95383). Phone 209/586-0757; toll-free 888/586-0757; fax 209/586-3689. www.mccaffreyhouse.com.* Adjacent to forest. 8 rooms, 3 story. Complimentary continental breakfast. Check-in 3-7 pm, check-out 11 am. Whirlpool. **$**

PALM HOTEL BED & BREAKFAST. *10382 Willow St, Jamestown (95327). Phone 209/984-*

3429; toll-free 888/551-1851; fax 209/984-4929. www.palmhotel.com. Built in 1890, remodeled in 1982. 8 rooms, 2 story. Complimentary full breakfast. Check-in 3-6 pm, check-out 11 am. **$**

Restaurant

★ ★ **CITY HOTEL.** *22768 Main St, Columbia (95310). Phone 209/532-1479; toll-free 800/532-1479; fax 209/532-7027. www.cityhotel.com.* Restored gold rush-era hotel (1856). American menu. Dinner, Sun brunch. Closed Mon; Dec 24-25. Bar. Reservations recommended. **$$**

South Lake Tahoe (D-3)

Population 23,609
Elevation 6,260 ft
Area Code 530
Web Site www.visitinglaketahoe.com

Limited-Service Hotels

★ ★ **BEST WESTERN STATION HOUSE INN.** *901 Park Ave, South Lake Tahoe (96150). Phone 530/542-1101; toll-free 800/528-1234; fax 530/542-1714. www.stationhouseinn.com.* 100 rooms, 2 story. Complimentary full breakfast. Check-in 3 pm, check-out noon. High-speed Internet access, wireless Internet access. Restaurant, bar. Outdoor pool, whirlpool. **$$**

★ ★ **BEST WESTERN TIMBER COVE LODGE.** *3411 Lake Tahoe Blvd, South Lake Tahoe (96150). Phone 530/541-6722; toll-free 800/972-8558; fax 530/541-7959. www.timbercovetahoe.com.* 262 rooms, 3 story. Pets accepted; fee. Complimentary full breakfast. Check-in 3 pm, check-out noon. High-speed Internet access. Restaurant, two bars. Fitness room. Outdoor pool, whirlpool. Business center. **$**

★ ★ **EMBASSY SUITES.** *4130 Lake Tahoe Blvd, South Lake Tahoe (96150). Phone 530/544-5400; toll-free 800/988-9820; fax 530/544-4900. www.embassytahoe.com.* This hotel is the perfect location to enjoy all that Lake Tahoe has to offer. It is within walking distance of all the major casinos and the lake. A free shuttle takes you to the Heavenly and Sierra-at-Tahoe ski resorts. 400 rooms, 9 story, all suites. Complimentary full breakfast. Check-in 4 pm, check-out noon. High-speed Internet access, wireless Internet access. Restaurant, bar. Fitness room. Indoor pool, whirlpool. Business center. **$**

★ **FANTASY INN.** *3696 Lake Tahoe Blvd, South Lake Tahoe (96150). Phone 530/541-4200; toll-free 800/367-7736; fax 530/541-6798. www.fantasyinn.com.* 52 rooms, 2 story. Check-in 3 pm, check-out 11 am. **$**

★ **FOREST SUITES RESORT.** *1 Lake Pkwy, South Lake Tahoe (96150). Phone 530/541-6655; toll-free 800/822-5950; fax 530/544-3135. www.forestsuites.com.* 116 rooms, 3 story. Complimentary continental breakfast. Check-in 4 pm, check-out 11 am. Bar. Fitness room. Outdoor pool, whirlpool. **$**

★ **HOLIDAY INN EXPRESS.** *3961 Lake Tahoe Blvd, South Lake Tahoe (96150). Phone 530/544-5900; toll-free 800/544-5288; fax 530/544-5333. www.holidayinnexpresstahoe.com.* 89 rooms, 2 story. Complimentary continental breakfast. Check-in 3 pm, check-out noon. Outdoor pool, whirlpool. **$$**

★ ★ **INN BY THE LAKE.** *3300 Lake Tahoe Blvd, South Lake Tahoe (96150). Phone 530/542-0330; toll-free 800/877-1466; fax 530/541-6596. www.innbythelake.com.* This inn is set among pine trees and offers scenic mountain views near Heavenly Ski Resort as well as Lake Tahoe water views. 100 rooms, 3 story. Pets accepted; fee. Complimentary continental breakfast. Check-in 3 pm, check-out noon. High-speed Internet access. Outdoor pool, whirlpool. Business center. **$**

★ **QUALITY INN.** *3838 Lake Tahoe Blvd, South Lake Tahoe (96150). Phone 530/541-5400; toll-free 800/245-6343; fax 530/541-7170. www.qualityinn.com.* 120 rooms, 2 story. Complimentary continental breakfast. Check-in 5 pm, check-out 11 am. Fitness room. Outdoor pool. **$**

Restaurants

★ ★ ★ **EVANS AMERICAN GOURMET CAFE.** *536 Emerald Bay Rd, South Lake Tahoe (96150). Phone 530/542-1990; fax 530/542-9111. www.evanstahoe.com.* Evans is an unexpected find in South Lake Tahoe. The creative menu offers choices like pan-seared foie gras with port wine glaze and roast Cervena venison with balsamic roast cherries, and the extensive wine list features selections from California and the Northwest. Don't forget to save room for dessert selections like tiramisu, crème brulee, and "chocolate obsession." American menu. Dinner. Closed Easter, Thanksgiving, Dec 25. **$$**

★★ **FRESH KETCH.** *2435 Venice Dr E, South Lake Tahoe (96150). Phone 530/541-5683; fax 530/541-6329. www.thefreshketch.com.* Seafood menu. Lunch, dinner. Closed Thanksgiving, Dec 25. Bar. Children's menu. Valet parking. Outdoor seating. **$$$**

★★ **NEPHELES.** *1169 Ski Run Blvd, South Lake Tahoe (96150). Phone 530/544-8130; fax 530/544-8131. www.nepheles.com.* Mountain house and cabins converted into restaurant and boutique shops. California menu. Dinner. Bar. Casual attire. **$$**

★★★ **SWISS CHALET.** *2540 Lake Tahoe Blvd, South Lake Tahoe (96150). Phone 530/544-3304; fax 530/544-0579.* This restaurant has been chef-owned and operated since 1957. Fondue menu. Dinner. Closed Mon; Easter, Thanksgiving, Dec 25; also three weeks in Nov. Bar. Children's menu. **$$**

St. Helena

See also Calistoga, Napa, Santa Rosa, Sonoma, Yountville

Founded 1853
Population 5,950
Elevation 257 ft
Information Chamber of Commerce, 1010 Main St, Suite A; phone 707/963-4456
Web Site www.sthelena.com

In a region rich with world-class dining and wine-tasting options, St. Helena reigns supreme as the ultimate wine country destination for connoisseurs of fine food and wine. The city is home to the Culinary Institute of America at Greystone, where the public can dine at the Wine Spectator Greystone Restaurant. St. Helena's notable vintners include Beringer Wine Estates, Charles Krug Winery, and V. Sattui Winery, among many others. With its location in the heart of Napa Valley, St. Helena serves as an ideal base for exploring attractions throughout the region. Not surprisingly, then, a wide range of accommodations can be found nearby. Downtown St. Helena offers a small-town atmosphere, with ice cream shops and antique stores situated alongside upscale boutiques and spas. Bargain shoppers should head north of town on Highway 29 to the St. Helena Premium Outlets.

What to See and Do

1351 Lounge. *1351 Main St, St. Helena (94574). Phone 707/963-1969. www.1351lounge.com.* Bringing a bit of urban nightlife into the quiet Napa Valley, 1351 Lounge keeps things hopping with music, dancing, occasional open mic nights for musicians, and theme parties like Mardi Gras and Halloween. The real draw, however, is the live music. On any given night, you might find funk, rock, soul, R&B, house, blues, acoustic, or retro '70s and '80s music. (Daily; closed Thanksgiving, Dec 25)

Beaulieu Vineyard. *1960 S St. Helena Hwy, St. Helena (94573). Phone 707/967-5230. www.bvwine.com.* Founded more than 100 years ago by venerable winemaker Georges de Latour, the Beaulieu Vineyard is one of Napa Valley's most historic wineries. It also was an early pioneer in developing premium chardonnay and pinot noir, resulting in the official designation of Carneros as a separate and unique appellation. Tours cover the historic production facilities and offer free tastings; samples of reserve wines are available for a small fee in the Georges de Latour Reserve Tasting Room. (Daily 10 am-5 pm; closed holidays) **FREE**

Beringer Vineyards. *2000 Main St, St. Helena (94574). Phone 707/963-4812. www.beringer.com.* The oldest continuously operating winery in the Napa Valley and the first to offer tours to visitors back in 1934, Beringer is a must-see. Because the tours are quite comprehensive—involving a tour of the hand-dug aging tunnels as well as informative talks about how wine is made and aged, followed, of course, by wine tastings—Beringer makes a good starting point for a Napa visit. Tours are available on a first-come, first-served basis. Also available are a vintage legacy tour, a reserve tasting room, and a food-and-wine-pairing demonstration. Be sure to spend some time on the lush grounds—the vineyard was placed on the National Register of Historic Places as a historic district, and it's easy to see why. (Daily 10 am-4 pm; closed Jan 1, Thanksgiving, Dec 25) **$$$$**

Charles Krug Winery. *2800 Main St, St. Helena (94574). Phone 707/967-2200; toll-free 888/747-5784. www.charleskrug.com.* The first winery founded in the Napa Valley (1861), Charles Krug has been owned by the Mondavi family since 1943. As the Napa Valley was making the transition from a regional to an international presence, this winery was considered a leader, building the first tasting room 50 years ago. Currently, it is undergoing a major restoration and tours may not be available, but visitors are welcome to explore the landmark facilities and sample the wines. (Daily 10:30 am-5 pm; closed holidays) **FREE**

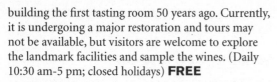

The Culinary Institute of America at Greystone. *2555 Main St, St. Helena (94574). Phone 707/967-2320. www.ciachef.edu.* Serious chefs and enthusiastic foodies will want to make the pilgrimage to the West Coast outpost of the famed Culinary Institute of America. Housed in a beautiful old stone building, the CIA specializes in professional development for chefs but also offers one-hour cooking demonstrations (daily 1:30 and 3:30 pm; also 10:30 am Sat-Sun, $$), several restaurants, including the Wine Spectator Greystone Restaurant, and the Spice Islands Marketplace, a store stocked with the latest kitchen equipment and more than 1,500 cookbooks. (Daily) **$$**

Dean & DeLuca. *607 S St. Helena Hwy, St. Helena (94574). Phone 707/967-9980. www.deandeluca.com.* This New York institution has done a marvelous job of adapting its brand of savvy marketing, quality foods, and exotic gourmet choices to the tastes of this region. You'll still find products from around the world, but especially in the prepared foods, you'll find fresh local ingredients and area specialties. The store features local produce, artisanal cheeses, 1,400 different kinds of California wine, an espresso bar, a catering service, and personal shopping. (Daily 9 am-7 pm; closed holidays)

Franciscan Oakville Estate. *1178 Galleron Rd, Rutherford (94574). 15 miles S via Hwy 29. Phone 707/963-7111; toll-free 800/529-9463. www.franciscan.com.* This award-winning, 25-year-old winery features a visitor center to better accommodate the vineyard's commitment to educating the public on all things wine. Besides offering visitors a choice of environments—a tasting bar, an open tasting room featuring an inviting fireplace, a private estate tasting room, and a shady patio—Franciscan sponsors private tastings, seminars, book signings, and a Taste Exploration series. (Daily 10 am-5 pm; closed holidays) **$$**

Louis M. Martini Winery. *254 St. Helena Hwy S, St. Helena (94574). Phone 707/963-2736; toll-free 800/321-9463. www.louismartini.com.* This third generation-owned family winery was one of the pioneering forces in putting Napa Valley on the international wine map. In addition to innovations in grape growing and winemaking, the Martini family was one of the first to venture into the Carneros region, now famous for its pinot noir. This low-key winery offers regular tours and tastings, a fine reserve tasting room, and charming gardens and picnic areas. (Daily 10 am-4:30 pm; closed holidays) **FREE**

Merryvale Vineyards. *1000 Main St, St. Helena (94574). Phone 707/963-7777. www.merryvale.com.* Specializing in wine education, this winery offers a variety of programs for both neophytes and connoisseurs. Popular are the Saturday and Sunday 10:30 am "Wine Component Tasting Seminars" ($$$), which include a tour of the historic winery with its spectacular cask room; the "Wine and Food in Balance" seminar ($$$) on the fourth Saturday of every month; and the "Barrel Tastings" ($) held the second Saturday of every month. There is a tasting room within a restored 1930s building, and 2,000- and 3,000-gallon oak casks on display. Merryvale produces distinct Chardonnays as well as Bordeaux-style red wine. Tours daily. (Daily 10 am-6:30 pm; closed holidays) **$**

Niebaum-Coppola Vineyards. *1991 St. Helena Hwy, St. Helena (94573). Phone 707/968-1100. www.niebaum-coppola.com.* More about commerce than wine, this vineyard is worth a visit only if you're a movie buff, where the adjoining museum displays owner Francis Ford Coppola's five Oscars, movie storyboards, and memorabilia from his films, including the desk from *The Godfather* and the car from *Tucker.* In the store, you'll find Coppola spaghetti sauce, movie T-shirts, and all sorts of logo-laden merchandise. That said, the grounds are gorgeous—including the old Inglenook Chateau—and wine tastings are available ($$$ and include a commemorative glass). (Daily; closed holidays) **FREE**

Silverado Museum. *1490 Library St, St. Helena (94574). Phone 707/963-3757. www.silveradomuseum.org.* Fans of Robert Louis Stevenson, the Scottish writer who penned such classics as *Treasure Island* and *Kidnapped,* will revel in the more than 8,000 items of memorabilia housed in this small museum. Among the treasures are the last words he ever wrote, his marriage license and wedding ring, first editions, photos, manuscript notes, galley proofs, and even the desk at which he worked while he lived in the area. (Tues-Sun noon-4 pm; closed holidays) **DONATION**

St. Helena Premium Outlets. *3111 N St. Helena Hwy, St. Helena (94574). Phone 707/226-9876.* In contrast to the one-of-a-kind boutiques and galleries found throughout the Napa Valley, the St. Helena Premium Outlets offer national and international brands at deep discounts. Though smaller than its sister outlet mall (see NAPA PREMIUM OUTLETS), St. Helena's still delivers bargains. The mall features Donna Karan, Joan and David, London Fog, Brooks Brothers, Movado, and Coach, among others. (Daily 10 am-6 pm; closed holidays)

V. Sattui Winery. *1111 White Ln, St. Helena (94574). Phone 707/963-7774. www.vsattui.com.* When you're tired of touring and ready to picnic, head to Sattui, a family-owned, 108-year-old winery that has one of the best gourmet food shops in the valley. While you can sample wines on the premises—and that's the only place you can, because the winery only sells directly to customers—it's better to build a picnic from its amazing assortments of cheeses, meats, breads, spreads, and sweets. You're also free to picnic on its lovely grounds. (Daily 8 am-5:30 pm; closed Dec 25)

Special Event

Napa Valley Wine Auction. *Napa Valley Vintner's Association, PO Box 141, St. Helena (94574). Phone 707/963-3388. www.napavintners.com.* Since it began in 1981, the Napa Valley Wine Auction has become the world's largest and most successful wine charity event, contributing more than $42 million to local social service agencies. More than 1,800 people from around the world attend to hunt bargains and pick up rare vintages from the 214 Napa Valley participating wineries. A limited number of day passes are available to the general public, as are individual tickets to the gala dinner. First weekend in June.

Full-Service Resort

★★★★ MEADOWOOD NAPA VALLEY. *900 Meadowood Ln, St. Helena (94574). Phone 707/963-3646; toll-free 800/458-8080; fax 707/963-3532. www.meadowood.com.* Guests drink in the best of the Napa Valley while staying at the casually refined Meadowood. From the esteemed John Thureen, who serves as resident wine tutor, to the guest services manager assigned to each arriving visitor, travelers are ensured an unforgettable experience. Rather like the home of a wealthy relative, Meadowood is nestled on more than 250 luscious acres in the renowned wine country. Country pursuits, such as croquet, tennis, and golf, are plentiful, while other guests prefer to get lost in a literary classic while poolside. The blend of Californian sensibilities and classic country style is perfect in the suites, cottages and lodges, where stone fireplaces and vaulted ceilings add to the timeless look. The Grill is available for casual dining under the shade of an umbrella, and the gastronomic pleasures of The Restaurant earn kudos from discriminating palates. 85 rooms, 2 story. Check-in 4 pm, check-out noon. High-speed Internet access. Two restaurants, two bars. Fitness room, fitness classes available, spa. Outdoor pool, children's pool, whirlpool. Golf, 9 holes. Tennis. Business center. **$$$$**

Full-Service Inn

★★★ INN AT SOUTHBRIDGE. *1020 Main St, St. Helena (94574). Phone 707/967-9400; toll-free 800/520-6800; fax 707/967-9486. www.innatsouthbridge.com.* Designed by renowned architect William Turnbull Jr., this inn was inspired by the small town squares of Europe. The upstairs guest quarters are spacious, with vaulted ceilings and fireplaces. French doors open onto private balconies, affording views of the courtyard, the rolling hills, and the town of St. Helena. Amenities include terry cloth bathrobes and down comforters. 21 rooms, 2 story. Complimentary continental breakfast. Check-in 4 pm, check-out noon. Restaurant, bar. Fitness room, spa. Outdoor pool, whirlpool. **$$$**

Specialty Lodgings

The following lodging establishments are approved by Mobil Travel Guide, but due to their unique and individualized nature have not been given a traditional Mobil Star rating. Included in this listing you may find bed-and-breakfasts, limited-service inns, guest ranches, and other unique hotel properties.

HARVEST INN. *1 Main St, St. Helena (94574). Phone 707/963-9463; toll-free 800/950-8466; fax 707/963-4402. www.harvestinn.com.* This renaissance of courtly English Tudor architecture is nestled among 8 acres of landscape and is reminiscent of the country gentry style. Even the meeting space at Harvest Inn has country inn charm. Hot air ballooning, gliding, Calistoga mud baths and winery tours are nearby. 57 rooms, 2 story. Pets accepted, some restrictions; fee. Complimentary continental breakfast. Check-in 4 pm, check-out 11 am. Two outdoor pools, whirlpool. **$$**

SHADY OAKS COUNTRY INN. *399 Zinfandel Ln, St. Helena (94574). Phone 707/963-1190; fax 707/963-9367. www.shadyoaksinn.com.* 5 rooms.

Complimentary full breakfast. Check-in 4-6 pm, check-out 11 am. **$$**

VINEYARD COUNTRY INN. *201 Main St, St. Helena (94574). Phone 707/963-1000; fax 707/963-1794. www.vineyardcountryinn.com.* 21 rooms, 2 story. Complimentary continental breakfast. Check-in 4 pm, check-out 11 am. Outdoor pool, whirlpool. **$$**

THE WINE COUNTRY INN. *1152 Lodi Ln, St. Helena (94574). Phone 707/963-7077; fax 707/963-9018. www.winecountryinn.com.* Perched on a knoll overlooking the vineyards and nearby hills, this inn offers individually decorated guest rooms. The personal touches include local antiques and handmade quilts. Most of the rooms have great vineyard views. To ensure total relaxation, televisions are not included in the rooms. 25 rooms, 3 story. Closed Dec 25. Complimentary full breakfast. Check-in 3 pm, check-out noon. Outdoor pool, whirlpool. **$$**

Restaurants

★ ★ ★ **PINOT BLANC.** *641 Main St, St. Helena (94574). Phone 707/963-6191; fax 707/963-6192. www.patinagroup.com.* California, Mediterranean menu. Lunch, dinner. Closed Mon. Bar. Outdoor seating. **$$**

★ ★ ★ ★ **TERRA.** *1345 Railroad Ave, St. Helena (94574). Phone 707/963-8931. www.terrarestaurant.com.* Chef/owner Hiro Sone has been wowing diners at Terra, his cozy, intimate Napa Valley dining room, since 1988. Set one block off the main drag on Railroad Avenue in St. Helena, Terra is located in a charming old stone building, rustically finished with vintage red-tiled floors, exposed stone walls, wood-beamed ceilings, and country floral arrangements. While many showy Napa Valley eateries scream "EAT HERE," Terra softly beckons diners to come in and have a seat. Terra inspires enjoyment and relaxation, so put your mind and your worries on hold and dig in. The food is spectacular, a successful blend of flavors from France, Asia, and northern California. Signatures change with the seasons and include red wine-braised veal cheeks, lobster tortelloni, and stone fruit *tarte tatin.* With gracious hospitality and warmth, the staff at Terra make you feel like you're dining at home. An evening here is simply a wonderful experience, one you will cherish long after your meal is over. French, Italian menu. Dinner. Closed Tues; holidays; also two weeks in early Jan. Reservations recommended. **$$$**

★ ★ ★ **TRA VIGNE.** *1050 Charter Oak Ave, St. Helena (94574). Phone 707/963-4444; fax 707/963-1233. www.travignerestaurant.com.* Located in the heart of California wine country, this restaurant offers inspiring views of the vineyards. Italian menu. Lunch, dinner. Closed July 4, Thanksgiving, Dec 25. Bar. Reservations recommended. Outdoor seating. **$$**

★ ★ ★ **WINE SPECTATOR GREYSTONE.** *2555 Main St, St. Helena (94574). Phone 707/967-1010; fax 707/967-2375.* Located within the Culinary Institute of America's western campus, the restaurant offers a view of the professional culinary staff (assisted by students from the Hyde Park, NY campus) at work in the open kitchen. The menu features local wine country-inspired cuisine, and an all-California wine list. California menu. Lunch, dinner. Closed holidays. Bar. Outdoor seating. **$$**

Stockton (E-2)

See also Lodi, Modesto

Founded 1849
Population 210,943
Elevation 13 ft
Area Code 209
Information Stockton/San Joaquin Convention and Visitors Bureau, 46 W Fremont St, 95202; phone 209/943-1987 or toll-free 800/350-1987
Web Site www.visitstockton.org

Connected to San Francisco Bay by a 78-mile deep water channel, Stockton is an important inland port with giant ore-loading facilities and grain terminals accessible to large ships. In its early days as the gateway to the Mother Lode country, it became a "city of a thousand tents." Many of the 49ers settled here and became rich when irrigation systems turned the surrounding countryside into fertile grain fields.

What to See and Do

Children's Museum. *402 W Weber Ave, Stockton (95203). Phone 209/465-4386. www.sonnet.com/usr/children.* Interactive displays covering 24,000 square feet; special events. (Tues-Sat 9 am-4 pm, Sun noon-5 pm; closed Sun in summer; also holidays) **$**

Haggin Museum. *1201 N Pershing Ave, Stockton (95203). Phone 209/462-4116. www.hagginmuseum.org.* State and local historical exhibits; 19th-century European and American paintings and decorative arts; Native American arts. Guided tours (Sat or by appointment); changing exhibits. (Tues-Sun 1:30-5 pm; closed holidays) Free the first Saturday of the month. **$**

Municipal recreation facilities. *Louis Park, 6 E Lindsay St, Stockton. Phone 209/937-8206.* The city maintains 50 parks, tennis courts, playgrounds, swimming pools, picnic areas; two golf courses; boat launching facilities and berths; ice arena; community and senior citizen centers. Fee for activities.

Pixie Woods. *Louis Park, 6 E Lindsay St, Stockton (95202). W end of Monte Diablo Blvd. Phone 209/937-8206.* Mother Goose and Fairyland characters; puppet shows in Toadstool Theatre; train, boat, and merry-go-round rides. (June-Labor Day: Wed-Sun; late Feb-May and after Labor Day-late Oct: Sat-Sun, holidays, including Easter week) **$**

World Wildlife Museum. *1245 W Weber Ave, Stockton (95203). Phone 209/465-2834.* More than 2,000 mounted zoological specimens represent wildlife from every continent. Includes deer, elk, African animals, wolves, antelope, bears, crocodiles and alligators, birds, and Arctic animals. (Wed-Sun) **$$**

Special Events

Asparagus Festival. *4520 W Eight Mile Rd, Stockton (95209). Phone toll-free 800/350-1987. www.asparagusfest.com.* Just about anything can be a reason for celebration, as demonstrated by the city of Stockton, which holds this annual three-day entertainment festival in honor of asparagus. Arts and crafts booths; food pavilions; cooking demonstrations; games and activities; and Asparagus Alley, a popular stop for deep-fried asparagus, are just a few of the goings-on at this event. Late Apr. **$$**

Greek Festival. *St. Basil Greek Orthodox Church, 920 W March Ln, Stockton (95207). Phone 209/478-7564. www.stbasilstockton.org.* Greek food, music, and dancing, games for kids. Weekend after Labor Day.

Obon Festival and Bazaar. *2820 Shimizu Dr, Stockton (95203). Phone 209/466-6701.* Street dance, food, exhibits, authentic Japanese costumes, colorful decorations at the Buddhist Temple. July.

San Joaquin County Fair. *County Fairgrounds, 1658 S Airport Way, Stockton (95206). Phone 209/466-5041. www.sanjoaquinfair.com.* Horse racing, agricultural and livestock displays, petting zoo, carnival, entertainment. June. **$$**

Limited-Service Hotels

★ HOWARD JOHNSON. *1672 Herndon Rd, Ceres (95307). Phone 209/537-4821; toll-free 800/446-4656; fax 209/537-1040. www.hojo.com.* 50 rooms, 2 story. Pets accepted. Complimentary continental breakfast. Check-in 2 pm, check-out 11 am. Outdoor pool. **$**

★★ RADISSON HOTEL STOCKTON. *2323 Grand Canal Blvd, Stockton (95207). Phone 209/957-9090; toll-free 800/932-3322; fax 209/473-0739. www.radisson.com.* 198 rooms, 5 story. Check-out 11 am. Restaurant, bar. Outdoor pool. **$**

Restaurant

★★ LE BISTRO. *3121 W Benjamin Holt Dr, Stockton (95219). Phone 209/951-0885; fax 209/320-3833. www.lebistrostockton.com.* French menu. Lunch, dinner. Closed holidays. Bar. **$$$**

Sunnyvale (E-2)

See also Santa Clara, Saratoga

Population 131,760
Elevation 130 ft
Area Code 408
Information Chamber of Commerce, 101 W Olive Ave, 94086; phone 408/736-4971
Web Site www.svcoc.org

What to See and Do

Sunnyvale Historical Museum. *235 E California Ave, Sunnyvale (94086). Phone 408/749-0220.* Houses historical artifacts and pictures of the area as well as information on pioneering families. (Tues, Thurs, Sun; closed holidays) **FREE**

Limited-Service Hotels

★★ COUNTRY INN & SUITES BY CARLSON *1300 Chesapeake Terrace, Sunnyvale (94089). Phone 408/747-0999; toll-free 800/456-4000; fax 408/745-0759. www.countryinns.com.* 180 rooms, 5 story. Check-in 3 pm, check-out noon. Restaurant, bar. Fitness room. Outdoor pool. Business center. **$$**

★ ★ FOUR POINTS BY SHERATON. *1250 Lakeside Dr, Sunnyvale (94085). Phone 408/738-4888; toll-free 800/543-3322; fax 408/737-7147. www.starwood.com/fourpoints.* Minutes from San Jose International Airport and nestled in the heart of Silicon Valley. 375 rooms, 3 story. Check-out noon. Restaurant, bar. Outdoor pool, whirlpool. Airport transportation available. **$**

★ MAPLE TREE INN. *711 E El Camino Real, Sunnyvale (94087). Phone 408/720-9700; toll-free 800/423-0243; fax 408/738-5665. www.mapletreeinn.com.* 18 rooms, 3 story. Pets accepted; fee. Complimentary continental breakfast. Check-in noon, check-out noon. Outdoor pool. **$**

★ STAYBRIDGE SUITES. *900 Hamlin Ct, Sunnyvale (94089). Phone 408/745-1515; toll-free 800/833-4353; fax 408/745-0540. www.staybridge.com.* 138 rooms, 3 story, all suites. Pets accepted, some restrictions; fee. Complimentary full breakfast. Check-out noon. Fitness room. Outdoor pool, whirlpool. Airport transportation available. **$**

Full-Service Hotel

★ ★ ★ SHERATON. *1100 N Mathilda Ave, Sunnyvale (94089). Phone 408/745-6000; fax 408/734-8276. www.sheraton.com.* 173 rooms, 2 story. Check-in 3 pm, check-out 1 pm. Restaurant, bar. Fitness room. Outdoor pool, whirlpool. Airport transportation available. **$**

Susanville (C-3)

See also Chester

Settled 1853
Population 13,541
Elevation 4,258 ft
Area Code 530
Zip 96130
Information Lassen County Chamber of Commerce, 84 N Lassen St, PO Box 338; phone 530/257-4323
Web Site www.lassencountychamber.org

Susanville is currently a trading center for an area producing livestock, lumber, alfalfa, garlic, and strawberries. There is fine hunting for deer, bear, antelope, pheasant, grouse, quail, ducks, and geese, and fishing in many lakes and rivers in the surrounding hills and mountains. Lassen National Forest headquarters and a Ranger District office are located here. In 1856, Susanville was the capital of the Republic of Nataqua, an area of 50,000 square miles. Isaac Roop, the town's first settler, helped establish the republic, which later joined the Nevada Territory. Roop was first Provisional Governor of Nevada and later senator. California surveys showed the area was part of Plumas County. The locals refused to join and holed up in Roop's house in 1864. After a day of gunfighting, California won back what is now Lassen County. Susanville was named by Roop in honor of his only daughter.

What to See and Do

Bizz Johnson Trail. *601 Richmond Rd, Susanville (96130). Begins 1/2 mile S via S Weatherlow St, left on Richmond Rd to Susanville Depot Trailhead; parking available. Phone 530/257-0456. www.recreation.gov.* Following the route of a long-defunct Southern Pacific railway, the Bizz Johnson National Recreation Trail is a 25-mile biking/hiking/riding/cross-country skiing trail that twists through spectacular scenery between Susanville and Westwood. The trail crosses the Susan River numerous times atop historic bridges and trestles, and even weaves through two tunnels. Remnants of the area's once proud logging industry dot the trailside, including a can't-miss monument to a dead mill: a 25-foot tall Paul Bunyan statue carved from a single redwood. **FREE**

Eagle Lake. *477-050 Eagle Rd, Susanville. 2 miles W on Hwy 36, then 15 miles N on County A1, in Lassen National Forest. Phone 530/257-4188.* Called by scientists "the lake that time forgot," this 26,000-acre lake was formed by the receding waters of a primeval lake larger than Lake Erie. It is the second-largest natural lake in California and home to Eagle Lake trout, a species averaging 3 to 5 pounds that has adapted to living in the lake's alkaline water. Gallatin Beach, at the south end of the lake, provides swimming and waterskiing. Five campgrounds available (fee). Marina has boat rentals. Contact Eagle Lake Resource Area.

Gallatin Marina. *Susanville. Phone 530/257-2151.* Adjacent to Lassen National Forest Campgrounds. Fishing, boating (ramps, rentals); groceries. (Late May-mid-Oct)

Lassen National Forest. *2550 Riverside Dr, Susanville (96130). 7 miles W on Hwy 36. Phone 530/257-*

2151. www.fs.fed.us/r5/lassen. More than 1 million acres. Swimming, excellent trout fishing in lakes and streams; hunting, cross-country and downhill skiing, snowmobiling. In the forest is

Wilderness Areas. *2550 Riverside Dr, Susanville. 35 miles W via Hwy 36 and County A21. Phone 530/257-2151.* All offer backpacking, primitive camping. (Daily) **Caribou Peak**. Gentle rolling forested terrain with many small crystal lakes. Many small cinder cones. **Thousand Lakes**. Contrasting topography; hiking trails. 25 miles E and S of Burney via Hwys 299, 89, Forest Rd 26. **Ishi Wilderness**. Dotted with rock outcroppings and bizarre pillar lava formations.

Roop's Fort & Lassen Historical Museum. *75 N Weatherlow St, Susanville (96130). Phone 530/257-3292.* Fort (1854), built by Isaac Roop, was the capitol of the Nataqua Republic. (May-Oct, Mon-Fri) **FREE**

Subway Cave. *1/4 mile N of the junction of Hwy 44 and 89, across from Cave Campground. Phone 530/336-5521.* Located just north of Lassen Volcanic National Park near the town of Old Station, Subway Cave is a 1,700-foot lava tube that was born out of a volcanic eruption about 20,000 years ago. Visitors are free to explore the cave on their own between May and October. Be sure to bring a lantern or other good light source; without one, the darkness is overwhelming.

Special Event

Lassen County Fair. *Fairgrounds, 195 Russell Ave, Susanville (96130). Off Russell Ave and Main St. Phone 530/257-4104.* Livestock and horse shows, rodeos, parade, livestock auction; entertainment. Third weekend in July.

Limited-Service Hotel

★★ BEST WESTERN TRAILSIDE INN. *2785 Main St, Susanville (96130). Phone 530/257-4123; toll-free 800/780-7234; fax 530/257-2665. www.bestwestern.com.* 90 rooms, 2 story. Complimentary continental breakfast. Check-out 11 am. Restaurant. Outdoor pool. **$**

Tahoe City (Lake Tahoe Area) (D-3)

See also Truckee

Population 2,500
Elevation 6,240 ft
Area Code 530
Zip 95730
Web Site www.visitinglaketahoe.com

What to See and Do

Tahoe State Recreation Area. *Near Tahoe City on Hwy 28. Phone 530/583-3074.* Less than a mile east of Tahoe City, this two-campground complex affords easy access to the restaurants and retailers in town and easier access to the fishing and swimming opportunities in the lake. The Lakeside campground is right on the shore, while the Hillside campground is across the highway. Though convenient, the highly developed location is not the spot to get away from it all.

Limited-Service Hotel

★ TRAVELODGE. *455 N Lake Blvd, Tahoe City (96145). Phone 530/583-3766; toll-free 800/578-7878; fax 530/583-8045. www.tahoetravelodge.com.* 47 rooms, 2 story. Complimentary continental breakfast. Check-in 2 pm, check-out 11 am. Outdoor pool, whirlpool. **$**

Full-Service Resort

★★★ RESORT AT SQUAW CREEK. *400 Squaw Creek Rd, Olympic Valley (96146). Phone 530/583-6300; toll-free 800/327-3353; fax 530/581-6632. www.squawcreek.com.* Situated in the heart of Lake Tahoe, the Resort at Squaw Creek is a skier's paradise. This full-service resort is just minutes by a private chair lift from the challenging peaks and scenic trails of Squaw Valley, the site of the 1960 Winter Olympics. The resort's outdoor skating rink, heated pools and hot tubs, and multitude of snowbound activities make it a natural choice for winter vacations, but with a terrific 18-hole golf course designed by Robert Trent Jones Jr., complete spa, tennis courts, and hiking and biking trails, it is an ideal destination year-round. Family-friendly, this mountain getaway has something for everyone with its variety of recreational opportunities, comfortable rooms and suites, and five dining outlets. 404 rooms, 9 story. Check-in 4 pm, check-out 11 am. High-speed Internet access, wireless Internet access. Five restaurants, five bars. Children's activity center. Fitness room, spa. Outdoor pool, children's pool, whirlpool. Golf. Tennis. Airport transportation available. Business center. **$$**

Specialty Lodgings

The following lodging establishments are approved by Mobil Travel Guide, but due to their unique and individualized nature have not been given a traditional Mobil Star rating. Included in this listing you may find bed-and-breakfasts, limited-service inns, guest ranches, and other unique hotel properties.

CHANEY HOUSE. *4725 W Lake Blvd, Tahoe City (96145). Phone 530/525-7333; fax 530/525-4413. www.chaneyhouse.com.* Built in 1928; original stone construction. 4 rooms, 2 story. Complimentary full breakfast. Check-in 3 pm, check-out 11 am. **$$**

THE COTTAGE INN. *1690 W Lake Blvd, Tahoe City (96145). Phone 530/581-4073; toll-free 800/581-4073; fax 530/581-0226. www.thecottageinn.com.* 22 rooms. Children over 12 years only. Complimentary full breakfast. Check-in 3-8 pm, check-out 11 am. High-speed Internet access. Rustic cabins in the woods. **$**

Restaurants

★ ★ ★ SWISS LAKEWOOD. *5055 W Lake Blvd, Homewood (96141). Phone 530/525-5211; fax 530/525-0947. www.swisslakewood.com.* French menu. Dinner. Closed Mon. Bar. Reservations recommended. **$$$**

★ WOLFDALE'S. *640 N Lake Blvd, Tahoe City (96145). Phone 530/583-5700. www.wolfdales.com.* California, Asian menu. Dinner. Bar. Outdoor seating. **$$**

Tahoe Vista (Lake Tahoe Area) (D-3)

See also Truckee

Population 1,668
Elevation 6,232 ft
Area Code 530
Web Site www.visitinglaketahoe.com

Limited-Service Hotel

★ CEDAR GLEN LODGE BEST VALUE INN & SUITES. *6589 N Lake Blvd, Tahoe Vista (96148). Phone 530/546-4281; toll-free 800/500-8246; fax 530/546-2250. www.tahoecedarglen.com.* 31 rooms, 2 story. Complimentary continental breakfast. Check-in 3 pm, check-out 11 am. Outdoor pool, children's pool, whirlpools. **$**

Specialty Lodging

The following lodging establishment is approved by Mobil Travel Guide, but due to its unique and individualized nature has not been given a traditional Mobil Star rating. Included in this listing you may find bed-and-breakfasts, limited-service inns, guest ranches, and other unique hotel properties.

SHORE HOUSE AT LAKE TAHOE. *7170 N Lake Blvd, Tahoe Vista (96148). Phone 530/546-7270; toll-free 800/207-5160; fax 530/546-7130. www.shorehouselaketahoe.com.* 9 rooms, 2 story. Complimentary full breakfast. Check-in 4-6 pm, check-out 11 am. **$$**

Restaurants

★ ★ CAPTAIN JON'S. *7220 N Lake Blvd, Tahoe Vista (96148). Phone 530/546-4819; fax 530/546-7963.* French, seafood menu. Dinner. Bar. Valet parking. Outdoor seating. On the lakefront. **$$**

★ ★ GAR WOODS GRILL & PIER. *5000 N Lake Blvd, Carnelian Bay (96140). Phone 530/546-3366; toll-free 800/298-2463; fax 530/546-2184. www.garwoods.com.* American menu. Lunch, dinner, Sun brunch. Bar. Children's menu. Outdoor seating. **$$**

Tiburon

See also Mill Valley, San Francisco, San Rafael, Sausalito

Population 8,666
Elevation 90 ft
Area Code 415
Zip 94920
Web Site www.tiburon.org

What to See and Do

China Cabin. *54 Beach Rd, Tiburon (94920). Belvedere Cove, near junction Tiburon Blvd. Phone 415/435-1853.*

Elegant social saloon of the 19th-century transpacific steamship SS *China*. The 20-by-40-foot cabin was removed in 1886 and used as a waterfront cottage until 1978. Completely restored; intricate woodwork, gold leaf, cut glass windows, brass and crystal chandeliers; period furnishings. Tours (Apr-Oct, Wed, Sun afternoons or by appointment). **DONATION**

Main Street. *Main St, Tiburon.* The quaint North Bay community of Tiburon offers great shopping and views of the San Francisco skyline on its charming Main Street, with its collection of lagoon-front eateries, galleries, and specialty stores. Near Sam's Anchor Café—a bar that was the Bay Area's bootlegging center during Prohibition—Main Street becomes Ark Row, a line of permanently moored houseboats that now lodge unusual shops and restaurants.

Limited-Service Hotel

★★ WATERS EDGE HOTEL TIBURON. *25 Main St, Tiburon (94920). Phone 415/789-5999; fax 415/789-5888. www.marinhotels.com.* 23 rooms, 2 story. Complimentary continental breakfast. Check-in 3 pm, check-out noon. Fitness room. **$$$**

Restaurants

★★ GUAYMAS. *5 Main St, Tiburon (94920). Phone 415/435-6300; fax 415/435-6802.* On the bay. Mexican menu. Lunch, dinner. Closed Thanksgiving, Dec 25. Bar. Children's menu. Outdoor seating. **$$**

★★ SERVINO RISTORANTE. *9 Main St, Tiburon (94920). Phone 415/435-2676; fax 415/435-4079. www.servino.com.* California, Italian menu. Lunch, dinner. Bar. Children's menu. Outdoor seating. **$$**

Trinidad (A-1)

See also Eureka

Population 311
Elevation 40 ft
Area Code 707
Zip 95570
Information Chamber of Commerce, PO Box 356; phone 707/677-1610
Web Site www.historictrinidad.com

When leaders of a Spanish expedition landed here on June 18, 1775, it was Trinity Sunday, so the leaders named the area Trinidad. The city was founded in 1850 and was a port of entry for supplies packed into the upriver gold country. Offshore is Prisoner Rock; in the old days, constables took drunks here and gave them two options: swim the sobering length ashore or dry out here.

What to See and Do

Cher-Ae Heights Casino. *27 Cher-Ae Ln, Trinidad (95570). Phone 707/677-3611; toll-free 800/684-2464. www.cheraeheightscasino.com.* One of a few gaming opportunities on California's north coast, Cher-Ae Heights is located in the quiet seaside town of Trinidad, about 10 miles north of Arcata via Highway 101. The casino wins points for variety, with scads of slots and other machines, a private poker room, and a cavernous bingo hall. There are several restaurants and lounges on-site, and a nonsmoking slot area. The casino operates a shuttle that runs to local hotels Wednesday through Saturday.

Patrick's Point State Park. *4150 Patrick's Point Dr, Trinidad (95570). 5 miles N on Hwy 101. Phone 707/677-3570. www.parks.ca.gov.* On 650 acres. Ocean fishing, beachcombing, tidepooling; hiking trails, picnicking, camping facilities in unusual rain-forest type of growth (reservations reccommended). Museum exhibits, naturalist programs, Yorok Village.

Telonicher Marine Laboratory. *570 Ewing St, Trinidad (95570). Ewing St at Edwards St. Phone 707/826-3671. www.humboldt.edu/~marinelb.* Marine teaching and research facility of Humboldt State University. Touch-tank with local tidepool marine life; display aquariums. Self-guided tours of hallway exhibits. (Sept-May: Mon-Fri 9 am-5 pm, Sat-Sun from 10 am; rest of year: Mon-Fri 9 am-5 pm; schedule may vary; closed school holidays) **FREE**

Specialty Lodging

The following lodging establishment is approved by Mobil Travel Guide, but due to its unique and individualized nature has not been given a traditional Mobil Star rating. Included in this listing you may find bed-and-breakfasts, limited-service inns, guest ranches, and other unique hotel properties.

LOST WHALE BED & BREAKFAST. *3452 Patrick's Point Dr, Trinidad (95570). Phone 707/677-3425; toll-free 800/677-7859; fax 707/677-0284.*

Historic Truckee

An Old West-style town tucked high in the Sierra Nevada near the northern shores of Lake Tahoe, Truckee offers not only atmosphere, but also a good aerobic workout—if you want to tackle a hill along the way. Park your car at one of the spaces or lots along Commercial Row, which is lined with Western-front, 19th-century stores and buildings. Head first for the town's visitor center, which is housed in the old railway depot built in 1896. A plaque marks the 1868 date when the first transcontinental railroad reached Truckee. Walking west along Commercial Row, you'll find an old loading dock once used by the Southern Pacific Railroad, the town's oldest railway structure. Lumber was shipped from here to San Francisco, Sacramento, and other cities. Walk north up Spring Street to Jibboom Street, site of the town's aptly named Old Jail; one of the oldest in the West, it was in use from 1875 to 1964. If you're feeling energetic, you can make the rather strenuous climb farther up Spring Street to High Street, then go west (left) along High Street to see the 17-ton rocking stone, which Native Americans once used for drying food. The stone no longer rocks—it has been stabilized to ward off vandals and protect sightseers from accidents. Walking back down the hill to Commercial Row, stay on the north side of the street (opposite the visitor center). Historic buildings here include the 601, where Truckee's "Vigilance Committee" once met to combat crime, and the Capitol, an 1870 building that is the oldest on the street and has served as a saloon, county courthouse, and theater. Charlie Chaplin is said to have hung out at the Capitol while filming his classic, *The Gold Rush*. Just across the Bridge Street intersection is the old Truckee Hotel, which dates to 1868—though it was rebuilt in the early 20th century following a fire and renovated again in 1977. Walking north up Bridge Street, turn right onto Church Street to find Gray's Log Waystation, Truckee's oldest building (1863). Return to Bridge Street and walk south. Across the railroad tracks, at East River Street, you'll find the gabled Swedish House, a rustic one-time boarding house that accommodated area lumbermen, ice cutters, railroad workers, and gold rush film crews. Go another block south, and cross the river via the walkway adjacent to the bridge. On Southeast River Street you'll see an old brick building that was once a Chinese herb shop. Returning north and recrossing the river, follow Bridge Street to West River Street where, to your left, you'll find the Victorian-style house of the man who owned the town's first lumber mill. From there, return up Bridge Street to Commercial Row, where several restaurants and cafés offer hearty cooking.

www.lostwhaleinn.com. 8 rooms. Complimentary full breakfast. Check-in 3-8 pm, check-out 11 am. Restaurant. Beach. **$$**

Truckee (D-3)

See also Mother Lode Country, Tahoe City, Tahoe Vista

Population 13,864
Elevation 5,820 ft
Area Code 530
Zip 96161
Information Truckee-Donner Chamber of Commerce, 10065 Donner Pass Rd; phone 530/587-2757
Web Site www.truckee.com

Once a lumbering camp, now a railroad and recreation center, Truckee becomes important in winter as the gateway to one of California's best winter sports areas. In 1913, the first California ski club was organized; today more than 20 ski clubs make their headquarters here. Truckee is surrounded by Tahoe National Forest; a Ranger District office of the forest is located here.

What to See and Do

Boreal. *19455 Boreal Ridge Rd, Soda Springs. 10 miles W on I-80, Castle Peak exit. Phone 530/426-3666. www.skiboreal.com.* Two quad, two triple, six double chairlifts; patrol, school, rentals, snowmaking; cafeteria, bar, lodge. Forty-one runs, longest run 1 mile; vertical drop 600 feet. (Nov-May, daily) Night skiing. **$$$$**

Donner Lake. *South Shore Dr, Truckee (96160). 3 miles W on Hwy 40.* Sparkling blue lake surrounded by the mountain slopes of the Sierras. Fishing, water sports.

Nearby is Donner Pass, the main route into California for more than a century.

Donner Memorial State Park. *12593 Donner Pass Rd, Truckee (96161). 2 miles W on Donner Pass Rd. Phone 530/582-7892. www.parks.ca.gov.* A 353-acre area that serves as a monument to the Donner Party, stranded here in October 1846 by early blizzards. Of a party of 81 who pitched camp, only 48 survived. The Emigrant Trail Museum has exhibits on the Donner Party, construction of first transcontinental railroad, geology of the Sierra Nevada, wildlife, and Native Americans (Memorial Day-Labor Day: daily 10 am-5 pm; Sept-May: daily 10 am-4 pm; closed Jan 1, Thanksgiving, Dec 25; fee). Swimming, fishing; nature trail, cross-country ski trail, picnicking, camping (Memorial Day-Labor Day). Ranger, naturalist programs (seasonal). Park (daily).

Donner Ski Ranch. *19320 Donner Pass, Truckee (95724). 10 miles W, 3 1/2 miles off I-80 at Soda Springs exit. Phone 530/426-3635. www.donnerskiranch.com.* Triple, five double chairlifts; patrol, school, rentals; bar, restaurant, cafeteria. Longest run 1 mile; vertical drop 750 feet. (Nov-May, daily) **$$$$**

Northstar. *6 miles S on Hwy 267 via I-80. Phone 530/562-1010; toll-free 800/466-6784. www.skinorthstar.com.* Two quad, three triple, three double chairlifts, gondola; patrol, school, rentals, snowmaking; cafeteria, restaurants, bars, lodging. Longest run 3 miles; vertical drop 2,280 feet. Cross-country skiing; rentals. (Nov-Apr, daily) Half-day rates. Summer activities include tennis, 18-hole golf, mountain biking, horseback riding, and swimming.

Royal Gorge Cross-Country Ski Resort. *9411 Hillside Dr, Soda Springs (95728). 12 miles W on I-80. Phone toll-free 800/500-3871. www.royalgorge.com.* Approximately 80 cross-country trails more than 200 miles of rolling terrain. Patrol, school, rentals; restaurants, two lodges. Longest trail 14 miles. (Mid-Nov-mid-May, Mon-Fri 9 am-5 pm, Sat-Sun, holidays 8:30 am-5 pm) **$$$$**

Sugar Bowl. *Old Hwy 40, Truckee (95724). 11 miles W on I-80. Phone 530/426-9000. www.sugarbowl.com.* Quad, six double chairlifts, gondola; patrol, school, rentals; restaurant, cafeterias, bar, nursery, lodging. Forty-seven runs, longest run 1 1/2 miles; vertical drop 1,500 feet. (Nov-Apr, daily) **$$$$**

Tahoe Donner. *11509 Northwoods Blvd, Truckee (96161). 6 miles NW off I-80. Phone 530/587-9444. www.tahoedonner.com.* One double chairlift, surface tow; patrol, school, rentals; cafeteria, restaurant, bar. (Dec-Apr, daily; closed Easter) Cross-country trails (fee). **$$$$**

Special Events

Donner Party Hike. Retraces the Donner Party's ill-fated passage. First weekend in Oct.

Truckee Championship Rodeo. *McIver Arena, 10695 Brockway Rd, Truckee (96161). Phone 530/582-9852. www.tdhorsemen.addr.com.* The PRCA rodeo caps off ten days of fun including mounted shooting, a rodeo queen pageant, and a parade. Second weekend in Aug.

Limited-Service Hotels

★★ BEST WESTERN TRUCKEE TAHOE INN. *11331 Hwy 267, Truckee (96161). Phone 530/587-4525; toll-free 800/824-6385; fax 530/587-8173. www.bestwesterntahoe.com.* 100 rooms, 2 story. Complimentary continental breakfast. Check-in 2 pm, check-out 11 am. Restaurant. Children's activity center. Fitness room. Outdoor pool. **$$**

★ DONNER LAKE VILLAGE RESORT. *15695 Donner Pass Rd, Truckee (96161). Phone 530/587-6081; toll-free 800/621-6664; fax 530/587-8782.* 57 rooms, 2 story. Check-in 3 pm, check-out 11 am. **$**

Restaurant

★ OB'S PUB & RESTAURANT. *10046 Donner Pass Rd, Truckee (96160). Phone 530/587-4164.* Built in early 1900s; many antiques, wood-burning stove. American menu. Lunch, dinner. Bar. Children's menu. Casual attire. Reservations recommended. **$$**

Ukiah (C-1)

See also Clear Lake Area (Lake County), Fort Bragg, Mendocino, Willits

Settled 1855
Population 15,497
Elevation 639 ft
Area Code 707
Zip 95482
Information Greater Ukiah Chamber of Commerce, 200 S School St; phone 707/462-4705
Web Site www.ukiah.com

In the center of a valley that Native Americans called Ukiah, or Deep Valley, this is the seat of Mendocino County. It is the trading place of an agricultural area that produces a $75 million annual crop of pears, grapes, and other products. Recreational activities include golf, tennis, and fishing.

What to See and Do

Dunnewood Vineyards. *2399 N State St, Ukiah (95482). Phone 707/462-2987. www.dunnewood.com.* Winery tours (by appointment). Tasting room (Mon-Thurs; closed holidays). Picnic area. **FREE**

Grace Hudson Museum. *431 S Main St, Ukiah (95482). Phone 707/467-2836. www.gracehudsonmuseum.org.* Permanent exhibits on Pomo people; regional artists and photographers; early 20th-century paintings by Mendocino County artist Grace Hudson. Changing exhibits. **The Sun House** (1911) is the six-room craftsman house of Grace and John Hudson. Tours. (Wed-Sat 10 am-4:30 pm, Sun from noon; closed holidays) **DONATION**

Lake Mendocino. *1160 Lake Mendocino Dr, Ukiah. 3 miles NE, off Hwy 101. Phone 707/462-7651. www.lakemendocino.com.* Nestled between the redwood forests and wine country near the crystalline Russian Rivers headwaters, Lake Mendocino is a manmade reservoir that is a popular destination for weekend warriors, water skiers, and other outdoor buffs. On or near the lake's shores, there are three campgrounds, a pair of boat ramps, and a wildlife area with deer, wild turkeys, and foxes. During the winter, bald eagles often nest just east of the lake. **FREE**

Parducci Wine Cellars. *501 Parducci Rd, Ukiah (95482). Phone 707/462-9463.* Wine tasting (Daily 10 am-5 pm; closed holidays). **FREE**

Special Event

Mendocino County Fair and Apple Show. *Boonville Fairgrounds, 14400 Hwy 128, Boonville (95415). Phone 707/895-3011. www.mendocountyfair.com.* Taste Anderson Valley apples, ciders, and local wines; browse the classic car show, 4-H displays, and craft areas; and take in the beautiful reds, golds, and oranges of fall flowers and foliage. Three days in mid- or late Sept. **$$**

Limited-Service Hotel

★ VICHY HOT SPRINGS RESORT AND INN. *2605 Vichy Springs Rd, Ukiah (95482). Phone 707/462-9515; fax 707/462-9516. www.vichysprings.com.* This unique historic hot springs resort offers the only naturally warm and carbonated mineral baths in North America. 25 rooms. Complimentary continental breakfast. Check-in 3 pm, check-out noon. Outdoor pool, whirlpool. **$$**

Vacaville (D-2)

See also Davis, Fairfield

Population 88,625
Elevation 179 ft
Area Code 707
Zip 95688
Web Site www.cityofvacaville.com

What to See and Do

Factory Stores at Vacaville. *321-2 Nut Tree Rd, Vacaville (95687). I-80, Orange Dr exit. Phone 707/447-5755. www.premiumoutlets.com.* Approximately 120 outlet stores. (Mon-Sat 10 am-9 pm, Sun to 6 pm)

Limited-Service Hotel

★ BEST VALUE INN. *950 Leisure Town Rd, Vacaville (95687). Phone 707/446-8888; toll-free 888/315-2378; fax 707/449-0109. www.bestvalueinn.com.* 118 rooms, 2 story. Complimentary continental breakfast. Check-in 3 pm, check-out 11 am. Outdoor pool, whirlpool. **$**

Vallejo (D-2)

See also Antioch, Berkeley, Concord, Fairfield, Martinez, Oakland

Founded 1851
Population 116,760
Elevation 50 ft
Area Code 707
Information Convention & Visitors Bureau, 495 Mare Island Way, 94590; phone toll-free 800/482-5535
Web Site www.visitvallejo.com

This was California's capital in 1852 for about a week; and again, a year later, for just over one month. Despite the departure of the legislature in 1853 for

Benicia, the town prospered because the United States purchased Mare Island for a Navy yard in 1854. The former Mare Island Naval Shipyard is a 2,300-acre spread of land between the Mare Island Strait and San Pablo Bay.

What to See and Do

Benicia Capitol State Historic Park. *115 W G St, Benicia. 6 miles SE. Phone 707/745-3385. www.parks.ca.gov.* A building has been restored and furnished in the style of 1853-1854, when it served as the state capitol. (Daily; closed Jan 1, Thanksgiving, Dec 25) **$**

Six Flags Marine World. *2001 Marine World Pkwy, Vallejo (94589). Phone 707/643-6722. www.sixflags.com/parks/marineworld.* Part of the Six Flags chain, this marine park specializes in animal and water shows, but also has enough rides to shake up the whole family. There are also plenty of tamer rides and a guided Sunset Safari where you can meet the animals up close. (Memorial Day-Labor Day: daily; Mar-Memorial Day and Labor Day-Oct: weekends; hours vary; call or visit Web site for schedule) **$$$$**

Vallejo Ferry. *495 Mare Island Way, Vallejo. Phone 707/643-3779. www.baylinkferry.com.* One-hour direct ferry service between Vallejo and San Francisco. Also to Angel Island State Park. Ferry packages include Marine World Package, Napa Valley Wine Tour, and Napa Valley Wine Train (schedules vary; fee). (Daily; closed Jan 1, Thanksgiving, Dec 25) **$$$**

Vallejo Naval and Historical Museum. *734 Marin St, Vallejo (94590). Phone 707/643-0077. www.vallejomuseum.org.* Located south of Napa on the San Pablo Bay, this museum documents the history of both the city of Vallejo and Mare Island, the US Navy's first Western outpost, from the 1850s to the present. Housed in the old city hall, it contains five galleries and includes a working periscope, a 1/4-scale model of the USS *Saginaw* (the first of 500 ships built at Mare Island), wall murals, and a Heritage Chamber for educational and cultural programs. (Tues-Sat 10 am-4:30 pm; closed holidays) **$**

Special Events

Solano County Fair. *Solano County Fairgrounds, 900 Fairgrounds Dr, Vallejo (94589). N off I-80. Phone 707/551-2000. www.scfair.com.* Horse races, children's rides and games, and a large variety of concerts entertain visitors at the fair. July.

Vallejo Shoreline Jazz, Art and Wine Festival. *42 Harbor Way, Vallejo (94590). Phone 707/642-3653. www.vallejojazzfestival.com.* Summer is the perfect time to relax with a glass of good wine and listen to the soothing sounds of jazz. And this festival, held over a weekend in late August, is exactly the place to do just that. Taking place along the municipal marina on Vallejo's harbor, this annual festival hosts world-famous jazz and blues musicians in addition to a gallery of fine art and wine tastings. Late Aug. **$$$**

Whaleboat Regatta. *Marina Vista Park, Vallejo. Phone 707/648-4217.* Early Oct.

Limited-Service Hotel

★ BEST WESTERN HERITAGE INN. *1955 E 2nd St, Benicia (94510). Phone 707/746-0401; toll-free 800/937-8376; fax 707/745-0842. www.bestwestern.com.* 91 rooms, 3 story. Pets accepted, some restrictions; fee. Complimentary continental breakfast. Check-in 2 pm, check-out 11 am. High-speed Internet access. Outdoor pool, whirlpool. **$**

Walnut Creek

See also Berkeley, Concord, Oakland

Population 64,296
Elevation 135 ft
Area Code 925
Web Site www.walnut-creek.com

What to See and Do

Diablo Ballet. *1601 Civic Dr, Walnut Creek. Phone 925/943-1775. www.diabloballet.org.* Launched in 1993 to fill the dance vacuum in the East Bay area, the Diablo Ballet has since entrenched itself as one of the top ballet ensembles in the American west. Blending innovation and tradition by putting modern spins on time-tested works, the troupe tours regionally and performs at numerous venues throughout the Bay Area, often at the Dean Lesher Regional Center for the Arts, Diablo's home base in Walnut Creek.

Lindsay Wildlife Museum. *1931 1st Ave, Walnut Creek (94597). Phone 925/935-1978. www.wildlife-museum.org.* This wildlife museum includes the nation's oldest and largest wildlife rehabilitation center. Birds and animals that can't be released back into the wild are displayed in creative habitats. (Tues-Sun; hours vary by season) **$$**

Limited-Service Hotel

★ ★ EMBASSY SUITES. *1345 Treat Blvd, Walnut Creek (94597). Phone 925/934-2500; toll-free 800/362-2779; fax 925/256-7233. www.embassysuites.com.* 249 rooms, 8 story, all suites. Pets accepted; fee. Complimentary full breakfast. Check-in 3 pm, check-out noon. High-speed Internet access. Restaurant, bar. Fitness room. Indoor pool, whirlpool. Business center. **$$**

Full-Service Hotels

★ ★ ★ LAFAYETTE PARK HOTEL & SPA. *3287 Mount Diablo Blvd, Lafayette (94549). Phone 925/283-3700; toll-free 800/368-2468; fax 925/284-1621. www.lafayetteparkhotel.com.* Lafayette Park Hotel & Spa, just a half hour from San Francisco, is one of the Bay Area's finest properties. This elegant European-style hotel recalls the grandeur of the past with its refined furnishings, priceless art and antiques, and white-glove service. The rooms and suites seduce guests with their French flair. Rich cherry furniture is set against cheerful French blue and striped fabrics, and fireplaces and vaulted ceilings in many rooms add additional charm. The hotel's spa is renowned for its unusual treatments and stylish setting, and the lushly landscaped pool deck is a tranquil spot. Casual noshes are to be had at the Bistro at the Park, while brunch at the Duck Club (see), consistently considered the best in the area, is a must. 139 rooms, 4 story. Check-in 3 pm, check-out noon. Restaurant, bar. Fitness room, spa. Outdoor pool, whirlpool. **$$**

★ ★ ★ MARRIOTT. *2355 N Main St, Walnut Creek (94596). Phone 925/934-2000; toll-free 800/228-9290; fax 925/934-6374. www.marriott.com.* 338 rooms, 6 story. Check-in 3 pm, check-out noon. High-speed Internet access. Restaurant, bar. Fitness room. Outdoor pool, whirlpool. Business center. **$$**

Restaurants

★ ★ ★ DUCK CLUB. *3287 Mount Diablo Blvd, Lafayette (94549). Phone 925/283-7108; fax 925/284-1621. www.lafayetteparkhotel.com.* The focal point upon entering this restaurant is a brass-trimmed, black-lacquered, eight-spit rotisserie oven imported from France and built to the specifications of chef John Townsend. Specializing in succulent, crisp-roasted duck and chicken, this elegant restaurant located inside the Lafayette Park Hotel (see), offers a feast for all the senses. American menu. Breakfast, lunch, dinner, Sun brunch. Closed Dec 31. Bar. Children's menu. Casual attire. Reservations recommended. Valet parking. **$$$**

★ ★ LARK CREEK. *1360 Locust St, Walnut Creek (94596). Phone 925/256-1234; fax 925/256-0503. www.larkcreek.com.* American menu. Lunch, dinner, Sun brunch. Closed Jan 1, July 4, Dec 25. Bar. Children's menu. Casual attire. Reservations recommended. Outdoor seating. **$$$**

★ ★ MUDD'S. *10 Boardwalk, San Ramon (94583). Phone 925/837-9387; fax 925/820-3663. www.mudds.com.* Cedarwood ceilings. Two-acre garden. California menu. Lunch, dinner, Sun brunch. Bar. Reservations recommended. Outdoor seating. **$$$**

★ ★ ★ POSTINO. *3565 Mount Diablo Blvd, Lafayette (94549). Phone 925/299-8700; fax 925/299-2433. www.postinorestaurant.com.* Postino (which means *postman*) is located in what was once Lafayette's post office, originally built in 1937. Choose from the smaller romantic rooms for dining, or the bustling main dining room that features an open kitchen. Italian menu. Lunch, dinner. Closed holidays. Bar. Casual attire. Reservations recommended. Outdoor seating. **$$$**

★ ★ PRIMA TRATTORIA E NEGOZIO-VINI. *1522 N Main St, Walnut Creek (94596). Phone 925/935-7780; fax 925/935-7955. www.primaristorante.com.* Italian menu. Lunch, dinner. Closed holidays. Bar. Casual attire. Valet parking. **$$$**

Weaverville (B-2)

See also Redding

Founded 1849
Population 3,554
Elevation 2,011 ft
Area Code 530
Zip 96093
Information Trinity County Chamber of Commerce, 210 N Main St, PO Box 517; phone 530/623-6101 or toll-free 800/487-4648
Web Site www.trinitycounty.com

Weaverville's birth was linked with the discovery of gold. Within a few years the town's population had jumped to 3,000—half of it composed of Chinese miners. A Ranger District office of the Shasta-Trinity National Forest (see REDDING) is located here.

What to See and Do

Highland Art Center. *530 Main St, Weaverville (96093). Phone 530/623-5111.* Exhibits by local and other artists include paintings, photography, sculpture, textiles, and pottery. (May-Dec: Mon-Sat 10 am-5 pm, Sun 11 am-4 pm; Jan-Apr: Mon-Sat 10 am-5 pm) **FREE**

J. J. Jackson Memorial Museum. *508 Main St, Weaverville. On Hwy 299. Phone 530/623-5211.* Local historical exhibits. (Apr-Nov: daily; rest of year: Tues, Sat) **DONATION**

Trinity Alps Wilderness Area. *210 Main St, Weaverville. 15 miles N in Shasta-Trinity National Forest (see REDDING). Resort areas on fringes. Phone 530/623-2121.* Wilderness permit necessary (free); obtain at Ranger District Office. Reached from Canyon Creek, Stuart Fork, Swift Creek, North Fork, New River, or Coffee Creek. Unsurpassed alpine scenery, called US counterpart of Swiss Alps. Backpacking, fishing, pack trips. **FREE**

Weaverville Joss House State Historic Park. *Oregon and Main sts, Weaverville. On Hwy 299. Phone 530/623-5284. www.parks.ca.gov.* Temple, built in 1874 by Chinese during gold rush, contains priceless tapestries and gilded wooden scrollwork. Hourly guided tours (Wed-Sun; closed Jan 1, Thanksgiving, Dec 25). **$**

Willits (C-1)

See also Fort Bragg, Mendocino, Ukiah

Founded 1888
Population 5,073
Elevation 1,364 ft
Area Code 707
Zip 95490
Information Chamber of Commerce, 239 S Main St; phone 707/459-7910
Web Site www.willits.org

Nestled in the Little Lake Valley, Willits is the hub of three railroads: the California Western "Skunk Train" (see FORT BRAGG), the North Coast Railroad, and the Northwestern Pacific. It's a great area to use as a home base if you're visiting the redwoods or touring the wineries of Mendocino County.

What to See and Do

Mendocino County Museum. *400 E Commercial St, Willits (95490). Phone 707/459-2736.* History of area depicted by artifacts, including unique collection of Pomo baskets; stagecoaches, redwood logging tools, antique steam engines. Special programs. (Wed-Sun; closed holidays) **FREE**

Willits Community Theatre. *37 W Van Ln, Willits. Phone 707/459-2281. www.allaboutwct.org.* Presents comedy, drama, and music productions as well as workshops year-round.

Limited-Service Hotel

★ BAECHTEL CREEK INN & SPA. *101 Gregory Ln, Willits (95490). Phone 707/459-9063; toll-free 800/459-9911; fax 707/459-0226. www.baechtelcreekinn.com.* This creekside inn sits on a quiet cul-de-sac, providing respite from the noise of Highway 101. Guest accommodations range from the rather plain standard rooms, reminiscent of a typical hotel, to the homier premium and deluxe rooms, which are set up more like private bedrooms and feature upgraded appointments like featherbeds and antique furnishings. The spa, which welcomes day users as well as hotel guests, offers massages, facials, and body treatments. 43 rooms, 2 story. Pets accepted; restrictions, fee. Complimentary continental breakfast. Check-in 2 pm, check-out 11 am. Spa. Outdoor pool, whirlpool. **$**

Willows (C-2)

Population 6,220
Elevation 135 ft
Area Code 530
Zip 95988
Information Willows Area Chamber of Commerce, 130 N Butte St; phone 530/934-8150

What to See and Do

Mendocino National Forest. *825 N Humboldt Ave, Willows (95988). Approximately 25 miles W via Hwy 162. Phone 530/934-3316. www.fs.fed.us/r5/mendocino.* More than 1 million acres. Swimming, fishing for steelhead and trout, boating at 2,000-acre Pillsbury

Lake; hiking, bridle and off-road vehicle trails, camping (fee at more developed sites; some water; high elevation sites closed in winter). Hang gliding.

Sacramento National Wildlife Refuge Complex. *752 County Rd 99W, Willows (95988). Sacramento Refuge: County Rd 68 (take Princeton Rd exit off I-5, about 6 miles S of Willows). Colusa Refuge: E of Williams off I-5. Phone 530/934-2801. sacramentovalleyrefuges.fws.gov.* Two-refuge complex attracts millions of migrating waterfowl, including ducks, geese, swans, pelicans, egrets, and herons; auto routes, hiking trails. (Daily) **$**

Limited-Service Hotel

★ ★ BEST WESTERN GOLDEN PHEASANT INN. *249 N Humboldt Ave, Willows (95988). Phone 530/934-4603; toll-free 800/338-1387; fax 530/934-4275. www.bestwestern.com.* 104 rooms. Pets accepted; fee. Complimentary continental breakfast. Check-out 11 am. Restaurant, bar. Two outdoor pools. Airport transportation available. **$**

Yosemite National Park (E-3)

See also Lee Vining

67 miles NE of Merced on Hwy 140; 62 miles N of Fresno on Hwy 41; 13 miles W of Lee Vining on Hwy 120.

Web Site www.nps.gov/yose

John Muir, the naturalist who was instrumental in the founding of this national park, wrote that here are "the most songful streams in the world...the noblest forests, the loftiest granite domes, the deepest ice sculptured canyons." More than 3 million people visit Yosemite year-round, and most agree with Muir. An area of 1,169 square miles, it is a park of lofty waterfalls, sheer cliffs, high wilderness country, alpine meadows, lakes, snowfields, trails, streams, and river beaches. There are magnificent waterfalls during spring and early summer. Yosemite's granite domes are unsurpassed in number and diversity.The entrance fee (good for seven days) is $20 per vehicle. Routes to Yosemite National Park involve some travel over steep grades, which may extend driving times. The portion of Tioga Pass (Hwy 120) that travels over Tioga Pass to Lee Vining/Hwy 395 is closed in winter. Highway 120 is open year-round to Crane Flat, where the Big Oak Flat Road continues into Yosemite Valley. For general park information, contact the Public Information Office, PO Box 577, Yosemite National Park; phone 209/372-0200. For lodging information, contact Yosemite Concession Services, Yosemite National Park; phone 559/252-4848. For recorded camping information, phone 209/372-0200. Camping reservations are taken by NPRS, the National Park Reservation System for Yosemite Valley (phone toll-free 800/436-7275) and other campgrounds.

What to See and Do

Badger Pass Ski Area. *Glacer Point Rd, Yosemite National Park. 23 miles from Yosemite Valley on Glacier Point Rd Phone 209/372-1000. www.badgerpass.com.* One triple, three double chairlifts, cable tow; patrol, rentals; snack stand, sun deck, nursery (minimum age 3 years); instruction (over 4 years old). Cross-country skiing. Ice skating (fee) in Yosemite Valley; scheduled competitions. Naturalists conduct snowshoe tours (fee) in the Badger Pass area. (Open mid-Dec-mid-Apr, daily 9 am-4:30 pm, weather permitting) **$$$$**

Boating. No motors permitted.

Campfire programs. At several campgrounds; in summer, naturalists present nightly programs on park-related topics and provide tips on how to enjoy the park. Evening programs are offered all year in the Valley only.

Camping. Limited to 30 days in a calendar year; May-mid-Sept, camping is limited to seven days in Yosemite Valley, in the rest of the park to 14 days. Campsites in the Valley campgrounds, Hodgdon Meadow, Crane Flat, Wawona, and half of Tuolumne Meadows campgrounds may be reserved through NPRS. Other park campgrounds are on a first-come, first-served basis. Winter camping in the Valley, Hodgdon Meadow, and Wawona only.

Fishing. California fishing regulations pertain to all waters. State license, inland waters stamp, and trout stamp are required. Special regulations for Yosemite Valley also apply.

Giant Sequoias. Located principally in three groves. Mariposa Grove is near the south entrance to the park; toured on foot or by 50-passenger trams (May-early Oct; fee). Merced and Tuolumne groves are near Crane Flat, northwest of Yosemite Valley. The Grizzly Giant in Mariposa Grove is estimated to be 2,700 years old and is 209 feet high and 34.7 feet in diameter at its base.

Glacier Point. Offers one of the best panoramic views in Yosemite. From here the crest of the Sierra Nevada can be viewed, as well as Yosemite Valley 3,214 feet below. Across the valley are Yosemite Falls, Royal Arches, North Dome, Basket Dome, Mount Watkins, and Washington Column; up the Merced Canyon are Vernal and Nevada falls; Half Dome, Grizzly Peak, Liberty Cap, and the towering peaks along the Sierran crest and the Clark Range mark the skyline. (Road closed in winter)

High Country. Tioga Road (closed in winter) crosses the park and provides the threshold to a vast wilderness accessible via horseback or on foot to mountain peaks, passes, and lakes. Tuolumne Meadows is the major trailhead for this activity; one of the most beautiful and largest of the subalpine meadows in the High Sierra, 55 miles from Yosemite Valley by way of Big Oak Flat and Tioga roads. Organized group horse and hiking trips start from Tuolumne Meadows (except winter), follow the High Sierra Loop, and fan out to mountain lakes and peaks. Each night's stop is at a High Sierra Camp; the pace allows plenty of time to explore at each camp.

Hiking and backpacking. On 840 miles of maintained trails. Wilderness permits are required for all overnight backcountry trips. Advance reservations for permits may be made up to 24 weeks in advance.

Nature Center at Happy Isles. *E end of Yosemite Valley.* Exhibits on ecology and natural history. (Summer, daily)

Pioneer Yosemite History Center. A few miles from Mariposa Grove in Wawona. Has a covered bridge, historic buildings, wagons, and other exhibits. Living history program in summer. (July-Aug Wed-Sun)

Swimming. Prohibited at Hetch Hetchy Reservoir and in some areas of the Tuolumne River watershed. Swimming pools are maintained at Camp Curry, Yosemite Lodge, and Wawona.

Visitor Center. *At Park Headquarters in Yosemite Valley. Phone 209/372-0265.* Orientation slide program on Yosemite (daily). Exhibits on geology and ecology; naturalist-conducted walks and evening programs offered throughout the year on varying seasonal schedules. Native American cultural demonstrators (summer, daily).

Indian Village (Ahwahnee). This reconstructed Miwok-Paiute Village is behind the Visitor Center and has a self-guided trail.

The Indian Cultural Museum. Located in the building west of the Valley visitor center, the museum portrays the cultural history of the Yosemite Native Americans. Consult *Yosemite Guide* for hours.

Yosemite Fine Arts Museum. The gallery features contemporary art exhibits and the Yosemite Centennial. (Daily 9 am-4:30 pm)

Walks and hikes. Conducted all year in the Valley and, during summer, at Glacier Point, Mariposa Grove, Tuolumne Meadows, Wawona, White Wolf, and Crane Flat.

★ **Waterfalls.** Reaching their greatest proportions in mid-May, they may, in dry years, dwindle to trickles or disappear completely by late summer. The Upper Yosemite Fall drops 1,430 feet; the lower fall drops 320 feet. With the middle Cascade they have a combined height of 2,425 feet and are the fifth-highest waterfall in the world. Others are Ribbon Fall, 1,612 feet; Vernal Fall, 317 feet; Bridalveil Fall, 620 feet; Nevada Fall, 594 feet; and Illilouette Fall, 370 feet.

Winter sports. *Phone 209/372-1000 for snow conditions.* Centered around the **Badger Pass Ski Area**, 23 miles from Yosemite Valley on Glacier Point Road. One triple, three double chairlifts, cable tow; patrol, rentals; snack stand, sundeck, nursery (minimum age three years); instruction (over four years). (Mid-Dec-mid-Apr, daily, weather permitting) cross-country skiing. Ice skating (fee) in Yosemite Valley; scheduled competitions. Naturalists conduct snowshoe tours (fee) in the Badger Pass area. **$$$$**

Yosemite Mountain-Sugar Pine Railroad. *4 miles S of south park entrance on Hwy 41. Phone 559/683-7273. www.ymsprr.com.* Four-mile historic narrow-gauge steam train excursion through scenic Sierra National Forest. Picnic area. Museum; gift shops. Logger steam train (mid-May-Sept, daily; early May and Oct, weekends). Jenny Railcars (Mar-Oct, daily). Evening steam train, outdoor barbecue, live entertainment (late May-early Oct, Sat evenings; reservations advised). **$$$$**

Yosemite Valley. Surrounded by sheer walls, waterfalls, towering domes, and peaks. One of the most spectacular views is from Tunnel View, looking up the Valley to Clouds Rest. El Capitan (7,569 feet) on the left, Bridalveil Falls on the right. The east end of the Valley, beyond Camp Curry, is closed to automobiles, but is accessible by foot, bicycle, and, in summer, shuttle bus (free); special placards permit the disabled to drive in a restricted area when the route is drivable. The placards are available at visitor centers and entrance stations.

Limited-Service Hotels

★ CEDAR LODGE. *9966 Hwy 140, El Portal (95318). Phone 209/379-2612; toll-free 888/742-4371; fax 209/379-2712. www.yosemite-motels.com.* 209 rooms, 2 story. Check-in 3 pm, check-out 11 am. Two restaurants, bar. Indoor pool, outdoor pool, whirlpool. **$**

★ ★ GROVELAND HOTEL AT YOSEMITE NATIONAL PARK. *18767 Main St, Groveland (95321). Phone 209/962-4000; toll-free 800/273-3314; fax 209/962-6674. www.groveland.com.* Built in 1849; European antiques. 17 rooms. Pets accepted; fee. Complimentary continental breakfast. Check-in 2 pm, check-out noon. Restaurant, bar. **$**

★ ★ PINES RESORT. *54449 Rd 32, Bass Lake (93604). Phone 559/642-3121; toll-free 800/350-7463; fax 559/642-3902. www.basslake.com.* 104 rooms, 2 story. Complimentary continental breakfast. Check-in 4 pm, check-out 11 am. Restaurant, bar. Outdoor pool, whirlpool. Tennis. **$$**

★ ★ WAWONA HOTEL. *Yosemite Valley National Park (95389). Phone 209/375-6556; fax 209/375-6601. www.yosemitepark.com.* Historic summer hotel. 104 rooms, 2 story. Check-in 4 pm, check-out 11 am. Restaurant, bar. Outdoor pool. Golf, 9 holes. Tennis. **$**

★ ★ YOSEMITE LODGE. *CA 41/140, Yosemite National Park (95389). Phone 559/252-4848; fax 209/372-1414. www.yosemitepark.com.* 245 rooms, 2 story. Check-in 5 pm, check-out 11 am. Two restaurants, bar. Outdoor pool. **$$**

★ ★ YOSEMITE VIEW LODGE. *11136 Hwy 140, El Portal (95318). Phone 209/379-2681; toll-free 888/742-4371; fax 209/379-2704. www.yosemite-motels.com.* 278 rooms, 3 story. Pets accepted, some restrictions; fee. Check-in 3 pm, check-out 11 am. Two restaurants, bar. Indoor pool, outdoor pool. **$**

Full-Service Resorts

★ ★ ★ THE AHWAHNEE. *Yosemite Valley (95389). Phone 559/253-5635; fax 559/372-1463. www.yosemitepark.com.* The Ahwahnee is a celebration of Native American and colonial American design. This luxurious hotel, located within Yosemite National Park, offers a one-of-a-kind experience to guests. This national landmark has been greeting visitors in its majestic halls since 1927. Its wooded, natural setting is perfectly complemented by the Native American décor, featuring the artifacts and artwork of the Yosemite Miwok. The rooms and suites are appropriately rustic in appearance but are complete with the amenities of a world-class hotel. The public spaces are especially glorious, with impressive stained-glass windows, intricate stonework, and mosaics gracing the lobby, great lounge, solarium, and dining room. 99 rooms, 6 story. Check-in 4 pm, check-out noon. Restaurant, bar. Children's activity center. Outdoor pool. Tennis. **$$$$**

★ ★ ★ TENAYA LODGE AT YOSEMITE. *1122 Hwy 41, Fish Camp (93623). Phone 559/683-6555; toll-free 888/514-2167; fax 559/683-8684. www.tenayalodge.com.* Travelers wanting to visit Yosemite National Park without having to put up with the spartan accommodations of a campsite head for the luxurious Tenaya Lodge. Situated on 35 acres adjacent to the Sierra National Forest and just 2 miles from Yosemite, this elegant mountain retreat is just the place to see the sights without forsaking the comforts of home. The chalet-style lobby, with its high ceilings and roaring fire, is instantly welcoming, and the guest rooms and suites share a similar rustic appeal. Activities are plentiful, both on property and off, and the resort offers a terrific children's program. Fine dining is to be discovered at Sierra, while Jackalope's Bar & Grill is ideal for the entire family. 244 rooms, 4 story. Pets accepted, fee. Check-in 3 pm, check-out 11 am. Three restaurants, bar. Children's activity center. Fitness room, spa. Indoor pool, outdoor pool, whirlpool. Business center. **$$**

Specialty Lodging

The following lodging establishment is approved by Mobil Travel Guide, but due to its unique and individualized nature has not been given a traditional Mobil Star rating. Included in this listing you may find bed-and-breakfasts, limited-service inns, guest ranches, and other unique hotel properties.

THE HOMESTEAD. *4110 Rd 600, Ahwahnee (93601). Phone 559/683-0495; toll-free 800/483-0495; fax 559/683-8165. www.homesteadcottages.com.* 4 rooms. Complimentary continental breakfast. Check-in 4-6 pm, check-out 11 am. **$$**

Restaurants

★★ CHARLES STREET DINNER HOUSE. *5043 Charles St, Mariposa (95338). Phone 209/966-2366. www.charlesstreetdinnerhouse.com.* Nineteenth-century house. American, California menu. Dinner, Sun brunch. Closed Thanksgiving, Dec 24-25. Children's menu. **$$**

★★ NARROW GAUGE INN. *48571 Hwy 41, Fish Camp (93623). Phone 559/683-7720; toll-free 888/644-9050; fax 559/683-2139. www.narrowgaugeinn.com.* Located in historic Fish Camp, this restaurant offers unique local cuisine in a rustic environment filled with antiques and a nightly fire in the fireplace. American menu. Dinner. Closed Mon-Tues. **$$**

★★ THE VICTORIAN ROOM. *18767 Main St, Groveland (95321). Phone 209/962-4000; toll-free 800/273-3314; fax 209/962-6674. www.groveland.com.* Victorian décor. California menu. Dinner. Closed Mon. Bar. Children's menu. Outdoor seating. **$$**

Yountville

See also Napa, Rutherford, St. Helena

Settled 1831
Population 2,916
Elevation 97 ft
Area Code 707
Zip 94599
Information Chamber of Commerce, 6516 Yount St, PO Box 2064; phone 707/944-0904
Web Site www.yountville.com

In the heart of Napa Valley, Yountville has retained the turn-of-the-century charm of a quiet farming community. The town dates from 1831 with the settlement of George Yount, a North Carolina trapper. Although now a major tourist destination, surrounded by world-famous wineries, the town has successfully protected its rural atmosphere and historic character, reflected in its quaint hotels, restaurants, and shops.

What to See and Do

Domaine Chandon. *1 California Dr, Yountville (94599). Phone 707/944-2280 (tour). www.chandon.com.* Founded in 1973 by the French Champagne maker Moet & Chandon, Domaine Chandon is one of the leading sparking wine producers in the United States. While the tours are fascinating, the setting alone is worth the visit—beautifully landscaped, tastefully appointed, and appropriately romantic. On the terrace adjacent to the Tasting Salon (tastings $$-$$$), you can sip some bubbly and enjoy lunch outdoors (weather permitting), which only heightens the romantic wine country experience. (May-Oct: 10 am-6 pm; Nov-Apr: 11 am-5 pm; closed Jan 1, Thanksgiving, Dec 25) **FREE**

Downtown Yountville. *Beard Plaza, 6540 Washington St, Yountville (94599). Phone 707/944-0850. www.yountville.com.* If you want to bring home more than wine from your visit to the Napa Valley area, spend an afternoon wandering through downtown Yountville, a charming area bursting with boutiques, art galleries, and antique shops. The main drag is Washington Street, where you'll find Beard Plaza, a showcase for high-end shops; Vintage 1870, a converted 130-year-old winery that now houses 36 specialty shops and galleries; and a host of home accessories and design stores.

Hot air ballooning. *PO Box 2290, Yountville (94599). www.nvaloft.com.* For those who can afford it, taking a hot air balloon ride over Napa Valley at sunrise is a breathtaking, once-in-a-lifetime experience. The company that started it all, the family-run Napa Valley Aloft, offers three different kinds of balloon experiences, all of which are piloted by experienced FAA-certified professionals with extensive knowledge of Napa Valley and its vineyards. All also offer pre-flight refreshments and a lavish post-flight breakfast. Above the West Ballooning (800/627-2759) offers the most personalized experience, limiting the size to four to six passengers, and provides shuttle service from local and downtown San Francisco locations ($220 to $260 per person). Adventures Aloft (800/944-4408) caters to individuals and small groups of up to eight and provides local hotel pickup ($205 per person). Balloon Aviation (800/367-6272) also holds no more than eight people per balloon but does not offer shuttle service ($195 per person). Most launches start from the landmark Groezinger Winery in Yountville, and all flights are weather permitting. (Year-round; closed holidays) **$$$$**

Napa Valley Museum. *55 Presidents Cir, Yountville (94599). Phone 707/944-0500. www.napavalleymuseum .org.* Dedicated to promoting the cultural and environmental heritage of the Napa Valley, this small museum features permanent exhibits on the valley's land and people, as well as the art and science of California wines. Upcoming special exhibits will cover the Arts and Crafts movement and the art of the Napa wine label. Though unprepossessing, this museum offers insight into the history and future of the Napa Valley community. (Daily 10 am-5 pm; closed holidays) **$**

Robert Mondavi Winery. *7801 St. Helena Hwy N, Oakville (94562). Phone 707/226-1335; toll-free 888/ 766-6328. www.robertmondaviwinery.com.* Graceful, mission-style building. Guided tours, wine tasting. Reservations are recommended. (Daily 10 am-5 pm; closed holidays)

Vintage 1870. *6525 Washington St, Yountville (94599). Phone 707/944-2451. www.vintage1870.com.* Restored brick winery complex houses five restaurants, a bakery, and more than 40 specialty shops. Wine-tasting cellar. Entertainment and holiday demonstrations in Dec. Picnic areas. (Daily 10 am-5:30 pm; closed holidays) **FREE**

Special Events

Napa Valley Mustard Festival. *Various venues, Yountville. Phone 707/259-9020. www.mustardfestival .org.* This winter festival celebrates the blooming of Napa Valley's golden wild mustard plants with food, wine, art, and entertainment. Highlights include the mustard recipe competitions, which attract contestants from around the world, as well as art and rare wine auctions. Although the festival was originally started to boost tourism during the winter months—a great time to experience Napa without the crowds—profits from the associated galas and fundraisers also support local arts organizations. Jan-Mar.

Robert Mondavi Winery Summer Music Festival. *7801 St Helena Hwy, Oakville (94562). Phone toll-free 888/769-5299. www.robertmondaviwinery.com/ summerfest.asp.* Since 1969, the Robert Mondavi Winery has hosted an outdoor summer music festival featuring top pop, jazz, and R&B performers—from Cassandra Wilson and Ella Fitzgerald to Boz Skaggs and Patti LaBelle. The festival has become one of the most beloved summer events for locals. You can enjoy a lawn picnic, music, and the magic of a Napa summer night against the backdrop of the winery's historic To Kalon Vineyard. Weekend nights in July. **$$$$**

Limited-Service Hotel

★ ★ NAPA VALLEY LODGE. *2230 Madison St, Yountville (94599). Phone 707/944-2468; toll-free 800/ 368-2468; fax 707/944-9362. www.napavalleylodge.com.* This Spanish-style lodge puts guests in the heart of the wine country. Elegantly furnished guest rooms have private terraces or balconies offering panoramic views of the Napa Valley, as well as large baths decorated with hand-painted Spanish tiles. The champagne breakfast buffet is served outdoors in the sunny pool area, and tea and cookies tempt guests in the lobby each afternoon. Conference facilities for up to 60 make this a good choice for a group meeting. 55 rooms, 2 story. Complimentary continental breakfast. Check-in 4 pm, check-out noon. High-speed Internet access. Fitness room. Outdoor pool, whirlpool. **$$$**

Full-Service Resort

★ ★ ★ VILLAGIO INN AND SPA. *6481 Washington St, Yountville (94599). Phone 707/944-8877; toll-free 800/351-1133; fax 707/944-8855. www.villagio .com.* 112 rooms, 2 story. Complimentary full breakfast. Check-in 4 pm, check-out noon. High-speed Internet access, wireless Internet access. Restaurant, two bars. Fitness room, fitness classes available, spa. Outdoor pool, whirlpool. Tennis. Business center. **$$$**

Full-Service Inns

★ ★ ★ VINTAGE INN. *6541 Washington St, Yountville (94599). Phone 707/944-1112; toll-free 800/351-1133; fax 707/944-1617. www.vintageinn.com.* Mountain and vineyard views. 80 rooms, 2 story. Pets accepted; fee. Complimentary full breakfast. Check-in 4 pm, check-out noon. High-speed Internet access, wireless Internet access. Restaurant, two bars. Fitness room, fitness classes available. Outdoor pool, whirlpool. Tennis. **$$$**

★ ★ ★ YOUNTVILLE INN. *6462 Washington St, Yountville (94599). Phone 707/944-5600; fax 707/944-5666. www.yountvilleinn.com.* 51 rooms. Pets accepted; fee. Check-in 3 pm, check-out noon. Outdoor pool, whirlpool. **$$$**

Specialty Lodgings

The following lodging establishments are approved by Mobil Travel Guide, but due to their unique and individualized nature have not been given a traditional Mobil Star rating. Included in this listing you may find bed-and-breakfasts, limited-service inns, guest ranches, and other unique hotel properties.

LAVENDER INN. *2020 Webber Ave, Yountville (94599). Phone 707/944-1388; toll-free 800/522-4140; fax 707/944-1579. www.lavendernapa.com.* 8 rooms. Complimentary full breakfast. Check-in 3 pm, check-out noon. **$$**

MAISON FLEURIE. *6529 Yount St, Yountville (94599). Phone 707/944-2056; toll-free 800/788-0369; fax 707/944-9342. www.maisonfleurienapa.com.* The gracious lifestyle of Napa Valley will leave you warmed and refreshed from bicycling through the wineries, touring the back roads, or simply shopping in Yountville. If you prefer to stay in, enjoy a bountiful breakfast or afternoon wine and hors d'oeuvres by the huge stone fireplace. 13 rooms, 2 story. Complimentary full breakfast. Check-in 3 pm, check-out noon. Outdoor pool, whirlpool. **$$**

PETIT LOGIS INN. *6527 Yount St, Yountville (94599). Phone 707/944-2332; toll-free 877/944-2332. www.petitlogis.com.* 5 rooms. Complimentary full breakfast. Check-in 3 pm, check-out 11 am. **$$**

Restaurants

★★ **BISTRO JEANTY.** *6510 Washington St, Yountville (94599). Phone 707/944-0103; fax 707/944-0370. www.bistrojeanty.com.* French Bistro menu. Lunch, dinner, late-night. Bar. Reservations recommended. Outdoor seating. **$$**

★★★ **BOUCHON.** *6534 Washington St, Yountville (94599). Phone 707/944-8037; fax 707/944-2769.* French bistro menu. Lunch, dinner, late-night. Closed Jan 1, Dec 25. Bar. Reservations recommended. Outdoor seating. **$$**

★★ **BRIX.** *7377 St. Helena Hwy, Yountville (94558). Phone 707/944-2749; fax 707/944-8320. www.brix.com.* California menu. Lunch, dinner, brunch. Closed Mon. Bar. Children's menu. Outdoor seating. **$$$**

★★★ **DOMAINE CHANDON.** *1 California Dr, Yountville (94599). Phone 707/944-2892; fax 707/944-1123. www.chandon.com.* California, French menu. Lunch, dinner. Closed Tues-Wed; Jan. Bar. Outdoor seating. **$$$**

★★★★★ **THE FRENCH LAUNDRY.** *6640 Washington Ave, Yountville (94599). Phone 707/944-2380. www.frenchlaundry.com.* There are dinners—the kind you go out for because you're hungry—and then there are destination dinners—the kind around which you build a trip. The French Laundry, a Napa Valley food mecca, belongs firmly to the latter few. Chef Thomas Keller has set the standard for fine dining in America from the circa-1900 rock and timber cottage, once a French steam laundry. Refined table appointments, including the house Limoges china, crystal stemware, and floor-length linens, set the tone for elegant five- and nine-course French tasting menus that change daily but always rely on seasonal produce and organic meats with a dose of comestible luxuries like foie gras and truffles. The country locale, warm interiors, and dignified enthusiasm of diners take the starch out of the well-paced experience. But do expect to plan for it well in advance. Restaurant reservation agents recommend calling two months in advance of dinner, but aficionados say you can't be too early. American, French menu. Dinner. Closed Mon; Thanksgiving, Dec 25; also first three weeks in Jan. Reservations recommended. **$$$$**

★★ **MUSTARDS GRILL.** *7399 St. Helena Hwy, Yountville (94599). Phone 707/944-2424; fax 707/944-0828. www.mustardsgrill.com.* A Napa Valley fixture for many years, Mustards Grill is one of the best known and most frequented of the area's many restaurants. It built its reputation on solid American food—fish, chops, steak, and ribs—cooked in wood-burning ovens and on grills, combined with innovative and international flavors. This approach is also reflected in the wine list, an eclectic blend of wines from around the world, not just the Napa Valley. Because of the restaurant's size and popularity, reservations are recommended. American menu. Lunch, dinner. Closed holidays. Bar. Children's menu. Reservations recommended. **$$**

★ **NAPA VALLEY GRILLE.** *6795 Washington St, Yountville (94599). Phone 707/944-8686; fax 707/944-2870.* This casual restaurant on Yountville's north end specializes in classic wine country recipes and features a wine list that reflects the diverse vineyards of the area. Diners are welcome to enjoy meals in the relaxed dining room, the friendly bar area, or out on the delightful patio under large umbrellas. California menu. Lunch, dinner, Sun brunch. Closed Dec 25. Bar. Outdoor seating. **$$**

Yreka (A-2)

See also Mount Shasta

Founded 1851
Population 7,290
Elevation 2,625 ft
Area Code 530
Zip 96097
Information Chamber of Commerce, 117 W Miner St; phone 530/842-1649 or toll-free 800/669-7352 (recording)
Web Site www.yrekachamer.com

Yreka (Why-RE-ka) was known in gold rush days as Thompson's Dry Diggings, later as Shasta Butte City, and finally, since 1852, as Yreka. Yreka today is the seat of Siskiyou County and a trade center for ranchers, loggers, and miners. Many historic buildings may be seen in the Historic Preservation District, in the vicinity of Miner and Third streets. Hunting and fishing are popular in the area.

What to See and Do

County Gold Exhibit. *County Courthouse, 311 4th St, Yreka. Phone 530/842-8340.* Extensive display of gold nuggets taken from mines in Siskiyou County. (Tues-Fri 9 am-5 pm, Sat to 4 pm; closed holidays) **FREE**

Iron Gate Dam and Lake. *Yreka. 13 miles NE on I-5, then 6 miles E on Klamath River Rd.* Water sports, fishing, boating (ramps, launching facilities); picnicking, camping.

Klamath National Forest. *1312 Fairlane Rd, Yreka (96097). E and W of town via Hwy 263, then turn left onto Hwy 96. Phone 530/842-6131. www.fs.fed.us/r5/klamath.* Approximately 1.72 million acres, of which 1.69 million acres are in California and the remainder in Oregon. Within the forest are the Klamath, Scott, Salmon, Siskiyou, and Marble mountain ranges and the Klamath, Scott, and Salmon rivers. Fishing, whitewater boating on the three rivers; camping, hunting, hiking, cross-country skiing. The western section of the forest includes

Marble Mountain Wilderness. *1312 Fairlane Rd, Yreka. Access off Hwy 96. Phone 530/842-6131.* On 241,000 acres. Once part of the flat bottom of a shallow ocean, volcanic upheaval and the erosive action of rivers and glaciers have since combined to form what is now one of the most attractive wilderness areas in California. Marble Mountain itself is composed primarily of prehistoric marine invertebrate fossils. Camping, hiking; fishing in many streams and 79 trout-stocked lakes. Fire permit for this wilderness area is required and may be obtained at the Supervisor's office or any Ranger District Office.

Northwest Interpretive Museum. *1312 Fairlane Rd, Yreka (96097). Phone 530/842-6131.* Lookout model; displays of wildlife, mining, timber production, fire management. (Mon-Fri; closed holidays) **FREE**

Siskiyou County Museum. *910 S Main St, Yreka. Phone 530/842-3836. www.siskiyou.ca.us/museum.* Exhibits of Siskiyou County from prehistoric era, Native Americans, trappers, gold rush, transportation, logging, agriculture. First and second floors include period rooms and environments. Research library on premises. (Tues-Sat 9 am-5 pm, Sat to 4 pm) **$**

Outdoor Museum. *530 S Main St, Yreka (96097). Phone 916/842-3836.* On 2 1/2 acres with pioneer cabin, schoolhouse, blacksmith shop, logging skid shack, miner's cabin, church, operating general store. (May-Sept, Tues-Sat 9:30 am-4:30 pm) **FREE**

Yreka Western Railroad. *300 E Miner St, Yreka (96097). Phone 530/842-4146; toll-free 800/973-5277. www.yrekawesternrr.com.* Steam engine-powered 1915 historic train takes visitors on a three-hour tour of the Shasta Valley. (Memorial Day-mid-June: weekends; mid-June-Sept: Wed-Sun; one departure 11 am) **$$$$**

Side Trips

While there is plenty to see and do in northern California, from wine tasting in Napa to rock climbing in Yosemite, the surrounding areas offer some different types of sites that you may want to include in your travels. The quaint beach town of San Luis Obispo and the historic whaling village of San Simeon are all within four hours of San Jose. If your schedule allows for a longer journey, Oregon has some beautiful areas worth seeing, including Bend, Coos Bay, Crater Lake National Park, Eugene, and Portland. If you hear slot machines calling your name, you can answer them in less than four hours in Reno, Nevada.

San Luis Obispo (G-2)

3 1/2 hours, 186 miles from San Jose

Founded 1772
Population 44,174
Elevation 315 ft
Area Code 805
Information Chamber of Commerce, 1039 Chorro St, 93401; phone 805/781-2777
Web Site www.slochamber.org

Father Fray Junipero Serra, who established the mission in 1772, saw a resemblance to a bishop's mitre in two nearby volcanic peaks and named the mission San Luis Obispo de Tolosa (St. Louis, Bishop of Toulouse). After the thatched mission roofs burned several times, a tile-making technique was developed that soon set the style for all California missions. Located in a bowl-shaped valley, the town depends on government employment, tourism, agriculture, retail trade, and its university population.

What to See and Do

Ah Louis Store. *800 Palm St, San Luis Obispo (93401). Phone 805/543-4332.* (1874) Leader of the Chinese community, Ah Louis was an extraordinary man who achieved prominence at a time when Asians were given few opportunities. The two-story building, which served as the Chinese bank, post office, and general merchandise store, was the cornerstone of the Chinese community. (Mon-Sat; closed holidays)

California Polytechnic State University. *1 Grand Ave, San Luis Obispo (93407). N edge of town. Phone 805/756-5734. www.calpoly.edu.* (1901) (17,000 students) On the campus are three art galleries; working livestock and farm units; and horticultural, architectural, and experimental displays. Campus tours (Mon, Wed, Fri; reservations required). **FREE** Also here are

Performing Arts Center of San Luis Obispo. *1 Grand Ave, San Luis Obispo (93407). Phone 805/756-2787. www.pacslo.org.* Center (91,500-square-feet) offers professional dance, theater, music, and other performances all year. The 1,350-seat Harmon Concert Hall is JBL Professional's exclusive North American test and demonstration site.

Shakespeare Press Museum. *California Polytechnic State University, Graphic Communications Building, San Luis Obispo (94301). Phone 805/756-1108. www.grc.calpoly.edu/pages/spm.html.* Features a collection of 19th-century printing presses, type, and related equipment; demonstrations for prearranged tours. (Mon, Wed; closed holidays) **FREE**

Children's Museum. *1010 Nipomo St, San Luis Obispo (93401). Phone 805/544-5437. www.kcbx.net/~slokids.* A hands-on museum for preschool through elementary school children (must be accompanied by an adult); houses many interactive exhibits; themes change monthly. (Tues 11:30 am-1 pm, Thurs 2-3:30 pm, Sat noon-2 pm; closed holidays) **$**

Mission San Luis Obispo de Tolosa. *751 Palm St, San Luis Obispo (93401). Phone 805/543-6850. www.missionsanluisobispo.org.* Fifth of the California missions, founded in 1772, still serves as the parish church. Eight-room museum contains extensive Chumash collection and artifacts from early settlers. First olive orchard in California planted here; two original trees still stand. (Daily 9 am-5 pm; closed holidays) **DONATION**

San Luis Obispo County Museum and History Center. *696 Monterey St, San Luis Obispo (93401). Near mission. Phone 805/543-0638. www.slochs.org.* (1905) Local history exhibits; decorative arts. (Wed-Sun 10 am-4 pm; closed holidays) **FREE**

Special Events

Madonnari Italian Street Painting Festival. *Mission Plaza, Monterey and Chorro Sts, San Luis Obispo (93401). Phone 805/781-2777.* Mission San Luis Obispo de Tolosa. Local artists decorate the streets around the mission with chalk drawings. Also music, Italian cuisine, and open-air market. Mid Sept. **$**

Mozart Festival. *1160 Marsh St, San Luis Obispo (93401). Phone 805/781-3008. www.mozartfestival.com.* Recitals, chamber music, orchestra concerts, and choral music. Held at various locations throughout the county, including Mission San Luis Obispo de Tolosa and California Polytechnic State University campus. Mid-July-early Aug. **$$$$**

Renaissance Festival. *1087 Santa Rosa St, San Luis Obispo (93408). Phone 707/864-5706.* Celebration of the Renaissance; period costumes, food booths, entertainment, arts and crafts. July.

SLO International Film Festival. *San Luis Obispo, 817 Palm St, San Luis Obispo. Phone 805/546-3456. www.slofilmfest.org.* This festival showcases the history and art of filmmaking with screenings of new releases, classics, short and long films, and documentaries. Additional events include seminars, a film competition, and the annual sing-along, where moviegoers dress up as characters from the featured musical and—you guessed it—sing along to the soundtrack. Early-mid-Mar. **$$$$**

Limited-Service Hotels

★ BEST WESTERN ROYAL OAK HOTEL. *214 Madonna Rd, San Luis Obispo (93405). Phone 805/544-4410; toll-free 800/545-4410; fax 805/544-3026. www.bestwestern.com.* 99 rooms, 2 story. Pets accepted; restrictions, fee. Complimentary continental breakfast. Check-in 3 pm, check-out noon. Outdoor pool. **$**

★ ★ EMBASSY SUITES. *333 Madonna Rd, San Luis Obispo (93405). Phone 805/549-0800; toll-free 800/864-6000; fax 805/543-5273. www.embassysuitesslo.com.* 196 rooms, 4 story, all suites. Complimentary full breakfast. Check-in 3 pm, check-out noon. High-speed Internet access. Restaurant, two bars. Fitness room. Indoor pool, outdoor pool, whirlpool. **$$**

★ HOLIDAY INN EXPRESS. *1800 Monterey St, San Luis Obispo (93401). Phone 805/544-8600; toll-free 800/465-4329; fax 805/541-4698. www.hiexpress.com.* 100 rooms, 3 story. Pets accepted; fee. Complimentary continental breakfast. Check-in 3 pm, check-out noon. Outdoor pool, whirlpool. **$**

★ ★ QUALITY SUITES. *1631 Monterey St, San Luis Obispo (93401). Phone 805/541-5001; toll-free 800/228-5151; fax 805/546-9475. www.qualitysuites.com.* 138 rooms, 3 story, all suites. Complimentary continental breakfast. Check-in 3 pm, check-out noon. High-speed Internet access. Outdoor pool, whirlpool. Business center. **$**

★ SANDS SUITES & MOTEL. *1930 Monterey St, San Luis Obispo (93401). Phone 805/544-0500; toll-free 800/441-4657; fax 805/544-3529. www.sandssuites.com.* 70 rooms, 2 story. Pets accepted; fee. Complimentary continental breakfast. Check-in 3 pm, check-out 11 am. Outdoor pool, whirlpool. **$**

Full-Service Hotel

★ ★ ★ APPLE FARM TRELLIS COURT. *2015 Monterey St, San Luis Obispo (93401). Phone 805/544-2040; toll-free 800/255-2040; fax 805/546-9495. www.applefarm.com.* 69 rooms, 3 story. Check-in 4 pm, check-out noon. Restaurant. Outdoor pool, whirlpool. Airport transportation available. **$**

Specialty Lodgings

The following lodging establishments are approved by Mobil Travel Guide, but due to their unique and individualized nature have not been given a traditional Mobil Star rating. Included in this listing you may find bed-and-breakfasts, limited-service inns, guest ranches, and other unique hotel properties.

GARDEN STREET INN. *1212 Garden St, San Luis Obispo (93401). Phone 805/545-9802; toll-free 800/488-2045; fax 805/545-9403. www.gardenstreetinn.com.* Restored Victorian house (1887) furnished with antiques. 13 rooms, 2 story. Complimentary full breakfast. Check-in 3-7 pm, check-out 11 am. **$$$**

MADONNA INN. *100 Madonna Rd, San Luis Obispo (93405). Phone 805/543-3000; toll-free 800/543-9666; fax 805/543-1800. www.madonnainn.com.* Odds are, you've never seen anything quite like the Madonna Inn, conveniently located halfway between Los Angeles and San Francisco. The hotel and its restaurants are shameless kitsch at its finest, and you may feel like you've stepped back in time to the 1940s or '50s. Flowers figure largely into the décor, as does ornately carved hardwood, brightly colored leather, and gold plating. Photographs of each uniquely decorated room are available for viewing on the inn's Web site, so you can decide exactly which color combination you want to wake up to. (Will it be the hot-pink carpeting and gold-and-crystal chandelier of Room 215, "Morning Star," or the solid-rock floors, walls, ceilings, and shower plus animal-print upholstery and bedding of Room 137, "Caveman Room"?) Even if you decide not to stay the night in San Luis Obispo, the Madonna Inn is worth a stop as you drive by it on Highway 101, if only to use the restroom and walk past the famed horseshoe-shaped bar and the Copper Café. 109 rooms, 4 story. Check-in 4 pm , check-out noon. Restaurant, bar. Airport transportation available. **$$**

Restaurants

★ ★ **1865 RESTAURANT.** *1865 Monterey St, San Luis Obispo (93401). Phone 805/544-1865; fax 805/541-5259. www.1865.com.* Seafood, steak menu. Lunch, dinner. Closed Sun. Bar. Business casual attire. Reservations recommended. **$$**

★ **APPLE FARM.** *2015 Monterey St, San Luis Obispo (93401). Phone 805/544-6100; fax 805/544-6890. www.applefarm.com.* American menu. Breakfast, lunch, dinner. Children's menu. Casual attire. **$$**

★ ★ **BENVENUTI.** *450 Marsh St, San Luis Obispo (93401). Phone 805/541-5393.* Italian menu. Lunch, dinner. Business casual attire. Reservations recommended. Outdoor seating. **$$**

★ ★ **CAFE ROMA.** *1020 Railroad Ave, San Luis Obispo (93401). Phone 805/541-6800; fax 805/786-2522.* Italian menu. Lunch, dinner. Closed Sun; holidays. Bar. Casual attire. Reservations recommended. **$$**

★ **CISCO'S.** *778 Higuera St, San Luis Obispo. Phone 805/543-5555.* American menu. Lunch, dinner. Children's menu. Casual attire. Outdoor seating. **$**

★ **SLO BREWING CO.** *1119 Garden St, San Luis Obispo (93401). Phone 805/543-1843. www.slobrew.com.* American menu. Lunch, dinner, late-night. Bar. Children's menu. Casual attire. **$**

San Simeon (C-2)

3 1/2 hours, 165 miles from San Jose

Population 250
Elevation 20 ft
Area Code 805
Zip 93452
Information Chamber of Commerce, 9255 Hearst Dr; phone 805/927-3500
Web Site www.sansimeon-online.com

San Simeon is a historical old whaling village. About 100 years ago, death-defying forays took place off these rocky shores when whales were spotted. Sea lion, sea otter, and whale-watching are popular during northward migration in March-May, and also during December-January, when southward migration occurs. Deep-sea fishing is especially popular all year.

What to See and Do

Hearst-San Simeon State Historical Monument (Hearst Castle). *750 Hearst Castle Rd, San Simeon (93452). Phone 805/927-2020. www.hearstcastle.com.* Crowning La Cuesta Encantada—the Enchanted Hill—is a princely domain of castle, guest houses, theater, pools, and tennis courts created by William Randolph Hearst as his home and retreat. After his death in 1951, the estate was given to the state as a memorial to the late publisher's mother, Phoebe Adderson Hearst. For years Hearst Castle could be glimpsed by the public only through a telescope at the nearby village of San Simeon, but today it is open to the public. A "carefully planned, deliberate attempt to create a shrine of beauty," it was begun in 1919 under the direction of noted architect Julia Morgan. An army of workers built the castle with its twin towers and surrounded it with formal Mediterranean gardens; construction continued for 28 years. And, though three guest houses and 115 rooms of the main house were completed, there was still much more Hearst had hoped to build.

Items collected by Hearst can be viewed in the castle and on the grounds. Features of the castle itself are the Refectory, an unbelievable "long, high, noble room" with a hand-carved ceiling and life-size statues of saints, silk banners from Siena, and 15th-century choir stalls from a Spanish cathedral; the Assembly Room, with priceless tapestries; and the lavish theater where the latest motion pictures were shown.

The estate includes three luxurious "guest houses"; the Neptune Pool, with a colonnade leading to an ancient Roman temple facade and an array of marble statuary; an indoor pool, magnificent gardens, fountains, walkways and, of course, the main house of 115 rooms.

Visitors may explore an exhibit on the life and times of William Randolph Hearst inside the Visitor Center at the bottom of the hill. Also here is an iWERKS giant-screen theater showing "Hearst Castle: Building the Dream," a 40-minute film detailing the rich history and architectural precedents of Hearst and his estate (phone 805/927-6811). Food and gift concessions are also located here. There is an area to observe artifact restoration in progress; entrance to the exhibit is free.

Parking is available in a lot near Highway 1, where buses transport visitors to the castle. Access to the castle and grounds is by guided tour only. Tour One takes in the grounds, a guest house, the pools, and the lower level of the main house; Tour Two visits the upper levels of the main house, which include Hearst's private suite; Tour Three covers the north wing and a guest house and includes a video about the construction of the castle; Tour Four (available April-October) is spent mostly outside in the gardens and around the pools, but also includes behind-the-scenes areas such as the wine cellar and two floors of the largest guest house. Evening tours are available for selected evenings in the spring and fall; these tours take in the highlights of the estate and include a living history program developed to give visitors a glimpse of life at the "Castle" in the early 1930s. All tours include the outdoor and indoor pools.

Day tours take approximately one hour and 45 minutes; evening tours take approximately two hours and 15 minutes. No pets. Reservations are recommended and are available up to eight weeks in advance by calling 800/444-4445. Tickets are also available at the ticket office in the visitor center. Tours entail much walking and stair climbing; wheelchairs can be accommodated under certain conditions and with ten days advance notice by calling 805/927-2020; strollers cannot be accommodated. (Daily; closed Jan 1, Thanksgiving, Dec 25) **$$$$**

Limited-Service Hotel

★ ★ BEST WESTERN CAVALIER OCEANFRONT RESORT. *9415 Hearst Dr, San Simeon (93452). Phone 805/927-4688; toll-free 800/826-8168; fax 805/927-6472. www.cavalierresort.com.* 90 rooms, 2 story. Pets accepted. Check-out noon. Restaurant, bar. Fitness room. Two outdoor pools, whirlpool. **$**

Bend, OR

10 hours, 492 miles from San Francisco

Settled 1900
Population 20,469
Elevation 3,628 ft
Area Code 541
Information Chamber of Commerce, 63085 N Hwy 97, 97701; phone 541/382-3221 or toll-free 800/905-2363
Web Site www.bendchamber.org

The early town was named Farewell Bend after a beautiful wooded area on a sweeping curve of the Deschutes River, where pioneer travelers had their last view of the river. The Post Office Department shortened it, but there was good reason for this nostalgic name. As westward-bound settlers approached, they found the first lush, green forests and good water they had seen in Oregon.

Tourists are attracted year-round to the region by its streams, lakes, mountains, great pine forests, ski slopes, and golf courses. There is also much of interest to geologists and rockhounds in this area. Movie and television producers often take advantage of the wild western scenery.

Two Ranger District offices of the Deschutes National Forest are located here.

What to See and Do

Deschutes National Forest. *1645 Hwy 20 E, Bend (97701). Phone 541/383-5300. www.fs.fed.us/r6/centraloregon/index.shtml.* The Deschutes National Forest encompasses 1.6 million acres of ruggedly scenic wilderness, a broad and diverse expanse of land marked by snowcapped mountains, craggy volcanic formations, old-growth forests, and deep rivers knifing through high-desert canyons. Established as a national forest in 1908, Deschutes has become one of the Pacific Northwest's most popular year-round tourist destinations, attracting over 8 million visitors annually. The winter months bring hordes of skiers and snowmobilers. Oregon's largest ski resort can be found alongside the 9,065-foot-high Mt. Bachelor. Hikers arrive after the spring thaw, eager to take advantage of the area's 1,388 miles of trails—including 60 miles of the Pacific Crest National Scenic Trail. Cars carrying strapped-down canoes and kayaks are a common sight, with paddlers headed to the Deschutes River, which has been designated both a National Scenic River and a National Recreational River. Anglers are drawn to the forest's 157 trout-filled lakes and reservoirs. Situated on the eastern side of the Cascade Mountains, the Deschutes National Forest gets significantly more sunshine than the rainier western side, but drier conditions also create a greater risk for forest fires. In the summer of 2003, the Booth and Bear Butte fires burned nearly 91,000 acres over the course of 39 days. The rapidly growing town of Bend lies just to the east of Deschutes, offering visitors a return to civilization after an exhausting day of outdoor adventure.

★ Driving Tour in Deschutes National Forest. *1645 Hwy 20 E, Bend (97701). Phone 541/388-2715.* An 89-mile paved loop (Century Dr, Cascade Lakes Hwy) provides a clear view of Three Sisters peaks, passes many mountain lakes and streams. Go west on Franklin Ave past Drake Park, follow the signs. Continue south past Mt. Bachelor, Elk Lake, Lava Lakes, and Cultus Lake. After passing Crane Prairie Reservoir, turn left (east) on Forest Road 42 to Highway 97, then left (north) for return to Bend. Also in the forest are Newberry National Volcanic Monument, the Lava Cast Forest and Lava Butte Geological Area, Mt. Bachelor Ski Area, Crane Prairie Osprey Management Area, as well as Mt. Jefferson, Diamond Peak, Three Sisters, and Mt. Washington wildernesses. Fishing, hiking, camping, picnicking, and rafting are popular. The forest includes 1.6 million acres with headquarters in Bend. Ten miles south of Bend, at the base of Lava Butte, is Lava Lands Visitor Center, operated by the US Forest Service, with dioramas and exhibits on history and geology of volcanic area. For further information contact Supervisor, 1645 Hwy 20 E, 97701.

High Desert Museum. *59800 S Hwy 97, Bend (97702). 6 miles S on Hwy 97. Phone 541/382-4754. www.highdesert.org.* A regional museum with indoor/outdoor exhibits featuring live animals and cultural history of Intermountain Northwest aridlands; hands-on activities; ongoing presentations. The galleries house wildlife, Western art, and Native American artifacts; landscape photography; and walk-through dioramas depicting the opening of the American West. The desertarium showcases seldom-seen bats, burrowing owls, amphibians, and reptiles. (Daily 9 am-5 pm; closed Jan 1, Thanksgiving, Dec 25) **$$**

LaPine. *15800 State Recreation Rd, Bend (97739). 22 miles S on Hwy 97, then 4 miles W. Phone 541/388-6055.* A 2,333-acre park on Deschutes River in Ponderosa pine forest. Scenic views. Swimming, bathhouse, fishing, boating; picnicking, improved trailer campsites (dump station).

Lava Butte and Lava River Cave. *58201 Hwy 97 S, Bend (97707). 11 miles S on Hwy 97. Phone 541/593-2421.* Lava Butte is an extinct cinder cone. Paved road to top provides view of Cascades; interpretive trails through pine forest and lava flow. One mile south, Lava River Cave offers a lava tube 1.2 miles long (fee); ramps and stairs ease walking. Visitor center has audiovisual shows (May-Sept, daily). **$$**

Mount Bachelor Ski Area. *Bend (97702). 22 miles SW on Century Dr. Phone 541/382-2442; toll-free 800/829-2442 (reservations). www.mtbachelor.com.* Panoramic, scenic view of forests, lakes, and Cascade Range. Facilities at base of 6,000 feet; 6,000 acres. Ten chairlifts; patrol, school, rentals; cafeterias, concession areas, bars, lodges; day care. Longest run 1 1/2 miles; vertical drop 3,365 feet; 56 miles of cross-country trails. (Mid-Nov-May, daily) **$$$$**

Newberry National Volcanic Monument. *1645 Hwy 20 E, Bend (97701). 24 miles S on Hwy 97, then 14 miles E on Forest Rd 21, in Deschutes National Forest. Phone 541/383-5300. www.fs.fed.us/r6/centraloregon/newberrynvm/index.shtml.* This monument, an active volcano, has a wide range of volcanic features and deposits similar to Mount Etna; obsidian flow, pumice deposits. On same road are East and Paulina lakes, both of which have excellent fishing as well as boat landings; hiking, picnicking (stoves, fireplaces), resorts, tent and trailer sites. You can get a view of the entire area from Paulina Peak, at nearly 8,000 feet. **$$**

Pilot Butte. *2880 NE 27th St, Bend (97701). 1 mile E on Hwy 20. Phone 541/388-6055.* A 101-acre park noted for a lone cinder cone rising 511 feet above the city. Summit affords an excellent view of the Cascade Range. No water, no camping.

Pine Mount Observatory. *26 miles SE near Millican, via Hwy 20, then 9 miles S. Phone 541/382-8331 (for appointment).* University of Oregon astronomical research facility. Visitors may view stars, planets, and galaxies through telescopes. (Memorial Day-Sept, Fri and Sat) **$$**

Tumalo. *5 1/2 miles NW off Hwy 20. Phone 541/382-3586.* A 320-acre park situated along the banks of the Deschutes River; swimming nearby, fishing; hiking, picnicking, tent and trailer campsites; solar-heated showers.

Tumalo Falls. *Skyliner Rd and Tumalo Falls, Bend (97701). W via Franklin Ave and Galveston Ave, 12 miles beyond city limits, then 2 miles via unsurfaced forest road. Phone 541/383-5300.* A 97-foot waterfall deep in pine forest devastated by 1979 fire.

Whitewater rafting. *Sun Country Tours, 531 SW 13th St, Bend (97702). Phone 541/382-6277. www.suncountrytours.com.* Choose from 2-hour or all-day trips. Also canoeing and special programs. (May-Sept) **$$$$**

Limited-Service Hotels

★ ★ MOUNT BACHELOR VILLAGE RESORT. *19717 Mount Bachelor Dr, Bend (97701). Phone 541/389-5900; toll-free 800/452-9846; fax 541/388-7404. www.mountbachelorvillage.com.* Woodland setting along Deschutes River. 130 rooms, 2 story. Check-out noon. Restaurant. Outdoor pool, children's pool. Tennis. Business center. **$$**

★ ★ RED LION. *1415 NE 3rd St, Bend (97701). Phone 541/382-7011; toll-free 800/733-5466; fax 541/382-7934. www.redlion.com.* 75 rooms, 2 story. Pets accepted. Check-out noon. Restaurant. Outdoor pool, whirlpool. **$**

★ ★ THE RIVERHOUSE. *3075 N Hwy 97, Bend (97701). Phone 541/389-3111; toll-free 800/547-3928; fax 541/389-0870. www.riverhouse.com.* This resort is located on the Deschutes River and features such amenities as refrigerators and microwaves, an indoor/outdoor pool, and golfing and skiing packages. 220 rooms, 2 story. Pets accepted. Check-out noon. Restaurant. Indoor pool, outdoor pool. Golf. **$**

★ ★ SHILO INN. *3105 NE O. B. Riley Rd, Bend (97701). Phone 541/389-9600; toll-free 800/222-2244; fax 541/382-4310. www.shiloinns.com.* On Deschutes River. 151 rooms, 2 story. Pets accepted, some restrictions; fee. Check-out noon. Restaurant, bar. Fitness room. Indoor pool, outdoor pool, whirlpool. Airport transportation available. **$**

Full-Service Resorts

★ ★ ★ INN OF THE SEVENTH MOUNTAIN. *18575 SW Century Dr, Bend (97702). Phone 541/382-8711; toll-free 800/452-6810; fax 541/382-3517. www.7thmtn.com.* With breathtaking views both in summer and winter, this beautiful oasis is set in Deschutes National Forest. Activities such as whitewater rafting, horseback riding, golfing, and canoeing make it Oregon's premier resort destination. 300 rooms, 3 story. Check-out noon. Restaurant, bar. Children's activity center. Two outdoor pools, children's pool, whirlpool. Tennis. **$**

★ ★ ★ SUNRIVER RESORT. *1 Center Dr, Sunriver (97707). Phone 541/593-1000; toll-free 800/801-8765; fax 541/593-4167. www.sunriverresort.com.* Central Oregon's Sunriver Resort is one of the state's best vacation destinations. This full-service, all-season resort on the sunny side of the scenic Cascade Mountain Range offers visitors a complete getaway with an endless supply of recreational opportunities, including sparkling pools, three 18-hole golf courses, a state-of-the-art fitness center, and an elegant spa. Recreational opportunities run the gamut from canoe and kayak trips to 30 miles of biking trails to a challenge ropes course, while the Sunriver Nature Center and Observatory offers stargazing, a botanical garden, and nature trails. Whether you plan to stay for just a few days or enjoy a longer visit, the accommodations range from deluxe rooms in the River Lodges and rooms and suites in the Lodge Village to private home and condominium rentals. Several restaurants entice diners with distinctive Northwestern cuisine or classic pub-food favorites, and regional beers and wines are a special highlight. 441 rooms, 2 story. Check-in 4 pm, check-out 11 am. Three restaurants, bar. Children's activity center. Fitness room, fitness classes available, spa. Three outdoor pools, children's pool, whirlpool. Golf, 54 holes. Tennis. Airport transportation available. Business center. **$**

Specialty Lodgings

The following lodging establishments are approved by Mobil Travel Guide, but due to their unique and individualized nature have not been given a traditional Mobil Star rating. Included in this listing you may find bed-and-breakfasts, limited-service inns, guest ranches, and other unique hotel properties.

DIAMOND STONE GUEST LODGE. *16693 Sprague Loop, LaPine (97739). Phone 541/536-6263; toll-free 800/600-6263. www.diamondstone.com.* This lodge sits adjacent to Quail Run Golf Course, at the gateway to Newberry National Volcanic Monument, with the Cascade Mountains as a backdrop. Surrounded by open meadows and pines, there are plenty of trails for hiking and exploring. 3 rooms, 2 story. **$**

ROCK SPRINGS GUEST RANCH. *64201 Tyler Rd, Bend (97701). Phone 541/382-1957; toll-free 800/225-3833; fax 541/382-7774. www.rocksprings.com.* 26 rooms. Check-in 4:30 pm, check-out 11 am. Restaurant. Children's activity center. Fitness room. Outdoor pool, whirlpool. Tennis. Airport transportation available. **$$**

Restaurants

★ ★ COWBOY DINNER TREE. *Hager Mountain Rd, Silver Lake (97638). Phone 541/576-2426. www.cowboydinnertree.homestead.com.* A very traditional Old West restaurant with a very limited menu and hours, but worth a visit for the great food and atmosphere. Located in a turn-of-the-century ranch. American menu. Dinner. Closed Mon-Tues, Thurs. No credit cards accepted. **$$**

★ ★ ★ ERNESTO'S ITALIAN RESTAURANT. *1203 NE 3rd St, Bend (97701). Phone 541/389-7274; fax 541/389-1686.* This former church is now a family restaurant featuring basic Italian fare. The service is courteous and helpful. Italian menu. Dinner. Bar. Children's menu. **$$**

★ ★ ★ MEADOWS. *1 Center Dr, Bend (97707). Phone 541/593-1000. www.sunriver-resort.com.* American menu. Dinner. Bar. **$$**

★ ★ PINE TAVERN. *967 NW Brooks St, Bend (97701). Phone 541/382-5581. www.pinetavern.com.* One hundred-foot pine tree in dining room. Seafood, steak menu. Lunch, dinner. Bar. Children's menu. Outdoor seating. **$$**

★ ROSZAK'S FISH HOUSE. *1230 NE 3rd St, Bend (97701). Phone 541/382-3173.* Seafood, steak menu. Lunch, dinner. Closed Memorial Day, Labor Day. Bar. Children's menu. **$$**

★ TONY'S. *415 NE 3rd St, Bend (97701). Phone 541/389-5858.* American, Italian menu. Breakfast, lunch, dinner. Closed Dec 25. Bar. Children's menu. **$$**

★ WESTSIDE BAKERY & CAFE. *1005 NW Galveston Ave, Bend (97701). Phone 541/382-3426.* American menu. Breakfast, lunch. Closed Thanksgiving, Dec 25. Children's menu. **$**

Coos Bay, OR

11 hours, 18 minutes, 488 miles from San Francisco

Founded 1854
Population 15,374
Elevation 11 ft
Area Code 541
Zip 97420
Information Bay Area Chamber of Commerce, 50 E Central, PO Box 210; phone 541/269-0215 or toll-free 800/824-8486
Web Site www.oregonsbayareachamber.com

This charming port town borders a bay that shares its name. The bay itself is the largest natural harbor between San Francisco and Seattle, and since the earliest pioneer days it has served as a key means of commercial passage to and from the sea. Coos Bay is the state's second-busiest maritime center, supported by such industries as forestry, shipbuilding, and fishing. Outdoor enthusiasts appreciate the area's mild climate (the temperature rarely falls below 45° F) and the terrific recreational opportunities available at three local state parks: Cape Arago, Shore Acres, and Sunset Bay. Anglers flock to the shores of the nearby Coos River, which is considered one of best places in Oregon to catch salmon and steelhead.

What to See and Do

Cape Arago. *Cape Arago Hwy, Coos Bay. 14 miles SW off Hwy 101 on Cape Arago Hwy. Phone 541/888-8867. www.oregonstateparks.org.* This 134-acre promontory juts 1/2 mile into the ocean. Two beaches, fishing; hiking (on Oregon Coast Trail), picnicking. Observation point (whale-and seal-watching).

Charleston Marina Complex. *63534 Kingfisher Dr, Charleston (97420). 9 miles SW. Phone 541/888-2548. www.charlestonmarina.com.* Charter boats; launching and moorage facilities (fee); car and boat trailer parking (free); dry boat storage, travel park; motel; marine fuel dock; tackle shops; restaurants. Office (Mon-Fri).

Oregon Connection/House of Myrtlewood. *1125 S 1st St, Coos Bay (97420). Just off Hwy 101 in S Coos Bay. Phone 541/267-7804.* Manufacturing of myrtlewood gift items. Tours. (Daily; closed holidays) **FREE**

Shore Acres. *89814 Cape Arago Hwy, Coos Bay (97420). 13 miles SW off Hwy 101 on Cape Arago Hwy. Phone 541/888-3732. www.shoreacres.net.* Former grand estate of Coos Bay lumberman, noted for its unusual botanical and Japanese gardens and spectacular ocean views (743 acres). Ocean beach; hiking (on the Oregon Coast Trail), picnicking.

South Slough National Estuarine Research Reserve. *61907 Seven Devils Rd, Charleston (97420). 4 miles S on Seven Devils Rd. Phone 541/888-5558. www.southsloughesturary.org.* A 4,400-acre area reserved for the study of estuarine ecosystems and life. Previous studies here include oyster culture techniques and water pollution. Special programs, lectures, and exhibits at Interpretive Center. Trails and waterways (daily); guided trail walks and canoe tours (June-Aug; fee). Interpretive Center (June-Aug: daily; rest of year: Mon-Fri). **FREE**

Sunset Bay. *Cape Arago Hwy, Coos Bay. 12 miles SW off Hwy 101 on Cape Arago Hwy. Phone 541/888-4902. www.oregonstateparks.org.* A 395-acre park with swimming beach on sheltered bay, fishing; hiking, picnicking, tent and trailer sites. Observation point.

Special Events

Bay Area Fun Festival. *Phone 541/267-3341; toll-free 800/738-4849.* This festival features activities for all ages including a quilt show, duck derby, sock hop, vendor booths, and car shows. Third weekend in Sept.

Blackberry Arts Festival. *Coos Bay. Phone 541/267-1022.* Features arts, crafts, jewelry, photography, paintings, and prints. Fourth weekend in Aug.

Oregon Coast Music Festival. *Phone toll-free 877/897-9350.* Variety of musical presentations ranging from jazz and dance to chamber and symphonic music. Also free outdoor picnic concerts. Last two full weeks in July.

Limited-Service Hotel

★★ RED LION HOTEL. *1313 N Bayshore Dr, Coos Bay (97420). Phone 541/267-4141; toll-free 800/733-5466; fax 541/267-2884. www.redlion.com.* Located at the north end of downtown Coos Bay on busy Highway 101, this motel-style facility offers comfortable guest rooms. Most have refrigerators and microwaves. For entertainment, there's an on-site putting green, and the lounge hosts stand-up comedy shows on weekend nights. 143 rooms, 2 story. Pets accepted. Check-in 3 pm, check-out noon. Restaurant, bar. Fitness room. Outdoor pool, whirlpool. Airport transportation available. **$**

Restaurant

★★ PORTSIDE. *8001 Kingfisher Rd, Charleston (97420). Phone 541/888-5544. www.portsidebythebay.com.* Seafood menu. Lunch, dinner. Bar. Children's menu. Outdoor seating. **$$**

Crater Lake National Park, OR

8 hours, 16 minutes, 423 miles from San Francisco

57 miles N of Klamath falls on Hwy 97, Hwy 62.

Web Site www.nps.gov/crla

One of Crater Lake's former names, Lake Majesty, probably comes closest to describing the feeling visitors get from the deep blue waters in the caldera of dormant Mount Mazama. More than 7,700 years ago, following climactic eruptions, this volcano collapsed and formed a deep basin. Rain and snow accumulated in the empty caldera, forming the deepest lake in the United States (1,932 feet). Surrounded by 25 miles of jagged rim rock, the 21-square-mile lake is broken only by Wizard and Phantom Ship islands. Entering by road from any direction brings you to the 33-mile Rim Drive (July-mid-Oct or the first snow), leading to all observation points, park headquarters, and a visitor center at Rim Village (June-Sept, daily). The Sinnott Memorial Overlook with a broad terrace permits a beautiful view of the area. On summer evenings, rangers give campfire talks at Mazama Campground (late June-Sept, phone 541/594-2211). The Steel Center located at Park Headquarters (open daily) has exhibits about the natural history of the park and shows a movie daily.

The park can be explored on foot or by car following spurs and trails extending from Rim Drive. Going clockwise from Rim Village to the west, The Watchman Peak is reached by a trail almost 1 mile long that takes hikers 1,800 feet above the lake with a full view in all directions; Mount Shasta in California, 105 miles away, is visible on clear days. The road to the north entrance passes through the Pumice Desert, once a flood of frothy debris from the erupting volcano.

On the northeast side, Cleetwood Trail descends 1 mile to the shore and a boat landing, where two-hour launch trips depart hourly each day in summer (fee). From the boats, Wizard Island, a small volcano, and Phantom Ship, a craggy mass of lava, can be seen up close.

Six miles farther on Rim Drive, going clockwise, is the start of a 2 1/2-mile hiking trail, 1,230 feet to Mount Scott, soaring 8,926 feet, the highest point in the park. Just to the west of the beginning of this trail is a 1-mile drive to the top of Cloudcap, 8,070 feet high and 1,600 feet above the lake. Four miles beyond this point, a road leads 7 miles from Rim Drive to The Pinnacles, pumice spires rising like stone needles from the canyon of Wheeler Creek.

Back at Rim Village, two trails lead in opposite directions. Counterclockwise, a 1 1/2-mile trek mounts the top of Garfield Peak. The other trail goes to Discovery Point, where in 1853 a young prospector, John Hillman, became the first settler to see the lake.

In winter, the south and west entrance roads are kept clear in spite of the annual 45-foot snowfall; the north entrance road and Rim Drive are closed from mid-October-June, depending on snow conditions. A cafeteria is open daily at Rim Village for refreshments and souvenirs.

Depending on snow, the campground (fee) is open from late June-mid-October. Mazama, at the junction of the south and west entrance drives, has a camp store, fireplaces, showers, laundry facilities, toilets, water, and tables; no reservations. There are six picnic areas on Rim Drive. The wildlife includes black bears—keep your distance and never feed them. There are also deer, golden-mantled ground squirrels, marmots, and coyotes. Do not feed any wildlife in park.

The park was established in 1902 and covers 286 square miles. For park information, contact Super intendent, Crater Lake National Park, PO Box 7, Crater Lake 97604; phone 541/594-2211, ext 402. Golden Eagle Passports are accepted (see MAKING THE MOST OF YOUR TRIP).

Note: conservation measures may dictate the closing of certain roads and recreational facilities. In winter, inquire locally before attempting to enter the park.

Full-Service Resort

★★★ **CRATER LAKE LODGE.** *565 Rim Village Dr, Crater Lake (97604). Phone 541/594-2255; fax 541/594-2342. www.crater-lake.com.* This grand lodge has been welcoming guests to its lakeside location since 1915. The lodge captures the essence of Pacific Northwest beauty and rusticity. Guests can relax with a good book in front of the Great Hall's massive stone fireplace. The Dining Room restaurant prepares dishes using Oregon-grown ingredients. It's also the perfect place to enjoy a cup of coffee as you watch the sun rise over Crater Lake, with the morning light reflecting on the placid blue surface of the second-deepest lake in the Western Hemisphere. Guest rooms are without TVs and phones, but, at a destination as blissful as this, you won't miss them. 71 rooms, 4 story. Closed mid-Oct-mid-May. Check-out 11 am. Restaurant. **$**

Eugene, OR

8 1/2 hours, 529 miles from San Francisco

Settled 1846
Population 112,669
Elevation 419 ft
Area Code 541
Information Lane County Convention & Visitors Association, 115 W 8th, Suite 190, PO Box 10286, 97440; phone 541/484-5307 or toll-free 800/547-5445
Web Site www.cvalco.org/travelguide/travelguide.html

Eugene sits on the west bank of the Willamette (Wil-AM-et) River, facing its sister city Springfield on the east bank. The Cascade Range rises to the east, mountains of the Coast Range to the west. Bicycling, hiking, and jogging are especially popular here, with a variety of trails to choose from. Forests of Douglas fir support a lumber industry that accounts for 40 percent of the city's manufacturing. Eugene-Springfield is at the head of a series of dams built for flood control of the Willamette River Basin. Willamette National Forest headquarters is located here.

What to See and Do

Armitage County Park. *90064 Coburg Rd, Eugene (97408). 6 miles N off I-5 on Coburg Rd. Phone 541/682-2000.* A 57-acre park on partially wooded area on the south bank of the McKenzie River. Fishing, boating (ramp); hiking, picnicking.

Camp Putt Adventure Golf Park. *4006 Franklin Blvd, Eugene (97403). Phone 541/741-9828.* An 18-hole course with challenging holes like "Pond O' Peril," "Thunder Falls," and "Earthquake." Lakeside patio with ice cream bar. (Late Mar-mid-Nov, daily) **$$**

Fall Creek Dam and Lake. *40386 W Boundary Rd, Lowell (97452). 20 miles SE on Hwy 58 to Lowell, then follow signs to Big Fall Creek Rd. Phone 541/937-2131.* Winberry Creek Park has swimming beach, fishing, boating (ramp); picnicking. (May-Sept) Some fees. North Shore Ramp has fishing, boat launching facilities; picnicking. (Daily with low-level ramp) Cascara Campground has swimming, fishing, boating (ramp); camping (May-Sept). Some fees.

Hendricks Park Rhododendron Garden. *Summit and Skyline drs, Eugene (97401). Phone 541/682-5324.* A 20-acre, internationally known garden features more than 6,000 aromatic plants, including rare species and hybrid rhododendrons from the local area and around the world (peak bloom mid-Apr-mid-May). Walking paths, hiking trails, picnic area. (Daily) **FREE**

Hult Center. *1 Eugene Ctr, Eugene (97401). 7th Ave and Willamette St. Phone 541/682-5000 (tickets).* Performing arts center offering more than 300 events each year ranging from Broadway shows and concerts to ballet.

Lane County Historical Museum. *740 W 13th Ave, Eugene (97402). Phone 541/682-4242. www.lchmuseum.org.* Changing exhibits depict history of county from mid-19th century to 1930s; includes artifacts of pioneer and Victorian periods; textiles; local history research library. (Wed-Fri 10 am-4 pm, Sat-Sun noon-4 pm) **$**

Lookout Point and Dexter Dams and Lakes. *40386 W Boundary Rd, Lowell (97452). 20 miles SE on Hwy 58. Phone 541/937-2131.* The 14-mile-long Lookout Point Lake has Black Canyon Campground (May-Oct; fee) with trailer parking. Fishing; picnicking. Hampton Boat Ramp with launching facilities and four camp sites (all year; fee) with trailer parking, picnicking; fishing, closed to launching during low water (usually Oct-Apr). Lowell Park on 3-mile-long Dexter Lake has swimming, water-skiing, boating (moorage, ramp), sailboating; picnicking. Dexter Park has water-skiing, fishing, boating (ramp), sailboating; picnicking. The Powerhouse at Lookout Point Dam is open to the public (by appointment).

Owen Municipal Rose Garden. *North Jefferson at the river, Eugene. N end of Jefferson St, along the Willamette River. Phone 541/682-5025.* A 5-acre park with more than 300 new and rare varieties of roses, as well as wild species (best blooms late June-early July); a recognized test garden for experimental roses. Also here is a collection of antiques and miniatures. Picnic area. (Daily) **FREE**

South Breitenbush Gorge National Recreation Trail. *Eugene. From Detroit Ranger Station, travel E on Hwy 22 for approximately 1 mile, turn left onto Breitenbush Rd 46, travel about 14 miles, turn right on Forest Rd 4685. Access 1 is 1/2 mile up Rd 4685. Access 2 is 2 miles on Rd 4685 at Roaring Creek, and access 3 is 1/4 mile past access 2. Phone 541/225-6301.* Meandering through giant trees in an old-growth grove, this popular trail follows the Wild & Scenic-eligible South Breitenbush River. A small Forest Service-operated campground is near the trailhead.

Spencer Butte Park. *Ridgeline and Willamette St, Eugene. 2 miles S of city limits on Willamette St. Phone 541/682-4800.* Park has 305 acres of wilderness, with Spencer Butte Summit, at 2,052 feet, dominating the scene. Hiking trails. Panoramic views of Eugene, Cascade Mountains. (Daily) **FREE** Starting at edge of park is

> **South Hills Ridgeline Trail.** *52nd St and Spencers Butte Park, Eugene (97405). Begins at 52nd and Willamette sts. Phone 503/325-7275.* A 5-mile trail extending from Blanton Road east to Dillard Road; a spur leads to top of Butte. The trail offers magnificent views of the Cascade Mountains, Coburg Hills, and Mount Baldy; the wildflowers along the trail reach their peak bloom in late Apr.

University of Oregon. *1205 University of Oregon, Eugene (97403). Bounded by Franklin Blvd and Agate St, Alder and 18th sts. Phone 541/346-3014. www.uoregon.edu.* (1876) (19,000 students) The 250-acre campus includes more than 2,000 varieties of trees. Points of interest include the Museum of Natural History, Robinson Theatre, Beall Concert

Hall, Hayward Field, and the Erb Memorial Union. Campus tours depart from Information and Tour Services, Oregon Hall (Mon-Sat). Also on campus are

Jordan Schnitzer Museum of Art. *1430 Johnson Ln, Eugene (97403). Phone 541/346-3027. uoma.uoregon.edu.* Diverse collections include large selection of Asian art representing cultures of China, Japan, Korea, Cambodia, and American and British works of Asian influence; official court robes of the *Ch'ing* dynasty (China, 1644-1911); Russian icon paintings from the 17th-19th centuries; Persian miniatures and ceramics; photography; works by contemporary artists and craftsmen from the Pacific Northwest, including those of Morris Graves. Special exhibits. Gift shop. (Wed-Sun afternoons; closed holidays) **FREE**

Knight Library. *University of Oregon Library, 1299 University of Oregon, Eugene (97403). Phone 541/346-3054. www.libweb.uorgon.egu.* With more than 2 million volumes, this is the largest library in Oregon. Main lobby features changing exhibits of rare books, manuscripts; Oregon Collection on second floor. Fine arts pieces, wrought iron gates and carved panels. (Daily)

Whitewater rafting. *Phone toll-free 800/547-5445.* Numerous companies offer trips on the McKenzie, Deschutes, and Willamette rivers. Trips range from two hours to five days. Contact Convention and Visitors Association for details.

Willamette National Forest. *211 E 7th Av, Eugene (97401). E via Hwy 20, Hwy 126. Phone 541/225-6300.* More than 1 1/2 million acres. Home to more than 300 species of wildlife; including Cascade Mountain Range summit; Pacific Crest National Scenic Trail with views of snowcapped Mt. Jefferson, Mt. Washington, Three Fingered Jack, Three Sisters, Diamond Peak; Koosah and Sahalie Falls on the Upper McKenzie River; Clear Lake; the lava beds at summit of McKenzie Pass; Waldo Lake near summit of Willamette Pass. Fishing; hunting, hiking, skiing, snowmobiling, camping (fee at some sites).

Willamette Pass Ski Area. *Cascade Summit. S via I-5, E on Hwy 58. Phone 541/345-7669. www.willamettepass.com.* Double, three triple chairlifts; patrol, school, rentals (ski and snowboard). Lodge, restaurant, lounge. Longest run 2.1 miles; vertical drop 1,583 feet. Also 20 kilometers of groomed nordic trails. Night skiing (late Dec-late Feb, Fri-Sat). (Late-Nov-mid-Apr) **$$$$**

Willamette Science and Technology Center. *2300 Leo Harris Pkwy, Eugene (97401). Phone 541/682-7888.* Participatory science center encourages hands-on learning; features exhibits illustrating physical, biological, and earth sciences and related technologies. Planetarium shows. (Wed-Sun) **$$**

Special Events

Bach Festival. *Phone toll-free 800/457-1486.* Numerous concerts by regional and international artists; master classes; family activities. Mid-June-early July.

Lane County Fair. *796 W 13th Ave, Eugene (97402). Phone 541/682-4292.* Features local talents in art, baking, photography, and livestock; also included is a Midway and entertainment. Mid-Aug.

Limited-Service Hotels

★ PHOENIX INN SUITES EUGENE. *850 Franklin Blvd, Eugene (97403). Phone 541/344-0001; toll-free 800/344-0131; fax 541/686-1288. www.phoenixinn.com.* 97 rooms, 4 story. Complimentary continental breakfast. Check-out noon. Fitness room. Indoor pool, whirlpool. **$**

★ ★ RED LION. *205 Coburg Rd, Eugene (97401). Phone 541/342-5201; toll-free 800/733-5466; fax 541/485-2314. www.redlion.com.* 137 rooms, 2 story. Pets accepted. Check-out noon. Restaurant, bar. Fitness room. Outdoor pool, whirlpool. Airport transportation available. **$**

Full-Service Hotels

★ ★ ★ HILTON EUGENE AND CONFERENCE CENTER. *66 E 6th Ave, Eugene (97401). Phone 541/342-2000; toll-free 800/445-8667; fax 541/342-6661. www.eugene.hilton.com.* In the heart of downtown Eugene, the Hilton is adjacent to the Hult Center for the Performing Arts (see), which holds Broadway shows, concerts, and other performances throughout the year. It's within walking distance of shops and restaurants. At the hotel, the Big River Grille serves Pacific Northwest cuisine, and the lobby bar offers local microbrews. 272 rooms, 12 story. Pets accepted, some restrictions; fee. Check-in 3 pm, check-out noon. High-speed Internet access. Restaurant, bar. Fitness room. Indoor pool, whirlpool. Airport transportation available. Business center. **$$**

★ ★ ★ WESTCOAST VALLEY RIVER INN. *1000 Valley River Way, Eugene (97401). Phone 541/587-0123; toll-free 800/543-8266; fax 541/687-0289. www.valleyriverinn.com.* This hotel is conveniently located downtown and minutes from the airport, shopping, the University of Oregon, and the convention center. Some rooms have views of the Willamette River. 257 rooms, 3 story. Pets accepted, some restrictions. Check-out 11 am. Restaurant, bar. Fitness room. Outdoor pool, children's pool, whirlpool. Airport transportation available. **$$**

Specialty Lodging

The following lodging establishment is approved by Mobil Travel Guide, but due to its unique and individualized nature has not been given a traditional Mobil Star rating. Included in this listing you may find bed-and-breakfasts, limited-service inns, guest ranches, and other unique hotel properties.

THE CAMPBELL HOUSE, A CITY INN. *252 Pearl St, Eugene (97401). Phone 541/343-1119; toll-free 800/264-2519; fax 541/343-2258. www.campbellhouse.com.* Comfort and elegance await you at this intimate bed-and-breakfast, which offers views of the city from a hill. Each room is tastefully and uniquely furnished. 19 rooms, 3 story. Complimentary full breakfast. Check-in 4 pm, check-out noon. **$$**

Restaurants

★ ★ AMBROSIA. *174 E Broadway, Eugene (97401). Phone 541/342-4141.* Italian menu. Lunch, dinner. Closed holidays. Bar. Outdoor seating. **$$**

★ ★ ★ CHANTERELLE. *207 E 5th Ave, Eugene (97401). Phone 541/484-4065.* European cuisine set in an intimate, relaxed atmosphere. Chef Ralf Schmidt creatively uses fresh, local ingredients to create such flawless dishes as lamb Provençale, tournedo of beef "Chanterelle," and sautéed prawns Maison. International/Fusion menu. Dinner. Closed Sun-Mon; holidays. **$$**

★ EXCELSIOR INN. *754 E 13th, Eugene (97401). Phone 541/342-6963. www.excelsiorinn.com.* Italian menu. Breakfast, lunch, dinner, Sun brunch. Bar. Children's menu. Outdoor seating. **$$**

★ ★ NORTH BANK. *22 Club Rd, Eugene (97401). Phone 541/343-5622.* Seafood, steak menu. Lunch, dinner. Closed Dec 25. Bar. **$$**

★ ★ OREGON ELECTRIC STATION. *27 E 5th Ave, Eugene (97401). Phone 541/485-4444; fax 541/484-6149. www.oesrestaurant.com.* Former train station (1912); memorabilia. American menu. Lunch, dinner. Closed July 4, Dec 25. Bar. Children's menu. Outdoor seating. **$$**

★ ★ ★ SWEETWATERS. *1000 Valley River Way, Eugene (97401). Phone 541/687-0123. www.valleyriverinn.com.* With a beautiful view of the Willamette River, this casually elegant restaurant delights guests with ample portions of Northwest cuisine and Mediterranean-inspired dishes. Fresh seafood, game meats, exotic fruits, and seasonal, local ingredients make up the majority of the menu. Breakfast, lunch, dinner, Sun brunch. Bar. Children's menu. Outdoor seating. **$$**

★ ★ ZENON CAFE. *898 Pearl St, Eugene (97401). Phone 541/343-3005.* American menu. Breakfast, lunch, dinner, Sun brunch. Closed Thanksgiving, Dec 25. Outdoor seating. **$$**

Portland, OR

10 hours 20 minutes, 635 miles from San Francisco

Founded 1851
Population 437,319
Elevation 77 ft
Area Code 503
Information Portland Oregon Visitors Association, 26 SW Salmon St, 97204; phone 503/222-2223 or toll-free 877/678-5263
Web Site www.pova.com
Suburbs Beaverton, Forest Grove, Hillsboro, Newburg, Oregon City; also Vancouver, WA.

Oregon's largest city sprawls across both banks of the Willamette River, just south of its confluence with the Columbia. The lush and fertile Willamette Valley brings it beauty and riches. Portland's freshwater harbor is visited by more than 1,400 vessels annually from throughout the world. The city enjoys plentiful electric power, captured from river waters, which drives scores of industries with minimal amounts of smoke or smog.

Portland is surrounded by spectacular scenery. The Columbia River Gorge, Mount Hood, waterfalls, forests, ski slopes, fishing streams, and hunting and camping areas are within easy access. It attracts many conventions, for which it is well equipped, with four

Portland's Outstanding Parks

The glory of Portland is its parks. Settled by idealistic New Englanders, Portland had an extensive park system in the 1850s, decades before other West Coast cities were even founded. Begin at Portland State University in the North Park Blocks, a swath of twenty blocks of parkland that cuts right through the heart of the city. The park was established in the 1850s and for generations was the best address for civic structures. Numerous historic churches, plus the Portland Art Museum, the Oregon History Center, the Portland Center for the Performing Arts, and the Schnitzer Concert Hall (home to the Oregon Symphony) flank the park. The park is also home to the largest remaining stand of American elm (killed elsewhere by Dutch elm disease), numerous heroic statues, and a farmers' market (on Wednesdays and Saturdays).

Drop down to Pioneer Courthouse Square at 6th and Morrison, often referred to as Portland's living room. This is where many outdoor festivals, concerts, and demonstrations take place. (Dan Quayle got such a raucous reception here that he thenceforward refused to visit Portland, referring to the city as "America's Beirut.") The Square is a great place for people-watching and sunbathing, and there are many food carts and cafés here. In the blocks around Pioneer Courthouse Square are many of Portland's major shopping venues. Adjacent is the Pioneer Courthouse itself, built in 1875.

Follow 5th Avenue south, noting the abundance of public art along the pedestrian-friendly bus mall. At 5th Avenue and Main Street is the Portland Building, a noted postmodern structure designed by Michael Graves. The front is surmounted by a massive statue called Portlandia. This is the second-largest hammered copper statue in the world, the largest being the Statue of Liberty.

Head over to the Willamette River waterfront. The park that runs the length of downtown along the river is recent. In the 1970s, the city ripped out a freeway that ran along the river and replaced it with this park, which in summer is loaded with joggers, sun worshipers, and any number of summer festivals. Also along the river are boat tour operators, a large marina with some shops and cafés, and, at the north end, a memorial to Japanese-American internment during World War II. Under the Burnside Bridge, adjacent to Waterfront Park, is the Portland Saturday Market (open both Saturday and Sunday), which is reputed to be the largest open-air crafts market in the nation.

Turn north along 3rd Avenue and walk through Portland's Old Town (most buildings date to the 1880s) to Chinatown. Here, between 2nd and 3rd avenues and Everett and Flanders streets is the Portland Chinese Garden, a traditional Chinese garden that is a joint project of Portland and the city of Suzhou. It is the largest Chinese-style garden outside of China itself.

large auditoriums: the Memorial Coliseum Complex, the Metropolitan Exposition Center, and the Oregon Convention Center. Portland's reputation as "The City of Roses" is justified by its leadership in rose culture, as seen in its International Rose Test Garden and celebrated during the annual Portland Rose Festival, which attracts visitors worldwide. Mount St. Helens, in Washington's Gifford Pinchot National Forest, 50 miles to the northeast, can be seen from numerous vantage points in Portland.

Portland is also an educational center, with Portland State University, the University of Portland (1901), Lewis & Clark College (1867), and Reed College (1911).

Public Transportation

Buses MAX light rail trains (Tri-County Metropolitan Transportation District), phone 503/238-7433.

Airport Portland International Airport. Phone 503/275-9792; cash machines, Main Terminal, N & S ends of Oregon Market Place.

Information Phone 503/460-4234

Lost and Found Phone 503/460-4277

Airlines Air Canada Jazz, Alaska Airlines, America West Airlines, American Airlines, Continental Airlines, Delta Air Lines, Frontier Airlines, Hawaiian Air, Horizon Air, Lufthansa, Mexicana Airlines, Northwest

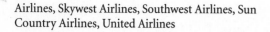

Airlines, Skywest Airlines, Southwest Airlines, Sun Country Airlines, United Airlines

What to See and Do

American Advertising Museum. *211 NW 5th Ave, Portland (97209). Phone 503/226-0000.* This museum is devoted to the history and evolution of advertising and its impact on culture. Boasting the industry's most comprehensive collection of advertising and business artifacts, the American Advertising Museum features permanent as well as changing exhibits. (Thurs-Sat 11 am-5 pm) **$**

Benson State Recreation Area. *30 miles E on I-84, exit 30. Phone 503/695-2261. www.oregonstateparks.org/park_147.php.* Thirty miles east of Portland, near Multnomah Falls, the Benson State Recreation Area has a lake that's perfect for fishing, swimming, and boating (nonmotorized boats only). Picnicking is also popular here, and the park even has a disc golf course. (Daily) **$**

Children's Museum 2nd Generation. *4015 SW Canyon Rd, Portland (97221). Off Hwy 26 opposite the Oregon Zoo. Phone 503/223-6500. www.portlandcm2.org.* CM2 offers plenty of hands-on play spaces, including the Vroom Room, where kids can race in a variety of wheeled objects, and KidCity Market, a children-sized grocery store with miniature carts and aisles of fake food. The museum also features temporary exhibits, one example being a replica of the television set of *Mister Rogers' Neighborhood.* (Sun 11 am-5 pm; Mon-Thurs, Sat 9 am-5 pm; Fri 9 am-8 pm; closed holidays) **$**

Council Crest Park. *SW Council Crest Dr, Portland (97201). S on SW Greenway Ave (follow the blue and white scenic tour signs). Phone 503/823-2223. www.parks.ci.portland.or.us/parks.* Council Crest Park is not just the city's highest park, it's the site of Portland's highest point, topping off at 1,073 feet above sea level. That may not sound all that high, but it's high enough to afford wonderful views of the Tualatin Valley, the Willamette River, Mount St. Helens, and the truly high and mighty Mount Hood. **FREE**

Crown Point. *40700 Historic Columbia River Hwy, Corbett (97019). E on I-84, exit 22; on Hwy 30. Phone 503/695-2230. www.oregonstateparks.org/park_150.php.* This 307-acre park possesses a 725-foot-high vantage point alongside the Columbia River Gorge, allowing for spectacular views of the gorge's rock walls, which rise 2,000 feet above the river. The historic Vista House, an octagonal building with a copper dome, is located here. **FREE**

Crystal Springs Rhododendron Garden. *SE 28th Ave, Portland (97202). N of SE Woodstock Blvd. Phone 503/823-2223. www.parks.ci.portland.or.us/parks/crysspringrhodgar.htm.* The pathways at Crystal Springs wind through a woodland setting, passing by some 2,500 rhododendrons, azaleas, and companion plants. A spring-fed lake attracts many species of birds and waterfowl. Admission is free from Labor Day through February. (Daily) **$**

Dabney State Recreation Area. *Portland. 19 miles E off I-84 exit 18, at Stark St Bridge on Hwy 30. Phone 503/695-2261. www.oregonstateparks.org.* East of Portland, this 135-acre park is a popular summertime destination, thanks to its idyllic swimming hole and picnic area. The park even offers electric cooking stations to fry up those hamburgers and tofu dogs. Other amenities include a reservable group shelter, walking trails, beach, boat ramp, and disc golf course. Many visitors enjoy fishing for salmon and steelhead in the Sandy River. **$**

Forest Park. *NW Skyline and Helens Rd, Portland. Off Hwy 30, NW of Fremont Bridge. Phone 503/228-8733. www.parks.ci.portland.or.us/parks/forestpark.htm.* Park encompasses over 5,000 wooded acres, making it the largest wilderness park within city limits in the United States. Visitors can take advantage of 74 miles of hiking, bicycling, and equestrian trails. Wildwood Trail begins at the Vietnam Veterans Living Memorial in Hoyt Arboretum and extends 27 miles, ending deep in the park, beyond Germantown Road. Some 100 bird species and 60 mammal species inhabit the park. (Daily) **FREE**

Gray Line bus tours. *4320 N Suttle Rd, Portland (97217). Phone 503/285-9845; toll-free 800/422-7042. www.grayline.com.* Gray Line offers seven tours that originate in Portland, including a three-hour tour of the city and a nine-hour tour that retraces Lewis and Clark's journey along the Columbia River. **$$$$**

The Grotto. *8840 N E Skidmore, Portland (97220). NE 85th Ave at Sandy Blvd, on Hwy 30. Phone 503/254-7371. www.thegrotto.org.* The National Sanctuary of Our Sorrowful Mother—commonly called The Grotto—is a 62-acre Catholic shrine and botanical garden. Created in 1924, The Grotto cuts into the side of a 110-foot cliff and is surrounded by beautiful plants and flowers. An elevator takes visitors to the Natural Gallery in the woods, where you'll find more than 100 statues. The landscaped upper level has a meditation chapel overlooking the Columbia River, with Mount St. Helens visible in the distance. (Daily; closed Thanksgiving, Dec 25) **DONATION**

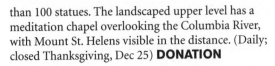

Guy W. Talbot State Park. *Columbia River Hwy, Troutdale (97062). E on I-84, exit 27; on Hwy 30. Phone 503/695-2261. www.oregonstateparks.org/park_154.php.* These 371 lush acres served as the estate of Guy Webster Talbot and his family until the property was donated to the state in 1929. The park is regarded as a wonderful picnicking destination, as it's rarely crowded and features beautiful natural surroundings, including 250-foot-high Latourell Falls, the second-highest falls along the Columbia River Gorge. **FREE**

Howell Territorial Park and the Bybee House. *13901 NW Howell Park Rd, Portland (97231). 12 miles N via Hwy 30, cross bridge to Sauvie Island, 1 mile W to Howell Territorial Park Rd. Phone 503/222-1741.* The Howell Territorial Park, occupying 93 pastoral acres on Sauvie Island, is home to the Bybee House, an impressive example of Greek Revival architecture. Originally a private home, the Bybee House was purchased in 1961 by Multnomah County and soon after restored to appear as it would have at the time of its construction in 1858. Guided tours of the home are conducted on the half-hour. (Park: daily; Bybee House: June-Labor Day, weekend afternoons) **DONATION**

Hoyt Arboretum. *4000 SW Fairview Blvd, Portland (97221). Phone 503/228-8733. www.hoytarboretum.org.* Within its 175 acres, the Hoyt Arboretum boasts more than 900 species of trees and shrubs, including one of the largest collections of conifers in the United States. The arboretum sits upon a ridge overlooking the Oregon Zoo. Guided tours are offered April-October on Saturdays and Sundays at 2 pm. The park and visitor center are open daily. **FREE**

Lewis and Clark College. *0615 SW Palatine Hill Rd, Portland (97219). 3 miles E of I-5 Terwilliger Exit. Phone 503/768-7000. www.lclark.edu.* The campus at Lewis and Clark College is simply gorgeous, highlighted by the floral display at the Memorial Rose Garden. Established in 1867, the college has an enrollment of about 3,000 students. Two campus buildings, the Manor House and Gatehouse, are listed in the National Register of Historic Places.

Lewis and Clark State Recreation Area. *16 miles E on I-84, exit 18. Phone 503/695-2261. www.oregonstateparks.org/park_159.php.* Situated near the confluence of the Columbia and Sandy rivers, this park offers picnic tables, a beach, and a boat ramp. Anglers and swimmers are a common sight in the cool waters of the Sandy River. Hiking also is popular here, particularly along a trail that leads to Broughton's Bluff. The park's namesakes camped and explored the area in November 1805. **FREE**

Lloyd Center. *2201 Lloyd Center, Portland (97232). Phone 503/282-2511. www.lloydcentermall.com.* Billing itself as the biggest mall in Oregon, the trilevel Lloyd Center features anchor stores such as Nordstrom and Meier & Frank, discount stores like Marshalls, numerous eateries, and an 18-screen movie theater.

Mount Hood-Columbia Gorge Loop Scenic Drive. *Phone toll-free 877/678-5263.* This 163-mile scenic drive along the Columbia River and through Mount Hood National Forest offers splendid views of the river basin, visits to waterfalls, many state parks, and spectacular mountain scenery. Drive east 17 miles on Highway 30, I-84 to Troutdale. At this point, for approximately 24 miles, there are two routes: you may turn right and take the mountainous upper-level scenic route or continue on the main river-level freeway. The two roads rejoin about 10 miles west of Bonneville Dam. Continue east on Highway 30, I-84 for 23 miles to Hood River, turning south on Highway 35 for 47 miles through Mount Hood National Forest to Highway 26. Drive northwest on Highway 26, 56 miles back to Portland. A description of this tour may be found in a free visitors guide from the Portland Visitors Association.

Mount Tabor Park. *SE 60th Ave and Salmon St, Portland (97215). Phone 503/823-2223. www.parks.ci.portland.or.us/Parks/MtTabor.htm.* This 195-acre park has something for everyone, with a basketball court, volleyball court, horseshoe pit, playground, picnic shelter, and tennis courts, as well as an off-leash area for dogs. The park contains an extinct volcano, making Portland one of only two US cities to have an extinct volcano within its city limits. (Daily)

Multnomah Falls. *I-84 to Multnomah Falls turnoff, Bridal Veil. 32 miles E on I-84. Phone 503/695-2372.* Chief among the 11 waterfalls along 11 miles of this highway; 620-foot drop in two falls, fourth-highest in United States. Hiking. Restaurant. Visitor center.

Oaks Park. *SE Spokane St, Portland (97202). SE Oaks Park Way, E end of Sellwood Bridge. Phone 503/233-5777. www.oakspark.com.* Opened in 1905, Oaks Park is one of the oldest continuously operating amusement parks in the United States. It features thrill rides, a children's area, a roller rink (Tues-Sun; rentals available), miniature golf, and waterfront picnicking. (Spring and fall: weekends; summer: daily).

Oregon Convention Center. *777 NE Martin Luther King Jr. Blvd, Portland (97232). Phone 503/235-7575; toll-free 800/791-2250. www.oregoncc.org.* Located within Portland's city center, the Oregon Convention Center (OCC) hosts conferences, exhibitions, and parties year round within its 255,000-square-foot facility. OCC provides Wi-Fi access throughout the property, a big plus for visitors seeking a high-speed connection to the Internet. The MAX light rail stops at OCC's front door.

Oregon Historical Society. *1200 SW Park Ave, Portland (97205). Phone 503/222-1741. www.ohs.org.* The Oregon Historical Society features a broad range of exhibits and collections within its museum and research library. The history of Oregon and the Pacific Northwest is documented through photographs, audio recordings, artifacts, and books. The library houses a book collection exceeding 35,000 titles (Wed-Sat). The museum offers permanent and changing exhibits. (Tues-Sun; closed holidays) **$$**

Oregon Museum of Science and Industry. *1945 SE Water Ave, Portland (97214). Phone 503/797-4000. www.omsi.edu.* The museum has six exhibit halls and labs, with an emphasis on putting the fun in such topics as astronomy, electronics, Earth science, biology, and dinosaurs. The museum is also home to a planetarium and Omnimax theater (daily, fee), as well as the USS *Blueback*, the Navy's last non-nuclear, fast attack submarine. (Labor Day-Memorial Day: Tues-Sun; rest of the year: daily; closed Dec 25) **$$**

Oregon Zoo. *4001 SW Canyon Rd, Portland (97221). Phone 503/226-1561. www.zooregon.org.* Specializing in breeding and protecting rare and endangered species, the Oregon Zoo has about 1,029 living specimens, 54 of which are considered either endangered or threatened. Opened as the Washington Park Zoo in 1887, the Oregon Zoo houses creatures large and small, ranging from elephants and giraffes to millipedes and scorpions. The botanical gardens have more than 1,000 species of exotic plants. The zoo is a five-minute ride from downtown Portland on the MAX light rail. A separate zoo railway links to the popular Washington Park. (Daily; closed Dec 25) **$$**

Peninsula Park and Community Center. *700 N Portland Blvd, Portland (97217). N Portland Blvd and Albina Ave. Phone 503/823-2223. www.parks.ci.portland.or.us/parks/peninsulapkrosegar.htm.* Home to Portland's first public rose garden and community center, Peninsula Park has extensive facilities, including softball, football, and soccer fields; a basketball court; an outdoor swimming pool; tennis courts; a horseshoe pit; a playground; and a picnic shelter. An amazing 8,900 plantings grow in the 2-acre rose garden. The park's community center (Mon-Fri; closed most holidays) is impressively fashioned as an Italian villa. (Daily) **FREE**

PGE Park. *1844 SW Morrison, Portland (97205). Take I-405 to the Salmon St exit. www.pgepark.com.* PGE Park serves as the home for two professional sports teams, the Portland Beavers and the Portland Timbers, as well as the football team at Portland State University. The Beavers are the AAA affiliate of the San Diego Padres, while the Timbers compete in the USL's A-League, soccer's highest level of play in the United States and Canada. PGE Park sits on a plot of land that has been used for athletic events since 1893, a time when it was known as Multnomah Field. Over the years, the versatile facility has hosted a wide range of athletic events, including tennis, cricket, and ski jumping. In 2001, PGE Park underwent a $38.5 million renovation, turning it into one of the most modern and comfortable stadiums of its size. Tickets may be purchased at the PGE Park box office or by calling Ticketmaster at 503/224-4400. **$$$**

Pittock Mansion. *3229 NW Pittock Dr, Portland (97210). Phone 503/823-3624. www.pittockmansion.com.* This restored and furnished French Chateau-esque mansion, dating to 1914, is surrounded by 46 forested and landscaped acres. Spectacular views of rivers, the city, and snowcapped mountains, including Mount St. Helens and Mount Hood, are an added bonus. (Summer: daily 11 am-4 pm; rest of year: noon-4 pm; closed holidays) **$$**

Police Historical Museum. *16th floor of Justice Center, 1111 SW 2nd Ave, Portland (97204). Phone 503/823-0019.* The museum features a collection of police uniforms, badges, photos, confiscated weapons, and other police memorabilia. One of the most popular museum pieces is a police motorbike with sidecar. (Mon-Thurs; closed holidays) **FREE**

★ Portland Art Museum. *1219 SW Park Ave, Portland (97205). At Jefferson St. Phone 503/226-2811. www.portlandartmuseum.org.* Founded in 1892, the Portland Art Museum holds a collection of more than 32,000 works of art, including European paintings and sculptures from the Renaissance to the present; 19th- and 20th-century American works; a noted collection of Northwest Coast Native American art; Asian, pre-Columbian, West African, and classical Greek and Roman art; British silver; and creative photography. The museum hosts lectures, films, concerts, and other arts-related special events. (Tues-Sun; closed holidays) **$$$**

Portland Fire (WNBA). *One Center Ct, Portland (97227). Phone 503/797-9622.* Team plays in the Rose Garden.

Portland Saturday Market. *108 W Burnside, Portland (97209). Under the Burnside Bridge. Phone 503/222-6072. www.portlandsaturdaymarket.com.* One of largest, oldest open-air community markets in the United States. More than 350 vendor booths feature arts and crafts made by Pacific Northwest artisans and a wide variety of foods, from sushi to curry. Street entertainers, face painters, and the like enliven the atmosphere and keep kids smiling. (Sat 10 am-5 pm, Sun 11 am-4:30 pm, Mar-Dec 24)

Portland State University. *724 SW Harrison St, Portland (97201). Visitor information center at SW Broadway and College sts. Phone 503/725-3000. www.pdx.edu.* Located in the woodsy South Park Blocks area, the university enrolls more than 21,000 students in its undergraduate and graduate programs. Art exhibits are often featured in the Smith Memorial Center and Neuberger Hall.

Portland Trail Blazers (NBA). *Rose Garden, 1 Center Ct, Portland (97227). Phone 503/797-9600. www.nba.com/blazers.* Portland loves its Trail Blazers, the city's lone major sports franchise. The Blazers, as they're better known, compete in the Pacific Division of the National Basketball Association, playing their home games in the 19,980-seat Rose Garden. Founded in 1970, the Blazers have made it to the NBA Finals on three occasions, taking home the championship in 1977 behind the stellar play of center Bill Walton and forward Maurice Lucas. The Blazers host 41 regular-season games, beginning in late October and finishing in mid-April. **$$$$**

Powell's City of Books. *1005 W Burnside, Portland (97209). Phone toll-free 866/201-7601. www.powells.com.* A must-stop for bibliophiles, Powell's City of Books stocks more than a million new and used titles within a sprawling 68,000-square-foot facility that occupies an entire city block in downtown Portland. First-time visitors should pick up a complimentary store map to help them navigate through nine color-coded rooms, perusing an inventory that's divided into 122 major subject areas and approximately 3,500 subsections. If you're a collector looking for, say, a signed first edition of *The Hobbit,* be sure to check out the Rare Book Room, which houses autographed first editions and other collectible volumes. (Daily 9 am-11 pm)

Rooster Rock State Park. *E on I-84, milepost 25. Phone 503/695-2261. www.oregonstateparks.org/park_175.php.* A short drive east of Portland, Rooster Rock offers 3 miles of sandy beaches along the Columbia River. The park is a popular destination for windsurfing, boating, fishing, swimming, hiking, and picnicking. One of Oregon's two designated nude beaches is located at the park's eastern edge. The nude beach is secluded, and it cannot be seen from the clothing-required area. **$**

Rose Quarter. *One Center Ct, Portland (97227). Phone 503/231-8000. www.rosequarter.com.* The Rose Quarter is Portland's home for big-name live entertainment. Two venues comprise the Rose Quarter: the Memorial Coliseum, which seats a shade under 13,000, and the Rose Garden, a modern arena with a capacity near 20,000. The Rose Garden serves as the home court for the NBA's Trail Blazers. The Portland Winter Hawks, a minor-league hockey team, take to the ice in both venues. Musical acts also perform in both venues, with more popular artists taking to the stage in the Rose Garden.

Sternwheeler *Columbia Gorge*. *1200 NW Naito Pkwy, Portland (97209). Cruises leave from Marine Park in Cascade Locks, E on I-84, exit 44. Phone 503/223-3928. www.sternwheeler.com.* Climb aboard the Sternwheeler *Columbia Gorge,* an authentic triple-deck paddle wheeler, and enjoy spectacular views as you journey along the Columbia River. A variety of excursions are offered, including champagne brunch cruises and dinner cruises. **$$$$**

★ Washington Park. *400 S W Kingston, Portland (97211). Accessible via W Burnside St, SW Park Pl, or Canyon Rd. Phone 503/823-2223 (weekdays). www.parks.ci.portland.or.us/Parks/Washington.htm.* Washington Park encompasses 129 scenic acres on a hill overlooking the city. On a clear day, the views are simply spectacular, with Mount Hood towering majestically in the east and Mount St. Helens visible in the northern horizon. The Shakespeare Garden, Lewis and Clark Memorial, and Sacajawea Memorial Statue can be found in the park, as well as the popular International Rose Test Garden and Japanese Garden. Washington Park facilities include softball and soccer fields, lighted tennis courts, covered picnic areas, a playground, and hiking trails. The MAX light rail stops at Washington Park. Also here are

International Rose Test Garden. *400 SW Kingston, Portland (97201). Phone 503/823-7529. www.parks.ci.portland.or.us/Parks/IntRoseTestGarden.htm.* In a city rich with natural wonders, perhaps no Portland location can match the beauty found at the International Rose Test Garden. The garden sits on a hillside in Washington Park, with a clear view of snowcapped Mount Hood rising majestically in the distance. The garden was created in 1917 by three prominent nurserymen, established, in part, to serve as a safe haven for hybrid roses grown in war-torn Europe. Today, the garden features more than 8,000 rosebushes, enhancing the city's reputation as the "City of Roses." Near the garden's parking lot, the Rose Garden Store offers an impressive array of rose-related arts and crafts. (Daily 7:30 am-9 pm)

Japanese Garden. *611 SW Kingston Ave, Portland (97205). Phone 503/223-1321. www.japanesegarden.com.* This 5-acre enclave of tranquility is considered one of the most authentic Japanese gardens outside of Japan. Masterly designed by Professor Takuma Tono, the garden opened in 1967 as a place for reflection and serenity within an environment of natural beauty and quietude. The Japanese Garden possesses five formal garden styles: Natural Garden, Sand and Stone Garden, Tea Garden, Strolling Pond Garden, and Flat Garden. The Japanese Garden Gift Store offers an eclectic array of arts and crafts merchandise, most of which comes from Japan. (Daily; closed holidays) **$$**

Water Tower at Johns Landing. *5331 SW MacAdam Ave, Portland (97239). Phone 503/242-0022.* Once a three-story furniture factory with a water tower used for fighting fires, this structure now houses specialty shops and restaurants. A cobblestone courtyard and rustic beamed ceilings make for a unique shopping experience. (Daily; closed holidays)

Willamette Stone State Heritage Site. *Skyline Blvd and W Burnside, Portland (97229). 4 miles W. Phone toll-free 877/678-5263. www.oregonstateparks.org/park_246.php.* The land in the United States is divided into a grid, and markers such as Willamette Stone are used as starting points from which grid lines are established. Willamette Stone serves as the "zero point" for the Willamette Meridian region, encompassing all of the land west of the Cascade Mountains in Oregon and Washington. A 500-foot trail cuts through dense forest as it leads to the actual marker and a plaque describing its relevance. **FREE**

World Forestry Center. *4033 SW Canyon Rd, Portland (97221). Phone 503/228-1367. www.worldforestry.org.* The World Forestry Center is highlighted by the Forest Discovery Center, a museum celebrating the importance and diversity of tree life. Opened in 1971, the museum features educational programs, gallery shows, and exhibits. The museum's most popular exhibit is a 70-foot-high talking tree, a replica Douglas fir that teaches tree biology in five different languages: English, French, Japanese, Spanish, and German. (Daily; closed Dec 25) **$$**

Special Events

Chamber Music Northwest. *522 SW 5th Ave, #725, Portland (97204). Phone 503/294-6400.* Catlin Gabel School and Reed College. Nationally acclaimed summer chamber music festival offers 25 concerts featuring 40-50 artists (Mon, Tues, Thurs-Sat). A catered picnic precedes each concert. Children under 7 only permitted at Family Concert. Mid-June-late July.

Elephant Garlic Festival. *Jessie Mayes Community Center, 30955 NW Hillcrest, North Plains (97133). Phone 503/647-2207. www.funstinks.com.* How can you go wrong with a festival whose motto is "Where fun stinks"? Garlic ice cream, garlic beer, and other delicacies dominate this yearly extravaganza that is almost surely devoid of vampires. Elephant garlic has been the theme only since 1998, when it was made the focus after almost ten years of lackluster attendance at "North Plains Days." Since then, the festival has blossomed, and attendance (which is still free) has increased almost every year. Third weekend in Aug.

Greyhound racing. *Multnomah Greyhound Park, 944 NE 223rd Ave, Wood Village (97060). NE 223rd Ave between NE Halsey and Glisan Sts, 12 miles E off I-84, exit 13 or 16A.Phone 503/667-7700.* Parimutuel betting. Matinee and evening races. Under 12 years not permitted at evening races. Call for schedule. May-Oct.

Holiday Parade of Christmas Ships. *Along Willamette and Columbia rivers.Phone 503/225-5555, ext 2065.* More than 50 boats cruise the two rivers in a holiday display. Early-mid-Dec.

Horse racing. *Portland Meadows, 1001 N Schmeer Rd, Portland (97217). 6 miles N on I-5.Phone 503/285-9144.* Parimutuel betting. Thoroughbred and quarter horse racing. (Fri evenings, Sat and Sun matinee) Under 12 years not permitted at evening races. Late Oct-Apr.

Mount Hood Jazz Festival. *Main and Powell sts, Gresham (97030). 15 miles E on I-84.Phone 503/219-9833.* International, national and local jazz acts presented in outdoor festival. First weekend in Aug.

Multnomah County Fair. *Phone 503/761-7577.* Agricultural and horticultural exhibits; entertainment. Mid-July.

Portland Center Stage. *Portland Center for the Performing Arts, 1111 SW Broadway, Portland (97205). Phone 503/274-6588.* Series of contemporary and classical plays. Daily except Mon. Call for fees, performance and title schedules. Sept-Apr.

Portland Marathon. *1221 SW 4th Ave, Portland (97204). Phone 503/226-1111. www.portlandmarathon.org.* World-class running event featuring international competition. Early Oct.

Portland Rose Festival. *220 NW 2nd Ave, #99, Portland (97209). Phone 503/227-2681.* Held for more than 90 years, this festival includes the Grand Floral Parade (reservations required for indoor parade seats) and two other parades; band competition; rose show; championship auto racing; hot air balloons; air show; carnival; Navy ships. Late May-June.

Portland Scottish Highland Games. *Mt. Hood Community College, 26000 SE Stark St, Gresham (97030). 15 miles E. Phone 503/293-8501.* Mid-July.

St. Patrick's Irish Festival. *Phone 503/227-4057.* One of the largest Irish festivals in the Pacific Northwest. Three days in Mar.

Limited-Service Hotels

★ ★ DAYS INN. *1414 SW 6th Ave, Portland (97201). Phone 503/221-1611; toll-free 800/544-8313; fax 503/226-0447. www.daysinn.com.* 173 rooms, 5 story. Check-out noon. Restaurant, bar. Outdoor pool. **$**

★ DAYS INN PORTLAND SOUTH. *9717 SE Sunnyside Rd, Clackamas (97015). Phone 503/654-1699; toll-free 800/241-1699; fax 503/659-2702. www.daysinn.com.* This hotel on the south side of Portland is across the street from the Clackamas Town Center Mall, which includes a movie theater. Several restaurants are within walking distance, and there's a public golf course one block away. 110 rooms, 3 story. Complimentary continental breakfast. Check-in 4 pm, check-out noon. Bar. Outdoor pool, whirlpool. **$**

★ ★ DOUBLETREE COLUMBIA RIVER HOTEL. *1401 N Hayden Island Dr, Portland (97217). Phone 503/283-2111; fax 503/283-4718. www.doubletree.com.* This hotel is located on the banks of the Columbia River. Located just 15 minutes from the Portland International Airport, free shuttle service is provided. 352 rooms, 3 story. Pets accepted; fee. Check-in 3 pm, check-out noon. Restaurant, bar. Fitness room, spa. Golf. Business center. **$$**

★ ★ DOUBLETREE HOTEL. *909 N Hayden Island Dr, Portland (97217). Phone 503/283-4466; toll-free 800/222-8733; fax 503/283-4743. www.doubletree.com.* This facility is conveniently located just 12 minutes from the Portland International Airport and provides guests with complimentary shuttle service. It is a sister property of the Doubletree Columbia River Hotel (see). 320 rooms, 4 story. Pets accepted; fee. Check-in 3 pm, check-out noon. Restaurant, bar. Fitness room. Outdoor pool, whirlpool. Tennis. Business center. **$$**

★ ★ DOUBLETREE HOTEL. *1000 NE Multnomah St, Portland (97232). Phone 503/281-6111; toll-free 800/222-8733; fax 503/284-8553. www.doubletree.com.* Located across from the Lloyd Center Mall and over 200 stores, 18 movie theaters, and an ice-skating rink. 476 rooms, 15 story. Check-in 3 pm, check-out noon. Restaurant, bar. Fitness room. Outdoor pool. Airport transportation available. Business center. **$**

★ FAIRFIELD INN. *11929 NE Airport Way, Portland (97220). Phone 503/253-1400; toll-free 800/228-2800; fax 503/253-3889. www.fairfieldinn.com.* 106 rooms, 3 story. Complimentary continental breakfast. Check-in 3 pm, check-out noon. Fitness room. Outdoor pool, whirlpool. **$**

★ **HAWTHORN SUITES.** *2323 NE 181st Ave, Portland (97230). Phone 503/492-4000; fax 503/492-3271. www.hawthorn.com.* 71 rooms, 3 story. Pets accepted, some restrictions; fee. Complimentary full breakfast. Check-out 1 pm. Fitness room. Indoor pool, whirlpool. **$**

★ ★ **HOLIDAY INN.** *1441 NE 2nd Ave, Portland (97232). Phone 503/233-2401; toll-free 800/465-4329; fax 503/238-7016. www.holiday-inn.com.* 238 rooms, 10 story. Check-out noon. Restaurant, bar. Outdoor pool. Airport transportation available. Business center. **$**

★ ★ **HOTEL LUCIA.** *400 SW Broadway at Stark, Portland (97205). Phone 503/225-1717; fax 503/225-1919.* 128 rooms, 9 story. Pets accepted. Check-out 2 pm. Restaurant, bar. **$**

★ ★ **MALLORY HOTEL.** *729 SW 15th Ave, Portland (97205). Phone 503/223-6311; toll-free 800/228-8657; fax 503/223-0522. www.malloryhotel.com.* 136 rooms, 8 story. Pets accepted; fee. Check-out 1 pm. Restaurant, bar. **$**

★ ★ **SWEET BRIER INN & SUITES.** *7125 SW Nyberg Rd, Tualatin (97062). Phone 503/692-5800; toll-free 800/551-9167; fax 503/691-2894. www.sweetbrier.com.* 131 rooms. Pets accepted; fee. Complimentary continental breakfast. Check-out noon. Restaurant, bar. Fitness room. Outdoor pool. **$**

Full-Service Hotels

★ ★ ★ **5TH AVENUE SUITES HOTEL.** *506 SW Washington St, Portland (97204). Phone 503/222-0001; toll-free 888/207-2201; fax 503/417-3386. www.5thavenuesuites.com.* This centrally located, full-service historic hotel dating to 1912 was once the Lipman, Wolf & Co. department store. Its guest rooms feature upholstered headboards, fluffy bedspreads, and Egyptian cotton robes to snuggle up in. The accommodations are decorated in soft colors, with subtle lighting and comfortable furniture adding to the cozy feel. The elegant lobby features soaring ceilings of molded plaster and wood, floor-to-ceiling windows, and a large corner fireplace surrounded by marble and topped with an antique mirror. Dine on Pacific Northwest cuisine at the Red Star Tavern & Roast House (see). 221 rooms, 10 story. Pets accepted, some restrictions. Check-in 2 pm, check-out noon. Restaurant, bar. Fitness room, spa. Business center. **$$**

★ ★ ★ **AVALON HOTEL & SPA.** *0455 SW Hamilton Ct, Portland (97239). Phone 503/802-5800; toll-free 888/556-4402; fax 503/802-5820. www.avalonhotelandspa.com.* Carefree yet sophisticated, Portland's Avalon Hotel & Spa is a unique destination. On the edge of downtown, this boutique hotel offers guests the best of both worlds. Its proximity to the city's attractions lures cosmopolitan travelers, while its location on the Willamette River draws those seeking a tranquil retreat. Blending styles from Asia and the Pacific Northwest, the hotel is a splendid contemporary showpiece. Dark and light woods combine to create a soothing space, while large windows capitalize on the superior setting. The two-story lobby is an inviting place to take in local artwork displays or to rest by the fire. When you enter the guest accommodations, an instant calm washes over you, largely due to the floor-to-ceiling windows that showcase the river's beautiful surroundings. Standard rooms feature marble baths, plush bathrobes, CD players, cordless phones, and private balconies; suites add fireplaces and double vanities. The Avalon Spa captures the essence of the region while paying tribute to Asian and European traditions. Dedicated to well-being, the spa's carefully selected treatment menu utilizes natural ingredients, ancient wisdom, and innovative therapies to completely relax you. The excellent Avalon Fitness Club offers cutting-edge classes like Pilates, kickboxing, and Neuromuscular Integrative Action (NIA) in addition to free weights and cardio equipment, with personal trainers on duty to help customize workouts for optimum results. 99 rooms, 6 story. Check-in 3 pm, check-out noon. High-speed Internet access. Restaurant. Fitness room (fee), fitness classes available, spa. **$$**

★ ★ ★ **BENSON HOTEL.** *309 SW Broadway, Portland (97205). Phone 503/228-2000; toll-free 888/523-6766; fax 503/471-3924. www.bensonhotel.com.* Presidents and celebrities alike have stayed in this landmark downtown hotel, whose owners have spared no expense since it was built in 1912. Feast your eyes on the lobby's paneling and Russian pillars, Austrian crystal chandeliers, and Italian marble staircase. The guest rooms are equally elegant, offering pleasantries like complimentary coffee, tea, and apples. With the hotel's one-to-one ratio of employees to guests, expect top service—from wine tastings to afternoon tea to the hotel's jazz club (the first ever to open in Portland). Don't miss the popular London Grill (see) restaurant, which offers an extensive wine collection and live jazz. 287 rooms, 14 story. Pets accepted; fee. Check-in 3 pm, check-out 1 pm. Restaurant, bar. Fitness room. Airport transportation available. Business center. **$$$**

★ ★ ★ CROWNE PLAZA. *14811 Kruse Oaks Blvd, Lake Oswego (97035). Phone 503/624-8400; toll-free 800/227-6963; fax 503/684-8324. www.crowneplaza.com.* Located just minutes from the downtown area, this hotel is quite convenient to the convention center as well as many of the area universities. 161 rooms, 6 story. Pets accepted; fee. Check-out noon. Restaurant, bar. Fitness room. Indoor pool, outdoor pool, whirlpool. Business center. **$$**

★ ★ ★ EMBASSY SUITES DOWNTOWN. *319 SW Pine St, Portland (97204). Phone 503/279-9000; toll-free 800/362-2779; fax 503/497-9051. www.embassyportland.com.* Unlike a typical Embassy Suites, the downtown Portland location is a historic hotel, originally opened in 1912. The restored lobby remains true to its origins, adorned with gold-leafed columns, marble stairways, and crystal chandeliers. The two-room suites have comfortable, traditional-style furnishings, as well as refrigerators and microwaves. Guests dine at Portland Steak and Chophouse, which offers more than 100 fine scotches and whiskies. Also on-site is the Salon Nyla Day Spa. 276 rooms, 8 story, all suites. Complimentary full breakfast. Check-in 4 pm, check-out noon. High-speed Internet access. Restaurant. Children's activity center. Fitness room, spa. Indoor pool, whirlpool. Airport transportation available. Business center. **$**

★ ★ ★ GOVERNOR HOTEL. *611 SW 10th Ave, Portland (97205). Phone 503/224-3400; toll-free 800/554-3456; fax 503/241-2122. www.govhotel.com.* The historic building sports a unique Lewis & Clark theme, with Native American flair throughout. The lobby, for example, features a totem pole, wood-burning fireplace, panoramic murals retracing Lewis & Clark's expedition, and turn-of-the-century frescoes. Some guest rooms have fireplaces, wet bars, and balconies offering panoramic city views. The clubby Jake's Grill (see) serves American food. 100 rooms, 6 story. Check-in 4 pm, check-out noon. Restaurant. Fitness room. Indoor pool, whirlpool. Business center. **$$**

★ ★ ★ THE HEATHMAN HOTEL. *1001 SW Broadway, Portland (97205). Phone 503/241-4100; fax 503/790-7110.* Dating to 1927, this grand "Arts Hotel of Portland" features a mix of artwork—from Art Deco mirrors in the Marble Bar to 18th-century French canvases in the historic Tea Court to silk-screens by Andy Warhol in the Heathman Restaurant (see). It's worth a tour for art lovers of any style and period. The guest rooms also have varied pieces of art. Personalized service at the front desk adds a warm and inviting touch. Distinguishing touches include a 400+ film library, afternoon tea, and nightly jazz in the Tea Court. 150 rooms, 10 story. Pets accepted; fee. Check-in 3:30 pm, check-out noon. Restaurant, bar. Fitness room. **$$**

★ ★ ★ HILTON PORTLAND. *921 SW Sixth Ave, Portland (97204). Phone 503/226-1611; toll-free 800/774-1500; fax 503/220-2565. www.portland.hilton.com.* Located in Portland's entertainment and cultural district, this hotel features fine dining and an athletic club with an indoor pool, tanning beds, sauna, and more. It is near the Performing Arts Center, shopping, and more than 60 restaurants. 782 rooms, 23 story. Check-in 4 pm, check-out noon. Restaurant, bar. Children's activity center. Fitness room. Indoor pool. Business center. **$$**

★ ★ ★ HOTEL VINTAGE PLAZA. *422 SW Broadway, Portland (97205). Phone 503/228-1212; toll-free 800/263-2305; fax 503/228-3598. www.vintageplaza.com.* What started out as the Imperial Hotel in 1894 is now the elegant Hotel Vintage Plaza, listed on the National Register of Historic Places. The hotel celebrates local winemaking by offering tastings of Oregon vintages in the evenings in the warm and inviting lobby. Guest accommodations feature Tuscan wine country décor, with Italian tapestries, ornately carved wooden mirrors, and bright colors and textures. Special rooms include the Garden Spa rooms, with their own outdoor patios and private spa tubs; and Starlight rooms, with slanted skylights and power shades. Pazzo Ristorante (see) offers fine Italian cuisine and wines. 107 rooms, 10 story. Pets accepted. Check-in 3 pm, check-out noon. Restaurant. Fitness room. Business center. **$**

★★★ MARRIOTT PORTLAND CITY CENTER. *520 SW Broadway, Portland (97205). Phone 503/226-6300; toll-free 800/228-9290; fax 503/227-7515. www.marriott.com.* 249 rooms, 20 story. Pets accepted; fee. Check-in 4 pm, check-out noon. Restaurant, bar. Fitness room. Whirlpool. Business center. **$**

★★★ MARRIOTT PORTLAND DOWNTOWN. *1401 SW Naito Parkway, Portland (97201). Phone 503/226-7600; toll-free 800/228-9290; fax 503/221-1789. www.marriott.com.* Enjoy a convenient location, lovely river views, and easy access to the waterfront in this friendly, stylish chain hotel that offers more than your typical Marriott. The guest rooms are decorated in warm tones of green, gold, and rust, and the lobby is equally inviting with its comfortable furniture and soft lighting. 503 rooms, 16 story. Check-in 4 pm, check-out noon. Restaurant, bar. Fitness room. Indoor pool, whirlpool. Business center. **$$**

★★★ PARAMOUNT HOTEL. *808 SW Taylor St, Portland (97205). Phone 503/223-9900; toll-free 800/663-1144; fax 503/223-7900. www.paramounthotel.net.* Fashioned in the neoclassical style, this 15-story boutique hotel is located smack dab in the middle of downtown Portland, within walking distance of Pioneer Square and the Center for the Performing Arts. The hotel's marble-tiled lobby creates a favorable first impression, with soaring ceilings, hand-loomed Persian rugs, and original artwork. Rooms are colored in warm tones, the walls adorned by black-and-white photography. Jetted tubs and private balconies are available in some rooms. Just off the hotel lobby, the Dragonfish Asian Café melds flavors and styles from all across East Asia, creating an eclectic Pan-Asian cuisine. 154 rooms. Pets accepted, some restrictions; fee. Check-in 3 pm, check-out noon. Wireless Internet access. Restaurant, bar. Fitness room. Business center. **$$**

★★★ RIVERPLACE HOTEL. *1510 SW Harbor Way, Portland (97201). Phone 503/228-3233; toll-free 800/227-1333; fax 503/295-6161. www.riverplacehotel.com.* Offering a full-service restaurant and bar, valet parking, and room service, this hotel is located in a quiet neighborhood next to a park and near downtown and its attractions. Also nearby is an athletic club and pool, for which guests receive passes. 84 rooms, 4 story. Pets accepted; fee. Complimentary continental breakfast. Check-out 1 pm. Restaurant, bar. Spa. Whirlpool. **$$**

★★★ SHERATON PORTLAND AIRPORT HOTEL. *8235 NE Airport Way, Portland (97220). Phone 503/281-2500; toll-free 800/325-3525; fax 503/249-7602. www.sheratonpdx.com.* This hotel is conveniently located on the grounds of the airport and offers many services and amenities. 218 rooms, 5 story. Pets accepted, some restrictions; fee. Check-in 3 pm, check-out noon. Restaurant, bar. Fitness room. Indoor pool, whirlpool. Business center. **$**

★★★ THE WESTIN PORTLAND. *750 SW Alder St, Portland (97205). Phone 503/294-9000; toll-free 800/937-8461; fax 503/241-9565. www.westin.com.* Located in the center of downtown Portland, this hotel is within walking distance to such area attractions as the Portland Convention Center. This facility offers guests Internet access, coffee makers, in-room safes, and dual-line direct-dial telephones with fax and data ports. 205 rooms, 18 story. Pets accepted; fee. Check-in 3 pm, check-out noon. Restaurant, bar. Fitness room. Business center. **$$**

Specialty Lodgings

The following lodging establishments are approved by Mobil Travel Guide, but due to their unique and individualized nature have not been given a traditional Mobil Star rating. Included in this listing you may find bed-and-breakfasts, limited-service inns, guest ranches, and other unique hotel properties.

HERON HAUS. *2545 NW Westover Rd, Portland (97210). Phone 503/274-1846; fax 503/248-4055. www.heronhaus.com.* 6 rooms, 3 story. Complimentary continental breakfast. Check-in 4-6 pm, check-out 11 am. High-speed Internet access. Outdoor pool. Restored house (1904) in the northwest hills overlooking city; library, morning room. **$$**

MCMENAMINS EDGEFIELD. *2126 SW Halsey St, Troutdale (97060). Phone 503/669-8610; toll-free 800/669-8610; fax 503/665-4209. www.mcmenamins.com/edge.* 103 rooms, 3 story. Complimentary full breakfast. Check-out 11 am. Restaurant, bar. Golf. Renovated in the style of a European village complete with theater, winery, distillery, and brewery. **$**

PORTLAND'S WHITE HOUSE BED AND BREAKFAST. *1914 NE 22nd Ave, Portland (97212). Phone 503/287-7131; toll-free 800/272-7131; fax 503/249-1641. www.portlandswhitehouse.com.* Located in a historic neighborhood within walking distance to shopping, dining, fitness facilities and local attractions, this bed-and-breakfast offers finely furnished rooms, each with a full bath. A white southern colonial mansion with Greek columns and a fountain at the entrance, it bears a striking resemblance to Washington, DC's White House. 9 rooms, 2 story. Complimentary full breakfast. Check-in 2 pm, check-out 11 am. Airport transportation available. **$**

Spa

★★★ **AVALON SPA.** *455 SW Hamilton Ct, Portland (97239). Phone 503/802-5900; toll-free 888/556-4402. www.avalonhotelandspa.com.* The Avalon Spa captures the essence of the Pacific Northwest while paying tribute to Asian and European traditions. Dedicated to well-being, the spa's carefully selected treatment menu utilizes natural ingredients, ancient wisdom, and innovative therapies to relax you. Warm and attentive, the exceptional staff enhances the experience. Whether you need help with a fitness machine or require more information to select the right spa treatment, the staff is there to assist you in every possible way. If you would like to run on a treadmill or to join a group exercise class, the state-of-the-art fitness center warrants a visit. The juice bar welcomes you to catch your breath and refuel yourself with a fresh drink. Pamper yourself with an Ayurvedic ritual or a body care therapy. Choose from rose, coastal evergreen, aromatherapy, chamomile, and Turkish aroma for your exfoliation treatment, or take advantage of the detoxifying benefits of a natural spirulina or moor mud body wrap. Relish a renew or a revitalize facial. Traditional European kurs, including Hungarian thermal mineral, thalasso, and Kräuter, are available to experience, or surrender to the heated waters of a themed bath. If stress has you tied up in knots, a heated stone, Swedish, sports, or reflexology massage can help melt away your tension. Expectant mothers in their second or third trimesters enjoy customized massages designed for them. The spa also offers salon services, including hair care, manicures, pedicures, waxing, and makeup instruction and applications.

Restaurants

★★ **AL-AMIR LEBANESE RESTAURANT.** *223 SW Stark St, Portland (97204). Phone 503/274-0010. www.alamirrestaurant.com.* Lebanese menu. Lunch, dinner. Bar. Children's menu. Casual attire. Reservations recommended. Valet parking. **$$**

★ **ALESSANDRO'S.** *301 SW Morrison, Portland (97204). Phone 503/222-3900; fax 503/224-9613.* Italian menu. Lunch, dinner. Closed Sun; holidays. Bar. **$$$**

★ **ALEXIS.** *215 W Burnside, Portland (97209). Phone 503/224-8577; fax 503/224-9354.* Greek menu. Lunch, dinner. Closed Sun. Bar. **$$**

★★ **BREWHOUSE TAP ROOM & GRILL.** *2730 NW 31st Ave, Portland (97210). Phone 503/228-5269. www.macsbeer.com.* American, German menu. Lunch, dinner. Closed holidays. Bar. Children's menu. Outdoor seating. **$$**

★★ **BUGATTI'S.** *18740 Willamette Dr, West Linn (97068). Phone 503/636-9555.* Italian menu. Dinner. Closed holidays. Children's menu. Outdoor seating. **$$**

★★ **BUSH GARDEN.** *900 SW Morrison, Portland (97205). Phone 503/226-7181; fax 503/226-7184.* Japanese menu. Lunch, dinner. Closed holidays. Bar. **$$$**

★★ **CAFE AZUL.** *112 NW 9th Ave, Portland (97209). Phone 503/525-4422.* Mexican menu. Dinner. Closed Sun-Mon; holidays. Bar. Outdoor seating. **$$$**

★★★ **CAFE DES AMIS.** *1987 NW Kearney St, Portland (97209). Phone 503/295-6487.* A quiet, intimate atmosphere with classic French bistro cuisine, offering excellent cooking, service, and wine selection. Try the not-to-be-missed steak or grilled scallops. French menu. Dinner, late-night. Closed Mon. **$**

★★ **CAPRIAL'S BISTRO.** *7015 SE Milwaukee Ave, Portland (97202). Phone 503/236-6457; fax 503/238-8554. www.caprial.com.* Mediterranean menu. Lunch, dinner. Closed Mon. Bar. Casual attire. Reservations recommended. **$$$**

★★ **CHART HOUSE.** *5700 SW Terwilliger Blvd, Portland (97201). Phone 503/246-6963. www.chart-house.com.* Seafood, steak menu. Lunch, dinner. Bar. Children's menu. Valet parking. **$$**

★ **CORBETT FISH HOUSE.** *5901 SW Corbett, Portland (97239). Phone 503/246-4434.* Seafood menu. Lunch, dinner. Bar. Children's menu. Outdoor seating. **$$**

★ **DAN & LOUIS OYSTER BAR.** *208 SW Ankeny St, Portland (97204). Phone 503/227-5906.* Seafood menu. Lunch, dinner. Closed holidays. Children's menu. **$$**

★ **ESPARZA'S TEX MEX CAFE.** *2725 SE Ankeny St, Portland (97214). Phone 503/234-7909; fax 503/232-3589.* Tex-Mex menu. Lunch, dinner. Closed Sun-Mon; holidays. Bar. Children's menu. **$$**

★ ★ **FERNANDO'S HIDEAWAY.** *824 SW First Ave, Portland (97204). Phone 503/248-4709; fax 503/248-0798. www.fernandosportland.com.* Spanish menu. Lunch, dinner, late-night. Bar. Casual attire. Outdoor seating. **$$**

★ ★ ★ **GENOA.** *2832 SE Belmont St, Portland (97214). Phone 503/238-1464; fax 503/238-9786. www.genoarestaurant.com.* Housed in a windowless, unassuming storefront that offers outsiders no clue as to the wonders just beyond the front door, Genoa is a hidden gem where glorious Italian feasts are served nightly. However, if you require predictability and control in your life, this restaurant may not be the place for you. There is no printed menu at Genoa. Your gracious waiter will offer you a choice of three entrées, but all other decisions rest with the chef. The menu is seven courses, prix fixe, and includes antipasto, soup, pasta, fish or salad, your chosen entrée, dessert, and then fruit. (A trip to the gym should be scheduled for the following day.) With this much food to consume, dinner at Genoa is a lengthy, leisurely, and lovely affair. The service is hospitable and knowledgeable, and nothing is rushed (a terrific concept), giving you time to savor the food and your company. Italian menu. Dinner. Casual attire. Reservations recommended. **$$$**

★ **GROLLA RESTAURANT & WINE BAR.** *2930 NE Killingsworth, Portland (97211). Phone 503/493-9521.* Mediterranean menu. Dinner. Closed Sun-Mon. Bar. Outdoor seating. **$$**

★ ★ ★ **HEATHMAN.** *1001 SW Broadway, Portland (97205). Phone 503/241-4100; fax 503/790-7110. www.heathmanhotel.com.* Executive chef Philippe Boulot offers classic French cooking, with an emphasis on Normandy, in a three-level dining room with a kitchen on one side and views of Broadway Street on the other. A prix fixe menu is offered for hurried theatergoers. American, French menu. Breakfast, lunch, dinner, late-night, brunch. Bar. Children's menu. Casual attire. Valet parking. Outdoor seating. **$$**

★ ★ ★ **HIGGINS.** *1239 SW Broadway, Portland (97205). Phone 503/222-9070; fax 503/222-1244.* Elegantly designed like a French bistro, this trilevel restaurant has taken special efforts to create an inviting atmosphere. Passionate about using local, organic ingredients, the chef creates a menu that leaves palates pleased. Northwestern regional cuisine. Lunch, dinner, late-night. Closed holidays. Bar. Children's menu. Casual attire. **$$$**

★ ★ **HUBER'S CAFE.** *411 SW 3rd Ave, Portland (97204). Phone 503/228-5686; fax 503/227-3922. www.hubers.com.* Originally a saloon established in 1879 that became a restaurant during Prohibition. Arched stained-glass skylight, mahogany paneling, and terrazzo floor. American menu. Breakfast, lunch, dinner, late-night. Closed Sun. Bar. Children's menu. Casual attire. Outdoor seating. **$$**

★ ★ **IL FORNAIO.** *115 NW 22nd Ave, Portland (97210). Phone 503/248-9400; fax 503/248-5678. www.ilfornaio.com.* Italian menu. Lunch, dinner, Sun brunch. Bar. Children's menu. Casual attire. Outdoor seating. **$$**

★ ★ ★ **JAKE'S FAMOUS CRAWFISH.** *401 SW 12th Ave, Portland (97205). Phone 503/226-1419; fax 503/220-1856. www.jakesfamouscrawfish.com.* At more than 110 years old, this downtown landmark restaurant doesn't hide its age; dark woods, turn-of-the-century décor, and scenes of old-time Portland give it a classic feel. An upbeat mood pervades the place, especially in the lively bar area, which is a local favorite. Jake's serves fresh regional seafood dishes as well as several varieties of the crawfish that made it famous. If you're feeling especially adventurous (not to mention hungry), try the 1-pound crawfish platter. Seafood menu. Breakfast, lunch, dinner, late-night. Bar. Children's menu. Casual attire. Outdoor seating. **$$**

★ ★ ★ **JAKE'S GRILL.** *611 SW 10th St, Portland (97205). Phone 503/220-1850; fax 503/226-8365. www.jakesgrill.com.* American menu. Breakfast, lunch, dinner, late-night, brunch. Bar. Children's menu. Casual attire. Valet parking. Outdoor seating. **$$$**

★ ★ **L'AUBERGE.** *2601 NW Vaughn St, Portland (97210). Phone 503/223-3302; fax 503/243-6600.*

www.laubergepdx.com. French menu. Dinner. Closed holidays. Bar. Outdoor seating. **$$$**

★ ★ ★ LONDON GRILL. *309 SW Broadway, Portland (97205). Phone 503/295-4110; fax 503/471-3924. www.bensonhotel.com.* With quiet elegance, this restaurant is set in The Benson Hotel. The chef prepares regional specialties such as Northwest salmon, rack of lamb, and ostrich. International/Fusion menu. Breakfast, lunch, dinner, Sun brunch. Bar. Children's menu. Casual attire. Valet parking. **$$**

★ ★ MANDARIN COVE. *111 SW Columbia, Portland (97201). Phone 503/222-0006; fax 503/274-9800.* Mandarin, Chinese menu. Lunch, dinner. Bar. Casual attire. **$**

★ ★ MARRAKESH MOROCCAN RESTAURANT. *1201 NW 21st Ave, Portland (97209). Phone 503/248-9442; fax 503/294-7191.* Moroccan menu. Dinner. Children's menu. Casual attire. **$$**

★ ★ MURATA. *200 SW Market St, Portland (97201). Phone 503/227-0080.* Japanese menu. Lunch, dinner. Closed Sun. Casual attire. Reservations recommended. Valet parking. **$$**

★ ★ NOHO'S HAWAIIAN CAFE. *2525 SE Clinton, Portland (97202). Phone 503/233-5301. www.nohos.com.* Hawaiian menu. Lunch, dinner. Casual attire. Outdoor seating. **$$**

★ ★ ★ PALEY'S PLACE. *1204 NW 21st Ave, Portland (97209). Phone 503/243-2403; fax 503/223-8041. www.paleysplace.citysearch.com.* Bistro fare featuring imaginative and beautifully presented entrées, using only the freshest local ingredients. Homemade chocolates arrive with the bill. Wine Wednesdays include wine tastings and a menu to match. French Bistro menu. Dinner. Bar. Casual attire. Outdoor seating. **$$$**

★ ★ PAPA HAYDN. *5829 SE Milwaukie, Portland (97202). Phone 503/232-9440; fax 503/236-5815. www.papahaydn.com.* American menu. Lunch, dinner, late-night, brunch. Children's menu. Casual attire. Outdoor seating. No credit cards accepted. **$$**

★ ★ ★ PAZZO RISTORANTE. *627 SW Washington, Portland (97205). Phone 503/228-1515; fax 503/228-5935. www.kimptongroup.com.* A cozy, friendly atmosphere is the setting for an authentically northern Italian restaurant that is a favorite among the locals. The open kitchen gives guests a preview of what's to come: handmade pastas and hearty dishes such as leg of lamb with goat cheese. Italian menu. Breakfast, lunch, dinner, brunch. Bar. Children's menu. Casual attire. Valet parking. Outdoor seating. **$$$**

★ ★ PERRY'S ON FREMONT. *2401 NE Fremont, Portland (97212). Phone 503/287-3655; fax 503/287-6216.* American menu. Dinner. Closed Sun. Bar. Children's menu. Casual attire. Valet parking. Outdoor seating. **$$**

★ ★ ★ PLAINFIELD'S MAYUR. *852 SW 21st Ave, Portland (97205). Phone 503/223-2995. www.plainfields.com.* Located in a historic Victorian house near Civic Stadium, this restaurant features East Indian food, an extensive wine list, and vegan and vegetarian entrées. Indian menu. Dinner. Casual attire. Reservations recommended. Outdoor seating. **$$$**

★ POOR RICHARDS. *3907 NE Broadway, Portland (97232). Phone 503/288-5285; fax 503/493-1449. www.poorrichardstwofer.com.* Seafood, steak menu. Lunch, dinner. Closed holidays. Bar. Children's menu. **$$**

★ ★ ★ RED STAR TAVERN & ROAST HOUSE. *503 SW Alder St, Portland (97204). Phone 503/222-0005; fax 503/417-3334. www.kimptongroup.com.* With views overlooking downtown Portland, this tavern turns out Northwestern fare that centers on spit-roasted meats, fresh seafood (especially shellfish) and great flatbread appetizers. Diners can watch their food being prepared in the semi-exposed kitchen. American menu. Breakfast, lunch, dinner, late-night, brunch. Bar. Children's menu. Casual attire. Valet parking. **$$**

★ ★ RHEINLANDER. *5035 NE Sandy Blvd, Portland (97213). Phone 503/288-5503. www.gutenfoods.com.* German menu. Lunch, dinner. Closed July 4, Dec 24-25. Bar. Children's menu. **$$**

★ ★ ★ RINGSIDE. *2165 W Burnside St, Portland (97210). Phone 503/223-1513; fax 503/223-6908. www.ringsidesteakhouse.com.* Seafood, steak menu. Dinner, late-night. Bar. Casual attire. Valet parking. **$$$**

★ RINGSIDE EAST. *14021 NE Glisan, Portland (97230). Phone 503/255-0750.* Seafood, steak menu. Lunch, dinner. Closed holidays. Bar. **$$$**

★ ★ SALTY'S ON THE COLUMBIA. *3839 NE Marine Dr, Portland (97211). Phone 503/288-4444; fax 503/288-3426. www.saltys.com.* Seafood, steak menu. Lunch, dinner, Sun brunch. Bar. Children's menu. Casual attire. Valet parking. Outdoor seating. **$$$**

★ **SANTORINI.** *11525 SW Barnes Rd, Portland (97201). Phone 503/646-6889.* Greek, Italian, Mediterranean menu. Lunch, dinner. Bar. Children's menu. Outdoor seating. **$**

★ ★ **SAUCEBOX.** *214 SW Broadway, Portland (97205). Phone 503/241-3393. www.saucebox.com.* Pan-Asian menu. Lunch, dinner. Closed Sun-Mon. Bar. Outdoor seating. **$$**

★ **SAYLER'S OLD COUNTRY KITCHEN.** *10519 SE Stark, Portland (97216). Phone 503/252-4171.* American menu. Dinner. Closed holidays. Bar. Children's menu. **$$$**

★ **SYLVIA'S.** *5115 NE Sandy Blvd, Portland (97213). Phone 503/288-6828. www.sylvias.net.* Italian menu. Dinner. Closed Thanksgiving, Dec 24-25. Bar. Children's menu. **$$**

★ **TASTE OF BALI.** *947 SW Broadway, Portland (97205). Phone 503/224-2254.* Indonesian, Malaysian menu. Lunch, dinner. Casual attire. Outdoor seating. **$**

★ ★ **TYPHOON!** *2310 NW Everett St, Portland (97210). Phone 503/243-7557; fax 503/243-7144.* Thai menu. Lunch, dinner. Closed holidays. Outdoor seating. **$$**

★ **WIDMER GASTHAUS.** *955 N Russell St, Portland (97227). Phone 503/281-3333. www.widmer.com.* German menu. Lunch, dinner. Closed Jan 1, Thanksgiving, Dec 25. Bar. Outdoor seating. **$$**

★ ★ ★ **WILDWOOD.** *1221 NW 21st Ave, Portland (97209). Phone 503/248-9663; fax 503/222-5153. www.wildwoodrestaurant.com.* This acclaimed Oregon restaurant serves the freshest seafood and seasonal Northwest ingredients in elegant combinations that highlight the indigenous flavors. A wood-burning oven turns out crisp pizzas and adds warmth to the dining room's comforting natural tones. American menu. Lunch, dinner, Sun brunch. Bar. Outdoor seating. **$$**

★ ★ **WINTERBORNE.** *3520 NE 42nd, Portland (97213). Phone 503/249-8486.* French menu. Dinner. Closed Sun-Tues; Dec 25. Children's menu. **$$**

Reno, NV (D-4)

3 1/2 hours, 218 miles from San Francisco

Founded 1868
Population 180,480
Elevation 4,498 ft
Area Code 775
Information Chamber of Commerce, 1 E First St, 16th Floor, 89501 775/337-3030. For information on cultural events, contact the Sierra Arts Foundation, 200 Flint St, 89501; 775/329-2787
Web Site www.reno-sparkschamber.org

Reno, "the biggest little city in the world," renowned as a gambling and vacation center, is an important distribution and merchandising area, the home of the University of Nevada-Reno, and a residential city. Between the steep slopes of the Sierra and the low eastern hills, Reno spills across the Truckee Meadows. The neon lights of the nightclubs, gambling casinos, and bars give it a glitter that belies its quiet acres of fine houses, churches, and schools. The surrounding area is popular for sailing, boating, horseback riding, and deer and duck hunting.

Reno was known as Lake's Crossing and was an overland travelers' camping place even before the gold rush. It grew with the exploitation of the Comstock Lode and became a city in May 1868, with a public auction of real estate by a railway agent. Within a month there were 100 houses. A railroad official named the town in honor of a Union officer of the Civil War, General Jesse Lee Reno. In 1871 it became the seat of Washoe County.

Many Nevadans resent Reno's reputation as a divorce capital. They point out that many more couples are married than divorced at the Washoe County Courthouse. A six-month divorce law had been on the books since 1861, before Nevada became a state. The six-week law became effective in the 1930s.

What to See and Do

Animal Ark. *Take Hwy 395 N to exit 78, turn right on Red Rock Rd and drive 11 1/2 miles, turn right on Deerlodge and drive 1 mile to 1265. Phone 775/970-3111. www.animalark.org.* Tucked amidst the forested hills north of Reno, Animal Ark is not a zoo, but a sanctuary for animals that cannot be returned to the wild—many were disabled or orphaned, and others were unwanted exotic pets. The residents include big cats (tigers, snow leopards, and cougars), gray wolves, black bears, and a few reptiles and birds. Each has a name and is presented as an "ambassador" for its species. (Apr-Oct, Tues-Sun 10 am-4:30 pm; open Mon holidays) **$$**

Blue Lamp. *125 W 3rd St, Reno (89501). Phone 775/329-6969.* A crowded, casual space laden with big couches and velvet art, this hip nightspot in downtown Reno has a vibe that's more San Francisco than northern Nevada. The stage here hosts live music, mainly jazz and rock, and DJs also hold court on regular theme nights.

Downtown Reno shopping district. Reno's neon-laden city center is not made up entirely of casinos and hotels. The downtown Riverwalk along the Truckee's banks (on Virginia, Sierra, First, and Second sts) is loaded with hip coffee shops and art galleries, and also is home to a number of chic eateries, eclectic boutiques, antique stores, salons, and theaters.

Foley's Irish Pub. *2780 S Virginia St, Reno (89502). Phone 775/829-8500. www.ripkord.com/foleys.* Authentically Irish and a favorite after-work hangout south of downtown Reno, Foley's is an agreeable place to sip on a pint and have a conversation. The food is good (the menu offers a nice mix of Irish standards and American pub grub), the bartenders are friendly, and there are both TVs for sports and video poker machines.

Great Basin Adventure. *Rancho San Rafael Regional Park, 1502 Washington St, Reno (89503). Phone 775/785-4319. www.maycenter.com.* Part of the Wilbur D. May Center in Rancho San Rafael Regional Park, Great Basin Adventure consists of several kids' attractions designed to educate and entertain simultaneously. At Wilbur's Farm, pint-sized visitors can take a pony ride or explore the 1 1/2-acre petting zoo. Guests can pan for gold at a replica mine building, with faux mine shafts that double as slides and displays on minerals and the area's mining history. Also on-site are the Discovery Room, a small "please touch" natural history museum with daily special events (storytelling, arts and crafts, and other kids' activities); a log flume ride on a man-made river (a great opportunity to cool off in the summer); and a colorful playground with swings and slides shaped like dinosaurs. (Tues-Sat 10 am-5 pm, Sun noon-5 pm) **$**

Humboldt-Toiyabe National Forest. *1200 Franklin Way, Sparks (89431). 10 miles W on I-80, then W on Hwy 27. Phone 775/331-6444. www.fs.fed.us/htnf.* At 6.3 million acres, this is the largest national forest in the lower 48 states. It extends across Nevada from the California border in a scattershot pattern, comprising ten ranger districts that encompass four distinct ecologies: meadows, mountains, deserts, and canyons. Just northwest of the Reno city limits, Peavine Mountain is crisscrossed by a number of old mining roads now reserved for hikers and mountain bikers. Other Humboldt-Toiyabe highlights include scenic Lamoille Canyon and the Ruby Mountains, southeast of Elko; the rugged, isolated Toiyabe Range, near the geographical center of Nevada; and, well southeast of Reno on the California-Nevada border, Boundary Peak, the state's highest point at 13,143 feet. Beyond hikers and bikers, off-road vehicles, snowmobiles, and campers flock to various areas in the vast forest. **FREE**

Meadowood Mall. *5515 Meadowood Mall Cir, Reno (89502). Phone 775/825-3955.* The most contemporary and posh shopping center in the region, Reno's Meadowood Mall is actually the city's most visited tourist attraction. The more than 100 stores under the mall's roof include anchors Macy's, JCPenney, and Sears, alongside a massive sporting goods store—Copeland's. There are also specialty stores like Brookstone and Victoria's Secret, and a number of restaurants.

Mount Rose Ski Area. *22222 Mt Rose Hwy, Reno (89511). 12 miles NE on Hwy 431. Phone 775/849-0704; toll-free 800/754-7673 (except in NV). www.mtrose.com.* Of all the ski resorts in the Reno-Tahoe area, Mount Rose has the highest base elevation (a precipitous 8,260 feet above sea level), making it the best bet for late-season skiing. Six lifts, including a six-person, high-speed chairlift, take skiers and snowboarders to the 9,700-foot summit, to 1,000 acres of terrain nearly evenly split among skill levels (30 percent beginner, 30 percent intermediate, and 40 percent advanced) and a pair of snowboarding parks. Located northwest of Lake Tahoe, Mount Rose is also known for its excellent "first-timer" program for beginners. There are no on-mountain accommodations. (Mid-Nov-mid-Apr, daily) **$$$$**

National Automobile Museum (The Harrah Collection). *10 Lake St S, Reno (89501). At the corner of Lake and Mill. Phone 775/333-9300. www.automuseum.org.* The brainchild of car collector and gaming titan Bill Harrah, this excellent facility covers more than a century of automotive history in fascinating detail. Four galleries house the museum's collection of more than 200 cars: The first details the late 19th and early 20th century (complete with a blacksmith's shop, the garage of the day); the second covers 1914 to 1931; the third, 1932 to 1954; and the fourth, 1954 to modern day. Also in the fourth gallery, the Masterpiece Circle Gallery accommodates temporary themed exhibits on subjects ranging from Porsches to pickup trucks. The oldest car in the museum dates to 1892, and there are a number of collector's trophies (such as the 1949 Mercury Coupe driven by James Dean in *Rebel Without a Cause*) and one-of-a-kind oddities (the steam-powered 1977 Steamin' Demon). (Mon-Sat 9:30 am-5:30 pm, Sun 10 am-4 pm; closed Thanksgiving, Dec 25) **$$**

Nevada Museum of Art. *160 W Liberty St, Reno (89501). Phone 775/329-3333. www.nevadaart.org.* The only nationally accredited art museum in the entire state, the Nevada Museum of Art would be a top-notch facility no matter where it was located. Perhaps the most distinctive architectural specimen in all of artsy Reno, the curved, sweeping structure is a work of art in and of itself: modern (it opened in 2003) and monolithic (60,000 square feet), evoking the image of the legendary Black Rock of the Nevada desert. The collection housed within is equally impressive, broken into five different themes: contemporary art, contemporary landscape photography (one of the best of its kind anywhere), regional art, American art from 1900 to 1945, and the E. L. Weigand Collection, American art with a "work ethic" theme. The museum also plays host to several temporary exhibitions every year, and has a café, a store, and an art school on-site. (Tues-Wed, Fri-Sun 11 am-6 pm, Thurs 11 am-8 pm; closed major holidays) **$$**

★ Reno Arch. *Virginia St, downtown, Reno.* In 1926, Reno commemorated the completion of the first transcontinental highway in North America—which ran through the city en route to San Francisco—with an arch that traverses Virginia Street downtown. Three years later, locals adopted the tagline "The Biggest Little City in the World" and added it to the landmark. The arch has since been replaced twice—in 1964 and in 1987—but remains one of the most photographed structures in the United States. The original arch was scrapped, but the 1964 arch found a new home across town at the National Automobile Museum (see).

Reno-Sparks Theater Coalition. *528 W First St, Reno (89503). Phone 775/786-2278. www.theatercoalition.org.* Consisting of more than 20 separate companies in the Reno-Sparks area, this organization is a cooperative effort to market a varied slate of theater, dance, and other performing arts. Member troupes range from the avant-garde to the kid-friendly, and the Coalition puts together an up-to-date events schedule for all of them.

Scruples Bar and Grill. *91 W Plumb St, Reno (89509). Phone 775/322-7171.* Nondescript on the exterior (it's tucked away in a strip mall), Scruples is cozier on the inside, just a good neighborhood bar, with rock on the jukebox and patio seating. It's a good bet for late night burgers and fries, and also the best place to watch a ballgame, especially those involving teams from the University of Nevada, Reno.

Sierra Nevada Bus Tours. *2050 Glendale Ave, Sparks (89431). Phone 775/331-1147; toll-free 800/822-6009.* To Virginia City, Ponderosa Ranch, Lake Tahoe, and other nearby points.

Sierra Safari Zoo. *10200 N Virginia St, Reno (89506). 8 miles N of downtown. Phone 775/677-1101. www.sierrasafarizoo.com.* The largest zoo in Nevada (but a fairly average one in national terms), Sierra Safari is home to 150 representatives of more than 40 species. The majority of the animals were selected for the rugged Reno climate, including a Siberian tiger and a number of other felines, but there are also tropical birds, a few reptiles, and a number of primates. A petting zoo and a picnic area are on-site. (Apr-Oct, daily 10 am-5 pm) **$**

University of Nevada, Reno. *1664 N Virginia St, Reno (89557). 9th and Virginia sts. Phone 775/784-4700 (tours). www.unr.edu.* (1874) (12,000 students) The campus covers 200 acres on a plateau overlooking the Truckee Meadows, in the shadow of the Sierra Nevada Mountains. Opened in Elko, it was moved to Reno and reopened in 1885. Tours of campus. On campus are

Fleischmann Planetarium and Science Center. *1650 N Virginia St, Reno (89503). Phone 775/784-4811. planetarium.unr.nevada.edu.* This facility projects public star shows on the inside of its 30-foot dome. The museum here houses all four of the meteorites that have landed in Nevada (including a massive specimen that weighs more than a ton) and scales rigged to reflect the gravity on Jupiter or a neutron star. On cloudless Friday nights, guests can peer through telescopes with members of the Astronomical Society of Nevada. (Mon-Fri 8 am-8 pm, Sat-Sun 11 am-8 pm) **$$**

Nevada Historical Society Museum. *1650 N Virginia St, Reno (89503). Phone 775/688-1190. dmla.clan.lib.nv.us/docs/museums/reno/his-soc.htm.* Founded in 1904, this is Nevada's oldest museum and one of its best. On permanent display is "Nevada: Prisms and Perspectives," which examines the Silver State's five biggest historical stories: the Native American perspective, the mining boom, the neon-lit story of gaming, transportation, and the "Federal Presence"—as the federal government owns 87 percent of Nevada's land. A store, changing exhibit gallery, and library are also on site. Galleries (Mon-Sat 10 am-5 pm; closed holidays) **$**

W. M. Keck Earth Sciences and Engineering Museum. *Mackay School of Mines Building, 9th and Virginia sts, Reno (89501). Phone 775/784-6987. mines.unr.edu/museum.* Located in the Mackay School of Mines Building, the Keck Museum focuses on the state's mining history. The collection of specimens originated from Nevada's most renowned mining districts—the Comstock Lode, Tonopah, and Goldfield—but exotic minerals from all over the world share the space. Rounding out the museum are displays of fossils, vintage mining equipment, and a collection of fine silver donated by the family of mining tycoon John Mackay. (Mon-Fri 9 am-4 pm; closed holidays) **FREE**

Special Events

Artown Festival. *Throughout the city. Phone 775/322-1538. www.artown.org.* Held annually in July (with a newer holiday counterpart in November and December), Reno's Artown Festival is a month-long extravaganza that includes more than 200 events and exhibitions and 1,000 artists in all. (That makes it the largest arts festival in the United States, and one that has won its fair share of national acclaim since it launched in 1996.) The artists span the disciplines of ballet, opera, theater, film, and the visual arts-there are flamenco dancers, comedy troupes, and internationally known performers of all stripes, not to mention the myriad gallery openings and historical tours. Multiple downtown venues host various aspects of the festival: Wingfield Park is the setting of an outdoor film every week, Rollin' on the River is a weekly concert series. Mondays are family nights, with entertainment ranging from science experiments to storytelling. July.

Best of the West Rib Cook-off. *John Ascuaga's Nugget Casino Resort, 1100 Nugget Ave, Sparks (89431). Phone 775/356-3300; toll-free 800/648-1177. www.janugget.com/events/ribcookoff.cfm.* Rack after gargantuan rack of baby-back ribs, slathered in sweet-hot sauce, lure nearly 300,000 barbecue fanatics to John Ascuaga's Nugget in Sparks every Labor Day weekend. In recent years, about 150,000 pounds of ribs have been consumed by the masses at this five-day event. (For those who are counting, that makes it the largest such event in the whole nation.) If you can pull yourself away from the addictive barbecue, there is also a lineup of live entertainment on numerous outdoor stages (ranging from rock to blues to zydeco), vendors hocking crafts and ribs at booths, and even karaoke. The "Best of the West" moniker is no joke: Just two dozen of the West's most revered barbecue pros (all invited) compete for the first-prize trophy and the judges are also culinary notables. The winner is presented with a pig-shaped check at the awards ceremony. Labor Day weekend.

Eldorado's Great BBQ, Brew, and Blues. *4th and Virginia sts, Reno (89505). Outside and inside of Eldorado Hotel and Casino.Phone 775/786-5700; toll-free 800/648-5966. www.eldoradoreno.com.* Held over the last weekend every June by the Eldorado Hotel and Casino, this street fair focuses on the three staples in its name: tangy barbecue, ice-cold beer, and a pair of stages featuring nonstop blues. The participating breweries hail from Nevada, California, and Oregon, and only those 21 years old and over are admitted. Last weekend in June.

Eldorado Great Italian Festival. *4th and Virginia sts, Reno (89501). Outside and inside the Eldorado Hotel and Casino.Phone 775/786-5700; toll-free 800/648-5966. www.eldoradoreno.com.* Red, white, and green streamers and flags blanket Virginia Street for two days in early October. The food runs the Italian gamut, from pasta, calamari, and risotto to gelato and, of course, vino. Put on by the Eldorado Hotel and Casino, the event includes several buffets, a farmers' market, and live entertainment, but the contests are the real attractions: a spaghetti sauce cook-off, a gelato-eating contest for kids, and the big event, the grape-stomping competition. Early Oct.

Hot August Nights. *1425 E Greg St, Reno (89431). Outside of Reno-Sparks Convention Center. Phone 775/356-1956. www.hotaugustnights.net.* Held over a weekend in early August, this retro event pays homage to the 1950s and '60s. Highlights include a series of concerts by nostalgia acts (past performers have included Chuck Berry, the Turtles, and Jan and Dean) and a classic car parade. There are street dances and sock hops, and casinos get in on the action by awarding a classic car or two to a few lucky winners. Early Aug.

National Championship Air Races. *Reno/Stead Airport, 4895 Texas Ave, Reno (89505). Phone 775/972-6663.*

www.airrace.org. Races (classes include Biplane, Formula One, Unlimited, Jet, Sport, and T-6), demonstrations, and fly-bys. Four days in mid-Sept. **$$$$**

Nevada Opera. *Pioneer Center for the Performing Arts, 100 S Virginia St, Reno (89501). Phone 775/786-4046. www.nevadaopera.com*. Founded in 1967 and surviving a tumultuous financial era in the late 1990s, the Nevada Opera stages several noteworthy operas each year in its fall/spring calendar. Recent productions have included *Madame Butterfly* and *Carmen*. While the group tours the entire state, its Reno home is the Pioneer Center for the Performing Arts. **$$$$**

Nevada State Fair. *1350 N Wells Ave, Reno (89512). Phone 775/688-5767 (tickets). www.nevadastatefair.org*. A Reno area tradition since 1874, the Nevada State Fair is held annually in late August, with rodeo events, livestock competitions, and a carnival midway. Beyond the expected fair diversions, the event also includes a kid-oriented science festival, an aerial motorcycle stunt show, and contests for the best homemade pies, cookies, and salsa. Late Aug.

Reno Basque Festival. *Wingfield Park, Reno. Phone 775/787-30309*. Basques from northern Spain and southern France immigrated to Nevada's Great Basin in the early 20th century to herd sheep, and they have been a visible part of the Reno community ever since. Held over a weekend in late July, the Reno Basque Festival started in 1959 with the goal of preserving Basque culture in the United States. Today, it's one of the largest events of its kind in the country, kicked off by a parade that snakes around downtown before coming to a stop at Wingfield Park along the Truckee River. From there, the festival takes over, with food, dancing, singing, and athletic competitions. Basque cuisine available for the sampling includes sheepherder bread, Basque beans, lamb stew, and other hearty staples, and there's also a market. Crowds gather for the traditional games: soka tira (a Basque tug-of-war), woodcutting, and weightlifting. Late July.

Reno Film Festival. *528 W First St, Reno Film Festival Office, Reno (89503). Phone 775/334-6707. www.renofilmfestival.com*. Drawing a handful of celebrities to downtown Reno every November, this film festival consists of Hollywood productions, independent features, world premieres, and retrospective revivals. Screenings are shown at various downtown venues (i.e., casinos, museums, and theaters), and there are also a number of film-related workshops, demonstrations, and lectures. Early Nov.

Reno Jazz Festival. *(89557). Phone 775/784-6847 (tickets)*. Held on the University of Nevada at Reno campus since 1963, this three-day event is one of the biggest of its kind, drawing hundreds of school bands (junior high to college) from Nevada, California, Oregon, Idaho, and Washington. The top bands and soloists play at a concluding encore performance, and the first two nights are highlighted by sets from nationally known jazz names. Late Apr. **$$$$**

Reno Philharmonic Orchestra. *Pioneer Center for the Performing Arts, 925 Riverside Dr #3, Reno (89503). Phone 775/323-6393. www.renophilharmonic.com*. Reno's symphony orchestra plays a September-to-April "Master Classics Series" (as well as a July 4th pops concert) at a number of venues in town, with Pioneer Center for the Performing Arts serving as its home stage. The orchestra plays works from composers such as Mozart, Beethoven, Copland, and Gershwin. "Preview from the Podium" is a free one-hour lecture given immediately before each concert. **$$$$**

Reno Rodeo. *Reno Livestock Events Center, 1350 N Wells Ave, Reno. Phone 775/329-3877; toll-free 800/225-2277 (tickets). www.renorodeo.com*. Known as the "Wildest, Richest Rodeo in the West"—with a total purse in excess of $1 million—the Reno Rodeo has been a big event since its inaugural year, 1919. The rodeo is one of the largest PRCA (Professional Rodeo Cowboys Association) events in the United States and features bull riding, barrel racing, and roping events. Late June. **$$**

Sparks Hometowne Farmers' Market. *Victorian Square, downtown, Sparks (89432). Phone 775/353-2291*. Every Thursday evening between June and August, Victorian Square in downtown Sparks comes alive with foods that will tempt even the most finicky tastes. More than 100 vendors furnish both fresh ingredients and finished meals, everything from rhubarb to pastries to tacos. Beyond the seemingly endless supply of good food, there is a nightly 6 pm cooking demonstration, a kids' area, and home and garden vendors.

Limited-Service Hotels

★ ★ BEST WESTERN AIRPORT PLAZA HOTEL. *1981 Terminal Way, Reno (89502). Phone 775/348-6370; toll-free 800/648-3525; fax 775/348-9722. www.bestwestern.com*. 270 rooms, 3 story. Check-out noon. Restaurant, bar. Fitness room. Outdoor pool, whirlpool. Airport transportation available. Business center. Casino. **$**

★ ★ FITZGERALD'S CASINO HOTEL. *255 N Virginia St, Reno (89504). Phone 775/785-3300; toll-free 800/535-5825; fax 775/785-3686. www.fitzgeralds.com.* 351 rooms, 16 story. Check-out 11 am. Restaurant, bar. Casino. **$**

★ LA QUINTA INN. *4001 Market St, Reno (89502). Phone 775/348-6100; toll-free 800/531-5900; fax 775/348-8794. www.laquinta.com.* 130 rooms, 2 story. Pets accepted, some restrictions. Complimentary continental breakfast. Check-out noon. Outdoor pool. Airport transportation available. **$**

Full-Service Hotels

★ ★ ★ ATLANTIS CASINO RESORT. *3800 S Virginia St, Reno (89502). Phone 775/825-4700; toll-free 800/723-6500; fax 775/826-7860. www.atlantiscasino.com.* What began as a 142-room hotel in the early 1970s underwent a significant face-lift in the 1990s. Now Atlantis, located about 3 miles south of downtown, is among Reno's top resorts, with several smoke-free gaming areas in the glass-enclosed casinos, a top-notch business center, and a dizzying array of rooms. Two highlights: the Sky Terrace restaurant, with sushi and oyster bars, and an excellent spa, featuring Ahava, Aveda, and Dermalogica products. 973 rooms, 27 story. Pets accepted, some restrictions; fee. Check-out 11 am. Restaurant, bar. Spa. Indoor pool, outdoor pool, whirlpool. Airport transportation available. Casino. **$**

★ ★ ★ ELDORADO HOTEL AND CASINO. *345 N Virginia St, Reno (89505). Phone 775/786-5700; toll-free 800/648-5966; fax 775/348-9269. www.eldoradoreno.com.* Of the casinos in downtown Reno, Eldorado is the one that attracts the youngest and hippest crowd, based primarily on its myriad nightspots: a microbrewery with live rock and blues, a martini/piano bar, and BuBinga, a popular dance club with DJs and live bands. Eldorado has some of the best-looking hotel rooms in town, airy and sunny with light tones, and the impressive "Fountain of Fortune" in the mezzanine plaza, a Baroque marvel adorned with dozens of ornate marble statues. The casino features 2,000 slots, boasts the best poker room in town, and is known for its generous comps, earned through Club Eldorado. Among the ten restaurants are eateries specializing in Chinese and Italian, as well as a seafood buffet. 817 rooms, 26 story. Check-out noon. Restaurant, bar. Outdoor pool, whirlpool. Airport transportation available. Casino. **$**

★ ★ ★ HARRAH'S HOTEL RENO. *219 N Center St, Reno (89520). Phone 775/786-3232; fax 775/788-2815. www.harrahs.com.* In the heart of downtown (right next to the Reno Arch), Harrah's Reno is one of the glitziest casinos in the city, a distinction it's held since opening in the early 1960s. The casino is immense and diverse, featuring 1,300 slot machines, table games of all kinds, and a sports book. Accommodations come in the form of nearly 1,000 sleek hotel rooms, ranging in style from standard rooms to skyline suites. There are seven restaurants, including the renowned Steak House at Harrah's Reno. Non-gamers can spend the day at Xtreme Park, a small amusement park featuring the hair-raising, 145-foot Xtreme Machine, which vaults passengers skyward at speeds up to 100 miles per hour. And entertainers work the crowd onstage at Sammy's Showroom, named after Sammy Davis Jr., who performed here 40 times. 952 rooms, 26 story. Pets accepted, some restrictions. Check-out noon. Restaurant, bar. Outdoor pool, whirlpool. Airport transportation available. Business center. Casino. **$**

★ ★ ★ HILTON RENO. *2500 E Second St, Reno (89595). Phone 702/789-2000; toll-free 800/648-5080; fax 702/789-1678. www.hilton.com.* With a 40,000-square-foot Fun Quest Center and a recreational vehicle park, this casino resort is for the whole family. Other activities available include hang gliding, bungee jumping, sky diving, bowling, a health and fitness center, aquatic driving range, an indoor golf and sports center, six restaurants, a comedy club and swimming pool. 2,000 rooms, 27 story. Check-out 11 am. Restaurant, bar. Fitness room. Outdoor pool, whirlpool. Airport transportation available. Business center. Casino. **$**

★ ★ ★ JOHN ASCUAGA' S NUGGET. *1100 Nugget Ave, Sparks (89431). Phone 775/356-3300; toll-free 800/648-1177; fax 775/356-4258. www.janugget.com.* An anchor in downtown Sparks, the Nugget has been one of the top resorts in the Reno area since opening in 1955. It's a few miles outside of the hubbub in downtown Reno, but right on the doorstep of Victorian Square, the site of numerous special events. (The Nugget itself hosts one of these big fiestas: the Best of the West Rib Cook-off.) The casino is loaded with all of the standards—slots, table games, a poker room, and a sports book. If food is your game, there are eight restaurants to choose from including a Basque restaurant and a long-standing steakhouse. The Celebrity Showroom is the place to go for fabulous entertainment. The hotel itself is a landmark, with a pair of 29-story towers flanking the casino—1,600 rooms in all—and a slate of amenities that includes everything from an arcade to a wedding chapel. 1,407 rooms, 29 story. Check-out 11 am. Restaurants, bars. Fitness room. Indoor pool, outdoor pool, whirlpool. Airport transportation available. Business center. Casino. **$**

★ ★ ★ PEPPERMILL HOTEL AND CASINO RENO. *2707 S Virginia St, Reno (89502). Phone 775/826-2121; toll-free 800/648-6992; fax 775/689-7127. www.peppermillcasino.com.* Consistently ranked near the top of the lists for best and hippest casinos in the city (and the country, for that matter), Peppermill's flagship resort, renovated for a tab of $300 million in 2000-2001, is a fixture in the entertainment district near the airport, about 2 miles south of downtown. The slick property features 1,100 rooms, 2,000 slot machines, the full spectrum of table gaming, poker, sports betting, and nightly live entertainment in the swanky Cabaret and the more intimate Piano Lounge. Among the amenities, the pool—replete with a man-made waterfall—stands out, as do the seven restaurants. The dozen themed nightspots are a prime lure; the highlights are the aquarium-laden Fish Bar and the domed, effects-laden ultra lounge at Romanza, one of the hippest, see-and-be-seen nightclubs in town. 1,070 rooms, 16 story. Check-out noon. Restaurant, bar. Fitness room. Outdoor pool, whirlpool. Airport transportation available. Casino. **$**

★ ★ ★ SIENA HOTEL SPA CASINO. *1 S Lake St, Reno (89505). Phone 775/337-6260; toll-free 877/743-6233; fax 775/337-6201. www.sienareno.com.* The Siena Hotel Spa Casino brings the romance of the Tuscan countryside to Reno. Located along the banks of the Truckee River, this comprehensive resort is at once restful and thrilling. A 23,000-square-foot casino invites gaming, while a full-service spa with a complete range of services caters to overworked individuals. Designed to resemble a Tuscan village, the resort carries the country Italian theme through to its delightful and soothing guest rooms and suites. Three dining establishments keep diners on their toes. Lexie's on the River shows off water views, although its exhibition kitchen captures the attention of many diners. Contrada Café satisfies hunger throughout the day with its informal fare, and Enoteca is an oenophile's fantasy with its extensive wine list and carefully chosen food and wine pairings. 214 rooms, 9 story. Check-out noon. Restaurants, bars. Fitness room, spa. Business center. Casino. **$**

★ ★ ★ SILVER LEGACY RESORT CASINO RENO. *407 N Virginia St, Reno (89501). Phone 775/329-4777; toll-free 800/687-7733; fax 775/325-7474. www.silverlegacyresort.com.* Located in downtown Reno, the Silver Legacy sports a Victorian theme, under an enormous steel and brass dome and behind a façade designed to resemble 1890s storefronts. Beyond the gaming—2,000 slots, table games, a sports book, and a keno lounge—there is a comedy club and a rum bar with dueling pianos. The showroom attracts big-name entertainers. 1,720 rooms, 38 story. Check-out 11 am. Restaurant, bar. Outdoor pool, whirlpool. Airport transportation available. **$**

Restaurants

★ ★ BRICKS RESTAURANT AND WINE BAR. *1695 S Virginia St, Reno (89502). Phone 775/786-2277; fax 775/786-3377.* American menu. Lunch, dinner. Closed Sun; holidays. Bar. **$$**

★ ★ FAMOUS MURPHY'S. *3127 S Virginia St, Reno (89502). Phone 775/827-4111; fax 775/824-2599. www.famousmurphys.com.* Seafood, steak menu. Lunch, dinner. Closed Sun. Bar. Children's menu. **$$**

★ ★ PALAIS DE JADE. *960 W Moana Ln #107, Reno (89509). Phone 775/827-5233.* Chinese menu. Lunch, dinner. Closed holidays. Bar. **$$**

★ ★ RAPSCALLION. *1555 S Wells Ave, Reno (89502). Phone 775/323-1211; fax 775/323-6096. www.rapscallion.com.* Seafood menu. Dinner, Sun brunch. Closed Thanksgiving, Dec 25. Bar. Outdoor seating. **$$**

★ ★ WASHOE GRILL. *4201 W 4th St, Reno (89503). Phone 775/786-1323.* Seafood, steak menu. Dinner. Closed Thanksgiving. Bar. **$$$**

Index

L

M

N

O

Q

R

S

T

U

Notes

Notes

Notes

Notes

Notes

Notes

Notes

Notes

Notes

Notes

Notes

Notes

Notes

Notes

Notes

Notes

Notes